MAR - - 2022

3124300 659 6448

D0872811

lone

Provence
& the Côte d'Azur

Alpes-de-Haute-
Provence
p278

Vaucluse
p219

The Luberon
p260

Côte d'Azur Monaco
p48   p110

The
Camargue
p197

Bouches-du-Rhône
p154

Var
p125

Hugh McNaughtan,
Oliver Berry, Gregor Clark, Regis St Louis

Contents

RIVER THOMPSON/LONELY PLANET ©

SOCCA P37

Contents

VILLEFRANCHE-SUR-MER
P65

COVID-19

We have re-checked every business in this book before publication to ensure that it is still open after the COVID-19 outbreak. However, the economic and social impacts of COVID-19 will continue to be felt long after the outbreak has been contained, and many businesses, services and events referenced in this guide may experience ongoing restrictions. Some businesses may be temporarily closed, have changed their opening hours and services, or require bookings; some unfortunately could have closed permanently. We suggest you check with venues before visiting for the latest information.

RIVER THOMPSON/LONELY PLANET ©

Right: Tapenade
(p38) and other
Provençal delicacies

WELCOME TO

Provence & the Côte d'Azur

As someone who values variety above all else, I couldn't help falling in love with Provence and the Côte d'Azur. You can spend your morning assembling farm-fresh produce from a sprawling open-air market, then head to the hinterlands for an afternoon of walking amid forested peaks – followed by dinner and drinks on the cobblestones of an ancient village. There's no wrong way to travel Provence: whether focusing on Roman ruins, birdwatching in the Camargue, white-knuckle adventures in the Gorges du Verdon, or visiting the landscapes that inspired so many artists over the years. The challenge is simply deciding where to begin.

By Regis St Louis, Writer

🐦 @regisstlouis 📷 regisstlouis

For more about our writers, see p352

Provence & the Côte d'Azur

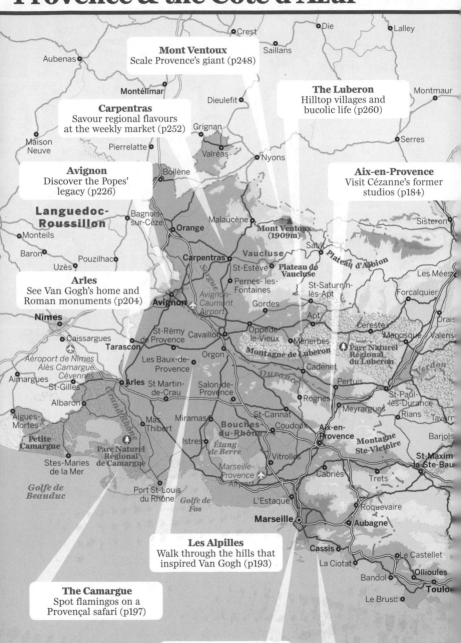

Mont Ventoux
Scale Provence's giant (p248)

The Luberon
Hilltop villages and
bucolic life (p260)

Carpentras
Savour regional flavours
at the weekly market (p252)

Avignon
Discover the Popes'
legacy (p226)

Aix-en-Provence
Visit Cézanne's former
studios (p184)

Arles
See Van Gogh's home and
Roman monuments (p204)

Les Alpilles
Walk through the hills that
inspired Van Gogh (p193)

The Camargue
Spot flamingos on a
Provençal safari (p197)

Marseille
Feast on bouillabaisse in this
vibrant harbour city (p155)

Les Calanques
Hike past stunning cliffs
and secret coves (p177)

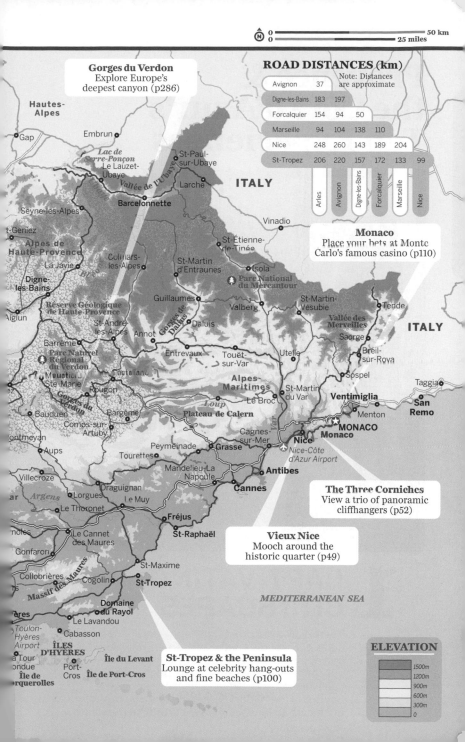

Gorges du Verdon
Explore Europe's deepest canyon (p286)

ROAD DISTANCES (km)
Note: Distances are approximate

	Arles	Avignon	Digne-les-Bains	Forcalquier	Marseille	Nice
Avignon	37					
Digne-les-Bains	183	197				
Forcalquier	154	94	50			
Marseille	94	104	138	110		
Nice	248	260	143	189	204	
St-Tropez	206	220	157	172	133	99

Monaco
Place your bets at Monte Carlo's famous casino (p110)

ITALY

ITALY

The Three Corniches
View a trio of panoramic cliffhangers (p52)

Vieux Nice
Mooch around the historic quarter (p49)

St-Tropez & the Peninsula
Lounge at celebrity hang-outs and fine beaches (p100)

MEDITERRANEAN SEA

ELEVATION

1500m
1200m
900m
600m
300m
0

50 km
25 miles

Provence & the Côte d'Azur's Top Experiences

1 CAPTIVATING CITYSCAPES

There's always something happening in the buzzing cities of France's southeast corner. You'll find fascinating museums, neighbourhoods ripe for exploring, and appealing dining and drinking options. Whatever your weakness — art, architecture, live music, cafes, boutiques, wine bars — you can find the best of the best on the urban lanes of Provence and the Côte d'Azur.

Above: Vieux Nice (p49)

Marseille

One of France's most ethnically diverse cities, Marseille crackles with life and atmosphere. The heart of town is the beautiful Vieux Port, the old harbour, which is lined with open-air seafood restaurants; a perfect spot for a meal with a side of people-watching. p155

Right: Vieux Port

Vieux Nice

The maze of Nice's old town is the most joyous part of this exquisite city. There's much to experience: browsing the morning market stalls along cours Saleya, afternoon wanders along boutique-lined alleyways, and evening all-ages merriment at bars, pubs and restaurants. p49

Monaco

With its skyscrapers, boutiques and yacht-packed harbour, high-rise Monaco has for decades been the favourite playground of Europe's elite. Don't miss the lavish belle-époque casino or the daily changing of the guard at the Palais Princier de Monaco. p110

Above: Casino de Monte Carlo (p113)

2 FLAVOURS OF PROVENCE

In Provence food is an all-consuming passion. The region's cuisine is guaranteed to be a highlight, whether that's savouring a simple bowl of soupe au pistou, trying candied fruits near Apt, tasting the season's first-press olive oil on a local farm, or indulging in a bowl of bouillabaisse on the seaside.

Above: Bouillabaisse (p38)

EDITA PLU/SHUTTERSTOCK ©

EVA-KATALIN/GETTYIMAGES ©

MARIA FUCHS/GETTY IMAGES ©

Seafood

Feast on bouillabaisse and
fruits de mer at Marseille,
home to world's best ver-
sions of its signature dish.
While you can find it at
harbourfront restaurants,
it's worth splashing out
for culinary masterpieces
at places like L'Epuisette.
p171

Niçois Cuisine

Nice's old town is awash
with places to try local
delicacies like *socca* (a
savoury, griddle-fried pancake made from chickpea
flour and olive oil), *petits
farcis* (stuffed vegetables),
pissaladière (onion tart
topped with black olives
and anchovies) and veg-
etable *beignets* (fritters).
p62

Top: *Salade niçoise*

Truffle Hunting

Plan an itinerary around
truffle season (mid-
November to mid-March).
You can look for fresh
truffles at weekly markets
in Vaison-la-Romaine and
Carpentras, and even go
truffle-hunting yourself
with a knowledgeable
guide. p245

Above: Truffles at Aups market (p149)

3 NATURAL WONDERS

Nature reveals its grandeur in countless ways in the south of France. You could spend many weeks exploring the coastline, hiking down to hidden coves, walking the craggy clifftops overlooking the Mediterranean and spying birdlife and thundering white stallions in its biologically rich wetlands. Inland offers even equally great rewards for travelers, with mountain peaks, dramatic river valleys and one massive canyon gouged out over millennia by the Verdon River.

Les Calanques

The coastline around Marseille is marked by high, rocky promontories rising like towers from the electric-blue waters of the Mediterranean. Its cliff-top trails, secret coves and powder-white beaches simply cry out for exploration. p177

Below: Calanque d' En-Vau (p178)

Gorges du Verdon

This massive canyon, 25km long and with cliffs that tower up to 900m high, is one of Provence's most impressive settings. There are so many ways to enjoy it: you can hike it, bike it, cruise along the cliffs, or thunder down the river on a raft or kayak. p286

Top left: Gorges du Verdon

The Camargue

Pan-flat and pocked with lagoons and salt-marshes, the Camargue is like a little world of its own. Head to this massive wetland for horse-riding along the trails, canoeing the reed-lined channels, or spotting the Camargue's famous flamingos. p197

Top right: Flamingos (p214)

4 MODERN MASTERPIECES

Many of the 20th century's great artists came to Provence for inspiration, and with so much bewitching scenery on show, it's not hard to see why. Some of the towns in southern France are intimately linked with the painters who put down roots: Van Gogh and Arles, Cézanne and Aix-en-Provence, Renoir and Cagnes-sur-Mer. And you can see some of the great works they produced in museums across the region.

Above: St-Paul de Vence (p74)

Atelier Cézanne

SYLVAIN SONNET/GETTY IMAGES ©

See the painstakingly preserved studio and home where the great master spent the final years of his life in Aix-en-Provence. It's all the more inspiring to arrive on foot from central Aix. p190

Below: Interior, Atelier Cézanne

TRABANTOS/SHUTTERSTOCK ©

ARTAZUM/SHUTTERSTOCK © BUILDING: © VILLE DE NICE

#JEVVICTOR/SHUTTERSTOCK ©

St-Paul de Vence

The small hilltop village has become an epicenter of the arts, thanks to the renowned painters who passed through. Highlights include the world-class collection of 20th-century artists at the Fondation Maeght, and the home and studio of Renoir. p74

Left: Musée Renoir (p74)

Nice

Allow a few days to take in the artistic trove, including the Matisse and Chagall museums. There's also the Musée d'Art Moderne et d'Art Contemporain, which pays tribute to home-grown neorealists such as Yves Klein, Niki de Saint Phalle and Arman. p49

Above: Musée d'Art Moderne et d'Art Contemporain (p54)

5 DRAMATIC DRIVES

Provence and the Côte d'Azur are made for explorers. One of the joys of travelling here is touring the back roads and soaking up the stunning variety of landscapes: fields of lavender, ancient olive groves, clifftop roads, maquis-cloaked hills and even snow-tipped mountains. It's home to France's deepest canyon, oldest road and some striking mountain passes — not to mention the cliff-backed Mediterranean. Take your time. Getting there is half the fun.

Route des Crêtes

Sweeping panoramas of the Calanques' mineral beauty unfold between Cassis and La Ciotat on a fabulous 16km drive. p286

Below: Cassis (p179), Route des Crêtes

LONGJON/SHUTTERSTOCK ©

Grande Corniche

Follow in the footsteps of Cary Grant and Grace Kelly on this famous clifftop coastal road. The views are spectacular at every turn as you wind your way from Nice to Monaco. p52

Above: Cap Ferrat peninsula view

Col de Restefond la Bonette

Crawl up and over one of the highest road passes in Europe at 2715m. The sky-high views through the French Alps is also a favourite of cyclists. p297

Right: Col de Restefond la Bonette

6 OUTDOOR ACTIVITIES

ALESSANDRO CRISTIANO/SHUTTERSTOCK ©

Home to soaring peaks, rugged coastline and meandering rivers, Provence and the Côte d'Azur offer tantalising options when it comes to outdoor adventures. You'll find myriad walking trails, cycling on backcountry roads, kayaking the turquoise seas near Marseille and even skiing in Haute-Provence. There's also great wildlife-watching, including flamingo-spotting in the Camargue.

Kayaking

Paddling your way along the maze of channels in the Camargue with Kayak Vert Camargue. You can make a 12km or 16km descent along the Petit Rhône, or hire a canoe or kayak for a more leisurely paddle. p211

Cycling

Tackle the trails around Provence's highest mountain, Mont Ventoux. You can even get a lift to the top and fire downhill on a mountain bike. p249

Hiking

Opportunities abound in Haute-Provence, especially around the Vallée de la Vésubie. There you'll find over a dozen marked trails coursing through the mountains. p282

Above: Parc National du Mercantour (p292)

7 HISTORICAL TREASURES

Two thousand years ago Provence was part of Roman Gaul, and the Romans left behind a fabulous legacy of monuments, structures and buildings. The area is littered with Roman remains, including amphitheatres, many bridges, and even whole towns near St-Rémy de Provence and Vaison-la-Romaine. Factor in a collection of prehistoric sites, medieval abbeys, elegant churches and art deco buildings, and Provence begins to feel like a living history book.

Les Arènes

Built in the first century AD, Arles' grand amphitheatre once held 21,000 spectators who packed in to watch gladiator battles and savage fights involving wild animals. p204

Top: Les Arènes

Papal Provence

For a time Avignon, not Rome, was the centre of Christendom – a legacy that lives on at the magnificent Palais des Papes, the largest Gothic palace ever constructed. p226

Above: Palais des Papes (p227)

Prehistoric Carvings

Bronze Age artists left their mark carved into the rock walls of the Vallée des Merveilles over 3500 years ago. p300

Above: Vallée des Merveilles carvings

8 DRINK OF THE GODS

JAG_CZ/GETTY IMAGES ©

Châteauneuf-du-Pape

Ocnophiles could spend many days (a lifetime?) tasting their way through the celebrated vineyards blanketing the Rhone Valley. Start off at the Caves du Verger des Papes. p238

Left: Vines, Châteauneuf-du-Pape

VIEW PICTURES/GETTY IMAGES ©

Château la Coste

The vine-clad slopes and forests of this Provençal estate are graced by harmonious examples of art and architecture, including work by Matisse. You can also taste delectable wines here. p185

Left: Art gallery by architect Tadao Ando, Château la Coste

La Part des Anges

Sip your way through some of France's finest organic and biodynamic wines at this delightful shop and wine bar in Nice. p62

Viticulture in southern France is an ancient art and tradition that bears its own unique trademark. The French thirst for wine goes back to Roman times, and *dégustation* (tasting) has been an essential part of French wine culture ever since. Vineyards carpet the landscape of Provence, with tasting opportunities galore, and you can join locals in the sacred *l'apero* tradition of pre-dinner drinking.

9 HILLTOP VILLAGES

Provence's *villages perchées* are a testament to the skill of medieval builders – and a sight to behold. For a laid-back getaway, you can forego city life altogether and make your base in tiny settlements. There you can immerse yourself in Provençal village life, exploring the shops and galleries, cafes and restaurants spread along the cobblestone lanes. You'll also enjoy fabulous views over the countryside from these lofty, once-strategic locales.

Les Baux-de-Provence

Sitting atop a limestone spur are the dramatic ruins of the 10th-century Château des Baux, providing a fabled vantage point over the car-free village and the rugged countryside beyond. p196

Below: Street scene, Les Baux-de-Provence

IVANFIRST/SHUTTERSTOCK ©

Èze

Spellbinding views of the Mediterranean attract throngs of visitors and yet Èze remains magical. It's worth making the trip just for the scenic drive from the coast. p68

Above: View of Èze

Bonnieux

With roots dating back nearly 2000 years, this striking village enjoys sweeping views from its soaring perch above the valley floor. It's a pure delight to wander, especially on market day (Friday). p274

Right: Church, Bonnieux

10 BOUNTIFUL MARKETS

AURÉLIEN LAFORET/SHUTTERSTOCK ©

Stalls groaning with fruit and vegetables, trays of cheese and *saucisson* (dry cured sausage) to sample, vendors loudly plying their wares – markets are an essential element of Provençal life. Practically every village has at least one weekly market, packed with locals shopping and gossiping, and with dozens of purveyors selling everything from locally farmed produce to spices, soaps and handmade crafts. It's worth planning your itinerary around market days.

Grand Marché d'Apt

Edible temptations come in many forms at this legendary Luberon market, which has been going strong since the Middle Ages. The action happens every Saturday morning. p272

Marché du Vendredi

Fridays are the best time to roll through the Vaucluse, as that's when you sure to score some of the world's best produce at the sprawling market of Carpentras. p254

Marché d'Aix-en-Provence

Every day is market day in lovely Aix — a clear indication of the food-minded mentality of this Provençal gem. Tuesdays, Thursdays and Saturdays are best, as various markets take over town. p189

Above: Food market, Aix-en-Provence

Need to Know

For more information, see Survival Guide (p321)

Currency
euro (€)

Language
French

Visas
Generally not required for stays of up to 90 days (or at all for EU nationals); some nationalities will require a Schengen visa.

Money
The euro (€) is the only legal tender in France and Monaco. ATMs are widely available, and most hotels and restaurants take credit cards.

Mobile Phones
Most modern smartphones will be able to pick up a signal from one of France's main carriers: Bouygues (www.bouyguestelecom.fr), Orange (www.orange.fr) and SFR (www.sfr.com).

Time
France uses Central European Time, one hour ahead of GMT/UTC.

When to Go

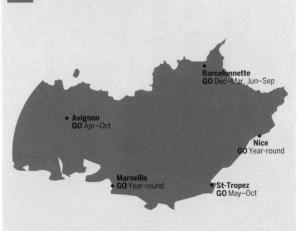

Warm to hot summers, mild winters

Barcelonnette
GO Dec–Mar, Jun–Sep

Avignon
GO Apr–Oct

Nice
GO Year-round

Marseille
GO Year-round

St-Tropez
GO May–Oct

High Season
(Jul & Aug)

➡ Hotels are full, often booked months in advance and at their priciest.

➡ It is hot: 35°C is fairly common at lunch time.

➡ A busy festival calendar, especially in July.

Shoulder Season (Apr–Jun, Sep & Oct)

➡ The best time of year to travel, with good weather and no school-holiday crowds.

➡ Spring blooms and autumn colours.

➡ Prices drop in many areas compared to the peak months of July and August.

Low Season
(Nov–Mar)

➡ Very quiet, especially in rural areas and coastal resorts, where many hotels close.

➡ Alpine resorts fill up with skiers and snowboarders.

➡ Attractions open shorter hours.

➡ Prices are at their lowest: 20% to 30% off summer rates.

Useful Websites

Provence–Alpes–Côte d'Azur Tourisme (www.decouverte-paca.fr) A wealth of info on what to do, where to go, where to stay and much more.

Côte d'Azur Tourisme (www.cotedazur-tourisme.com) General information on the Riviera.

Visit Provence (www.visitprovence.com) Covers Marseille, Arles and the Camargue.

Tourisme Alpes Haute-Provence (www.tourism-alps-provence.com) Guide to the mountains.

Provence Verte (www.la-provence-verte.net) Website of a cooperative of tourist offices in the Haut Var.

Lonely Planet (www.lonelyplanet.com/france) Sights, activities, accommodation and much more.

Important Numbers

France country code	🖉33
International dialling code	🖉00
Europe-wide emergency	🖉112
Ambulance (SAMU)	🖉15
Police	🖉17

Exchange Rates

Australia	A$1	€0.63
Canada	C$1	€0.64
Japan	¥100	€0.75
New Zealand	NZ$1	€0.59
UK	£1	€1.15
US	US$1	€0.81

For current exchange rates, see www.xe.com.

Daily Costs

Budget: Less than €120

➡ Dorm bed: €20–30

➡ Double room in a budget hotel: €60–90

➡ Bistro lunch €10–15

➡ Bus and train tickets €5–10

Midrange: €120–220

➡ Double room in a hotel: €90–190

➡ Set menus in restaurants: €20–40

➡ Car hire €25 per day

Top end: More than €220

➡ Double room in luxury hotel: more than €190

➡ À la carte meal: €50–100

➡ Luxury car hire: €40–50 per day

Opening Hours

Most businesses, sights and museums close over lunch between noon and 2pm. In rural Provence, many places open only from Pâques (Easter) to Toussaint (1 November). Standard hours are as follows:

Banks 9am–noon and 2pm–5pm Monday to Friday

Cafes 8am–11pm Monday to Saturday

Post offices 8.30am–5pm Monday to Friday, 8am–noon Saturday

Restaurants Lunch noon–2.30pm, dinner 7pm–11pm

Shops 10am–noon and 2pm–6.30pm Monday or Tuesday to Saturday

Supermarkets 8.30am–7pm Monday to Saturday, 8.30am–12.30pm Sunday

Arriving in Provence & the Côte d'Azur

Aéroport Nice Côte d'Azur (Nice) Buses run to the Nice city centre every 20 minutes, and to Cannes, Antibes, Monaco and Menton every 30 minutes. Budget €25 to €30 for a taxi to Nice.

Aéroport Marseille Provence (Marseille) Buses run to Marseille and Aix-en-Provence every 20 minutes. Direct trains run to various destinations, including Marseille, Arles and Avignon. Allow €50 for a taxi to Marseille.

Getting Around

Public transport in Provence is generally good value and reasonably reliable. The excellent French-language website **PACA Mobilité** (www.pacamobilite.fr) offers handy planning tools for getting around by public transport in the PACA region.

Car Allows maximum freedom, especially in rural areas. Cars can be hired in most towns and cities. Driving is on the right, but automatic transmissions are rare. *Autoroutes* (motorways) are fast, but many charge tolls. Beware the *priorité à droite* rule, which means you have to give way to vehicles entering on the right.

Train France's state-owned trains are fast, efficient and great value. High-speed TGVs connect major cities; smaller towns are served by slower TER trains, sometimes supplemented by buses. Remember to time-stamp your ticket before boarding.

Bus Useful for remote villages, but timetables revolve around school-term times; fewer services run on weekends and school holidays.

For much more on **getting around**, see p331

Accommodation

Provence–Côte d'Azur has a huge and varied range of accommodation, from cosy rural cottages to swish pamper pads. It's wise to book well ahead everywhere in summer (online is easiest); prices are at their highest in July and August.

Where to Stay

Provence and the Côte d'Azur region has perhaps the most varied range of accommodation anywhere in France, spanning the spectrum from super-luxury hotels with dreamy views of the coast to cosy little cottages nestled among vineyards and lavender fields. There's somewhere to suit all tastes and budgets – unfortunately, the region's charms are no secret, and in summer, prices skyrocket and rooms are scarce.

Hotels

Hotels in France are rated from one to five stars: one and two stars are basic, while four and five stars offer luxury services such as pools, room service and a concierge. Elevators *(ascenseurs)* are generally only found in bigger hotels. Triples and quads are widely available, and good for families. Breakfast is nearly always extra, costing anything from €7 to €30 per person. Wi-fi (pronounced wee-fee) is available nearly everywhere, and generally provided for free.

Note that, in France, 'ground floor' *(rez de chaussée)* refers to the floor at street level; the '1st floor' is the floor above that.

Logis de France (www.logishotels.com) An umbrella organisation for small, independent hotels, often with a decent restaurant.

iGuide (www.iguide-hotels.com) Charming, quirky hotels and B&Bs.

Relais & Châteaux (www.relaischateaux.com) Luxury and historic hotels.

Chambres d'Hôte (B&Bs)

Chambres d'hôtes are the French version of a B&B. Many are on farms, wineries and historic properties, and the top places now rival hotels in terms of luxury and design. Breakfast is included in the price, and many places serve dinner (known as *table d'hôte*).

Fleurs de Soleil (www.fleursdesoleil.fr) Quality *chambres d'hôte*.

Bienvenue à la Ferme (www.bienvenue-a-la-ferme.com) Farmstays.

Hostels

Hostels in France vary in standard from hip to threadbare. You don't have to be young to stay in one, although rates are cheaper if you're under 26.

Sheets are provided, but sleeping bags are not allowed. In big cities, hostels are sometimes quite a long way from the city centre. Most hostels have a kitchen for guests' use.

Two other types of hostels are *gîtes d'étape* (basic lodges for hikers) and *gîtes de refuge* (high mountain huts).

The following are France's two official organisations.

Fédération Unie des Auberges de Jeunesse (www.fuaj.org)

Ligue Française pour les Auberges de la Jeunesse (www.auberges-de-jeunesse.com)

Camping

The French are big on camping, but they favour sites that are more like holiday parks, with swimming pool, shop, playground for the kids and (most importantly) a decent

CELLO7/SHUTTERSTOCK ©

Hostel, Vence (p75)

restaurant. Most cities and large towns have a *camping municipal* (municipal campsite) – basic, but good for cutting costs.

Most campgrounds only open between April and October. Standard rates quoted are usually for two adults with a tent and car. Electric hook-ups are available at many sites; some also have chalets or bungalows for hire. *Camping sauvage* (wild camping) is illegal.

Camping en France (www.camping.fr) Pan-France campsite listings.

HPA Guide (http://camping.hpaguide.com) Good family-friendly campsite guide.

Cabanes de France (http://www.cabanes-de-france.com) Treehouses for wannabe Tarzans.

Reservations

Advance reservations are essential in July and August. Booking online is easiest.

Out of season, many hotels and B&Bs close for a few weeks for their *congé annuel* (annual closure). From Easter onwards, things get busier, making advance booking essential. In July and August don't even contemplate the coast unless you have a reservation or are prepared to pay a fortune for the few rooms still available.

Tourist offices can invariably tell you where rooms are available; some run accommodation-reservation services.

PRICES

The following price ranges apply to a standard double room with private bathroom, breakfast not included.

➡ € less than €90

➡ €€ €90–190

➡ €€€ more than €190

First Time Provence & the Côte d'Azur

For more information, see Survival Guide (p321)

Checklist

➡ Check passport validity and visa requirements

➡ Book hotels, car-hire and big-name restaurants

➡ Organise travel insurance

➡ Check airline baggage restrictions and customs regulations

➡ Get a chip-and-PIN credit card (magnetic strips do not work)

➡ Inform your credit-card company that you will be travelling abroad

What to Pack

➡ Passport and driving licence

➡ Adaptor plug – France uses two-pin EU plugs

➡ Sunglasses, hat and sunscreen

➡ Towel, swimsuit and sandals for the beach

➡ Sturdy shoes for hiking and walking

➡ Corkscrew with bottle opener

➡ Smart clothes for eating out

➡ French phrasebook

➡ An adventurous appetite

Top Tips for Your Trip

➡ For atmosphere, you can't beat a morning market: nearly every town and village has one at least once a week.

➡ If you're driving, the autoroutes (motorways) are fast, but regional roads (designated D and N on maps) generally have better scenery.

➡ Most shops, businesses and museums close for lunch (between noon and 2pm). Do as the locals do and head for the nearest restaurant.

➡ Don't underestimate the heat. Temperatures of 35°C are routine in summer. Schedule sightseeing for early morning or late afternoon.

➡ Overseas cards occasionally don't work in French chip-and-PIN readers (automated gas stations are a frequent culprit). Bring a spare.

What to Wear

➡ Outside Monaco, Cannes and St-Tropez, fashion is pretty relaxed. Dress up rather than down for dinner (avoid jeans, shorts or trainers).

➡ Sturdy shoes are essential for walking, and a pack-down raincoat comes in handy.

➡ Going topless is routine on Côte d'Azur beaches, but it's a no-no anywhere else. Save bare chests and bikinis for the beach.

Sleeping

Provence–Côte d'Azur has a huge and varied range of accommodation, from cosy rural cottages to swish pamper pads. It's wise to book well ahead everywhere in summer (online is easiest); prices are at their highest in July and August.

Hotels Range from basic one-star inns right up to five-star luxury hotels. Breakfast is generally not included; many older buildings don't have lifts.

Chambres d'hôtes The French version of a B&B; in terms of luxury, can range from rustic to regal. Breakfast is nearly always included.

Mas The Provençal word for farmhouse. These properties tend to be rural and secluded, but standards vary widely.

Camping Campsites tend to be more like holiday parks, with pools, playgrounds, activities etc. Wild camping (including on the beach) is illegal.

Gîtes Simple hostels geared towards walkers.

Cutting Costs

Eat cheap Lunchtime *formules* (two courses) and *menus* (three courses) are cheaper than dinner menus. Self-catering and shopping at the market keep costs down. At restaurants, order *une carafe d'eau* (a jug of water) rather than bottled water.

Family travel Many hotels have triple, quad and family rooms. Buy family tickets and travel passes (usually for two adults and two kids).

Free sites Though most sights charge admission for visitors over 12, public parks, green spaces, coastline and national parks are free.

Bargaining

With the exception of haggling at flea markets, bargaining is not the norm in France.

Tipping

By law, restaurants and cafes are *service compris* (15% service included), thus there's no need to leave a *pourboire* (tip). If satisfied with the service, leave a euro or two on the table.

Bar Round to nearest euro

Hotel housekeepers €1 to €1.50 per day

Porters €1 to €1.50 per bag

Restaurants Generally 2% to 5%

Taxis 10% to 15%

Toilet attendant €0.20 to €0.50

Tour guide €1 to €2 per person

Language

It's a good idea to learn some useful phrases before you go; the French will appreciate the effort. Most people can speak at least a few words of English, but fluency is rare in rural areas.

 What are the opening hours?
Quelles sont les heures d'ouverture?
kel son lay zer doo·vair·tewr

French business hours are governed by a maze of regulations, so it's a good idea to check before you make plans.

 I'd like the set menu, please.
Je voudrais le menu, s'il vous plaît.
zher voo·dray ler mer·new seel voo play

The best-value dining in France is the two- or three-course meal at a fixed price. Most restaurants have one on the chalkboard.

 Which wine would you recommend?
Quel vin vous conseillez?
kel vun voo kon·say·yay

Who better to ask for advice on wine than the French?

 Can I address you with 'tu'?
Est-ce que je peux vous tutoyer?
es ker zher per voo tew·twa·yay

Before you start addressing someone with the informal 'you' form, it's polite to ask permission first.

 Do you have plans for tonight/tomorrow?
Vous avez prévu quelque chose ce soir/demain?
voo za·vay pray·vew kel·ker shoz ser swar/der·mun

To arrange to meet up without sounding pushy, ask friends if they're available rather than inviting them directly.

Etiquette

Greetings When entering or leaving a shop, it's polite to say *bonjour* and *au revoir*. When greeting friends, it's usual to give a kiss on both cheeks and ask *Comment ça va?* (How are you?)

Conversation Use *vous* (you) when speaking to people you don't know well, or who are older than you; use *tu* (also you) with friends, family and children.

Asking for help Say *excusez-moi* (excuse me) to attract attention; say *pardon* (sorry) to apologise.

Religious buildings Dress modestly and be respectful when visiting.

Eating & drinking When dining in a French home, wait for your host to start first. Always clear the plate. When you're finished, line up your fork and knife on top of your plate towards the right.

Waiters Never, ever call waiters *garçon* – use *Monsieur* (Mr), *Mademoiselle* (Miss) or *Madame* (Mrs), or attract their attention by saying *s'il vous plaît* (please).

Month by Month

January

Even in winter, Provence and the Côte d'Azur has its charms. The Provençal Alps are carpeted in snow, while crisp winter days flatter the Riviera. However, many hotels and attractions close, making travel harder.

✕ Truffles

Provence's black diamond is picked from November to February (restaurants make the most of it, and so should you!), but the season culminates in January with the **Messe de la Truffe** in Richerenches and the Journée de la Truffe in Aups (p150).

🏃 Skiing

Provence and the Côte d'Azur's ski resorts are excellent: small, family-friendly, dotted with trees, sunny and easily accessible by public transport (just €2 return from Nice).

☆ Festival International du Cirque de Monte-Carlo

The world's best circus artists compete every year for the 'Golden Clown' Award in Monte Carlo (www.montecarlofestival. mc). Winners then put on a week of performances.

February

February can be divine on the Riviera: the days are bright, the sky is blue and it's often mild. French school kids get two weeks off to tear down the *pistes*.

🎭 Carnaval de Nice

Both the decorated floats and the crowds are gigantic at this flamboyant Mardi Gras street parade (www. nicecarnaval.com) in Nice, celebrated since 1293. Don't miss the legendary flower battles.

✕ Fête du Citron

Monumental sculptures and floats crafted from a zillion and one lemons make the two-week Fête du Citron (www.feteducitron. com) in Menton the French Riviera's most exotic (and eccentric!) fest.

April

April weather in Provence is full of surprises. Easter holidays can be spent on the beach as much as on the slopes. Many towns and villages hold ancestral religious celebrations strong on folklore and colour.

🎭 Feria Pascale

Held each year over Easter in Arles to open the bull-fighting season (www. feriaarles.com), the *féria* is four days of exuberant dancing, music, concerts and bullfighting.

May

The sea remains cold and the mistral (northern wind) can be howling in Provence. May is also bank-holiday-tastic in France, with no fewer than four of them, so plan well in advance for reservations.

◉ Flowers

Provence's gardens look lush at this time of year. Visit a flower farm (p79) or stroll in the sumptuous gardens of Villa Ephrussi de Rothschild (p67).

🌠 Fête des Gardians

The traditional Camargue cowboy and his bullish and equestrian skills are the focus of this vibrant festival on 1 May in Arles.

☆ Cannes Film Festival

The world's premier film event (www.festival-cannes.org) sees cinematic luminaries star on La Croisette in Cannes.

☆ Monaco Grand Prix

Formula One's most anticipated race, the Monaco Grand Prix (www.acm.mc) tears around the tiny municipality in a haze of glamour, Champagne, VIPs and after-parties.

July

July is Provence at its most picturesque: cicadas fill the air with incessant song, and lavender fields stretch in all their purple glory; it's hot, and to cool off you have a choice between pool, sea and rosé.

☆ Festival d'Avignon

Theatre in every guise takes to the stage at this renowned festival (www.festival-avignon.com) in Avignon; the fringe event (called Off) parallels the official fest.

☆ Chorégies

France's oldest festival (www.choregies.fr) stages operas at the incredible Roman theatre in Orange, an unforgettable night if you can get tickets.

☆ Jazz on the Riviera

The Riviera swings to the music of two great jazz festivals: Jazz à Juan in Antibes-Juan-les-Pins (www.jazzajuan.com) and the Nice Jazz Festival (www.nicejazzfestival.fr). Be sure to book tickets well in advance.

☆ Festival d'Aix-en-Provence

A month of world-class opera, classical music and ballet is what this prestigious festival (www.festival-aix.com) offers.

August

This is the busiest time to come to Provence, with every hotel fully booked, but it's also the liveliest, with events galore, night markets and an infectious party atmosphere.

🌠 Fireworks

Cannes and Monaco both hold free international fireworks festivals in July and August when pyrotechnicians from around the world compete for the 'ooohs' and 'aaahs' of the crowd.

☆ Dance Music in Cannes

Cannes is *the* party spot in August. Le Palais nightclub opens for 50 nights of dancing under the stars, and two great dance-music festivals set up shop: Festival Pantiero (www.festivalpantiero.com) and Les Plages Électroniques (www.plages-electroniques.com).

October

The days may be shortening, but in the glow of the autumn sun they're a delight. You can still swim on warm days, and what's more, you're likely to have the beach to yourself.

✕ Chestnuts

Head to Collobrières in the Massif des Maures to pick, feast on and learn about chestnuts. The forest is at its loveliest for long walks too. Harvest celebrations culminate in the Fête de la Châtaigne (p140).

🌠 La Transhumance

Sheep and their shepherds descend from their summer pastures and crowd the roads of Haute-Provence, from the Verdon to Col d'Allos. The same happens in reverse in June.

December

Families celebrate Christmas with midnight Mass, Provençal chants, 13 desserts (yes) and nativity scenes full of *santons* (terracotta figurines). Outside of Christmas and New Year's Eve parties, however, it is a quiet month.

Itineraries

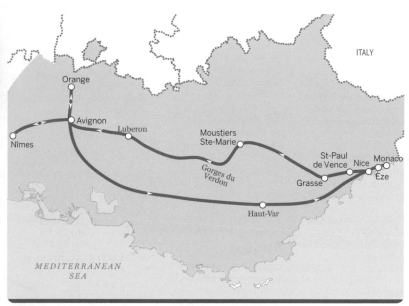

 Essential Provence–Côte d'Azur

All the classics in one easy itinerary: along the coast, into the hills and back again, via gorges, villages, vineyards, Roman ruins and lavender fields.

Fly to **Nice**. On day two, mooch around Vieux Nice and amble along the Promenade des Anglais. On day three, catch a bus to stunning **Èze** to feast on views; head to **Monaco** for lunch and enjoy the rest of the day in the principality. Catch a train back to Nice. On day four, pick up a rental car and drive to the medieval wonder of **St-Paul de Vence** and its art galleries. On day five, drive to **Moustiers Ste-Marie** along the scenic N85, stopping in **Grasse** on the way for an insight into the town's perfume industry. Spend the following day in **Gorges du Verdon**.

Explore the villages of the **Luberon** on days seven and eight, and on day nine head to **Avignon**. Enjoy the city for a day, and take a day trip to **Orange** or **Nîmes** on day 11. On days 12 and 13, head to the **Haut-Var** for hilltop villages and vineyards, before returning to Nice.

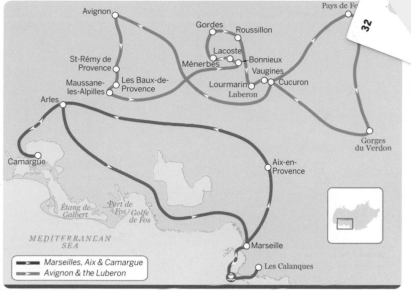

Marseilles, Aix & Camargue

Avignon & the Luberon

Marseille, Aix & the Camargue
1 WEEK

Mix city with countryside, starting in bustling Marseille and following with clifftop hiking, art appreciation, Roman history and flamingo spotting.

Spend your first day exploring **Marseille**: the Vieux Port, the historic Le Panier quarter and the art scene. Go to cours Julien for a night out. On day two, take a boat trip to **Les Calanques** or visit Château d'If before heading up to Basilique Notre Dame de la Garde for panoramic views of the city and the sea. Dine in the picturesque Vallon des Auffes. On day three, head to **Aix-en-Provence** to visit Cézanne's studio, his family house and the Bibemus quarries where he painted. Treat yourself at one of Aix's fine restaurants.

On day four, head to **Arles** and discover the places that inspired Van Gogh. Book a table at one of the city's Michelin-starred establishments. On day five, immerse yourself in the town's fine Roman heritage – the amphitheatre, theatre, baths and Musée Départemental Arles Antique. Take a day trip to **Camargue** on day six: hire bikes, and don't forget your binoculars for birdwatching. Head back to Marseille. This entire itinerary can be done by public transport.

Avignon & the Luberon
1 WEEK

This trip captures the essence of Provence, starting in bustling Avignon and ending in the mighty Gorges du Verdon, with stops at some of the area's dreamiest villages and most photogenic sights en route.

Spend day one in **Avignon**, exploring the old town and the Palais des Papes. On day two, drive down to **St-Rémy-de-Provence** in Les Alpilles. Explore the town's stupendous Roman site Glanum and visit the asylum where Van Gogh spent the last – but most productive – year of his short life. On day three, take a day trip to **Les Baux-de-Provence**: visit the ruined castle and go olive-oil tasting around **Maussane-les-Alpilles** in the afternoon.

On day four, drive to the **Luberon** and explore a trio of lovely villages: **Bonnieux**, **Lacoste** and **Ménerbes**. On day five, visit **Gordes** and its Abbaye Notre-Dame de Sénanque and the ochre-coloured village of **Roussillon**. On day six, pack a picnic and head to the gorges, forests and lavender fields around **Lourmarin**, **Vaugines** and **Cucuron**. On day seven, drive back to Avignon or carry on to **Pays de Forcalquier** and the **Gorges du Verdon** for another three days.

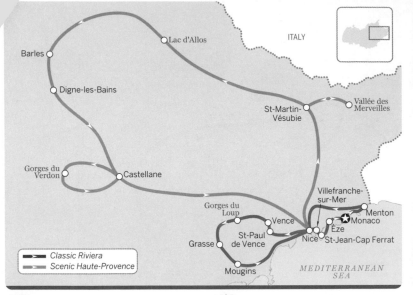

10 DAYS Scenic Haute-Provence

It's time to tear yourself away from the coast and explore the mighty, majestic Alps. Amazingly, just an hour's drive north of Nice, you'll find yourself surrounded by mountain scenery – perfect for hiking, biking and wildlife spotting.

Start in **Nice** – enjoy a day of urban delight in Vieux Nice before hitting the road on day two. Drive to **St-Martin-Vésubie** and watch semi-wild wolves in the Alpha wildlife reserve. On day three, organise a guided hike to see the amazing ancient rock art of the **Vallée des Merveilles**, then head west to explore the many hiking trails around **Lac d'Allos** on days four and five.

On day six, drive to **Digne-les-Bains**, stopping in **Barles** along the way for fossil hunting in the Réserve Géologique de Haute-Provence. Organise a lavender walk on day seven, and on day eight drive down to **Castellane**, and take a scenic tour of the **Gorges du Verdon**. Explore the canyon in a different way on day nine: go rafting, canyoning or just trekking. On day 10, drive back to Nice or carry on along the Riviera.

10 DAYS Classic Riviera

This tour captures all the Côte d'Azur's unmissable sights. You can do the first part by bus and train, but for the full Riviera experience, a car is preferable – and a convertible would be better still.

Dedicate your first couple of days to the belle of the Côte d'Azur: **Nice**. Stroll in Vieux Nice and browse the market stalls of cours Saleya; visit Cimiez' wonderful Musée National Marc Chagall and Musée Matisse; and party till dawn in Vieux Nice's bars.

On day three, take a day trip along the Corniche Inférieure, stopping at **Villefranche-sur-Mer** and **St-Jean-Cap-Ferrat**. On day four, head to hilltop **Èze** for sensational views of the Med; carry on to **Monaco** for the rest of the day. Spend the following day in **Menton**.

On day six, rent a car and head for the hills: stop in **St-Paul de Vence** and **Vence**, and spend day seven motoring around the beautiful **Gorges du Loup**. On day eight, visit **Grasse** and its museums and perfumeries; leave your last day for the pretty village of **Mougins**. Drive back to Nice on day 10, continue in Haute-Provence or head west along the coast.

Plan Your Trip
Activities

With its varied landscapes – alpine mountains and cavernous gorges, flamingo-pink wetlands, and a world-famous coastline of sparkling white sand and turquoise water – Provence has an outdoor activity to match every mood, moment and energy level.

Land
Walking

Provence is a great place to strap on your boots, especially once you escape the searing heat of the coast and head up into the mountains of Provence and the Parc National du Mercantour. The region is crossed by a number of long-distance GR *(Grande Randonnée)* trails, and a whole host of *sentiers balisés* (marked paths).

The little town of St-Martin-Vésubie in the Vallée de la Vésubie is a popular hub for hikers in the Mercantour, with regular guided walks into the remote Vallée des Merveilles, famous for its Bronze Age rock carvings. Neighbouring valleys also have hundreds of trails to explore; tourist offices stock maps, guidebooks and leaflets. This is the best region for summer walking – the altitude means that temperatures remain cooler than at the coast, although snowfall makes hiking here impractical between October and March.

Further south, trails run along the clifftops and coves of the Parc National des Calanques, with glittering views of the Mediterranean accompanying every step. It's best saved for spring or autumn, as hiking in the summer heat here is more punishment than pleasure.

France's national map publisher, IGN, publishes the best maps for walkers, with all trails and topographical features clearly marked.

Between 1 July and 15 September forested areas are closed due to the high risk

Top Outdoor Sites

Parc National du Mercantour (p292)
The mountains and valleys of this national park provide some of southern France's most spectacular hiking.

Luberon Valley (p260)
From rural roads to backcountry trails, Provence seems to be made for cycling – and the lovely Luberon is a great place to start.

Rafting on the Verdon (p286)
Braving the bucking Gorges du Verdon rapids aboard a raft is a white-knuckle experience.

Domaine du Rayol (p138)
Get acquainted with the Côte d'Azur's submarine residents at this underwater snorkelling park.

Parc National des Calanques (p177)
Paddle a sea kayak beneath the cliffs of the Calanques, and access some of the Côte d'Azur's most beautiful – and quietest – coves.

Mont Ventoux (p248)
Provence's highest peak often has skiable snow until April.

DAY WALKS

Île Ste-Marguerite (p95) Picnic in cool pine forests and on deserted shores on this Cannois island.

Sentier du Littoral (p96) Walk the seashore from St-Raphaël to Agay; lunch at **Villa Matuzia** (☎04 94 82 79 95; www.matuzia.com; 15 bd Ste Guitte, Agay; mains €22, menus €28-49; ⊙noon-2pm Tue & Thu-Sun, 7.30-9.30pm Tue-Sat; ✿☎).

Gorges d'Oppedette (p273) Explore this little-known canyon system near Rustrel.

Mourre Nègre Climb up to the Luberon's highest viewpoint for stunning scenery.

Calanque de Morgiou (p178) Treat yourself to a *garrigue*-scented stroll from Marseille to one of these rocky little coves.

Gigaro (p109) Lap up the Sentier du Littoral's breathtaking coastal views around Cap Lardier, Cap Taillat and L'Escalet, near St-Tropez.

Colorado Provençal (p268) Hike through crimson gorges in Rustrel.

of forest fire. Always check with the local tourist office before setting off.

Take bottled water and snacks and wear good boots (even on a hot day). Don't rely on being able to get a mobile-phone signal, especially in the mountains.

Fédération Française de Randonnée Pédestre (www.ffrandonnee.fr) Has the most comprehensive walking guides; some are now available as ebooks.

Guides RandOxygène (https://randoxygene. departement06.fr/randoxygene-8938.html) Publishes three walking guides to the region, which are sold in local tourist offices; ebook versions can be downloaded from their website.

Escapado (www.escapado.fr) Publishes downloadable routes for road cyclists, mountain-bikers and walkers.

Rando Alpes Haute Provence (www.rando-alpes-haute-provence.fr) A great resource, with dozens of suggested routes.

Cycling & Mountain Biking

There's no shortage of sunshine, and let's face it – you're not going to get away without tackling a few hills. The best regions for cycling tend to be away from the busy coastal roads: the quiet country roads of the Luberon, the villages of the Var and the hills of Haute-Provence are all good areas to explore.

Road bikes (*vélo de route*) and mountain bikes (VTT, *vélo tout-terrain*) can be widely hired for around €15 a day including helmet and puncture-repair kit. Children's bikes (around €12 per day) and toddler seats (around €5 per day) are also

widely available. Some outlets deliver to your door.

Your first port of call for routes should, as always, be the local tourist office – it always has a range of leaflets and guides to give away, as well as suggestions on local bike shops and rental outfits.

Keen to make the best of their ski lifts and cable cars in summer, ski resorts have developed a brilliant mountain-biking infrastructure, whereby you and your bike are ferried up the mountain so that you can enjoy two hours of uninterrupted, thrilling descent.

Mont Ventoux is a key centre for downhillers and mountain-bikers.

Skiing & Snowboarding

The few ski resorts in Haute-Provence are refreshingly low-key. Slopes are best suited to beginner and intermediate skiers and costs are lower than in the Northern Alps.

Resorts include Pra Loup (1500m to 1600m), Valberg (1600m to 1700m), Foux d'Allos (1800m) and the concrete-block Isola 2000 (2450m).

The ski season runs from December to March/April (depending on the snow conditions). As always, buying a package is the cheapest way to ski and/or snowboard. Otherwise allow €25 to €30 for a daily lift pass, and about the same again for equipment rental.

Horse Riding

With its famous cowboys, creamy-white horses and expansive sandy beaches to gallop along, the Camargue is a wonderful, windswept spot to ride. Aspiring cowboys and cowgals can learn the ropes on week-long *stages de monte gardiane* (Camargue cowboy courses).

Dramatically different but equally inspiring are the donkey and horse treks through lyrical chestnut and cork oak forests in the Massif des Maures, set up by the **Conservatoire du Patrimoine du Freinet** (☑04 94 43 08 57; www.conservatoiredufreinet. org; Chapelle St-Jean, place de la Mairie, La Garde-Freinet; ☺9am-1pm & 2-5pm Mon-Sat Apr-Oct, Tue-Sat Nov-Mar). Donkey treks and horse rides are also offered around the Parc National du Mercantour.

Elsewhere in Provence, tourist offices have lists of stables and riding centres where you can saddle up.

Terre Equestre (www.terre-equestre. com) is a useful French-language listings site with details of horse-riding schools all over the region and further afield.

Wildlife Watching

Perhaps the easiest way to see some wildlife is to grab some flippers and a snorkel mask and go swimming – shoals of colourful fish can be spotted at practically any beach on the Côte d'Azur. For more exotic species, head for Monaco's excellent Musée Océanographique (p113).

The prime area for animal spotting is definitely the Parc National du Mercantour, where with a bit of luck and a good pair of binoculars, you might be able to spy anything from a mouflon (big-horn sheep) to a golden eagle soaring through the skies. There's also a wild wolf reserve to visit.

Ornithologists flock to see clouds of pink flamingos in the protected Camargue delta and between pink-hued salt pans on the Presqu'île de Giens near Hyères. The Gorges du Verdon is another great area thanks to its population of reintroduced griffin vultures, while sea-birds can be spied in the Parc Naturel Départemental de la Grande Corniche and the Parc National des Calanques (p177), both on the Côte d'Azur.

LPO PACA (☑04 94 12 79 52; http://paca. lpo.fr) organises guided birdwatching expeditions near Hyères.

Water
Sailing, Snorkelling & Sea Sports

With such a beautiful coastline, it's no surprise there is so much to do on the water. Note that there is often a minimum-age restriction for many watersports.

➡ In summer you'll find the usual fun rides of jet skiing, waterskiing and wakeboarding (€30 to €50) at a number of beaches along the Côte d'Azur.

➡ Hiring a kayak is the best way to explore the turquoise rocky coves of the Calanques near Marseille.

➡ Canoes are ideal for paddling along the rivers Gard and Sorgue.

EXTREME SPORTS

There are even more extreme ways to get your thrills and spills in Provence. *Parapente* (parasailing) is a particularly popular pastime in the high mountains; local guide schools offer initiation flights and longer courses.

In the Gorges du Verdon, canyoning (which involves scrambling over rocks and jumping into rivers) is popular too, along with a whole smorgasbord of weird and wonderful watersports: cano-raft, airboating, tubing and plenty more besides. You can also throw yourself off Europe's highest bungee-jump site here: the Pont de l'Artuby, a dizzying 182m above the Verdon river.

Rock-climbing is excellent thanks to the surfeit of sheer faces available in Provence: Les Alpilles, the Dentelles de Montmirail and the Buoux valley are just a few of the best-known areas.

If you fancy trying out a few of these sports, the flashy Vésubia (p298) activity centre in St-Martin-Vésubie is a great one-stop-shop, with fibreglass environments that simulate the experience of caving, rock-climbing, canyoning and so on.

WEATHER CHECK

Whatever activity you're planning on, check the latest weather forecast on **Météo France** (www.meteofrance. com), or ask at the tourist office. Even on a sunny day in midsummer, storms, heavy rainfall and mistral winds can appear out of nowhere – so it pays to be prepared.

Swimming

You couldn't come to the coast and not get wet – whether that means a quick paddle or a proper snorkelling session.

➡ The sea is warm enough for swimming without a wetsuit between June and October.

➡ Flippers, masks and goggles are widely available from sport and dive shops along the coast.

➡ Underwater nature trails and guided snorkelling tours are available at many beaches.

➡ Local dive clubs offer courses (€300 to €500) as well as single dives (€50) to seek out the many shipwrecks that lie at the bottom of the Med.

➡ The latest craze on the Côte d'Azur is stand-up paddleboarding, which involves standing on a surfboard and steering yourself around with a long paddle. Paddleboard providers are springing up on many beaches; budget on €10 for a half-hour, €15 to €18 per hour.

Canoeing, Kayaking & Rafting

For a white-knuckle ride, the Gorges du Verdon is famous for its foaming white-water rapids. Dozens of operators offer trips from their main base in Castellane (p289), along with related river activities such as floating and canyoning. Allow €35/60 for a half/full day.

For a more tranquil trip, try paddling beneath the arches of the Pont du Gard, or along the River Sorgue between the towns of L'Isle-sur-la-Sorgue and Fontaine de Vaucluse.

Air
Ballooning

Drifting across Provence's patchwork fields in a hot-air balloon is a seductive way to take in the captivating countryside. Balloon flights last one to 1½ hours (allow three to four hours in all for getting to and from the launch pad, inflating the balloon etc) and cost from €230 per person. Flights run year-round but are subject to weather forecasts.

Operators include **Montgolfière Vol-Terre** (☏06 03 54 10 92; www.montgolfiere -luberon.com) near Roussillon, with flights in the Avignon and Luberon areas; and **Les Montgolfières du Sud** (www.sud montgolfiere.com), west of Nîmes, whose balloons fabulously float above the Pont du Gard.

Plan Your Trip
Eat & Drink Like a Local

Whether it's feasting on freshly caught fish in Marseille or tucking into a rich country stew in Haute-Provence, this is one corner of France where food isn't just an important part of everyday life – it's often the main event.

Food Experiences
Meals of a Lifetime

Le Vivier (p257) Sophisticated but unpretentious dining in L'Isle-sur-la-Sorgue.

L'Arôme (p172) Seek out this little local Marseille gem for classic Provençal dishes.

Arazur (p85) A Michelin-trained chef works wonders in Vieil Antibes.

La Table de Ventabren (p192) A wonderfully creative restaurant near Aix-en-Provence.

À Côté (p209) Try renowned chef Jean-Luc Rabanel's food without the premium price-tag.

Le Champ des Lunes (☑04 13 98 00 00; www.domainedefontenille.com; lunch menu €35, dinner €42-108; ⊙noon-2pm & 7-9.30pm Wed-Sat, noon-2pm Sun) Stellar restaurant in the heart of the Luberon.

Cheap Treats

Pissaladière The Niçois equivalent of pizza, topped with caramelised onions, olives, garlic and anchovies.

Socca Another classic Niçois street snack, a savoury pancake made with chickpea flour.

Petits farcis Vegetables (tomatoes, onions, courgettes, courgette flowers) filled with a stuffing of mince, cheese, breadcrumbs, egg yolk and herbs.

The Year in Food
Spring (March–May)

Spring lambs are a traditional Easter meat across Provence; in Camargue, bull meat (stewed or cured as *saucissons*) is another favourite.

Summer (June–August)

Peak food season in Provence, when olives and grapes ripen, tomatoes and peppers explode with flavour, and peaches, cherries and nectarines dangle from the trees. It's a time of year made for alfresco eating – and the locals take full advantage.

Autumn (September–November)

Harvest time: this is when the year's wines and olive oils are bottled. It's also chestnut harvest in Collobrières, just in time to make *marrons glacés* (glazed chestnuts) for Christmas.

Winter (December–February)

Truffle season: locals head out in their droves to seek these precious wild fungi. A Christmas tradition in Provence is to serve 13 desserts; you're supposed to try them all to have luck for the coming year. In February, Menton celebrates all things citrus with its lemon festival.

Tapenade Olive dip, a common accompaniment to pre-dinner drinks, eaten on crusty bread.

Anchoïade Like tapenade, but made with salty anchovies and garlic.

Fromage de chèvre Goats cheese is the staple *fromage* of Provence – the best comes from Banon, in the Luberon.

Omelette aux truffes Truffle-tasting on the cheap – a classic omelette flavoured with fragrant black truffles.

Calissons d'Aix Aix-en-Provence's signature cakes are sweet and irresistible.

Dare to Try

Oursin Sea urchin is an acquired taste – eaten raw from the shell with a squeeze of lemon, it's pungent and very, very fishy.

Pieds paquets For the adventurous diner: lambs' feet and stomachs simmered together in white wine.

Saucisson de taureau Bull sausage is a common sight on menus around the Camargue. Trust us, it's meaty and delicious!

Saucisson de sanglier Wild-boar sausage is cured, and it's much lower in fat than pig sausage.

Escargots Snails are popular in rural Provence; they're very tasty doused in lashings of garlic butter, a bit like cockles or winkles.

BLACK DIAMONDS

Prized by chefs and connoisseurs alike, *la truffe noir* (black truffle, *Tuber melanosporum*) is the most illustrious ingredient of Provençal cuisine. Growing wild on the roots of oak trees, these mushrooms were traditionally snouted out by pigs but these days are mostly hunted by dogs. It's a lucrative business: depending on their quality, black truffles can fetch as much as €1000 per kilo, so it's no wonder they're often known in France as *la diamant noir* (black diamond).

Peak truffle season runs from November to March; truffles also grow in summer (when they're known as *truffes d'été*) but fetch lower prices, as they're thought to lack the fine flavour of their winter cousins.

Local Specialities

As befits a rural region, Provence's culinary specialities are rooted in *cuisine paysanne* (peasants' dishes), using unwanted fish and cheap cuts of meat to make sure that nothing is wasted.

Bouillabaisse

This pungent yellow fish stew has been brewed by Marseillais for centuries. It requires a minimum of four types of fresh fish (favourites include scorpion fish, white scorpion fish, weever, conger eel, chapon and tub gurnard) cooked in a rockfish stock with onions, tomatoes, garlic, *herbes de Provence* – a mix of thyme, rosemary, marjoram, oregano and a few other herbs – and saffron (hence the colour).

The name bouillabaisse is derived from the French *bouillir* (to boil) and *baisser* (to lower, as in a flame), reflecting the cooking method required: bring it to the boil, let it bubble ferociously for 15 minutes, then serve it: the *bouillon* (broth) first as a soup, followed by the fish flesh, in the company of a local wine, a white Cassis or dry Bandol rosé.

Authentic bouillabaisse has to be ordered a day in advance, and usually comes in a pot for two or more people to share.

Soupe de Poissons

A rich, velvety fish soup, *soupe de poissons* is made by boiling down fish, trimmings and bones into a thick broth. It's usually served with *rouille* (a spicy tomato condiment), crispy croutons and grated Gruyère cheese.

Bourride

The fish stew *bourride* is similar to bouillabaisse but has fewer ingredients, a less prescriptive recipe and often a slightly creamier sauce. It's customarily served with aïoli (garlic mayonnaise).

Ratatouille

Provence is the spiritual home of the filling vegetable stew *ratatouille*, typically made with tomatoes, onions, courgettes, aubergines and red and green peppers, which have been cooked with aromatic *herbes de Provence*.

Daube

A rich meaty stew, *daube* consists of beef braised in red wine, onions, celery, carrot, garlic and herbs. Like all stews, it must cook slowly for several hours; ideally, it is prepared the day before it's served.

Aïoli

Most people are familiar with this garlicky mayonnaise, but in Provence, the word also refers to a dish (sometimes known as *le grand aïoli*): a generous fishy stew that's usually made with salt cod, vegetables, boiled potatoes and usually a boiled egg, served with lashings of the eponymous aïoli sauce.

Soupe au Pistou

More stew than soup, the classic peasant dish *soupe au pistou* consists of a filling vegetable broth (beans, carrots, potatoes, courgettes, tomatoes and onions are all common ingredients), laced with lashings of olive oil, garlic and basil. Sometimes it comes with croutons, sometimes not.

Brouillade de Truffes

A humble dish (scrambled eggs) with a gourmet twist (black-truffle shavings), *brouillade de truffes* allows the fungi's delicate flavour to shine through. It's a common course on truffle menus.

How to Eat & Drink

When to Eat

➡ The classic French breakfast is a cup of coffee and a bit of yesterday's baguette with jam; croissants and *pains au chocolats* are reserved for weekend treats but usually feature as part of a hotel breakfast alongside cheeses, yoghurts, fruit and charcuterie. Breakfast is usually served from around 7.30am to 9.30am.

➡ Lunch is often the main meal of the day; nearly everyone takes a couple of hours for lunch between noon and 2pm, often taking advantage of the *plat du jour* at a local brasserie.

➡ Although most restaurants open around 7pm, diners generally start trickling in around 8pm and often linger till 10.30pm or later.

TABLE ETIQUETTE

➡ Forget balancing your bread on your main-course plate; crumbs on the table are fine.

➡ Using the same knife and fork for your starter and main is common-place in many informal restaurants.

➡ *Santé* is the toast for alcoholic drinks; *bon appétit* is what you say before tucking in.

➡ The French generally end their meal with a short, sharp espresso coffee.

➡ Splitting the bill is seen as crass – except among young people.

➡ Service is generally included, so leaving a tip is optional.

Where to Eat & Drink

Dining *à la provençal* can mean anything from lunch in a village bistro to dining in a star-studded gastronomic temple. Irrespective of price, a *carte* (menu) or *ardoise* (blackboard) is usually hanging up outside, allowing you to check what's on offer before committing.

Bookings are always advisable in summer, particularly if you'd like a table *en terrasse* (outside).

Auberge Inn serving traditional country fare, often in rural areas. Some also offer rooms.

Bistro (also spelled *bistrot*) Anything from an informal bar serving light meals to a fully fledged restaurant.

Brasserie Very much like a cafe, except that it serves full meals (generally non-stop from 11am to 11pm) as well as drinks and coffee.

Cafe Serves basic food (cold and toasted sandwiches), coffees and drinks.

Restaurant Most serve lunch and dinner five or six days a week.

Menu Decoder

Plat du jour The dish of the day, usually great value.

Formule A two-course menu, often served only at lunch. You can usually choose either starter and main or main and dessert.

L'APERO

•••••••••••••••••••••••••••••••••••

L'apéro (short for *l'apéritif*, an alcoholic drink taken before dinner) is a national pastime in France, particularly in Provence–Côte d'Azur. It's a pre-dinner drink accompanied by snacks; a classic is a shot of pastis or a glass of chilled rosé, served with marinated olives, crusty bread and tapenade.

Menu Usually two or three courses, with a more limited choice of dishes compared to the à la carte menu.

Entrées Starters.

Plats Main dishes – sometimes divided into *viandes* (meats) and *poissons* (fish).

Desserts Desserts.

À la carte Always the most expensive way to dine.

Provence through the Seasons

It was through the humble rhythm and natural cycle of the land that a distinctly Provençal cuisine – laden with sun-filled tomatoes, melons, cherries, peaches, olives, Mediterranean fish and alpine cheese – emerged several centuries ago. Nothing has changed. Farmers still gather at the weekly morning market to sell their fruit and vegetables, olives, garlic plaits, and dried herbs displayed in stubby coarse sacks. *À la Provençal* continues to involve a generous dose of garlic-seasoned tomatoes; while a simple filet mignon, sprinkled with olive oil and rosemary fresh from the garden, makes the same magnificent Sunday lunch it did a generation ago.

Vegetarians & Vegans

In a country where *viande* (meat) once meant 'food' too, it comes as no surprise that vegetarians and vegans are not well catered for. Here are some tips to help you make the best of Provençal cuisine:

➡ Starters are often vegetarian, so order two or three starters instead of the usual starter and main.

➡ Dishes that can easily be customised include pasta, pizza and salads, all very common across Provence–Côte d'Azur.

➡ Small restaurants serving just a few daily specials will find it harder to accommodate dietary requirements, so opt for larger establishments instead.

➡ Note that most cheeses in France are made with *lactosérum* (rennet), an enzyme derived from the stomach of a calf or young goat.

➡ Larger towns often have a *restaurant bio* (organic restaurant). These tend to have a better choice for vegetarians, but even here you'll often struggle to find anything without dairy or cheese.

Musée Océanographique de Monaco (p113)

Plan Your Trip
Family Travel

Provence–Côte d'Azur is a wonderful place to travel with children. It offers swimming and snorkelling galore, cycling through lavender fields, kayaking in the Camargue, visiting Roman ruins, walking along the Calanques and wildlife-watching in the Parc National du Mercantour, to name a few.

Best Regions for Kids

Nice, Monaco & Menton

Riviera glamour isn't just for grown-ups: skate or scooter along Nice's promenade des Anglais; hop on a boat for a scenic cruise or a dolphin excursion; and in Monaco, watch the changing of the guard, ogle the yachts and slurp milkshakes at Stars 'n' Bars.

St-Tropez to Toulon

Buckets and spades, beachcombing, swimming, snorkelling – it's all about the beach here.

Arles & the Camargue

Quiet roads, bountiful nature, long beaches and activities galore make the Camargue one of the easiest places to visit *en famille*. Add evocative Roman ruins in Arles and you have the perfect holiday.

Haute-Provence & the Southern Alps

White-water activities in the Verdon, snow fun in the mountains, dinosaurs in Digne and indoor adventures at Vesubia in St-Martin-Vésubie – nature is Haute-Provence's drawcard.

Provence & the Côte d'Azur for Kids

Museums & Activities

Many museums and monuments are free for kids, but rules vary – sometimes 'kids' refers to children aged under 18, sometimes to children aged under six or 12. Family tickets, covering two adults and two children, are often available.

Note that for many outdoor activities (rafting, canoeing, horse riding etc), there is often an age minimum, generally six or seven years. Check in advance to avoid disappointed faces on the day.

Food & Drink

Eating out *en famille* is commonplace, but the French will expect children to behave properly at the table – so don't let the kids run wild. Most restaurants don't open for dinner before 7.30pm, so brasseries (which serve food continuously) are often a more useful option for families.

There is usually a *menu enfant* (children's menu) – pizza, pasta and *steak haché-frites* (bun-less hamburger and fries) are staples. Don't be shy about ordering a starter or half-portion as a child's meal; most restaurants will happily oblige.

Drinks can be pricey in restaurants (€5 for a soft drink is not unusual); save money by ordering *une carafe d'eau* (a jug of tap water) or *un sirop* (syrup; €2 at most), diluted with water. If you want a straw, ask for *une paille*.

Children's Highlights

Activities

Sentier de Littoral, Cap d'Antibes (p86) Clamber among rocks, in caves and on cliffs.

Véloroute du Calavon, Luberon Valley (p261) Cycle through this lovely Provençal valley.

Château des Baux, Les-Baux-de-Provence (p196) Relive medieval battles at this hilltop castle.

Colorado Adventures, near Apt (p268) Tackle the adventure course near these old ochre mines.

Nature Lovers

Alpha, St-Martin-Vésubie (p298) See semi-wild wolves in the mountains.

Gorges du Verdon (p286) Look out for vultures in the skies.

Village des Tortues, Carnoules (p142) Spot native French tortoises.

Camargue (p214) Go horse-riding and flamingo-watching.

Domaine du Rayol, Corniche des Maures (p138) Snorkel with colourful fish in the Med.

Rainy Days

Vesúbia, St-Martin-Vésubie (p298) Try canyoning, rock-climbing and more.

Musée Océanographique de Monaco (p113) Watch sharks, fish, and octopuses.

Musée International de la Parfumerie, Grasse
(p79) Test your sense of smell.

Observatoire de Haute-Provence (p279) Learn
about the stars at this small observatory.

Planning
When to Go

➡ For swimming and sunshine, the best times
are from May to September; for skiing in the
mountains, the season runs from December to
March.

➡ Be careful of the heat – especially in
midsummer, when the sun is fierce. It's very
easy to get sunburned, even on overcast days;
cover up and slap on the suncream.

➡ Be especially wary on cool days in the
mountains – the air often feels deceptively cool,
but the sun can be extremely strong, making
sunburn a certainty without protection.

Accommodation

Most hotels have quadruple or family
rooms with extra beds for the kids. *Chambres d'hôte* are a great family option; many
offer dinner on the premises, which takes
care of babysitting arrangements: just
bring a baby monitor to wine and dine in
peace.

Renting your own *gîte* (self-catering
cottage) is the best idea if you don't mind
staying in one place; it feels more like
home, and you can cook your own meals.

Camping is popular too. Book ahead,
as tent pitches and mobile homes get
snapped up fast. Most larger French campsites tend to be busy, holiday-park-style
affairs, with shops, playgrounds, activities
and so on.

What to Pack

Don't panic if you forget something: you
will find everything you need in French
shops and supermarkets.

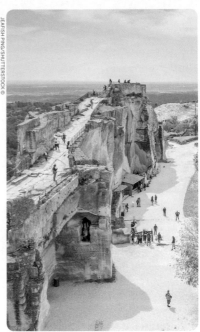

JEAFISH PING/SHUTTERSTOCK ©

Château des Baux (p196)

Babies & Toddlers

➡ A carry sling: pushchairs are a pain on
cobbled lanes.

➡ A portable changing mat (changing facilities
are rare)

➡ A screw-on seat for toddlers (restaurants
don't always have high chairs)

➡ Inflatable armbands for the sea or pool

➡ Baby sunscreen and mosquito repellent

Six to 12 Years

➡ Entertainment for car journeys – tablets, DVD
players, activity books, sketchpads (remember
to pack chargers and extra plug adapters)

➡ Swimming gear, goggles, snorkel and flip-
flops for the beach

➡ Binoculars for spotting wildlife

➡ Camera and batteries

Regions at a Glance

The Provence and the Côte d'Azur region packs in the most incredible diversity of sights, landscapes and activities.

The coast tends to be relatively built up, with exceptions around the Camargue, the Calanques and the unspoilt Îles d'Hyères. To get away from the crowds, head inland to the sparsely populated Haute-Provence, the majestic southern Alps, the vineyards of the Var or the storybook Luberon.

Back in town, Nice is utterly delightful, its old town teeming with life and the Mediterranean lapping the shores of its promenade, whereas Marseille, France's second-biggest city, blends urban grit with culture on the rise.

And then there's Monaco, a law unto itself, with its skyscrapers, tax-haven residents, scandal-prone royal family and hedonistic fun.

Côte d'Azur

Architecture
Gardens
Views

Belle Époque History

The French Riviera was all the rage in the 19th century and we can thank wintering royals and high-society divas for their legacy: meringue-like buildings, operas, casinos and promenades.

Parks & Gardens

With its mild, sunny climate, the Côte d'Azur has always been a gardener's heaven. Cue the region's many exotic, botanical and themed gardens, which reach their prime in spring.

Panoramas

The coast rises abruptly from the sea along the Riviera, reaching 800m in places, with mind-bending views along the way. Drive the Grande Corniche or visit Ste-Agnès or Èze for knock-out vistas.

p48

Monaco

Nightlife
Culture
Sports

Nightlife

It may be pint-sized, but little Monaco knows how to party – whether that means dressing to the nines and placing a bet at the famous casino, attending the opera or partying till late at a portside bar.

Monaco's Monarchy

Monaco's royal family is a constant source of fascination: peek behind the curtain by visiting the fabulous royal palace and watching the pomp of the changing of the guard.

Motor Racing

The highlight of Monaco's calendar is its annual grand prix, held every May. At other times, you can trace the famous circuit on foot, or visit Prince Rainier's private collection of classic cars.

p110

Var

Beaches
Wine
Islands

Beaches

The western end of the fabled Côte d'Azur brings yet more golden beaches, from the celeb-heavy, nudist-friendly sands around St-Tropez to the lesser-known coves of the Corniche des Maures.

Wine

This is the home of Provence's signature rosé wines, so spare an afternoon to visit the vineyards of Côtes de Provence, Bandol or Correns organic wine makers.

Islands

A few miles offshore lies the little archipelago of the Îles d'Hyères, where you should be able to escape the summer hustle of the coast – and with luck, find a deserted patch of sand.

p125

Bouches-du-Rhône

Food
Nature
Culture

Eating Out

You won't go hungry in this part of Provence. Dine on just-landed seafood and authentic bouillabaisse in Marseille, or seek out one of the excellent Provençal restaurants dotted along the backstreets of Aix-en-Provence.

Outdoors

The rugged, mineral beauty of the Massif de la Ste-Baume, Les Alpilles and the Calanques has captivated painters and writers; follow in their footsteps with a walk, paddle or drive.

Museums

From Marseille's museums (such as the Musée des Civilisations de l'Europe et de la Méditerranée) to the many impressive galleries and artistic sights of Aix-en-Provence, this is a region that's awash with history and culture.

p154

The Camargue

Food
Nature
History

Food

Camargue's specialities its red rice, bull meat and seafood – are reminiscent of Spain. Try them, as well as modern French cuisine, in one of the area's mighty fine restaurants.

Wildlife-Watching

More than 500 species of bird regularly visit the Camargue, chief among them the colourful flocks of pink flamingos. The mosquitoes seem just as abundant as the birds, so pack repellent along with your binoculars!

Roman Sights

Arles flourished under Julius Ceasar, and the town's past prosperity is still awe-inspiring: amphitheatre, theatre, necropolis and a leading mosaic-renovation centre.

p197

Vaucluse

Nature
Wine
History

Outdoors

Ascend giant Mont Ventoux, hike the stunning Dentelles de Montmirail, paddle below Pont du Gard or along the glassy Sorgue and breathe Provence's fresh air.

Wine Tasting

With three of the region's most famous wines – reds Châteauneuf-du-Pape and Gigondas, and Muscat de Beaumes-de-Venise – the Avignon region is a must for wine connoisseurs.

Romans & Popes

The Romans and the popes all decided to call the area home: find out why by exploring the ancient town of Glanum, Orange's theatre and Avignon's imposing Palais des Papes.

p219

The Luberon

History
Activities
Villages

Churches & Abbeys

Long a Protestant stronghold in a Catholic country, the Luberon is steeped in religious history, from glorious churches to peaceful abbeys.

Cycling

With its rolling hills, postcard landscapes and light traffic, the Luberon is prime cycling territory. And, happily, there is plenty of help out there to facilitate your journey, from itinerary planning to luggage-carrying services.

Villages

Gordes, Ménerbes, Lacoste, Bonnieux: this is the Provence of your dreams. There are 101 ways to enjoy these stunning villages: stroll, cycle, browse the weekly market or stop for a long lunch.

p260

Alpes-de-Haute-Provence

Nature
Scenery
Activities

Wildlife

The grey wolf made a much publicised comeback to the Mercantour from Italy in the 1990s, but as well as wolves you could see vultures, eagles, mountain ibexes and cute marmots.

Scenery

From Europe's deepest canyons to some of its highest peaks, Haute-Provence's alpine scenery is majestic and unspoilt. Even the night sky will bowl you over with its incredible clarity.

Activities

Adrenalin junkies, Haute-Provence is for you: you can go rafting, canyoning, skydiving, bungee-jumping, mountain biking, cycling, paragliding and climbing. Hiking, in comparison, will look meek, but make no mistake: trekking here is tough.

p278

On the Road

Côte d'Azur

Best Places to Eat

➡ Le Mirazur (p73)

➡ Peixes (p61)

➡ Bistrot Gourmand Clovis (p78)

Best Places to Stay

➡ Château de Valmer (p109)

➡ Les Rosées (p82)

➡ Hôtel La Pérouse (p59)

Why Go?

Once upon a time, everyone called this glamorous stretch of Mediterranean coast the French Riviera; then in 1888 author Stéphen Liégeard dubbed it *La Côte d'Azur,* the name stuck and the rest is history.

Whatever you prefer to call it, the seashore that extends from St-Tropez to the French-Italian border is one of the world's great seaside destinations, packed with gorgeous beaches, luxury hotels, designer bars, belle-époque villas, coastal trails, red-rock headlands and offshore islands. From Monte Carlo's casino to Nice's Promenade des Anglais to the Cannes film festival and St-Tropez's yacht harbour, the Côte d'Azur is home to some of the most iconic spots in Europe's collective consciousness.

Beyond the coast, the region is also home to some spectacular hilltop villages and mountain scenery, along with vineyards, flower farms that feed the French perfume industry and more than its fair share of great art museums.

Driving Distances (km)

	Antibes	Cannes	Eze	Fréjus	Menton	Monaco	Nice
Cannes	15						
Eze	35	50					
Fréjus	50	35	75				
Menton	55	65	20	95			
Monaco	45	60	10	90	10		
Nice	25	35	15	75	30	20	
St Tropez	85	85	125	35	135	130	105

ℹ Getting There & Away

International flights arrive at two airports in the region, the more important being **Nice-Côte d'Azur Airport** (p329) between Nice and Antibes. The much smaller **Toulon-Hyères Airport** (p329) is a convenient gateway to the western Côte d'Azur, as is **Marseille Provence Airport**, 112km further west.

The A8 autoroute runs east–west through the region, granting access to coastal cities between Menton and Cannes, then continuing inland towards Aix-en-Provence, where it joins the A7 to Lyon. The smaller D559 hugs the coast west of Cannes along the Corniche de l'Esterel to St-Raphaël, then turns south to St-Tropez before continuing west towards Toulon and Marseille.

SNCF trains runs east–west along the coast, from Menton near the Italian border through Monaco, Nice, Cannes and Antibes to St-Raphaël. Beyond St-Raphaël, fast trains continue west to Marseille, Aix-en-Provence, Avignon, Lyon and Paris, while local trains go southwest to Toulon, bypassing St-Tropez.

ℹ Getting Around

There aren't many places in this area that you can't access by public transport. The Arrière-Pays Niçois, the Grande Corniche, the Gorges du Loup and the villages around Menton are the only places where you'll really need a car; elsewhere, you should make the best of the fantastic – and very cheap – trains and buses. They also run at night, so you'll be able to keep the wine flowing!

NICE

POP 342,522

With its mix of real-city grit, old-world opulence, year-round sunshine, vibrant street life and stunning seaside location, no place in France compares with Nice.

◎ Sights

★**Vieux Nice**   HISTORIC SITE
(🚌1 to Opéra-Vieille Ville/Cathédrale-Vieille Ville) Getting lost among the dark, narrow, winding alleyways of Nice's old town is a highlight. The layout has barely changed since the 1700s, and it's now packed with delis, restaurants, boutiques and bars, but the centrepiece remains **cours Saleya**: a massive market square that's permanently thronging in summer. The **food market** (cours Saleya; ◎6am-1.30pm Tue-Sun) is perfect for fresh produce and foodie souvenirs, while the **flower market** (cours Saleya; ◎6am-5.30pm

Tue-Sat, 6.30am-1.30pm Sun) is worth visiting just for the colours and fragrances. A **flea market** (Marché à la Brocante; cours Saleya; ◎7am-6pm Mon) is held on Monday.

Baroque aficionados will adore architectural gems **Cathédrale Ste-Réparate** (📞04 93 92 01 35; place Rossetti; ◎2-6pm Mon, 9am-noon & 2-6pm Tue-Sun), honouring the city's patron saint; exuberant 16th-century **Chapelle de la Miséricorde** (📞04 92 00 41 90; cours Saleya; ◎2.30-5pm Tue Sep-Jun); and 17th-century **Palais Lascaris** (📞04 93 62 72 40; 15 rue Droite; museum pass 24hr/7 days €10/20, guided visit adult/child €6/free; ◎10am-6pm Wed-Mon late Jun–mid-Oct, from 11am mid-Oct–late June), a frescoed riot of Flemish tapestries, faience (tin-glazed earthenware), gloomy religious paintings and 18th-century pharmacy.

There's also a lively – and very smelly – **fish market** (place St-François; ◎6am-1pm Tue-Sun) on place St-François.

★**Promenade des Anglais**   ARCHITECTURE
(🚌8, 52, 62) The most famous stretch of seafront in Nice – if not France – is this vast paved promenade, which gets its name from the English expat patrons who paid for it in 1822. It runs for the whole 4km sweep of the Baie des Anges with a dedicated lane for cyclists and skaters; if you fancy joining them, you can rent skates, scooters and bikes from **Roller Station** (📞04 93 62 99 05; www.roller-station.fr; 49 quai des États-Unis; skates, boards & scooters per hour/day €5/12, bicycles €5/15; ◎9am-8pm Jul & Aug, 10am-7pm May, Jun, Sep & Oct, to 6pm Nov-Apr).

A more unusual way to cruise along is an electric Segway from **Mobilboard Nice** (📞04 93 80 21 27; www.mobilboard.com/nice-promenade; 2 rue Halévy, Batiment Ruhl Méridien; 30min/1hr/2hr tour €20/30/50; ◎9.30am-6pm; 🚌8, 52, 62 to Massenet); the same agency also rents bikes.

Along the way, keep an eye out for a few of the promenade's landmarks, including the **Hôtel Negresco** (📞04 93 16 64 00; www.hotel-negresco-nice.com; 37 promenade des Anglais; 🚌8, 52, 62 to Gambetta/Promenade), the art-deco Palais de la Méditerranée (p59; 1929) and Niçoise sculptor Sabine Géraudie's giant iron sculpture *La Chaise de SAB* (2014), which pays homage to the city's famous blue-and-white beach chairs.

In 2015 the city of Nice submitted the Promenade des Anglais as a candidate for Unesco World Heritage status – the process can take up to 10 years to complete.

CÔTE D'AZUR NICE

Côte d'Azur Highlights

❶ Tour du Cap-Ferrat (p67) Walking past billionaires' mansions and dramatic rocky coves.

❷ Nice (p49) Splitting your time between beaches, bistros, museums and festivals in the Côte d'Azur's unofficial capital.

❸ Sentier du Littoral (p69) Taking a dramatic cape-to-cape walk along Roquebrune-Cap Martin's high.drama coastal path.

❹ St-Tropez (p100) Sipping pastis and watching *pétanque* players under the plane trees in picturesque place des Lices.

❺ St-Paul de Vence (p74) Prowling the backstreets of this stunning hilltop village.

❻ Antibes (p82) Visiting the Musée Picasso and viewing the Alps across the sparkling Mediterranean.

❼ Grasse (p78) Retracing three millennia of perfume-making at museums, factories and fragrant flower farms.

❽ Corniche de l'Estérel (p95) Losing yourself in the scarlet sunset glow of this seaside massif.

❾ Les Gorges du Loup (p76) Navigating the hairpin turns of this dramatic river gorge.

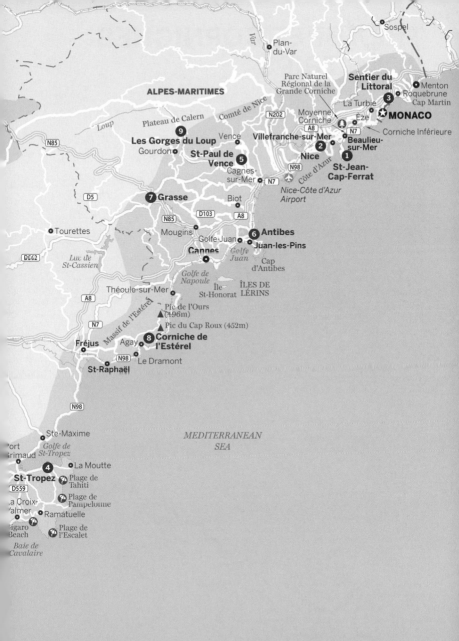

THE THREE CORNICHES ROAD TRIPS

This trio of corniches (coastal roads) hugs the cliffs between Nice and Monaco, each higher than the last, with dazzling views of the Med. For the grandest views, it's the Grande Corniche you want, but the Moyenne Corniche runs a close scenic second. The lowest of all, the Corniche Inférieure, allows access to a string of snazzy coastal resorts.

❶ Corniche Inférieure

Skimming the villa-lined waterfront between Nice and Monaco, the Corniche Inférieure, built in the 1860s, passes through the towns of Villefranche-sur-Mer, St-Jean-Cap-Ferrat, Beaulieu-sur-Mer, Èze-sur-Mer and Cap d'Ail.

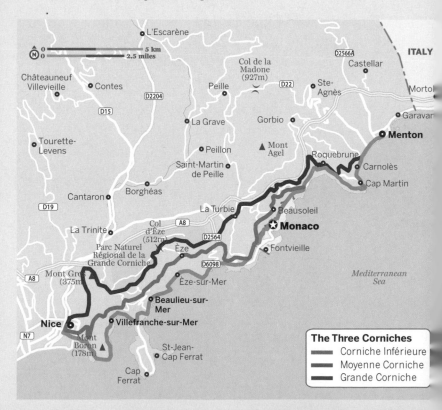

ZM_PHOTO/SHUTTERSTOCK ©

Moyenne Corniche

② Moyenne Corniche

Cut through rock in the 1920s, the Moyenne Corniche takes drivers from Nice past the Col de Villefranche (149m), Èze and Beausoleil (the French town bordering Monaco's Monte Carlo).

Walk down from the hilltop village of Èze to its coastal counterpart, Èze-sur-Mer, via the steep Sentier Nietzsche, a 45-minute footpath named after German philosopher Friedrich Nietzsche, who started writing *Thus Spake Zarathustra* while staying in Èze (and enjoying this path).

③ Grande Corniche

Views from the spectacular cliff-hanging Grande Corniche are mesmerising, and if you're driving, you'll probably want to stop at every bend to admire the unfolding vistas. Hitchcock was sufficiently impressed by Napoléon's Grande Corniche to use it as a backdrop for his film *To Catch a Thief* (1956), starring Cary Grant and Grace Kelly. Ironically, Kelly died in 1982 after crashing her car on this very same road.

There are no villages of note along the Grande Corniche until you reach hilltop La Turbie, best known for its imposing Roman triumphal monument. There's pretty much nowhere to stay along the road between Nice and La Turbie.

★Colline du Château   PARK
(Castle Hill; ⊘8.30am-8pm Apr-Sep, to 6pm Oct-Mar) FREE For the best views over Nice's red-tiled rooftops, climb the winding staircases up to this wooded outcrop on the eastern edge of the old town. It's been occupied since ancient times; archaeological digs have revealed Celtic and Roman remains, and the site was later occupied by a medieval castle that was razed by Louis XIV in 1706 (only the 16th-century **Tour Bellanda** remains). There are various entrances, including one beside the tower, or you can cheat and ride the free **lift** (Ascenseur du Château; rue des Ponchettes; ⊘9am-8pm Jun-Aug, to 7pm Apr, May & Sep, 10am-6pm Oct-Mar).

★Musée Matisse   GALLERY
(☑04 93 81 08 08; www.musee-matisse-nice.org; 164 av des Arènes de Cimiez; museum pass 24hr/7 days €10/20; ⊘10am-6pm Wed-Mon late Jun–mid-Oct, from 11am rest of year; 🚌15, 17, 20 or 22 to Arènes/Musée Matisse) This museum, 2km north of the city centre in the leafy Cimiez quarter, houses a fascinating assortment of works by Matisse, including oil paintings, drawings, sculptures, tapestries and Matisse's famous paper cut-outs. The permanent collection is displayed in a red-ochre 17th-century Genoese villa in an olive grove. Temporary exhibitions are in the futuristic basement building. Matisse is buried in the **Monastère Notre Dame de Cimiez** (place du Monastère; ⊘8.30am-12.30pm & 2.30-6.30pm; 🚌15, 17, 20 or 22 to Arènes/Musée Matisse) cemetery, across the park from the museum.

★Musée Masséna   MUSEUM
(☑04 93 91 19 10; 65 rue de France; museum pass 24hr/7 days €10/20; ⊘10am-6pm Wed-Mon late Jun–mid-Oct, from 11am rest of year; 🚌8, 52, 62 to Congrès/Promenade) Originally built as a holiday home for Prince Victor d'Essling (the grandson of one of Napoléon's favourite generals, Maréchal Massena), this lavish belle-époque building is another iconic architectural landmark. Built between 1898 and 1901 in grand neoclassical style with an Italianate twist, it's now a fascinating museum dedicated to the history of the Riviera – taking in everything from holidaying monarchs to expat Americans, the boom of tourism and the enduring importance of Carnaval.

It was built by the Danish architect Hans-Georg Tersling (1857–1920), who was responsible for several other important buildings during the belle époque. The ground floor can still be used for official occasions, so the museum sometimes closes at short notice.

★Musée d'Art Moderne et
d'Art Contemporain   GALLERY
(MAMAC; ☑04 97 13 42 01; www.mamac-nice.org; place Yves Klein; museum pass 24hr/7 days €10/20; ⊘10am-6pm Tue-Sun late Jun–mid-Oct, from 11am rest of year; 🚌1 to Garibaldi) European and American avant-garde works from the 1950s to the present are the focus of this sprawling multilevel museum. Highlights include many works by Christo and Nice's neorealists: Niki de Saint Phalle, César, Arman and Yves Klein. The building's rooftop also works as an exhibition space (with knockout panoramas of Nice to boot).

Musée National Marc Chagall   GALLERY
(☑04 93 53 87 20; www.musee-chagall.fr; 4 av Dr Ménard; adult/child €10/8; ⊘10am-6pm Wed-Mon May-Oct, to 5pm Nov-Apr; 🚌15 or 22 to Musée Chagall) The strange, dreamlike and often unsettling work of the Belarusian painter Marc Chagall (1887–1985) is displayed at this museum, which owns the largest public collection of the painter's work. The main hall displays 12 huge interpretations (1954–67) of stories from Genesis and Exodus. From the city centre, allow about 20 minutes to walk to the museum (signposted from av de l'Olivetto), or take the bus.

Port Lympia   ARCHITECTURE
(🚌2 to Port Lympia) Nice's Port Lympia, with its beautiful Venetian-coloured buildings, is often overlooked. But a stroll along its quays is lovely, as is the walk to get here: come down through Parc du Château or follow quai Rauba Capeu, where a massive **war memorial** hewn from the rock commemorates the 4000 Niçois who died in both world wars.

**Cathédrale Orthodoxe
Russe St-Nicolas**   CATHEDRAL
(☑09 81 09 53 45; av Nicolas II; ⊘9am-noon & 2-6pm Apr-Oct, 9.30am-noon & 2-5.30pm Nov-Mar; 🚌64, 75 to Tzaréwitch/Gambetta) Built between 1902 and 1912 to provide a big enough church for the growing Russian community, this cathedral, with its colourful onion domes and rich, ornate interior, is the biggest Russian Orthodox church outside Russia. The cathedral boasts dozens of intricate icons – unfortunately, there is very little in the way of explanation for visitors.

⚡ Activities & Tours

⭐ **Train des Pignes**   RAIL

(Pine Cone Train; www.trainprovence.com; single/return Nice to Digne €24.10/48.20; 🚌1 to Libération) Chugging between the mountains and the sea, the Train des Pignes is one of Provence's most picturesque train rides. The 151km track between Nice and Digne-les-Bains rises to 1000m for breathtaking views as it passes through Haute-Provence's scarcely populated backcountry. The service runs four times daily from Gare de Nice-CF de Provence and is ideal for a day trip inland.

Trans Côte d'Azur   BOATING

(www.trans-cote-azur.com; quai Lunel; ⊘Apr-Oct; 🚌2 to Port Lympia) Trans Côte d'Azur runs one-hour boat cruises along the Baie des Anges and Rade de Villefranche (adult/child €18/13) from April to October. From late May to September it also sails to Île Ste-Marguerite (€40/31, one hour), St-Tropez (€65/51, 2½ hours), Monaco (€38.50/30, 45 minutes) and Cannes (€40/31, one hour).

⚡ Festivals & Events

⭐ **Carnaval de Nice**   CARNIVAL

(www.nicecarnaval.com; ⊘Feb-Mar) Held over a two-week period in late February and early March since 1294. Highlights include the *batailles de fleurs* (battles of flowers), and the ceremonial burning of the carnival king on Promenade des Anglais, followed by a fireworks display.

Nice Jazz Festival   MUSIC

(www.nicejazzfestival.fr; ⊘Jul) France's original jazz festival has taken on a life of its own, with a jam-packed six-night calendar of performances on two stages in Jardin Albert 1er, and fringe concerts popping up all around town, from Vieux Nice to Massena and the shopping streets around rue de France.

🛏 Sleeping

⭐ **Hostel Meyerbeer Beach**   HOSTEL €

(📞04 93 88 95 65; www.hostelmeyerbeer.com; 15 rue Meyerbeer; dm €25-50, s €80-90, d €90-100; 🚌7, 9, 22, 27, 59, 70 to Rivoli) It's easy to see why this cosy little hostel got voted Best in France in 2018. A welcoming mood prevails throughout, thanks to the congenial, international staff of four, a kitchen small enough to make you feel like you're cooking at home, and a cheerful, immaculate mix of

GUIDED TOURS
⋯⋯⋯⋯⋯⋯⋯⋯⋯⋯⋯⋯⋯⋯⋯⋯⋯

Nice has a few companies offering hop-on, hop-off bus tours, but ultimately walking is the best way to appreciate the city. The city-run **Centre du Patrimoine** (📞04 92 00 41 90; www.nice.fr/fr/culture/patrimoine; 14 rue Jules Gilly; tours adult/child €5/free; ⊘9am-1pm & 2-5pm Mon-Thu, to 3.45pm Fri) leads an excellent variety of well-priced walking tours throughout the city, while companies such as **French Way** (📞06 27 35 13 75; www.thefrenchway.fr) organise themed walks focusing on specialised topics like Niçois food and drink, perfume or history.

private rooms and four- to eight-bed dorms, each with its own en-suite bathroom.

Villa Saint-Exupéry Beach Hostel   HOSTEL €

(📞04 93 16 13 45; www.villahostels.com; 6 rue Sacha Guitry; dm €30-50, d €100; ❄@🛜; 🚌1 to Masséna) Five blocks in from the beach, this long-standing, centrally located city hostel has plenty of pluses: bar, kitchen, gym, sauna, ping pong, games room, and a friendly multilingual staff. Dorms sleeping four to 16 all come equipped with private en-suite bathrooms, and there's a host of activities on offer, including yoga, sailing, scuba diving, canyoning, and free city walking tours.

Hôtel Wilson   HOTEL €

(📞04 93 85 47 79; www.hotel-wilson-nice.com; 39 rue de l'Hôtel des Postes; s €35-57, d €42-82; 🛜; 🚌7, 9 to Wilson or Pastorelli) Generations of travellers have passed through Jean-Marie's rambling 3rd-floor apartment, where all the rooms have been decorated with potted plants, items collected on his travels and a faintly bohemian, hippie-hangover style (one room's styled after Frida Kahlo, another stuffed with '70s kitsch, while others have African and Asian flavours). It's faded but winningly friendly and family-run. Cheaper rooms share bathrooms.

Hôtel Villa St-Hubert   HOTEL €

(📞04 93 84 66 51; www.villasainthubert.com; 26 rue Michel-Ange; s €60-70, d €72-80; 🛜; 🚌1 to Borriglione) This two-star in a blue-shuttered villa north of the train station offers good value for money. It's closer to the centre than you might think at first glance, thanks to the

Nice

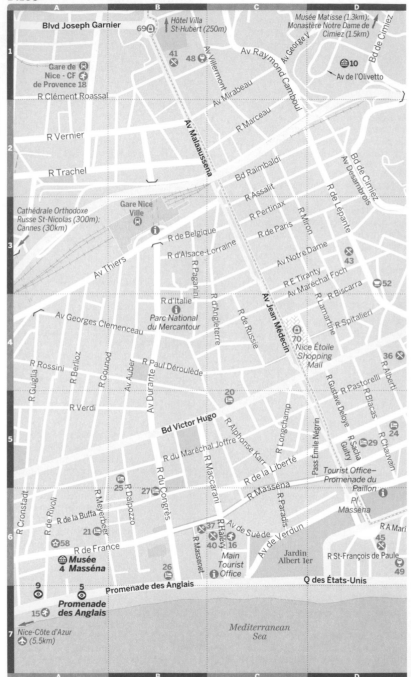

Blvd Joseph Garnier

69

Hôtel Villa St-Hubert (250m)

Musée Matisse (1.3km); Monastère Notre Dame de Cimiez (1.5km)

Bd de Cimiez

41

48

Av Villermont

Av Raymond Camboul

Av George V

10

Av de l'Olivetto

Gare de Nice - CF de Provence 18

R Clément Roassal

Av Mirabeau

R Marceau

R Vernier

R Trachel

Av Malaaussena

Bd Raimbaldi

Bd de Cimiez

Av de Desambrois

R Assalit

R Pertinax

R de Paris

R Miron

R de Lépante

Cathédrale Orthodoxe Russe St-Nicolas (300m); Cannes (30km)

Gare Nice Ville

R de Belgique

R d'Alsace-Lorraine

Av Notre Dame

43

Av Thiers

R Paganini

R E Tiranty
Av. Maréchal Foch

R Biscarra

52

R d'Italie

R d'Angleterre

Av Jean Médecin

R Lamartine

R Spitalieri

Av Georges Clemenceau

Parc National du Mercantour

R de Russie

70

Nice Étoile Shopping Mall

36

R Rossini

R Berlioz

R Gounod

Av Auber

R Paul Déroulède

R Gustave Deloye

R Pastorelli

R Blacas

R Alberti

R Guglia

R Verdi

Av Durante

20

Bd Victor Hugo

R Alphonse Karr

R Longchamp

Pass Émile Négrin

24

R Sacha Guitry

29

R Chauvain

R du Maréchal Joffre

R de la Liberté

Tourist Office– Promenade du Paillon

25

27

R Dalpozzo

R du Congrès

R Maccarani

R Masséna

R Paradis

Pl Masséna

R Cronstadt

R de Rivoli

R Meyerbeer

R de la Buffa

R A Mari

45

21

58

R de France

37

R Haléy

Av de Suède

Av de Verdun

R St-François de Paule

49

26

40

16

R Massenet

Main Tourist Office

Jardin Albert Ier

Musée Masséna 4

9

5

15

Promenade des Anglais

Q des États-Unis

Promenade des Anglais

Nice-Côte d'Azur (5.5km)

Mediterranean Sea

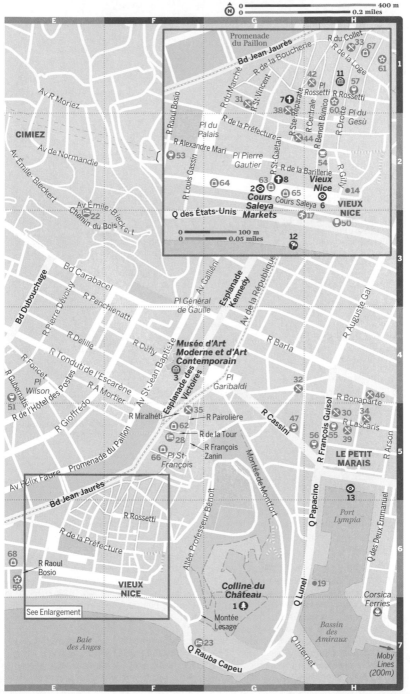

Map labels:

N
0 — 400 m
0 — 0.2 miles

Promenade du Paillon
Bd Jean Jaurès
R du Collet
R de la Boucherie
R de la Loge
33
67
61
42
11
57
Pl Rossetti
R Rossetti
R du Marché
R St-Vincent
31
7
38
R Centrale
R Benoît Bunico
60
R Droite
Pl du Gesù
R de la Préfecture
R Raoul Bosio
R Ste-Réparate
44
Pl du Palais
R Alexandre Mari
53
Pl Pierre Gautier
R St-Gaëtan
R de la Barillerie
54
R Louis Gassin
64
63
2
8
Vieux Nice
R Gilly
14
65
Cours Saleya
6
VIEUX NICE
Cours Saleya Markets
Q des États-Unis
17
50
0 — 100 m
0 — 0.05 miles
12

CIMIEZ

Av R Moriez
Av de Normandie
Av Émile-Bieckert
Av Émile-Bieckert
Chemin du Bois
22

Bd Dubouchage
Bd Carabacel
R Penchienatti
R Pierre Dévoluy
R Delille
Av Gallieni
Pl Général de Gaulle
Esplanade Kennedy
Av de la République
R Foncet
Pl Wilson
R Tondutit de l'Escarène
R Defly
Musée d'Art Moderne et d'Art Contemporain
3
R Barla
Av Auguste Gal
51
R de l'Hôtel des Postes
R Gioffredo
R A Mortier
Av St-Jean Baptiste
Esplanade des Victoires
Pl Garibaldi
32
R Gubernatis
R Miralhéti
35
R Pairolière
R Cassini
46
R Bonaparte
30
34
62
28
R de la Tour
47
56
R François Guisol
55
39
66
Pl St-François
R François Zanin
R Lascaris
LE PETIT MARAIS
R Arson
Promenade du Paillon
Av Félix Faure
Bd Jean Jaurès
R Rossetti
R de la Préfecture
R Raoul Bosio
68
59
VIEUX NICE
See Enlargement
Allée Professeur Benoît
Montée de Montfort
Q Papacino
13
Port Lympia
Q des Deux Emmanuel
Colline du Château
1
Montée Lesage
19
Q Lunel
Corsica Ferries
Baie des Anges
23
Q Rauba Capeu
Q Internet
Bassin des Amiraux
Moby Lines (200m)

Nice

tram line right outside your door; friendly, attentive owner Sophie makes guests feel right at home.

★ **Hôtel Windsor**   BOUTIQUE HOTEL €€
(☑ 04 93 88 59 35; www.hotelwindsornice.com; 11 rue Dalpozzo; d €92-290; ❄ @ ⊛ ☎; ☐ 7, 9, 22, 27, 59, 70 to Grimaldi or Rivoli) Don't be fooled by the staid stone exterior: inside, owner Odile Redolfi has enlisted the collective creativity of several well-known artists to make each of the 57 rooms uniquely appealing. Some are frescoed, others are festooned with experimental chandeliers or photographic murals. The garden and pool out back are

delightful, as are the small bar and attached restaurant.

★ **Nice Garden Hôtel**   BOUTIQUE HOTEL €€
(☑ 04 93 87 35 62; www.nicegardenhotel.com; 11 rue du Congrès; s €75-85, d €110-140; ⊙ reception 8.30am-9pm; ❄ ☎; ☐ 7, 9, 22, 27, 59, 70 to Grimaldi) Behind heavy iron gates hides this gem: the nine beautifully appointed rooms – the work of the exquisite Marion – are a subtle blend of old and new and overlook a delightful garden with a glorious orange tree. Amazingly, all this charm and peacefulness is just two blocks from the promenade. Breakfast costs €9.

Villa La Tour
BOUTIQUE HOTEL €€

(☑ 04 93 80 08 15; www.villa-la-tour.com; 4 rue de la Tour; d €86-210, junior ste €380; ❋ ⊛) This old-town favourite has 17 rooms, each individually decorated to evoke a different artist – Niki de Saint Phalle, Vaco, Klein and so forth. Riviera history buffs will appreciate the Queen Victoria room. A diminutive flower-decked roof terrace is complemented by a street terrace, ideal for watching Vieux Nice go by. The continental breakfast buffet costs €7.50.

★Hôtel La Pérouse
BOUTIQUE HOTEL €€€

(☑ 04 93 62 34 63; www.hotel-la-perouse.com; 11 quai Rauba Capeu; d €247-665; ❋ @ ⊛ ☒) A prime seaside location and boutique style put La Pérouse in a league of its own. Built into the rock cliff-face of Colline du Château, it evokes the spirit of a genteel villa. Lower-floor rooms face a shaded courtyard and pool; upper-floor rooms have magnificent sea vistas. Smart accent colours and Italian marble bathrooms add flair to the traditional decor.

Hôtel du Petit Palais
HISTORIC HOTEL €€€

(☑ 04 93 62 19 11; www.petitpalaisnice.com; 17 av Émile Bieckert; d €130-350; ⊛ ☒; ◻ 37 to Montée de Cimiez) A refined retreat at the fringes of the city, this early-20th-century hillside mansion gazes down over Nice's rooftops and the distant Mediterranean. Gracious reception, elegant ambience, and sea views from 10 of the 25 rooms all make for a delightful stay, as do the outdoor terraces and small pool. Onsite parking and breakfast cost €12 and €20, respectively.

Hyatt Regency Nice Palais de la Méditerranée
LUXURY HOTEL €€€

(☑ 04 93 27 12 34; www.lepalaisdelamediterranee.com; 13 promenade des Anglais; d €149-879; ❋ @ ⊛ ☒; ◻ 8, 52, 62 to Congrès/Promenade) This opulent edifice is spectacularly recessed behind the massive pillars of its majestic 1929 art-deco façade. Rooms are well-appointed (king-sized beds, separate shower and bath) and all have balconies, though it's worth noting that the sea views tend to be obstructed by the façade's pillars. It all feels indulgently upscale, with starchy tablecloths and starchy service to match.

Exedra
DESIGN HOTEL €€€

(☑ 04 93 16 75 94; http://nice.boscolohotels.com; 12 bd Victor Hugo; d from €299; ❋ @ ⊛ ☒; ◻ 1 to Jean Médecin) Crusted with curlicues, swashes and balconies, this magnificent belle-époque mansion looks like the Austro-Hungarian equivalent of a wedding cake. But behind its old-world exterior, inside it's one of Nice's sexiest, smartest design hotels. Everything from the furniture and fabrics to the guest rooms, art works and pared-down spaces is white with the odd hint of gold, including a super-chic spa and pool.

🍴 Eating

Gelateria Azzurro
ICE CREAM €

(☑ 04 93 13 92 24; www.facebook.com/Gelateriaazzurro; 1 rue Ste-Réparate; ice cream from €2.70; ⊙ 11am-midnight) Next door to the cathedral, this venerable Vieux Nice *gelateria* is beloved for its ice cream, yes – but even more so for its home-made waffle cones, made here on the hot griddle right before your eyes!

★Chez Palmyre
FRENCH €

(☑ 04 93 85 72 32; 5 rue Droite; 3-course menu €18; ⊙ noon-1.30pm & 7-9.30pm Mon, Tue, Thu & Fri) Look no further for authentic Niçois cooking than this packed, cramped, convivial little space in the heart of the old town. The menu is very meat-heavy, with plenty of tripe, veal, pot-cooked chicken and the like, true to the traditional tastes of Provençal cuisine. It's a bargain, and understandably popular. Book well ahead, even for lunch.

★La Rossettisserie
FRENCH €

(☑ 04 93 76 18 80; www.larossettisserie.com; 8 rue Mascoïnat; mains €16.50-19.50; ⊙ noon-2pm & 7-10pm Mon-Sat) Roast meat is the order of the day here: make your choice from beef, chicken, veal or lamb, and pair it with a choice of mashed or sautéed potatoes, ratatouille or salad. Simple and sumptuous, with cosy, rustic decor and a delightful vaulted cellar.

★Mama Baker
BAKERY €

(☑ 06 23 91 33 86; www.facebook.com/Mamabakernice; 13 rue de Lépante; items from €2; ⊙ 7am-2pm & 3-7pm Mon-Fri, 7am-6pm Sat; ◻ 4 to Toselli) Great bakeries abound in France, but even here, truly creative artisanal ones stand out. Witness Mama Baker, where organic grains and specialty ingredients go into a host of unique goodies. Don't miss the delectable *bouchées aux olives,* soft and crispy bite-sized bits of olive-studded cheesy dough, or *pompe à l'huile,* a semi-sweet roll flavoured with olive oil and orange blossoms.

Badaboom
VEGAN €

(☑ 06 71 48 24 01; www.badaboom-nice.net; 11 rue François Guisol; plat du jour €14, with juice €17;

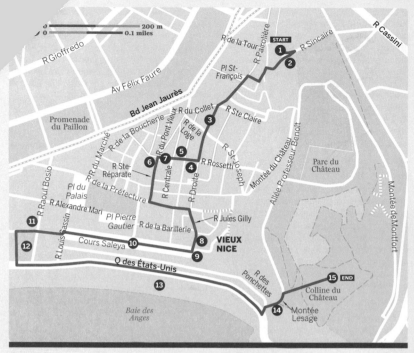

Walking Tour
Vieux Nice & Colline du Château

START PLACE ST-AUGUSTIN
END COLLINE DU CHÂTEAU
LENGTH 2KM; ONE HOUR

Begin exploring in **1** **place St-Augustin**, at the foot of Colline du Château (Castle Hill). Before you, written in Nice's Italian-influenced Nissart dialect, is a **2** **plaque honouring Catarina Segurana**, the city's 16th-century washerwoman heroine, who brandished her washing paddle to rebuff a 1543 Franco-Turkish siege and save the hill from capture.

Head south on **3** **rue Droite**, the main 13th-century thoroughfare for Nice's lucrative salt trade into the Alps. Turn right on rue Rossetti, noticing the sneaky **4** **trompe l'œil windows** to your left. Some shutters here are real, others are fake – can you tell which? One block west, notice the sign for **5** **Carriera de la Judarìa**, the heart of Nice's medieval Jewish quarter.

6 **Cathédrale Ste-Réparate** (p49) soon comes into view. This 17th-century Baroque beauty is the centrepiece of Vieux Nice. **7** **Place Rossetti**, the square before the

church, shows strong Italian stylistic influences in its tall shutters and red-and-yellow colour scheme.

Zigzag south to the eastern end of cours Saleya. At 14 rue Gilles Jilly, the **8** **Centre du Patrimoine** (p55) leads tours of Vieux Nice; to its right at 1 place Charles Felix is the grand golden-hued **9** **Palais Caïs de Pierlas**, where Matisse had his studio from 1921 to 1938. Walk west down cours Saleya, enjoying the colours, sights and smells of Nice's favourite **10** **produce and flower markets** (p49). Further down on the right, glance in at **11** **Maison Auer** (p63), a fifth-generation confectioner's shop famous for its chocolates and candied fruits. On the left is Nice's venerable late-19th-century **12** **opera house** (p63).

Turn left towards the Mediterranean and follow quai des États-Unis east to Nice's popular public beach, **13** **Plage Publique des Ponchettes**. Across the street, hop aboard the **14** **lift** (p54) for a free ride to hilltop **15** **Colline du Château** (p54), where you can enjoy bird's-eye views of every place you just walked.

⏲ 8.30am-6pm Mon-Wed, to 10pm Thu & Fri, 10am-5pm Sat; 🖉 ; 🚌 1 to Garibaldi, 2 to Port Lympia) Vegans and vegetarians are in heaven at this little cafe specialising in fresh cold-pressed juices, whole grains, local organic produce and raw desserts. The menu features salads, wraps and daily *plats du jour,* each served with juice for an extra €3.

⭐**Peixes**   SEAFOOD €€
(🖉 04 93 85 96 15; 4 rue de l'Opéra; small plates €12-19, mains €17-35; ⏲ noon-10pm Tue-Sat) This chic modern seafood eatery is the latest jewel in the crown of Niçois master restaurateur Armand Crespo. All done up in white-and-turquoise nautical decor, with dangling fish eyeball light fixtures and murals of a tentacle-haired mermaid ensnaring a fishing boat, it specialises in fresh local fish turned into scrumptious *ceviches, tartares* and *ta takis* by chefs in the open kitchen.

⭐**Bar des Oiseaux**   FRENCH €€
(🖉 04 93 80 27 33; 5 rue St-Vincent; 3-course lunch menu €20, dinner menus from €30; ⏲ noon-1.45pm & 7.15-9.45pm Tue-Sat) Hidden down a narrow backstreet, this old-town classic has been in business since 1961, serving as a popular nightclub before reincarnating itself as a restaurant (some of its original saucy murals have survived the transition). Nowadays it's a lively bistro serving superb traditional French cuisine spiced up with modern twists. The weekday lunch special offers phenomenal value. Book ahead.

⭐**Franchin**   FRENCH €€
(🖉 04 93 87 15 74; www.franchin.fr; 10 rue Massenet; mains €24-31; ⏲ noon-2pm & 7-10pm Wed-Sun; 🚌 8, 52, 62 to Massenet) White linen tablecloths give this upscale brasserie an air of formality, but the friendly service dispels any notions of stuffiness, and the food is simply divine. Don't miss the octopus salad with potatoes and chorizo (one of the best appetisers you'll find anywhere on the Côte d'Azur), and ask about the €16 weekday specials (excellent value for money when available).

⭐**La Femme du Boulanger**   BISTRO €€
(🖉 04 89 03 43 03; www.facebook.com/femmeduboulanger; 3 rue Raffali; mains €20-25, tartines €16-22; ⏲ 9am-3pm & 7-11pm; 🚌 8, 52, 62 to Massenet) This back-alley gem with sidewalk seating is a vision of French bistro bliss. Mains like duck *à l'orange*, honey-balsamic glazed lamb shank, or perfect *steak au poivre* with *gratin dauphinois* (cheesy potatoes) and perfectly tender veggies are followed up

with raspberry clafoutis, tiramisu and other scrumptious desserts. *Tartines* (open-faced sandwiches) on wood-fired home-made bread are the other house specialty.

Olive et Artichaut   PROVENÇAL €€
(🖉 04 89 14 97 51; www.oliveartichaut.com; 6 rue Ste-Réparate; 3-course menu €32, mains €16-28; ⏲ noon-2pm & 7.30-10pm Wed-Sun) There's barely enough room to swing a pan in this tiny street bistro, especially when it's full of diners (as it often is), but it doesn't seem to faze young Niçois chef Thomas Hubert and his friendly team. He sources as much produce as possible from close-to-home suppliers (Sisteron lamb, Niçois olives, locally caught fish) and likes to give the old classics his own spin. Wise diners reserve.

Café Paulette   TAPAS €€
(🖉 04 92 04 74 48; 15 rue Bonaparte; tapas €6-10, mains €11-29; ⏲ 8am-12.30am Wed-Sat; 🚌 1 to Garibaldi) Chilled and classy Café Paulette has become one of the Petit Marais's favourite hangouts since opening in 2017. Part cafe, part convivial lunch spot and part evening wine bar, it's especially beloved for its tasty international tapas such as roast squid and barley 'risotto' or sesame-crusted tuna tataki. An ample array of cocktails supplements the solid wine list.

La Gauloise   BRASSERIE €€
(🖉 04 93 62 07 90; www.restaurant-lagauloise.fr; 28 av Malausséna; mains €14-24; ⏲ 9am-11pm Tue-Sat, to 3pm Sun; 🚌 1 to Libération) With red and black booths and lashings of exposed brick, this cheerful place in the heart of the Libération neighbourhood serves up solid brasserie food in a lively setting. Go for appetisers such as *beignets de crevettes* (shrimp fritters), followed by lamb chops grilled with thyme, or ravioli with *pistou* sauce. Service is friendly and everything is dependably home-made.

Flaveur   GASTRONOMY €€€
(🖉 04 93 62 53 95; www.restaurant-flaveur.com; 25 rue Gubernatis; 2-course lunch menus €62, 3-/4-course dinner menus €85/99; ⏲ noon-2pm Tue-Fri, 7.30-10pm Tue-Sat; 🚌 3, 7, 9, 27 to Pastorelli) Run by brothers Gaël and Mickaël Tourteau, this small restaurant has big culinary ambitions (and a second Michelin star as of 2018). In a zen dining room with bold fabrics and wooden platters artfully arranged on the walls, it's a haute-cuisine temple, with dishes dressed in foams, creams, reductions and snows, and presented with the precision of museum exhibits.

DON'T MISS

NIÇOIS SPECIALITIES

Niçois specialities include *socca* (a savoury, griddle-fried pancake made from chickpea flour and olive oil, sprinkled with a liberal dose of black pepper), *petits farcis* (stuffed vegetables), *pissaladière* (onion tart topped with black olives and anchovies) and the many vegetable *beignets* (fritters). Try them at **Chez René Socca** (📞04 93 92 05 73; 2 rue Miralhéti; small plates €3-6; ⏱9am-9pm Tue-Sun, to 10.30pm Jul & Aug, closed Nov; 📞), **Socca d'Or** (📞04 93 56 52 93; www.restaurant-soccador-nice.fr; 45 rue Bonaparte; socca €3; ⏱11am-2pm & 6-10pm Mon, Tue & Thu-Sat; 🚌1 to Garibaldi, 2 to Port Lympia) or **Chez Pipo** (📞04 93 55 88 82; www.chezpipo.fr; 13 rue Bavastro; socca €2.90; ⏱11.30am-2.30pm & 5.30-10pm Wed-Sun; 🚌1 to Garibaldi, 2 to Port Lympia).

Jan
GASTRONOMY €€€

(📞04 97 19 32 23; www.restaurantjan.com; 12 rue Lascaris; 3-course lunch menus €55, dinner menus €98-118, incl wine pairings €137-164; ⏱7-10pm Tue-Sat, noon-2pm Fri & Sat; 🚌1 to Garibaldi, 2 to Port Lympia) For the full-on fine-dining experience, make a pilgrimage to the Michelin-starred restaurant of South African chef Jan Hendrik van der Westhuizen. Dishes here are laced with Antipodean and New World flavours and crackle with artistic and culinary flair. There's nothing à la carte – Jan decides his *menus* on the day. It's high-end (dress smart) and sought after; reservations essential.

🍷 Drinking & Nightlife

Cafe terraces on cours Saleya are lovely for an early-evening aperitif. Vieux Nice's bounty of pubs attracts a noisy, boisterous crowd; most bars have a happy hour from 6pm to 8pm. The trendy area to drink these days is Le Petit Marais in the Port Lympia area, where a clutch of new bars and bistros have opened up.

Les Distilleries Idéales
CAFE

(📞04 93 62 10 66; www.facebook.com/ldinice; 24 rue de la Préfecture; ⏱9am-12.30am) The most atmospheric spot for a tipple in the old town, whether you're after one of the many beers on tap or a local wine by the glass. Brick-lined and set out over two floors (with a little balcony that's great for people-watching), it's packed until late. Happy hour is from 6pm to 8pm.

El Merkado
BAR

(📞04 93 62 30 88; www.el-merkado.com; 12 rue St-François de Paule; ⏱11am-1.30am Oct-Apr, 10am-2.30am May-Sep) Footsteps from cours Saleya, this hip tapas bar (strapline: 'In Sangria We Trust') struts its vintage stuff on the ground floor of a quintessential Niçois townhouse. Lounging on its pavement terrace or a sofa with an after-beach cocktail is the thing here.

La Movida
COCKTAIL BAR

(📞04 93 80 48 04; www.movidanice.com; 41 quai des États-Unis; ⏱10am-2am) No place in Vieux Nice offers better people-watching than the beach-facing tables on La Movida's streetside deck and upstairs terrace. Snag one in time for sunset if you can, and stick around for cocktails, tapas, DJs and live music.

Snug & Cellar
PUB

(📞09 63 08 02 12; www.facebook.com/TheSnugAndCellar; 22 rue Droite; ⏱4pm-12.30am Mon-Thu, to 2am Fri, noon-2am Sat, noon-12.30am Sun) A more chilled retreat than many of the pubs in the old town, especially if you can bag one of the prime tables in the eponymous cellar. Weekly open mics, Sunday game nights, televised rugby and football, and occasional live bands keep the interest going.

Le 6
LGBTIQ+

(📞04 93 62 66 64; www.le6.fr; 6 rue Raoul Bosio; ⏱10pm-5am Wed-Sat) Primped and pretty A-gays crowd shoulder to shoulder at Nice's compact, perennially popular gay bar. Le 6 keeps a busy event and party schedule: guest DJs, karaoke and shower shows.

★ La Part des Anges
WINE BAR

(📞04 93 62 69 80; www.lapartdesanges-nice.com; 17 rue Gubernatis; ⏱10am-8.30pm Mon-Thu, to midnight Fri & Sat; 🚌7, 9 to Pastorelli or Wilson) The focus at this classy wine shop–bar is organic wines – a few are sold by the glass, but the best selection is available by the bottle, served with home-made tapenades and charcuterie platters. The name means 'the Angel's Share', referring to the alcohol that evaporates as wines age. There are only a few tables, so arrive early or reserve ahead.

★ La Ronronnerie
CAFE

(📞09 51 51 26 50; www.laronronnerie.fr; 4 rue de Lépante; ⏱11.30am-6pm Tue-Sat; 🚌4 to Sasserno) Kitties rule the roost at this one-of-a-kind cafe, an absolute must for cat-lovers. Five free-range felines roam about the tables, seeking the right lap to sit in, yawning and stretching on plush pedestals or climbing the tree branch overhead. Meanwhile, humans sip hot beverages and nibble on bagels and cake. It's all squeaky clean, without a flea in sight.

★ **Beer District** CRAFT BEER

(📞06 75 10 26 36; www.beerdistrict.fr; 13 rue Cassini; ⊗6pm-1am Tue-Sat; 🚊1 to Garibaldi, 2 to Port Lympia) One of Nice's coolest nightspots, Beer District pours a regularly rotating line-up of 16 draught microbrews and 50 bottled beers from all over the world. The vibe is chilled and friendly, with free tastes cheerfully offered and little bowls of peanuts for snacking.

Rosalina Bar BAR

(📞04 93 89 34 96; www.facebook.com/bar.rosalina; 16 rue Lascaris; ⊗6.30pm-12.30am Mon-Sat; 🚊1 to Garibaldi, 2 to Port Lympia) Way back before Le Port-Garibaldi became so trendy, Rosalina was the neighbourhood's nightlife pioneer. A decade later, it's still an inviting, friendly spot for drinks or dinner, whether you're sipping wine and nibbling complimentary crostini with killer olive tapenade on the outdoor terrace, or downing a cocktail beside the piano and the swing in the whimsically decorated interior.

Rosé WINE BAR

(📞04 93 07 68 40; www.bar-rose.com; 22 rue François Guisol; ⊗6pm-midnight Tue-Sun; 🚊2 to Port Lympia) The concept is simple and the results agreeable at this wine bar. The extensive wine list skews heavily towards the top-quality rosés for which southern France is famous (though reds and whites are also available if you really *must*). Friends congregate for after-work aperitifs and late-afternoon snacks such as *barbajuans* (deep-fried ravioli stuffed with chard and cheese).

Brasserie Artisanale de Nice BREWERY

(📞09 73 59 20 30; www.brasserie-nice.com; 14 av Villermont; 5-7pm Tue-Fri, 10am-noon & 4-7pm Sat; 🚊1 to Libération) Taste some of southern France's most interesting beers at this neighbourhood microbrewery, which opens to the public a few hours per week. Don't miss the flagship Zytha, a Niçois classic brewed with chickpeas, or the Blùna, made with bitter-orange peel and coriander.

☆ **Entertainment**

Nice has a strong live-music tradition, from pop rock to jazz and cabaret; many bars regularly host bands. Vieux Nice is the hotspot, with multiple venues packed together on streets such as rue de la Préfecture and rue Benoît Bunico. Other dynamic neighbourhoods include Le Port-Garibaldi and la Promenade des Anglais in summer.

Opéra de Nice OPERA

(📞04 92 17 40 79; www.opera-nice.org; 4-6 rue St-François de Paule) The vintage 1885 grande dame hosts opera, ballet and orchestral concerts.

Shapko LIVE MUSIC

(📞06 15 10 02 52; www.shapkobar.fr; 5 rue Rossetti; ⊗6pm-2.30am) Near the cathedral square, Shapko stages live music nightly in a variety of genres: blues, funk, jazz, R&B, soul, rock and more. Happy hour is from 6pm to 9pm.

Théâtre Francis Gag THEATRE

(📞04 92 00 78 50; www.theatre-francis-gag.org; 4 rue de la Croix) This community theatre in the heart of Vieux Nice has an active following and still produces some plays in *Nissart,* the local Niçois dialect.

Cinéma Rialto CINEMA

(www.lerialto.cine.allocine.fr; 4 rue de Rivoli; 🚊7, 9, 22, 27, 59, 70 to Rivoli) Undubbed films, with French subtitles.

🛍 **Shopping**

Shops abound in Nice, ranging from the boutiques of Vieux Nice to the New Town's designer fashion temples to the enormous Nice Étoile (www.nicetoile.com; 30 av Jean Médecin; ⊗10am-7.30pm Mon-Sat, 11am-7pm Sun; 🚊1 to Jean-Médecin) shopping mall.

★ **Maison Auer** FOOD

(📞04 93 85 77 98; www.maison-auer.com; 7 rue St-François de Paule; ⊗9am-6pm Tue-Sat) With

LOCAL KNOWLEDGE

LE PETIT MARAIS

Parisians might scoff at the idea, but Le Petit Marais in Nice is nicknamed after the trendy Marais district in Paris for good reason. The Niçois *quartier* – the area of town wedged between place Garibaldi and Port Lympia – buzzes with happening eating, drinking and boutique shopping addresses, firmly off the tourist radar but in the address book of every trendy local. Stroll the lengths of rue Bonaparte, rue Bavestro, rue Lascaris and surrounding streets to catch the city's latest hot new opening.

CÔTE D'AZUR NICE

its gilded counters and mirrors, this opulent shop – run by the same family for five generations – looks more like a 19th-century boutique than a sweet shop, but this is where discerning Niçois have been buying their *fruits confits* (crystallised fruit) and *amandes chocolatées* (chocolate-covered almonds) since 1820.

★ **Marché de la Libération** MARKET
(pl du Général de Gaulle; ⊘6am-12.30pm Tue-Sun; 🚋1 to Libération) After the cours Selaya market, this is Nice's largest outdoor display of fresh fruit and veggies – and an authentically local experience. When it's in full swing, its dozens of stalls fill several city blocks along av Malausséna, place du Général de Gaulle, place de la Gare du Sud, rue Clément Roassal, rue Veillon and bd Joseph Garnier.

Friperie Caprice VINTAGE
(📱09 83 48 05 43; www.facebook.com/Caprice VintageShop; 12 rue Droite; ⊘2-7pm Mon, 11am-1.30pm & 2.30-7pm Tue-Sat) Nice's favourite vintage shop is a treasure trove of clothing, jewellery and accessories spanning much of the 20th century; what really sets it apart is the generous advice and assistance of amiable owner Madame Caprice, who knows every piece in the store.

Cave de la Tour WINE
(📱04 93 80 03 31; www.cavedelatour.com; 3 rue de la Tour; ⊘7am-8pm Tue-Sat, to 12.30pm Sun) Since 1947, locals have been trusting this atmospheric *cave* (wine seller) to find the best wines from across the Alpes-Maritimes and Var. It's a ramshackle kind of place, with upturned wine barrels and blackboard signs, and a loyal clientele, including market traders and fishmongers getting their early-morning wine fix. Lots of wines are available by the glass.

ℹ️ Information

Police Station (Commissariat Nice Central; 📱04 92 17 22 22, for non-French speakers 04 92 17 20 31; 1 av Maréchal Foch; ⊘24hr; 🚋15, 22 to Désambrois) Translators are on hand for non-French speakers.

Hôpital St-Roch (📱04 92 03 77 77; www. chu-nice.fr; 5 rue Pierre Dévoluy; ⊘24hr; 🚋3, 7, 9, 27 to Hôpital St-Roch)

Main Tourist Office (📱04 92 14 46 14; www. nicetourisme.com; 5 Promenade des Anglais; ⊘9am-7pm daily Jun-Sep, to 6pm Mon-Sat Oct-May; 🎧; 🚋8, 52, 62 to Massenet) Nice's main tourist office has handy smaller branches outside the **train station** (📱04 92 14 46 14;

av Thiers; ⊘9am-7pm daily Jun-Sep, to 6pm Mon-Sat, 10am-5pm Sun Oct-May; 🚋1 to Gare Thiers) and on **Promenade du Paillon** (Promenade du Paillon; ⊘10am-8pm Jun-Sep, to 5pm Dec; 🚋1 to Masséna or Opéra-Vieille Ville).

ℹ️ Getting There & Away

Nice-Côte d'Azur Airport is 7km west of the city, with direct flights to many cities in France and Europe, including London in only two hours. Excellent, low-cost public transport connects the airport to downtown, and its location near the A8 autoroute on Nice's western outskirts makes this a convenient place to pick up or drop off a rental car.

Nice-Ville train station, at the north end of Nice's city centre (1.5km inland from the waterfront), is the other main point of entry, with speedy rail connections to cities throughout France, including Paris in less than six hours. Train connections to neighbouring Italy are made through Ventimiglia, 55 minutes away on the French-Italian border.

For drivers, the A8 autoroute offers fast, convenient connections to the rest of France and the Italian border, but parking costs can make a car an expensive liability if you're planning a longer stay in downtown Nice.

ℹ️ Getting Around

Nice's excellent public transport system, operated by **Lignes d'Azur** (📱08 10 06 10 06; www. lignesdazur.com), includes a modern, dependable fleet of trams and buses, with the new tram line 2 radically improving access to the port and airport since 2019.

Tram The tram is generally your best best for journeys between the train station, the airport, the port and the city centre.

Bus Buses are more convenient for destinations along the beachfront and in outlying neighbourhoods such as Cimiez.

On foot Since the weather is often good, and the city beautiful and pedestrian-friendly, walking is also an efficient and enjoyable way to get around, especially in Vieux Nice and Le Port-Garibaldi, and along the Promenade des Anglais.

Bicycle The city's bike-share program **Vélo Bleu** (📱04 93 72 06 06; www.velobleu.org) offers another low-cost option for exploring the city.

ARRIÈRE-PAYS NIÇOIS

This quiet, little-known corner of the Côte d'Azur, 20km inland from Nice, is where Niçois come for weekends away from the urban rush. Attractions are low-key: a walk in the hills (consult www.randoxygene.org for itinerary ideas), a stroll in isolated villages, or a long lunch in an *auberge* (country inn). There is a bus to Peille, but your own wheels are best.

Peillon

POP 1483

This spectacular hilltop village has long been prized by local populations for its defensive characteristics: the first houses date to the 10th century. When you first catch a glimpse of Peillon's improbable perch from the valley below, it's hard to imagine how anyone ever made it up here. Even with the benefit of 21st-century transportation, the dizzying series of hairpin curves that zigzags up the mountain is downright daunting – but once up top, it's pure heaven, with a tight labyrinth of streets to explore and hiking trails leading off into the surrounding mountains.

Rooms at **Auberge de la Madone** (☑04 93 79 91 17; www.auberge-madone-peillon.com; 3 place Auguste Arnulf; r €77-185; 🐾) are nothing to write home about, but the setting of this three-star hotel at the entrance to Peillon village is truly spectacular, with sweeping views over the valley from the lovely outdoor terrace and from private balconies on several of the rooms. The attached **restaurant** (lunch menus €19-25, dinner menus €40-65; ⊙noon-2pm & 7.30-10pm Thu-Tue Feb-early Nov; 🐾) is another drawcard, especially for its good-value lunches.

Peille

Peille may not be quite as spectacular as Peillon, but it makes up for it with history. The village's excellent **Point Info Tourisme** (☑04 93 82 14 40; 15 rue Centrale; ⊙10am-noon & 1-6pm Wed-Sun) offers free, tailor-made guided tours depending on how much time you have (available in English and Italian). Highlights include the medieval centre, the village museum, the church and old photographs of the village.

Bus 116, operated by Lignes d'Azur, links Peille with La Turbie (€1.50, 20 minutes) and Nice (€1.50, one hour) three times a day. SNCF trains run to Nice's Pont Michel station (€3.30, 25 minutes) eight times daily. If you're driving, Peille is 35 minutes from either Nice or Menton.

VILLEFRANCHE-SUR-MER

POP 5112

Heaped above an idyllic harbour, this picturesque village with imposing citadel overlooks the Cap Ferrat peninsula and, thanks to its deep harbour, is a prime port of call for cruise ships. The 14th-century old town, with its tiny, evocatively named streets broken by twisting staircases and glimpses of the sea, is a delight to amble (preferably broken with a long lazy lunch on the water's edge or bijou old-town square). Especially outside of summer season, Villefranche offers a vision of small-town Mediterranean life that's totally unexpected so close to Nice.

◉ Sights & Activities

Chapelle St-Pierre CHURCH
(€3; ⊙10am-noon & 3-7pm Wed-Mon Apr-Sep, 9.30am-12.30pm & 2-6pm Wed-Sun Oct-Mar) Villefranche was a favourite of Jean Cocteau (1889–1963), who sought solace here in 1924 after the death of his companion Raymond Radiguet. Several years later, Cocteau convinced locals to let him paint the neglected, 14th-century Chapelle St-Pierre, which he transformed into a mirage of mystical frescoes. Scenes from St Peter's life are interspersed with references to Cocteau's cinematic work (notably the drivers from *Orpheus*) and friends (Francine Weisweiller, whose **Villa Santo Sospir** (☑04 93 76 00 16; www.villasantosospir.fr; 14 av Jean Cocteau; guided tour €12; ⊙by appointment only) in St-Jean-Cap-Ferrat Cocteau also decorated).

La Citadelle FORTRESS
(Fort St-Elme; ☑04 93 76 33 27; place Emmanuel Philibert; ⊙10am-noon & 2-5.30pm Oct & Dec-May, 10am-noon & 3-6.30pm Jun-Sep, closed Sun morning & Nov) FREE Villefranche's imposing citadel is worth visiting for its impressive architecture. Built by the duke of Savoy between 1554 and 1559 to defend the gulf, its walls today shelter the town hall, well-combed public gardens and several free museums. The **Musée Volti** (☑04 93 76 33 27; ⊙10am-noon & 2-5.30pm Oct & Dec-May, 10am-noon & 3-6.30pm Jun-Sep, closed Sun morning & Nov) FREE displays voluptuous bronzes by Villefranche sculptor Antoniucci Volti; the **Musée Goetz-Boumeester** features modern art in the citadel's former living quarters; and the **Collection Roux** comprises several hundred ceramic figurines depicting life in medieval and Renaissance times.

BOATING

www.amv-sirenes.com; Port de
) Since the creation of an
ne mammal sanctuary be-
naco and Italy in 1999, a
riviera waters. Dolphins are common; more
occasional are sperm whales and fin whales.
Keep your eyes peeled during a half-day dol-
phin- and whale-watching expedition (adult/
child €50/36). The company also organises
two-hour boat trips to Monaco (€22/15).

🛏 Sleeping

Hôtel La Villa Patricia HOTEL €€
(📞 04 93 01 06 70; www.hotel-patricia.riviera.fr;
310 av de l'Ange Gardien; d €85-135; ❄ 🐾) What a
charmer this little hotel is, five minutes from
the beaches. The 10 rooms, though small,
have lots of character – colourful fabrics
on the bed, vintage posters of boats on the
walls, freestanding sinks in the bathroom,
and a few even have dinky balconies.

Welcome Hôtel BOUTIQUE HOTEL €€€
(📞 04 93 76 27 62; www.welcomehotel.com; 3
quai Amiral Courbet; d €235-398, ste from €425;
⊗ Jan-Oct; ❄ 🐾 🖥) Boasting an unbeatable
location on Villefranche's waterfront promenade, this burnt-orange beauty has 35 nauti-
cally themed rooms, all with balcony and sea
view. Those on the 6th floor are predictably
the best, but watching the fishermen pull
into harbour to sell their catch is an early-
morning joy from every room. Guests can
rent out the hotel's 12-man boat (complete
with skipper).

🍴 Eating

La Grignotière BRASSERIE €
(📞 04 93 76 79 83; 3 rue Poilu; pizzas €11-14, mains
€15-23; ⊗ noon-2pm & 7.30-9.30pm; 🚸) For a
cheap and cheerful fill, there is no finer address along the coast than La Grignotière,
known far and wide for its generous portions
of grilled fish and veg, lasagne, pizza and
other crowd-pleasers. Decor is old-fashioned
and nothing to rave about, but the place is
charming and unpretentious. It has a few tables on the pedestrian street.

★ L'Aparté BISTRO €€
(📞 04 93 01 84 88; 1 rue Obscure; mains €22-32;
⊗ 7-10pm Tue-Sun) Slick modern decor and
an adorable canine mascot (Charlie) greet
you at the door of this wonderful backstreet
bistro, where the two-woman team dazzles

with superb food and effortlessly efficient
service. Dishes such as the *parrillada de la
mer*, a mixed grill of fresh seafood, come accompanied by beautifully presented sides. A
class act all around.

★ Les Garçons MEDITERRANEAN €€
(📞 04 93 76 62 40; 18 rue du Poilu; mains €21-28;
⊗ noon-2pm & 7.30-10.30pm Thu-Tue) Gourmets
in the know flock to this stylish address,
buried in Villefranche's rabbit warren of
ancient old-town backstreets. In summer
tables sprawl elegantly across a bijou stone
square, romantically lit by twinkling lights
after dark. Cuisine is creative, local and driv-
en by the market and local fishers' catch.

La Mère Germaine SEAFOOD €€€
(📞 04 93 01 71 39; www.meregermaine.com; 7
quai Amiral Courbet; menus €48, mains €33-65;
⊗ noon-2.30pm & 7-10pm) In business since
1938, La Mère Germaine is an upmarket
waterfront address for seafood, fish and
more seafood, washed down with a splendid
choice of wine.

ℹ Information

Tourist Office (📞 04 93 01 73 68; www.ville
franche-sur-mer.com; Jardins François Binon;
⊗ 9am-6.30pm Jul & Aug, 9am-noon & 2-5pm
Mon-Sat Sep-Jun) April to September the tourist office runs Friday-morning guided tours (€5,
1½ hours) of the citadel museums and old town.
It also has information on family workshops
(adult/child €5/3) held in the citadel museums.

ℹ Getting There & Away

Villefranche is only a 15-minute drive from Nice,
but it's even faster by bus or train, which saves
you the hassle of searching for a parking spot.

The coastal train line runs to Nice (€1.90,
seven minutes) and Monaco (€3.10, 15 minutes).

Bus 81, operated by **Lignes d'Azur** (p64), runs
from Nice's Promenade des Arts stop (just north
of Vieux Nice) to Villefranche every 20 to 25
minutes (€1.50, 10 minutes).

ST-JEAN-CAP-FERRAT

POP 1628

A world unto itself, the prosperous seaside
village of St-Jean-Cap-Ferrat sits aloof from
the hustle and bustle of the main coast road,
astride a dreamy peninsula that juts into
the Mediterranean midway between Nice
and Monaco. Away from the town centre,
the Cap-Ferrat peninsula is dotted with the
villas of billionaires, and laced with 14km of

eucalyptus-scented walking paths affording magnificent views of the rugged coastline. There are various walking itineraries, all easy going; tourist offices have maps.

◉ Sights & Activities

★ Villa Ephrussi de Rothschild
HISTORIC BUILDING

(📞 04 93 01 33 09; www.villa-ephrussi.com/en; adult/child €14/11; ⊙ 10am-6pm Feb-Jun, Sep & Oct, to 7pm Jul & Aug, 2-6pm Mon-Fri, 10am-6pm Sat & Sun Nov-Jan) An over-the-top, belle-époque confection, this villa was commissioned by Baroness Béatrice Ephrussi de Rothschild in 1912. She was an avid art collector and the villa is filled with Fragonard paintings, Louis XVI furniture and Sèvres porcelain. From its balcony, nine exquisite themed gardens appear like a ship's deck. Stunning in spring, the Spanish, Japanese, Florentine, stone, cactus, rose and French gardens are delightful to stroll through – sea views are supreme and fountains 'dance' to classical music every 20 minutes. An audioguide helps make sense of the show.

★ Tour du Cap-Ferrat
WALKING

Encompassing the heart and soul of Cap-Ferrat's coastline, this 7km loop circumnavigates the most rugged and scenic part of the peninsula, with one trailhead starting from **Plage de Passable** behind St-Jean's tourist office and another just south of the village of St-Jean-Cap-Ferrat. Highlights include the series of rocky, secluded coves on the peninsula's western shoreline and the **Cap Ferrat Lighthouse** at the far southern tip. Allow about two hours to walk the trail in either direction.

Tour de la Pointe St-Hospice
WALKING

Starting from **Jardin de la Paix**, a pretty park at the edge of St-Jean-Cap-Ferrat village, this 3km trail loops around the pine-fringed easternmost spur of the Cap Ferrat peninsula and returns to town via beautiful **Plage Paloma** (av Jean Mermoz), where you can stop for a swim, a drink or a meal. Along the way, side paths leads up to the serene Chapelle Ste-Hospice and a WWI cemetery where dozens of Belgian soldiers lie buried. Allow 40 minutes to complete the entire loop.

✗ Eating & Drinking

La Buvette de Jean-Marc
SANDWICHES €

(plage Cros deï Pin; sandwiches €4.50-5.90; ⊙ 7.30am-8.30pm May-Sep) This humble *buvette* (snack bar) has a noble history. Proprie-

tor Jean-Marc is the son of local legend Billy Allari, who ran his own popular *buvette* on this same beach until 1982, when zoning laws forced him to close. Years later, in response to public nostalgia, Jean-Marc was allowed to open this seasonal stand selling reasonably priced sandwiches, beer and coffee.

Le Pacha du Sloop
SEAFOOD €€

(📞 04 93 01 48 63; Port de Plaisance; mains €16-26, lunch menus €28; ⊙ noon-1.30pm & 7-9.30pm Thu-Tue) With its elegant red-and-blue nautical decor and portside terrace within grasp of the bobbing yachts, Le Sloop is a cut above the rest on this popular restaurant strip. Its seafood and shellfish are uberfresh and good value.

La Civette
CAFE

(📞 04 93 76 04 14; 1 place Clemenceau; ⊙ 10am-7pm) In business for nearly 100 years, this cafe boasts a spacious terrace fronting St-Jean's central square. It's popular for morning coffee and afternoon glasses of wine – but most of all for people-watching.

❶ Information

St-Jean-Cap-Ferrat Tourist Office (📞 04 93 76 08 90; www.saintjeancapferrat-tourisme. fr; 5 av Denis Séméria; ⊙ 9.30am-6.30pm Mon-Sat, 9am-1pm & 2-5pm Sun May-Sep, shorter hours rest of year) Down by the port, St-Jean-Cap-Ferrat's efficient tourist office has well-informed staff, with lots of information on walks, activities and water sports. There's also a branch office (59 av Denis Séméria; ⊙ 9am-1pm & 2-5pm Mon-Sat May-Sep, 9am-noon & 1-5pm Mon-Fri Oct-Apr) along the main road in the centre of the peninsula.

❶ Getting There & Away

Bus 81, operated by **Lignes d'Azur** (p64), provides direct service from Nice's Promenade des Arts stop to the centre of St-Jean-Cap-Ferrat (€1.50, 30 minutes).

BEAULIEU-SUR-MER

POP 3726

The seaside holiday town of Beaulieu-sur-Mer is known for its well-preserved belle-époque architecture and its spectacular setting, backed by cliffs that rise abruptly from the Mediterranean east of town. Throw in some nice beaches and a splendid historic villa-museum in the heart of town, and you've got one of the Côte d'Azur's most appealing destinations. Beaulieu also serves as the gateway to Cap-Ferrat.

TIER NIETZSCHE

This incredibly steep downhill hike takes you all the way from the hilltop village of Èze (elevation 427m) to the seaside village of Èze-sur-Mer in just 45 minutes, with some spectacular views en route. Bring sturdy hiking shoes and plenty of water, and take care with loose rocks underfoot. The trail is clearly signposted near the bottom of Èze village.

Beaulieu's open-air produce **market** (place du Général de Gaulle; ⊙8.30am-1pm) takes place in the town centre every morning of the year.

◎ Sights

Villa Grecque Kérylos HISTORIC BUILDING
(☑04 93 01 01 44; www.villakerylos.fr; Impasse Gustave Eiffel; adult/child €11.50/free; ⊙10am-7pm May-Aug, to 5pm Sep-Apr) This magnificent dwelling is a reproduction of a 1st-century Athenian villa, complete with baths, stunning mosaic floors and furniture such as dining recliners. It was designed by scholar-archaeologist Théodore Reinach in 1902, at a time when the must-have for well-to-do socialites was an eccentric house on the Côte d'Azur.

🛏 Sleeping

Hôtel Riviera HOTEL €€
(☑04 93 01 04 92; www.hotel-riviera.fr; 6 rue Paul Doumer; d €79-130; ⊙reception 7.30am-7pm Jan-Oct; 🅿🕸) A breath of fresh air, this tasteful two-star hotel with wrought-iron balconies and a hibiscus-laden summer patio perfect for breakfasting is hard to resist. Rooms are immaculate and comfortable. Probably the best value on the coast.

ⓘ Information

Beaulieu-sur-Mer Tourist Office (☑04 93 01 02 21; www.otbeaulieusurmer.com; place Georges Clémenceau; ⊙9am-6.30pm Mon-Sat, to 12.30pm Sun Jul & Aug, shorter hours rest of year) Beaulieu's tourist office is town-focused, with info on current events and accommodation.

ⓘ Getting There & Away

Beaulieu-sur-Mer is on the coast railway between Nice (€2.30, 10 minutes) and Monaco (€2.70, 10 minutes). Buses 81 and 100, both operated by **Lignes d'Azur** (p64), also run frequently to/from Nice (€1.50, 20 minutes).

ÈZE

POP 2343

This rocky little village perched on an impossibly steep peak is the jewel in the Riviera's crown. The main attraction is the medieval village itself, with small higgledy-piggledy stone houses and winding lanes (and plenty of galleries and shops), and the mesmerising views of the coast.

The village gets very crowded during the day; for a quieter wander, come early in the morning or late afternoon.

◎ Sights

Fort de la Revère VIEWPOINT
Sitting just below Èze, this fort is the perfect place to revel in 360-degree views. An orientation table helps you get your bearings. The fort was built in 1870 to protect Nice (it served as an allied prisoner camp during WWII). There are picnic tables under the trees for an alfresco lunch and dozens of trails in the surrounding Parc Naturel Départemental de la Grande Corniche, a protected area that stretches along the D2564 from Col d'Èze to La Turbie.

Jardin Exotique d'Èze GARDENS
(☑04 93 41 10 30; www.jardinexotique-eze.fr; rue du Château; adult/child €6/3.50; ⊙9am-7.30pm Jul-Sep, to 6.30pm Apr-Jun & Oct, to 4.30pm Nov-Mar) The best panorama in Èze village is from this cactus garden right at the top of the craggy hilltop village. Take time to relax in the ruins of Èze's castle and contemplate the stunning view from the garden's Zen area – few places offer such a wild panorama.

🛏 Sleeping & Eating

Domaine Pins Paul B&B €€
(☑04 93 41 22 66; www.domainepinspaul.fr; 4530 av des Diables Bleus; d/ste €190/290; 🅿🕸) Swimming in the panoramic pool of the Domaine Pins Paul comes complete with views of the sea and Èze village. Rooms in the grand Provençal *bastide* (country house) are beautiful (each with their own little wine fridge), and the surrounding fragrant woods are perfect for a stroll.

★ Château Eza LUXURY HOTEL €€€
(☑04 93 41 12 24; www.chateaueza.com; rue de la Pise; d from €370; 🅿🕸) If you're looking for a place to propose, well, there can be few more memorable settings than this wonderful clifftop hotel, perched dramatically above the glittering blue Mediterranean.

There are only 12 rooms, so it feels intimate, but the service is impeccable, and the regal decor (gilded mirrors, sumptuous fabrics, antiques) explains the sky-high price tag.

Even if you're not staying, it's worth experiencing a sundowner at the stylish bar or a meal at the hotel's luxurious **restaurant** (lunch menus €52-62, tasting menus €120).

ROQUEBRUNE-CAP-MARTIN

POP 12,679

Beautiful Cap Martin nestles its languid shores into the sea of crystalline water between Monaco and Menton. The village of Roquebrune-Cap-Martin is actually centred on the medieval village of Roquebrune, which towers over the cape (the village and cape are linked by innumerable *very* steep steps). The amazing thing about this place is that, despite Monaco's proximity, it feels a world away from the urban glitz of the principality: the coastline around Cap Martin remains relatively unspoiled and it's as if Roquebrune had left its clock on medieval time.

◎ Sights

★**Cabanon Le Corbusier** ARCHITECTURE
(✆ 06 48 72 90 53; www.capmoderne.com; Promenade Le Corbusier; guided tours adult/child €18/free; ⊗ guided tours 10am & 2pm May-Sep) The only building French architect Le Corbusier (1887–1965) ever built for himself is this rather simple – but very clever – beach hut on Cap Martin. The *cabanon* (small beach hut), which he completed in 1952, became his main holiday home until his death. The hut can be visited on excellent two-hour guided tours run by the Association Cap Moderne; tours depart on foot from Roquebrune-Cap-Martin train station and must be reserved in advance by email.

★**Villa E-1027** ARCHITECTURE
(✆ 06 48 72 90 53; www.capmoderne.com; guided tours adult/child €18/free; ⊗ tours 10am & 2pm May-Sep) Irish modernist architect Eileen Gray designed this tour de force of a Mediterranean villa, complete with highly inventive furniture and fixtures, in the late 1920s. Nearly a century later, after an extensive renovation, it is once again open to the public for guided tours. Other noteworthy features of the villa include its beautiful landscaping and seaside location, along with the murals

added by Le Corbusier against Gray's wishes in the 1930s. Reserve ahead online; tour size is limited to 12 people.

Roquebrune HISTORIC SITE
The medieval chunk of Roquebrune-Cap-Martin, Roquebrune sits 300m high on a pudding-shaped lump crowned by the 10th-century **Château de Roquebrune** (✆ 04 93 35 07 22; www.rcm-tourisme.com; place William Ingram; adult/child €5/3; ⊗ 10am-1pm & 2-7pm Jun-Sep, 10am-12.30pm & 2-6pm Feb-May, to 5pm Oct-Jan). Of all the steep and tortuous streets leading up to the château, rue Moncollet, with its arcaded passages and rock-carved stairways, is the most impressive. Architect Le Corbusier is buried in the village cemetery (section J; he designed his own tombstone). Sensational sea views unfold from place des Deux Frères.

🛏 Sleeping & Eating

Hôtel Victoria DESIGN HOTEL €€€
(✆ 04 93 35 65 90; www.hotel-victoria.fr; 7 promenade du Cap Martin; d €133-291; ❀ @ 🛜) Well placed on the waterfront, between Roquebrune's urban attractions and the wilder shores of Cap Martin, this remodelled four-star features immaculate blue and white rooms, with balconies on the sea-facing units. It's next to the bus 100 stop (going to Menton, Nice and Monaco) and 500m from Roquebrune-Cap-Martin train station (on the Nice–Ventimille route). Rates are cheaper online.

Fraise et Chocolat CAFE €
(✆ 06 67 08 32 20; place des Deux Frères; sandwiches/panini €4/5; ⊗ 8am-6pm; 🖋) Strawberry

---

WALKING FROM CAP-MARTIN TO CAP D'AIL

With the exception of a 4km stretch through Monaco, you can walk the entire 13km coastal strip between Roquebrune-Cap-Martin and Cap d'Ail without passing a car. Starting west of Menton, the **Sentier du Littoral** follows Cap Martin's rugged coastline past beaches and wooded shores, including beautiful Plage Buse, all the way to Monaco's Plage Larvotto. Resuming at Plage Marquet near Monaco's western edge, the path skirts dramatic coastal bluffs all the way to hedonistic Plage Mala in Cap d'Ail.

...olate is a delightful cafe with an ...ioned-deli feel on Roquebrune's main ... Stop for a drink, an ice cream or a ... bite (sandwiches and quiches) on the ...et back terrace and swoon over the sweeping sea view.

Les Deux Frères MODERN FRENCH €€
(☑ 06 80 86 22 41, 04 93 28 99 00; www.lesdeux freres.com; 1 place des Deux Frères; lunch/dinner menus €28/53; ☺ noon-1.30pm & 7.30-9.30pm Wed-Sun; 🛜) This gourmet hotel-restaurant with panoramic terrace is super stylish. Eight chic boutique rooms (doubles €75 to €110) – two with sea view – slumber up top, while waiters in black serve magnificent dishes (huge pieces of meat or whole fish for two, delicate fish fillets in hollandaise sauce or spinach and basil olive oil) hidden beneath silver domed platters.

ℹ Information

Tourist Office (☑ 04 93 35 62 87; www.roque brune-cap-martin.com; 218 av Aristide Briand; ☺ 9am-12.30pm & 2-5.30pm Mon-Sat) Local information on the Roquebrune area.

ℹ Getting There & Away

Bus 100 (€1.50) goes to Monaco (15 minutes), Nice (1¼ hours) and Menton (15 minutes); it stops on av de la Côte d'Azur, which lies below Roquebrune and above Cap Martin (you'll see steps near the bus stop).

The Roquebrune-Cap-Martin train station is at the western end of Cap Martin, adjacent to the coastal path and steeply downhill from Château de Roquebrune. Destinations include Monaco (€1.60, four minutes), Nice (€4.80, 30 minutes), Menton (€1.40, six minutes) and Ventimiglia (€3.90, 25 minutes). Trains run half-hourly.

MENTON

POP 28,231

Last stop on the Côte d'Azur before Italy, the seaside town of Menton offers a glimpse of what the high life on the Riviera must have been like before the developers moved in. With its sunny climate, shady streets and pastel mansions – not to mention a lovely old port – it's one of the most attractive towns on the entire coast. Menton's old town is a cascade of pastel-coloured buildings. Add a fantastic museum dedicated to the great artist and film director Jean Cocteau, as well as several excellent restaurants, and Menton really is a must.

To French people, the town is also known for its lemons, which are renowned for their flavour and celebrated every February with a big lemon-themed party.

◉ Sights

★ **Musée Jean Cocteau Collection Séverin Wunderman** GALLERY
(☑ 04 89 81 52 50; www.museecocteaumenton.fr; 2 quai de Monléon; adult/child Jun-Oct €10/free, Nov-May €8/free; ☺ 10am-6pm Wed-Mon) Art collector Séverin Wunderman donated some 1500 Cocteau works to Menton in 2005 on the condition that the town build a dedicated Cocteau museum. And what a museum Menton built: this futuristic, low-rise building is a wonderful space to make sense of Cocteau's eclectic work. Its collection includes drawings, ceramics, paintings and cinematographic work, with exhibits rotating annually. Admission includes the Cocteau-designed Musée du Bastion. At the time of research this museum had suffered from flood damage and was slated to re-open in 2023.

Musée du Bastion GALLERY
(quai Napoléon III; adult/child Jun-Oct €10/free, Nov-May €8/free; ☺ 10am-6pm Wed-Mon) Cocteau loved Menton. It was following a stroll along the seaside that he got the idea of turning a disused 17th-century bastion (1636) on the seafront into a monument to his work. He restored the building himself, decorating the alcoves, outer walls, reception hall and floors with pebble mosaics. The works on display change regularly. Admission includes entry to the Musée Jean Cocteau.

Salle des Mariages ARCHITECTURE
(Registry Office; ☑ 04 92 10 50 00; www.menton. fr/La-Salle-des-Mariages.html; place Ardoïno; adult/ child €2/free; ☺ 8.30am-noon & 2-4.30pm Mon-Fri) In 1957 Jean Cocteau decorated the marriage registry office inside Menton's town hall from floor to ceiling, covering the walls with swirly drawings, and installing leopard-print carpet, aloe-vera lampshades and red armchairs. In 2018 the hall was reopened to the public after a complete renovation that has left it gleaming. A multilingual audioguide runs you through the symbolism of Cocteau's designs.

Basilique St-Michel Archange CHURCH
(place de l'Église St-Michel; ☺ 10am-noon & 4-6pm Mon-Fri Jul & Aug, 10am-noon & 3-5pm Mon-Fri Sep-Jun) From place du Cap a ramp leads to southern France's grandest Baroque church, the 17th-century Italianate Basilique St-Michel Archange. Its olive green and ochre

Menton

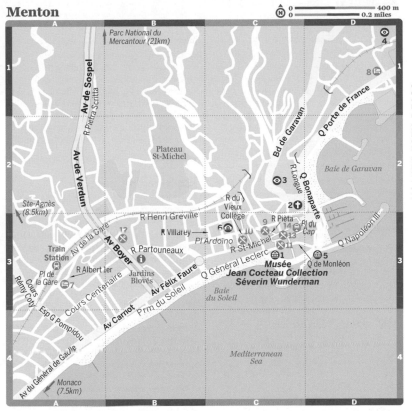

Menton

façade is flanked by a 35m-tall clock tower and 53m-tall steeple (1701–03) and fronted by an attractive square decorated in pretty black-and-white pebble mosaics. The whole ensemble is breathtaking – especially when seen from above, with the Mediterranean glinting in the distance.

Cimetière du Vieux Château   CEMETERY

(montée du Souvenir; ⏰ 7am-8pm Apr-Oct, 8am-5pm Nov-Mar) For great views of the old town and the port, meander all the way up through the historic quarter to this hilltop cemetery. It's something of a pilgrimage site for rugby fans, who come to pay their

WORTH A TRIP

VENTIMIGLIA

Menton literally sits on the border with Italy and there is no finer reason to dash across for a dose of *la dolce vita* than the all-day Friday market in Ventimiglia (Vintimille in French), the border town on the Italian side. The market sprawls over 1km along the seafront and is popular among French shoppers for its cheap fruit and veg, tasty deli counters (mozzarella-stuffed peppers, sun-dried tomatoes etc), bargain leather goods and cheap fashion. Watch out for counterfeits here; French customs take it very seriously and you risk a fine and confiscation of your goods.

Ventimiglia is at the end of the French SNCF network; there are half-hourly trains to/from Menton (€2.70, 10 minutes), Monaco (€4.60, 30 minutes), Nice (€8, one hour) and Cannes (€13.20, 1¾ hours).

respects at the tomb of William Webb Ellis, legendary inventor of the sport.

Jardin de la Serre de la Madone
GARDENS

(☑04 93 57 73 90; www.serredelamadone.com; 74 rte de Gorbio; adult/child €8/4; ☺10am-6pm Tue-Sun Apr-Oct, to 5pm Jan-Mar, closed Nov & Dec) Beautiful if slightly unkempt, this garden was designed by American botanist Lawrence Johnston. He planted dozens of rare plants picked up from his travels around the world. Abandoned for decades, it has been mostly restored to its former glory. Guided tours (1½ hours) take place daily at 3pm. Take Zest (p73) bus 7 (€1.50, 15 minutes) from Menton's train or bus station to the Serre de la Madone stop.

Jardin Botanique Exotique du Val Rahmeh
GARDENS

(☑04 93 35 86 72; www.mnhn.fr/fr/visitez/lieux/jardin-botanique-exotique-menton; av St-Jacques; adult/child €7/5; ☺9.30am-12.30pm & 2-6pm Wed-Mon Apr-Sep, 10am-12.30pm & 2-5pm Wed-Mon Oct-Mar) Laid out in 1905 for Lord Radcliffe, governor of Malta, the terraces of the Val Rahmeh overflow with exotic fruit-tree collections, including the only European specimen of the Easter Island tree *Sophora toromiro,* now extinct on the island.

☆☆ Festivals & Events

Fête du Citron
CARNIVAL

(Lemon Festival; www.fete-du-citron.com; ☺Feb) Menton's quirky two-week Fête du Citron sees sculptures and decorative floats made from tonnes of lemons weave along the seafront. Afterwards, the monumental lemon creations are dismantled and the fruit sold off at bargain prices in front of Palais de l'Europe. Each year the festival follows a different theme.

🛏 Sleeping

Hôtel Lemon
HOTEL €

(☑04 93 28 63 63; www.hotel-lemon.com; 10 rue Albert 1er; s €65, d €73-85; ☎) Hôtel Lemon sits in an attractive 19th-century villa with a pretty garden, opposite a school. Its spacious minimalist rooms are decked out in shades of white with bright red or lemon-yellow bathrooms. Breakfast costs €9.

★ Hôtel Napoléon
BOUTIQUE HOTEL €€

(☑04 93 35 89 50; www.napoleon-menton.com; 29 porte de France; d €95-330, junior ste €149-450; ❀@☎☀) Standing tall on the seafront, the Napoléon is Menton's most stylish sleeping option. Everything from the pool to the restaurant-bar and the back garden (a heaven of freshness in summer) has been beautifully designed. Rooms are decked out in white and blue, with Cocteau drawings on headboards. Sea-facing rooms have balconies but are a little noisier because of the traffic.

✕ Eating & Drinking

Halles Municipales
MARKET €

(quai de Monléon; ☺6am-1pm Tue-Sun) Menton's covered food market near the seafront bursts with local colours, scents and flavours.

Fleur de Sel
FRENCH €

(☑04 93 44 87 34; 2 rue du Vieux Collège; crêpes €8-12; ☺noon-2.30pm & 7-10pm) Genuine, reasonably priced Breton crêpes make for a low-key lunch or dinner at this backstreet restaurant in the heart of Menton's old town. Everything, from ham and cheese to house specialties like crab and avocado, comes with a side salad, and free-flowing cider contributes to the convivial atmosphere.

Maison Martin et Fils
MODERN FRENCH €€

(☑04 93 35 74 67; www.maison-martin-et-fils.com; 7 rue des Marins; mains €15-31, menus €26-31;

⊘noon-3pm & 7-9.15pm Tue-Sat) Tucked behind Menton's covered market, Maison Martin serves a good-value *plat du jour* (€11.90) and a house-made menu that highlights local specialities such as zucchini-flower *beignets* and *socca* (chickpea fritter)-wrapped burgers.

Le Bistrot des Jardins PROVENCAL €€
(☑ 04 93 28 28 09; www.le-bistrot-des-jardins.fr; 14 av Boyer; 2-/3-course menus lunch €27/33, dinner €33/40; ⊘noon-2pm & 7.30-9.30pm Tue-Sat, noon-2pm Sun) Reservations are required at this delightful patio garden restaurant with tables clothed in lilac languishing alfresco between flowering magnolias and aromatic pots of thyme, sage and other Provençal herbs. The traditional, market-inspired cuisine is equally attractive.

★**Le Mirazur** GASTRONOMY €€€
(☑ 04 92 41 86 86; www.mirazur.fr; 30 av Aristide Briand; lunch menus €80-110, dinner menus €110-210; ⊘12.15-2pm & 7.15-10pm Wed-Sun Mar-Dec) Design, cuisine and sea views (the full sweep of the Med above Menton town below) are all spectacular at this 1930s villa with a twinset of Michelin stars. This is the culinary kingdom of daring Argentinian chef Mauro Colagreco, who flavours dishes not with heavy sauces, but with herbs and flowers from Le Mirazur's dazzling herb and flower garden, citrus orchard and vegetable patch.

Vinum Veritas WINE BAR
(☑ 04 93 78 97 69; www.facebook.com/vinum.veritas.5; 32 rue St-Michel; ⊘5-11pm Sun-Thu, to midnight Fri & Sat) The stone-vaulted back room at this Italo-Albanian-run wine bar makes a cosy spot for an evening tipple, accompanied by boards of cheese and charcuterie.

❶ Information

Tourist Office (☑ 04 92 41 76 76; www.tourisme-menton.fr; 8 av Boyer; ⊘9am-7pm Jul & Aug, 9am-12.30pm & 2-6pm Mon-Sat Sep-Jun) Information on Menton.

❶ Getting There & Away

Bus 100, operated by **Lignes d'Azur** (p64), runs frequently to Nice (€1.50, 1½ hours) via Monaco (40 minutes) and the Corniche Inférieure. Bus 110 links Menton with Nice–Côte d'Azur airport (one way/return €22/33, 1¼ hours, hourly). **Zest** (☑ 04 93 35 93 60; www.zestbus.fr) offers additional bus service to inland villages such as Gorbio, Roquebrune and Ste-Agnès.

There are regular train services (half-hourly, to Ventimiglia in Italy (€2.70, 10 minutes), Monaco (€2.30, 11 minutes) and Nice (€5.50, 40 minutes).

GORBIO

POP 1387

Drop-dead-gorgeous Gorbio, just a few kilometres inland from Menton and the Mediterranean coast, is a classic Provençal *village perché* (hilltop village). Strolling through the town's narrow medieval streets is the main entertainment here, along with the scenic climb to the neighbouring village of Ste-Agnès.

✖ Eating

★**Le Beauséjour** MODERN FRENCH €€
(☑ 04 93 41 46 15; 14 place de la République; lunch/dinner menus €29/47, mains €20-28; ⊘noon-2.30pm Thu-Tue Apr-Oct, 7.15-9.30pm Jul-Sep) The stuff of Provençal lunch dreams, 'Beautiful Stay' serves delicious local fare in a buttermilk house with front terrace overlooking Gorbio's village square. The interior dining room, straight out of a design magazine, proffers panoramic views of the tumbling vale. Every item, from *salade niçoise* to duck breast glazed with local honey, is a work of art. No credit cards.

❶ Getting There & Away

Bus 7, operated by **Zest** (☑ 04 93 35 93 60; www.zestbus.fr), runs four to six times daily between Gorbio and Menton's train and bus stations (€1.50, 30 minutes). With a car, the drive takes 20 minutes from Menton or 45 minutes from Nice.

LOCAL KNOWLEDGE

THE BAKER'S KISS

Au Baiser du Mitron (The Baker's Kiss; ☑ 04 93 57 67 82; www.aubaiserdumitron.com; 8 rue Piéta; items from €1; ⊘8am-7pm Tue-Sun) is a one-of-a-kind *boulangerie* showcasing breads from the Côte d'Azur, inland Provence and other favourite spots from baker-owner Kevin Le Meur's world travels. Everything is baked in a traditional *four à bois* (wood bread oven) from 1906, using 100% natural ingredients and no preservatives. The *tarte au citron de Menton* (Menton lemon tart) is the best there is.

...t itself is what most people associate with the Côte d'Azur, but the *arrière-pays* (hinterland) has a charm of its own. Less crowded and delightfully varied, it has something for everyone – from walkers to culture vultures to foodies.

St-Paul de Vence

POP 3451

Once upon a time, St-Paul de Vence was a small medieval village atop a hill looking out to sea. Then came the likes of Picasso in the postwar years, followed by showbiz stars such as Yves Montand and Roger Moore, and St-Paul shot to fame. The village is now home to dozens of art galleries as well as the renowned Fondation Maeght.

Among the many artists who have lived in or passed through St-Paul over the years are Soutine, Léger, Cocteau, Matisse and Chagall. The latter is buried with his wife, Vava, in the cemetery at the village's southern end (immediately to the right as you enter).

St-Paul's tiny cobbled lanes get overwhelmingly crowded in high season – come early or late to beat the rush.

◉ Sights

Fondation Maeght   MUSEUM
(☏ 04 93 32 81 63; www.fondation-maeght.com; 623 chemin des Gardettes; adult/child €15/10; ⊙10am-7pm Jul-Sep, to 6pm Oct-Jun) St-Paul's renowned art museum features works by a who's-who of 20th-century artists – including many who found inspiration along the Côte d'Azur. From pieces by Georges Braque, Vassily Kandinsky and Marc Chagall to spooky sculptures by Giacometti and glassworks by Miró, it's a treasure trove – although works from the permanent collection are often disappointingly confined to a single room to make room for temporary exhibits. The innovative building designed by Josep Lluís Sert is fittingly experimental, and the gardens are delightful.

Musée Renoir   MUSEUM
(☏ 04 93 20 61 07; www.cagnes-tourisme.com; chemin des Colettes, Cagnes-sur-Mer; adult/child €6/free; ⊙10am-1pm & 2-6pm Jun-Sep, 10am-noon & 2-6pm Apr & May, to 5pm Oct-Mar, closed Tue year-round) Immersed in greenery 6km southeast of St-Paul de Vence, Le Domaine des Collettes in Cagnes-sur-Mer was home and studio to an arthritis-crippled Renoir (1841–1919) from 1907 until his death. He lived there with his wife and three children, and the house is wonderfully evocative, despite being sparsely furnished. On display are a handful of original paintings, including a version of *Les Grandes Baigneuses* (The Women Bathers; 1892), as well as a number of sculptures, letters, photos, documents and the artist's wheelchair.

🛏 Sleeping & Eating

Villa St Paul   B&B €€
(☏ 04 93 72 58 71; www.villasaintpauldevence.com; 293 Chemin Fontmurado; r €78-150, apt €98-240; 🛜🏊) At this attractive oasis 1km below St-Paul, friendly young hosts David and Jeannette welcome guests with three spacious, comfortable rooms and a grassy pool area for lounging. Days begin with abundant breakfasts featuring fresh-squeezed orange juice, croissants, a variety of cheeses and eggs cooked to order. The pricier adjoining Étoile de St-Paul features six more rooms and its own *hammam*.

★ Les Cabanes d'Orion   B&B €€€
(☏ 06 75 45 18 64; www.orionbb.com; Impasse des Peupliers, 2436 chemin du Malvan; d €230-285; 🛜🏊) Dragonflies flit above water lilies in the natural swimming pool, while guests slumber amid a chorus of frogs and cicadas in luxurious cedar-wood treehouses at this enchanting, ecofriendly B&B. Children are well catered for with mini-*cabanes* in two of the tree houses. There's a minimum two- to four-night stay from May to September.

La Colombe d'Or   HOTEL €€€
(☏ 04 93 32 80 02; www.la-colombe-dor.com; place de Gaulle; d €250-430; 🅿🛜🏊) This world-famous inn could double as the Fondation Maeght's annexe: the 'Golden Dove' was party HQ for dozens of 20th-century artists (Chagall, Braque, Matisse, Picasso etc) who paid for their meals in kind, resulting in an extraordinary private art collection. Rooms are strung with unique pieces, as are the **restaurant** (mains €29-49; ⊙noon-2.30pm & 7.30-10.30pm late Dec-Oct) and garden.

★ Le Tilleul   MODERN FRENCH €€
(☏ 04 93 32 80 36; www.restaurant-letilleul.com; place du Tilleul; menus €25-29, mains €15-32; ⊙8.30am-10.30pm; ☏) Considering its location on the *remparts,* this place could have easily plumbed the depths of a typical

A CULINARY PILGRIMAGE

Filling three floors of the childhood home of Auguste Escoffier (1846–1935), the **Musée Escoffier de l'Art Culinaire** (Escoffier Museum of Culinary Arts; ☑ 04 93 20 80 51; http://fondation-escoffier.org; 3 rue Auguste Escoffier, Villeneuve-Loubet; adult/child €6/free; ⊙10am-1pm & 2-7pm daily Jun-Sep, to 6pm Oct-May) celebrates the life of France's most legendary chef. Exhibits include a reconstructed 19th-century Provençal kitchen, giant chocolate sculptures and vintage menus. Escoffier's culinary techniques and global celebrity were responsible for establishing the reputation of French cuisine across the world, and still form the basis for many a brasserie menu – although some of his more outlandish creations (tortoise consommé, bacon-wrapped larks) seem a tad peculiar today.

The museum is 6.5km south of St-Paul de Vence, in the village of Villeneuve-Loubet.

tourist trap. But it hasn't. Instead, divine and beautifully presented dishes grace your table, complemented by an all-French wine list and blissful terrace seating under the shade of a big lime-blossom tree. Open for breakfast and afternoon tea too.

❶ Information

Tourist Office (☑ 04 93 32 86 95; www.saint-pauldevence.com; 2 rue Grande; ⊙10am-7pm Jun-Sep, to 6pm Oct-May, closed 1-2pm Sat & Sun) The dynamic tourist office runs a series of informative, themed guided tours that delve into the village's illustrious past. Some tours are also available in English. Book ahead.

❶ Getting There & Away

Bus 400, operated by **Lignes d'Azur** (p64), serves St-Paul once or twice hourly, running between Nice (€1.50, one hour) and Vence (€1.50, seven minutes). The town is closed to traffic, but there are several car parks (€2.70 per hour) surrounding the village.

Vence

POP 18,393

Some visitors only come to Vence to see Matisse's otherworldly Chapelle du Rosaire at the edge of town. Yet Vence deserves more than a flying visit. It's well worth lingering a while to explore the city's charming and well-preserved medieval centre, much of which dates back to the 13th century. Sample some of Vence's gastronomic talent on restaurant-fringed place du Peyra, stroll through lovely place du Frêne with its 500-year-old ash tree, or take time to appreciate the Marc Chagall mosaic in Vieux Vence's cathedral. A fruit-and-veg market fills place du Jardin several mornings a week, with antiques on Wednesday.

◉ Sights

★ **Chapelle du Rosaire**　ARCHITECTURE
(Rosary Chapel; ☑ 04 93 58 03 26; www.vence.fr/the-rosaire-chapel; 466 av Henri Matisse; adult/child €7/4; ⊙10am-noon & 2-6pm Tue, Thu & Fri, 2-6pm Wed & Sat Apr-Oct, to 5pm Nov-Mar) An ailing Henri Matisse moved to Vence in 1943 to be cared for by his former nurse and model, Monique Bourgeois, who'd since become a Dominican nun. She persuaded him to design this extraordinary chapel for her community. The artist designed everything from the decor to the altar and the priests' vestments. From the road, you can see the blue-and-white ceramic roof tiles, wrought-iron cross and bell tower. Inside, light floods through the glorious blue, green and yellow stained-glass windows.

Musée de Vence　MUSEUM
(Fondation Émile Hugues; ☑ 04 93 24 24 23; www.museedevence.com; 2 place du Frêne; adult/child €6/3; ⊙11am-6pm Tue-Sun) With its wonderful 20th-century art exhibitions, this daring art museum inside the imposing Château de Villeneuve offers a nice contrast to Vence's historic quarter. Matisse-lovers will appreciate the permanent exhibit on the 2nd floor, which showcases the city of Vence's private collection of six dozen works by the great artist, displayed on a rotating basis.

Cathédrale Notre-Dame de la Nativité　CATHEDRAL
(www.vence.fr/notre-dame-de-la-nativite; place Clemenceau; ⊙9am-6pm) Vence's Romanesque cathedral was built in the 11th century on the site of an old Roman temple. It contains Chagall's mosaic of Moses (1979), appropriately watching over the baptismal font.

🛏 Sleeping

★ La Maison du Frêne   B&B €€
(📞 06 88 90 49 69; www.lamaisondufrene.com; 1 place du Frêne; d €135-170; ☺Feb-Dec; ❋ 🗢) Named for the gorgeous 500-year-old ash tree out front, this arty guesthouse is a labor of love for avid art collectors Thierry and Guy. Yes, that Niki de Saint Phalle is an original. And yes, the César too. It's an essential sleepover for true art-lovers, who will thoroughly appreciate the superb, sprawling rooms that boldly mix classic and contemporary styles.

Le 2   B&B €€
(📞 06 15 37 22 40, 04 93 24 42 58; www.le2avence. fr; 2 rue des Portiques; d incl breakfast €108-128; ❋ 🗢) This 'bed and bistro,' as it's tagged itself, is a welcome addition to staid Vence. Nicolas and his family have turned this medieval townhouse into a hip establishment offering four very modern rooms upstairs and a popular vegetarian restaurant down below. Value and atmosphere guaranteed.

✗ Eating

La Onda   TAPAS €
(📞 04 93 32 90 97; www.la-onda.fr; 3 rue Place Vieille; tapas €6-12; ☺noon-2.30pm & 7-10pm Tue-Sat) Bright artwork covers the walls and the scent of garlic fills the air at this exuberant, Spanish-run tapas bar on one of Vence's prettiest squares. Everything is authentic and exceptionally tasty, from *gambas al ajillo* (shrimp sautéed in garlic and olive oil) to *txistorra* (Basque sausage with peppers) to the Catalan-inspired garlic-rubbed toast topped with tomato and Iberian ham.

★ Restaurant La Litote   MODERN FRENCH €€
(📞 04 93 24 27 82; www.lalitote-vence.com; 5 rue de l'Évêché; 2-/3-course lunch menus €18/22, dinner menus €29/34; ☺noon-2.30pm & 7-10pm, closed Tue Jun-Sep, closed Sun evening & Mon Oct-May) In the heart of Vence's old town, La Litote is the very picture of a village bistro, with tables set out on the square and blackboard menus filled with seasonal classics. Expect stews, supremes and steaks in winter, grilled fish and salads in summer, and delicious desserts year-round. Homey and lovely.

Le Michel Ange   MEDITERRANEAN €€
(📞 04 93 58 32 56; 1 place Godeau; 2-/3-course lunch menus €19/23, dinner menus €26/30; ☺noon-2pm Tue-Sun, 7-9.30pm Fri & Sat) With tables beneath a leafy tree on a fountain-clad square behind the cathedral, this casual restaurant gets top billing among locals. Families with kids swarm here at weekends for its car-free outdoor space and easy, excellent-value cuisine. The menu abounds in Niçois specialties such as *petits farcis* (meat-stuffed vegetables), *daube de boeuf* (Provençal-style beef stew), and codfish aioli every Friday.

ℹ Information

Tourist Office (📞 04 93 58 06 38; www. vence-tourisme.fr; 8 place du Grand Jardin; ☺9am-6pm Mon-Sat) Has several good leaflets on self-guided tours in and around Vence.

ℹ Getting There & Away

Lignes d'Azur (p64) bus 400 to/from Nice (€1.50, 1¼ hours, once or twice hourly) stops on place du Grand Jardin. Medieval Vence is pedestrianised; park in the paid lot underneath place du Grand Jardin or in the streets leading to the historical centre.

Les Gorges du Loup

A combination of perilously perched villages, sheer cliffs, waterfalls, densely wooded slopes and gushing rivers, the Gorges du Loup is a scenic, unspoiled part of the world, known for spectacular drives and walking trails.

The highlight of the gorge's western side (reached via the D3) is the fortified village of Gourdon, which teeters on a rocky summit. From place Victoria at the top of the souvenir-shop-riddled village, a magnificent coastal panorama sweeps 80km from Nice to Théoule-sur-Mer.

Down below, along the D2210, bitter-orange trees are cultivated on terraces around the beautifully intact medieval village of Le Bar-sur-Loup. Further north along the rushing river's edge, tucked beneath the remnants of an old railway bridge (bombed during WWII) you'll find the hamlet of Le Pont du Loup.

On the eastern side, off the D2210, the isolated hamlet of Courmes is reached by a single, winding lane.

◎ Sights & Activities

Confiserie Florian   FACTORY
(📞 04 93 59 32 91; www.confiserieflorian.com; chemin de la Confiserie, Le Pont du Loup; ☺9am-noon & 2-6.30pm Sep-Jun, 9am-7pm Jul & Aug) **FREE** At this sweet factory jams, candied fruits and crystallised violets, roses and

verveine leaves are cooked in a 19th-century flour mill. Free 20-minute tours show you how clementines and other fruits are candied by being simmered in syrup for three minutes every second day over a 45-day period; visit weekdays to see the kitchens in action. Tours end in the boutique, where you can taste and buy.

Ascendance PARAGLIDING
(☑ 04 93 09 44 09, 06 61 42 08 64; www.ascendance06.com; Auberge de Gourdon, rte de Caussol, Gourdon) This paragliding school in Gourdon, on the western side of the scenic Gorges du Loup, organises 10-/20-/30-minute maiden flights in tandem (€70/90/120), as well as piloting lessons.

Chemin du Paradis WALKING
(www.terresetpierresdazur.com/paradis) This popular hiking trail follows the old mule track used by villagers from Gourdon who descended into the Gorges du Loup to cultivate flowers and fruit trees. Count on 80 minutes from Gourdon to Le Pont du Loup, or 90 minutes to Le Bar-sur-Loup.

🛏 Sleeping & Eating

⭐**La Cascade** B&B €
(☑ 04 93 09 65 85; www.gitedelacascade.com; 635 chemin de la Cascade, Courmes; d €65-75, q €95-130; ❄ 🎧 ≋) This rural idyll sits snug in a 4-hectare former sheepfold, with forest, ponds, swimming pool, *pétanque* pitch and majestic views of the Gorges du Loup and surrounding mountains. In summer it feels like the edge of the world, while winter is about cosying up by the fire. Dinner (€27 for three courses, including drinks) is another highlight.

Château de Grasse RENTAL HOUSE €€€
(☑ 06 82 53 66 96, 04 93 42 06 29; www.chateaudegrasse.com; 6 place Francis Paulet, Le Bar-sur-Loup; 6-bedroom home €449; 🅿 🎧) It's hard to imagine that Le Bar-sur-Loup's majestic 13th-century castle, perched right at the top of the village, once lay in ruins. It's now an appealing vacation rental with irresistible wooden-deck terrace out front and German owner Heinrich at the helm. Six huge rooms sleeping up to 14 people ooze 'country-chic' elegance, with soft-toned fabrics and sweeping valley views.

Au Vieux Four BISTRO €€
(☑ 04 93 09 68 60; www.facebook.com/auvieuxfour gourdon; 4 rue Basse, Gourdon; lunch menus €22-28, dinner menus €38-42; ⊙ noon-2pm Fri-Tue, 7.15-9pm Fri & Sat) With stone walls, whitewashed beamed ceilings, vintage Laughing Cow posters and colourful mismatched napkins, this bistro in medieval Gourdon wins instant cosiness points. But the real highlight is chef Stephan Lucas' splendid home cooking. The short, market-fresh menu bursts with flavour in dishes such as chicken and vegetable risotto or pork ribs with creamy polenta, garlicky mushrooms and caramelised carrots.

Hôtel Particulier des Jasmins FRENCH €€
(☑ 04 93 60 42 05; www.lesjasmins.fr; 938 av des Écoles, Le-Bar-sur-Loup; mains €14, lunch menus €18-24.50; ⊙ 9am-9pm Tue-Sat, to 2.30pm Sun) With panoramic views over the valley, Bruce and Julien's shiny restaurant – its façade cleverly stencilled to give the appearance of a much older enterprise – fills the ground floor of a high-ceilinged historic perfumemaker's home. The seasonally sourced menu changes every Tuesday, ushering in three new entrées, three main courses and three desserts weekly. We loved the lavender crème brûlée!

❶ Getting There & Away

Exploring the Gorges du Loup is much easier with your own vehicle. Main access roads in the region include the D2210, which loops along the river between Pont du Loup and Le-Bar-sur-Loup; the D3, which climbs the valley's western side to Gourdon; and the D6 and D503 along the eastern side to Courmes. Driving times from Nice are 40 minutes to Pont du Loup, 45 minutes to Le-Bar-sur-Loup, 50 minutes to Gourdon and 55 minutes to Courmes.

Lignes d'Azur (p64) provides limited bus service in the area on its route 511, which connects Pont du Loup with Vence (€1.50, 30 minutes) and Grasse (€1.50, 25 minutes) four to eight times daily.

Tourrettes-sur-Loup
POP 3995

Dubbed the 'city of violets' after its signature flower, Tourrettes is a postcard-perfect, 15th-century hilltop village with a substantial community of artists and international expatriates. Walking around the town won't take you more than half an hour or so, but it's a delightful place to kick back for a couple of days. There are some fine restaurants, galleries and artisans' shops in town, and a smattering of other attractions in the surrounding hills.

s & Activities

Violettes FARM
06 97; www.facebook.com/musee
ttes; chemin de la Ferrage; ⊘10am-
Tue-Sat Apr-Sep) **FREE** To find out
more about Tourrettes' famous violet and
see the fields where it is cultivated, head to
the Bastide aux Violettes, 10 minutes' walk
from the centre of town. This modern space
takes you through the history of the flower
and its many uses.

Fromagerie des Courmettes FARM
(⊘04 93 59 39 93; rte des Courmettes; ⊘9am-
12.30pm & 4-6pm Mar-Dec) 🐾 High in the hills
above Tourrettes-sur-Loup, this organic
goats-cheese producer welcomes visitors.
To see its 70 goats being milked, arrive
sharp at 8am. Farm tours (one hour, €63
for up to 10 people, available in English)
include tastings of the cheese – divine and
incredibly diverse in taste. You can also buy
cheese direct from the onsite shop without
taking a tour. Find the farm 4.4km along
the perilously steep and hairpin-laced rte
des Courmettes, signposted off the D2210
to Tourrettes.

★ **Domaine des Courmettes** WALKING
(⊘04 92 11 02 32; www.courmettes.com; rte des
Courmettes; donation requested; ⊘8am-8pm Mar-
Dec) 🐾 This peaceful nature reserve with
sweeping Mediterranean views protects
millennia-old holly oaks and rare birds on
the lofty Plateau des Courmettes. There are
three circular *sentiers de randonée* (walking trails), ranging from an easy 1.2km to
a steep 5.5km hike uphill to the top of the
Pïc des Courmettes (1280m). Grab a map
and work out trailheads at the visitors centre. There's no entrance fee, but visitors are
asked to donate what they can to help maintain the reserve.

🛏 Sleeping & Eating

★ **Le Mas des Cigales** B&B €€
(⊘04 93 59 25 73; www.lemasdescigales.com;
1673 rte des Quenières; d €140; ❄🛜🏊) With
its pretty Provençal *mas* (farmhouse), tumbling garden, picture-perfect pool and feast
of a breakfast, you'll never want to leave this
five-room *chambre d'hôte*, run with care and
passion by friendly Belgian couple Stefaan
and Véronique. Active types will adore the
tennis courts, *pétanque* pitch and bicycles.
Dinner (€39 including aperitif and wine) is
cooked up three nights a week.

Tom's ICE CREAM €
(⊘04 93 24 12 12; 25 Grand Rue; ice cream 1/2/3
scoops €2.50/4/5) No visit to Tourrettes is
complete without a cup or cone of violet ice
cream topped with a candied violet from
Tom's. The town's beloved *glacier* (ice cream
shop) features plenty of other floral flavours
such as jasmine, along with traditional favourites such as chocolate, strawberry etc.

★ **Bistrot**
Gourmand Clovis MODERN FRENCH €€€
(⊘04 93 58 87 04; www.clovisgourmand.fr; 21
Grand Rue; 2-/3-/4-course menus €40/49/58,
tasting menus with/without wine €105/67; ⊘12.30-
1.30pm & 7.30-9.30pm Wed-Fri & Sun, 7.30-9.30pm
Sat; 🐾) This bistro in the cobbled heart of
Tourrettes is a stunner – for its stylish contemporary decor and its creative cuisine,
honoured with a Michelin star. Chef Julien
Bousseau works with only the best seasonal produce from the region and the results
are superb. The wine list stays very much in
Provence and is equally appealing. Bookings
essential.

ℹ Information

Tourist Office (⊘04 93 24 18 93; www.
tourrettessurloup.com/office-de-tourisme;
2 place de la Libération; ⊘9am-1pm &
2-5.30pm Mon-Sat) Mountains of information,
including itineraries, on walking in the scenic
hills and flower fields around Tourrettes-sur-
Loup.

ℹ Getting There & Away

Bus 510-511, operated by **Lignes d'Azur** (p64),
runs from Tourrettes-sur-Loup to Vence (€1.50,
15 minutes) and Grasse (€1.50, 35 minutes) four
to eight times daily. With your own wheels, Tourrettes is 35 minutes west of Nice or 40 minutes
north of Antibes.

Grasse

POP 50,937
Up in the hills to the north of Nice, the town
of Grasse has been synonymous with perfumery since the 16th century, and the town
is still home to around 30 makers – a few of
which offer guided tours of their factories,
and the chance to hone your olfactory skills.
The perfumes of Provence are something
that linger long after you leave for home –
especially if you happen to have bought a
few soaps, body sprays and *eaux de toilette*
to take home with you.

◉ Sights & Activities

★ **Musée International
de la Parfumerie** MUSEUM

(MIP; ☑ 04 97 05 58 11; www.museesdegrasse.com;
2 bd du Jeu de Ballon; adult/child €4/free, combo
ticket incl Les Jardins du MIP €6/free; ⊙ 10am-7pm
May-Sep, to 5.30pm Oct-Apr; ▣) This whizz-
bang museum is a work of art: housed in an
18th-century mansion enlarged with a modern glass structure, it retraces three millennia
of perfume history through beautifully presented artefacts (including Marie Antoinette's
travelling case), bottles, videos, vintage posters, olfactive stations and explanatory panels.
The museum offers interesting insights into
how the industry developed in Grasse. Kids
are well catered for with dedicated multimedia stations, a fragrant garden, a film testing
sense of smell as well as a reconstructed
19th-century perfume shop.

Musée d'Art et d'Histoire
de Provence MUSEUM

(☑ 04 93 36 80 20; www.museesdegrasse.com; 2
rue Mirabeau; adult/child €2/free; ⊙ 10am-7pm
May-Sep, to 5.30pm Oct-Apr) This local-history
museum, at home since 1921 in an aristocratic *hôtel particulier* (mansion), is a wonderful evocation of life in the 18th century.
Rooms are laid out pretty much as they were
when the marquise of Clapiers-Cabris lived
here – he loathed his mother, who lived opposite, so much that he had a Gorgon's head
carved over his door to leer through her
windows. Don't miss the ground-floor kitch-
en, decorative art collection and gardens
with beautiful springtime wisteria. Admission also includes entry to the **Villa Musée
Jean-Honoré Fragonard** (☑ 04 93 36 52 98;
www.museesdegrasse.com/vmjhf/presentation; 23
blvd Fragonard; adult/child €2/free; ⊙ 1-7pm Jul,
Aug & school holidays).

Musée Fragonard MUSEUM

(Collection Hélène et Jean-François Costa; ☑ 04
93 36 02 07; www.fragonard.com/fr/usines/
musee-fragonard; 14 rue Jean Ossola; ⊙ 10am-6pm)
FREE On Grasse's main pedestrian street, this
small museum explores the work of Grassois
painter Fragonard (1732–1806), whose risqué
paintings of love scenes shocked and titillat-
ed 18th-century France with their licentious
love scenes. Paintings by Marguerite Gérard
(1761–1837), Fragonard's sister-in-law and
protégée, and Jean-Baptiste Mallet (1759–
1835), another Grasse native, fill other rooms
on the 1st floor.

Fragonard's Usine Historique
& Musée du Parfum MUSEUM

(☑ 04 93 36 44 65; www.fragonard.com/fr/usines/
musee-du-parfum; 20 bd Fragonard; ⊙ 9am-6pm)
FREE At the entrance to the old town, next
to the Jardin des Plantes, this ochre-coloured
mansion is where the Fragonard perfumery
began in 1926 – though perfumers were at
work here as early as 1782. Guided visits take
in the original equipment used for extraction
and distilling, and end at the shop where you
can buy Fragonard scents. Upstairs there's a
small, self-guided Musée du Parfum (Perfume
Museum) tracing perfume's history. Fragonard offers 90-minute English-language
perfume-making workshops (€65; book
ahead).

Domaine de Manon FARM

(☑ 06 12 18 02 69; www.lo domaine de manon.
com; 36 chemin du Servan, Plascassier; adult/child
€6/free) ✿ For a different spin on Grasse's
perfume production, plan a trip to this lovely flower farm 7km southeast of the centre
of Grasse. Centifolia roses and jasmine have
been cultivated here for three generations,
and the farm now supplies Dior exclusively. Tours only take place during flowering:
Tuesday at 9am early May to mid-June for
roses, and late August to mid-October for jasmine; contact Carole Biancalana at domaine
demanon@yahoo.fr or ring to reserve and
verify times, which vary from year to year.

🛏 Sleeping & Eating

There is a dire lack of decent accommodation in Grasse town, but there are some
lovely options in the surrounding countryside, especially around the nearby villages
of Mougins, Mouans-Sartoux, Le Rouret and
Cabris.

Le Mas du Naoc B&B €€

(☑ 04 93 60 63 13; www.lemasdunaoc.com; 580
chemin du Migranié, Cabris; d €160-220, tr €230;
🛜 ❄) This vine-covered, 18th-century *chambre d'hôte* 6km west of Grasse slumbers in the
shade of century-old olive, jasmine, fig and orange trees. Soft natural hues dress Sandra and
Jérôme Maingret's three lovely rooms – all
with access to fully equipped kitchens – and
the coastal panorama from the pool is inspirational. No children under seven; minimum
two-night stay April to October.

★ Hotel du Clos HOTEL €€€

(☑ 04 93 40 78 85; www.hotel-du-clos.com;
3 Chemin des Écoles, Le Rouret; r €169-260;

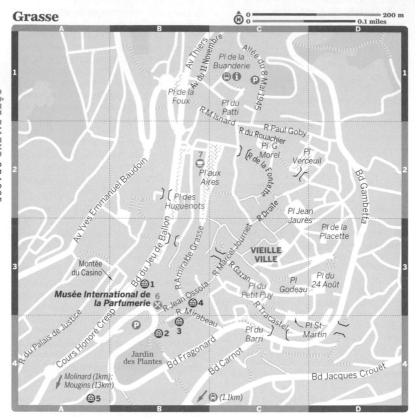

Grasse

CÔTE D'AZUR GRASSE

Grasse

🅿 ❄ 🛜 ⛵) Hidden in the hills 10km east of Grasse, this village retreat began as a restaurant (now Michelin-starred) and has since expanded with a second bistro and this lovely hotel, housed in a 17th-century farmhouse and barn. It's effortlessly tasteful, with chic rooms, cosy country decor and swanky bathrooms. The best rooms have views over gardens and olive trees.

Les Comptoirs NamasThé CAFE
(27 place aux Aires; ⊘ 9am-7pm Mon-Sat) First-class coffee and chocolate.

Café des Musées MODERN FRENCH €
(1 rue Jean Ossola; lunch specials from €11; ⊘ 9am-6.30pm Mon-Sat, to 6pm Sun) This stylish, well-situated cafe is the perfect stop between sights for lunch (creative salads, carefully crafted daily specials, soup or pasta of the day) or a gourmet coffee break (€6 for crepes with coffee, tea or *chocolat chaud*).

🛈 Information

Tourist Office (📞 04 93 36 66 66; www. grasse.fr; place de la Buanderie; ⊘ 9am-1pm

& 2-5pm Mon-Fri, from 10am Sat; 🕾) Takes reservations for guided tours and workshops of the perfume factories, and provides maps and information on the town. Adjacent to the Grasse bus station.

ℹ️ Getting There & Around

BUS

Local bus company **Lignes d'Azur** (p64) departs regularly from Grasse's **bus station** (place de la Buanderie). Fares for all destinations are a flat-rate €1.50. Bus 600 goes to Cannes (one hour, every 20 minutes) via Mouans-Sartoux (30 minutes) and Mougins (35 minutes). Bus 500 goes to Nice (1½ hours, hourly).

CAR

Grasse's one-way street system is maddening and often congested, so park as soon as you can and walk. If arriving from Nice, park at **Parking Notre Dame des Fleurs** (place Mai telly). If arriving from Cannes, park at **Parking Honoré Cresp** (cours Honoré Cresp). Rates range from €1.90 for the first hour to €15 for 24 hours.

TRAIN

The station is a short distance downhill from the centre; shuttle buses (€1.50) to 'Centre Ville' depart from in front of the train station. There are regular rail services to Nice (€9.60, one hour, hourly) via Cannes (€4.60, 25 minutes).

Mougins

Spiralling up its hilltop in the shape of a snail shell, pinprick Vieux Mougins looks almost too perfect to be real. Picasso discovered the medieval village in 1935 with lover Dora Marr and lived here with his final love, Jacqueline

Roque, from 1961 until his death. Mougins has since become something of an elite location, with prestigious hotel-restaurants, the country's most-sought-after international school and Sophia Antipolis (France's Silicon Valley) nearby.

Nearby Mouans-Sartoux (population 10,490) is equally charming and more down to earth, with a cluster of popular eateries and its own excellent museum to explore.

⊙ Sights

★ Musée d'Art Classique de Mougins   GALLERY

(MACM; 🖉 04 93 75 18 22; www.mouginsmusee. com; 32 rue Commandeur; adult/child €12/5; ⊙ 10am-6pm Oct-Jun, to 8pm Jul-Sep) The brainchild of compulsive art collector and British entrepreneur Christian Levett, this outstanding museum contains 600 works spanning 5000 years. The collection aims to show how ancient civilisations inspired neoclassical, modern and contemporary art, thus the collection is organised by civilisations – Roman, Greek and Egyptian – with antiquities juxtaposed with seminal modern works. The top floor is dedicated to armoury, with excellent interactive displays bringing to life the helmets, spears and shields. There's also a fascinating Roman and Greek coin collection.

★ Les Jardins du MIP   GARDENS

(🖉 04 92 98 62 69; www.museesdegrasse.com; 979 chemin des Gourettes, Mouans-Sartoux; adult/child €4/free, combo ticket incl MIP €6/free; ⊙ 10am-7pm May-Aug, to 5.30pm Apr & Sep-Nov, closed Dec-Mar) 🖋 These gorgeous gardens belonging to Grasse's Musée International de la

---

CREATE YOUR OWN SCENT

It can take months for a *nez* (nose or perfumer who, after 10 years' training, can identify up to 3000 smells) to create a perfume. And you'll understand why the instant you plant yourself in front of a nose's organ – a line-up of miniature ginger-glass bottles containing 127 'notes' ranging from green amber, vanilla, hyacinth, lily of the valley and civet (nose shock or what) to hare, rose petals and sandalwood. The fact that many bottles contain not one but several essences pre-mixed only adds to the olfactory bewilderment. The number of combinations is dizzying.

Perfume workshops won't turn you into a perfumer overnight, but the olfactory education they offer is fascinating – and great fun for adults and kids alike. **Molinard** (🖉 04 92 42 33 21; www.molinard.com; 60 bd Victor Hugo, Grasse; 20min/1hr/2hr workshops €30/69/189; ⊙ 9.30am-6.30pm) runs several different workshops, ranging in length from 20-minute sessions to two-hour epics, during which you get to create your own custom perfume from the essences on offer; you get to take it home with you at the end.

Galimard (🖉 04 93 09 20 00; www.galimard.com; 73 rte de Cannes, Grasse; workshops from €49; ⊙ 9am-12.30pm & 2-6pm) and **Fragonard** (p79) offer similar workshops, which include a bottle of bespoke *eau de parfum* at the end.

Parfumerie (p79) showcase plants used in scent-making. Half the garden is displayed as fields to show how roses, jasmine and lavender are grown; the other half is organised by olfactory families (woody, floral, amber etc), which you can rub and smell on your way around. The gardens are 5km northwest of Mougins and 10km southwest of Grasse on the edge of the Mouans-Sartoux village.

Musée de la Photographie André Villers
MUSEUM
(☑ 04 93 75 85 67; Porte Sarrazine; ⊕ 10am-12.30pm & 2-6pm) **FREE** The small but perfectly formed Musée de la Photographie has some fascinating black-and-white photos of Picasso, snapped by celebrated photographers such as André Villers and Jacques Henri Lartigue. It also hosts regular exhibitions on anything from fashion to war photography.

Espace de l'Art Concret
GALLERY
(www.espacedelartconcret.fr; Château de Mouans, Mouans-Sartoux; adult/child €7/free; ⊕ 11am-7pm daily Jul & Aug, 1-6pm Wed-Sun Sep-Jun) Modern-art and architecture lovers should not miss Mouans-Sartoux's contemporary-art centre, housed in the 16th-century Château de Mouans and the purpose-built Donation Albers-Honegger extension, a brilliant and brilliantly controversial lime-green concrete block ferociously clashing with its historic surroundings. All the old familiars (Eduardo Chillida, Yves Klein, Andy Warhol, César, Philippe Starck) are here, along with lesser-known practitioners and temporary exhibitions. It's 4km northwest of Mougins.

🛏 Sleeping & Eating

★ Les Rosées
B&B €€€
(☑ 04 92 92 29 64; www.lesrosees.com; 238 chemin de Font Neuve; d €280-360; **P ❄ 🛜 ❄**) You know that dreamy Provençal getaway you've been looking for? The one in the little village, set among gardens filled with lavender and honeysuckle, and peaceful wood-beamed rooms looking out over Provençal hills? Well, this place is it. Throw in luxuries including Bose sound systems, designer bathrooms, home-cooked food and a gorgeous pool, and you really won't ever want to leave.

★ Le Sot l'y Laisse
PROVENCAL €€
(☑ 04 93 75 54 50; www.sotlylaisse.fr; 1 place Suzanne de Villeneuve, Mouans-Sartoux; lunch menus €20-25, dinner menus €25-35, mains €17-28; ⊕ noon-2pm & 7-10pm Thu-Mon) You won't find a more authentic Provençal restaurant than this place, on the shady town square of Mouans-Sartoux, 4km northwest of Mougins. The signature dish, a hearty chicken stew, gives the place its name (it means 'the fool leaves it there,' referring to the juicy oyster of meat most people miss in poultry). Fish, meats and desserts are all superb.

★ L'Amandier
MODERN FRENCH €€€
(☑ 04 93 90 00 91; www.amandier.fr; 48 av Jean-Charles Mallet; lunch menus €22, dinner menus €35-55; ⊕ noon-2pm & 7-9.30pm; ❄) Young chef Denis Fétisson has brought Roger Vergé's baby back to its former glory. Set in an old mill, it's considered casual in these parts, but comes with chandeliers and breathtaking views. Various fixed-price meals let you shape your culinary experience, but the underlying theme is classic French. Lunch menus (€22 including wine, coffee and mini-desserts) offer outstanding value.

🍷 Drinking & Nightlife

La Cave de Mougins
WINE BAR
(☑ 04 92 28 06 11; www.cavedemougins.fr; 50 av Jean-Charles Mallet; ⊕ 11.30am-11pm Thu-Tue) A fantastic spot for oenophiles, stocking hundreds of local vintages with cheese and pâté platters to match.

ℹ Information

Tourist Office (☑ 04 92 92 14 00; www.mougins-tourisme.com; 39 place des Patriotes; ⊕ 10am-7pm daily Jul & Aug, to 6pm daily Jun & Sep, to 6pm Mon-Sat Apr & May, to 5pm Mon-Sat Oct-Mar) Located at the entrance of the old village. Pick up the free map to the town's historic centre, and borrow a free set of boules to play *pétanque* with the locals (or your friends); just leave an ID.

ℹ Getting There & Away

Bus 600 (€1.50), operated by **Lignes d'Azur** (p64), runs every 20 minutes, connecting Mougins and Mouans-Sartoux with Cannes (20 minutes) and Grasse (35 minutes). Drivers can park free at the **Moulin de la Croix** lot at the foot of town.

ANTIBES
POP 76,119

With its boat-bedecked port, 16th-century ramparts and narrow cobblestone streets festooned with flowers, it's little wonder that lovely Antibes has stolen the hearts of so many artists and writers: including Graham

Greene, Max Ernst and Picasso, who featured the town in many paintings and now has a museum dedicated to him here.

Only Antibes' attractive old town would be recognisable to any of its famous former residents. The modern town, like many along the Riviera, has sprawled rather unbecomingly along the coast and inland, so the best vantage point is from the sea – ideally in one of the many posh yachts that pull into port throughout summer, or from the long series of beaches south of town.

Beyond the city limits, save some time to explore beautiful **Cap d'Antibes**, a wooded cape studded with seaside mansions and pretty walking trails.

⊙ Sights & Activities

Musée Picasso   MUSEUM
(☑ 04 92 90 54 26, www.antibes-juanlespins.com/culture/musee-picasso; Château Grimaldi, 4 rue des Cordiers; adult/concession €6/3; ⊙ 10am-6pm Tue-Sun mid-Jun–mid-Sep, 10am-1pm & 2-6pm Tue-Sun rest of year) Picasso himself said, 'If you want to see the Picassos from Antibes, you have to see them in Antibes'. The 14th-century Château Grimaldi was Picasso's studio from July to December 1946 and now houses an excellent collection of his works and fascinating photos of him. The sheer variety – lithographs, paintings, drawings and ceramics – shows how versatile and curious an artist Picasso was. The museum also has a room dedicated to Nicolas de Staël, another painter who adopted Antibes as home.

Bastion St-Jaume   MONUMENT
(quai Henri Rambaud; ⊙ 10am-11pm Jun-Aug, to 6pm Sep-May) FREE Stroll along the rampart walkway to the harbour, where luxury yachts jostle for the limelight with *Nomade* (2010), an 8m-tall sculpture of a man looking out to sea. The work of Catalan artist Jaume Plensa, the mirage-like piece is built from thousands of white letters and is lit at night – a magnificent sight. It squats on the terrace of the Bastion St-Jaume, the former site of a Roman temple, a 17th-century fortified tower and, until 1985, a shipyard.

Vieil Antibes   HISTORIC SITE
Ringed by sturdy medieval walls and crisscrossed with lanes and shady squares, old Antibes is a delightful place for a wander. The wonderful Marché Provençal (p85) is old Antibes' beating heart, sheltered by a 19th-century cast-iron roof and packed with stalls selling olives, cheese, vegetables, tapenades and other Provençal goodies until around 1pm every day.

Fort Carré   MONUMENT
(☑ 04 92 90 52 13; av 11 Novembre; guided tour adult/child €3/free; ⊙ 10am-1pm & 2-6pm Tue-Sun Jun-Oct, 10am-12.30pm & 1.30-4.30pm Tue-Sun Nov-May) The impregnable 16th-century Fort Carré, enlarged by Vauban in the 17th century, dominates the approach to Antibes from Nice. It served as a border defence post until 1860, when Nice, until then in Italian hands, became French. Tours depart half-hourly; some guides speak English.

Plage de la Gravette   BEACH
(quai Henri Rambaud) Right in the centre of Antibes, you'll find Plage de la Gravette, a small patch of sand by the *remparts* (ramparts).

Pointe Bacon   SNORKELLING, SWIMMING
The stretch of coast between Plage de la Salis and Cap d'Antibes, especially the section around Pointe Bacon, is fringed with rocky coves, where snorkellers frolic in clear waters.

⚑ Festivals & Events

Jazz à Juan   MUSIC
(www.jazzajuan.com; Les Jardins du Jazz, bd Baudoin; ⊙ mid-Jul) This major festival has been running for more than 50 years. Every jazz great has performed here, and the festival continues to attract big music names.

🛏 Sleeping

★Mademoiselle   BOUTIQUE HOTEL €€
(☑ 04 93 61 31 34; www.hotelmademoisellejuan.com; 12 av du Docteur Dautheville; d €135-200, ste €175-230; ☜) This vibrantly colourful place two blocks in from the Med puts Juan-les-Pins' staider beach hotels to shame. Each of the 14 rooms has its own theme, with an abundance of playful, quirky details: fibreglass animal heads, dangling teapots, vintage prints and exuberantly bold tile and wallpaper choices. Free coffee, tea, soft drinks and fruit are another nice touch.

Hôtel La Jabotte   B&B €€
(☑ 04 93 61 45 89; www.jabotte.com; 13 av Max Maurey; d €154-214, q €254; ❋ @ ☜) Just 150m inland from Plage de la Salis and 2km south of the old town towards Cap d'Antibes, this pretty little hideaway makes a cosy base. Hot pinks, sunny yellows and soothing mauves dominate the homey, feminine decor, and

Antibes

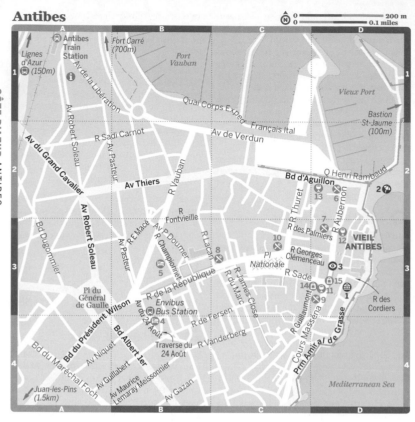

Antibes

⊙ Sights
 1 Musée Picasso D3
 2 Plage de la Gravette D2
 3 Vieil Antibes...D3

🛏 Sleeping
 4 Hôtel La Place B4
 5 Le Relais du Postillon B3

✖ Eating
 6 La Ferme au Foie Gras D2
 7 l'Arazur..D3

 8 L'Atelier Jean-Luc Pelé..........................C3
 9 Le Zinc..D3
 10 Nacional...C3

⊙ Drinking & Nightlife
 11 Absinthe Bar D3
 12 Drinkers Club D3
 13 Hop Store..D2

⌂ Shopping
 14 Fromagerie L'Etable.............................D3
 15 Marché Provençal D3

there's a sweet patio where breakfast is served on sunny days. There's a minimum stay of three nights in summer.

Le Relais du Postillon   HOTEL €€
(✆ 04 93 34 20 77; www.relaisdupostillon.com; 8 rue Championnet; s from €65, d €85-149; ⊙ reception 7.30am-11pm; ✵🕸) This stone-walled

former coaching hotel has got a great location opposite a small park and square on the edge of the old town. Rooms are rather charming, especially if you bag one at the front, which have their own dinky balconies overlooking the square. The ground-floor cafe is a lovely spot for breakfast, too.

Hôtel La Place HOTEL €€
(☑ 04 97 21 03 11; www.la-place-hotel.com; 1 av du 24 Août; d €89-205; ❋@☎) It's rare to find contemporary chic decor and a warm, professional welcome next to a city bus station, but La Place does it awfully well. Its 14 rooms are spacious, stylish and dressed in soothing taupe and aubergine or aniseed green. Three have bijou balconies. Breakfast (€14.50) is served in the airy lounge and there's discount public parking available for €12 per day.

✖ Eating

Vieil Antibes is the place to eat, both for atmosphere and for its diversity of restaurants. To build your own picnic, hit Antibes' **Fromagerie l'Etable** (☑ 04 93 34 51 42; 1 rue Sade; ☺8am-1pm & 4-7pm Tue-Sat, 8am-1pm Sun) for cheese and deli products, and dazzling morning market **Marché Provençal** (cours Masséna; ☺7am-1pm Tue-Sun Sep-Jun, daily Jul & Aug) for everything else. If you've got access to your own kitchen, head down to the wa terfront quai des Pêcheurs, where fishers sell their morning's catch from 9am to 12.30pm.

★ **L'Atelier Jean-Luc Pelé** SANDWICHES €
(☑ 04 92 95 78 21; www.jeanlucpele.com; 27 rue de la République; sandwiches from €5; ☺7am-7pm) This branch of Jean-Luc Pelé's stellar Cannes bakery is a welcome addition to Antibes' lunch line-up. Gourmet bagels, wraps, soups, quiches and sandwiches come in all kinds of creative combos (€7.50 to €11) including a drink and a sinful cake from the patisserie counter. There's also a divine array of chocolates.

La Ferme au Foie Gras DELI €
(☑ 04 93 34 26 50; www.vente-foie-gras.net; 35 rue Aubernon; sandwiches €4-9; ☺8am-7pm Tue-Sun) Just down the hill from the Marché Provençal, this heartwarming deli sells local goodies like charcuterie, cheeses and jams, and makes delicious gourmet sandwiches – with ingredients ranging from foie gras to smoked duck and salmon, mozzarella, camembert and more.

★ **Nacional** INTERNATIONAL €€
(☑ 04 93 61 77 30; www.restaurant-nacional-antibes.com; 61 place Nationale; tapas €8-21, mains €21-38; ☺noon-2pm & 7-10pm Tue-Thu, to 10.30pm Fri & Sat) 'Beef & Wine' is the strapline of this contemporary wine-bar-styled space, so that should give you some idea of the focus here. It's popular for its burgers, steaks in pepper or port sauce, and other grilled meats. The in-crowd adores it for aperitifs and tapas, best sampled on the walled patio garden hidden away at the back.

Le Zinc FRENCH €€
(☑ 04 83 14 69 20; 15 cours Masséna; mains €16-29; ☺noon-2pm Tue-Sun, 7-10pm Tue-Sat) Head uphill from the market and you shouldn't miss this titchy little bistro-cum-wine-bar – the tiny street terrace is usually full of diners, especially at lunchtime. It's good for classic bistro food, plus some great cheese and charcuterie platters, but it's the fantastic local wine list that draws in many diners.

l'Arazur FRENCH €€€
(☑ 04 93 34 75 60; www.larazur.fr; 8 rue des Palmiers; lunch menus €29-34, dinner menus €60; ☺12.15-2pm Thu-Sun, 7.15-10pm Wed-Sun) After years polishing his skills in double- and triple-starred Michelin restaurants, young chef Lucas Marini launched his own gastronomic venture in Vieil Antibes' pedestrian zone. Fresh seafood, local veggies and classic Provençal ingredients are incorporated into dishes such as grilled squid with artichokes, candied lemon and olive powder. The stone-walled cellar is especially cosy; come at lunchtime for best value.

☙ Drinking & Nightlife

Pedestrian bd d'Aguillon heaves with merry Anglophones falling out of the busy 'English' and 'Irish' pubs.

Drinkers Club BAR
(☑ 04 93 34 08 12; www.facebook.com/drinkers club06; 12 rue Aubernon; ☺4pm-2am Mon-Fri, from 1pm Sat & Sun; ☎) The in-crowd flops off the beach (or yacht they're crewing on) and onto the pavement terrace of this buzzing

---

JUAN-LES-PINS

The beach resort of Juan-les-Pins, 2km southwest of Antibes, was famously the home of F Scott Fitzgerald, who lived here with his wife Zelda and daughter Scottie in 1926–27 (their house is now a posh hotel). The waterfront draws steady crowds of beachgoers in summer, along with music fans who descend en masse for the Jazz à Juan festival in July. In winter it's a much sleepier place, where groups of locals play boules under the eponymous pines in Jardin de la Pinède, the city's favourite park.

CAP D'ANTIBES: A WALK AROUND BILLIONAIRE'S BAY

You feel like a shrunken Alice in Wonderland on this select peninsula: larger-than-life villas and parasol pine trees loom high above you at every turn, and the frenzied sound of cicadas provides an unearthly soundtrack in summer. A walk around 'Billionaires Bay' – naturally majestic and packed with millionaires' mansions – is a Riviera highlight.

The easiest way to access the lush green cape is aboard **Envibus** bus 2 from the Envibus bus station to the 'Phare du Cap' bus stop. From here, cross the road and follow in pilgrims' footsteps along ave Malespine (bear left where the road forks) and rte du Phare uphill to Chapelle de la Garoupe. The tiny, renovated chapel, filled with poignant offerings from fishing families, crowns the highest point of Cap d'Antibes. Sweeping views of the coastline, from St-Tropez to Italy, mesmerise. The neighbouring **Phare de la Garoupe**, a square brick lighthouse with scarlet beacon, can't be visited.

Panorama celebrated, walk back downhill to bd du Cap and head along chemin de la Garoupe. A 10-minute walk past high-walled properties and towering pines brings you down to the bright-turquoise, crystal-clear water of the pretty, relentlessly popular **Plage de la Garoupe**. At the far end of the sandy beach, pick up the signposted **Sentier Littoral** (coastal footpath) that ducks and dives along the shoreline to Eilenroc (1¼ hours, 3.2km) on the cape's southern tip. The path is partly paved, very rocky in places and riddled with steep steps and the occasional scary drop (wear decent shoes). It provides a superb lookout on the rugged coastline and is memorable for its many tiny sundecks and picnic spots, considerately crafted into the stone. Weave your way around the cape, past solitary fishers tucked into the rocks and knowing locals lunching with five-star views, until you reach the start of chemin des Douaniers, an inland-bound footpath wedged between the high stone walls of Villa Eilenroc and neighbouring **Château de la Croë**. Famously home to the Duke of Windsor and Wallis Simpson in the late 1930s, the pearly white Victorian-style château was originally built for an English aristocrat in 1927 and renovated most recently by its current owner, Russian billionaire Roman Abramovich.

Duck through the doorway at the foot of chemin des Douaniers and continue for another 800m along the signposted footpath to **Villa Eilenroc** (📞04 93 67 74 33; av Mrs Beaumont, Cap d'Antibes; adult/child €2/free; ⊘2-5pm Wed, plus 1st & 3rd Sat of month). The villa, designed in 1867 by Charles Garnier for a Dutchman who scrambled the name of his wife, Cornélie, to come up with the villa's name, has clearly seen better days – its scantily furnished interior lacks its history's glamour. But a stroll around the 11-hectare park with rosary, olive grove and aromatic garden goes some way towards evoking the beauty of the villa's belle-époque heyday. On the shore below the villa, **Plage de Galets** is a bijou pebble cove well worth a dip and/or sun-kissed siesta. From Eilenroc, it is a five-minute walk along av Mrs Beaumont to the 'Fontaine' bus stop on bd JF Kennedy.

The southwestern tip of Cap d'Antibes, also linked by bus 2 from Antibes, is graced with the legendary **Hôtel du Cap Eden Roc**. Dating from 1870, it hit the big time just after WWI when a literary salon held here one summer (previous guests had come for the winter season only) was attended by Hemingway, Picasso et al. The icing on the cake was the immortalisation of the hotel (as the thinly disguised Hôtel des Étrangers) by F Scott Fitzgerald in his novel *Tender Is the Night* (1934).

In the centre of Cap d'Antibes, the serene **Jardin Botanique de la Villa Thuret** (📞04 97 21 25 00; www6.sophia.inra.fr/jardin_thuret; 90 chemin Raymond; ⊘8am-6pm Mon-Fri Jun-Sep, 8.30am-5.30pm Mon-Fri Oct-May) **FREE** is a 3.5-hectare botanical garden created in 1856 and showcasing 2500 species. It provides the perfect opportunity to study the sun-rich cape's lush and invariably exotic flora up close.

lounge bar for early-evening cocktails, wine and bruschetta.

Absinthe Bar   BAR
(📞04 93 34 93 00; www.facebook.com/Absinthe Antibes; 25 cours Masséna; ⊘10.30am-7.30pm

Tue-Thu, to 12.30am Fri & Sat) Flirt with the green fairy in this convivial cellar, with original 1860 zinc bar, a few round tables and all the accessories (four-tapped water fountain, sugar cubes etc). Live piano music on

Friday and Saturday evenings enhances the ambiance.

Hop Store
PUB

(☎ 04 93 34 15 33; 38 bd Aguillon; ⊗ 10am-midnight) On a lively street lined with pubs, just inside the old ramparts, this grungy boozer is the place for a late-night pint. It's a favourite for expat crews working on the fancy yachts moored up in Antibes' harbour.

La Siesta Beach Club
CLUB

(☎ 04 93 33 31 31; www.joa.fr/casinos/antibes-la-siesta; 2000 rte du Bord de Mer; ⊗ 6pm-1am Sun-Thu, to 2am Fri & Sat mid-Jun–early Sep) This legendary establishment is famous up and down the coast for its summer beachside nightclub and late-night dancing under the stars. There are DJs nightly, plus live music on Fridays and Saturdays. Find it 4km north of Vieil Antibes on the D6000.

ℹ Information

Tourist Office (☎ 04 22 10 60 10; www.antibesjuanlespins.com; 42 av Robert Soleau; ⊗ 9am-7pm daily Jul & Aug, 9.30am-12.30pm & 2-5pm Mon-Sat, 9am 1pm Sun Sep-Jun) Antibes' main tourist office is a bit of a walk from the old town, up by the train station. It's efficient and runs guided walking tours of old Antibes and 'Painters on the French Riviera' (adult/child €7/3.50).

ℹ Getting There & Away

BUS

The Nice–Cannes bus service (route 200, €1.50) operated by **Lignes d'Azur** (p64) has a **stop** (bd Général Vautrin) just west of Antibes' train station (cross the tracks via the pedestrian overpass).

Envibus (☎ 04 89 87 72 00; www.envibus.fr) operates local bus services for Cap d'Antibes, Biot, Vence and St-Paul de Vence from a separate **bus station** (Gare Routière d'Antibes; place Guynemer; ⊗ ticket office 9am-12.30pm & 2-5pm Mon-Sat) on the western edge of Vieil Antibes, 700m south of Antibes' train station. Tickets cost €1 from machines, €1.50 from the bus driver.

CAR & MOTORCYCLE

Vieil Antibes is mostly pedestrianised; park outside the centre and walk. There are several paying car parks along the port on av de Verdun.

TRAIN

Antibes' train station is on the main line between Nice (€4.80, 15 to 30 minutes, four hourly) and Cannes (€3.10, 10 to 15 minutes, four hourly).

BIOT
POP 9876

This 15th-century hilltop village was once an important pottery-manufacturing centre specialising in earthenware oil and wine containers. Metal containers brought an end to this, but Biot is still active in handicraft production, especially glassmaking.

You can see the blowers in action and pick up some premium glassware at the renowned **Verrerie de Biot** (☎ 04 93 65 03 00; www.verreriebiot.com; chemin des Combes; guided tour adult/child €6/3, museum adult/child €3/1.50; ⊗ 9.30am-8pm Mon-Sat, 10.30am-1.30pm & 2.30-7.30pm Sun May-Sep, to 6pm Oct-Apr) **FREE**, at the foot of the village. One and a half kilometres south of town, there's also a **museum** (☎ 04 92 91 50 20; www.musee-fernandleger.fr; chemin du Val de Pôme; adult/child inol audioguide €5.50/free, special exhibitions additional €2; ⊗ 10am-6pm Wed-Mon May-Oct, to 5pm Nov-Apr) devoted to the experimental artist Fernand Léger, a major inspiration for pop art.

CANNES
POP 74,285

Glamorous Cannes sets camera flashes popping at its film festival in May, when stars pose in tuxes and full-length gowns on the red carpet. But the glitz doesn't end there. Throughout the year, as you walk among the designer bars, couture shops and palaces of La Croisette, the wealth and glamour of this city cannot fail to impress. Admiring Ferraris and Porsches and celebrity-spotting on the chic sunlounger-striped beaches and liner-sized yachts moored at the port are perennial Cannes pastimes.

Whether Cannes' soul has managed to survive its celebrity-playground status is another question, but there's still enough natural beauty to make a trip worthwhile: the harbour, the bay, the clutch of offshore islands and the old quarter, Le Suquet, all spring into life on a sunny day. And with the city's famous beaches benefiting from a serious facelift in 2019, there's suddenly lots more space to lay your towel!

◉ Sights

★ La Croisette
ARCHITECTURE

The multi-starred hotels and couture shops lining the iconic bd de la Croisette (aka La Croisette) may be the preserve of the rich and famous, but anyone can enjoy strolling the palm-shaded promenade – a favourite pastime among Cannois at night, when it twinkles with bright lights. Views of the Baie de Cannes and nearby Estérel mountains are beautiful, and seafront hotel palaces dazzle in all their stunning art-deco glory.

Palais des Festivals et des Congrès
LANDMARK

(Festival & Congress Palace; 1 bd de la Croisette; guided tour adult/child €6/free) Posing for a selfie on the 22 steps leading up to the main entrance of this concrete bunker – unlikely host to the world's most glamorous film festival – at the western end of La Croisette is an essential Cannes experience. Afterwards, wander along the **Allée des Étoiles du Cinéma**, a footpath of 46 celebrity hand imprints in the pavement; it begins with the hands of Meryl Streep in front of the tourist office.

The only way to enter the festival building and walk into the auditorium, tread the stage and learn about cinema's most glamorous event is with a **Palais des Festivals guided tour** (☑ 04 92 99 84 22; www.cannes-destination.com/guided-tour/visit-palais-festival-cannes; adult/child €6/free) organised by the Cannes tourist office. Check dates and get booking instructions on the tourist office website.

Vieux Port
PORT

(Old Port) The celebrity yachts that line the port are here to remind you of Cannes' celebrity status, lest you forget it.

Le Suquet
HISTORIC SITE

Follow rue St-Antoine and snake your way up through the narrow streets of Le Suquet, Cannes' oldest district. Up top you'll find the site of Cannes' medieval castle, place de la Castre, flanked by the 17th-century Église Notre-Dame de l'Esperance. Climb the adjacent ramparts for great views of the bay.

Activities

Cannes is blessed with sandy beaches, although much of the bd de la Croisette stretch is taken up by private enterprises, leaving just a small strip of free sand near the Palais des Festivals for the bathing hoi polloi.

Plage du Midi
BEACH

(bd Jean Hibert) This urban beach just west of Vieux Port enjoys gorgeous sunset views across to the red rock formations of the Corniche de l'Esterel.

Plage de la Bocca
BEACH

Cannes' westernmost beach is this narrow strip of sand about 5km outside the city centre.

Plage Vegaluna
BEACH

(☑ 04 93 43 67 05; www.vegaluna.com; La Croisette; sunloungers €15-25; ☺ 9.30am-7pm; 🖈) Family-friendly private beach.

Z Plage
BEACH

(☑ 04 93 90 12 34; 73 bd de la Croisette; ☺ 9.30am-6pm Apr-Sep, to 7pm Jul & Aug) Expect to pay €60/45/70 in July and August (€40/30/50 in other months) for the blue sunloungers on the front row/other rows/pier of the super-stylish Z Plage, the beach of Hôtel Martinez. Booking ahead is advised.

👉 Tours

Trans Côte d'Azur Cruises
BOATING

(☑ 04 92 98 71 30; www.trans-cote-azur.com; quai Max Laubeuf) From June to September this boat company offers all-day cruises to St-Tropez (adult/child return €50/40) and Monaco (€54/40). Shorter two-hour cruises set sail for the Corniche d'Or (€27/18), where you can take in the dramatic contrasts of the

---

VALLAURIS

Picasso (1881–1973) discovered ceramics in the small potters village of Vallauris in 1947. Attracted by its artistic vibe, he settled in the village between 1948 and 1955, during which time he produced some 4000 ceramics. He also completed his last great political composition, the *Chapelle La Guerre et La Paix* (War and Peace Chapel), a collection of dramatic murals painted on plywood panels and tacked to the walls of a disused 12th-century chapel, now the **Musée National Picasso 'La Guerre et la Paix'** (☑ 04 93 64 71 83; www.musee-picasso-vallauris.fr; place de la Libération; adult/child €5/free; ☺ 10am-12.15pm & 2-5pm Wed-Mon Sep-Jun, longer hours Jul & Aug).

Picasso left Vallauris another gift: a dour bronze figure clutching a sheep, *L'Homme au Mouton,* now on place Paul Isnard (adjoining place de la Libération). But his biggest legacy was the revival of the ceramics industry in Vallauris, an activity that might have died out had it not been for the 'Picasso effect'.

STARRING AT CANNES

For 12 days in May, all eyes turn to Cannes, centre of the cinematic universe, where 33,000 producers, distributors, directors, publicists, stars and hangers-on descend to buy, sell or promote more than 2000 films. As the premier film event of the year, the **Festival de Cannes** (www.festival-cannes.com; ☉May) attracts around 4000 journalists from all over the world.

At the centre of the whirlwind is the colossal, 60,000-sq-metre **Palais des Festivals**, where the official selections are screened. The palace opened in 1982, replacing the original Palais des Festivals – since demolished. The inaugural festival was scheduled for 1 September 1939, as a response to Mussolini's fascist-propaganda film festival in Venice, but Hitler's invasion of Poland brought the festival to an abrupt end. It restarted in 1946 – and the rest is history.

Over the years the festival split into 'in competition' and 'out of competition' sections. The goal of 'in competition' films is the prestigious Palme d'Or, awarded to the festival's best film as chosen by the jury and its president. Notable winners include Francis Ford Coppola's *Apocalypse Now* (1979), Quentin Tarantino's cult *Pulp Fiction* (1994) and American activist Michael Moore's anti-Bush-administration polemic *Fahrenheit 9/11* (2004). More recent winners include *La Classe* (2008), a film by Laurent Cantet about teaching in tough Parisian suburbs; *Dheepan* (2015) by French director Jacques Audiard, which tells the tale of how a former Tamil Tiger from Sri Lanka gains asylum in France, and *Shoplifters* (2018), by Japanese director Hirokazu Kore-eda, about an impoverished family that takes in an abused girl.

The vast majority of films are 'out of competition'. Behind the scenes the Marché du Film (www.marchedufilm.com) sees nearly $1 billion worth of business negotiated in distribution deals. And it's this hard-core commerce, combined with all the televised Tinseltown glitz, that gives the film festival its special magic.

Tickets to the film festival are off limits to average Joes. What you can get are same-day free tickets to selected individual films, usually after their first screening. Availability is limited, and all arrangements must be made through **Cannes Cinéma** (☑04 97 06 45 15; www.cannes-cinema.com; 10 av de Vallauris; ☉10am-noon & 2-4pm).

Estérel's red cliffs, green forests and intense azure waters.

★⌣ Festivals & Events

Festival d'Art Pyrotechnique FIREWORKS
(www.festival-pyrotechnique-cannes.com; ☉Jul & Aug) Around 200,000 people cram onto La Croisette every summer to admire the outstanding fireworks display over the Baie de Cannes. Magical. Held on six nights in July and August (see the website for exact dates).

Les Plages Électroniques MUSIC
(www.plages-electroniques.com; 1-day pass €30-37, 2-/3-day pass €57/77; ☉Aug) DJs spin on the sand at the Plage du Palais des Festivals during this relaxed festival, held over a three-day weekend in mid-August.

🛏 Sleeping

Cannes is an important conference centre, and when an event swings into town (there are a dozen or so during the year, including the film festival), hotels book up and prices soar. Many hotels sell out in summer as well, so plan ahead. During film-festival season you won't be able to find a bed for love nor money, but you can always stay in nearby Nice and catch the train to Cannes.

★Hôtel de Provence HOTEL €€
(☑04 93 38 44 35; www.hotel-de-provence.com; 9 rue Molière; s €93-140, d €110-247, ste €246-340; ☉closed mid-Jan–early Mar; ❄🛜) This traditional Provençal townhouse with buttermilk walls, lavender-blue shutters and a palm-lined entryway disguises a minimalist-chic interior. Almost every room sports a balcony, climaxing with a 7th-floor suite with stunning rooftop terrace. The Provence also has self-catering studios in the neighbourhood for three to six people. Breakfast costs €10.80.

7th Art Hotel BOUTIQUE HOTEL €€
(☑04 93 68 66 66; www.7arthotel.com; 23 rue du Maréchal Joffre; s €85-120, d €98-145; ❄🛜) This cinema-themed hotel is styled after the 'seventh art' (as French people call film), with the rooms divided into three filmic categories (Short Film, Long Film and Palme d'Or). Space is tight, but additions like iPod docks

Cannes

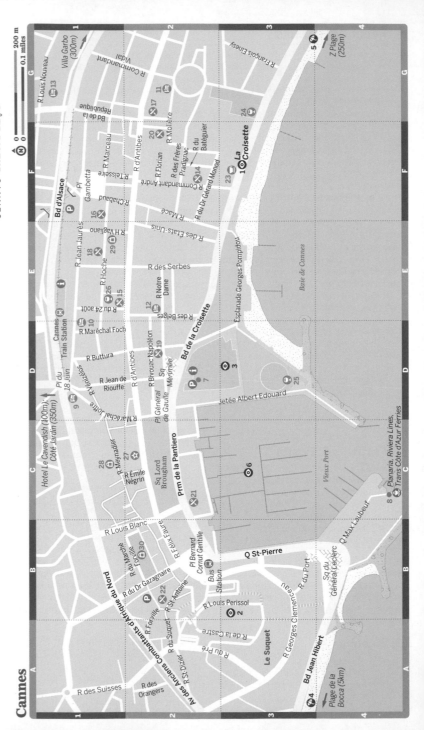

200 m
0.1 miles

R Louis Nouveau
Villa Garbo (300m)
13
R Commandant Vidal
Bd de la République
11
17
R Marceau
20
R d'Antibes
R Florian
R Molière
R des Frères Pradignac
R du Batéguier
24
R Teisseire
R Chabaud
R du Dr Gérard Monod
14
23
1 La Croisette
R Macé
R Commandant André
Pl Gambetta
Bd d'Alsace
16
R H Vagliano
18
R Jean Jaurès
29
R des États-Unis
R Hoche
26
15
R Notre Dame
R des Serbes
Esplanade Georges Pompidou
Baie de Cannes
R du 24 août
12
R des Belges
Cannes Train Station
10
R Maréchal Foch
19
R Bivouac Napoléon
Sq Mérimée
Bd de la Croisette
R Buttura
R d'Antibes
Pl du 18 Juin
R Venizelos
9
R Jean de Riouffe
R Maréchal Joffre
Pl Général de Gaulle
7
3
Jetée Albert Edouard
25
Hotel Le Cavendish (100m); Côte Jardin (350m)
27
R Meynadier
R Émile Négrin
Sq Lord Brougham
Prm de la Pantiero
28
21
6
Vieux Port
R Louis Blanc
R du Marché Forville
30
R Félix Faure
Pl Bernard Cornut Gentille
Q St-Pierre
8
Planaria, Riviera Lines; Trans Côte d'Azur Ferries
Bus Station
Q du Max Laubeuf
R du Port
22
R St-Antoine
R Forville
R du Dr Gazagnaire
R du Suquet
R St-Dizier
R Louis Perissol
2
R de la Castre
Le Suquet
Sq du Général Leclerc
Av des Anciens Combattants d'Afrique du Nord
R du Pré
R des Orangers
R des Suisses
R Georges Clemenceau
Bd Jean Hibert
4
Plage de la Bocca (5km)

R François Einesy
5
Z Plage (250m)

Cannes

and vintage film posters add character. The noisy road outside is a major drawback. Book direct with the hotel to save 15%.

Colette BOUTIQUE HOTEL €€
(☑ 04 93 39 01 17; www.hotelcolette.com; 5 place de la Gare; d €120-580; ❄ @ ☎) Right opposite the swish train station, this zingy little hotel makes a great Cannes choice. Rooms are imaginative and fun, and full of interesting touches such as pop-art prints, shabby-chic furniture, art-deco mirrors and Anglepoise lamps. Rates vary widely from one week to the next, so check online for the best deals.

Hôtel Le Mistral BOUTIQUE HOTEL €€
(☑ 04 93 39 91 46; www.mistral-hotel.com; 13 rue des Belges; r €89-159; ❄ ☎) For super-pricey Cannes, this little three-star offers amazing value. The 10 rooms are small but decked out in flattering red and plum tones – Privilege rooms have quite a bit more space, plus a fold-out sofa bed. There are sea views from two rooms on the fourth floor, and the hotel is just 50m from La Croisette. There's no lift, though.

La Bastide de l'Oliveraie BOUTIQUE HOTEL €€
(☑ 04 92 99 35 00; www.bastidedeloliveraie.fr; 7 allée des Oliviers; d €147-283, junior ste €245-330; ❄ ☎ ⊠) Fairly recently converted into a four-star boutique hotel, this former *mas* (farmstead) on a residential hillside north of town offers a refuge from Cannes' urban bustle. While its historic charms have been entirely obliterated by modern renovations, the rooms are dependably comfortable, the views over Cannes are splendid and the pool is very welcome indeed on a hot summer day.

Hôtel Villa Claudia HOTEL €€
(☑ 04 93 38 34 33; www.villa-claudia-cannes.com; 37 bd d'Alsace; d €100-190; ❄ ☎) Completely renovated in 2018, this dusky rose villa just east of the train station offers comfortable, refined digs within easy walking distance of everything. The high-ceilinged rooms are hung with photos of film stars, and there's a pleasant outdoor patio for soaking up the sun. Reserve ahead for hassle-free parking in the enclosed courtyard (per night €10).

Hotel Le Cavendish HERITAGE HOTEL €€€
(☑ 04 97 06 26 00; www.cavendish-cannes.com; 11 bd Carnot; d €170-310) With its rotunda rooms and Napoleon III–era architecture, this grand dame of a hotel can't fail to impress. It's classic in style – plenty of taffeta, tassels and swags, and a monumental marble staircase – but there's a civilised air of old-world grandeur about the place, with special touches such as complimentary evening aperitifs and a private beach on La Croisette.

Rooms are well soundproofed too, so don't fret about busy bd Carnot nearby.

Villa Garbo   BOUTIQUE HOTEL €€€

(✆ 04 93 46 66 00; www.villagarbo-cannes.com; 62 bd d'Alsace; d €250-650; ❄@🛜) For a taste of Cannes' celeb lifestyle, this indulgent stunner is hard to beat. Rooms are more like apartments, offering copious space, plus kitchenettes, king-size beds, sofas and more. The style is designer chic – acid tones of puce, orange and lime contrasted with blacks and greys, supplemented by quirky sculptures and objets d'art. Unusually, rates include breakfast.

✗ Eating

Most private beaches have restaurants, particularly delightful on warm sunny days, although you pay for the privilege of eating *les pieds dans l'eau* (on the waterfront). Expect to pay around €25 to €30 for a main of grilled fish or meat, or a gourmet salad.

Several streets just inland, such as rue Hoche, are filled with restaurants and bistros. Cheaper eats can be found in and around Cannes' atmospheric food market, Marché Forville.

★ PhilCat   SANDWICHES €

(✆ 04 93 38 43 42; promenade de la Pantiéro; sandwiches & salads €3.50-5.50; ⊘ 7am-7pm mid-Mar–Oct; ✐) Phillipe and Catherine's prefab cabin on the waterfront is a perfect lunch spot. This is fast-food, Cannes-style – giant salads, toasted panini and the best *pan bagna* (€5.30; a gargantuan bun filled with tuna, onion, red pepper, lettuce and tomato, and dripping in olive oil) on the Riviera. The 'super' version (€5.50) throws anchovies into the mix.

La Boulangerie par Jean-Luc Pelé   BAKERY €

(✆ 04 93 99 45 82; www.jeanlucpele.com; 3 rue du 24 Août; sandwiches €5, lunch menus €5.50-10.50; ⊘ 7.30am-7.30pm Mon-Sat) This swanky bakery by Cannois *chocolatier* and *pâtissier* Jean-Luc Pelé casts a whole new spin on eating cheap in Cannes. Creative salads, sandwiches, wraps and bagels – to eat in or out – burst with local flavours and provide the perfect prelude to the utterly sensational cakes and desserts Pelé is best known for.

La Casa di Nonna   ITALIAN €

(✆ 04 97 06 33 51; 41 rue Hoche; mains €12-19; ⊘ 8.30am-7.30pm Mon-Sat) Flowers on the tables, fresh floral decor, Italian food just like an Italian *nonna* (grandmother) makes and delicious home-made cakes make this

hybrid restaurant-tearoom a real hit in Cannes. Be it breakfast, mid-morning coffee, lunch or early-evening drinks, Grandma's House is gourmet gold.

Côté Jardin   BISTRO €

(✆ 04 93 38 60 28; www.facebook.com/pg/cote jardinbychristopheferre; 12 ave St-Louis; plats du jour €12-14, other mains €12-22; ⊘ noon-2pm & 7-9.30pm Tue-Sat) Craving a break from Cannes' glitz and grandiosity? This down-to-earth bistro on a residential backstreet is the perfect antidote. Enjoy superb-value *plats du jour* in an enclosed garden overhung with flowering trees, the menu changing based on what chef Christian Ferré finds at the market: Provençal beef stew, chicken curry, codfish aïoli...all updated daily on the Facebook page.

★ Bobo Bistro   MEDITERRANEAN €€

(✆ 04 93 99 97 33; www.facebook.com/Bobo BistroCannes; 21 rue du Commandant André; pizzas €14-20, mains €18-31; ⊘ noon-3pm & 7-11pm) Predictably, it's a 'bobo' (bourgeois bohemian) crowd that gathers at this achingly cool bistro in Cannes' fashionable Carré d'Or. Decor is stylishly retro, with attention-grabbing objets d'art including a tableau of dozens of spindles of coloured yarn. Cuisine is local, seasonal and invariably organic: artichoke salad, tuna carpaccio with passion fruit, roasted cod with mash *fait masion* (home-made).

Le Grain de Sel   BISTRO €€

(✆ 04 93 38 83 65; www.legraindesel-cannes. com; 25 rue Hoche; lunch menus €19, mains €24-32; ⊘ noon-2pm Mon-Sat, 7-10pm Tue-Sat) French-trained, Vietnamese-born chef Nhut Nguyen is at the helm of this delightful bistro on Cannes' pedestrianised restaurant row. The high-ceilinged interior dining room, done up with modern lighting and faux bookshelves, creates a relaxed backdrop for inventive offerings such as shrimp tempura with Provençal zucchini fritters or roast lamb with herbes de Provence, parsnip mousse, dates and candied lemon.

Noisette Café et Cuisine   ITALIAN €€

(✆ 04 93 39 70 35; www.noisettecannes.fr; 6 rue Tony Allard; mains €15-28; ⊘ noon-2.30pm & 7-9.30pm Tue-Sat) There's not a soupçon of pretension about this cosy little Italian tucked away between La Croisette and rue d'Antibes. With its sea-blue furniture and sunny walls, the setting feels summery and the food is authentically Italian – fresh home-made pasta, meat and cheese platters and proper osso bucco with crispy saffron risotto, followed by the frothiest cappuccino in Cannes.

Le Roof
FUSION €€

(☑ 04 63 36 05 06; www.fiveseashotel.com/le-roof-five-seas-hotel; 1 rue Notre Dame; lunch menus €19, street-food platters €15, mains €22-32; ⊘ noon-2pm & 7.30-11.30pm Mon-Fri, noon-3pm & 7.30-11.30pm Sat & Sun; 🕸) Perched on the Five Seas Hotel's 5th floor, this bistro with sublime panoramic views regularly gives its menu a makeover. Highlights may include lunchtime 'roofbowls', health-conscious mixes of fresh veggies, rice, nuts, fish and other lighter fare; after-work street-food platters accompanied by glasses of Provençal rosé, and evening meals for sharing, from steak to salmon to shepherd's pie.

★ Table 22
MODERN EUROPEAN €€€

(Mantel; ☑ 04 93 39 13 10; www.restaurantmantel.com; 22 rue St-Antoine; menus €39-65, mains €35-46; ⊘ noon-2pm Wed-Sun, 7.30-10pm daily) Discover why Noël Mantel is the hotshot of the Cannois gastronomic scene at his refined old-town restaurant. Service is stellar and the seasonally inspired cuisine divine – Mantel's food maximises local ingredients but isn't afraid to experiment with unusual flavours and cooking techniques. Spot the classic film stars on the walls, from Cary Grant to Alfred Hitchcock.

L'Affable
MODERN FRENCH €€€

(☑ 04 93 68 02 09; www.restaurant-laffable.fr; 5 rue la Fontaine; lunch/dinner menus €29/46, mains €40-44; ⊘ noon-2pm & 7-10pm Mon-Fri, 7-10pm Sat) Fine dining with a price to match, run by experienced chef Jean-Paul Battaglia. The setting is formal – beige chairs and banquette seats, tasteful art on the walls – and suited to Battaglia's intricate modern food, which scores as highly on presentation as on flavour. Leave room for the signature Grand Marnier soufflé. Bookings essential.

🍷 Drinking & Nightlife

Going out in Cannes is taken seriously: dress to impress.

Bars around Carré d'Or (Golden Sq) – bordered by rue Commandant André, rue des Frères Pradignac, rue du Batéguier and rue du Dr Gérard Monod – tend to be young, trendy and busy. Beach and hotel bars are more upmarket. Download the free **Cannes Agenda app** (www.cannes.com/fr/mairie/espace-communication/le-mois-a-cannes.html) for listings.

★ L'Epicurieux
WINE BAR

(☑ 04 93 99 93 94; 6 rue des Frères Casanova; ⊘ 10am-10pm Mon-Thu, to 11pm Fri & Sat) A cosy little spot for a glass or two of a local vintage – the wine list here is great, with hand-picked choices from local domains including Côtes de Provence and Côtes du Rhône. Bistro snacks and live bands at weekends make it doubly attractive.

Gotha Club
CLUB

(☑ 04 93 45 11 11; www.gotha-club.com; place Franklin Roosevelt, Casino Palm Beach; cover €25-50; ⊘ midnight-dawn May, Jul & Aug) Only open in May during the film festival and again in July and August, this club is a hot ticket in DJ land. Bringing together some of the most happening names in music with a spectacular setting at the seafaring end of La Croisette, Gotha is a glitzy VIP favourite. Door policy is tight: no guys without girls and only fabulous-looking people.

Armani Caffè
CAFE

(☑ 04 93 99 44 05; www.armanirestaurants.com/cannes-armani-caffe; 42 bd de la Croisette; ⊘ 8.30am-7pm Mon-Sat) The alfresco café of Italian fashion design house Armani is predictably chic, stylish and full of panache. Sit beneath taupe parasols in a prettily manicured garden and enjoy the comings and goings of La Croisette over a chilled glass of prosecco (€10). Salads, pasta and panini too.

JW Grill
LOUNGE

(☑ 04 92 99 70 92; 50 bd de la Croisette; ⊘ 10am-2am) This dazzling white lounge bar on the ground floor of the Marriott hotel is possibly the most beautiful on the Croisette, with designer sofas facing out to sea. Come dusk, indulge in an €18 glass of Champagne and revel in the chic five-star location.

Bâoli
CLUB

(☑ 04 93 43 03 43; www.baolicannes.com; Port Pierre Canto, bd de la Croisette; ⊘ 8pm-6am Fri & Sat) This is Cannes' coolest, trendiest and most selective nightspot – so selective, in fact, that your entire posse might not get in unless you're dressed to the nines. It's part club, part restaurant, so one way to ensure you'll get in is to book a table and make a night of it. Located at the eastern end of La Croisette.

LOCAL KNOWLEDGE

SHOP LIKE A LOCAL

When it comes to shopping with taste, forget Chanel, Gucci and the gaggle of other designer fashion houses strutting their desirable stuff down Cannes' catwalk-like streets.

The insider scoop is **Fromagerie Ceneri** (☑ 04 93 39 63 68; www.fromagerie-ceneri. com; 22 rue Meynadier; ⊙ 10am-6pm Mon, 8am-7pm Tue-Sat, 8.30am-12.30pm Sun) – the only place in Cannes to shop for cheese and dairy products. With cowbells strung from the wooden ceiling and a stunning array of cheeses, this master *fromager-affineur* (cheesemonger and ripener), in business since 1968, is a rare and precious breed on the Riviera. Its selection of *chèvre* (goats cheese) from Provence is second to none, as is its cheese board from elsewhere in France.

For local folklore, hit **Marché Forville** (11 rue du Marché Forville; ⊙ 7.30am-1pm Tue-Fri, to 2pm Sat & Sun), Cannes' busy food market, a couple of blocks back from the port. It dates to 1934 and remains one of the region's key markets. On Monday the fresh fruit, veg, fish and meat stalls are replaced by an all-day *brocante* (flea market).

Simultaneously indulge your inner fashionista and your inner foodie with a pair of chocolate stiletto heels from **JP Paci** (☑ 04 93 39 47 94; www.paci-chocolatier.com; 28 rue Hoche; ⊙ 9.30am-7pm Mon-Sat). Artisan *chocolatier* Jean-Patrice also crafts perfectly formed rounds of Camembert cheese, ravioli squares, red roses, tool boxes and flower pots out of chocolate – all to sweet realist perfection.

☆ Entertainment

Cinéma Les Arcades   CINEMA
(www.arcadescannes.cine.allocine.fr; 77 rue Félix Faure) Catch a movie in English.

ℹ Information

Tourist Office (☑ 04 92 99 84 22; www. cannes-destination.fr; 1 bd de la Croisette; ⊙ 9am-7pm Mar-Oct, to 8pm Jul & Aug, 10am-6pm Nov-Feb; 🛜) Runs the informative 'Once Upon a Time: Cannes' guided walking tour (€6) in English at 9.15am (June to September) or 2.30pm (October to May) every Monday, as well as a host of fun themed tours (in English).

Tourist Office – Train Station Annexe (8 bis place de la Gare; ⊙ 9am-1pm & 2-6pm Mon-Sat)

ℹ Getting There & Away

BUS

From bus stops in front of Cannes' train station, **Lignes d'Azur** (p64) runs express services to Nice (bus 200; €1.50, 1¾ hours, every 15 minutes), Nice-Côte d'Azur airport (bus 210; one way/return €22/33, 50 minutes, half-hourly), Mougins (bus 600; €1.50, 25 minutes, every 20 minutes) and Grasse (bus 600; €1.50, one hour).

Palmbus (☑ 08 25 82 55 99; www.palmbus. fr) operates local buses serving Cannes and the surrounding region from a separate **bus station** (place Bernard Cornut Gentille) near the waterfront.

BICYCLE

Mistral Location (☑ 06 20 33 87 64, 04 93 39 33 60; www.mistral-location.com; 4 rue Georges Clémenceau) rents out bicycles/scooters for €20/30 per day.

CAR

Find all the big car-hire companies at the train station. Local company **Mistral Location** also rents cars, starting at €74 per day.

Street parking is limited to two hours in the town centre. Car parks such as **Parking Palais** (Port Canto, 1 bd de la Croisette), **Parking Suquet-Forville** (7 rue Pastour) or the train station's **Parking SNCF Gare** (1 rue Jean Jaurès) have no maximum time restriction, but costs mount quickly (first hour free, then €2.70 per hour).

TRAIN

Cannes' gleaming white train station is well connected with other towns along the coast.
Antibes (€3.10, 12 minutes, twice hourly)
Marseille (€33, 2¼ hours, half-hourly)
Monaco (€10, one hour, at least twice hourly)
Nice (€7.20, 40 minutes, every 15 minutes)
St-Raphaël (€7.60, 30 minutes, hourly)

ÎLES DE LÉRINS

The two islands making up Lérins – Île Ste-Marguerite and Île St-Honorat – lie within a 20-minute boat ride of Cannes. Tiny and traffic free, they're oases of peace and tranquillity, a world away from the hustle and bustle of the Riviera.

Île Ste-Marguerite is home to an impressive 17th-century bastion, the Fort Royal, which once served as a remote holding cell for prisoners, including the famous Man in the Iron Mask. It now houses a maritime-themed museum. Île St-Honorat is best known for its Cistercian abbey, whose two dozen monks still cultivate vineyards on the island.

Camping is forbidden, and aside from Ste-Marguerite's intermittent hostel, there is no other accommodation on either island. Eating options are also limited, so bring a picnic and a good supply of drinking water. Annoyingly, there's no ferry between the two islands, so you have to return to the mainland if you want to visit both.

❶ Getting There & Away

Boats for the islands leave Cannes from quai des Îles, at the end of quai Laubeuf on the western side of the harbour. **Riviera Lines** (⬚ 04 92 98 71 31; www.riviera-lines.com; quai Max Laubeuf), **Horizon** (⬚ 04 92 98 71 36; www.horizon-lerins. com; quai Laubeuf) and **Trans Côte d'Azur** (⬚ 04 92 98 71 30; www.trans-cote-azur.com; quai Max Laubeuf) run ferries to Île Ste-Marguerite (return adult/child €15/9.50), while **Planaria** (⬚ 04 92 98 71 38; www.cannes-ilesdelerins. com; quai Max Laubeuf) operates boats to Île St-Honorat (return adult/child €16.50/8).

Île Ste-Marguerite

Covered in sweet-smelling eucalyptus and pine, Ste-Marguerite makes a wonderful day trip from Cannes. Its shores are a succession of castaway beaches ideal for picnics, and there are numerous walking trails.

An easy half-hour loop around the island's western tip passes a WWII German bunker, an elevated viewing platform and **Étang du Batéguier**, a wetland teeming with birdlife. The island served as a strategic defence post for centuries. Fort Royal, built in the 17th century by Richelieu and later fortified by Vauban, today houses a **museum** (⬚ 04 89 82 26 26; www.cannes.com/fr/culture/musee-de-la-mer.html; Fort Royal, Île Ste-Marguerite; adult/child €6/free; ◷ 9.30am-5.45pm Apr-Sep, 10.30am-4.45pm Oct-Mar, closed 1.15-2.15pm Tue-Sun & all day Mon Oct-May) with exhibits on the island's Greco-Roman history, artefacts from numerous shipwrecks, and a small aquarium focusing on Mediterranean fauna and flora. Museum admission also includes the former state prison, where the famous Man in the Iron Mask was held.

Even without a museum ticket, you can wander the fort's ramparts, which boast grand views of the coast.

Île St-Honorat

Forested St-Honorat (at 1.5km by 400m, the smaller of the two Lérins islands) was once the site of a powerful monastery founded in the 5th century. Today 25 Cistercian monks still live in the walled, 19th-century Abbaye Notre Dame de Lérins, built around a medieval cloister. At the island's southern tip are the ruins of an earlier fortified monastery dating to the 11th century and designed to ward off pirate attacks.

Visitors can wander the island's trails freely. Amid the Aleppo pines, olive trees and vineyards, you'll find seven chapels and two late-18th-century Napoleonic furnaces once used to heat cannonballs.

CORNICHE DE L'ESTEREL

A walk or drive along the winding Corniche de l'Estérel, opened by the Touring Club de France in 1903, is an attraction in its own right. Also known as the Corniche d'Or, 'Golden Coast', and signposted as the N98 or the D559, it offers spectacular views of rugged red rock formations juxtaposed against the blue-green Mediterranean. Small summer resorts and dreamy inlets (perfect for swimming), all accessible by bus or train, dot its 30km length. The most dramatic stretch is between Anthéor and Théoule-sur-Mer, where the tortuous, narrow road skirts through sparsely built areas.

🏃 Activities

With its lush green Mediterranean forests, intensely red peaks and sterling sea views, the Massif de l'Estérel is a walker's paradise. Local tourist offices have leaflets detailing the most popular walks, including Pic de l'Ours (496m) and Pic du Cap Roux (452m). Buy IGN's Carte de Randonnée (1:25,000) No 3544ET *Fréjus, Saint-Raphaël & Corniche de l'Estérel* for more serious walks.

Those preferring a more informed hike can sign up for a three-hour guided walk with a forest ranger from the Office National des Forêts (National Forestry Office) or nature guide at St-Raphaël tourist office (p97). Access to the range is prohibited on windy or particularly hot days because of fire risks; check with the tourist office before setting off.

With its 30km of coastline, the corniche has more than 30 beaches running the gamut of possibilities: sandy, pebbly, nudist, cove-like, you name it. But wherever you go, the sea remains that crystal-clear turquoise and deep blue, an irresistible invitation to swim.

The Estérel is also a leading dive centre, with numerous WWII shipwrecks and pristine waters. Much of the coast is protected, meaning its fauna and flora are among the best around.

Sentier du Littoral
HIKING

Running 11km between Port Santa Lucia (the track starts behind the naval works) and Agay, this coastal path (yellow markers) takes in some of the area's most scenic spots. It takes roughly 4½ hours to complete, but from May to October you could make a day of it by stopping at some of the idyllic beaches scattered along the way.

You can choose to walk smaller sections; the most scenic is around **Cap du Dramont**, crowned by a signal station, which you can do as a loop from **Plage du Débarquement**. This long, sandy beach is where the US 36th Infantry Division landed on 15 August 1944 as part of Operation Dragoon (Provence landing). The large memorial park has a car park easily accessible from the N98/D559.

Plage d'Agay
SWIMMING

One of the best beaches along the Corniche de l'Estérel for activities (beach volleyball, kids' clubs, water sports etc).

Plage Beaurivage
SWIMMING

An easy walk from the centre of St-Raphaël, this city beach is a popular spot for swimming and sunbathing, with a mini-golf course thrown in for good measure.

Anthéor–Le
Trayas Coast
SNORKELLING, SWIMMING

The section of the Corniche de l'Estérel between Anthéor and Le Trayas is famed for its jewel-like *calanques* (tiny coves) and brilliant snorkelling. The landscape here is especially rugged, with many coves only accessible by boat.

Euro Plongée
DIVING, SNORKELLING

(☑ 04 94 19 03 26, 06 09 18 53 74; www.europlongee. fr; Port de Boulouris) A reputable and family-friendly dive club with CMAS accreditation. Offers individual dives and courses, as well as great two-hour snorkelling tours (€30). They're fantastic for families: kids will love spotting starfish, sea anemones, urchins and other colourful Mediterranean residents.

🛏 Sleeping & Eating

La Villa Mauresque
LUXURY HOTEL €€€

(☑ 04 94 83 02 42; www.villa-mauresque.com; 1792 route de la Corniche; r €289-842; ✳ 🛜 ⛱) A whitewashed vision of Mediterranean luxury, this castle-like 19th-century villa 3km southeast of St-Raphaël features a sea-facing pool and beautiful perspectives on the Bay of St-Tropez from its attached restaurant, Le Bougainvillier. Many of the elegant rooms come with private terraces, hot tubs and/or views of the water.

★ Les Flots Bleus
SEAFOOD €€

(☑ 04 94 44 80 21; www.hotel-cote-azur.com; 83 rte St-Barthélémy, Anthéor; menus €25-32; ⊙ noon-2.30pm Tue-Sun, 7-9.30pm daily) Midway along the Corniche de l'Esterel, Les Flots Bleus fits the dream vision of a roadside Mediterranean eatery, with fine sea views from its terrace and a wide-ranging seafood menu. Favourites include oysters, catch-of-the-day specials and the trademark Marmite des Flots Bleus, a tempting stew of sea bream, red mullet, scallops, razor clams, octopus, shrimp and cuttlefish.

ℹ Getting There & Away

Bus 8, operated by **AggloBus** (☑ 04 94 44 52 70, 04 94 53 78 46; www.agglobus-cavem.com), runs between St-Raphaël and Agay, stopping at Le Dramont on the way; four daily runs (one on Sunday) go all the way to Le Trayas. Tickets cost €1.50.

ST-RAPHAËL

POP 35,296

Just along the shoreline from the neighbouring town of Fréjus, St-Raphaël briefly flourished as a jazz-age hang-out during the 1920s and '30s, but urban sprawl has somewhat obscured its charm. Still, it's looking better since the port was spruced up, and it's a handy base for exploring the Estérel – and a lot cheaper than Cannes.

◎ Sights & Activities

Musée Archéologique
de St-Raphaël
MUSEUM

(☑ 04 94 19 25 75; www.musee-saintraphael.com; parvis de l'Église, rue des Templiers; ⊙ 10am-6pm Tue-Sat Jul-Sep, 9am-12.30pm Wed-Sat & 2-5pm Tue-Sat Mar-Jun & Oct, 10am-12.30pm Wed-Sat & 2-5pm Tue-Fri Nov-Feb) FREE The waters off St-Raphaël are home to the largest number of antique shipwrecks in France, and this museum explores the town's maritime heritage. You'll therefore be able to see a 1928 scuba system developed in St-Raphaël and the first commercial equipment developed by Jacques-Yves Cousteau in the 1940s, as well as numerous artefacts rescued from local wrecks. Visitors can also access the adjoining medieval church and panoramic tower.

Les Bateaux de St-Raphaël BOATING
(☑04 94 95 17 46; www.bateauxsaintraphael. com; quai Nomy; ☺Apr-Oct) This boat company offers some great coast trips, including one to explore the coves of the Corniche de l'Estérel (adult/child €20/10). It also offers a ferry service to Île Ste-Marguerite (adult/child return €23/12, one hour 10 minutes) and St-Tropez (adult/child return €26/15, one hour).

🛏 Sleeping & Eating

Hôtel le 21 HOTEL €€
(☑04 94 19 21 21; www.le21-hotel.com; 21 place Galliéni; r €69-149; ❄🌐) Handy for both the train station and the town centre, this small hotel is one of the better-value options in St-Raphaël. Rooms are plain and proper, with laminate floors, spacious bathrooms and a vaguely Scandi feel. There's a lift, but it's tiny. It's set back above a cafe, on the way down to the seafront from the train station.

Chez Gaston MEDITERRANEAN €€
(☑04 94 53 77 13; www.facebook.com/chezgaston ruecharabois; 36 rue Charabois; lunch menus €17, mains €23-28; ☺noon-3pm Tue-Fri, 7-11pm Tue-Sat) Blackboard menus, pavement tables, a wall of wines and hearty dishes such as steak béarnaise, fish soup and slow-roasted lamb: really, what more do you want from a French bistro? It's family-run, too, and a thoroughly cosy place for a thoroughly French lunch. Or dinner, for that matter.

Elly's GASTRONOMY €€€
(☑04 94 83 63 39; www.elly-s.com; 54 rue de la Liberté; menus €65; ☺noon-1.30pm & 7-9.30pm Tue-Sat) Overseen by chef Franck Chabod, a veteran of several Michelin-starred establishments, this attractive restaurant feels a little out of place in St-Raphaël: its glitzy food, glam presentation and garish modern art all feel like they deserve to be located somewhere a little flashier. Still, if you're in the mood for fine French food, Elly's rates E for excellent.

ℹ Information

Tourist Office (☑04 94 19 52 52; www. saint-raphael.com; 99 quai Albert 1er; ☺9am-12.30pm & 2-6.30pm Mon-Sat Sep-Jun, 9am-7pm Jul & Aug) Can help you book activities in the area, among other things.

ℹ Getting There & Away

Bus 4, operated by **AggloBus**, goes to Fréjus' old town (€1.50, 10 minutes) from St Raphaël bus station. Bus 8 links St Raphaël with villages along the coast between Boulouris and Le Trayas (€1.50). **Varlib** (☑09 70 83 03 80; www. varlib.fr) offers service to St-Tropez on its line 7601 (€3, 1¼ to 1½ hours, eight daily, more in summer).

There are hourly trains to Nice (€11.90, one hour), Cannes (€7.60, 30 to 45 minutes) and Marseille (€28.30, 1¾ hours). Some services stop at the villages along the Corniche de l'Estérel.

FRÉJUS

POP 52,897

Once an important province of Roman Gaul (when it was known as Forum Julii), the little town of Fréjus is a quiet spot that has some surprisingly big attractions – including some Roman ruins, a chapel decorated by the filmmaker-artist Jean Cocteau (of *Les Enfants du Paradis* fame), and an impressive Gothic cathedral whose cloister houses a unique collection of medieval ceiling frescoes.

It's particularly worth a visit on Wednesday and Saturday morning, when the old-town market is in full swing.

⊙ Sights

If you're visiting several sights in Fréjus, it's worth buying a **Fréjus Pass** (€6), which grants entry to all municipal museums, or the **Fréjus Pass Integral** (€9), which also includes the town's top attraction, the cathedral cloister. You can buy the pass at the first sight you visit.

★**Cloître de la Cathédrale de Fréjus** CATHEDRAL
(☑04 94 51 26 30; www.cloitre-frejus.fr; 48 rue de Fleury; adult/child €6/free; ☺10am-12.30pm & 1.45-6.30pm Jun-Sep, 10am-1pm & 2-5pm Tue-Sun Oct-May) Fréjus' star sight is its 11th- and 12th-century cathedral, one of the region's first Gothic buildings. Its **cloister** features rare 14th- and 15th-century painted wood-

Fréjus

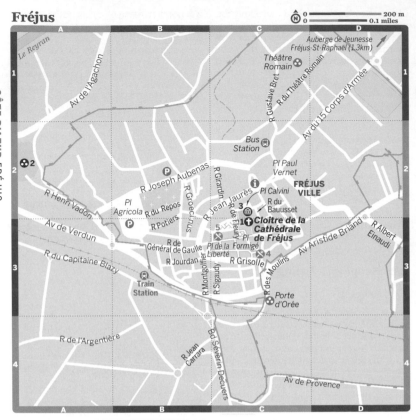

Fréjus

◎ **Top Sights**
1 Cloître de la Cathédrale de Fréjus......C3

◎ **Sights**
2 Les Arènes...A2
3 Musée Archéologique.........................C2

✖ **Eating**
4 L'Entrée des Artistes...........................C3
5 Mon Fromager.......................................C3

en ceiling panels depicting angels, devils, hunters, acrobats and monsters in vivid comic-book fashion. Both the meaning and origin of these are unknown. Only 500 of the original 1200 frames survive. Afterwards, peek at the octagonal 5th-century **baptistery**, which incorporates eight Roman columns; it's one of the oldest Christian buildings in France and is exceptionally well preserved.

Musée Archéologique   MUSEUM
(☑ 04 94 52 15 78; 3 place Calvini; adult/child €3/ free; ⊙ 9.30am-12.30pm & 2-6pm Tue-Sun Apr-Sep, 9.30am-noon & 2-4.30pm Tue-Sat Oct-Mar) Fréjus' Roman remains have seen better days, so the town's archaeological museum makes a useful accompaniment. There are some fascinating treasures on display dating all the way back to the town's Grecian and Roman beginnings, from everyday objects to rare finds, such as a double-faced marble statue of Hermes, a head of Jupiter and a stunning 3rd-century mosaic depicting a leopard.

Les Arènes   RUINS
(Amphitheatre; ☑ 04 94 51 34 31; rue Henri Vadon; adult/child €3/free; ⊙ 9.30am-12.30pm & 2-6pm Tue-Sun Apr-Sep, 9.30am-noon & 2-4.30pm Tue-Sat Oct-Mar) In comparison to some of Provence's other Roman ruins, Fréjus' amphitheatre is a little underwhelming – it was badly damaged during archaeological

digs, and some half-hearted reconstruction doesn't quite recapture the atmosphere of what was once one of Gaul's largest amphitheatres (seating 10,000 spectators). Plans have been mooted to rebuild it properly, but so far no joy.

Chapelle Cocteau GALLERY
(Chapelle Notre-Dame-de-Jérusalem; ☑ 04 94 51 34 31; rte de Cannes; adult/child €3/free; ◷ 9.30am-12.30pm & 2-6pm Tue-Sun Apr-Sep, 9.30am-noon & 2-4.30pm Tue-Sat Oct-Mar) This was one of the last pieces of work embarked upon by Jean Cocteau (1889–1963), best known for the fishermen's chapel he decorated in Villefranche-sur-Mer. Cocteau began work on Chapelle Notre Dame in Fréjus in 1961, but it remained incomplete until the artist's legal heir, Édouard Dermit, finished his former companion's work in 1988. The chapel is about 5km northeast of the old town, in the quarter of La Tour de Mare (served by bus 13), on the N7 towards Cannes.

🛏 Sleeping

Auberge de Jeunesse Fréjus-St-Raphaël HOSTEL €
(☑ 04 94 53 18 75; www.fuaj.org; chemin du Counillier; dm €19-24; ◷ Mar-Oct; 🛜) A rambling, basic HI-affiliated hostel set in 10 hectares of pine trees and parkland, where you can also pitch your tent. Take bus 2 or 3 from St-Raphaël or Fréjus train stations to stop Les Chênes, then cross the roundabout and take chemin du Counillier on your left (600m). Daily lockout between noon and 5.30pm; rates include breakfast and sheets.

Hôtel Les Calanques HOTEL €€
(☑ 04 98 11 36 36; www.hotel-les-calanques.com; rue du Nid au Soleil, Les Issambres; s €72-104, d €83 148, tr €118-145, f €149-168) Thirteen kilometres south of Fréjus towards St-Tropez along the winding coast road, this family-run three-star sits on the rocks above its own quiet cove, accessed via the hotel's palm-filled garden. Many of the 12 rooms sport renovated bathrooms and other upgrades from a fairly recent makeover, and 10 boast stunning sea views – don't even consider the two facing the busy road.

🍴 Eating

⭐Mon Fromager DELI €
(☑ 04 94 40 67 99; www.mon-fromager.fr; 38 rue Siéyès; plat du jour €15.60, 5-cheese platter €12.70; ◷ shop 9.30am-12.30pm & 2-7pm Tue-Sat, lunch noon-2pm Tue-Sat; ☑) Enterprising cheesemonger Philippe Daujam not only sells cheese – he also cooks it into tasty lunches in his deli-style restaurant by the cheese counter and on the street outside. Locals flock for the excellent-value *plat du jour* and can't-go-wrong cheese platters with salad. The faux cow-skin table mats are a fun touch, and Philippe is a font of *fromage* knowledge.

L'Entrée des Artistes BISTRO €
(☑ 04 94 40 11 60; 63 place St-François de Paule; lunch menus €17.50, mains €17-20; ◷ noon-2pm & 7.30-9.30pm Tue-Sat) Brothers Seb and Chris Terrier run this intimate bistro with its pleasant front terrace overlooking a square in the historic centre. The lunchtime *plats du jour* (€12) and *formules* (€17.50 including wine, dessert and coffee) are a steal – better yet, they're available Saturday too.

ℹ Information

Tourist Office (☑ 04 94 51 83 83; www.frejus. fr; 249 rue Jean Jaurès; ◷ 9.30am-7pm Jul & Aug, 9.30am-12.30pm & 2.30-6.30pm Mon-Sat Jun & Sep, 9.30am-noon & 2-6pm Mon-Sat Oct-May) Runs French-language guided tours (€8) of the town covering history, architecture and natural history.

ℹ Getting There & Away

Bus 4, operated by **AggloBus** (p96), links Fréjus' little **bus station** (rue Gustave Bret) with St-Raphaël (€1.50).

From Fréjus' small train station, in summer there are hourly services to/from St-Raphaël (€1.40, three minutes), Cannes (€8.10, 30 to 45 minutes) and Nice (from €12.40, one hour).

PRESQU'ÎLE DE ST-TROPEZ

Jutting out into the sea between the Golfe de St-Tropez and the Baie de Cavalaire, you'll find the Presqu'île de St-Tropez (St-Tropez peninsula). From swanky St-Tropez on the northern coast, fine-sand beaches of buttercream yellow and gold – easily the loveliest on the Côte d'Azur – ring the coast. The golden sands of France's chicest beach, Plage de Pampelonne, line the peninsula's eastern side, where you'll also find St-Tropez's storied beach-club scene.

South of St-Tropez unfurl manicured vineyards and quiet, narrow lanes dotted with châteaux, solitary stone *bastides*

BEST BEACHES OF THE PRESQU'ÎLE DE ST-TROPEZ

Plage de Pampelonne The 5km-long, celebrity-studded Plage de Pampelonne sports a line-up of exclusive beach restaurants and clubs in summer. Find public entries (and parking for €5.50) at one of six access points: rte de Tahiti, chemin des Moulins, chemin de Tamaris, bd Patch, chemin des Barraques and rte de Bonne Terrasse. The northern edge of the beach begins 4km southeast of St-Tropez with **Plage de Tahiti** (p100).

Plage des Salins (chemin des Salins) Just east of St-Tropez, Plage des Salins is a 600m-wide pine-fringed beach at the southern foot of Cap des Salins. At the northern end of the beach, on a rock jutting out to sea, is the tomb of Émile Olivier (1825–1913), who served as first minister to Napoleon III until his exile in 1870. It looks out towards **La Tête de Chien**, named after the legendary dog who declined to eat St Torpes' remains.

Plage de Tahiti This famous nudist beach is also a naturally magnificent stretch of sandy beach, about 4km southeast of St-Tropez.

(country houses) and private villas. Inland, the flower-dressed hilltop villages of Gassin and Ramatuelle charm the socks off millions.

St-Tropez

POP 4305

Pouting sexpot Brigitte Bardot came to St-Tropez in the 1950s to star in *Et Dieu Créa la Femme* (*And God Created Woman;* 1956) and overnight transformed the peaceful fishing village into a sizzling jet-set favourite. Tropeziens have thrived on their sexy image ever since: at the Vieux Port, yachts like spaceships jostle for millionaire moorings, and infinitely more tourists jostle to admire them.

Yet there is a serene side to this village trampled by 60,000 summertime inhabitants and visitors on any given day. In the low season, the St-Tropez of mesmerising quaint beauty and 'sardine scales glistening like pearls on the cobblestones' that charmed Guy de Maupassant (1850–93) comes to life. Meander cobbled lanes in the old fishing quarter of La Ponche, sip pastis at a place des Lices cafe, watch old men play *pétanque* beneath plane trees, or walk in solitary splendour from beach to beach along the coastal path.

◎ Sights & Activities

★ **Musée de l'Annonciade**   GALLERY
(04 94 17 84 10; www.saint-tropez.fr/fr/culture/musee-de-lannonciade; place Grammont; adult/child €6/free; 10am-6pm daily mid-Jun–Sep, Tue-Sun Oct–mid-Jun) In a gracefully converted 16th-century chapel, this small but famous museum showcases an impressive collection of modern art infused with that legendary Côte d'Azur light. Pointillist Paul Signac bought a house in St-Tropez in 1892 and introduced other artists to the area. The museum's collection includes his *St-Tropez, Le Quai* (1899) and *St-Tropez, Coucher de Soleil au Bois de Pins* (1896). Vuillard, Bonnard and Maurice Denis (the self-named 'Nabis' group) have a room to themselves.

★ **La Ponche**   HISTORIC SITE
Shrug off the hustle of the port in St-Tropez's historic fishing quarter, La Ponche, northeast of the Vieux Port. From the southern end of quai Frédéric Mistral, place Garrezio sprawls east from 10th-century **Tour Suffren** to place de l'Hôtel de Ville. From here, rue Guichard leads southeast to iconic **Église de St-Tropez** (Eglise Notre Dame de l'Assomption; rue Commandant Guichard). Follow rue du Portail Neuf south to **Chapelle de la Miséricorde** (1-5 rue de la Miséricorde; 10am-6pm).

★ **Citadelle de St-Tropez**   MUSEUM
(04 94 97 59 43; www.saint-tropez.fr/fr/culture/citadelle; 1 montée de la Citadelle; adult/child €3/free; 10am-6.30pm Apr-Sep, to 5.30pm Oct-Mar;) Built in 1602 to defend the coast against Spain, the citadel dominates the hillside overlooking St-Tropez to the east. The views are fantastic, as are the exotic peacocks wandering the grounds. Its dungeons are home to the excellent **Musée de l'Histoire Maritime**, an interactive museum that traces the history of humans at sea through fishing, trading, exploration, travel and the navy. The particular focus, of course, is Tropezienne and Provençal seafarers.

Vieux Port   PORT

Yachts line the harbour (as their uniformed crews diligently scrub them) and visitors stroll the quays at the picturesque old port. In front of the sable-coloured townhouses, the **Bailli de Suffren statue** (quai Suffren) of a 17th-century naval hero, cast from a 19th-century cannon, peers out to sea. Duck beneath the archway, next to the tourist office, to uncover St-Tropez' daily morning fish market, on place aux Herbes.

Place des Lices   SQUARE

St-Tropez' legendary and very charming central square is studded with plane trees, cafes and *pétanque* players. Simply sitting on a cafe terrace watching the world go by or jostling with the crowds at its twice-weekly **market** (place des Lices; ⊙8am-1pm Tue & Sat) extravaganza, jam-packed with everything from fruit and veg to antique mirrors and sandals, is an integral part of the St-Tropez experience.

Les Bateaux Verts   BOATING

(📞04 94 49 29 39; www.bateauxverts.com; 7 quai Jean Jaurès) Les Bateaux Verts offers trips around Baie des Cannebiers (dubbed 'Bay of Stars' after the celebrity villas dotting its coast) from April to September (adult/child from €11/0), as well as seasonal boats to Cannes (€39/25, 1½ hours) and Porquerolles (€43/28, two hours), and regular shuttle boats to Marines de Cogolin, Port Grimaud, Ste-Maxime and Les Issambres.

⚑ Festivals & Events

Bravade de Saint-Tropez   RELIGIOUS

(⊙May; www.bravade-saint-tropez.fr) Since 1558 Tropeziens have turned out in traditional costume to watch an ear-splitting army of 140 musket-firing *bravadeurs* parade with a bust of St Torpes, the namesake and patron of the town. La Bravade (Provençal for 'bravery') is held from 16 to 18 May.

Bravade des Espagnols   CULTURAL

(⊙Jun) The place des Lices is invaded with musket-wielding historical re-enactors as processions and martial displays celebrate victory over the 21 Spanish galleons that attacked Marseille on 15 June 1637.

🛏 Sleeping

St-Tropez is home to celebrity-studded hangs, with prices to match – this is no shoestring destination, though campgrounds do sit southeast along Plage de Pampelonne.

Most hotels close in winter; the tourist office lists what's open, and also has a list of B&Bs. If you're driving, double-check the parking arrangements.

Hôtel Lou Cagnard   HOTEL €€

(📞04 94 97 04 24; www.hotel-lou-cagnard.com; 30 av Paul Roussel; r from €95; ⊙Apr-Oct; P❄🖥) This old-school hotel stands in stark contrast to most of the swanky hotels around St-Tropez. Located in an old house shaded by lemon and fig trees, its 18 rooms are unashamedly frilly and floral, but some have garden patios, and the lovely jasmine-scented garden and welcoming family feel make it a home away from home. The cheapest rooms share toilets.

Hôtel Le Colombier   HOTEL €€

(📞04 94 97 05 31; http://lecolombierhotel.free.fr; impasse des Conquettes; d/tr €131/274; ⊙mid-Apr–mid-Nov; ❄🖥) An immaculately clean converted house, five minutes' walk from place des Lices, the Colombier's fresh, summery decor is inherently relaxing. Rooms are in shades of white and furnished with vintage pieces.

Hôtel Les Palmiers   HOTEL €€

(📞04 94 97 01 61; www.hotel-les-palmiers.com; 26 bd Vasserot; d €165; ❄🖥) What a great spot this simple hotel has, in an old villa on the edge of place des Lices. It's so perfectly situated that you don't mind the plainness of the (bright) rooms, the best of which overlook the hotel's gated courtyard. Choose one in the main building rather than the annexe.

Hôtel Ermitage   BOUTIQUE HOTEL €€€

(📞04 94 81 08 10; www.ermitagehotel.fr; 14 av Paul Signac; r from €320; ❄🖥) Well, if you really want to hang with the jet set, the hip Hôtel Hermitage is your kind of place. Self-consciously retro, the decor draws inspiration from St-Tropez's midcentury heyday: bold primary colours, vintage design pieces and big prints of '60s icons on the walls. The bar's as cool as they come, with sweeping views over St-Trop.

B Lodge Hôtel   HOTEL €€€

(📞04 94 97 58 72; www.hotel-b-lodge.com; 23 rue de l'Aïoli; r from €220; ⊙Dec-Oct; ❄🖥) Just downhill from the Citadelle, this swanky design pad looks oldish from the outside, but inside it's a model modern hotel: minimalist furniture, exposed stone walls, muted tones and touches of black-and-white zebra decor. Obviously rooms with balconies and

St-Tropez

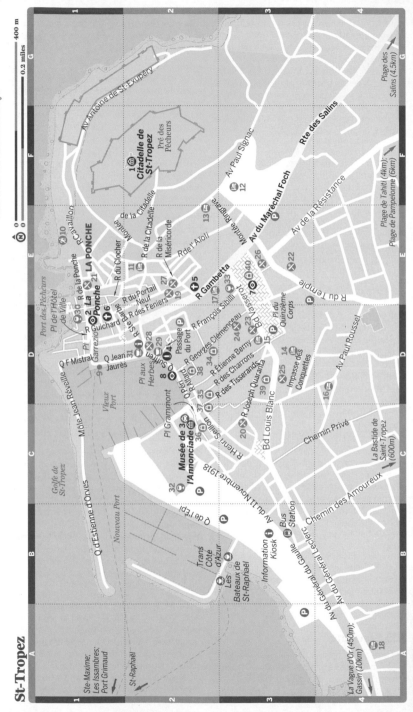

St-Tropez

CÔTE D'AZUR ST-TROPEZ

Citadelle views are fabulous. Prices drop significantly in winter.

Eating

Prices are high: the glamour dust sprinkled on fish and chips doesn't come cheap! Quai Jean Jaurès is lined with mediocre restaurants with great portside views. Cheaper eats cluster near quai de l'Épi and the new port. Reservations are essential in high season; many restaurants close in winter.

Don't leave town without sampling *tarte Tropézienne,* an orange-blossom-flavoured double sponge cake filled with thick cream, created by Polish baker A Mickla in 1955.

La Tarte Tropézienne　　CAFE €
(☑04 94 97 94 25; www.latartetropezienne.fr; place des Lices; tarts/snacks from €5.50/3; ☉6.30am-10pm; 🐾) This smart, bustling cafe-bakery is the creator of St Tropez' eponymous sugar-crusted, orange-perfumed cake, but also does decent breads and light meals. There are smaller branches on **rue Clémenceau** (☑04 94 97 71 42; 36 rue Clémenceau; tarts/snacks €5.50/3; ☉7am-10pm) and near the **new port** (☑04 94 97 19 77; 9 bd Louis Blanc; tarts/snacks €5.50/3; ☉6.30am-7.30pm), plus

various other towns around Provence and the Île de France.

Le Gorille　　CAFE €
(☑04 94 97 03 93; www.legorille.com; 1 quai Suffren; sandwiches/mains €7/17; ☉7am-7pm) This portside hang-out gets its name from its previous owner – the short, muscular and apparently very hairy Henri Guérin! Stop here for breakfast or a post-clubbing *croque-monsieur* and fries. It's anything but pretentious.

La Pesquière　　SEAFOOD €
(☑04 94 97 05 92; http://pesquiere.mazagran. free.fr; 1 rue des Remparts; menus adult/child €29/14; ☉9am-midnight late Mar-Oct) It's no surprise this old-fashioned place survives in restless, modish St Tropez: since 1962 the one family has made an art of buying the day's freshest catch – whether that be dourade, red mullet, bass or prawns – and cooking it to simple perfection. Locals love it, as do visitors, and you feel you've had your money's worth.

★Le Café　　CAFE €€
(☑04 94 97 44 69; www.lecafe.fr; Traverse des Lices; 2-course lunch menu €18, mains €22-29;

THE ST-TROPEZ BEACH LIFE

St-Tropez' seaside scene revolves around sandy clubs and restaurants, all with their own style. Most are open May to September; advance bookings are highly recommended.

Pearl Beach (☑ 04 98 12 70 70; www.thepearlbeach.com; quartier de la Bouillabaisse; mains €27-31; ⊘ 9am-6pm mid-Feb–Dec) A good bet for beachside dining, this pan-European bistro-bar is on the way out of town. With its wood deck and swaying palms, it's perfect for a sundowner cocktail, or something more substantial – perhaps burrata with green beans and olive powder, or seared parmesan-crusted tuna with cumin and vegetables.

La Plage des Jumeaux (☑ 04 94 58 21 80; www.plagedesjumeaux.com; rte de l'Épi, Plage de Pampelonne; mains €27-32; ⊘ noon-5pm; P ☑ ⊞) The pick of Pampelonne's beach restaurants, Jumeaux serves beautiful seafood (including fabulous whole fish, ideal to share) and sun-busting salads on its dreamy white-and-turquoise-striped beach. Families are well catered for, with playground equipment, beach toys and a kids' menu.

Nikki Beach (☑ 04 94 79 82 04; www.nikkibeach.com/sttropez; 1093 rte de l'Epi, Plage de Pampelonne; ⊘ 11.30am-8pm Apr-Sep) Favoured by dance-on-the-bar celebs, and those who just want to be seen, Nikki can become a beachside bacchanal to match most fantasies. The debauchery ends surprisingly early.

Le Club 55 (☑ 04 94 55 55 55; www.leclub55.fr; 43 bd Patch, Plage de Pampelonne; ⊘ 10am-7pm Mar-Oct; ☎) The longest-running Pampelonne beach club dates to the 1950s and was originally the crew canteen during the filming of *And God Created Woman*. Now it caters to celebs who do *not* want to be seen. The food is – remarkably – nothing special.

Shellona (C'est la Vie; ☑ 04 94 79 84 35; www.shellonabeach.com; rte de l'Épi, Plage de Pampelonne; mains €41-47; ⊘ Feb-Oct; P ☎) A Greek restaurant and beach club, Shellona is a little more relaxed than some of its immediate neighbours. Burrata, fish in Provençal herbs and *chimichurri* may have you wondering how strictly Hellenic the kitchen is, but the food's good, the sea's bright, and the vibe's right.

Couleurs Jardin (☑ 04 94 79 59 12; www.restaurantcouleursjardin.com; 142 bd de Gigaro, La Croix-Valmer; mains €25-35; ⊘ noon-2.30pm & 7.30-11pm Apr-Sep; P ☎) Eclectic and hip, this imaginative beachside space is *the* place to dine and/or drink. Loll on cushioned seating beneath the trees or pick a table on the terrace with nothing between you and the deep blue sea. Cuisine is market- (and fashion-) fuelled: swordfish with *yuzu*, or grilled prawns with Sichuan pepper.

La Vigneraie 1860 (☑ 04 94 97 17 03; www.la-vigneraie-1860.fr; chemin des Moulins; site for 2 people €53.50, apt per week from €800; ⊘ Apr-Oct, reception 8am-noon & 5-8pm; P) This simple caravan and camping ground just off of Plage de Pampelonne offers one of the few ways to live cheaply and still get a chance to hang out in one of the most exclusive locales in the region. Surrounded by vineyards, it has basic showers and apartments.

Le Refuge (☑ 04 94 79 67 38, 06 17 95 65 38; www.lerefuge-cotedazur.fr; plage de Gigaro, La Croix-Valmer; d/tr from €83/98; ⊘ Apr-Sep; ☎) This rustic seaside house sits back off the sand. Ten humble rooms and five studios with kitchenettes open onto private little tabled terraces. Proprietors cook up tasty grills at the restaurant of the same name at the start of the coastal path. Wi-fi is available downstairs.

⊘ 8am-11pm) Whetting whistles since 1789, this historic cafe is where artists and painters preferred to hang out back in the days when St-Trop was still a sleepy port. Happily, it has clung on to its no-nonsense roots – you'll find solid dishes such as pot-roasted chicken, mussels and grilled fish on the menu.

Le G'Envie
BISTRO €€

(📞 07 86 31 11 22, 04 94 79 85 09; www.facebook. com/LeGRestaurant/ 67 rue du Portail Neuf; menu lunch/dinner from €20/39; ⊙ noon-2pm & 7.30-11pm Tue-Sun) Run by ebullient owners Alain and Nuno, this pint-sized restaurant has so much skill and enthusiasm expended on making diners happy. There are only a few tables, so expect to queue – but the wonders issuing from the little open-plan kitchen make it worth the wait. Fresh market ingredients drive the menu, which changes regularly.

La Ramade
PROVENCAL €€€

(📞 04 94 81 58 67; 3 rue du Temple; menus €50; ⊙ noon-3pm & 7-11pm Feb–mid-Nov) A lovely slice of old-fashioned Provençal hospitality, this terraced (or fire-warmed, on chilly days) bistro does great French service: few frills, great ingredients treated with skill, good wine, and a general sense that life is being lived right. The *onglet* (skirt steak) with eschalot sauce couldn't be more satisfying, while anything grilled on the open fire is bound to delight carnivores.

Au Caprice des Deux
FRENCH €€€

(📞 04 94 97 76 78; www.aucapricedesdeux.com; 40 rue du Portail Neuf; mains from €39; ⊙ 7.30-10.30pm daily Jul & Aug, Wed-Mon Apr-Jun & Sep, Thu-Sat Oct-Mar) This traditional *maison de village* (old stone terraced house) with coffee-coloured wooden shutters is a fancy-night-out favourite with locals, who know what award-winning chef Stéphane Avelin can do with good produce, and are prepared to pay. Its intimate interior is as traditional as its French cuisine: grilled veal liver or truffle risotto. For St-Tropez, the prices aren't too extreme

Auberge des Maures
PROVENCAL €€€

(📞 04 94 97 01 50; www.aubergedesmaures.fr; 4 rue du Docteur Boutin; mains €35-45; ⊙ 6.45pm-12.30am Apr-Oct) The town's oldest restaurant remains the locals' choice for always-good, copious portions of earthy Provençal cooking, like *daube* (braised-beef stew), tapenade-stuffed lamb shoulder, lobster and *onglet* (skirt steak) grilled over the fire with eschalot sauce. Book a table (essential) in the leafy courtyard. The wine selection is pretty special, too.

🍷 Drinking & Nightlife

Dress to kill. And bring more money than you think you'll need. Many places close in winter, but in summer it's party central seven days a week.

To tap into the local LGBTIQ+ scene, hit L'Esqui Club (p105).

★ Sénéquier
CAFE

(📞 04 94 97 20 20; www.senequier.com; quai Jean Jaurès; ⊙ 8am-1am; 🛜) Sartre wrote parts of *Les Chemins de la Liberté* (Roads to Freedom) at this portside cafe – in business since 1887 – which is popular with boaties, bikers and tourists. Look for the terrace crammed with pillar-box-red tables and director's chairs. Be warned, however, that a mere coffee costs €8, so be prepared for a shock when you see the menu...

★ Les Caves du Roy
CLUB

(www.lescavesduroy.com; Hôtel Byblos, av Paul Signac; ⊙ 10pm-6am Fri & Sat Apr-Oct, daily Jul & Aug) The star-studded bar at the infamous Hôtel Byblos remains the perennial champion of nightclubs in St-Tropez, if not the whole Riviera. Dress to impress if you hope to get in and mingle with starlets and race-car drivers.

Café de Paris
CAFE

(📞 04 94 97 00 56; www.cafedeparis.fr; 15 quai Suffren; ⊙ 8am-2am) The terrace is *the* place to sport your new strappy sandals at afternoon aperitifs. Service is the friendliest along the port.

Bar du Port
BAR

(📞 04 94 97 00 54; www.barduport.com; 7 quai Suffren; ⊙ 7am-3am; 🛜) Young, happening harbour-side bar for beautiful people, with chichi decor in shades of white and silver. It's been run by the same family for 50 years, who maintain its antique sense of dignity.

L'Esqui Club
CLUB

(📞 04 94 79 83 42, 5 rue du Four; ⊙ midnight-7am daily Jun-Sep, Thu-Sat Oct-May) Where the party winds up when you want to dance until dawn. The Tropéziens' top choice, it's also distinctly LGBTIQ+ friendly.

VIP Room
CLUB

(📞 04 94 97 14 70; www.facebook.com/VipRoom StTropez; residence du Nouveau Port; ⊙ 8pm-6am Jun-Sep) New York loft–style club at the Nouveau Port; around for aeons and still lures in the occasional VIP.

White 1921
BAR

(📞 04 94 45 50 50; www.white1921.com; place des Lices; ⊙ 8pm-late mid-May–mid-Oct) Blindingly white and appropriately expensive, White 1921 is owned by Louis Vuitton. It's a chic alfresco champagne lounge in a renovated

CÔTE D'AZUR ST-TROPEZ

townhouse on place des Lices. Can't make it home? Stay over in one of the swank rooms (from €345).

Bar at l'Ermitage
BAR

(www.ermitagehotel.fr; Hôtel Ermitage, av Paul Signac; ⊙ 5pm-midnight Apr-Oct) Escape the crowds at the laid-back Ermitage, kitted out in distressed '50s-modern furniture, with enchanting views of the rooftops of old St-Tropez and the sea.

🛍 Shopping

St-Tropez is loaded with couture boutiques, gourmet food shops and art galleries.

Atelier Rondini
SHOES

(☑ 04 94 97 19 55; www.rondini.fr; 18 rue Georges Clémenceau; ⊙ 10.30am-1pm & 3-6.30pm Tue-Sun) Colette brought a pair of sandals from Greece to Atelier Rondini (open since 1927) to be replicated. It's still making the iconic sandals today (from about €145).

K Jacques
SHOES

(☑ 04 94 97 41 50; www.kjacques.com; 39bis rue Allard; ⊙ 10am-1pm & 2.30-8.30pm Mon-Sat, 10.30am-1pm & 3-8.30pm Sun) Hand-crafting sandals (from €240) since 1933 for such clients as Picasso and Brigitte Bardot. There's another branch (p106) nearby.

Benoît Gourmet & Co
FOOD & DRINKS

(☑ 04 94 97 73 78; 6 rue des Charrons; ⊙ 9am-noon & 2-6pm Mon-Sat) Everything gourmet (caviar, Champagne and foie gras included).

La Pause Douceur
FOOD

(☑ 04 94 97 27 58; 11 rue Allard; ⊙ 9am-1pm & 2-8.30pm) Run by local girl Delphine and her mother, this irresistible little shop sells delicious home-made chocolates, biscuits and sweet treats. The praline chocolate is a favourite of chef and cookery writer Nina Parker.

K Jacques
SHOES

(☑ 04 94 97 41 50; www.kjacques.fr; 16 rue Seillon; ⊙ 10am-1pm & 2.30-8.30pm Mon-Sat, 10.30am-1pm & 3-8.30pm Sun) Outlet for St-Tropez hand-crafted sandals (from €240). K Jacques has been around since 1933, serving such clients as Picasso and Brigitte Bardot.

Le Dépôt
CLOTHING

(☑ 04 94 97 80 10; www.ledepot-saint-tropez.com; 12 bd Louis Blanc; ⊙ 10am-noon & 2-6.30pm daily Apr-Oct, Tue & Thu-Sat Nov-Mar) Since 1999 this chic boutique has sold secondhand and vintage designer clothes and accessories.

ℹ Information

Tourist Office (☑ 08 92 68 48 28; www.sainttropeztourisme.com; quai Jean Jaurès; ⊙ 9.30am-1.30pm & 3-7.30pm Jul & Aug, 9.30am-12.30pm & 2-7pm Apr-Jun, Sep & Oct, to 6pm Mon-Sat Nov-Mar) Runs 1½-hour walking tours April to October (adult/child €6/free) and rents iPods with an interactive discovery town tour (€3). The **kiosk** (⊙ 9am-6pm Jul & Aug) in Parking du Port operates in July and August.

ℹ Getting There & Away

BOAT

Trans Côte d'Azur (☑ 04 92 98 71 30; www.trans-cote-azur.co.uk; ⊙ May-Oct) Ferries from Nice and Cannes.

Les Bateaux Verts (p101)

Les Bateaux de St-Raphaël (☑ 04 94 95 17 46; www.bateauxsaintraphael.com; ⊙ Apr-late Nov) Seasonal boats between St-Tropez (Nouveau Port) and St-Raphaël (one-way adult/child €15/10, one hour).

Sea Taxi (☑ 06 12 40 28 05; www.taxi-boat-saint-tropez.com) Taxi boat for hire around St-Tropez. A crossing from St Tropez to Ste-Maxime is €80 during the day, and €100 after 10pm.

BUS

VarLib (☑ 09 70 83 03 80; www.varlib.fr) tickets cost €3 from the **bus station** (Gare Routière; ☑ 04 94 56 25 74; av du Général de Gaulle) for anywhere within the Var département (except Toulon-Hyères airport). Destinations include Ramatuelle (35 minutes, up to six daily) and St-Raphaël (1¼ to three hours, depending on traffic, hourly) via Grimaud and Port Grimaud and Fréjus.

Buses to Toulon (two hours, seven daily, fewer in summer) stop at Le Lavandou (one hour) and Hyères (1½ hours).

Buses serve Toulon-Hyères airport (€15, 1½ hours), but some require a transfer.

CAR

During high season, those in the know avoid horrendous four-hour traffic bottlenecks on the one road into St-Tropez (and €40 parking, which is nonetheless hard to find) by parking in Port Grimaud or Ste-Maxime and taking a **Les Bateaux Verts** (p101) shuttle boat.

TRAIN

By train, the most convenient station is in St-Raphäel, which is served by **Les Bateaux de St-Raphaël** boats in high season, or a slower **VarLib** bus. There is no luggage storage at the train station (or any public place in the Var).

ST-TROPEZ HIGH LIFE

St-Tropez is riddled with high-class digs and fancy tables. If your wallet's feeling plump, consider one of the following.

Hôtel Byblos (☏04 94 56 68 00; www.byblos.com; av Paul Signac; d/ste from €480/910; ☉mid-Apr–Oct; P@⏼⊠) Hôtel Byblos remains a perennial favourite among Hollywood A-listers, who come for the exclusive atmosphere, uphill from the more 'mixed' parts of St-Tropez. Renowned Alain Ducasse restaurant Rivea, and Byblos' **Les Caves du Roy** (p105) club scene round out the fun. Expect an extra whack of €40 per person in high season, which gives you an idea of the kind of place it is.

Pastis (☏04 98 12 56 50; www.pastis-st-tropez.com; 75 av du Général Leclerc; d from €575; ⏼⊠) This stunning townhouse-turned-hotel is the brainchild of an English couple besotted with Provence and passionate about modern art. You'll love the pop-art-inspired interior (if that's your thing) and long for a swim in the emerald-green pool. Every room is beautiful, although those overlooking av du Général Leclerc are noisy. Low-season deals make it much more affordable.

Pan Deï Palais (☏04 94 17 71 71; www.pandei.com; 52 rue Gambetta; d from €410) This elegant town house with a lush central courtyard is decked out along luxe Indian themes. Swan about like a raja.

La Bastide de Saint-Tropez (☏04 94 55 82 55; www.bastidesaint-tropez.com; 25 rte des Carles; r/ste from €600/1200; ☉Feb-Dec; P⏼⊠) Staying at La Bastide de Saint-Tropez is like living in your own sprawling country villa. Rooms are centred on a lovely pool, there's a shuttle to whisk you into town, and even a 22m yacht for hire. Naturally there's a spa, a Michelin-starred restaurant, and everything else the St-Trop elite expect as a matter of course.

La Vague d'Or (☏04 94 55 91 00; www.residencepinede.com; Résidence de la Pinède, Plage de la Bouillabaisse; menus from €130; ☉7.30-10pm mid-Apr–mid-Oct; ⏼) Triple-starred chef Arnaud Donckele has established a gastronomic temple at the Résidence de la Pinède: expect exquisite ingredients treated with the utmost cheffy cleverness. But with offerings such as the Balade Epicurienne setting you back half a grand for seven courses, with matched wines, expectations can rise to dangerous heights. Then again, this *is* St Tropez.

ⓘ Getting Around

Rolling Bikes (☏04 94 97 09 39; www.rolling-bikes.com; 50 av du Général Leclerc; per day bikes/scooters/motorcycles from €17/46/120; ☉9am-12.30pm & 3-7pm Tue-Sat Sep-Jun, daily Jul & Aug) Do as the locals do and opt for two wheels.

There's a **taxi** (☏04 94 97 05 27) rank at the Vieux Port, in front of the Musée de l'Annonciade.

Grimaud

POP 4300

Surrounded by vineyards, olives and the oak-and-beech-clad foothills of the Massif des Maures, this atmospheric medieval hilltop village sits inland from the Golfe de St-Tropez. Seven kilometres distant lies Port Grimaud, on the edge of the Golfe de St-Tropez. A mosquito-filled swamp in the 1960s, this modern pleasure port is now barricaded from the busy N98 by high walls. Its yacht-laden waterways comprise 12km of quays, but the town is best used as an access point for shuttle boats to St-Tropez.

⚑ Festivals & Events

Les Grimaldines MUSIC
(www.les-grimaldines.com; ☉Jul & Aug) World music comes to the atmospheric shell of Château du Grimaud on Tuesday evenings in July and August, during this popular festival. There are also performances in the streets of the town.

✗ Eating

★**Fleur de Sel** FRENCH €€
(☏04 94 43 21 54; www.fleurdeselgrimaud.wixsite.com/fleur-de-sel-grimaud; 4 place du Cros; lunch/dinner menus €17/39-49; ☉noon-2pm & 7-10pm Tue-Fri & Sun, noon-2pm Sat Apr-Oct) Young

couple Audrey and Thomas have built up a following with fresh, local produce treated in modern Provençal style. The bistro is housed in the town's former bakery, in the midst of the old village; outdoor seating is under an olive tree. The emphasis is on seafood (prawns in spices with cucumber and green apple) but there are terrestrial options.

Gassin

POP 2576

In medieval Gassin, 11km southwest of St-Tropez atop a rocky promontory, narrow streets wend up to the village church (1558). The village's most compelling feature is its 360-degree view of the peninsula, St-Tropez bay and the Maures forests.

🛏 Sleeping & Eating

Hôtel Bellovisto   HOTEL €€
(☏ 04 94 56 17 30; www.bellovisto.eu; place dei Barri; d from €165; ☉ Apr-Sep; ❉ 🛜) This hilltop hotel's charm is largely due to the cafe-clad square with panoramic view on which it resides. The hotel itself is dead simple: local bar on the ground floor displaying *pétanque* club trophies, a fine restaurant (mains €32) and nine rooms up top. Lop off €15 per person if you eschew breakfast, and expect big reductions outside high season.

Au Vieux Gassin   PROVENCAL €€
(☏ 04 94 56 14 26; www.auvieuxgassin-restaurant. com; place dei Barri; mains €22-24, menus €34;

☉ 11.30am-2pm & 6.30-9.30pm Mar-Oct) When the sun's out and you have nowhere pressing to be, there can be few sweeter terraces to enjoy a prolonged Provençal meal than Au Vieux Gassin's. With commanding views of the St Tropez Peninsula and its vineyards, cobbled alleys and antique buildings as your backdrop, and dishes such as beef fillet with *cèpes* (porcini mushrooms) to enjoy, it's all pretty joyous.

Ramatuelle

POP 2094

High on a hill, this labyrinthine walled village with a tree-studded central square got its name from 'Rahmatu'llah', meaning 'Divine Gift' – a legacy of 10th-century Saracen rule. Jazz and theatre fill the tourist-packed streets during August's **Festival de Ramatuelle** (☏ 04 94 79 25 63; www.festivalderamatuelle.com; ☉ Jul-Aug) and **Jazz Fest** (☏ 04 94 79 10 29; www.jazzaramatuelle.com; ☉ Aug).

If you follow the road (rte des Moulins de Paillas) up over the hilltop the 2.5km towards Gassin, you'll take in grand views and historic windmills.

The fruits of the peninsula's vineyards – Côtes de Provence wine – can be tested at various châteaux along the D61; the **tourist office** (☏ 04 98 12 64 00; www.ramatuelle-tourisme.com; place de l'Ormeau; ☉ 9am-1pm & 2-6.30pm Mon-Sat, 10am-1pm & 2-6pm Sun) has a list of estates where you can taste and buy. Most require an advance RDV (rendez-vous; appointment).

SIPPING THE PRESQU'ÎLE DE ST-TROPEZ

The St-Tropez hinterland is rich with wine-tasting opportunities, from vignerons' cooperatives to cellar doors.

Les Maîtres Vignerons de la Presqu'île de St-Tropez (☏ 04 94 56 32 04; www. vignerons-saint-tropez.com; 270 rte Départementale, D98, La Foux; ☉ 9am-7pm Mon-Sat) Shop for Côtes de Provence AOC wine at this clearinghouse of regional vineyards, near the giant roundabouts to the west of St-Tropez.

Caves des Vignerons de Grimaud (☏ 04 94 43 20 14; www.lesvigneronsdegrimaud.fr; 36 av des Oliviers, D61; ☉ 9am-7pm Mon-Sat Jun-Sep, plus 9am-12.30pm Sun mid-Jul–mid-Aug, 9am-12.30pm & 2-6pm Mon-Sat Oct-May) The Grimaud vignerons cooperative stretches back to 1932, when eight producers banded together to improve and market their wines. South of Grimaud along the St-Tropez-bound D61, this is the ideal place to stock up on Vin de Pays du Var for little more than €2.50 a litre.

Mas de Pampelonne (☏ 04 94 97 75 86; www.masdepampelonne.com; 912 chemin des Moulins; ☉ 9am-1pm Mon, Tue, Thu, Fri) Excellent, crisp rosé from 15 hectares of the verdant St-Tropez Peninsula. Find it a few hundred metres inland from Pampelonne beach.

🛏 Sleeping & Eating

Ferme Ladouceur
B&B €€

(✆ 04 94 79 24 95; www.fermeladouceur.com; D61, Quartier Les Roullière; d from €129; ⊙ Apr-Sep; 🅿) Have breakfast beneath a fig tree at this lovely *chambre d'hôte*, housed in a 19th-century *bastide* (country house). The rustic restaurant (menu including wine €47) is open to anyone who fancies an evening taste of good old-fashioned farm cuisine. Find it north of Ramatuelle, signposted off the D61 to St-Tropez.

Auberge de l'Oumède
B&B €€€

(✆ 04 94 44 11 11; www.aubergedeloumede.com; Chemin de l'Oumède, Ramatuelle; d from €360; ⊙ May-Sep; ✹ 🛜 ⊠) Far removed from St-Trop's swagger, this sweet country hideaway sits at the end of a dusty lane near the village of Ramatuelle, 3.5km west of town. It has rooms in an old stone *bastide* (country house) and auberge, all stylishly tinted in ochres and taupes; a few have quirky design touches, like a Native American print and faux-cowskin fabrics.

Chez Camille
SEAFOOD €€€

(✆ 04 98 12 68 98; www.chezcamille.fr; rte de Bonne Terrasse, Ramatuelle; menus €44-79; ⊙ 12.30-2pm & 8-9.30pm Wed-Sun Apr-Sep; 🅿) Deep terracotta walls hide this blue-and-white-tiled fishing cottage, dating from 1913. Now onto its fourth generation, the beachside restaurant is famous for wood-grilled fish, but is also capable of turning out great bouillabaisse, steak and other treats. From the D93 follow signs for Bonne Terrasse: it's 6km east of Ramatuelle, just south of Plage de Pampelonne.

ⓘ Getting There & Away

VarLib (www.varlib.fr) offers bus connections to St Tropez (€3, 30 minutes, up to six daily) and Gassin (€3, 10 minutes, up to six daily).

Gigaro

On the southeastern coast of the Presqu'île de St-Tropez, seaside hamlet Gigaro harbours a sandy beach, some lovely eating and sleeping options, and a water-sports school. From the far end of the beach, a board maps the **Sentier du Littoral** that works its way around the coast to Cap Lardier (4.7km, 1½ hours) and past Cap Taillat to L'Escalet (9km, 2¾ hours). From Gigaro, the narrow but drop-dead-gorgeous D93 winds inland over the **Col de Collebasse** (129m) to Ramatuelle – a good ride for mountain bikers.

🛏 Sleeping

Château de Valmer
HOTEL €€€

(✆ 04 94 55 15 15; www.chateauvalmer.com; 81 bd de Gigaro; d/treehouse from €419/621; ⊙ May-Sep; ✹ @ 🛜 ⊠) This fabulous 19th-century wine-producer's mansion is for nature bods with a penchant for luxury. Sleep above the vines in a *cabane perchée* (tree house), stroll scented vegetable and herb gardens, and play hide-and-seek around century-old palm and olive trees. It's located between La Croix-Valmer and Gigaro.

Les 3 Îles
B&B €€€

(✆ 04 94 49 03 73; www.3iles.com; 1779 bd du Littoral, Quartier du Vergeron; r from €225; ⊙ Apr–mid-Oct; ✹ 🛜 ⊠) The same seductive view, of the sea and the golden Îles d'Hyères, awaits you in each of the five carefully thought-out rooms (and from the infinity pool). Tropézienne Catherine and husband Jean-Paul are the creative energy behind this faultless, oh-so-chic *maison d'hôte*. Located between La Croix-Valmer and Gigaro. Minimum stays of three to five nights apply.

Monaco

POP 37,550

Best Places to Eat

➡ La Montgolfière (p121)

➡ Marché de la Condamine (p120)

➡ La Marée (p121)

Best Places to Stay

➡ Hôtel Port Palace (p120)

➡ Hôtel de France (p116)

➡ Novotel Monte Carlo (p120)

Why Go?

Squeezed into just 200 hectares, Monaco might be the world's second-smallest country (only the Vatican is smaller), but what it lacks in size it makes up for in attitude. A magnet for high-rollers and hedonists since the early 20th century, it's also renowned as one of the world's most notorious tax havens and home to the annual Formula One Grand Prix.

Despite its prodigious wealth, Monaco is far from being the French Riviera's prettiest town. World-famous Monte Carlo is basically an ode to concrete and glass, dominated by high-rise hotels, super yachts and apartment blocks that rise into the hills like ranks of dominoes, plunked into an utterly bewildering street layout seemingly designed to confound lowly pedestrians.

In dramatic contrast, the rocky outcrop known as Le Rocher, jutting out on the south side of the port, is crowned by a rather charming old town, home to the principality's royal palace.

Driving Distances (km)

	Beaulieu-sur-Mer	Èze	La Turbie	Menton	Monaco	Nice
Èze	5					
La Turbie	12	7				
Menton	19	19	15			
Monaco	11	10	8	10		
Nice	10	15	20	30	21	
Roquebrune-Cap-Martin	18	16	11	4	9	25

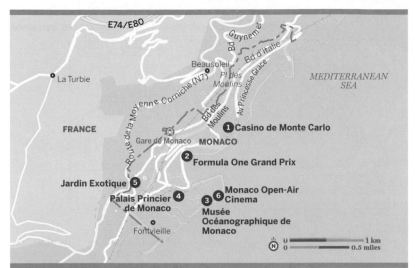

Monaco Highlights

❶ Casino de Monte Carlo (p113) Soaking up the casino's glitzy history on a day tour, or rubbing elbows with the highrollers on an evening gambling spree.

❷ Formula One Grand Prix (p116) Thrilling to the rhythm of revving engines at the world's most iconic motor sports event.

❸ Musée Océanographique de Monaco (p113) Watching fish frolic, and diving into the history of underwater exploration.

❹ Palais Princier de Monaco (p114) Whetting your appetite for royal living in the Grimaldi family's sprawling ancestral residence.

❺ Jardin Exotique (p113) Wandering in a wonderland of exotic cacti, high above the sparkling Mediterranean.

❻ Monaco Open Air Cinema (p122) Celebrating balmy summer evenings with movies in a dramatic outdoor setting.

History

Since the 13th century Monaco's history has been that of the Grimaldi family, whose rule began in 1297. Charles VIII, king of France, recognised Monégasque independence in 1489. But during the French Revolution, France snatched Monaco back and imprisoned its royal family. Upon release, they had to sell the few possessions they still owned and the palace became a warehouse.

The Grimaldis were restored to the throne under the 1814 Treaty of Paris. But in 1848 they lost Menton and Roquebrune to France, and Monaco swiftly became Europe's poorest country. In 1860 Monégasque independence was recognised for a second time by France and a monetary agreement in 1865 sealed the deal on future cooperation between the two countries.

Rainier III (r 1949–2005), nicknamed *le prince bâtisseur* (the builder prince), ex-

panded the size of his principality by 20% in the late 1960s by reclaiming land from the sea to create the industrial quarter of Fontvieille. In 2004 he doubled the size of the harbour with a giant floating dyke, placing Port de Monaco (Port Hercules) among the world's leading cruise-ship harbours. Upon Rainier's death, son Albert II became monarch.

◉ Sights

Monaco's sights include spectacular gardens, a variety of museums, a real-life prince's palace, and of course the Monte Carlo Casino at the centre of it all. When we visited a major construction project was underway on the the north side of the port – a brand new location for Prince Rainier's personal collection of cars (and a large car park). The museum of sorts is expected to open in this location during 2022.

Monaco

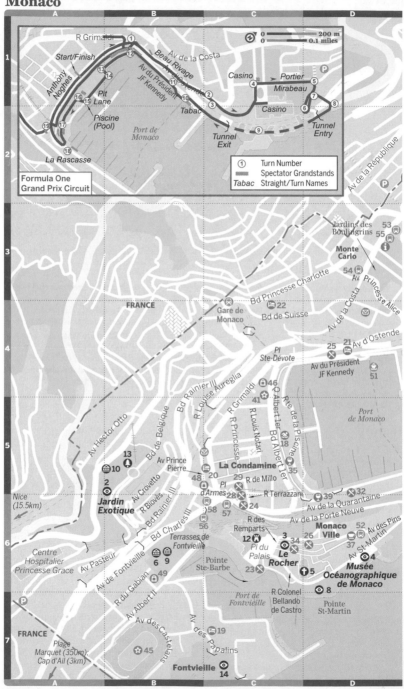

Formula One
Grand Prix Circuit

Map labels (circuit inset):
R Grimaldi · Start/Finish · Anthony Noghes · Av de la Costa · Beau Rivage · Av Ostende · Av du Président JF Kennedy · Pit Lane · Piscine (Pool) · Port de Monaco · Tabac · Tunnel Exit · La Rascasse · Casino · Portier · Mirabeau · Casino · Tunnel Entry

200 m
0.1 miles

① Turn Number
▮ Spectator Grandstands
Tabac Straight/Turn Names

Main map labels:
Jardins des Boulingrins · Monte Carlo · Av Princesse Alice · Av de la Costa · Av de la République · FRANCE · Gare de Monaco · Bd Princesse Charlotte · Bd de Suisse · Av d'Ostende · Av du Président JF Kennedy · Pl Ste-Dévote · Port de Monaco · Bd Rainier III · R Louise Aureglia · R Grimaldi · R Louis Notari · Bd Albert 1er · Rte de la Piscine · Av Hector Otto · Bd de Belgique · Av Prince Pierre · R Princesse · La Condamine · R de Millo · R Terrazzani · Av de la Quarantaine · Av de la Porte Neuve · Av Crovetto · R Biovés · Bd Rainier III · Pl d'Armes · Monaco Ville · Av des Pins · Av St-Martin · Jardin Exotique · Nice (15.5km) · Bd Charles III · R des Remparts · Pl du Palais · Le Rocher · Musée Océanographique de Monaco · Centre Hospitalier Princesse Grace · Av Pasteur · Terrasses de Fontvieille · Av de Fontvieille · R du Gabian · Pointe Ste-Barbe · Pointe St-Martin · R Colonel Bellando de Castro · R Albert II · Port de Fontvieille · Av des Castelans · Av des Papalins · FRANCE · Plage Marquet (350m); Cap d'Ail (3km) · Fontvieille

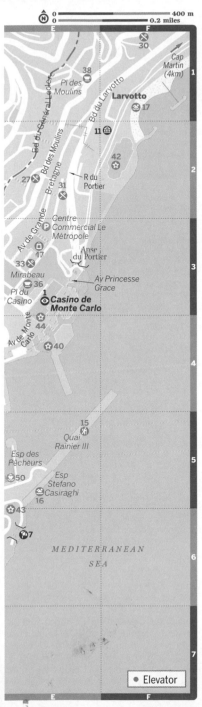

★ **Casino de Monte Carlo** CASINO

(🖉 98 06 21 21; www.casinomontecarlo.com; place du Casino; morning visit incl audioguide adult/child Oct-Apr €14/10, May-Sep €17/12; salons ordinaires gaming Oct-Apr €14, May-Sep €17; ⊙ visits 9am-1pm, gaming 2pm-late) Peeping inside Monte Carlo's legendary marble-and-gold casino is a Monaco essential. The building, open to visitors every morning, including the exclusive *salons privés,* is Europe's most lavish example of belle-époque architecture. Prince Charles III spearheaded the casino's development and in 1866, three years after its inauguration, the name 'Monte Carlo' – Ligurian for 'Mount Charles' in honour of the prince – was coined. To gamble here, visit after 2pm (when a strict over-18s-only admission rule kicks in).

★ **Musée Océanographique de Monaco** AQUARIUM

(🖉 93 15 36 00; www.oceano.mc; av St-Martin; adult/child high season €16/12, low season €11/7; ⊙ 9.30am-8pm Jul & Aug, 10am-7pm Apr-Jun & Sep, to 6pm Oct-Mar) Stuck dramatically to the edge of a cliff since 1910, the world-renowned Musée Océanographique de Monaco, founded by Prince Albert I (1848–1922), is a stunner. Its centrepiece is its aquarium with a 6m-deep lagoon where sharks and marine predators are separated from colourful tropical fish by a coral reef. Upstairs, two huge colonnaded rooms retrace the history of oceanography and marine biology (and Prince Albert's contribution to the field) through photographs, old equipment, numerous specimens and interactive displays.

★ **Le Rocher** HISTORIC SITE

Monaco Ville, also called Le Rocher, is the only part of Monaco to have retained its original old town, complete with small, windy medieval lanes. The old town thrusts skywards on a pistol-shaped rock, its strategic location overlooking the sea that became the stronghold of the Grimaldi dynasty. There are various staircases up to Le Rocher; the best route up is via Rampe Major, which starts from place d'Armes near the port.

★ **Jardin Exotique** GARDENS

(🖉 93 15 29 80; www.jardin-exotique.mc; 62 bd du Jardin Exotique; adult/child €7.20/3.80; ⊙ 9am-7pm mid-May–mid-Sep, to 6pm rest of year) Home to the world's largest succulent and cactus collection, from small echinocereus to 10m-tall African candelabras, the gardens tumble down the slopes of Moneghetti through a maze of paths, stairs and bridges.

Monaco

Views of the principality are spectacular. Admission includes the **Musée d'Anthropologie**, which displays prehistoric remains unearthed in Monaco, and a 35-minute guided tour of the **Grotte de l'Observatoire**. The prehistoric, stalactite- and stalagmite-laced cave is the only one in Europe where the temperature rises as you descend.

Bus 2 links Jardin Exotique with the town centre.

Palais Princier de Monaco　　PALACE
(☑93 25 18 31; www.palais.mc; place du Palais; adult/child €8/4, incl car museum €11.50/5, incl Oceanographic Museum €19/11; ⊙10am-6pm Apr-Jun & Sep–mid-Oct, to 7pm Jul & Aug) Built as a fortress atop Le Rocher in the 13th century, this palace is the private residence of the Grimaldi family. It is protected by the blue-helmeted, white-socked Carabiniers du Prince; changing of the guard takes place

daily at 11.55am, when crowds gather outside the gates to watch.

Most of the palace is off limits, but you can get a glimpse of royal life on a tour of the glittering **state apartments**, where you can see some of the lavish furniture and priceless artworks collected by the family over the centuries. It's a good idea to buy tickets online in advance to avoid queuing.

Combined tickets including Monaco's oceanographic museum (p113) or the Prince's classic car collection are also available.

Cathédrale de Monaco
CATHEDRAL

(4 rue Colonel Bellando de Castro; ⊙8.30am-6.45pm) `FREE` An adoring crowd continually shuffles past Prince Rainier's and Princess Grace's flower-adorned graves, located inside the cathedral choir of Monaco's 1875 Romanesque-Byzantine cathedral.

Nouveau Musée National de Monaco – Villa Paloma
GALLERY

(☑98 98 48 60; www.nmnm.mc; 56 bd du Jardin Exotique; adult/child €6/free incl Villa Sauber, free admission Sun; ⊙10am-6pm) This pearly-white villa, built for an American in 1913 on a hillside near the Jardin Exotique, is part of Nouveau Musée National de Monaco, along with Villa Sauber. It hosts seasonal contemporary art exhibitions with an environmental theme (oceans, apocalypse etc). Also sells a combo ticket (€10) which includes entry to the Jardin Exotique (p113).

Roseraie Princesse Grace
GARDENS

(av des Papalins; P) `FREE` Thoroughly revamped in 2014, this exuberant collection of over 4000 rose bushes – along with the adjacent Parc Fontevieille – stands out in dramatic contrast to the otherwise sterile highrise environment of Fontevieille. The garden bursts with colour in springtime, with multi-hued roses climbing up arbours and encircling the trunks and branches of olive trees.

Jardins St-Martin
GARDEN

(⊙9am-sunset) `FREE` The steep-sided, statue-studded Jardins St-Martin runs round the coast outside the Musée Océanographique.

Collection de Voitures Anciennes
MUSEUM

(Monaco Top Cars Collection; ☑92 05 28 56; www.mtcc.mc; Terrasses de Fontvieille; adult/child €6.50/3, incl Palais Princier de Monaco €11.50/5; ⊙10am-6pm) Starting in the early 1950s, car-mad Prince Rainier amassed an impressive array of over 100 classic automobiles, which he opened to the public in 1993. His

haul includes various F
Lamborghinis, Rolls Roy
and rally cars, along wit
carried the current prir
in 2011. The museum i
exhibition hall, but wi
purpose-built home by
it's completed in 2022.

Nouveau Musée National de Monaco – Villa Sauber
GALLERY

(☑98 98 91 26; www.nmnm.mc; 17 av Princesse Grace; adult/child €6/free including Villa Paloma, free admission Sun; ⊙10am-6pm) Part of Nouveau Musée National de Monaco, this sumptuous belle-époque villa with lush garden hosts seasonal contemporary art exhibitions focusing on a performing-arts theme (Serge Diaghilev, stage designs etc). Also sells a combo ticket (€10) which includes entry to the Jardin Exotique (p113).

Musée des Timbres et des Monnaies
MUSEUM

(☑98 98 41 50; www.mtm-monaco.mc; 11 terrasses de Fontvieille; adult/child €3/1.50; ⊙9.30am-5pm Sep-Jun, to 6pm Jul & Aug) This one-room museum traces the history of stamps and coins minted in Monaco. The stamp collection, spanning many decades, is especially fun, with images of everyone from Dante to Grace Kelly and everything from circus animals to 1950s movies. The attached boutique offers a wide variety of stamps for sale.

 Activities

Stade Nautique Rainier III
SWIMMING, ICE SKATING

(☑93 30 64 83; quai Albert 1er; morning/afternoon/evening/full day €3.20/4/2.40/5.70; ⊙9am-8pm Jun-Aug, to 6pm Sep-mid-Oct & May, closes at 6pm Mon year-round) Smack in the middle of Monaco's port area, this Olympic-sized outdoor sea-water pool has diving boards and a curly water slide. In winter it becomes an ice rink.

Digue de Monaco
WALKING

(Monaco Dyke) A serene alternative to the sweaty hike with the crowds up Rampe Majeur to Le Rocher is a panoramic stroll along the port's dyke, the world's largest floating dyke, 28m wide and 352m long. Scale the steps at the end of quai Antoine 1er and bear left to the viewpoint at the dyke's far end, next to the cruiseship terminal, for an outstanding Monte Carlo panorama.

Backtrack to **Esplanade Stefano Casiraghi** for a quick flop in the sun on the

MONACO FESTIVALS & EVENTS

AL EXPERIENCES

Morning market Chat with a local lemon grower or sit down for fresh-baked socca at bustling Marché de la Condamine (p120).

Kid-friendly diversions Take the kids for a romp at the minigolf course or fit-for-royalty playground in **Parc Princesse Antoinette** (⊙ 8.30am-6pm).

Hidden refuges Catch some rays, hit the beach, and soak up the spectacular city and coastal views at Digue de Monaco (p115) and Crique Ciappaira .

contemporary sun deck here; ladders allow you to dip into the water. Then weave your way along the coastal path and up through the shady Jardins St-Martin to Le Rocher. Look out for stone steps leading down to a **secret shingle beach** (Plage des Pêcheurs) only locals know about.

Plage du Larvotto   SWIMMING
At Monaco's eastern edge, this sandy crescent – dotted with beach chairs and umbrellas, crisscrossed with volleyball nets and backed by a palm-fringed boardwalk – is a favourite summer hang-out.

★ Festivals & Events

Formula One Grand Prix   SPORTS
(www.formula1monaco.com; ⊙ late May) Formula One's most iconic event spans four days in late May, when Monaco goes completely car crazy and every street in town is closed for the race. At other times of the year, fans can walk the 3.2km circuit through town; the tourist office has maps. Friday's cheapest tickets go for €30, but figure €1400 for a prime casino-side Sunday spot.

Grand Prix Historique de Monaco   SPORTS
(www.monacograndprixticket.com/grand-prix-historique; ⊙ May) Held every other year (in even-numbered years), this fun event features vintage racing cars navigating Monte Carlo's twists and turns two weeks before the Formula One Grand Prix begins.

Monaco ePrix   SPORTS
Starting in 2015, Monaco joined the ePrix (electric racing car) circuit. At this biannual event, held every May in odd-numbered

years, drivers navigate a shorter, less hilly circuit than in the traditional Grand Prix.

International Fireworks Festival   EVENT
(www.monaco-feuxdartifice.mc/en; ⊙ Jul & Aug) This showdown of pyrotechnic expertise lights up the port area for four Saturdays in July and August. The winner gets to organise the fireworks on 18 November, eve of Monaco's national holiday.

Rolex Monte-Carlo Masters   SPORTS
(www.montecarlotennismasters.com; Monte-Carlo Country Club, 155 av Princesse Grace, Roquebrune-Cap-Martin; ⊙ Apr) This annual tournament, held at the Monte-Carlo Country Club, is fast becoming a key fixture on the professional circuit.

🛏 Sleeping

Accommodation in Monaco – which ranges from uninspiring cheapies to luxurious old-school resort hotels – is always expensive. During the Grand Prix nearly every hotel within a 50km radius is booked up months in advance. At any time of year, it's much better value to stay at nearby Nice or Menton and take the train into Monaco.

Include Monaco's country code +377 when calling hotels in Monaco from outside the principality.

Relais International de la Jeunesse Thalassa   HOSTEL €
(☑ 04 93 78 18 58; www.clajsud.com/relaisclajcapdail.html; 2 av Gramaglia, Cap d'Ail; dm €20; ⊙ Apr-Oct) Perched at the Mediterranean's edge, this hostel in Cap d'Ail, France (2km from Monaco, or five minutes by bus or train) has a fab beachside location, clean four- to 10-bed dorms, home-cooked meals (€12), takeaway picnics (€9), and a handy location 300m from the station. The one possible downside? Large school groups occasionally overrun the place.

Hôtel de France   HOTEL €
(☑ 93 30 24 64; www.hoteldefrance.mc; 6 rue de la Turbie; s €95-125, d €115-170, tr €145-190; 🛜) Anywhere else this stalwart hotel would be way overpriced, but in sky-high Monaco it qualifies as a bargain. The older rooms are nothing special – plain furniture, basic beds – but some have been renovated with a sleeker and more contemporary look; ask to see a few before committing. The Condamine market (p120) right next door is paradise for affordable eats.

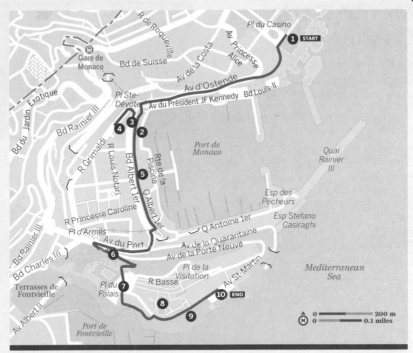

City Walk
Monte Carlo Casino to Monaco-Ville

START CASINO DE MONTE CARLO
END MUSÉE OCÉANOGRAPHIQUE
LENGTH 2KM; TWO HOURS

Starting in front of Monte Carlo's legendary **1 casino** (p113), walk towards Monaco's medieval old town, Le Rocher, which beckons from a hilltop across the water. As you make a curving descent to the **2 port of La Condamine**, you're tracing the route of Monaco's iconic **3 Formula One Grand Prix**.

If Grand Prix swag tickles your fancy, cross bd Albert 1er upon arrival at the waterfront to reach **4 La Boutique** (p123). This official shop of Monaco's automobile club can sell you everything from model cars to racing jackets. Back on the waterfront, watch crowds frolic at **5 Stade Nautique Rainier III** (p115), home to an Olympic-sized pool in summer and an ice-skating rink in winter.

At the port's far end, follow signs for the Palais Princier and climb the zigzag **6 Rampe Majeur** into Le Rocher. If you time things right, you'll reach Place du Palais, the square in front of the **7 prince's palace** (p114), in

time to see the 11.55am changing of the guard. The knee-sock wearing crew hasn't had to do much actual defending of the principality in recent memory, but their daily drum-beating spectacle is still good fun.

Next, follow the signposted clifftop path towards **8 Cathédrale de Monaco** (p115), where you can pay your respects to Grace Kelly, the movie-star turned princess who died tragically in a 1982 car accident. Her tomb in the cathedral's apse is often covered in fresh flowers from the queues of admirers.

Enjoy views of Monaco's Fontvieille harbour as you enter the gorgeous **9 Jardins St-Martin** (p115), draped in greenery and adorned with statues and fountains. From up here, it's easy to perceive the principality's dual strategy for growth: build up (skyscrapers) and out (landfill). The latter technique has increased Monaco's 'land' area by 25%.

At the far end of the park is the extraordinary **10 Musée Océanographique de Monaco** (p113), which towers over the Mediterranean. After lunch in the old town, spend the afternoon exploring the fine aquarium and historic collection of marine artifacts inside.

Monte Carlo Casino

TIMELINE

1863 Charles III inaugurates the first Casino on Plateau des Spélugues. The **❶ atrium** is a small room with a wooden podium from which an orchestra entertains while punters purchase entrance tickets.

1864 Hôtel de Paris opens and the area becomes known as the 'Golden Square'.

1865 Construction of **❷ Salle Europe**. Cathedral-like, it is lined with onyx columns and lit by eight Bohemian crystal chandeliers weighing 150kg each.

1868 The steam train arrives in Monaco and **❸ Café de Paris** is completed.

1878–79 Gambling moves to Hôtel de Paris while Charles Garnier is charged with building a new casino with a miniature replica of the Paris Opera House, **❹ Salle Garnier**.

1890 The advent of electricity casts a glow on architect Jules Touzet's newly added **❺ gaming rooms** for high rollers.

1903 Inspired by female gamblers, Henri Schmit decorates **❻ Salle Blanche** with caryatids and the painting *Les Grâces Florentines*.

1904 Smoking is banned in the gaming rooms and **❼ Salon Rose**, a new smoking room, is added.

1910 **❽ Salle Médecin**, immense and grand, hosts the high-spending Private Circle.

1966 Celebrations mark 100 years of uninterrupted gambling despite two world wars.

HORIZON IMAGES/MOTION/ALAMY STOCK PHOTO ©

Atrium
The casino's 'lobby', so to speak, is paved in marble and lined with 28 Ionic columns, which support a balustraded gallery canopied with an engraved glass ceiling.

Hôtel de Paris

HÔTEL DE PARIS
Notice the horse's shiny leg (and testicles) on the lobby's statue of Louis XIV on horseback? Legend has it that rubbing them brings good luck in the casino.

Salon Rose
Smoking was banned in the gaming rooms following a fraud involving a croupier letting his ash fall on the floor. The Salon Rose (Pink Room; today a restaurant) was therefore opened in 1903 for smokers – the gaze of Gallelli's famous cigarillo-smoking ladies follows you around the room.

Salle Garnier
Taking eight months to build and two years to restore (2004–06), the opera's original statuary is rehabilitated using original moulds saved by the creator's grandson. Individual air-con and heating vents are installed beneath each of the 525 seats.

EMPEROROSARY/SHUTTERSTOCK ©

TOP TIPS

➡ After 2pm when gaming begins, admission is strictly for 18 years and over. Rooms beyond the Salle Europe are closed to the general public. Photo ID is obligatory.

➡ Don't wear trainers. A jacket for men is not obligatory (but is recommended) in the gaming rooms.

➡ In the main room, the minimum bet is €5/25 for roulette/blackjack.

➡ In the *salons privés*, there is no maximum bet.

Salle Europe
The oldest part of the casino, where they continue to play *trente-et-quarante* and European roulette, which have been played here since 1865. Tip: the bull's-eye windows around the room originally served as security observation points.

Café de Paris
With the arrival of Diaghilev as director of the Monte Carlo Opera in 1911, Café de Paris becomes the go-to address for artists and gamblers. It retains the same high-glamour ambience today. Tip: snag a seat on the terrace and people-watch.

Jardins des Boulingrins

Place du Casino

Jardins du Casino

Salles Touzet
This vast partitioned hall, 21m by 24m, is decorated in the most lavish style: oak, Tonkin mahogany and oriental jasper panelling are offset by vast canvases, Marseille bronzes, Italian mosaics, sculptural reliefs and stained-glass windows.

Salle Médecin
Also known as Salle Empire because of its extravagant Empire-style decor, Monégasque architect François Médecin's gaming room was originally intended for the casino's biggest gamblers. Part of it still remains hidden from prying eyes as a Super Privé room.

Terraces, Gardens & Walkways

Fairmont Monte Carlo

Salle Blanche
Today a superb bar-lounge, the Salle Blanche (White Room) opens onto an outdoor gaming terrace. The caryatids on the ceiling were modelled on fashionable courtesans such as La Belle Otéro, who placed her first bet here aged 18.

BEST VIEWS
Wander behind the casino through manicured gardens and gaze across Victor Vasarely's vibrant op-art mosaic, *Hexagrace*, to views of the harbour and the sea.

Hexagrace Mosaic

Novotel Monte Carlo HOTEL €€
(☑99 99 83 00; www.novotel.com/5275; 16 bd Princesse Charlotte; d from €225; ✳@🅰🏊) Yes, we realise it's a chain, but this Novotel really is rather special. It's far from the usual bland, faceless place: rooms are bright and sleek, there are artworks and sculptures dotted around, and a spankingly smart pool. Needless to say, port views command a premium.

Hôtel Port Palace LUXURY HOTEL €€€
(☑97 97 90 00; www.portpalace.net; 7 av du Président JF Kennedy; r from €327; ✳🅰) Built into the hillside overlooking the yacht harbor, this discreetly sexy boutique hotel is decked out in fine silks, soft leather and Carrara marble. All rooms have king-size beds, walk-in showers and super views of the port and Le Rocher. There's also a very good seafood restaurant on the roof.

Columbus BOUTIQUE HOTEL €€€
(☑92 05 90 00, reservations 92 05 92 22; www.columbushotels.com; 23 av des Papalins; d €180-452; ✳@🅰🏊) Hi-tech urban chic best describes this large boutique hotel in Fontvieille. Rooms are beautifully decorated in designer greys, striped fabrics and 'back to nature' bathrooms with bamboo towel racks and elegant wooden furniture. All rooms have little balconies and good views (the higher the better), and there's an outdoor pool (heated from May to October).

✖ Eating

Restaurants in Monaco range from touristy pizza joints to top-quality gastronomic venues catering to a well-heeled clientele. French and Italian cuisine prevail, though you'll find a full line-up of international fare. Don't miss the quintessential Monégasque specialty, *barbajuans* (deep-fried ravioli). Key restaurant zones include bd des Moulins near the Casino, the Les Condamines port and market, and the narrow streets behind the cathedral in Le Rocher.

★ Marché de la Condamine MARKET €
(www.facebook.com/marche.condamine; 15 place d'Armes; ⊙7am-3pm Mon-Sat, to 2pm Sun) For tasty, excellent-value fare around shared tables, hit Monaco's fabulous food court, tucked beneath the arches behind the open-air place d'Armes market. Rock-bottom budget faves include fresh pasta from **Maison des Pâtes** (☑93 50 95 77; Marché de la Condamine, 15 place d'Armes; pasta €6.40-12;

⊙7am-3.30pm) and traditional Niçois *socca* from **Chez Roger** (☑93 50 80 20; Marché de la Condamine, 15 place d'Armes; socca €3; ⊙10am-3pm); there's also pizza and seafood from Le Comptoir, truffle cuisine from Truffle Bistrot, a deli, a cafe, a cheesemonger and more.

U Cavagnetu MEDITERRANEAN €€
(☑97 98 20 40; www.facebook.com/cavagnetu.monaco; 14 rue Comte Félix Gastaldi; plat du jour €16.50, menu €27.50; ⊙11am-10pm) The crush of tourist-oriented restaurants in the narrow streets of Le Rocher may make you want to run screaming, but U Cavagnetu is worth sticking around for. The tasty line-up of authentic Monégasque treats includes *barbajuans* (deep fried ravioli), *beignets de courgettes* (zucchini fritters) and *poulpe à la monégasque* (octopus stewed with tomatoes, onion, garlic, parsley and wine).

Ristorante Mozza ITALIAN €€
(☑97 77 03 04; www.mozza.mc; 11 rue du Portier; lunch menus €19-24, pizzas €14-24, mains €18-39; ⊙noon-2.30pm & 7.30-10.30pm Mon-Thu, to 11.30pm Fri-Sun; ☑) As its name suggests, Mozza's speciality is its eponymous cheese – directly imported from Italy, with multiple varieties to taste at the mozzarella bar. Otherwise, it's fine traditional Italian fare: sophisticated pizza and pastas, antipasti and (rather curiously) hamburgers.

Tip Top INTERNATIONAL €€
(☑93 50 69 13; www.facebook.com/TipTop Monaco; 11 av des Spélugues; pizza €15-20, mains €16-38; ⊙9am-5am Mon-Sat, 6.15pm-midnight Sun; 🅰) A favourite haunt of Monaco's night owls, this tiny, check-clothed bistro sticks out like a sore thumb, just a stone's throw from the fancy Café de Paris and the casino. It's been going for donkey's years and still draws in a loyal local crowd for its reliable, no-fuss pizzas and pastas and its daily *plat du jour*.

Le Loga INTERNATIONAL €€
(☑93 30 87 72; www.loga.mc; 25 bd des Moulins; lunch menus €15-22, dinner menu €38, mains €16-42; ⊙8am-11pm Mon, Tue & Thu-Sat, 8am-7pm Wed) On the main drag above the casino, Loga really shines on weekdays, when its wine-inclusive lunch menus are among the best deals in Monaco. Specialities include steaks, meal-sized salads and exquisite homemade gnocchi, along with other Italian fare.

Stars 'n' Bars
AMERICAN €€

(☎ 97 97 95 95; www.starsnbars.com; 6 quai Antoine 1er; burgers €15.50-24, mains €17.50-35; ⊙ 11am-midnight; ⓘ) Sophisticated it ain't, but Monaco's take on an American-style sports bar draws crowds (especially families) with its burgers, ribs, steaks, milkshakes, ice cream and apple pie. It's worth visiting just for its F1 memorabilia, including photos of famous drivers who've eaten here, and a full-size F1 car suspended from one wall, driven to victory by Mika Häkkinen in 1998 and 1999.

★ La Montgolfière
FUSION €€€

(☎ 97 98 61 59; www.lamontgolfiere.mc; 16 rue Basse; 3-/4-course menu €47/54; ⊙ noon-2pm & 7.30-9.30pm Mon, Tue & Thu-Sat) Monégasque chef Henri Geraci has worked in some of the Riviera's top restaurants, but he's now happily settled at his own establishment down a shady alleyway near the palace. Escoffier-trained, he's faithful to the French classics, but his travels have inspired a fondness for Asian flavours, so expect some exotic twists. The restaurant's small and sought after, so reserve ahead.

Le Train Bleu
ITALIAN €€€

(☎ 98 06 24 24; http://fr.montecarlosbm.com/restaurant-monaco; place du Casino; mains €25-68; ⊙ 2pm-5am) For one of Monaco's most atmospheric dining experiences, head for Le Train Blue in the Casino de Monte Carlo (p113). The menu is high-end Italian, served in a replica vintage belle-époque train car.

La Marée
SEAFOOD €€€

(☎ 377 97 97 80 00; www.lamaree.mc; 7 av du Président JF Kennedy; mains €22-82; ⊙ noon-11pm Mon-Fri, noon-midnight Sat & Sun) La Marée's 'fish & chic' tagline says it all: if you're after seafood with a stunning sea view, then this swish rooftop restaurant at the Hotel Port-Plage is the place. From turbot, red mullet, sea bass and monkfish to seafood platters loaded with lobster and crustaceans, pescatarians will be properly pampered here. Monaco's jet-set turn out in force for Sunday brunch.

Castel Roc
FRENCH €€€

(☎ 93 30 36 68; www.castelrocmonaco.com; 1 place du Palais; 2-/3-course lunch menu €24/32, 3-/4-course dinner menu €48/59; ⊙ 12.30-2pm & 7.30-9.30pm Tue-Sun) This fine-dining stalwart has perhaps the most princely location in all of Monaco – it's literally steps from the

LOCAL KNOWLEDGE

THE MAÎTRE GLACIER

It's a bit of a local's secret: Monaco's best ice creams and sorbets are made by the eponymous Corsican *maître glacier* at **Pierre Geronimi** (☎ 97 98 69 11; www.glacespierregeronimi.com; 36 bd d'Italie; 1/2/3 scoops €3.80/6/8; ⊙ 8am-7pm Mon-Sat Oct-Apr, 7.30am-7.30pm Mon-Sat & 10am-6pm Sun May-Sep). The flavours are exciting – try the chestnut flour, beetroot, matcha tea or honey-and-pine nut – and for the ultimate indulgence, ask for it to be served cocktail-style in a glass *verrine*. He also creates delicious ice-cream cakes and patisseries. Don't say we didn't warn you...

palace's main gates, with a suntrap patio to boot. Well-heeled patrons come here for rich, traditional French food like stuffed rabbit saddle and slow-cooked lamb, served on sparkly china plates and starchy white tablecloths. The lunch menu is surprisingly good value.

🍸 Drinking & Nightlife

Much of Monaco's superchic drinking goes on in its designer restaurants and the bars of luxury hotels. For a lower-key ambience, head to the relaxed bars located behind the port. Monégasque people are fond of wine and will drink it almost anytime of day. The signature after-dinner drink is *limoncello*, sometimes home-made with lemons grown in the region.

Chocolaterie de Monaco
CAFE

(☎ 97 97 88 88; www.chocolateriedemonaco.com; place de la Visitation; ⊙ 9.30am-6.30pm Mon-Sat, 10am-noon & 12.30-5.30pm Sun) For a sweet pick-me-up between the Palais Princier and the Musée Océanographique, this chocolate shop with attached cafe couldn't be better placed. Various drinks are on the menu, but hot chocolate (€5.20 to €5.90) is naturally the star.

Rascasse
BAR

(☎ 98 06 16 16; www.larascassemontecarlo.com; 1 quai Antoine; ⊙ 4pm-5am) This two-storey lounge bar down by the port draws the crowds at apéritif time, then morphs into Monaco's liveliest nightspot, with live music Monday through Friday and all-night DJs on weekends.

Brasserie de Monaco
MICROBREWERY

(☑ 97 98 51 20; www.facebook.com/brasseriede monacomc; 36 rte de la Piscine; ⊙ noon-2am) Having Monaco's only microbrewery gives this bar down by La Condamine a useful USP, and its organic lagers and ales pack the punters in. Inside it's all chrome, steel and big-screen TVs, and live sports and DJs keep the weekends extra busy. For a more chilled experience, head for the portside patio out the front. Happy hour's from 6pm to 8pm.

Café de Paris
CAFE

(☑ 98 06 76 23; www.facebook.com/cafedeparis montecarlo; place du Casino; ⊙ 8am-2am) The *grande dame* of Monaco's cafes (founded in 1882), perfect for *un petit café* and a spot of people-watching. Everything else is chronically overpriced, and the waiters can be horrendously snooty, but it's the price you pay for a front-row view of Monte Carlo's razzamatazz.

Le Teashop
TEAROOM

(☑ 97 77 47 47; www.leteashop.com; place des Moulins; ⊙ 9am-7pm Mon-Sat) This super-stylish tea bar is all the rage with Monaco's ladies who lunch. There are more than 130 loose-leaf teas to choose from, served classically in a china pot, as a frothy latte or Asian-style with bubbles. The home-made cakes are too good to resist.

☆ Entertainment

The Grimaldis have a long tradition of art patronage. Even back in the 18th century, the palace regularly opened its doors to offer music performances to its subjects.

Monaco Open Air Cinema
CINEMA

(☑ 93 25 86 80; www.cinemas2monaco.com; av de la Quarantaine; adult/child €12/9; ⊙ mid-Jun–mid-Sep) Watch crowd-pleasing blockbusters, mostly in English, beneath the stars at the world's only 3D open-air cinema. Films start at 10pm nightly in June and July, and at 9.30pm in August and September. There are 500 seats but no advance reservations, so arrive when the doors open at 8.45pm (8.30pm August and September).

Opéra de Monte Carlo
OPERA

(Salle Garnier; ☑ ticket office 98 06 28 28; www. opera.mc; Casino de Monte Carlo, place du Casino) Also known as the Salle Garnier, Monaco's opera house is an 1892 confection of neo-

---

THE MONACO GRAND PRIX

If there's one trophy a Formula One driver would like to have on the mantelpiece, it would have to be from the most glamorous race of the season, the Monaco Grand Prix. This race has everything. Its spectators are the most sensational: the merely wealthy survey the spectacle from Hôtel Hermitage, the really rich watch from their luxury yachts moored in the harbour, while the Grimaldis see the start and finish from the royal box at the port. Then there's the setting: the cars scream around the very centre of the city, racing uphill from the start/finish line to place du Casino, then downhill around a tight hairpin and two sharp rights to hurtle through a tunnel and run along the harbourside to a chicane and more tight corners before the start/finish.

But despite its reputation, the Monaco Grand Prix is not really one of the great races. The track is too tight and winding for modern Formula One cars, and overtaking is virtually impossible. The Brazilian triple world champion Nelson Piquet famously described racing at Monaco as like 'riding a bicycle around your living room'. Piquet clearly rides a much faster bicycle than most of us; Monaco may be the slowest race on the calendar, but the lap record is still over 160km/h, and at the fastest point on the circuit, cars reach 280km/h. Even the corner in the gloom of the tunnel is taken at 250km/h.

The 78-lap race happens on a Sunday afternoon in late May, the conclusion of several days of practice, qualifying and supporting races. Tickets (€30 to €1400) are theoretically available from the Automobile Club de Monaco (www.acm.mc) online or in Monaco at its **billetterie** (ACM; ☑ 93 15 26 00; www.acm.mc; 23 bd Albert 1er), but in practice the best seats sell out months in advance.

If you can't make the big event but are still eager to see car racing on the streets of Monaco, come in mid-May for the biannual **Grand Prix Historique de Monaco** (p116), featuring vintage race cars.

classical splendour adjoining Monte Carlo Casino, designed by Charles Garnier (who also designed the Paris operahouse). The season runs from October through April. It also serves as a venue for concerts by the Monte Carlo Philharmonic Orchestra (www.opmc.mc) and dance performances by Les Ballets de Monte Carlo (www.balletsdemontecarlo.com).

Stade Louis II   SPECTATOR SPORT
(☑92 05 40 21; www.stadelouis2.mc; 7 av des Castelans; guided tour adult/child €5.20/2.60; ⏰tours 10.30am, 11.30am, 2.30pm, 3.30pm, 4.30pm Mon-Fri Apr-Sep) The stadium is home to the AS Monaco football team. Buy match tickets from the ticket office inside or view the stadium as part of a 20-minute guided tour; just turn up at the respective time and buy a ticket.

Auditorium Rainier III   CLASSICAL MUSIC
(☑93 10 85 00; bd Louis II) Well regarded for its acoustics, this auditorium is the main venue for classical music concerts by the Monte Carlo Philharmonic Orchestra.

Grimaldi Forum   LIVE PERFORMANCE
(☑ticket office 99 99 30 00; www.grimaldiforum.mc; 10 av Princesse Grace; ⏰noon-7pm Tue-Sat) This large auditorium hosts expos, trade shows, concerts by the Monte Carlo Philharmonic Orchestra (www.opmc.mc), dance performances by Les Ballets de Monte Carlo (www.balletsdemontecarlo.com) and more.

🛍 Shopping

Monaco's streets drip with couture and designer shops; many congregate in Monte Carlo on av des Beaux Arts and av de Monte Carlo. For vaguely more mainstream (read less expensive) fashion boutiques, try Le Métropole (☑93 50 15 36; www.metropoleshoppingmontecarlo.com; 17 av des Spélugues; ⏰10am-7.30pm Mon-Sat). Mid-July to mid-August, boutiques open on Sunday. Note that sky-high rents discourage the presence of smaller boutiques run by local artists, artisans or designers.

L'Orangerie   DRINKS
(☑99 90 43 38; www.orangerie.mc; 9 rue de la Turbie; ⏰9.30am-12.30pm & 2.30-5.30pm Mon-Fri) The brainchild of expatriate Dubliner Philip Culazzo, l'Orangerie is an artisanal liqueur made with bitter oranges harvested from the citrus trees lining some of Monaco's streets. Grab a taste and bring home

a bottle from this cute-as-a-button, bright orange boutique.

Office des Émissions de Timbres-Poste   GIFTS & SOUVENIRS
(☑98 98 41 41; www.oetp-monaco.com; 23 av Albert II; ⏰9am-5pm Mon-Fri) Collectors – and anyone else smitten with the quirky allure of stamps issued in the world's second smallest country – should stop in at this official government office, which sells a wide variety of Monaco stamps, both past and present.

La Boutique de l'Automobile Club de Monaco   GIFTS & SOUVENIRS
(☑97 70 45 35; www.monaco-grandprix.com; 46 rue Grimaldi; ⏰9.30am-7pm Mon-Fri, from 10.30am Sat) At this boutique run by Monaco's automobile club, you can buy the official T shirt, along with zillions of other Monaco Grand Prix–themed accessories: shirts, bags, jeans, watches, model cars, noise-cancelling headphones, baby clothes... You get the idea.

ℹ Information

Centre Hospitalier Princesse Grace (Hospital; ☑97 98 99 00; www.chpg.mc; 1 av Pasteur) Medical care.

Police Station (☑112; 3 rue Louis Notari)

Tourist Office (☑92 16 61 16; www.visitmonaco.com; 2a bd des Moulins; ⏰9am-7pm Mon-Sat, 11am-1pm Sun) Get maps and info – along with your semi-official Monaco passport stamp – at this helpful office just above the casino. From mid-June through mid-September, it also runs a tourist information kiosk down by the Port de la Condamine.

ℹ Getting There & Away

AIR
Monaco has no airport of its own, but **Nice-Côte d'Azur Airport** (p329) is nearby and well serviced by local buses. **Héli-Air Monaco** (☑92 05 00 50; www.heliairmonaco.com; per person Nice airport transfer from €144, panoramic flight 10/20/30min from €60/100/150) and **MonacAir** (☑97 97 39 00; www.monacair.mc; per person Nice airport transfer one-way/return from €140/260, scenic flight per group 10/20min from €350/650) run helicopter flights between Nice airport and Monaco's **Héliport** (av des Ligures) several times a day (per person from €140, seven minutes).

BUS
Lignes d'Azur (www.lignesdazur.com) runs bus 100 (€1.50, every 15 minutes from 6am to

9pm) to/from Nice (45 minutes) and Menton (40 minutes) along the Corniche Inférieure; bus 110 (one way/return €22/33, hourly) goes to/from Nice-Côte d'Azur airport (45 minutes). Eastbound, both services stop at the tunnel entrance near **place d'Armes** and the **Monte Carlo Casino bus stop** in front of the tourist office. Westbound, the **casino stop** is diagonally opposite the tourist office near Jardins des Boulingrins, and the **place d'Armes stop** is on bd Charles III. Night services run Thursday to Saturday.

CAR

Only Monaco and Alpes-Maritimes (06) registered cars can access Monaco Ville. If you decide to drive, park in one of the numerous underground car parks (first hour free, €2.40 next 15 minutes, €0.10 to €1 per 15 minutes thereafter, daily maximum €25).

TRAIN

Services run about every 20 minutes east to Menton (€2.30, 12 minutes) and west to Nice (€4.10, 25 minutes). Access to the **station** (av Prince Pierre) is through pedestrian tunnels, elevators and escalators from **allée Lazare Sauvaigo**, **pont Ste-Dévote**, **place Ste-Dévote** (place Ste-Dévote) and **bd de Belgique/bd du Jardin Exotique**. There are no trains between midnight and 5.30am.

ⓘ Getting Around

BUS

Monaco's urban bus system, operated by Compagnie des Autobus de Monaco (CAM; www.cam.mc), has six lines. Tickets cost €1.50 if purchased from machines at bus stops, €2 on board (day ticket €5.50).

Lines 1, 2, 4 and 6 are especially useful for visitors, along with the Bus de Nuit. Key stops are at **place d'Armes**, **Monaco Ville** and **Monte-Carlo Tourisme**.

➡ Line 1 links Monaco Ville (Le Rocher) to Monte Carlo and then continues east up bd des Moulins.

➡ Line 2 links Monaco Ville (Le Rocher) to Monte Carlo and then loops back to the Jardin Exotique.

➡ Line 3 links Fontvieille with Villa Paloma near the Jardin Exotique.

➡ Line 4 links the train station with the tourist office, the casino and Plage du Larvotto.

➡ Line 5 links the hospital with the tourist office, the casino and Plage du Larvotto.

➡ Line 6 links Fontvieille with the tourist office, the casino and Plage du Larvotto.

After 9.20pm the Bus de Nuit (9.30pm to 12.30am) follows one big loop around town; service is extended to 4am on Friday and Saturday.

BOAT

The solar-powered **Bateau Bus** (http://monaco-navigation.com/bateau-bus-tarif-monaco.html; quai des États-Unis) sails back and forth across the harbour between **quai Antoine 1er** (quai Antoine 1er) (Monaco Ville) and **quai des États-Unis** (quai des États-Unis) (Monte Carlo). Boats make the four-minute crossing every 20 minutes from 8am to 7.50pm; buy tickets on board (€2) or from machines at the docks (€1.50).

CAR

Driving is not the best way to get around Monaco; major thoroughfares are crowded, traffic patterns are convoluted and on-street parking is limited. You're generally better off walking or taking public transport. Park at one of the many well-signposted garages around town.

TAXI

Call **Taxis Monaco** (☑ 93 15 01 01; www.taxi monaco.com; ⊙ 24h).

Var

Best Places to Eat

➡ Chez Bruno (p148)

➡ Le Clos des Vignes (p151)

➡ La Pescalune (p147)

➡ La Rastègue (p139)

Best Places to Stay

➡ Le Mas du Langoustier (p135)

➡ Hôtel des Deux Rocs (p148)

➡ Hôtel de la Tour (p129)

Why Go?

Sizzling shoreline hogs the headlines here, and the coast is undeniably magnetic, but there's so much more to Var than super-yachts and overpriced *bouillabaisse*. A string of stunning islands, magnificent secluded monasteries, and uplands dotted with memorable villages make this *département* one of the most varied and enticing in Provence.

By all means, spend time on the area's many capes, people-watching on a terrace and sipping a cappuccino alongside a yacht-lined quay. Then head out to explore the region's soul-stirring coastal paths, chichi beach clubs and vine-knitted capes. When you're ready to move out of the limelight, you'll be enveloped by nature in the Massif des Maures, where thick chestnut groves harbour small villages and unforgettable vistas. The main trio of islands in the Îles d'Hyères offers splendid, quiet coastal escapes. Inland, in the Haut-Var, meander through stone villages, each with its own character and history.

Driving Distances (km)

	Bandol	Collobrieres	Draguignan	Hyères	St-Tropez
Collobrieres	72				
Draguignan	103	56			
Hyères	39	30	82		
St-Tropez	97	30	52	50	
Toulon	20	38	83	18	68

Var Highlights

❶ Monastère de la Verne (p142) Finding your way through the Massif des Maures to this serene monastery.

❷ Haut-Var (p145) Roaming the tranquil back roads and tiny hilltop villages.

❸ Domaine du Rayol (p138) Spending the day wandering (or snorkelling) at this lush Mediterranean garden.

❹ Île de Porquerolles (p133) Walking the cliff-side tracks and sipping the wines of this island paradise.

❺ Collobrières (p142) Going nuts on sweet chestnuts.

❻ Sanary-sur-Mer (p129) Promenading on the quay and tasting Bandol wines.

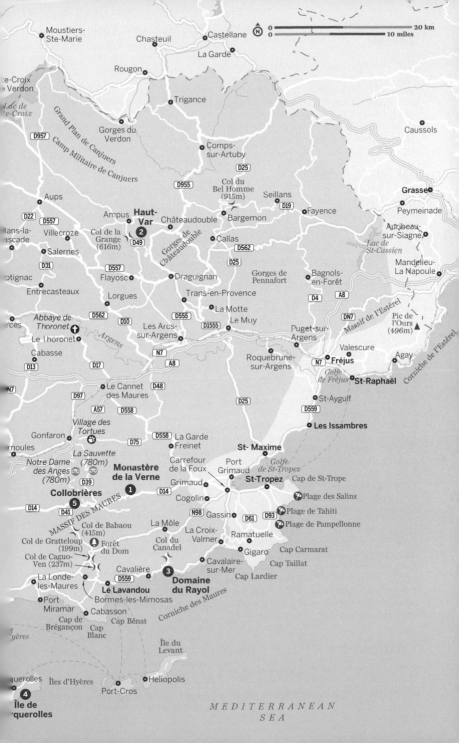

Toulon

POP 167,479

Built around a *rade* (a sheltered bay lined with quays), France's second-largest naval port stands distinct from the glitter of the Côte d'Azur. It has a certain rough charm, and although it's getting progressively more attractive, most visitors just pass through. Above the town rises Mont Faron, accessible by téléphérique.

◉ Sights & Activities

Musée de la Marine   MUSEUM

(☑ 04 94 02 02 01; www.musee-marine.fr; place Monsenergue; adult/child €6.50/free; ☺ 10am-6pm daily Jun-Aug, Wed-Mon Sep-May) Toulon has a long naval history, and remains an important commercial and military port. This historic portside building holds a very good, modern seafaring museum with exhibits, models and paintings illustrating the town's rich naval pedigree. Audioguides are included (and recommended) to get the most out of Toulon's most compelling attraction.

Mont Faron   MOUNTAIN

North of the city, Mont Faron (589m) towers over Toulon, and the views are, as you would expect, epic. Near the summit the **Mémorial du Débarquement de Provence** (☑ 04 94 88 08 09; 8488 rte du Faron Mont Faron; adult/child €4/free; ☺ 10am-12.30pm & 1.15-7.15pm) commemorates the Allied landings of Operation Dragoon, which took place along the coast here in August 1944. There are pleasant walks in the surrounding forest. To get here, catch a ride on the **Téléphérique du Mont Faron** (☑ 04 94 92 68 25; www.telepherique-faron. com; return adult/child €7.50/5.50; ☺ 10am-8pm Jul & Aug, shorter hours rest of year) cable car.

Les Bateliers de la Rade   BOATING

(☑ 04 94 46 24 65; www.lesbateliersdelarade.com; quai de la Sinse; adult/child €13/8; ☺ May-Sep) From the port you can take a guided boat tour around the *rade*, with a commentary (in French) on the local events of WWII (there are also leaflets in English). Also runs trips to the Île de Porquerolles (€29, May to September).

TOULON PASS

The one-day **Toulon Pass** (www.reseau mistral.com; per person €6) includes a trip on the Mont Faron cable car plus public transport travel.

🍴 Sleeping & Eating

Toulon's hotel choices leave a bit to be desired. You'll find a few cheap options clustered around the station.

Hôtel Little Palace   HOTEL €

(☑ 04 94 92 26 62; www.hotel-littlepalace.com; 6 rue Berthelot; s/d €59/74; ✳ @ ☎) The over-the-top, Italian-inspired decor is slightly risible and the lighting could be nicer, but Little Palace is well run, friendly and has 23 great-value rooms in the centre of town. No lift.

Les P'tits Pins   FRENCH €€

(☑ 04 94 41 00 00; www.lesptitspins.com; 237 place de la Liberté; 2-/3-course menus €22/29; ☺ 11.30am-2pm Mon-Thu, 11.30am-2pm & 7.30-10pm Fri & Sat; ✐) This is the restaurant that shows Toulon is slowly but surely shaking its down-at-heel image. With crisp white tablecloths, sparkling glasses and banquette seats, it's an elegant setting for elegant food: tomato and strawberry gazpacho, angus *bavette* and whatever the fish markets provide that morning.

L'Aromate Provençale   PROVENCAL €€

(☑ 04 94 29 73 87; www.aromate-provencal.fr; 32 rue Gimelli; mains €18-19, menus €27; ☺ noon-1.30pm & 7-10pm Tue-Sat) Traditional Provençal flavours get a modern twist at this little side-of-the-street brasserie, run by young entrepreneurs Pierre Andreini and Martial Merlino. The space is small, but the flavours are big: zingy tomato sauces, citrus and herbal overtones, lashings of olive oil. The location is great too, near the opera house.

ℹ Information

Tourist Office (☑ 04 94 18 53 00; www.toulon tourisme.com; 12 place Louis Blanc; ☺ 9am-6pm Mon-Wed & Fri-Sat, from 10am-5pm Tue, 9am-1pm Sun) Has maps and walking-tour brochures, and sells tickets for sights including the Mont Faron cable car.

ℹ Getting There & Away

AIR

Toulon-Hyères Airport (p329), 25km east of Toulon, offers flights (some seasonal) to Brussels, Rotterdam, Southampton and Copenhagen, as well as French cities including Paris, Brest, Lyon, Bordeaux and Ajaccio in Corsica.

Reseau Mistral bus 102 runs at least five times daily from the airport to Toulon's train and bus stations (30 minutes) via Hyères' port and bus stations (10 minutes); the fare is €1.40. VarLib (www.varlib.fr) runs a shuttle bus to St-Tropez (€3, 1½ hours).

BOAT

Corsica Ferries (www.corsica-ferries.fr; Port de Commerce, 2 av de l'Infanterie-de-Marine) has services to both Corsica and Sardinia.

In summer **Bateliers de la Côte d'Azur** (☑ 04 94 93 07 56; www.bateliersdelacotedazur. com; quai Cronstadt) goes to the Îles d'Hyères, including Porquerolles (adult/child €29/19, 30 minutes), Port-Cros (€30/20, 45 minutes) or a combined two-island cruise (€36/19). Ferry services also run to St-Tropez in high season, and there are cruises around the bay too.

BUS

VarLib (www.varlib.fr) buses (€3) operate from the **bus station** (Gare Routière; ☑ 04 94 24 60 00; bd de Tessé), next to the train station. Buses to St-Tropez (two hours, up to 13 daily) go via Hyères (35 minutes) and Le Lavandou (one hour).

The tourist office sells a one-day **Toulon Pass** that includes unlimited travel on local **Le Réseau Mistral** (☑ 04 94 03 87 00; www.reseau mistral.com) buses and commuter boats, and a return ticket for the Mont Faron *téléphérique*.

TRAIN

Toulon has frequent connections to Marseille (€10, 50 minutes), St-Raphaël (€12, 50 minutes), Cannes (€14.50, 1¼ hours) and Nice (€17, 1¾ hours). Fastest trips are as always by TGV. The **station** (Toulon Station; Place de l'Europe) is in the centre of town.

Sanary-sur-Mer

POP 16,168

Pretty as a picture, seaside Sanary-sur-Mer is a stroller's dream. Watch the fishers unload their catch on the quay, or admire the traditional fishing boats from one of the seafront cafes. Wednesday's colourful market draws crowds from miles around, and shops line interior streets. Novelist Aldous Huxley (1894–1963) called Sanary home in the early 1930s.

One kilometre off the Presqu'île du Cap Sicié is the Île des Embiez, home to the **Institut Océanographique Paul Ricard** (☑ 04 94 34 02 49; www.institut-paul-ricard.org; Six-Fours-les-Plages, Île des Embiez; Institiute & Museum adult/child €5/2.50; ◷ 10am–noon & 1.30-5.30pm Mon-Fri, 10am-12.30pm & 2-5.30pm Sat & Sun Jun-Sep; shorter hours rest of year).

The rest of the 95-hectare island is occupied by a vast pleasure port, pine forest, maquis, vineyards, apartment blocks and a couple of posh hotels. Boats sail year-round from the small port at Le Brusc (10 minutes), a beach resort 5km south of Sanary-sur-Mer. From June to September four daily boats (adult/child return €10/6) sail to and from Bandol.

VAR ONLINE

Visit Var (www.visitvar.fr) Information on the Var region.

Vins de Provence (www.vinsde-provence.com) Online winery directory and information.

Maisons d'Hôtes du Var (www.mh-vprovence.com) Stylish B&Bs.

Provence Verte (www.provenceverte.fr) Co-operative of tourist offices covering 43 towns in the Haut Var.

👉 Tours

Croix du Sud V TOURS
(☑ 06 75 71 81 76; www.croixdusud5.com; quai Charles de Gaulle, Sanary-sur-Mer, ◷ Apr-Sep) From mid-April to September, boat tours explore the *calanques* east of Marseille, leaving from the Quai Général de Gaulle in Sanary-sur-Mer (adult/child from €26/16, depending on the number of *calanques* visited). The company also runs trips to Île de Porquerolles (€40/23).

🍴 Sleeping & Eating

Sanary-sur-Mer makes a lovely seaside base. There are a few nice hotels to choose from, but prices are inevitably high.

⭐**Hôtel de la Tour** HOTEL €€
(☑ 04 94 74 10 10; www.sanary-hoteldelatour.com; 24 quai Charles de Gaulle; s/d €75/126; ❄️🛜) This charming, fin-de-siècle hotel offers 24 large, dignified rooms, some with awesome portside views. The charming decor is clean and inviting, and the restaurant with harbourside terrace offers delicious Provençal meals and elegant service. Parking is €12 per day.

Hostellerie La Farandole BOUTIQUE HOTEL €€€
(☑ 04 94 90 30 20; www.hostellerielafarandole. com; 140 chemin de la Plage; d from €388; ❄️🛜🏊) There is something of the old Riviera glamour in the rooms of this uber-stylish modern hotel, with their patterned wallpaper, oversized B&W posters of Hollywood stars and plush soft furnishings. And then there is the location: west-facing, on a secluded beach, with a panoramic roof terrace. Along with a pool, restaurant, jacuzzi and general swankiness, you know you're here to be pampered.

Le Bard'ô MEDITERRANEAN €€
(☑ 04 94 88 42 56; www.le-bardo.com; 210 Bis esplanade Frédéric Dumas, Plage de Portissol; mains

€22-24, menus €35; ⊙ 9am-11pm Mon-Thu, to 3pm Fri & Sat) Just west of Sanary, on Portissol beach, this seafront restaurant/club is perfect for everything from leisurely coffees and delicious meals to late-night DJs and live music. The lunch menu is a bargain but available in limited quantities – arrive early.

ℹ️ Information

Tourist Office (☏ 04 94 74 01 04; www.sanary surmer.com; 1 quai du Levant; ⊙ 9am-7pm Jul & Aug, 9am-6pm Mon-Fri, 9am-1pm & 2-5pm Sat Apr-Jun & Sep-Oct, shorter hours Nov-Mar) Plenty of info on the village and boat timetables.

ℹ️ Getting There & Away

The nearest train station is in nearby Ollioules, which is inconvenient as it means you have to catch a taxi from town (around €10).

Several VarLib buses stop here; the most useful is Line 8805 (€3, 10 daily Monday to Saturday, seven on Sunday), which stops en route from Bandol (15 minutes) to Toulon (30 minutes).

Bandol

POP 8122

Bandol's old fishing-port charm has long since been swallowed up by its high-rise seaside apartment blocks. But the plentiful restaurants, cheap-and-cheerful shops and copious beach facilities make it a favourite for holidaymakers from nearby Toulon and Marseille. For everyone else, it's probably best for a quick lunch stop or a spot of wine tasting, rather than an overnight stay.

◉ Sights & Activities

Île de Bendor   ISLAND
(www.lesilespaulricard.com) A place of exile during the 17th century, once-desolate pinprick Bendor was subsequently abandoned for 250 years. Then in 1951 along came Paul Ricard, a pastis millionaire, who transformed the islet into one of the most fashionable spots on the south coast. The islet, 300m offshore from Bandol, 19km east of Toulon, is now filled with structures that look like a Disney set, such as Mediterranean-style villas and neo-classical statuary.

The port itself, with its shrunken toy-town buildings and meticulously planned alleys and squares, is quite surreal. Seasonal exhibitions (check www.bendor.com) are held on the island and its shallow-sloping beach, with lifeguards, is great for tiny kids. **Les Îles Paul Ricard** (☏ 04 94 10 65 20; www.lesilespaulricard. com; Port de Bandol; adult/child return €14/9) ferries cross from Bandol (five minutes, at least hourly June to mid-September; less frequent at other times).

Sentier du Littoral   WALKING
This yellow-marked coastal trail runs 12km (allow 3½ to four hours) from Bandol's port to La Madrague in St-Cyr-les-Lecques, with the beautiful Calanque de Port d'Alon roughly halfway.

🛏️ Sleeping & Eating

There are plenty of seafood restaurants and brasseries along the seafront. Look behind the waterfront promenade into the network of streets just inland for better options, and be sure to reserve in advance.

Golf Hôtel   HOTEL €€
(☏ 04 94 29 45 83; www.golfhotel.fr; 10 promenade de la Corniche; d/q from €123/190; ⊙ Jan-Nov; ❄️🍽️) A prime address for beachside sleeping; some of the rooms have terraces facing the sea, and are accordingly more pricey. Half-board is available (adult/child €41/28)

VINS DE BANDOL

Bandol's 49 vineyards carefully manage their prized production of red, rosé and white. The Bandol appellation comprises eight neighbouring communities, including Le Castellet, Ollioules, Évenos and Sanary-sur-Mer. Most vineyards require an appointment; for tastings and sales during regular hours, try the following:

The cooperative of Bandol *vignerons*, from the 16 sq km of the renowned Bandol appellation, showcase their wares at the **La Maison des Vins de Bandol** (☏ 04 94 90 29 59; www.vinsdebandol.com; 238 chemin de la Ferrage, Le Castellet; ⊙ 9am-12.30pm & 3-7pm Mon-Sat, 9.30am-noon Sun) boutique and information centre.

Affiliated with the Maison des Vins de Bandol, 12km to the north, **Oenothèque de Bandol** (☏ 04 94 29 45 03; www.maisonsdesvins-bandol.com; place Lucien Artaud, Bandol; ⊙ 10am-1pm & 3-7pm Mon-Sat, 10am-1pm Sun) is a little oenophile's playground providing tastings. It keeps a fascinating range of Bandol wines, and can direct you to surrounding vineyards.

and the in-house Golf Restaurant has lovely access to the beach.

Key Largo
HOTEL €€

(🖉04 94 29 46 93; www.hotel-key-largo.com; 19 corniche Bonaparte; s/d from €102/112; ✳🖀) Bandol's hotels can be short on charm, but this small place on the point between the port and Renécros beach is one of the better options. Rooms are decorated in mauves, greys and sea blues, and the out-of-town setting ensures a peaceful vibe. Good-value golf and accommodation packages, playing at the seaside Dolce Fregate course, are available.

L'Ardoise
MEDITERRANEAN, BISTRO €€

(🖉04 94 32 28 58; 25 rue du Dr Marçon; lunch menu €16, dinner menus €27-41; ⊙noon-1.30pm & 7.30-9.30pm Wed-Sun) Set back from the port's hustle, this stylish place is good for gourmet Mediterranean cuisine. The best tables are on the streetside terrace, or there's a cosy dining room for chilly nights. Try the stuffed prawns with ratatouille.

L'Espérance
BISTRO €€

(🖉04 94 05 85 29; www.lesperance-bandol.com; 21 rue du Dr Marçon; menus €32-45; ⊙noon-1pm & 7-9pm Wed-Sun) Reserve ahead to get a spot in this tiny Provençal restaurant run ably by a husband and wife team. Expect dishes such as mushroom-stuffed rabbit leg with polenta or a *pot au feu* made with monkfish. The stone arches at the front of house provide perfect portals for watching people promenade down rue du Dr Marçon.

ⓘ Information

Tourist Office (🖉04 94 29 41 35; www.bandoltourisme.fr; allée Alfred Vivien; ⊙9am-7pm Jun-Sep, 10am-6pm Oct-May) Offers the usual information on hotels, restaurants and activities, plus a town guide in English.

ⓘ Getting There & Away

Trains run once or twice per hour from Bandol to Marseille (Blancarde or St-Charles, €10, 50 minutes), stopping at Toulon (€4.10, 20 minutes) and Hyères (€8.10, 45 minutes). Other destinations include Les Arcs (€16, 1½ hours, once daily) and Cassis (€5.70, 18 minutes, hourly). Bandol's Gare SNCF (train station) is in the centre of town.

Bandol also has several useful bus services, leaving from the *gare routière* (bus station) near the Gare SNCF, including VarLib (www.varlib.fr) buses to Sanary-sur-Mer (8805, €3, one hour, up to 10 daily) and La Ciotat (8001, €3, 30 minutes, up to four daily).

Cap de Carqueiranne

Immediately west of Hyères, Cap de Carqueiranne is a partly forested stretch of headland, criss-crossed by tiny lanes. The coastal path that edges its way from the town of Carqueiranne is a scenic means of exploring the pretty cape. Just below and to the north is the sweet little fishing port of Oursinières, with a small beach and a marina.

✗ Eating

★ **L'Oursinado**
SEAFOOD €€€

(🖉04 94 21 77 06; www.oursinado.com; chemin du Pas dei Garden; mains/bouillabaisse €29/61; ⊙noon-1.30pm & 7-9.30pm Tue-Sun Jul & Aug, noon-1.30pm & 7-9.30pm Thu-Mon & noon-1.30pm Tue mid-Feb–Jun & Sep–mid-nov; Ⓟ🖀) Dreams of perfect Provençal holidays centre around places like L'Oursinado, a secluded fantasy of a restaurant tucked amongst the pines on a cliff above the tiny port of Les Oursinières. The sea views are pure Med magic, the cicadas sing in summer, and the seafood is sublime: roasted scallops, freshly grilled fish, stewed octopus and *bouillabaisse* (order in advance).

Afterwards, walk off your excesses on the Sentier Côtier (coastal path), high above the pounding waves of the Pointe du Bau Rouge.

ⓘ Getting There & Away

To explore the cape properly, you'll need either a car, or good walking shoes.

Bus 91 runs between Oursinières and Planquette, via La Pradet (€3.90, 20 minutes, up to 14 per day). Catch it from the corner of place des Oursinières and quai Pierre Cocciante.

Hyères

POP 56,478

Hyères, once a rightly acknowledged gem of the southern Var, has somehow slipped back a little in the travelling consciousness. It has too many attractions to disappear entirely, but there's no doubt it has become underappreciated in the glamour-seeking mind of today's Provençal sun-chaser. Odd, when you consider Hyères' thriving, compact medieval *vieille ville*, garden-clad heights above town, and proximity to the further delights of the Presqu'île de Giens, and Îles d'Hyères.

Driving down the busy streets of modern Hyères, lined by stately palm trees and a big casino, you could be forgiven for completely missing the medieval old town above. Make sure you don't.

◉ Sights & Activities

★ Vieille Ville   HISTORIC SITE

(www.hyeres-tourisme.com) Over 2000 years of human habitation are layered in Hyères' attractive old town, which begins on the western side of place Georges Clemenceau at the 13th-century **Porte Massillon**. West along cobbled rue Massillon is rue des Porches, with its polished flagstones and shady arcades.The rambling hillside grove of **Parc St-Bernard** abuts the striking Villa Noailles. Back downhill, **Parc Castel Ste-Claire**, a 17th-century convent converted into a private residence with delightful gardens, was home to American writer Edith Wharton from 1927.

Villa Noailles   HISTORIC BUILDING

(📞04 98 08 01 98; www.villanoailles-hyeres.com; montée de Noailles; ⊙1-6pm Wed, Thu, Sat & Sun, 2-8pm Fri) FREE A cubist maze of concrete and glass, the villa was designed by Robert Mallet-Stevens in 1923 as a winter residence for devoted lover of modern art Vicomte Charles de Noailles. It now hosts art and photography exhibitions, and is worth seeing in its own right. The Jardin Remarquable, just below the house, repays a ramble, too. Be warned: it's a steep walk from the centre of Hyères.

Presqu'île de Giens   OUTDOORS

If you don't have time to visit the Camargue, this beach-fringed peninsula might well be your next-best bet for some flamingo-spotting. Several large lagoons lie at its centre, visited by many seasonal species including herons, egrets, teals, cormorants and Provence's famous flamingos. A **Sentier du Littoral** (Coastal Path) loops the peninsula; bring binoculars. The peninsula is well signposted from Hyères' old town. It's about a 9km drive to the end of the point along the D197.

La Capte   BIRDWATCHING

Pink flamingos add a splash of colour to the otherwise barren landscape of La Capte, two narrow sand bars supporting the Salins des Presquiers salt pans and a lake, 4km south of Hyères' centre. A 1½-hour cycling itinerary (12.5km) loops the salt pans, and the Hyères tourist office runs guided bird-discovery **nature walks** (adult/child €5/free).

🛏 Sleeping & Eating

Hôtel Le Méditerranée   HOTEL €€

(📞04 94 00 52 70; www.hotel-lemediterranee.com; 8 av de la Méditerranée, Hyères Beach Rd; d €83-107, 5-night min in high season; ⊙Feb-Nov; ❄🤶) Run by a friendly Swedish couple, this pleasant little hotel abuts Hyères' racing track, so you may be able to see (or hear) horses thundering past as you enjoy an afternoon prosecco. There are 10 pretty rooms in stylish greys, taupes and whites, some with balconies. It's just a short walk to the beach and the port's abundance of restaurants.

Hôtel Bor   BOUTIQUE HOTEL €€

(📞04 94 58 02 73; www.hotel-bor.com; 3 allée Émile Gérard, Hyères Beach; d from €150; ⊙Mar-Oct; ❄@🤶🏊) Beside Plage Bona, this Scandi-tinged, palm-fringed hotel is a stylish place to stay, with its cedar-clad exterior, sun-loungers, potted plants and seafront deck. Rooms are modern and minimal, with gloss-wood floors, monochrome photos and steel-grey walls. The on-site bar and restaurant (mains €26 to €28) is good for a burger or grilled seafood.

★ Le Béal   PROVENCAL €€

(📞04 94 20 84 98; www.lebeal.com/; 24 rue de Limans; lunch/dinner menus €26/30; ⊙noon-2pm & 7-9.30pm Thu-Mon) The Béal is the name of the 15th- to 16th-century canal that brought water 10km to Hyères, which still functions and can be seen at points around the old town. Its namesake restaurant also nourishes the citizens of Hyères, with delightful modern French food such as octopus salad, and chorizo-crusted cod on creamy risotto. It's friendly, tastefully designed, and generally joyful.

Ola Le Rêve   FRENCH €€

(📞04 94 38 59 34; 4 Port la Gavine, batiment B; mains €26-39; ⊙noon-2pm & 7-11pm Wed-Sun) This friendly, busy spot on Hyères' pleasure port provides a wonderful backdrop of gleaming waves and gently rocking yachts for a relaxed meal on the terrace. While there's naturally plenty of seafood on the menu (grilled dorade, mullet and bass, or plump mussels), there are also pastas, burgers and steaks to keep everyone happy. It's open year-round.

❶ Information

Tourist Office (📞04 94 01 84 50; www.hyeres-tourisme.com; Rotonde du Park Hôtel, av de Belgique; ⊙9am-6pm Mon-Fri, to 4pm Sat year-round, plus 9am-4pm Sun Jul & Aug) This well-stocked, multilingual and very friendly office offers guided birdwatching walks to Hyères' lagoons, and can help with trips to the islands.

❶ Getting There & Around

AIR

Toulon-Hyères Airport (p329) is 3km south of Hyères and 25km east of Toulon. It has direct daily flights to Paris, with less regular seasonal links to Brest, Bordeaux, Bastia and Ajaccio, as well as Brussels, London, Southhampton and Bournemouth.

From the airport, Le Réseau Mistral (www.reseaumistral.com) bus 102 runs to the town hall in Hyères (10 minutes) and to the train and bus station in Toulon (40 minutes); tickets cost €1.40. You can also catch bus 63 into Hyères.

VarLib (www.varlib.fr) runs a shuttle bus to St-Tropez (€3, 1½ hours, five daily).

BOAT

Transport Littoral Varois (☎04 94 58 21 81; www.tlv-tvm.com) Runs year-round ferries from Tour Fondue to the Île de Porquerolles (return €20, 20 minutes) and less-frequent services from Port d'Hyères to Île de Port-Cros (return €28.10, one hour) and Île du Levant (return €28, 1½ hours). There's also a two-island day-trip (return €32) to Port-Cros and Le Levant from the Port d'Hyères.

BUS

From the **bus station** (place du Maréchal Joffre), bus 67 goes to the train station (€1.40, five minutes), Port d'Hyères (€1.40, 15 minutes) and La Tour Fondue (€1.40, 35 minutes). Buy tickets on board.

TAXI

Taxis Radio Hyerois (☎04 94 00 60 00; www.taxis-hyeres.com)

TRAIN

Gare de Hyères (Hyères Train Station; place de l'Europe) Destinations served by trains from Hyères include Toulon (€4.80, 20 minutes) and Marseille Blancarde (€16, 1¼ hours). Most trains stop in Cassis, La Ciotat, Bandol and Ollioules-Sanary.

ÎLES D'HYÈRES

Lying intriguingly offshore from the coast between Toulon to Hyères, the Îles d'Hyères are also known as the Îles d'Or (Islands of Gold) – not just due to their mica-rich rock, but also for the golden beaches that fringe their forested hinterland. They're overrun in July and August, but for much of the rest of the year you might have them largely to yourself, with plenty of good weather, too.

Île de Porquerolles is the largest; Île de Port-Cros is a national park with fantastic snorkelling; and Île du Levant is both an army camp and a nudist colony. Wild camping and cars are forbidden in the archipelago.

ⓘ Getting There & Away

The main ports for travelling to the islands are La Tour Fondue (at the southern end of the

REGIONAL MARKETS

Most Var villages hold a market once a week. For travellers, they're an ideal window into local life, and the best way to build a picnic lunch. Markets are morning affairs, usually setting up from around 7am, and beginning to pack up around noon or 1pm.

Monday Bormes-les-Mimosas

Tuesday Bandol, Callas, Cotignac, Fayence, Hyères, Lorgues

Wednesday Bormes-les-Mimosas, La Garde Freinet, Salernes, Sanary-sur-Mer, Tourtour

Thursday Aups, Bargemon, Callas, Collobrières (July and August), Fayence, Hyères, Ramatuelle

Friday Entrecasteaux, La Motte

Saturday Carcès, Claviers, Cogolin, Draguignan, Fayence, Hyères, Tourtour

Sunday Ampus, Cavalière, Collobrières, Gassin (April to October), La Garde Freinet, Ramatuelle, Salernes, Vidauban

Presqu'île de Giens), Port d'Hyères (further north) and Le Lavandou (east of Hyères). From June to September seasonal ferries also run from other locations, including Toulon and St-Tropez.

Transport Littoral Varois runs year-round ferries to Porquerolles (from La Tour Fondue) and Port-Cros and Le Levant (from Port Hyères). Naturally there are more services in high season.

Vedettes Îles d'Or et Le Corsaire (☎04 94 71 01 02; www.vedettesilesdor.fr; quai des Îles d'Or, Le Lavandou, Gare Maritime; ⊙8.30am-12.15pm & 2-6.30pm Mon, Tue, Thu, Sat & Sun, from 1.15pm Wed & Fri) runs boats to the Îles d'Hyères from its bases at Le Lavandou, Cavalaire and La Croix-Valmer.

Vedettes also runs multi-island cruises (adult/child €48/39) on high-speed La Croisière Bleue vessels, which leave from Le Lavandou and stop at both Porquerolles and Port-Cros. You can catch these from either Le Lavandou or Cavalaire, running from June to September.

Île de Porquerolles

POP 345

Despite the huge influx of day trippers (up to 6000 a day in July and August, joining similar numbers staying on the island), beautiful Porquerolles somehow remains unspoilt.

Two-thirds of its sandy white beaches, pine woods, maquis and eucalyptus are protected by the Parc National de Port-Cros, and a wide variety of indigenous and tropical flora thrive, including Requien's larkspur, which grows nowhere else in the world. April and May are the best months to spot some of the 114 bird species.

Pottering along the island's rough unpaved trails on foot or by bicycle, breaking with a picnic lunch on the beach and a dip in crystal-clear turquoise water, is heavenly. The southern edge of the island is the most dramatic and uncluttered, but the inland vineyards and olive groves have a magic of their own, as do the gorgeous beaches of the northern coast.

◉ Sights & Activities

Porquerolles' northern coast is laced with beautiful sandy beaches. Cliffs line the island's more dangerous southern coast, where swimming and diving are restricted to Calanque du Brégançonnet to the east and Calanque de l'Oustaou de Diou to the west. Get maps at the tourist office.

The tourist office map also has four cycling itineraries, from 6.5km to 13.8km long. More detail is included in a cyclo-guide (€6) in French, available at the Maison du Parc. Bike-hire outfits line the port and place d'Armes.

Porquerolles' vineyards cover a square kilometre of the western part of the island, and are tended by three wine producers. Each offers *dégustation* (tasting) sessions of their predominantly rosé wines.

Place d'Armes   SQUARE
A eucalypt-shaded *pétanque* pitch dominates central place d'Armes, which, as its name suggests, was once a parade ground. Music concerts fill Église Ste-Anne on its southern side in summer. Day in, day out, this hub of Porquerollais life buzzes with outdoor cafes, ice-cream stands, and cyclists pedalling to and fro. Once the last of the day-tripper boats has sailed, a peaceful lull falls across the square.

Fort Ste-Agathe   FORT
(☑04 94 58 07 24; www.portcrosparcnational.fr; adult/child €3/2; ☺Apr–mid-Sep, by guided tour only) This 16th-century fort contains historical and natural-history exhibits, and its tower has lovely island views. Much of the building dates from between 1812 and 1814, when Napoléon had it rebuilt after the British destroyed it in 1793. From place d'Armes, walk uphill along chemin Ste-Agathe (between Villa Ste-Anne and Auberge des Glycines) to reach the fort. Admission is only with timed, guided national-park tours. There are also tours of nearby windmill Moulin du Bonheur (€2).

Jardin Emanuel Lopez & Conservatoire Botanique National Méditerranéen   GARDENS
(☑04 94 58 07 24; chemin de la Pépinière; ☺9.30am-12.30pm & 2-6pm Apr-Oct) This wonderful ornamental garden is planted with palms, cypresses, vanilla and grenadier trees, cactus and bamboo, sweetly scented jasmine, and every herb known to grow under the Provençal sun. It's also home to the Parc National de Port-Cros Maison du Parc.

LES PLAGES DE PORQUEROLLES

The Porquerolles coastline is stunning: a mix of sheer, wave-washed cliffs and delightful beaches. Here are some of the best places for a dip.

Plage de la Courtade Voted the most beautiful beach in Europe, this gorgeous crescent of sand is a mere 800m walk east from the port (follow the track uphill behind the tourist office).

Plage d'Argent West of the village, Plage d'Argent, a good 2km along a potholed track past vineyards, is popular with families because of its summer beachside cafe-restaurant, lifeguards and toilets.

Plage de Notre Dame Porquerolles' largest and (some say) most beautiful beach, Plage de Notre Dame, is about 3.5km east of the port (follow the track uphill behind the tourist office).

Plage du Langoustier About as remote as anywhere can be on tiny Porquerolles, secluded Plage du Langoustier is located at a former lobster farm 4.5km from the village on the northern shores of the Presqu'île du Langoustier.

Locamarine 75 BOATING
(☑ 06 08 34 74 17, 04 94 58 35 84; www.locamarine
75.com; speedboats per day from €95, double kayak
half-/full-day €35/45; ⊙ 9am-7pm) Speedboat
rental outlet at the port; also has kayaks.
More powerful boats require permits to hire.

Base Nautique KAYAKING
(☑ 04 34 34 02 33; www.ileo-porquerolles.fr; kayak rental 1/3/6hrs €20/35/45) On Plage de la
Courtade; has kayaks, windsurfers, catama-
rans and scuba diving.

🛌 Sleeping

Accommodation is pricey and limited, and
it gets booked months in advance. The tourist office has details on self-catering apart-
ments/villas and three B&Bs. Prices plummet in the low season, when most places
close for an annual break.

Villa Ste-Anne INN €€
(☑ 04 94 04 63 00; www.sainteanne.com; place
d'Armes; r from €160; ⊙ Apr-Nov; ❋) The main
draw of this typical Porquerollais inn on
the square is its terracotta-tiled restaurant
terrace that overlooks the *pétanque* pitch.
Borrow a set of *boules* should you fancy a
toss. Indulge in an aperitif and *petit friture*
(tiny deep-fried fish dipped in spicy *rouille*).
There are three apartments if your party
won't fit into one of the 25 rooms.

Auberge des Glycines PENSION €€
(☑ 04 94 58 30 36; www.auberge-glycines.com; 22
place d'Armes; d €160-280, 1-week min in high season; ❋ 📶) This inn overlooking the village
square ranks as highly in the dining stakes
as it does in sleeping. Decor is traditional
(note the cicada collection hanging on the
wall in reception) and dining is Porquerol-
laise – in other words, shoals of fish. Three-
course *menus* are €35.

★ Le Mas du Langoustier HOTEL €€€
(☑ 04 94 58 30 09; www.langoustier.com; chemin
du Langoustier; s/d per person €270/540; ⊙ May-
Sep; ❋ 📶 ☲) The 'to die for' choice: guests
have been known to drop in by helicopter
at this exceptional hotel with a glamorous
history (dating to 1931), vineyards, and
stunning views from its seaside perch.
Everything, from the rooms to the Michelin-starred restaurant, is impeccable. Some
apartments are available for families.

★ L'Oustaou PENSION €€€
(☑ 04 94 58 30 13; www.oustaou.com; place
d'Armes; d/tr from €200/255; ⊙ Apr-Nov; ❋ 📶)

ℹ️ WHEN TO GO TO PORQUEROLLES

Avoid July and August, when the risk of
fire closes the interior of the island and
makes some trails inaccessible. Smoking
is generally forbidden outside the village.

Superclean rooms with modern decor either
face the village square or have marvellous
port views. It's lovely for couples, with a hint
of romance. Downstairs, tuck into modern
French standards or burgers (mains €16 to
€26). Half-board is available (€35).

Les Mèdes HOTEL €€€
(☑ 04 94 12 41 24; www.hotel-les-medes.fr; 2 rue
de la Douane; d/tr/q €195/215/245; ⊙ Jan-Oct;
❋ @ 📶 ☲) This hotel mixes traditional
rooms with self-catering apartments. The
icing on the cake: a terraced garden with
fountain pool and sunloungers.

🍴 Eating

An admirable picnic of juicy cherries, peaches, cold meats, fresh goats-milk cheese and
so on can easily be built from the fruit
stands on place d'Armes, and the small
grocery store here or at the port; note that
just after noon they all close for a two-hour
lunch break. Most hotels also have restaurants, and bistros ring the place d'Armes.

L'Escale BRASSERIE €
(☑ 04 94 58 30 18; 2 rue de la Ferme; menus from
€18; ⊙ noon-2pm & 7-9.30pm Apr-Aug, noon-2pm
Sep-early Jan & mid-Feb–Mar; 📶 🚷) With a huge
deck overlooking the swaying masts and
wooded cove beyond, L'Escale draws the
freshly disembarked like bees to honey. And
they're not disappointed: friendly, energetic
service, local wines by the glass, a menu long
on fresh seafood and a general sense of luck
at being somewhere so lovely make it an all-
round winner. There are plenty of tapas options to share (€10 to €12) in summer.

ℹ️ Information

Tourist Office (☑ 04 94 58 33 76; www.
porquerolles.com; Carré du Port; ⊙ 9am-
6.15pm Mon-Sat, to 1pm Sun Jul & Aug, shorter
hours rest of year) Brochures and maps, one
marked with cycling and walking paths (€3).

Parc National de Port-Cros Maison du Parc
(☑ 04 94 58 07 24; www.portcrosparcnational.
fr; chemin de la Pépinière, Jardin Emanuel
Lopez; ⊙ 9.30am-12.30pm & 2-6pm Apr-Oct)

PORQUEROLLES OUT THE BARREL

Tiny Porquerolles supports some very fine Côtes de Provence wineries.

Domaine de la Courtade (☑ 04 94 58 31 44; www.lacourtade.com; chemin Notre Dame; ⊘ by appointment) offers tastings of its predominantly rosé wines.

Domaine de l'Île (☑ 04 98 04 62 30; www.domainedelile.com; ⊘ Mon-Fri, by appointment), focusing on rosé, offers tastings by appointment.

Domaine Perzinsky (☑ 04 94 58 34 32; www.domaine-perzinsky.com; chemin de la Pépinière; ⊘ 8am-noon & 2-5pm) Framed by a fabulous formation of parasol pines, Domaine Perzinsky is an easy stop en route to Plage d'Argent and, unusually, requires no advance reservation for tastings. As with many Porquerolles producers, its rosé is particularly fine.

National park office with maps, information and guided tours.

🛈 Getting There & Away

Transport Littoral Varois (p133) Runs year-round ferries to the Île de Porquerolles (return €20, 20 minutes), leaving from La Tour Fondue at the southern end of Presqu'île de Giens.

Vedettes Îles d'Or et Le Corsaire (p133) Runs boats to Porquerolles from its bases at Le Lavandou, Cavalaire and La Croix-Valmer. From Le Lavandou, the trip is 45 to 75 minutes (adult/child return €36/28). Trips from Cavalaire and La Croix-Valmer cost about €5 extra.

🛈 Getting Around

BICYCLE

There's an abundance of places hiring bikes in town. Prices are pretty uniform; we recommend **Le Cycle Porquerollais** (☑ 04 94 58 30 32; www.cycle-porquerollais.com; 1 rue de la Ferme; half-/full-day from €13/16; ⊘ 9.30am-12.30pm & 2.30-4.30pm).

TAXI

Bateaux-Taxi Le Pélican (☑ 06 09 52 31 19; www.bateaux-taxi.com) This boat taxi can circle Porquerolles or go to the mainland.

Luggage Taxi (☑ 06 81 67 77 12; Embarcadère du Port; ⊘ mid-Feb–Dec) A limited luggage-carting service.

Île de Port-Cros

France's smallest national park, **Parc National de Port-Cros** (☑ 04 94 12 82 30; www.portcrosparcnational.fr; 🛍), was created in 1963 to protect the 7-sq-km island of Port-Cros and a 13-sq-km zone of water around it. Industry and agriculture once flourished here, and their atmospheric remains can be seen while walking the island's trails.

Until the end of the 19th century the islanders' vineyards and olive groves ensured their self-sufficiency. Today, high-season tourism is their sustenance. If on a day trip, it's a good idea to bring picnic supplies and drinking water; the few port bistros open April to October, but there's nothing elsewhere but beauty (and a picnic in a secluded calanque can be truly magical). Don't forget the portion of the park that lies offshore: there's some fantastic diving, snorkelling and boating to be had.

⊙ Sights & Activities

Walkers (and birdwatchers) must remain on the 30km of marked trails. Fishing, fires, camping, dogs, motorised vehicles and bicycles are not allowed, nor is smoking outside the village. Snorkelling and diving are permitted, accompanied by licensed operators.

Fort de l'Estissac   FORT
(www.portcrosparcnational.fr; ⊘ 10.30am-12.30pm & 2-5pm May-Oct; 🛍) FREE This 17th-century fort, strengthened by Napoleon after being partly destroyed by the English, crowns the northwestern part of Port-Cros. You can climb its tower and sometimes catch exhibitions in summer, when it opens.

Sentier Sous-Marin   SNORKELLING
(Underwater Trail; ☑ 04 94 01 40 70; Plage de la Palud; ⊘ mid-Jun–mid-Sep; 🛍) FREE This 35-minute underwater circuit is marked by buoys with explanatory panels – the bay is home to 500 algae species and 180 types of fish. The Maison du Parc at the port sells a waterproof leaflet (€5). Rent equipment from portside outfit **Sun Plongée** (☑ 04 94 05 90 16, 06 80 32 14 16; www.sun-plongee. com; promenade de la Rade; 3 dives €190; ⊘ mid-Mar–mid-Nov). And check to see if there are any jellyfish before diving in!

Sentier des Plantes   WALKING
(Botanical Trail) The 15th-century **Fort du Moulin** is the starting point for the Sentier des Plantes (4km, 1½ to two hours), a lovely

aromatic trail that wends its way past wild lavender and rosemary to **Plage de la Palud** (30 minutes), a beautiful beach on the island's northern shore. Small plaques inform walkers about some of the plant species.

Circuit de Port-Man   WALKING
From Plage de la Palud, the Circuit de Port-Man (four hours) follows the coastline to secluded Plage de Port-Man on the island's far northeastern tip, before looping back inland. It offers forts, forest and dramatic coastline.

Sentier des Crêtes   WALKING
The demanding Sentier des Crêtes (7.5km; three hours) explores the southwestern corner of the island and climaxes atop Mont Vinaigre (194m). Along the way you'll see old chapels, manor houses and stunning coastline.

🛏 Sleeping & Eating

Accommodation requires booking months in advance, and is limited to the small port area: consider a day trip. There are some very pleasant restaurants, concentrated around the port. Be aware that they're seasonal, however, and may not be open when you visit. A packed picnic lunch is an excellent insurance policy.

Hôtel Le Manoir de Port-Cros   PENSION €€€
(☑ 04 94 05 90 52; www.hotel-lemanoirportcros.com; rte du Barrage; d with half-board €380; ☺ Apr-Oct; ❄ ≋) This enchanting 21-room manor with white turreted facade 300m from Port-Cros' port is the exclusive option. Find it nestled in a sweet-smelling eucalyptus grove with outdoor pool, upmarket restaurant and the elegant air of bygone island life. The delightful sea-facing terraced restaurant turns out fresh fish à la Niçoise, monkfish with crayfish infusion, and other marine delights.

Hostellerie Provençale   PENSION €€€
(☑ 04 94 05 90 43; www.hostellerie-provencale.com; promenade de la Rade; d incl half-board €298; ☺ Apr-mid-Nov; ❄ 🛜 ≋) Run since 1921 by the island's oldest family, this bustling portside *hostellerie* (inn) sports five bright rooms facing the water; the best have balconies. The eye-catching cocktail bar and restaurant sit on the waterfront with canary-yellow sun umbrellas.

La Trinquette   BISTRO €€
(☑ 04 94 05 93 75; www.restaurant-trinquette-port-cros.fr; menus €22-28; ☺ 8am-midnight Apr-Oct) At the edge of the harbour sand, dine on steaks, seafood or pasta before walking out across the island. The day's catch, sold by weight and simply grilled, is hard to pass up.

ℹ Information

At the port, the **Maison du Parc** (☑ 04 94 01 40 70; www.portcrosparcnational.fr) opens to meet freshly arrived boats, providing information on the island and its attractions.

Île du Levant

Île du Levant, an 8km strip of an island, has a split personality. Ninety per cent of it is a closed military camp, and the remaining pocket of **Héliopolis** (on the island's southwestern edge) is a nudist colony.

The post office, cafes and hotels are clustered around the central square, place du Village, 1km uphill from the port along rte de l'Ayguade. From there a nature trail leads east into the **Domaine des Arbousiers**, a nature reservation sheltering rare island plants. The **tourist office** (☑ 04 94 05 93 52; www.iledu levant.com.fr; ☺ Easter–mid-Sep) has information on guided tours. There are no ATMs on the island.

🛏 Sleeping & Eating

Most accommodation options close over winter, but in season there are perhaps a dozen places, from camping to expensive hotels, in the main settlement. In-season eating options are also plentiful; out of season, they're almost nil. There is mainly casual dining, with a few higher-end places too.

ℹ Getting There & Away

Boats dock at Port de l'Ayguade, near the tourist information hut.
Transport Littoral Varois (p133) Runs ferries to Le Levant (from Port Hyères, adult/child €28/25, one hour). Naturally there are more services in high season.

LA LONDE-LES-MAURES

POP 10,173

La Londe-les-Maures is a town in two parts: the major, inland settlement is the hub of a small but highly respected wine-growing region; while the seaside section, the port area of Miramar and Maravelle, is 3km distant. Both offer varied and distinct attractions: inland you can explore olive groves, vineyards and flower gardens, or hire a bike and taste wine via pedal power; at the seaside you can swim, take boat tours and ferries, or enjoy a sundowner with the Îles d'Hyères as a not-unpleasant backdrop.

ℹ Information

Tourist Office (☑ 04 94 01 53 10; www.ot-la londelesmaures.fr; 60 bd du Front de Mer, Port Miramar; ⊙10am-1pm & 3-7pm Mon-Fri, 3-7pm Sat-Sun Jul & Aug; shorter hours rest of year) This harbourside office is larger and more-often open than the one in central La Londe.

ℹ Getting There & Away

La Londe benefits from multiple coastal bus routes including regular services to St-Tropez (€3, 60 to 70 minutes), Toulon (€3, one hour) and Hyères (€3, 30 minutes).

CORNICHE DES MAURES

The Corniche des Maures (D559) unwinds beautifully southwest from La Croix-Valmer to Le Lavandou along a shoreline trimmed with sandy beaches ideal for swimming, sunbathing and windsurfing. Slightly inland, Bormes-les-Mimosas is the jewel in its crown (and appropriately popular in summer).

◉ Sights

★**Domaine du Rayol**   GARDENS
(Le Jardin des Méditerranées; ☑ 04 98 04 44 00; www.domainedurayol.org; av des Belges, Rayol-Canadel-sur-Mer; adult/child €11/8; ⊙9.30am-7.30pm Jul & Aug, to 6.30pm Apr-Jun, Sep & Oct, to 5.30pm Nov-Mar; 🅿🚼) 🏊 Growing continuously since its conception in 1910, this stunning garden, with plants from all Mediterranean climates, is wonderful for a stroll or a themed nature walk. The dense flora cascades down the hillside to the sea, and while the flowers are at their best in April and May, it's always worth a visit. In summer, at the estate's petite gem of a beach, you can snorkel around underwater flora and fauna with an experienced guide (adult/child €28/20; bookings essential).

Also reserve ahead for open-air musical concerts or in-depth workshops (program online). The estate's relaxed **Café des Jardiniers**, open from noon, serves light organic lunches and refreshing hibiscus-peach infusions.

🛏 Sleeping & Eating

There are a few hotels dotted along the coastal road, but the hillside village of Bormes-les-Mimosas makes a more pleasant base.

Le Relais des Maures   INN €€
(☑ 04 94 05 61 27; www.lerelaisdesmaures.fr; av Charles Koecklin, Rayol-Canadel-sur-Mer; s/d €135/145; ⊙Apr-Sep; 🅿🚼🛜) This inn, tucked just off the D559, has homey guest rooms, some with sea views (it's just a short walk to the Plages du Royal). The excellent restaurant (*menus* €37) is worth a stop in its own right for its seasonal, locally sourced dishes. The inn was completely renovated in 2018.

★**Chez Jo**   SEAFOOD €€
(Restaurant Plage du Layet; ☑ 04 94 05 85 06; Plage du Layet, Cavalière; mains €20-30; ⊙noon-3pm May-Sep) The ultimate summer seafood, suntan and socialisation shack, Chez Jo buzzes with tanned, barefoot beach-lovers, sipping Bandol whites and devouring the fresh seafood. The restaurant is bare bones, unsigned and not that easy to find (search the southwestern end of the nudist Plage du Layet). It's all tables in the sand (or on the deck), beach umbrellas, and long, happy lunches.

ℹ Getting There & Away

BOAT

Vedettes Îles d'Or et Le Corsaire (p133) runs boats to the Îles d'Hyères from Le Lavandou, Cavalaire and La Croix-Valmer.

From Le Lavandou, boats go to Île du Levant (return adult/child €28/23, 35 to 55 minutes), Île de Port-Cros (€28/€23, 35 to 55 minutes) and Île de Porquerolles (€36/28, 45 to 75 minutes). Trips from Cavalaire and La Croix-Valmer cost about €5 extra.

There are also multi-island cruises (adult/child €48/39) on high-speed La Croisière Bleue vessels, which stop at both Île de Porquerolles and Île de Port-Cros. The company also runs a summer-only ferry to St-Tropez from Le Lavandou (adult/child €47/37), Cavalaire (€32/26) and La Croix-Valmer. In winter, boats only connect Le Lavandou, Île du Levant and Île de Port-Cros.

BUS

The coastal D559 is served by **VarLib** (www.varlib.fr) buses 7801 and 7802, running between St-Tropez and Toulon (€3, two hours, up to 20 per day).

Bormes-les-Mimosas

POP 7862 / ELEV 180M

The old cobbled streets of this 12th-century village are lined with art galleries and boutiques selling traditional Provençal products. The town is spectacularly flowered with bougainvilleas in summer and bright-yellow mimosas in winter (despite the name, the mimosa is actually an invasive species from Australia, known as the yellow wattle).

◎ Sights & Activities

The tourist office takes bookings for botanical walks (€9) and hikes (€7) with a forest warden in the nearby Forêt du Dom.

Fort de Brégançon   FORT
(☑04 94 01 38 38; www.bormeslesmimosas.com; av Guy Tezenas, Cap de Brégançon; adult/child €10/free, parking €6-9; ☺9.15am-4.15pm late-Jun–late Sep, shorter hours rest of year) A private residence of the president from 1968 to 2013, the Fort de Brégançon is now an accessible national monument. Located on a scenic peninsula 20 minutes' drive from Bormes-les-Mimosas, the imposing fort dates back to the 11th century and has featured in numerous conflicts since, from the tensions between Provence and France to the French Revolution and WWI. Tickets must be booked in advance via the Bormes tourist office, either in person or online.

🛏 Sleeping & Eating

Seasonal bars and brasseries make great use of stone niches in the medieval streets.

★Hôtel Bellevue   HOTEL €
(☑04 94 71 15 15; www.bellevuebormes.com; 14 place Gambetta; d/q from €61/136; ☺Jan-Oct; ❄🛜) Excellent value for such a centrally located, welcoming and comfortable hotel, this charming salmon-pink hostelry justifies its name with sensational views over the village's jumbled rooftops all the way to the glittering blue. Not-yet-renovated rooms are cheaper, some are wheelchair-accessible, and there's also a pleasant terraced restaurant – arrive early for a prime valley-view table. You'll save €10.50 by skipping breakfast.

Hostellerie du Cigalou   HOTEL €€€
(☑04 94 41 51 27; www.hostellerieducigalou.com; place Gambetta; d/q €200/266; ❄🛜🏊) Occupying an unimprovable central location in Borne-les-Mimosas, the Cigalou offers 20 plush rooms and a dreamy pool, plus a very good traditional French restaurant. Several rooms have freestanding bath tubs, and a few have their own private terraces overlooking the village. Room rates are €11 less per person if you're not having breakfast there.

★La Rastègue   GASTRONOMY €€€
(☑04 94 15 19 41; www.larastegue.com; 48 bd du Levant; menus €49; ☺7.30-9pm Tue-Sat, noon-1.45pm Sun Apr-Nov) Jérôme Masson rules over the kitchen; his wife, Patricia, over the dining room – and they sure do excel. La Rastègue has earned a Michelin star with its ever-changing menu of superb Provençal fare, inviting dining room and sensational sea-view terrace. The open kitchen allows you to see the chef at work.

ℹ Information

Tourist Office (☑04 94 01 38 38; www.bormeslesmimosas.com; 1 place Gambetta; ☺9am-12.30pm & 2.30-6.30pm Jul & Aug, 9am-12.30pm & 2-5pm Mon-Sat Oct-Mar; 🛜) Renovated in 2018, this office organises local walks and is a wealth of information. Good hiking maps are available for €5.

ℹ Getting There & Away

Several **VarLib** (www.varlib.fr) buses run via Bormes-les-Mimosas, but they are dependent on school term times. Most destinations cost a flat-rate €3. The most useful is Line 7801, which travels to/from St-Tropez (one hour, six to eight daily) via Le Rayol-Canadel-sur-Mer (30 minutes) and Le Lavandou (15 minutes) en route to Hyères (30 minutes) and Toulon (one hour).

MASSIF DES MAURES

A wild range of wooded hills rumpling the landscape inland between Hyères and Fréjus, the Massif des Maures is a pocket of surprising wilderness just a few miles from the hustle of the Côte d'Azur. Shrouded by pine, chestnut and cork oak trees, its near-black vegetation gives rise to its name, derived from the Provençal word *mauro* (dark pine wood).

Traditional industries (chestnut harvests, cork, pipe-making) are still practised here, and the area is criss-crossed by hiking trails that offer spectacular views of the surrounding coastline.

◎ Sights & Activities

Local tourist offices can supply hiking guides and route suggestions, but note that from June to September, access to many areas is limited due to the risk of forest fire.

LE PASS SITES VAR

Le Pass Sites Var is a free pass with discounts on admission to 28 abbeys, chapels, gardens and museums in the Var. Get the online coupon for the sights you are interested in at www.visitvar.fr.

CLAUDIOBEDUSCHI/GETTY IMAGES ©

1. Île de Porquerolles (p133)
Two thirds of this Îles d'Hyères island is protected national park.

2. Monastère de la Verne (p142)
This 12th century monastery features a Romanesque church, a formal garden and a prior's workshop.

3. Sanary-sur-Mer (p129)
Picturesque fishing boats are a key attraction on this pretty Var island.

4. Domaine du Rayol (p138)
Thsi seaside garden displays plants from all around the Mediterranean.

IVAN BASTIEN/SHUTTERSTOCK ©

Depending on the risk, trails are graded yellow, orange, red and black, with yellow meaning some minor restrictions at certain times of day, and black meaning total closure. Ask at a tourist office before you set out.

★ Monastère de la Verne   MONASTERY

(Chartreuse de la Verne; ☑ 04 94 43 45 51; off D14; adult/child €6/3; ⊙ 11am-6pm Wed-Mon Jun-Aug, to 5pm Feb-May & Sep-Dec; Ⓟ) The majestic 12th-century Monastère de la Verne sits on a forested ridge in the Massif des Maures, rising like an island of honeyed stone in a sea of green. The Carthusian institution was founded in 1170, possibly on the site of a temple to the goddess Laverna, protector of the bandits who hid in the Maures. It has been ravaged by fire and rebuilt several times over the years (much of the reconstruction dates to the 17th- and 18th-centuries).

After falling into further disrepair, the monastery has been painstakingly restored over past decades (a 20-minute video details the work) and now houses a community of the Sisters of Bethlehem. Highlights include the austere Romanesque church, the prior's cell – with small formal garden and workshop – the bakery and the olive mill. The shop (closed Sunday) is full of excellent artisanal food, soaps, art and crafts made by the nuns. Walking trails lead from the monastery through ancient *châtaigneraies* (chestnut groves) into the forested surroundings.

From Collobrières, follow rte de Grimaud (D14) east for 6km, then turn right (south) on to the D214 and drive another 6km to the monastery. Park at the lot and walk the final 700m section, which is unpaved.

Village des Tortues   WILDLIFE RESERVE

(☑ 04 89 29 14 10; www.villagedestortues.fr; 1065 route du Luc (D97), Carnoules; adult/child €15/10; ⊙ 9am-7pm mid-Mar–mid-Oct, 9.30am-5pm mid-Oct–mid-Mar; Ⓟ) This sanctuary protects one of France's most endangered species, the Hermann tortoise *(Testudo hermanni)* today found only in the Massif des Maures and on Corsica. In summer, the best time to see the tortoises is in the morning and late afternoon. Watch them hatch from mid-May to the end of June; they hibernate from November through early March. Guided tours at 10.30am and 2pm are enlightening.

The **Station d'Observation et de Protection des Tortues des Maures** (SOPTOM; Maures Tortoise Observation and Protection Station) runs the tortoise clinic, where wounded tortoises are treated and then released into the Maures. Young tortoises also spend the first three of their 60 to 100 years in SOPTOM's hatcheries and nurseries, safe from the predations of magpies, rats, foxes and wild boars. Check the website for many other events and educational opportunities.

🛏 Sleeping & Eating

There are only a handful of hotels in the hills, but if you're after peace and quiet, you should be able to find it.

Traditional country cuisine dominates local menus. In season, you might have the chance to sample some wild boar.

Relais du Vieux Sauvaire   MEDITERRANEAN €€€

(☑ 04 94 22 02 32; www.relaisduvieuxsauv aire.com; rte des Crêtes, corniche de la pierre d'Avenoun; menu €45, mains €32-38; ⊙ noon-2.30 & 7-9.30pm Mon-Sat, noon-12.30pm Sun May-Nov; Ⓟ) There are few more dramatic approaches to a restaurant than the rough, superbly scenic rte des Crêtes, with its alternating glimpses of the coast and inland Provence. It's worth the drive even if you can't get a table, but it would be a shame to miss out on Relaix du Vieux Sauvaire's superb Provençal food in a setting beyond superlatives.

Auberge de la Môle   FRENCH €€€

(☑ 04 94 49 57 01; place de l'Église, La Môle; lunch/dinner menus €23/55; ⊙ 9am-3pm & 7-10.30pm Wed-Sun, 9am-3pm Tue) Tradition rules fierce and strong at this no-frills village inn, which doubles as the local *bar-tabac* (cafe-tobacconist). For locals, this is *the* place to appease hearty appetites with legendary terrines, pâtés and feisty jars of pickles. Find the inn next to the church in the hamlet of La Môle.

ⓘ Getting There & Away

Public transport is pretty much non-existent up in the hills. You'll need your own wheels.

Collobrières

POP 1919

Hidden in the forest, the leafy village of Collobrières is *the* place to taste chestnuts. Across the 11th-century bridge, the tourist office can help you participate in the October chestnut harvest, celebrated with the Fête de la Châtaigne, or join a guided forest walk.

🥾 Activities

Fôret des Maures   HIKING

Walking in the Fôret des Maures is delightful. The Collobrières tourist office (p144) has details on hikes, including one to the **Châtaignier**

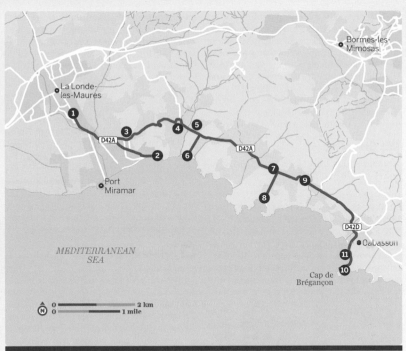

Cycling Tour
Pedal-Powered Wine Tasting

START LA LONDE
END PLAGE DE CABASSON
LENGTH 11 KM

Start at ❶ **Syril Bike Azur** (☎ 04 94 15 92 99; www.facebook.com/syrilbikeazur.locationvelo) in La Londe: find it by following the main street south; at the traffic lights, turn onto av Général de Gaulle, then continue for 400m, cross the roundabout, and carry on for 700m. There you can pick up wheels and La Londe's pea-green cycling track. Soon scenic views of perfectly symmetrical rows of vines kick in. At the next roundabout, detour 1km to ❷ **Plage d'Argentière** for a swim and snorkel along an aquatic nature trail, or continue east along the D42a following signs for Fort de Brégançon.

You're now on Route des Vins de la Londe. ❸ **Château des Bormettes** (☎ 04 94 66 81 35; www.chateaudesbormettes.com) is framed by palm trees; pedalling 2km further, you'll come to another dreamy château, where ❹ **Clos Mireille** (☎ 04 94 01 53 50; www.domaines-ott. com), one of the region's most highly regarded wines, has been produced since 1896.

At the next junction, bear right towards the fort and Bormes-les-Mimosas. Two needle pines mark the entrance to ❺ **Domaine de la Sanglière** (☎ 04 94 00 48 58; www.domaine-sangliere.com), where you can nibble wild boar with your wine. Some 200m further east is the entrance to ❻ **Plage du Pellegrin**, the private beach of Château de Léoube, 1.7km further down the road. Stock up on fresh fruit at the ❼ **fruit stall** 700m east of the château and carry on 200m to ❽ **Parc de l'Esagnot** for a picnic on its white sandy beach. Lunch done, pedal 500m to ❾ **Château de Brégançon** (☎ 04 94 64 80 73; www.chateau-de-bregancon.fr), a shabby old château with 40-year-old vines facing the sea. Its Reserve du Château white makes a brilliant marriage with shellfish.

Don't confuse the château with 16th- to 18th-century ❿ **Fort de Brégançon**, sign-posted 500m further east down the D42d on the western side of Cap de Brégançon. Once you're in front of the heavily guarded entrance to the fort, where the president of France summers (and has since 1968), park up and flop out on the rocky cape's gorgeous beach, sandy ⓫ **Plage de Cabasson**.

de Madame (the biggest chestnut tree in Provence, with a mighty 10.4m circumference, still appreciable and popular despite largely burning down in 1980). Another walk visits the two biggest menhirs in the Var, heritage-listed monuments raised between 3000 and 2000 BCE and each over 3m in height.

Be warned – both walks are four hours, one-way: three shorter walking trails are mapped on the noticeboard outside the office.

🛏 Sleeping

The tourist office lists local *gîtes* (cottages), hotels and B&Bs online.

Hôtel Les Maures HOTEL €

(☑ 04 94 48 07 10; www.hoteldesmaures.fr; 19 bd Lazare Carnot; d from €65, half-/full-board €20/35; ❄ 🖥) The same family has run this hub, Collobrières' most popular watering-hole, since 1886. Above the convivial bar there are 15 excellent-value, very comfortable rooms. There's also a perfectly decent restaurant (menus €16 to €25) and a river terrace for warm weather.

Hôtel Notre Dame HOTEL €€

(☑ 04 94 48 07 13; www.hotel-collobrieres.com; 15 av de la Libération; d from €101; ❄ 🖥 🏊) Occupying an ochre-painted 18th-century townhouse, Collobrières' most high-end option has 10 rooms individually decorated around jewel themes (coral, amethyst, topaz, rose and pearl). There's a restaurant and a very small pool. Breakfast is €12 if you don't pay for it when you book.

🍴 Eating

★La Petite Fontaine FRENCH €€

(☑ 04 94 48 00 12; 6 place de la République; menus €27-33; ⊙ noon-1.30pm & 7.30-9pm Tue-Sat, noon-1.30pm Sun) Locals travel from miles around to sit at a tree-shaded table on place de la République and feast on *daube de boeuf* (beef stew), forest mushrooms and house-made terrine, at one of southern France's most charming, relaxed village inns. The walls inside are exposed stone, and the fruit tarts are out of this world. Reservations are essential, as is cash.

We dare you to try the *broussain:* leftover cheeses mixed with Marc de Provence liqueur, olive oil and garlic – pungent!

Ferme de Peïgros FRENCH €€

(☑ 04 94 48 03 83; http://fermedepeigros.pagesperso-orange.fr; Col de Babaou; menus €29; ⊙ noon-2pm Jan-Dec, 7-9.30pm Jul & Aug; 🅿) Treat yourself to real mountain food: wild boar, pheasant, capon, kid, *cèpes* (porcini

mushrooms) and other delicacies. Finish with chestnut ice cream and superb views at this goat farm, 1.8km along a gravel track from the top of the Col de Babaou (8km from Collobrières). You can also stay at one of two *gîtes* (per week €305). Bring cash.

La Farigoulette FRENCH €€

(☑ 04 94 36 64 26; www.restaurantlafarigoulette. over-blog.com; 2 bd Lazare Carnot; lunch/dinner menus €27/35; ⊙ noon-2pm & 7.30-9pm Thu-Tue mid-Jan–mid-Dec; 🌱) Local produce – especially chestnuts, which appear in soups, crème brûlée, and many other dishes when they're in season – is a feature of the excellent cooking at this small, welcoming restaurant. Decor features tiled floors, yellow photo-covered walls and homely bric-a-brac. There are also simple guest-rooms upstairs (from €70).

🛍 Shopping

Meni & Fils FOOD

(☑ 04 94 48 08 63; 9 place de la République; ⊙ 6am-noon & 3.30-7.30pm Tue-Sun) Meni (Gerard) and son make an astonishing array of sausages, terrines, cured meats and pre-prepared dishes in this tiny shop, the very image of an artisanal French *charcuterie/boucherie*. If you have access to a kitchen, pick up some *daube de sanglier* (Provençal wild-boar stew) for a great meal in.

Confiserie Azuréenne FOOD

(☑ 04 94 48 07 20; www.confiserieazureenne.com; bd Kœnig; marrons glacés from €6.80; ⊙ 9.30am-12.30pm year-round; 1.30-7.30pm summer, 2-6pm winter) This local producer of chestnut products has a well-stocked shop of *marrons glacés* (candied chestnuts), chestnut ice cream, *crème de marrons* (chestnut cream) and chestnut liqueur. There's also a small, free museum showing how chestnuts are processed. Great for presents.

ℹ Information

Tourist Office (☑ 04 94 48 08 00; www. collobrieres-tourisme.com; bd Charles Caminat; ⊙ 9am-12.30pm & 2-5.30pm Mon-Wed & Fri-Sat, 2-5.30pm Thu, 9am-12.30pm Sun Jul & Aug, shorter hours rest of year) Has maps for local walks, and lists *gîtes* and B&Bs in the area online. Also has display-only examples of the wines, terrines, chestnut preserves and other typical products available in the village.

ℹ Getting There & Away

VarLib (www.varlib.fr) buses go to/from Hyères (€3.50 minutes, up to four daily) and Toulon (€3, 1¾ hours, up to five daily).

HAUT-VAR

The northern half of the Var *département* (north of the A8), known as the Northern or Upper Var, is vastly different from its coastal counterpart. Peaceful hilltop villages drowse beneath the midday sun, and are within easy reach of the wild Gorges du Verdon. Skip Draguignan, the hard-nosed main town where the French army maintains its largest military base, and head for the hills: lush vineyards, earthy black truffles and a bounty of gastronomic delights await.

🛏 Sleeping & Eating

All of the Haut-Var's larger and/or more popular villages offer accommodation – often traditional and good-value. Check ahead for seasonal closures. You won't find anything especially luxurious in some (Correns), whereas others (Cotignac) have some lovely rural accommodation in the surrounding vineyards and olive groves.

The Haut-Var is famous truffle, chestnut and wild game territory. Across the region plenty of highly respected restaurants (both in the towns and surrounding countryside) are able to turn these ingredients into something truly memorable. Always plan and book ahead, as many places are seasonal.

ℹ Information

Most villages in the Haut-Var have excellent tourist offices, which have pooled resources to create the co-operative **Provence Verte** (www. la-provence-verte.net). Check **Visit Var** (www. visitvar.fr) for details on the entire region. The Haut-Var is divided into sections served by their own tourist boards and governments.

For area **winemakers**, visit www.vinsde provence.com. **Le Var Campsites** booklets are available at tourist offices, while **Gîtes de France** (www.gites-de-france-var.fr) has country rentals.

ℹ Getting There & Away

The best way to get around the Haut-Var is with your own wheels.

Draguignan is the main hub for buses in the Haut-Var, running to many of the towns you may wish to visit.

East of Draguignan

The hills and villages to the east and south of Draguignan fall into the Dracénie region. As you depart the more built-up areas, you'll emerge into picturesque country graced with vineyards and handsome hilltop villages.

DON'T MISS

DELIGHTFUL DRIVES

The D14 runs through Collobrières, the largest town in the massif and the chestnut capital of the universe, and is graced with superb panoramas. It's a particularly popular route for cyclists. Similarly dramatic, the D39 from Collobrières soars north to Notre Dame des Anges (780m) before plunging down to Gonfaron. Running parallel to the D14, the N98 skims through vineyards and cork oak plantations from St-Tropez to Bormes-les-Mimosas.

From La Môle – where you can find a delicious meal at Auberge de la Môle (p142) – the breathtakingly narrow Col du Canadel (D27) dives to the coast, dishing up unbeatable views of the Massif des Maures, coastline and islands.

Les Arcs-sur-Argens

POP 7143

The extended urban development around Les Arcs is about as exciting as you'd expect, but the nearby area (such as the stretch along the D25) is rich in vineyards and wine-tasting opportunities. There are some great restaurants, and the medieval summit of Les Arcs is an unexpected highlight. St Rosaline was born there in 1263 in the 12th-century **château** where she later performed the 'miracle of roses': turning bread into roses.

◉ Sights & Activities

★ **Chapelle Sainte-Roseline**   CHURCH
(☑ 04 94 73 30 13; www.diocese-frejus-toulon.com; rte de Ste-Roseline (D91); ⊙ 2.30-6.30pm Thu-Sun Jun-Sep, shorter hours rest of year; ℗) A 1975 mosaic by Marc Chagall illuminates this 13th-century Romanesque chapel, 4.5km east of Les Arcs-sur-Argens. The church contains a crystal shrine holding the corpse of St Roseline (1263–1329), who was born at the château in Les Arcs and eventually became a Carthusian nun and mother superior here. She experienced visions and was said to be able to curtail demons. Other artists' work also graces the chapel, and concerts are held here in July and August.

★ **Maison des Vins Côtes de Provence**   WINE
(☑ 04 94 99 50 20; www.caveaucp.fr; N7; ⊙ 10am-7pm Mon-Sat, to 6pm Sun Apr-Sep) This bacchanalian House of Wines, 2.5km southwest of

Les Arcs-sur-Argens on the N7, is a one-stop shop to taste, learn about and buy (at producers' prices) Côtes de Provence wines. Each week 16 of the 800 wines from 250 wine estates are selected for tasting. Knowledgeable multilingual staff advise you on the perfect dish to eat with each wine.

Château Ste-Roseline   WINE
(☏04 94 99 50 36; www.sainte-roseline.com; D91; ⊙9am-12.30pm & 2-6.30pm Mon-Fri, 10am-12.30pm & 2-6pm Sat & Sun) Sample and buy a prestigious *cru classé* (top vintage) wine, produced here since the 14th century. The château adjoins the Chapelle de Ste-Rosaline. Tasting and sales are available whenever the *cave* is open.

🛏 Sleeping & Eating

The medieval crown atop Les Arcs has some lovely sleeps, not necessarily evident from the urban sprawl below. If you're just looking for a cheaper modern place to rest before you move on, then stay in the lower town; if you want something special, prepare to climb up the steep cobbled streets to the medieval town.

★Logis du Guetteur   FRENCH €€€
(☏04 94 99 51 10; www.logisduguetteur.com; place du Château; menus €40-110; ⊙noon-2pm & 7.15-9.30pm Feb-Dec; 🅿❄📶) This serious restaurant perches at the summit of Les Arcs in a 12th-century château. In winter, dine in the renovated *cave* beneath paintings of white peacocks and cornucopia; in summer, sit on the terrace, with views all around. Dishes such as confit duckling with truffled potato are sublime, service is attentive, and the ambience is carefully created.

You can also stay over in simple, stylish rooms (from €130).

❶ Getting There & Away

Les Arcs is a very handy hub for onward bus connections within Var, including to Aups (€3, 70 minutes, up to five daily), Toulon (€3, 1¾ hours, up to five daily) and Draguignan (€3, 10 minutes, up to six daily). Buses leave from the same area as the train station: av de la Gare.

Les Arcs Draguignan train station has up to two services per hour to Marseille (€24, two hours).

La Motte

POP 2931

Its red-tiled roofs framed by green hillsides, La Motte is a flourishing centre of viticulture, surrounded by 11 different wineries. The town

itself is quintessentially Provençal and well worth a stop for its quiet tangle of streets, convivial squares, limestone houses and bubbling fountains. Watered by the Nartuby and Endre Rivers, the area has been inhabited at least since Celtic times, although the oldest remaining building is the parish church, which dates to the 11th century and was largely reconstructed in the 18th. La Motte has the distinction of being the first town in Provence liberated (by paratroopers) in WWII – a fact celebrated in the naming of the av du 15 Août 1944, which runs through the centre of town.

🛏 Sleeping & Eating

There are only a handful of eating options in La Motte, but they're generally a cut above (plus the unavoidable pizza place). It's in the surrounding vineyards, however, that you'll find the most rewarding dining.

Le Mas du Péré   B&B €€
(☏04 94 84 33 52; www.lemasdupere.com; 280 chemin du Péré, La Motte; d €117, studio per week €930; ❄@🏊) In a quiet area to the north of La Motte village, this is a very pleasant spot from which to go wine tasting in the region. Perfectly clean, well-appointed rooms in muted tones look out on the pool. Some have dappled terraces; studios have kitchenettes.

★Domaine de la Maurette   BISTRO €€
(☏04 94 45 92 82; www.restaurant-lamaurette. com; 2290 rte de Callas, D25; mains €24-28, menus €29-37; ⊙noon-2pm Mon, Thu & Sun, noon-2pm & 7.30-9.30pm Fri & Sat; 🚗) For an authentic Provençal feast, head east out of La Motte along the D47 to this rustic wine estate on the intersection of the D47 and D25. Taste and buy wine, and dine on a vine-covered terrace next to the vines, enjoying *onglet* (skirt) steak in shallot sauce, scallops with truffle cream and other indulgences.

❶ Getting There & Away

Bus 2602 passes through La Motte up to seven times a day: all fares are €3, with destinations including Draguignan (20 minutes) and Fréjus (40 minutes).

Callas

POP 1851

The largely 18th-century streetscapes of this small hill town, which sits 400m above prime olive- and grape-growing country, are a charm to wander, admiring fountains of pitted stone and venerable churches. Beyond the ancient centre are the natural beauty of the **Pennafort Gorge** and re-markable religious buildings such as the **Chapelle Ste-Auxile,** 1.5km from town.

From the central village square in Callas you get a stunning panorama of the red-rock **Massif de l'Estérel**. The village lanes wind up the hill in a warren of bends.

⊙ Sights

Moulin de Callas   FARM
(📞 04 94 39 03 20; www.moulindecallas.com; Les Ferrages, just off D25; ⊙ 10am-noon & 3-7pm Mon-Sat Jun-Sep, 10am-noon & 2-6pm Mon-Sat Oct-Apr) FREE Picturesque plantations spread out around this farm at the foot of Callas, where Andrew, Mathieu and Anthony Bérenguier are the fourth generation of an olive-growing dynasty stretching back to 1928. Admire the old water-wheel, learn about olive oil production and then purchase some in the on-site shop, which also carries a broad array of regional soaps, honeys and other products. In-depth tours and tastings can be pre-arranged (some are free, others very reasonable).

ⓘ Information

Callas Tourist Office (📞 04 94 39 06 77; www.tourisme-dracenie.com; place du 18 Juin 1940; ⊙ 9.30am-12.30pm & 1.30-5pm Tue-Thu, 9.30am-12.30pm Mon & Fri) A friendly and well-resourced source of information on Callas and the Haut-Var.

ⓘ Getting There & Away

Callas is not currently served by any bus lines. It's 24km along the D54 from Les Arcs, or 18km from Draguignan along the Vieille Route de Grasse.

Bargemon

POP 1429

Sitting pretty on a monumental rock in a sea of olive fields, the medieval village of Bargemon is quiet and well preserved, offering excellent views across the valley to the neighbouring town of Claviers. Testament to the hill-town's former prominence are in its twisting streets, powerful ramparts, imposing churches (of which 15th-century **St-Etienne** and 17th-century **Notre Dame de Montaigu** are the most significant), beautifully maintained 14th-century **Château Reclos** and late-16th-century artillery **Tour du Clos**. But it's really the relaxed, well-preserved town itself, interspersed with quiet, fountained squares, rather than any stand-out attraction, that's worth exploring. Market day is Thursday.

✖ Eating

★ **La Pescalune**   INTERNATIONAL €€
(📞 06 29 94 66 64; www.la-pescalune.fr; 13 rue de la Résistance; mains €19-22; ⊙ 6.30pm-1am Tue-Sat, 11am-3pm Sun) Presiding over one of the region's top kitchens, Virginie Martinelli ensures the menu is tailored to the best of what is seasonally available. Expect dishes inspired as much by world cuisines as her own upbringing in Haute-Savoie and Provence: Vietnamese salads, bream with lemongrass-mussel broth, and other dishes as intriguing as they are delicious.

ⓘ Information

Bargemon Tourist Office (📞 04 94 47 81 73; www.ot-bargemon.fr; av Pasteur; ⊙ 9.15am-12.15pm & 1.45-5pm Mon-Fri Sep-Jun, 9.30am-12.30pm & 2.30-6pm Jul & Aug) Rents bikes for those who fancy a day cycling (bikes/e-bikes €20/25).

ⓘ Getting There & Away

There's no public transport to Bargemon. If you're driving, it's 18km northeast of Draguignan along the D25.

Seillans

POP 2600

Possibly settled by the Greek colonists who made lives for themselves in Provence 500 years before Christ, Seillans is a steeply cobbled hill town that retains much of its medieval layout, and is well worth a few hours' exploration. It's crowned by a 13th-century castle and chapel, which can only be admired externally. Like so many of Haut-Var's best preserved old towns, Seillans' primary joy lies in just wandering and admiring its character and beauty. Probably the most famous recent resident of this archetypal hill town was the surrealist artist Max Ernst, who lived here from 1953 until his death in 1976.

⊙ Sights

Tanning-Ernst Collection   GALLERY
(📞 04 94 76 85 91; www.seillans.fr; Maison Waldberg, place du Thouron,; adult/child €3/free; ⊙ 2-5.30pm Wed, Thu & Sat, 10am-1pm & 2.30-5.30pm & 10am-1pm Thu-Fri) FREE Sharing the Maison Waldberg with the Seillans tourist office is this gallery of work by Dorothea Tanning and surrealist Max Ernst, who lived in Seillans from 1964 until his death in 1976. They bequeathed their collection of lithographs and other work to the city.

VAR EAST OF DRAGUIGNAN

🛏 Sleeping & Eating

Seillans' popularity with French holidaymakers means a good range of options, and higher prices. Book ahead, especially in summer.

The town also hides some very pleasant restaurants in its twisting medieval streets. Definitely reserve ahead in high season.

★**Hôtel des Deux Rocs** INN €€
(📞 04 94 76 87 32; www.hoteldeuxrocs.com; 1 place Font d'Amont; s/d €95/150; mains €19-23; ⊗ restaurant noon-2pm & 7-9.30pm Wed-Sun Feb-Dec; 🛜) This boutique hotel with fig-flower Fragonard soap in the bathrooms, a fine collection of old black-and-white family photos and a gourmet restaurant, wins the prize hands down for most atmospheric village inn in Seillans. The soulful *bastide* is home to the Malzacs, who run their 13-room hotel with admirable panache. Summer dining is alfresco around a fountain. Scipion, knight of the Flotte d'Agout, lived here in the 17th century.

ℹ️ Information

Tourist Office (📞 04 94 76 85 91; www.paysdefayence.com; Maison Waldberg, place Thouron; ⊗ 10am-12.30pm & 2.30-6.30pm Mon-Sat, 2.30-5.30pm Sun mid-Jun–mid-Sep, shorter hours rest of year) Small but useful source of advice on Seillans and surrounds.

ℹ️ Getting There & Away

Seillans is well connected by bus to Cannes (€5, 1½ hours, up to six on school days), Draguignan (€3, 30 minutes, up to four on school days), St Raphael (€3, 1½ hours, up to five on school days) and several other local destinations.

West of Draguignan

The quaint villages and folded hills west of Draguignan roll north towards the Gorges du Verdon. They fall across the regions known as Provence Verte and the Coeur de Var: wine and truffle country.

Lorgues

POP 9042

Lorgues is a hub within great wine country, with an exceptional number of respected vineyards and winemakers in its immediate surrounds, including some plantings of great antiquity. It naturally makes a good base for a day or two of oenophilic tourism, and offers great opportunities to buy something special for those at home, without paying retail prices.

It's also ensconced between two rivers and low, attractive hills, the perfect backdrop for its harmoniously coloured stone buildings. Throw in some lovely old fountains, churches and oil mills, one of France's best-preserved and most ravishingly handsome abbeys, and a truly great truffle restaurant, and the case for making a detour to this quiet town becomes near impossible to dismiss. If you're in town on Tuesday morning, the weekly market is one of the region's biggest and best.

⊙ Sights

★**Abbaye de Thoronet** ABBEY
(📞 04 94 60 43 90; www.le-thoronet.fr; off the D79, Le Thoronet; adult/child €8/free; ⊗ 10am-6.30pm Jun-Sep, shorter hours Oct-May; 🅿️) The simplest but most beautiful of 'The Sisters' (a trio of great Provençal Cistercian abbeys including Silvacane and Notre-Dame de Sénanque), Thoronet, built between 1160 and 1190, is a masterpiece of sacred architecture. It's remarkable for its ultra-austere style: pure proportions, perfectly dressed stone and the subtle fall of light and shadow on unadorned, but never severe, geometry. It's so well preserved that it's easy to imagine the strict lives the monks (and particularly the lay brothers) led.

There's so much to see, but highlights include the graceful cloisters, the deliberately unadorned church, the chapter house, lavabo and cellars. Definitely fork out for the enlightening €3 audioguide. It's 14km from Lorgues, concealed in beech woods.

Domaine de l'Abbaye WINERY
(Franc Petit; 📞 04 94 73 87 36; Quartier Pugette, off rte de Carcès, D84, Le Thoronet; ⊗ 9am-noon&1-6pm Mon-Sat, other times by appointment; 🅿️) Excellent wines are produced using traditional methods, in vineyards originally cultivated by monks in the 12th century. Ring the bell if it seems no one is around during opening hours.

🍴 Eating

★**Chez Bruno** GASTRONOMY €€€
(📞 04 94 85 93 93; www.restaurantbruno.com; rte des Arcs, D10; menus €78-195; ⊗ 12.30-2.30pm & 7.30-9.30pm mid-Jun–mid-Sep, shorter hours rest of year; 🅿️) If truffles are the most divine of ingredients, then Chez Bruno is their high temple. It's just 2.5km southeast of Lorgues; drive through giant truffle-sculptured gates to the grounds of an

18th-century estate that belonged to the eponymous Bruno's grandmother. Now a Michelin-starred restaurant, it gets through 5000kg of the little delicacies each year.

Chef Bruno largely leaves the cooking to son Benjamin now, but is still intimately involved. The grounds themselves are a delight, and you may be tempted to stay in one of the lovely rooms, amidst olive groves and kitchen gardens (rooms from €200).

ⓘ Information

Lorgues Tourist Office (☑ 04 94 73 92 37; www.lorgues-tourisme.fr; 12 rue du 8 Mai; ☉9am-12.15pm & 2.30-6pm Mon-Sat, 9am-12.15pm Sun Jul & Aug, shorter hours rest of year) Has maps of walks and a list of hotels. Lorgues itself isn't the most fascinating Provençal town, but there are plenty of vineyards, medieval villages and other delights in the area that the generous staff are happy to advise on.

ⓘ Getting There & Away

Lorgues is well connected, with multiple local bus services, including to Tourtour (€3, 30 minutes, one to two daily), Draguignan (€3, 20 minutes, two to three daily during school terms), Le Thoronet (€3, 15 minutes, one to two daily during school terms) and other destinations.

Tourtour

POP 587

Tourtour is a beautiful amber-stoned village, with a churchyard stretching across a promontory offering panoramic views. It makes a handy place to break your journey, stroll the cobbled lanes filled with galleries and shops, or indulge your truffle fancy. **Market days** are Wednesday and Saturday mornings.

✗ Eating

Restaurants congregate on the shady place des Ormeaux on the upper edge of town. Most offer great regional cuisine.

L'Alechou   BISTRO €
(☑ 04 94 70 54 76; 16 rue Grande; mains €9-15; ☉11.30am-10.30pm) The petite dimensions and flower-baskets of this attractive place on the main street probably draw more custom than the crêpes and salads, but they're perfectly acceptable, so no need to feel hard done by.

★ **Les Chênes Verts**   GASTRONOMY €€€
(☑ 04 94 70 55 06; rte de Villecroze, D51; menus €60-160; ☉noon-1.30pm & 7.30-9pm Mon & Thu-Sat, noon-1.30pm Sun Aug-May; Ⓟ) On the road

between Tourtour and the equally lovely Haut-Var village of Villecroze is a turn-off you might easily miss, unawares. Yet the 'The Green Oaks' holds a Michelin star, courtesy of chef Paul Bajade's way with truffles and other top-notch ingredients. Such is his attachment to the fungus that the restaurant closes in the hot months unconducive to truffles.

ⓘ Information

Tourist Office (☑ 04 94 70 59 47; www.tourisme-tourtour.com; montée de St-Dénis; ☉10am-12.30pm & 3-6.30pm Jun-Aug, shorter hours rest of year) Stocked with accommodation and activity listings.

ⓘ Getting There & Away

VarLib (www.varlib.fr) buses run to Lorgues (€3, 30 minutes, one to two per day) and Aups (€3, 30 minutes, one daily).

Aups

POP 2134

Amber-hued Aups has a history that goes back much further than even its antique streets suggest, having been a Celtic *oppidum* (fortified settlement), Roman town, and even a Moorish stronghold. Now it would be best known as a gateway to the Gorges du Verdon to the north, if not for the period from November to late February that precious black gold – *Tuber melanosporum* (black truffles) – matures beneath its frigid ground. These alien-looking nuggets of black fungus are revered throughout France, ending up on many a Michelin-starred table. They can be viewed (and bought, if you have the coin) at the Thursday-morning **truffle market** on Aups' central plane-tree-studded square.

Truffle hunts and truffle-hunting demonstrations lure a crowd in January during Aups' annual Journée de la Truffe Noir (p150).

◉ Sights

Maison de la Truffe   MUSEUM
(Truffle House; ☑ 04 94 84 00 69; www.maisondelatruffe-verdon.fr; place Martin Bidouré; Truffle Adventure adult/child €2.50/1.50; ☉9am-noon & 2-5pm Mon-Sat Sep-Jun, to 6.30pm Jul & Aug) Attached to Aups tourist office you'll find this shop selling the 'black diamond' of Aups in various forms (whole, in pastes and pastas). It's also home to the Truffle Adventure, an interactive and multisensory space exploring the precious fungus, its history and gastronomy. Truffle-hunting and -eating can be arranged.

🎊 Festivals & Events

Journée de la Truffe Noire FOOD & DRINK
(☑ 06 84 81 48 41; place Frédéric Mistral; ☺ late Jan) For 25 years now Aups, the epicentre of the Haut-Var's prized black truffle, has turned its largest public space into a day-long celebration of the knobbly delicacy. There are tastings of all sorts of truffle concoctions, music, truffle-dog competitions, and plenty of truffle dishes cooked up by local restaurateurs.

🛏 Sleeping & Eating

There are only a handful of hotels in Aups' traditional centre, but what there are offer good value. The eating is good in Aups, with a number of higher-class restaurants devoted to local cuisine, especially truffles.

Restaurant des Gourmets PROVENCAL €€
(☑ 04 94 70 14 97; www.restaurantdesgourmets. fr; 5 rue Voltaire; menus €24-39; ☺ noon-1.30pm & 7-9pm Tue & Thu-Sat, noon-1.30pm Wed & Sun Dec-Oct) One of the best places in Aups to try the famous local truffles, Des Gourmets serves up fantastic regional fare beneath frescoes of the Provençal seasons.

ℹ Information

Aups Tourist Office (☑ 04 94 84 00 69; www. aups-tourisme.com; place Martin Bidouré; ☺ 9am-12.30pm & 2.30-6.30pm Mon-Sat, 9am-12.30pm Sun mid-Jul—mid-Aug, to 5.30pm Mon-Sat May—mid-Jul & mid-Aug—Oct, shorter hours rest of year) Lists of local truffle producers, hotels and activities. They can connect you with local truffle hunters who can take you on a hunt.

ℹ Getting There & Away

VarLib (www.varlib.fr) runs buses connecting Aups with Les Arcs (line 1201, €3, one hour, up to four daily), Brignoles (line 1404, €3, 1¼ hours, up to two daily), and multiple lesser destinations.

Entrecasteaux

POP 1105

Entrecasteaux, with its elegant château, fountain-clad square, and old stone houses, perches dramatically over a river. The village is known for its honey, and the wines produced in the surrounding hills. Wandering the streets, admiring 16th-century buildings, ducking into the 13th-century Église Saint-Sauveur and snapping pictures of the two 18th-century bridges all make for a pleasant afternoon.

◉ Sights

Château d'Entrecasteaux CHATEAU
(☑ 04 94 04 43 95; www.chateau-entrecasteaux. com; 2 rue le Courtil; adult/child €10/5; ☺ tour 4pm Sun Easter-Jun, 4pm Sun & Mon Jul-Sep) While there's been a fortress on this site since the 11th century, the present handsome pile was assembled piecemeal between the 15th and 18th centuries. Its *oubliettes* (bottle-necked dungeons), vaulted ceilings, ornamental gardens and period furniture represent a melange of styles, but are no less impressive for it.

🍴 Eating

Drink something local with your meal at one of Entrecasteaux's cafe-bars. Most are unpretentious, unadorned, and aimed at locals, but the *vin ordinaire* can always be trusted.

Bar Central CAFE
(☑ 04 94 04 43 53; 2 cours Gabriel Péri; ☺ 6am-9.30pm Tue-Sun) Grab a coffee at the green-canopied Bar Central – you won't get more local and unfussy than this.

Chez Ellie INTERNATIONAL €€
(☑ 06 33 66 06 66; www.chezelliegrignotage.com; 9bis cours Gabriél Péri; mains €18-20; ☺ noon-3pm & 7-10pm Tue-Sat, noon-3pm Sun summer, noon-3pm Tue-Sun winter) A real passion for produce and the world's full palette of flavours shines through in this modern bistro – a clean-lined, innovative alternative to the sweet traditionalism that prevails in Entrecasteaux. Owner-chef Ellie Grignotage, having cooked in Asian restaurants in the States, is very comfortable with eastern flavours and techniques, and plugged in to great local suppliers.

ℹ Getting There & Away

You'll need your own wheels for Entrecasteaux. It's 14 km along the D50 from Lorgues, or 8km along the D562 and D31 from Carcès.

Cotignac

POP 2254

Huddled picturesquely into the shelter of a towering 400m-long tufa (limestone) cliff-face, the quiet stone village of Cotignac is a real picture. The River Cassole and the tree-lined promenade of the cours Gambetta run through its 'modern' heart, but above this there are 'troglodyte' dwellings cut directly into the rock face. The Tuesday-morning market is lively, and the tourist office has maps of walks to the village's chapels (including the Shrine of Our Lady of Graces, a minor place of pilgrimage), fountains and squares.

🏃 Activities

Les Vignerons de Cotignac   WINE
(📋 04 94 04 60 04; www.vigneronsdecotignac.com; 1 rue Arnoux Borghino; ⊕9am-12.30pm & 2-6pm Tue-Sat, 2-6pm Mon Sep-Jun, to 7pm Jul & Aug) The 330 hectares of Cotignac's appellation produce some very nice wines, of which their producers are justly proud. This collective is the spot to taste and buy some local rosé.

🛏️ Sleeping & Eating

With recent closures, there's nowhere to sleep within Cotignac at present, but some very pleasant options are in the nearby countryside. These out-of-town lodgings make for such peaceful and reviving options that you won't mind the dearth of choices in town.

Les Fouguières   CAMPGROUND €
(📋 04 94 59 96 28; www.camping-les-fouguieres.com; 165 chemin des Fouguières; 2-person site/cottage €30/100; ⊕mid-Mar–mid-Nov; P 🛜 🏊) Pleasantly sited near the town of Carcès, in the bucolic wine country between Thoronet and Cotignac, this family-oriented campground offers bungalows and shady sites by the Caramy River. There's plenty to do in the surrounding countryside, from wine-tasting to horse-riding. Prices drop outside high summer.

Mas de l'Olivette   B&B €€
(📋 04 94 80 28 73; www.masdelolivette.com; 1779 chemin de Blain, rte d'Entrecasteaux, D50; d per 2 nights €210, studio per week €800; 🏊 🛜 🏊) The lovely Jean-Claude and Yannick welcome you so warmly to their tiny B&B that it feels like home. The two impeccable, beautifully appointed guest rooms – decked out in pleasing terracotta, stone, whitewash and Provençal decor, with L'Occitane products in the bathrooms – can adjoin for families. The spotless, freestanding studio has a kitchen, terrace and views across the olive groves. There's a one-week minimum stay for the studio, and a two-night minimum for the guest rooms.

🍴 Le Clos des Vignes   FRENCH €€
(📋 06 87 82 30 11, 04 94 04 72 19; www.restaurant-le-clos-des-vignes.fr; rte de Monfort, D22; menus €26-39; ⊕noon-2pm & 7.30-9.30pm Tue-Sat; P) Seek out this farmhouse for the home-cooked cuisine (by husband Jean-Luc) and the warm welcome (by wife Dany). House-made *foie gras* features frequently, as do veal and fresh seafood. It's at its best in summer, when you can dine on the terrace by the vines.

La Table des Coquelicots   FRENCH €€
(📋 04 94 69 46 07; 10 cours Gambetta; menus €23-35; ⊕noon-3pm & 7-9.30pm Tue-Sat, noon-3pm Sun) Choose between the elegant, muted dining room or the people-watching terrace under the plane trees. Open year-round, 'The Poppy Table' offers classic bistro food (entrecôte, rack of lamb, hot goats-cheese salad and numerous fish dishes) and enormous profiteroles. Not much for vegetarians, unfortunately.

ℹ️ Information

Tourist office (📋 04 94 04 61 87; www.ot-cotignac.provenceverte.fr; Pont de la Cassole, rte de Carcès, D13; ⊕9am-12.30pm & 2-7pm Mon-Sat, 9am-1pm Sun Jul & Aug, shorter hours rest of year) Near the bridge at the south of the village.

ℹ️ Getting There & Away

VarLib (www.varlib.fr) offers bus connections to Brignoles (line 1404, €3), Carcès (line 1404, €3) and Lorgues (line 4223, €3).

Correns

POP 893

Spreading out from the 12th-century Fort Gibron (a monastic building adapted and fortified over the years), Correns is a charming if sleepy village straddling the Argens River with a handsome arched bridge. Surrounded by vineyards, wine is Correns' lifeblood. It makes a lovely place to top and stretch your legs, but there are few sights likely to fascinate.

In 1997 the mayor of Correns, on the banks of the River Argens, decided to make the village's 200 hectares of AOC Côtes de Provence vineyards organic. Local farmers have also since turned organic to produce honey, chicken, eggs, olive oil and goats cheese.

⊙ Sights & Activities

★ Vallon Sourn   NATURE RESERVE
(www.provenceverte.co.uk; D45) The protected Vallon Sourn, where the swift waters of the Argens have cut a picturesque canyon from the soft rock, is a haven for for walking, cycling, canoeing, wild swimming and even rock climbing (although be warned – these rock faces are for serious climbers only). A scenic drive/ride from Correns, north on the D45 towards Châteauvert, will get you there.

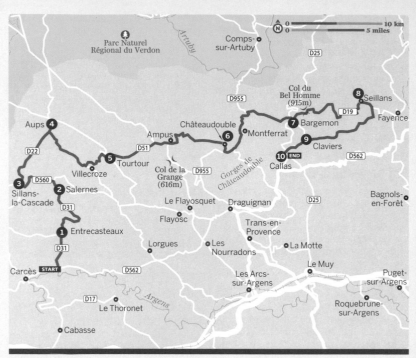

Driving Tour
Haut-Var Hilltop Villages

START ENTRECASTEAUX
END CALLAS
LENGTH 91KM; ONE DAY

Start with a wander around gorgeous hilltop **1 Entrecasteaux**, its giant 17th-century château the centrepiece of formal gardens perching dramatically along the river.

Bear right along the D31 and drive another wiggly 6km to **2 Salernes**, where hand-made terracotta tiles called *terres cuites* (literally 'baked earth') have been manufactured since the 18th century. The tourist office has a list of workshops to visit.

From Salernes, pick up the westbound D2560 and subsequent D560 to **3 Sillans-la-Cascade**, a gem of a fortified village with a waterfall, on the banks of the River Bresque. Then it's 9km north along the D22 to **4 Aups**, an unhurried village that's ground zero for Haut-Var's famous truffles. From here, it's a genuinely stunning 10km drive south-east past olive groves and lavender gardens to the 'eagle nest' gold-stone village of

5 Tourtour. Buy olive oil in the village and, in mid-December, watch olives being pressed in its 17th-century *moulin à huile;* the tourist office runs guided tours of the mill.

Six kilometres further east along the D51 you'll encounter Ampus; continue east 9km to **6 Châteaudouble**, an astonishing village clinging to a cliff of the Gorges de Châteaudouble.

Just 7km east of here is **7 Bargemon**, a village with a maze of medieval streets and ramparts to stroll and an excellent bistro, La Pescalune, in which to dine.

8 Seillans, a scenic 12km drive east, is an irresistibly pretty, typical Provençal village with cobbled lanes coiling to its crown, and a village inn, Hôtel des Deux Rocs, that only the stone-hearted will be able to resist.

If you have any gas left in your proverbial tank, you can circle back south to **9 Claviers** and **10 Callas**, yet more picturesque villages.

Château de Miraval
WINERY

(www.miraval-provence.com) Sitting in a delightful valley planted with ancient vines and olive groves, Château de Miraval was a monastery in the 13th century, then legendary Miraval recording studio (where Pink Floyd recorded part of *The Wall* in 1979). It shut its doors in 2008 when Brad Pitt, Angelina Jolie and kids moved into the gold-stone property on the vast 400-hectare estate, but it still makes some of the most valued wine in the region.

Vignerons de Correns
WINE

(☑ 04 94 59 59 46; www.vigneronsdecorrens.fr; rue de l'Église; ⊙ 2.30-7pm Mon-Fri, 9.30am-12.30pm & 2.30-7pm Sat) Taste and buy Château de Miraval and other big Correns wine names such as Domaine de la Grande Pallière at this producers' cooperative and shop on the outskirts of Correns. Founded in 1935, the co-op also has branches in Lo Val and Aups.

Les Caves du Commandeur
WINE

(☑ 04 94 59 59 02; www.caves-du-commandeur.fr; 18 rue des Moulins, D22, Montfort-sur-Argens; ⊙ 9am-12.30pm & 2.30-6.30pm Mon-Sat) This *domaine* of AOC Côtes de Provence and IGP Var wines has a giant facility for tasting and sales. It's in Montfort-sur-Argens, 6km east of Correns.

✖ Eating

You may need to drive, but you'll find some pleasant places to eat in the wine country surrounding Correns. The town itself has a pizza restaurant, a bistro/*auberge* and little else.

Auberge de Correns
FRENCH €€

(☑ 04 94 59 53 52; www.aubergedecorrens.fr; 34 place du Général de Gaulle; 2-/3-course menus €18/23; ⊙ noon-1.45pm & 7-8.45pm Jul & Aug, Thu-Mon Mar-Jun, Fri-Mon Nov-Feb; 🐾) Lunch well, and mostly organically, here, where the cuisine is innovative and market-driven, the wine list features local varieties, and mains are as sizeable as the elegant (if slightly outmoded) guest rooms (doubles with breakfast €99).

ℹ Information

Correns Tourist Office (☑ 04 94 37 21 95; www. correns.fr; 5 place Général de Gaulle, Mairie; ⊙ 9am-noon Tue-Sat) Now housed in the Town Hall, Correns' Tourist Office dispenses information about the town, the region and its wine.

ℹ Getting There & Away

VarLib (www.varlib.fr) buses 1404, 1424 and 4423 pass through Correns to Aups, Brignoles and Cotignac. Fares are only €3 and travel times less than 20 minutes, but services are rare.

MASSIF DE LA STE-BAUME

Dividing the *départements* of Bouches-du-Rhône and Var is the Massif de la Ste-Baume, a mountainous ridge 1147m high. Declared a Regional Natural Park in 2017, its 847 sq km are mostly covered in beech, oak and yew forest, and contain the mythical last resting place of Mary Magdalene. But it's not just a place of religious pilgrimage: honeycombed with caves, sheltering an abundance of flora and fauna, and offering glorious walking, it's a destination for nature-lovers, too. The views from the summit of the massif are incredible.

Other than wilderness and holy sites, there's the village of Plan-d'Aups-Sainte-Baume, an extremely quiet and pleasant Provençal mountain village.

⊙ Sights

Grotte de Ste-Madeleine
CAVE

(www.saintebaume.org/grotte; ⊙ hostel 7.30am-10pm) **FREE** A 40-minute forest trail leads from La Ste-Baume to the Grotte de Ste-Madeleine (950m), a mountain cave where Mary Magdalene is said to have spent the last years of her life. Its entrance offers a breathtaking panorama of Montagne Ste-Victoire, Mont Ventoux and the Alps. Dominican Friars have developed the grotto as a place of pilgrimage for over 700 years, building the Hostellerie de la Sainte-Baume in 1835 to welcome pilgrims.

🛏 Sleeping & Eating

Either stay in the Dominican hostel at the Grotte de Ste-Madeleine, or find a room in one of Plan-d'Aups-Sainte-Baume's three hotels. The hostel serves three meals a day at the Grotte de Ste-Madeleine. Other than that, Plan-d'Aups-Sainte-Baume has three hotel/restaurants.

Hôtel Le Couvent Royal
FRENCH €€

(☑ 04 94 86 55 66; www.hotel-lecouventroyal.fr; place Jean Salusse, St-Maximin-la-Ste-Baume; menus €20-55, d €80; 🅿🐾) This former Dominican convent has been converted into a sumptuous hotel, which has an elegant restaurant serving traditional French cuisine based on fresh Provençal produce. Its 13th- and 14th-century architecture has been repurposed delightfully. Parking is €10 per day.

ℹ Getting There & Away

You'll need your own car to mount the Massif de la Ste-Baume. It's a little over an hour's drive from Marseille.

Bouches-du-Rhône

Best Places to Eat

➜ L'Epuisette (p171)

➜ La Table de Ventabren (p192)

➜ La Table de Pierre Reboul (p191)

➜ Le Petit Verdot (p189)

Best Places to Stay

➜ Villa Gallici (p188)

➜ Intercontinental Marseille – Hôtel Dieu (p170)

➜ Hôtel les Quatre Dauphins (p188)

➜ Hôtel Edmond Rostand (p169)

Why Go?

The 'mouths-of-the-Rhône', where one of Europe's great rivers splits before spilling its Swiss-Alpine snowmelt into the Mediterranean, is Provence's most populous *département*. Its palpitating heart is Marseille, a gritty former Greek colony, France's second-largest city, and a place of real cultural energy. Centred on the bristling masts and bluff forts of the Vieux Port, it has a strong Maghrebian flavour – imported from nearby Tunisia, Algeria and Morocco – and the idiosyncratic pride of a long-established seafaring city, which runs counterpoint to the restless energy of its arts, dining and cultural scenes. Spreading out from Marseille's concrete margins are pine-swaddled coastal uplands cut by ravishingly beautiful *calanques* (coves), while inland is the still-thriving Roman spa town of Aix-en-Provence, reposing handsomely in the Pays d'Aix (Aix Country) so beloved of Cézanne.

Driving Distances (km)

	Cassis	Marignane (Airport)	Marseille	Salon de Provence
Marignane (Airport)	55			
Marseille	25	25		
Salon de Provence	80	30	30	
St-Remy-de-Provence	120	75	70	35

ⓘ Getting There & Away

The Bouches-du-Rhône *département* is well-connected by air, road, rail and sea to the rest of Provence, as well as to France, the Mediterranean and several countries beyond. The **Aéroport Marseille-Provence** (p329), 25km from its namesake city, is the principal point of entry for those arriving by air, with select connections to North America, Africa and the Middle East, and excellent connections to European cities.

High-speed TGV trains link Marseille with Paris, Lyon and Lille, while slower services head west (to Montpellier), north (to Avignon) and east (to Nice and Italy).

The A7, A8, A9 and A51 are the principal *autoroutes* for those travelling by road.

The main ferry port is located in the Joliette area of Marseille, with regular services to Corsica, Sardinia (Italy), Algeria and Tunisia.

ⓘ Getting Around

Unlike most of Provence, which is best seen with your own wheels, you will be grateful *not* to have a car in Marseille and Aix-en-Provence. Driving is difficult, parking is expensive and public transport is great in both cities (especially Marseille). Yet some of Marseille's outlying jewels – such as the wild coastline of the Parc National des Calanques and the ridge-top Route des Crêtes – do require a car. Or, better still, a motorbike (provided you know what you're doing and conditions are good).

MARSEILLE

POP 861,635

Grit and grandeur coexist seamlessly in Marseille, an exuberantly multicultural port city with a pedigree stretching back to classical Greece and a fair claim to the mantle of France's second city. Once seen as somewhat dirty and dangerous, and lacking the glamour of Cannes or St-Tropez, this black sheep of the Provençal coastline has blossomed in cultural confidence since its 2013 stint as the European Capital of Culture. The addition of a brace of swanky museums is just the outward sign of an optimism and self-belief that's almost palpable.

Marseille's heart is the vibrant Vieux Port (old port), mast-to-mast with yachts and pleasure boats. Just uphill is the ancient Le Panier neighbourhood, the oldest section of the city. Also worth an explore is the République quarter, with its stylish boutiques and Haussmannian buildings, and the Joliette area, centred on Marseille's totemic Cathédrale de Marseille Notre Dame de la Major (p159).

History

Around 600 BCE, Greek mariners founded Massilia, a trading post, at what is now Marseille's Vieux Port. In the 1st century BCE the city lost out by backing Pompey the Great rather than Julius Caesar: Caesar's forces captured Massilia in 49 BCE and directed Roman trade elsewhere.

Marseille became part of France in the 1480s. Its citizens embraced the French Revolution, sending 500 volunteers to defend Paris in 1792. Heading north, they sang a rousing march, ever after dubbed 'La Marseillaise' – now the national anthem. Trade with North Africa escalated after France occupied Algeria in 1830 and the Suez Canal opened in 1869. After the World Wars, a steady flow of migration from North Africa began and with it the rapid expansion of Marseille's periphery. Since 1995 the Marseille-Euroméditerranée urban renewal and economic development project has worked wonders, improving the city geographically and culturally.

◉ Sights

Bear in mind that a majority of museums close on Mondays.

★**Vieux Port**   PORT
(Old Port; Map p166; Ⓜ Vieux Port) Ships have docked for millennia at Marseille's birthplace, the vibrant Vieux Port. The main commercial docks were transferred to the Joliette area in the 1840s, but the old port remains a thriving harbour for fishing boats, pleasure yachts and tourist boats. Guarded by the forts St-Jean (p158) and **St-Nicolas** (Map p166; 1 bd Charles Livon; ◲ 83), both sides of the port are dotted with bars, brasseries and cafes, with more to be found around place Thiars and cours Honoré d'Estienne d'Orves, where the action continues until late. (For more details, see p164).

★**Le Panier**   AREA
(Map p166; Ⓜ Vieux Port) 'The Basket' is Marseille's oldest quarter – site of the original Greek settlement and nicknamed for its steep streets and buildings. Its close, village-like feel, artsy ambience, cool hidden squares and sun-baked cafes make it a delight to explore. Rebuilt after destruction in WWII, its mishmash of lanes hide artisan shops, *ateliers* (workshops) and terraced houses strung with drying washing. Its centrepiece is La Vieille Charité (p158).

BOUCHES-DU-RHÔNE MARSEILLE

Bouches-du-Rhône Highlights

1 Marseille (p155) Appreciating world-class museums, 2600 years of history and an innovative cultural scene.

2 Parc National des Calanques (p177) Hiking through sun-warmed pines, before plunging into secluded *calanques* (coves).

3 Bouillabaisse (p171) Submitting to the full, five-course fish extravaganza in classic coastal restaurants like Le Rhul.

4 Aix-en-Provence (p184) Revelling in elegant architecture and arts in this former Roman spa town.

5 Cassis (p181) Visiting this charming village for a glass of Provence's finest.

6 Montagne Ste-Victoire (p190) Climbing the Pays d'Aix stark limestone centrepiece, immortalised by Cézanne.

7 Îles du Frioul (p163) Stalking seabirds across these dramatic islands off Marseille, then exploring the forbidding Château d'If, fictional prison of the Count of Monte Cristo.

8 Route des Crêtes (p179) Gripping 15km of hairpin turns on this seasonal, coastal road, metres above the rocks and wild breakers below.

9 St-Rémy-de-Provence (p193) Exploring the Roman town of Glanum and visiting an asylum where Van Gogh lived.

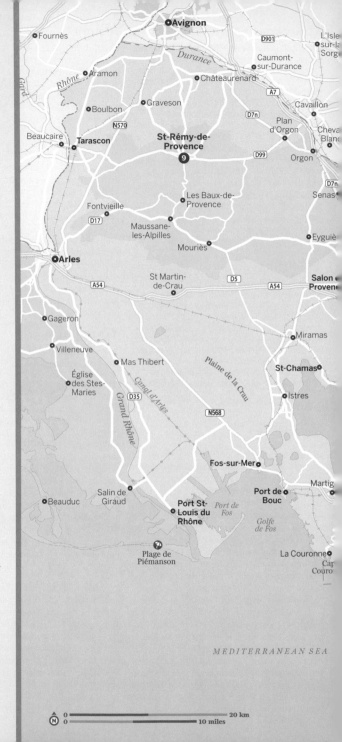

...tions de
...terranée   MUSEUM
...an & Mediterranean Civ-
...4 35 13 13; www.mucem.
...font; adult/child incl ex-
...m-8pm Wed-Mon Jul &
...y-Jun & Sep-Oct, 11am-
...   M Vieux Port, Joliette)
...seille, this stunning
...history, culture and
civilisation of the Mediterranean region
through anthropological exhibits, rotating
art exhibitions and film. The collection sits in
a bold, contemporary building designed by
Algerian-born, Marseille-educated architect
Rudy Ricciotti, and Roland Carta. It is linked
by a vertigo-inducing footbridge to the 13th-
century **Fort St-Jean** (Map p166; M Vieux Port),
from which there are stupendous views of
the Vieux Port and the surrounding sea. The
fort grounds and gardens are free to explore.

★ Basilique Notre Dame
de la Garde   BASILICA
(Montée de la Bonne Mère; Map p160; ☑ 04 91 13
40 80; www.notredamedelagarde.com; rue Fort du
Sanctuaire; ◷ 7am-8pm Apr-Sep, to 7pm Oct-Mar;
🚌 60) Occupying Marseille's highest point,
La Garde (154m), this opulent 19th-century
Romano-Byzantine basilica is Marseille's most-
visited icon. Built on the foundations of a
16th-century fort, which was itself an enlargement of a 13th-century chapel, the basilica is
ornamented with coloured marble, superb
Byzantine-style mosaics, and murals depicting ships sailing under the protection of La

Bonne Mère ('The Good Mother'). The campanile supports a 9.7m-tall gilded statue of said
Mother on a 12m-high pedestal, and the hilltop gives 360-degree panoramas of the city.

Villa Méditerranée   MUSEUM
(Map p166; ☑ 04 95 09 42 70; www.villa-mediterra
nee.org; esplanade du J4, off bd du Littoral; ◷ noon-
6pm Tue-Fri, from 10am Sat & Sun; 🚻; M Vieux Port,
Joliette) **FREE** This eye-catching white structure next to MuCEM is no ordinary 'villa'.
Designed by architect Stefano Boeri in 2013,
the sleek edifice sports a spectacular cantile-
ver overhanging an ornamental pool. Inside, a
viewing gallery with glass-panelled floor (look
down if you dare!), and two or three temporary multimedia exhibitions evoke aspects of
the Mediterranean, be they aquatic, historical
or environmental. Not unlike MuCEM, the
building itself is the undisputed highlight.

★ La Vieille Charité   HISTORIC BUILDING
(Map p166; ☑ 04 91 14 58 80; www.vieille-charite-mar
seille.com; 2 rue de la Charité; museums adult/child
€6/free; ◷ 10am-6pm Tue-Sun mid-Sep–mid-May,
longer hours in summer; M Joliette) In the heart of
Marseille's Le Panier quarter is this grand and
gorgeous almshouse, built by Pierre Puget
(1620–94), an architect and sculptor born just
a couple of streets away who rose to become
Louis XIV's architect. With its neoclassical
central chapel and elegant arcaded courtyard,
it's a structure of great harmony and grace.
Entry is free, although there's a charge to visit
the excellent **Musée d'Archéologie Méditer-
ranéenne** (Museum of Mediterranean Archeology;

MARSEILLE IN FOUR DAYS

Breakfast quayside, watching the fish market (p176) before an early Frioul If Express
ferry to Château d'If (p163) and the Îles du Frioul (p163). You may be back in port for
tagine at La Goulette (p171).

On the Vieux-Port's northern side, you'll be kept busy by MuCEM, Fort St-Jean, the
Villa Méditerranée, Notre Dame de Major, La Vieille Charité and the bars and boutiques
of Le Panier (p155). A great dinner at intimate L'Arôme (p172) awaits.

Next morning, climb to the iconic Basilique Notre Dame de la Garde, snap superb
views from the Jardin du Pharo (Map p160; 58 bd Charles Livon; ◷ 8am-9pm; 🚌 81, 82, 83),
then sample real bouillabaisse at Michel (p171). Don't miss the Abbaye St-Victor (p162),
or the Musée Cantini as you head back to rest.

Day three is for exploring the further-flung delights of La Cité Radieuse (p159), Parc
Borély (p163) and the Vallon des Auffes (p162), ideal for a seafood lunch. Bus 83 will
carry you back to Opéra Municipal de Marseille (p175), where nearby bars, boutiques
and restaurants should account for the rest of your day.

Day four is where things get contemporary: make the trip out to La Friche La Belle de
Mai (p174), eating at its superb restaurant Les Grandes Tables (p170), then head to bohemian cours Julien for drinks at Waaw (p173).

Map p166; ☑04 91 14 58 59; www.culture.marseille.
fr) and **Musée d'Arts Africains, Océaniens
et Amériden** (Museum of African, Oceanic &
American Indian Art; Map p166; ☑04 91 14 58 38;
www.marseille.fr/node/630), both housed within.
There's also a nice cafe just inside the gateway.

Cathédrale de Marseille
Notre Dame de la Major   CATHEDRAL
(Map p166; ☑04 91 90 52 87; www.marseille.
catholique.fr/La-Major-cathedrale; place de la Major;
◷10am-6.30pm Wed-Sun Apr-Sep, to 5.30pm Oct-
Mar; ⓜJoliette) Standing guard between the
old and new ports is the striking 19th-century
Cathédrale de la Major. After its foundation
stone was laid by Napoleon III in 1852, the
'New Major' took over 40 years to complete. It
boasts a Byzantine-style façade made of local
Cassis stone and green Florentine marble.

La Joliette   AREA
(Map p160; ⓜJoliette, ⓡJoliette) The old maritime neighbourhood of La Joliette, mori-
bund since the decline of the 19th-century
docks, has been revitalised by bars, boutiques and restaurants. Ferries still depart
for ports around the Med, but the long sweep
of 19th-century commercial facades along
Quai de la Joliette has been given an impressive scrub. Here you'll find Marché de la Joliette (p176), one of Marseille's buzziest markets, and **Les Docks** (Map p160, ☑04 91 44
25 28; www.lesdocks-marseille.com; ◷10am-7pm)
– abandoned 19th-century warehouses now
filled with shops, boutiques and galleries.

Musée Cantini   GALLERY
(Map p166; ☑04 91 54 77 75; www.culture.marseille.
fr; 19 rue Grignan; adult/child €6/free; ◷10am-
7pm Tue-Sun mid-May–mid-Sep, to 6pm mid-Sep–
mid-May; ⓜEstrangin-Préfecture) Donated to
the city by the sculptor Jules Cantini on his
death in 1916, this 17th-century mansion-
turned-museum holds some superb art. The
core collection boasts fantastic examples of
17th- and 18th-century Provençal art, including André Derain's *Pinède à Cassis* (1907) and
Raoul Dufy's *Paysage de l'Estaque* (1908). Another section is dedicated to work about Marseille, with pieces by Max Ernst, Joan Miró,
André Masson and others.

Musée des Beaux Arts   MUSEUM
(☑04 91 14 59 30; www.marseille.fr/node/639; 7 rue
Édouard Stephan; adult/child €6/free; ◷10am-7pm
Tue-Sun mid-May–mid-Sep, to 6pm mid-Sep–mid-
May; ⓹; ⓜCinq Avenues-Longchamp, ⓡLong-
champ) Set in the lavish, colonnaded Palais de
Longchamp, Marseille's oldest museum owes

DON'T MISS

MARSEILLE'S GALLERIES & MUSUEMS

Marseille's galleries and museums have
flourished in recent years. In addition to
the many makeovers of local institutions
like La Friche La Belle de Mai (p174), the
Musée des Beaux Arts and the Musée
Cantini, spectacular facilities have been
built for MuCEM and the **Fonds Régional d'Art Contemporain** (FRAC;
Map p160; ☑04 91 91 27 55; www.fracpaca.
org; 20 bd de Dunkerque; adult/child €5/
free; ◷noon-7pm Tue-Sat, 2-6pm Sun mid-
Mar–Nov, 11am-6pm Tue-Sat, 2-6pm Sun rest
of year; ⓜJoliette).

The outstanding arts organisation
Marseille Expos (www.marseilleexpos.
com) sponsors the festival **Printemps
de l'Art Contemporain** each May,
and also distributes an excellent map of
hot galleries. Copies can be obtained at
the Tourist Office, La Friche La Belle de
Mai and most theatres and museums.

its existence to an 1801 decree of pre-Napo-
leonic France's short-lived Consulate, which
established 15 museums across the country.
A treasure trove of 16th- to 19th century Italian and Provençal painting and sculpture, it's
set in parkland popular with local families
seeking shade in Marseille's treeless centre.
The spectacular fountains, constructed in
the 1860s, in part disguise the water tower at
which the Roquefavour Aqueduct terminates.

Musée d'Histoire de Marseille   MUSEUM
(History Museum of Marseille; Map p166; ☑04 91 55
36 00; http://musee-histoire.marseille.fr; 2 rue Hen-
ri-Barbusse; adult/child €6/free; ◷10am-7pm Tue-
Sun mid-May–mid-Sep, to 6pm mid-Sep–mid-May;
ⓜVieux Port) This intriguing 15,000-sq-metre
museum traces the story of 'France's Oldest
City' from prehistory (the paintings of the
Cosquer Cave) to the present day, across 12
chronological exhibitions. The complex was
built beside the remains of a Greek harbour
uncovered during construction of the Bourse
shopping centre. Highlights include the
remains of a 3rd-century merchant vessel discovered in the Vieux Port in 1974: to preserve
the soaked and decaying wood, it was freeze-
dried where it now sits, behind glass.

La Cité Radieuse   ARCHITECTURE
(Unité d'Habitation; ☑04 91 16 78 00; www.mar
seille-citeradieuse.org; 280 bd Michelet; ◷9am-6pm;
ⓡ83 or 21, stop Le Corbusier) **FREE** Visionary

BOUCHES-DU-RHÔNE MARSEILLE

Marseille

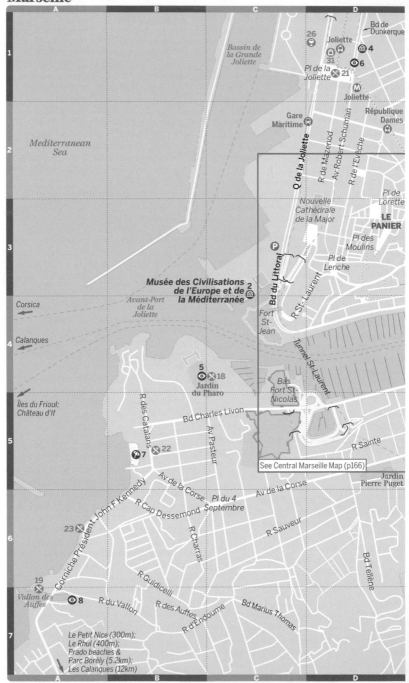

Bd de Dunkerque

26

Joliette

4

31

6

Pl de la Joliette

21

Joliette

République Dames

Gare Maritime

Q de la Joliette

R de Mazenod

Av Robert Schuman

R de l'Evêche

Pl de Lorette

Nouvelle Cathédrale de la Major

LE PANIER

Pl des Moulins

Mediterranean Sea

Bassin de la Grande Joliette

Pl de Lenche

Bd du Littoral

Musée des Civilisations de l'Europe et de la Méditerranée

2

Avant-Port de la Joliette

Fort St-Jean

R St-Laurent

Tunnel St-Laurent

Corsica

Calanques

5

18

Jardin du Pharo

Bas Fort St-Nicolas

Îles du Frioul; Château d'If

R des Catalans

Bd Charles Livon

See Central Marseille Map (p166)

R Sainte

7

22

Av Pasteur

Av de la Corse

Jardin Pierre Puget

Av de la Corse

Corniche Président John F Kennedy

R Cap Dessemond

Pl du 4 Septembre

R Charras

R Sauveur

Bd Tellene

23

19

Vallon des Auffes

8

R du Vallon

R des Auffes

R Guidicelli

R d'Endoume

Bd Marius Thomas

Le Petit Nice (300m);
Le Rhul (400m);
Prado beaches &
Parc Borély (5.2km);
Les Calanques (12km)

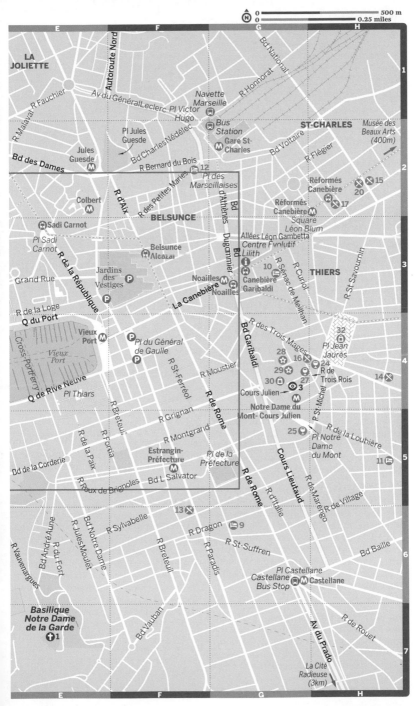

Marseille

modernist architect Le Corbusier redefined urban living in 1952 with the completion of this vertical 337-apartment tower, popularly known as La Cité Radieuse ('The Radiant City'). Its purpose was to increase residential density to allow for more green space. Today the apartments are joined by the Hôtel Le Corbusier, the high-end restaurant Le Ventre de l'Architecte and a rooftop terrace. English-language tours (10am Friday and Saturday; adult/child €10/5) can be booked through the tourist office (p176).

Abbaye St-Victor CHURCH
(Map p166; 3 rue de l'Abbaye; ◎9am-7pm; Ⓜ Vieux Port) To the west of the Vieux Port lies Abbaye St-Victor, the birthplace of Christianity in Marseille, built on a 3rd century BCE necropolis. It's €2 to visit the crypts, with guided tours available from 4pm to 6pm on Tuesdays and Thursdays (or download a 'tour' from www.saintvictor.net).

Cours Julien STREET
(Map p160; www.coursjulien.marsnet.org; Ⓜ Notre Dame du Mont-Cours Julien) Marseille's most vibrant bohemian quarter centres on Cours Julien, an elongated concrete square shaded by palm trees. It's lined with great bars, cafes and music venues, and its street-art-slathered sidestreets are home to a wealth of bookshops, galleries, tattoo parlours and ethnic restaurants. Markets are held in the square on several days of the week: flowers on Wednesday and Saturday, antique books alternate Saturdays, and stamps or antique books on Sunday.

◉ Along the Coast

Mesmerising views of another Marseille unfold along **corniche Président John F Kennedy**, the coastal road that cruises south to the small, beach-volleyball-busy **Plage des Catalans** (Map p160; 3 rue des Catalans; ◎8.30am-6.30pm; 🚌81, 82) and the fishing cove of **Vallon des Auffes** (Map p160; 🚌83).

Further south, the vast **Prado beaches** are marked by Jules Cantini's 1903 marble replica of Michelangelo's *David*. The beaches, all gold sand, were created from backfill from the excavations for Marseille's metro. They have a world-renowned **skate park**. Nearby lies expansive Parc Borély.

Promenade Georges Pompidou continues south to **Cap Croisette**, from where the beautiful Parc National des Calanques (p177) can be reached on foot.

To head down the coast, take bus 83 from the Vieux Port. At av du Prado switch to bus 19 to continue further. Espace Infos RTM (p177) sells tickets for ferries between the

Vieux Port and La Pointe Rouge, just to the south of the Prado beaches; the City Pass does not cover the ticket.

Musée d'Art Contemporain   GALLERY
(Museum of Contemporary Art, MAC; ☑ 04 91 25 01 07; www.culture.marseille.fr; 69 av de Haïfa; adult/child €9/free; ⊗ 10am-7pm Tue-Sun mid-May–mid-Sep, to 6pm mid-Sep–mid-May; ☐ 23 or 45) Creations of Marseille-born sculptor César Baldaccini (1921–98) jostle for space with works by Christo, Andy Warhol, Jean-Michel Basquiat and Nice New Realists Yves Klein and Ben in this repository for the most modern works held by the Musée Cantini. From the Prado metro station, take bus 23 or 45 to the Haïfa-Marie-Louise stop.

Château d'If   CASTLE
(☑ 06 03 06 25 26; www.if.monuments-nationaux. fr; Île d'If; adult/child €6/free; ⊗ 10am-6pm Apr-Sep, to 5pm Tue-Sun Oct-Mar) Commanding access to Marseille's Vieux Port, this photogenic island-fortress was immortalised in Alexandre Dumas' 1844 classic *The Count of Monte Cristo*. Many political prisoners were incarcerated here, including the Revolutionary hero Mirabeau and the Communards of 1871. Other than the island itself there's not a great deal to see, but it's worth visiting just for the views of the Vieux Port. **Frioul If Express** (Map p166; ☑ 04 96 11 03 50, www. frioul if-express.com; 1 quai de la Fraternité) runs boats (return €11, 20 minutes, up to 10daily) from Quai de la Fraternité.

Îles du Frioul   ISLAND
Around nine kilometres west of Marseille lie the dyke-linked limestone islands of Ratonneau and Pomègues, known jointly as the the Îles du Frioul. Seabirds and rare plants thrive on these tiny outcrops, which measure around 200 hectares combined. The remains of old fortifications add interest, and the islands offer excellent rambling. Frioul If Express boats to Château d'If also serve the Îles du Frioul (one/two islands return €11/16, 35 minutes, up to 21 daily).

Parc Borély   PARK
(av du Parc Borély; ☐ 19 or 83, stop Parc Borély) Five kilometres south of central Marseille, this 17th-century park encompasses a lake, a miniature of the Notre-Dame de la Garde cathedral, a botanical garden and the graceful 18th-century Château Borély, which houses the **Musée des Arts Décoratifs, de la Faïence et de la Mode** (Museum of Decorative Arts, Ceramics and Fashion; ☑ 04 91 55 33 60; www.

culture.marseille.fr; 134 av Clot Bey, Château Borély, Parc Borély; adult/child €6/free; ⊗ 10am-7pm Tue-Sun mid-May–mid-Sep, to 6pm mid-Sep–mid-May).

🏃 Activities

Marseille is a natural launch pad for exploring the nearby Parc National des Calanques (p177). Several boat tours depart from the Vieux Port.

Raskas Kayak   KAYAKING
(☑ 04 91 73 27 16; www.raskas-kayak.com; impasse du Dr Bonfils, Auberge de Jeunesse Marseille; half/full day €40/70) This well-established outfit is a great option for sea-kayaking excursions around the Vieux Port, islands, Cap Croisette and Les Calanques, leaving either from Marseille or Cassis. Trips are season- and weather-dependent, and can be booked online.

👉 Tours

Marseille Provence Greeters   WALKING
(www.marseilleprovencegreeters.com) A great idea: free walking tours led by locals, covering street art, history, food shops, football culture and lots more. Sign up in advance online and check whether your guide speaks English.

Guided Tours   TOURS
(☑ 08 26 50 05 00; www.marseille-tourisme.com; from €10; ⊙ Apr–Oct; Ⓜ Vieux Port) Run by the tourist office, these tours take in everything from the city's history to Le Corbusier's architectural experiments at La Cité Radieuse. There's an English-language tour of the Vieux Port and Le Panier every Saturday at 2pm. You can also download maps for self-guided walks from the tourist office website.

Croisières Marseille Calanques   BOATING
(Map p166; ☑ 04 91 58 50 58; www.croisieres-mar seille-calanques.com; 1 La Canebière, Vieux Port; Ⓜ Vieux Port) Runs 2¼-hour trips from the Vieux Port taking in six *calanques* (adult/child €23/18); 3¼-hour trips to Cassis passing

---

CITY PASS

The **Marseille City Pass** (www.resa-marseille.com; 24/48/72hr €26/33/41) covers admission to city museums and public transport, and includes a guided city tour and a Château d'If boat trip, plus other discounts. It's not necessary for children under 12, as many attractions are greatly reduced or free. Buy it online or at the tourist office.

Vieux Port

AN ITINERARY

Start with an early-morning coffee on the balcony at La Caravelle, with views of the boats bobbing in the harbour and Basilique Notre Dame de la Garde across the way.

Mosey down the quay to the sparkling ❶ **MuCEM** and its cantilevered neighbour ❷ **Villa Méditerranée** for a morning of art and culture. You'll enter through Fort St-Jean, and wind through rooftop gardens to reach the state-of-the-art museums.

Alternatively, take in green-and-white striped ❸ **Cathédrale de la Major** then explore the apricot-coloured alleys of ❹ **Le Panier**, browsing the exhibits at the ❺ **Centre de la Vieille Charité**, and shopping in the neighbourhood's tiny boutiques.

In the afternoon, hop on the cross-port ferry to the harbour's south side and take a ❻ **boat trip** to Château d'If, made famous by the Dumas novel *The Count of Monte Cristo*.

Or stroll under Norman Foster's mirrored pavilion, then wander into the ❼ **Abbaye St-Victor**, to see the bones of martyrs enshrined in gold.

As evening nears, you can catch the sunset from the stone benches in the ❽ **Jardin du Pharo**. Then as the warm southern night sets in, join the throngs on cours Honoré d'Estienne d'Orves, where you can drink pastis and people-watch beneath a giant statue of a lion devouring a man – the ❾ **Milo de Croton**.

Cathédrale de la Major
The striped façade of Marseille's cathedral is made from local Cassis stone and green Florentine marble. Its grand north staircase leads from Le Panier to La Joliette quarter

Villa Méditerranée ❷

MuCEM ❶

Palais & Jardin du Pharo

Musée des Civilisations de l'Europe et de la Méditerranée (MuCEM)
Explore the icon of modern Marseille. This stunning museum was designed by Rudy Ricciotti and Roland Carta, and is linked by a vertigo-inducing footbridge to 13th-century Fort St-Jean. You'll get stupendous views of the Vieux Port and the Mediterranean.

© ARCHITECTS RUDY RICCIOTTI & ROLAND CARTA/MUCEM. PHOTO BY LISA RICCIOTTI ©

Centre de la Vieille Charité

Before the 18th century, beggar hunters rounded up the poor for imprisonment. The Vieille Charité almshouse, which opened in 1749, improved their lot by acting as a workhouse. It's now an exhibition space and only the barred windows recall its original use.

Le Panier

The site of the Greek town of Massilia, Le Panier woos walkers with its sloping streets. Grand Rue follows the ancient road and opens out into place de Lenche, the location of the Greek market. It is still the place to shop for artisanal products.

LUCKY-WATER/SHUTTERSTOCK ©

Frioul If Express

Catch the Frioul If Express to Château d'If, France's equivalent to Alcatraz. Prisoners were housed according to class: the poorest at the bottom in windowless dungeons, the wealthiest in paid-for private cells, with windows and a fireplace.

Quai des Belges

La Caravelle →

Quai du Port

Cross-Port Ferry

Quai de Rive Neuve

Cours Honoré d'Estienne d'Orves

ort St-Jean

Bas Fort St-Nicolas

Milo de Croton

Subversive local artist Pierre Puget carved the savage *Milo de Croton* for Louis XIV. The statue, whose original is in the Louvre, is a meditation on human pride and shows the Greek Olympian being devoured by a lion, his Olympic cup cast down.

Abbaye St-Victor

St-Victor was built (420–30) to house the remains of tortured Christian martyrs. On Candlemas (2 February) the black Madonna is brought up from the crypt and the archbishop blesses the city and the sea.

Jardin du Pharo

Built by Napoléon III for the Empress Eugénie, the Pharo Palace was designed with its 'feet in the water'. Today it is a congress centre, but the gardens with their magnificent view are open all day.

Central Marseille

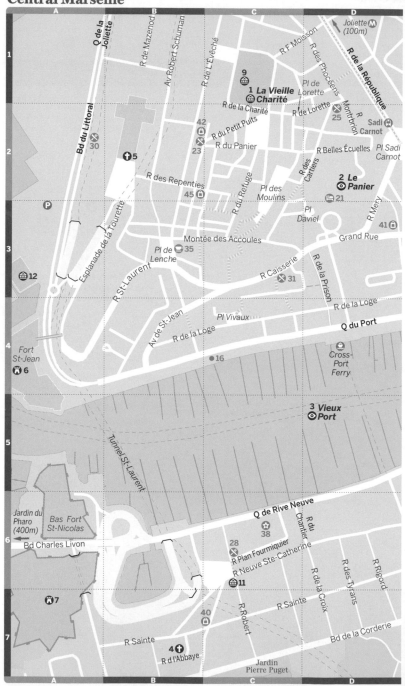

Q de la Joliette

Joliette Ⓜ (100m)

R de Mazenod

Av Robert Schuman

R de L'Évêché

R F Moisson

R des Phocéens

R de la République

9

1 La Vieille Charité

R de la Charité

Pl de Lorette

R de Lorette

25

Montbrion

Sadi Carnot

Bd du Littoral

30

5

42

R du Petit Puits

R du Panier

R Belles Écuelles

R des Cartiers

Pl Sadi Carnot

23

R des Repenties

45

R du Refuge

Pl des Moulins

2 Le Panier

21

R Mery

41

Pl Daviel

Montée des Accoules

35

Grand Rue

Pl de Lenche

R Caisserie

R de la Prison

31

R St-Laurent

Av de St-Jean

Pl Vivaux

R de la Loge

R de la Loge

Q du Port

Fort St-Jean

6

16

Cross-Port Ferry

3 Vieux Port

Tunnel St-Laurent

Jardin du Pharo (400m)

Bas Fort St-Nicolas

Q de Rive Neuve

38

Bd Charles Livon

28

R Plan Fourmiguier

R du Chantier

7

R Neuve Ste-Catherine

11

R de la Croix

R des Tyrans

R Rigord

40

R Robert

R Sainte

Bd de la Corderie

R Sainte

4

R d'l'Abbaye

Jardin Pierre Puget

12

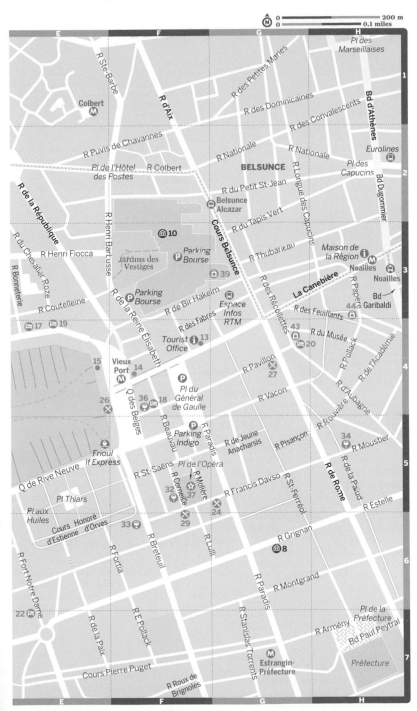

Central Marseille

BOUCHES-DU-RHÔNE MARSEILLE

12 *calanques* (adult/child €29/22); and 1¾-hour trips around the Baie de Marseille (€10), including Château d'If (add €6).

Tourist Train TOURS
(Map p166; ☑ 04 91 25 24 69; www.petit-train-marseille.com; 174 quai du Port; adult/child €8/4; ⊙ 10am-12.30pm & 2-6pm Apr–mid-Oct; shorter hours rest of year; ⊞; Ⓜ Vieux Port) These electric 'trains' trace two circular routes: to Notre Dame basilica and Old Marseille and the Terrasses du Port (April to December only). Tours last from 1¼- to 1¾-hours, with stops, and leave every 20 to 30 minutes in high season (less frequently from November to March).

Balades en Tuk-Tuk TOURS
(Map p166; ☑ 06 25 35 47 21; www.tuktukmarseille.com; Office du Tourisme et des Congrés, 11 La Canebière; 3-person tuk-tuk hire per 1/2/3 hrs €47/77/115) See Marseille's sights from the back of a buzzing tuk-tuk, then hop aboard

a boat to explore the surrounding coastline. There are various prearranged itineraries, including an option to visit Notre Dame de la Garde and Vallon des Auffes en route to a swim in the Calanque de Sormiou. Drivers speak English. Enquire at the tourist office.

✷✷ Festivals & Events

Carnaval de Marseille STREET CARNIVAL
(⊙ Mar or Apr) Marseille's version of Carnival centres on a parade and Saturday-afternoon *fête* (party) in Parc Borély (p163), with mad costumes, decorated floats and strolling circus acts.

Festival de Marseille PERFORMING ARTS
(www.festivaldemarseille.com; ⊙ Jun & Jul) Held over three weeks and four weekends in high summer, this international festival brings dance, theatre, music and art (and tens of thousands of visitors) to Marseille.

Five Continents Jazz Festival   MUSIC
(Marseille Jazz de Cinq Continents; www.marseille
jazz.com; ☺ Jul) International guests of the
calibre of Tony Allen, Branford Marsalis
and Herbie Hancock play alongside French
and European artists in this high-summer
celebration of jazz, held at venues across
town including MuCEM and the Palais
Longchamp.

Foire aux Santons   CHRISTMAS MARKET
(www.foire-aux-santons-de-marseille.fr;   ☺ 10am–
7pm 18 Nov to 31 Dec) Since 1803, *santonniers*
(traditional ceramic-figurine makers) have
displayed their creations at this fair, held in
the place du Général de Gaulle, just behind
the Vieux Port. Once purely religious icons,
the *santons* now take on a variety of forms.

🛏 Sleeping

There are modest hotels close to the train
station, but the good local-transit system
means that it's easy to reach the hotels scattered around the Vieux Port. Few hotels
have their own parking facilities, but most
central ones offer discounted rates at one of
the city's car parks.

★ **Vertigo Vieux-Port**   HOSTEL €
(Map p166; ☎ 04 91 54 42 95; www.hotelvertigo.
fr; 38 rue Fort Notre Dame; dm/tw €26/70; 🔲,
Ⓜ Vieux Port) This award-winning hostel
shows a swanky sleep is possible on a shoestring budget – for your euro you can expect
breakfast, murals by local artists, vintage
furniture, stripped wooden floors and original architectural details such as exposed
wooden beams and stone arches. All rooms
have their own modern bathrooms, and
there are lockers, a good kitchen and a TV
lounge.

Vertigo Saint-Charles   HOSTEL €
(Map p160; ☎ 04 91 91 07 11; www.hotelvertigo.fr;
42 rue des Petites Maries; dm/tw €31/86; @ 🛜;
Ⓜ Gare St-Charles) This snappy boutique
hostel kisses dodgy bunks and hospital-like
decor goodbye. Here it's 'hello' to vintage
posters, a designer chrome kitchen, contemporary communal spaces (including a bar
and outdoor area) and polite multilingual
staff. Double rooms are particularly good;
some have private terraces. No curfew (or
lift, alas).

★ **Hôtel Edmond Rostand**   DESIGN HOTEL €€
(Map p160; ☎ 04 91 37 74 95; www.hoteledmond
rostand.com; 31 rue Dragon; s/d/tr €100/110/135;
❉ @ 🛜; Ⓜ Estrangin-Préfecture) Push past the

unassuming façade of this great-value hotel
in the Quartier des Antiquaires to find a stylish interior with a communal lounge area, a
cafe and 15 rooms dressed in crisp white and
soothing natural hues. Some rooms overlook
a tiny private garden and others the Basilique Notre Dame de la Garde.

★ **Mama Shelter**   DESIGN HOTEL €€
(Map p160; ☎ 04 84 35 20 00; www.mamashelter.
com; 64 rue de la Loubière; d from €113; 🅿 ❉ 🛜;
Ⓜ Notre Dame du Mont-Cours Julien) Part of a
funky mini-chain of design-forward hotels,
Marseille's Mama Shelter offers 125 Philippe
Starck-imagined rooms over five floors.
It's all about keeping the cool kids happy
here – with sleek white-and-chrome colour
schemes, a live stage and bar and a giant
babi foot (fussball) table. Smaller rooms are
oddly shaped, however, and it's a walk from
the Vieux Port.

★ **Hôtel St-Louis**   HISTORIC HOTEL €€
(Map p166; ☎ 04 91 54 02 74; www.hotel-st-louis.
com; 2 rue des Récollettes; d €113; ❉ 🛜;
Ⓜ Noailles, 🚋 Canebière Garibaldi) The stuc-
coed façade, wrought-iron balconies and
'mini-museum' of this charming hotel pay
homage to its 19th-century origins. Each of
the rooms is unique – from the 'Kenya' (dedicated to Satao, a Kenyan elephant killed by
poachers in 2014) to the 'Yorkshire', inspired
by an English cottage – and a few have little
balconies. Continental breakfasts can be up-
graded to full English on request.

Hotel Carré Vieux Port   HOTEL €€
(Map p166; ☎ 04 91 33 02 33; www.hotel-carre-
vieux-port.com; 6 rue Beauvau; s/d/tr €97/111/151;
❉ 🛜) Sitting pretty between the quai des
Belges and place Général de Gaulle, this
well-maintained hotel rates as one of the old
port's top choices. Its rooms are bright, spacious and comfortable, and you'll enjoy nice
touches like frying-pan-sized shower heads,
cube-shaped bath goodies, complimentary
tea, coffee and biscuits and (naturally) the
fibreglass bull in reception.

Le Ryad   BOUTIQUE HOTEL €€
(Map p160; ☎ 04 91 47 74 54; www.hoteldemar
seille.fr; 16 rue Sénac de Meilhan; d/ste €111/191;
🛜; Ⓜ Noailles, 🚋 Canebière Garibaldi) Morocco comes to Marseille at this stylish hotel,
which takes its inspiration from the *riads*
of North Africa, all woven cushions, patterned rugs and colourful throws. There's
a lovely garden, the top-floor room ('Mog-
ador') has its own mini roof terrace, and the

BOUCHES-DU-RHÔNE MARSEILLE

Moroccan breakfast – with North African pancakes and fresh fruit – is worth the extra €7 per person.

Hotel Bellevue
HOTEL €€

(Map p166; ☑ 04 96 17 05 40; www.hotelbelle vuemarseille.com; 34 quai du Port; s/d €95/155; ❄@☺; Ⓜ Vieux Port) Rooms at this enduring 1950s hotel are tastefully decorated with midrange simplicity, but the portside views are million-dollar. Breakfast can be delivered to your room for €15, but selecting it from the buffet (€10) on the pocket-sized balcony of the hotel's portside cafe La Caravelle (p173) is a Marseille highlight. Prices can hike during special events.

Villa Monticelli
B&B €€

(☑ 0491221520, 0627427403; www.villamonticelli. com; 96 rue du Commandant Rolland; r from €125; ℙ❄☺; ☐ 86, Ⓜ Rond-Point du Prado) English-speaking host Sébastien is passionate about Marseille, and the five exquisite *chambres d'hôte* in his beautifully-restored villa are worth the slightly outer-city location, in quiet streets favoured by consulates. Breakfast is a delight of homemade local specialities, served on the terrace, with lovely views.

Intercontinental Marseille – Hôtel Dieu
LUXURY HOTEL €€€

(Map p166; ☑ 04 13 42 42 42; http://marseille. intercontinental.com; 1 place Daviel; r from €230; ℙ❄@☺☼; Ⓜ Colbert, ☐ Sadi Carnot) Occupying a heritage-listed 18th-century hospital, the Hôtel Dieu, the Intercontinental Marseille has a commanding position in Le Panier overlooking the Vieux Port. The grand U-shaped pile features tall arched windows framed by local golden-hued stone and masonry. Within, the 179 rooms and 15 suites are suitably polished, while the best have either harbour views or private terraces.

Hôtel La Résidence du Vieux Port
DESIGN HOTEL €€€

(Map p166; ☑ 04 91 91 91 22; www.hotel-resi dence-marseille.com; 18 quai du Port; d from €219; ❄@☺; Ⓜ Vieux Port) Externally as attractive as a multistorey car park, this portside hotel scores big on interior design and views. Its rooms are self-consciously retro – think bold primary colours, art in the styles of Miró and Mondrian, '50s-style furniture and Anglepoise lamps – and most come with port-view balconies. The ultimate is the 8th-floor Suite Ciel (Sky Suite).

 Eating

The Vieux Port and surrounding pedestrian streets teem with cafe terraces, but choose carefully (some rely on tourists to pay too much for average food). For world cuisine, try cours Julien and nearby rue des Trois Mages. For pizza, roast chicken, and Middle Eastern food under €10, nose around the streets surrounding Marché des Capucins (p176).

★ El Santo Cachon
CHILEAN €

(Map p160; ☑ 06 95 99 45 93; 40 rue Ferrari; mains €16-18; ☺ 7.30pm-midnight Mon-Sat; ☐ Eugene Pierre) Arrive early or reserve a table at Marseille's only Chilean restaurant, because this place fills fast – and after a pisco sour (or three), you'll see why. If you want to make it out of the door walking, combat the frothy cocktail's effects with deliciously heavy fried cheese empanadas. The *ceviche mixto* of fresh fish and octopus is great too.

★ Les Grandes Tables
INTERNATIONAL €

(☑ 04 95 04 95 85; www.lesgrandestables.com; 41 rue Jobin, La Friche La Belle de Mai; mains €16; ☺ noon-2pm Sun-Wed, noon-2pm & 8-10pm Thu-Sat; ☐ 49, 52) The vast former canteen at the vibrant La Friche La Belle de Mai cultural centre manages to pull off the trick of seeming both intimate and stylish. Working with local producers, a young and friendly team serve imaginative food, such as candied lamb shank with parmesan polenta, or seared tuna with thyme, sesame and chickpea puree, to clued-up diners at communal tables.

Vanille Noire
ICE CREAM €

(Map p166; ☑ 07 77 33 68 19; www.vanillenoire. com; 13 rue Caisserie; ice cream €2; ☺ 12.30pm-6.45pm; Ⓜ Vieux Port) There are plenty of ice-cream shops around Marseille, but there's only one that sells black ice cream (coloured by vanilla pods, which lend a unique, bitter-sweet, custardy flavour). There are around 30 other flavours of ice cream and sorbet to try, all made on-site with organic ingredients. Go for the pastis or lavender to keep it Provençal.

Le Bar à Pain
BAKERY €

(Map p160; ☑ 06 45 17 37 33; 18 cours Joseph Thierry; lunch €4-5; ☺ 8am-8pm Tue-Fri, to 6pm Sat; ☐ Canebière) Selling arguably the best baguettes in the city, this charming organic bakery in the Chapitre neighbourhood also rustles together tasty midday snacks like flaky courgette tarts and toasty tomato pizzas, all to be enjoyed on their suntrap of a terrace. The coffee is excellent too, and don't leave without trying a Ti Coco, their rum-laden coconut ball.

La Goulette
TUNISIAN €

(Map p166; ☑ 04 91 33 39 90; 1 rue Pavillon; mains €7-14; ☺ 9am-11pm) Locals in the know and homesick Tunisians flock to this bustling, tiled restaurant, named for the main port of Tunis. A *couscous maison* of vegetables, *brochettes* (skewers), *côtelettes d'agneau* (lamb chops), *merguez* (sausage) and *kefta* (meatballs) is best followed with sweet mint tea and a pastry from the bounty in the window.

La Cantine de Nour d'Egypte
EGYPTIAN €

(Map p160; ☑ 09 80 63 06 56; www.nourdegypte.com; 10 rue Bernex; mains €14-16; ☺ 11.30am-11pm Mon-Thu & Sat, to 4.30pm Sun, 3.30pm-11pm Fri; 🚇 National) Nestled within a welcoming Egyptian cultural centre, this cheery restaurant serves dishes of thick Egyptian flatbread, chunky hummus, creamy aubergine caviar and crispy felafel, all from an open kitchen. Choose from a menu scrawled on the window each day, and finish with a dessert of nutty pastries and fresh mint tea among cushions, blankets and Egyptian mosaics.

Chez Étienne
PIZZA €

(Map p166; 43 rue de Lorette; pizza €13-15, mains €16-18; ☺ noon-2pm & 8-11pm Mon-Sat; 🚻; Ⓜ Colbert) Family photos and veteran service staff hint at the longevity of this Le Panier favourite, known for authentic, hand-thrown pizza, topped with homemade tomato sauce, fresh herbs and mozzarella. You can't book (there's no phone), and you need to bring cash, but the atmosphere and food (not just pizza, but seafood and Marsellais standards) are worth the effort.

Bar des 13 Coins
BRASSERIE €

(Map p160; ☑ 04 91 91 56 49; 45 rue Sainte-Françoise; mains €13-16; ☺ 9am-11pm; Ⓜ Vieux Port) Night and day, this corner bar is a classic Le Panier hang-out whether you're old, young, hip or in need of a hip replacement. It's on a quiet backstreet with tables on the square, and serves bistro standards like

DON'T MISS

BOUILLABAISSE

Originally cooked by fisherfolk from the scraps of their catch, bouillabaisse is Marseille's signature dish. True bouillabaisse includes at least four kinds of fish, and sometimes shellfish. Don't trust tourist traps that promise cheap bouillabaisse; the real deal costs at least €50 per person. It's served in two parts: the *soupe de poisson* (broth), rich with tomato, saffron and fennel; and the cooked fish, de-boned tableside and presented on a platter. On the side are croutons, *rouille* (a bread-thickened garlic-chilli mayonnaise) and grated cheese, usually Gruyère. Spread *rouille* on the crouton, top with cheese and float it in the soup. Be prepared for a huge meal and tons of garlic.

Le Rhul (☑ 04 91 52 01 77; www.hotel-restaurant-le-rhul.com/le-restaurant; 269 corniche Président John F Kennedy; mains/bouillabaisse €36/58; ☺ noon-2pm & 5-9pm; 🚌 83) This long-standing classic in a 1940s seaside hotel with Mediterranean views has plenty of atmosphere, however kitschy. Although this is one of the most reliable spots for authentic bouillabaisse, consider ordering the other Marseillais seafood classic, *bourride* (per person €63, minimum two people), a garlicky close cousin brimming with aioli.

Michel (Brasserie Catalans; Map p160; ☑ 04 91 52 30 63; www.restaurant-michel-13.fr; 6 rue des Catalans; bouillabaisse €75; ☺ noon-1.30pm & 8-9.30pm; 🚌 83) This deceptively shabby-looking restaurant opposite Plage des Catalans has been the culinary pride and joy of the Michel family since 1946. Contrary to appearances, it serves some of Marseille's most authentic bouillabaisse, *bourride* and grilled catch of the day (€90 per kg).

L'Epuisette (Map p160; ☑ 04 91 52 17 82; www.l-epuisette.com; 158 rue du Vallon des Auffes; lunch/bouillabaisse menu €75/98; ☺ noon-1.30pm & 7.30-9.30pm Tue-Sat; 🚌 83) This swanky restaurant has a Michelin star and knockout water-level views from an elegant dining room. Many splurge on what may be Marseille's top bouillabaisse – which comes as part of a four-course *menu* – and on the superb cellar, which leans heavily towards French whites.

BOUCHES-DU-RHÔNE MARSEILLE

LOCAL KNOWLEDGE

A PERFECT SUNSET

Only Marseillais and the cognoscenti are privy to **Le Chalet du Pharo** (Map p160; ☑04 91 52 80 11; www.le-chalet-du-pharo.com; 58 bd Charles Livon, Jardin du Pharo; menus €39-47; ⊗noon-3pm & 7.30-11pm Mon-Sat, noon-3pm Sun; M Vieux Port), a little chalet with a very big view, secreted in the Jardin du Pharo. Its hillside terrace, shaded by pines and parasols, stares across the water to Fort St-Jean, MuCEM and the Villa Méditerranée beyond. Grilled fish and meat dominate the menu. Online reservations are essential, and cards aren't accepted.

entrecôte, bruschetta and charcuterie plates – but it's the chilled vibe you come for, best tasted over an evening pastis.

Longchamp Palace
BISTRO €

(Map p160; ☑04 91 50 76 13; 22 bd Longchamp; mains €15-17; ⊗8am-12.30am Mon-Wed, to 2am Thu-Sat, 11am-12.30am Sun; ☖National) A classic neighbourhood bar and bistro, the Longchamp Palace teems with convivial locals, especially after work. Stained glass windows that might have been made by Henri Matisse and brightly-coloured mosaics provide an 'art-deco' environment in which to enjoy bistro classics such as beef tartare or just to sip an apéritif. Arrive early to get a table.

Le Pain de l'Opéra
BAKERY €

(Map p166; ☑04 91 33 01 05; http://lepaindelopera.free.fr; 61 rue Francis Davso; lunch €4-5; ⊗7am-7.30pm Mon-Sat; M Vieux Port) Baking some of the best pastries near the Vieux Port, Le Pain de l'Opéra also has plenty of savoury options.

Boulangerie Aixoise
BAKERY €

(Map p166; ☑04 91 33 93 85; www.biscuiterie marseillaise.fr; 45 rue Francis Davso; lunch €6-8; ⊗6.30am-7.30pm Mon-Sat; M Vieux Port) The Aixoise has given locals their daily bread, in all its forms – *pain de campagne* (country bread), crunchy *ficelle* (minibaguettes) or a classic baguette – since 1920. It also bakes great *navettes* (traditional boat-shaped Provençal biscuits) and other sweet treats.

★ L'Arôme
FRENCH €€

(Map p160; ☑04 91 42 88 80; 9 rue de Trois Rois; menus €23-28; ⊗7.30-11pm Mon-Sat; M Notre Dame du Mont) Reserve ahead to snag a ta-

ble at this fabulous little restaurant just off cours Julien. From the service – relaxed, competent, friendly without over familiarity – to the street art on the walls and the memorable food, it's a complete winner. Well-credentialled chef-owner Romain achieves sophisticated simplicity in dishes such as roast duckling served with polenta and a pecorino *beignet* (doughnut).

La Passarelle
PROVENCAL €€

(Map p166; ☑04 91 33 03 27; www.restaurantla passarelle.fr; 52 rue Plan Fourmiguier; mains €16-22; ⊗noon-2.30pm & 8-10.30pm Mar-Oct, shorter hours rest of year; ☖82, 83, M Vieux Port) This admirably unpretentious bistro grows most of its organic veggies in its own *potager* (kitchen garden), from tomatoes to courgettes, salad leaves and aubergines. It's a cosy, friendly place for sampling delicious Mediterranean flavours, with mix-and-match tables and chairs arranged on a decked terrace beneath a spreading sail. Charming and simple.

Café Populaire
BISTRO €€

(Map p160; ☑04 91 02 53 96; 110 rue Paradis; mains €19-24; ⊗noon-2pm & 8-10.30pm Mon-Fri, 8-10.30pm Sat, noon-3pm Sun; M Estrangin-Préfecture) Vintage furniture, latticed blinds, old books and antique soda bottles lend a retro air to this style-conscious, 1950s-styled *jazz comptoir* (counter) – a restaurant in all but name. The crowd is chic, and smiling chefs in the open kitchen churn out international dishes like *tagliata* (steak strips with rocket and parmesan) and black cod with miso and *yuzu* (Japanese citrus).

L'Entre Pots
ARGENTINE €€

(Map p160; ☑09 50 78 40 05; www.lentre-pots.com; 22 cours Joseph Thierry; mains €17-20; ⊗6-11pm Mon-Sat; M Réformés Canebière) Doing double duty as a *bar à vin* (wine bar) and Argentinian restaurant, L'Entre Pots is a great place to snack on plump empanadas, juicy entrecôte and plump sausages with *chimichurri*, whilst selecting from towering shelves of Côtes du Rhône, Beaujolais and South American malbec. Tables spill out onto cours Joseph Thierry in fine weather, and there's occasional live music.

Chez Jeannot
INTERNATIONAL €€

(Map p160; ☑04 91 52 11 28; www.pizzeriachezjean not.com; 129 rue du Vallon des Auffes; mains €16-22; ⊗noon-2.30pm & 7-10.30pm; ☖83) Occupying a magical spot on the little harbour of Vallon des Auffes, this old favourite has a split-level layout and picture windows overlooking the boats (try for a table on the upper floor for maximum atmosphere). The pizzas are decent, as are pasta and seafood dishes such as seared gnocchi with *ceps* (porcini), but it's the setting that's the true attraction.

Le Môlé Passédat
FRENCH €€€

(Map p160; ☑ 04 91 19 17 80; www.passedat.fr; 1 esplanade du J4, MuCEM; La Table lunch/dinner menus €55/75, La Cuisine 2-/3-course menus €25/35; ☺ La Table noon-2.30pm & 7.30-10.30pm Wed-Mon; La Cuisine noon-4pm Wed-Mon; Ⓜ Vieux Port, Joliette) On the top floor of Marseille's flagship museum, MuCEM, Michelin-starred chef Gérald Passedat cooks up exquisite French fare alongside big blue views of the Mediterranean and Marseillais coastline. **La Table** is the gastronomic restaurant; **La Cuisine**, with buffet dining around shared tables (no sea view), is the cheaper choice. Reserve both online.

Le Petit Nice
SEAFOOD €€€

(☑ 04 91 59 25 92; www.passedat.fr; 17 rue des Braves; menus from €240; ☺ 7.30-10.30pm Tue-Sat 🚍 83) The flagship restaurant of Marseille-born gastronomic star Gérald Passedat, Le Petit Nice is a true dining destination. Set in a 1917 seafront villa on the Anse de Maldormé, this three-star Michelin icon sets the benchmark for seafood cookery in Provence. Expect *oursin* (sea-urchin), *langouste* (crayfish), *rouget* (red mullet) and other freshly caught Mediterranean delights at their very best.

Restaurant Peron
SEAFOOD €€€

(Map p160; ☑ 04 91 52 15 22; www.restaurant-peron. com; 56 corniche Président John F Kennedy; lunch/dinner menus from €55/72; ☺ noon-2pm & 8-10.15pm; 🚍 83) Peron is a premium address for seafood in Marseille, with the advantage of a stunning cliftop perch and views over the water to the Îles du Frioul. Expect vast seafood platters, proper bouillabaisse (€56) and various fish dishes, served in a slightly starchy, timber-floored setting.

⬤ Drinking & Nightlife

In the best tradition of Mediterranean cities, Marseille embraces the cafe-lounger lifestyle. Near the Vieux Port, head to place Thiars and cours Honoré d'Estienne d'Orves for cafes that bask in the sun by day and buzz into the night. Cours Julien is a fine place on a sunny day to watch people come and go at the many characterful shops, cafes and restaurants in one of Marseille's most inter-

esting neighbourhoods. Le Panier, place de Lenche and rue des Pistoles are ideal places to while away an afternoon soaking up the area's boho charms.

★ Waaw
BAR

(Map p160; ☑ 04 91 42 16 33; www.waaw.fr; 17 rue Pastoret; ☺ 4pm-midnight Wed & Sat, from 6pm Tue, Thu & Fri; Ⓜ Notre Dame du Mont) Marseille's creative chameleon and the heart of the cours Julien scene, Waaw ('What an Amazing World') has everything you could possibly want for a night out. Whether that's a cold cocktail, a late-night dancehall DJ set or an innovative dinner made from local market produce, the city's unofficial cultural headquarters offers music, film, festivals and much more.

La Caravelle
BAR

(Map p166; ☑ 04 91 90 36 64; www.lacaravelle-mar seille.com; 34 quai du Port; ☺ 7am-2am; 🛜; Ⓜ Vieux Port) On the first floor of Hôtel Bellevue, this lovely little bar is styled with rich wood and leather, with a zinc bar and yellowing murals that hint of its 1920s pedigree. If it's sunny, snag a coveted spot on the portside terrace, and sip a pastis as you watch the throng below. On Friday there's live jazz from 9pm.

La Dame du Mont
BAR

(Map p160; ☑ 04 91 47 35 76; 30-32 place Notre Dame du Mont; ☺ 4.30pm-1.30am; Ⓜ Notre Dame du Mont-Cours Julien) Regular DJs bring reggae, soul, funk, rock and much else besides to this friendly, bustling hang-out on place Notre Dame du Mont. Craft beers, cocktails and bonhomie are in ample supply, especially during happy hours (7pm to 9pm).

Le Montmartre
CAFE

(Map p166; ☑ 04 91 56 03 24; 4 place de Lenche; ☺ noon-10.30pm Wed-Mon; Ⓜ Vieux Port, Joliette) Le Montmartre is beautifully situated on a charming, small square with glimpses of the Vieux Port. Among several cafes here, this one perhaps best captures the Le Panier vibe and is a fine place to hang out with a drink on a lazy afternoon. Also serves steak, seafood and Provençal standards (mains €17 to €18).

Bistrot L'Horloge
BAR

(Map p166; ☑ 04 88 08 33 03; 11 cours Honoré d'Estienne d'Orves; ☺ 9.30am-1am Mon-Sat, from 4pm Sun; Ⓜ Vieux Port) A local favourite with parasol-shaded table and chairs at the lion-statue end of cours Honoré d'Es-

LGBTIQ+ MARSEILLE

Visit www.actu-gay.com for information on Marseillais LGBTIQ+ life. It's a small scene that is in constant flux and only really converges on weekends, but the city is generally gay friendly.

Le Trash (☑ 04 91 25 52 16; www.letrashbar.com; 28 rue du Berceau; ☺ 8.30pm-2am Mon & Wed, from 9.30pm Fri & Sat, from 3pm Sun; Ⓜ Baille) Southwest of the cours Julien nightlife area, Le Trash bills itself as Marseille's cruising bar, for good reason. There's a cover charge most nights (from €10).

Caffè Noir (Map p166; ☑ 04 91 04 08 66; 3 rue Moustier; ☺ 9am-7pm Mon-Tue & Thu-Sat, to midnight Wed; Ⓜ Vieux Port) Caffè Noir, with its severe charcoal façade and black pavement terrace staggering down the street in three steps, more than lives up to its name. Inside and out, a young, mixed, hard-drinking crowd gathers. It's affiliated with Cargo, a sauna at nearby 9 rue Moustier.

L'Endroit (Map p166; ☑ 04 91 33 97 25; 8 rue Bailli de Suffren; ☺ 7pm-5am Tue-Sat; Ⓜ Vieux Port) Dive through the tiny door to discover the Vieux Port's only LGBTIQ+ bar. Theme nights include karaoke.

tienne d'Orves, this *bistrot*-bar rocks. In summer live music entertains in the early evening while punters chat over mint and ice-jammed mojitos, pots of black olive tapenade and charcuterie platters. The food (mains €16 to €18) is good too.

Baby Club　　　　　　　　　CLUB
(Map p160; ☑ 06 48 48 64 17; 2 rue André Poggioli; ☺ midnight-6am Wed-Sun; Ⓜ Notre Dame du Mont) Located in the bohemian neighborhood of La Plaine, Baby Club offers the perfect atmosphere for an abandoned after-hours party. Look for its garish zebra-striped exterior, then head inside to catch top French and European house DJs. Some nights are free, but a cover of €10 is more common.

R2　　　　　　　　　COCKTAIL BAR
(Map p160; ☑ 04 91 91 79 39; www.airdemarseille. com; 9 quai du Lazaret; ☺ 7pm-2am Tue-Sun Apr-Sep; Ⓜ Joliette) Together, **Le Rooftop** – a spectacular open-air cocktail bar with rotating DJs playing house, electro, disco and rock – and **Reverso** – the restaurant space below it, serving from 7pm – make up R2, a slick waterside spot in Joliette.

Au Son des Guitares　　　　　　CLUB
(Map p166; ☑ 04 91 33 11 47; 18 rue Corneille; ☺ 10.30pm-4am Thu-Sun; Ⓜ Vieux Port) Popular with Corsican locals, this small club next to the opera was once a favourite of Spanish refugees in Franco's era. It has limited dancing, lots of (pricey) drinking and performances on most nights, including the occasional Corsican singer. Look sharp to get in.

☆ Entertainment

Cultural events are covered in *L'Hebdo* (€1.20), available around town, and at www.marseille bynight.com and www.journalventilo.fr.

Espace Julien　　　　　　　LIVE MUSIC
(Map p160; ☑ 04 91 24 34 10; www.espace-julien. com; 39 cours Julien; Ⓜ Notre Dame du Mont-Cours Julien) Rock, *opérock,* alternative theatre, reggae, hip hop, Afro groove and other cutting-edge entertainment all appear on the bill at this mainstay of the cours Julien scene. See the website for the program and tickets.

★ La Friche La Belle de Mai　　ARTS CENTRE
(☑ 04 95 04 95 04; www.lafriche.org; 41 rue Jobin; ☺ ticket kiosk 11am-6pm Mon, to 7pm Tue-Sat, from 12.30pm Sun; 🚌 49, 52) This 45,000-sq-metre former tobacco factory is now a vibrant arts centre with a theatre, cinema, bar, bookshop, artists' workshops, multimedia displays, skateboard ramps, electro- and world-music parties and much more. Check the program online. The on-site restaurant, Les Grandes Tables (p170), is a great bet for interesting, locally sourced food.

★ Videodrome 2　　　　　　CINEMA
(Map p160; ☑ 04 88 44 41 84; www.videodrome2. fr; 49 cours Julien; tickets from €3; ☺ 5pm-2am Tue & Thu-Fri, from 3pm Wed & Sat, to 12.30am Sun; Ⓜ Notre Dame du Mont) Fewer video shops would have gone the way of the dodo if they'd followed the lead of Videodrome 2: a DVD rental store, bar/bistro and tiny arthouse movie theatre, it's a treat for gregarious cinephiles. As well as stocking some

excellent local beers, the cinema shows rare and cult films and runs retrospectives on notable auteurs.

Le Moulin — LIVE MUSIC

(⟳ 04 91 06 33 94; www.lemoulin.org; 47 bd Perrin; tickets from €9; 📟 42, 53) Despite the name, this live-music venue is actually a repurposed 1950s cinema, not a windmill (which would have made for interesting gigs). Scheduling indie and alternative acts in the main, it's a vital proving ground for young talent from Marseille and around (although it also books more established acts).

Opéra Municipal de Marseille — OPERA

(Map p166; ⟳ 04 91 55 11 10; http://opera.marseille.fr; ⊙ box office 10am-5.30pm Tue-Sat; Ⓜ Vieux Port) Built in the 1920s on the site of its 18th-century predecessor, this 1800-seat neoclassical theatre has seen the French premieres of many notable operas, and hosted some of its most famous performers. The season runs from September to June.

Dock des Suds — LIVE MUSIC

(⟳ 04 91 99 00 00; www.dock-des-suds.org; 12 rue Urbain V; ⊙ box office 9am-1pm & 2-5pm Mon-Fri, closed Aug; Ⓜ National, 🚋 Arenc le Silo) With a 1400-capacity club and concert space for 2800, this eclectic music venue is in the Joliette neighbourhood north of the Vieux Port. Check out the program and book online.

Théâtre National de Marseille — THEATRE

(La Criée; Map p166; ⟳ 04 91 54 70 54; www.theatre-lacriee.com; 30 quai de Rive Neuve; Ⓜ Vieux Port) Since 1981, this 280-seat theatre has presented dance and drama. The name 'Criée' refers to the fish-auctions once held on the site.

🛍 Shopping

For chic shopping and large chains, stroll west of the Vieux Port to the 6th *arrondissement,* especially pedestrianised rue St-Ferréol. Cours Julien has more creative boutiques and vintage shops; bohemian Le Panier is the go-to spot products by local artisans.

★ Maison Empereur — HOMEWARES

(Map p166; ⟳ 04 91 54 02 29; www.empereur.fr; 4 rue des Récollettes; ⊙ 9am-7pm Mon-Sat; 📟 2, 3) If you only have time to visit one store in Marseille, make it this one. Run by the same family since 1827, France's oldest hardware store remains a one-stop shop for beautifully made homeware items including Opinel

cutlery, Savon de Marseille soaps, wooden toy sailing boats and ceramic shaving bowls.

★ Maison de la Boule — GIFTS & SOUVENIRS

(Map p166; ⟳ 04 88 44 39 44; www.museedelaboule.com; 4 place des 13 Cantons; ⊙ 10am-7pm Mon-Sat, to 6pm Sun; 📟 49, Ⓜ Vieux Port) Pick up a set of handmade boules (complete with carry bag), plus plenty of other souvenirs of France's iconic game. There's also an indoor court and a little museum exploring the history of the sport, including the curious figure of Fanny (tradition dictates if you lose a game 13 to nil, you must kiss her bare bum cheeks).

Four des Navettes — FOOD

(Map p166; ⟳ 04 91 33 32 12; www.fourdesnavettes.com; 136 rue Sainte; ⊙ 7am-8pm Mon-Sat, 9am-1pm & 3-7.30pm Sun; Ⓜ Vieux Port) Opened in 1781, this is the oldest bakery in Marseille; it's been passed down between three families, and it still uses the original 18th-century oven. It is *the* address to pick up Marseille's signature biscuits, the orange-perfumed *navettes de Marseille,* as well as *calissons* (Provençal almond biscuits), nougat and other delights.

UndARTground — ART

(Map p166; ⟳ 06 50 08 28 21; www.undartground.com; 21 rue des Repenties; ⊙ 11am-7pm Wed-Mon; 📟 49) As the street-art daubed walls of this concept store and gallery suggest, it showcases the work of local underground artists. As well as posters by eBoy and prints by Oaï of Life, expect anything from urban t-shirts and thick coffee table books to ghetto blaster pillow cases designed by AK-LH.

La Grande Savonnerie — COSMETICS

(Map p166; ⟳ 09 50 63 80 35; www.lagrandesavonnerie.com; 36 Grande Rue; ⊙ 9am-6pm Tue-Sun; Ⓜ Vieux Port) Soap making in Marseille has been traced by some to the 14th century, but much of the stuff for sale at the city's markets is made elsewhere. That's not the case at this little soap maker, which specialises in the genuine Marseillais article, made with olive oil and no added perfume, and shaped into cubes.

Atelier du Santon — ARTS & CRAFTS

(Map p166; ⟳ 04 91 13 61 36; www.santonsmarcelcarbonel.com; 49 rue Neuve Ste-Catherine; ⊙ 10am-12.30pm & 2-6.30pm Mon-Sat; Ⓜ Vieux Port) Head to the boutique of Santons Marcel Carbonel, within the **Musée du Santon,** (⟳ 04 91 54 26 58) **FREE**, for tiny kiln-fired figures – or *santons* (from *santoùn*, meaning 'little saint') – handcrafted in Carbonel's nearby workshop. The custom of creating a nativity scene with figurines dates from the Avignon papacy of John XII (1319–34).

ℹ Information

Hôpital de la Timone (☑ 04 91 38 00 00; http://fr.ap-hm.fr; 264 rue St-Pierre; Ⓜ Timone) Round-the clock accident and emergency; located 1.5km southeast of place Jean Jaurès.

Maison de la Région (Map p166; ☑ 04 91 57 50 57; www.regionpaca.fr; 27 place Jules Guesde; ⊗ 11am-6pm Mon-Sat; Ⓜ Noailles) Info on Provence and the Côte d'Azur.

Marseille Expos (www.marseilleexpos.com) This outstanding arts organisation distributes an excellent map of hot galleries and sponsors the festival Printemps de l'Art Contemporain each May. Its website lists what's on.

Police (☑ 04 88 77 58 00; 66-68 La Canebière; ⊗ 24hr; Ⓜ Noailles) Central police station.

Tourist Office (Map p166; ☑ 08 26 50 05 00; box office 04 91 13 89 16; www.marseille-tour isme.com; 11 La Canebière; ⊗ 9am-6pm; Ⓜ Vieux Port) Marseille's tourist office has plenty of information on everything, including guided city tours (by foot, bus, electric tourist train or boat) and trips to Les Calanques. There's free wi-fi too.

ℹ Getting There & Away

For local transport information in and around Marseille, see www.lepilote.com.

AIR

Aéroport Marseille-Provence (p329) is located 25km northwest of Marseille in Marignane. There are regular year-round flights to nearly all major French cities, plus major hubs in the UK, Germany, Belgium, Italy and Spain.

BOAT

Gare Maritime de la Major (Marseille Fos; www.marseille-port.fr; Quai de la Joliette; Ⓜ Joliette), the passenger ferry terminal, is located just south of place de la Joliette.

Corsica Linea (☑ 08 25 88 80 88; www.corsicalinea.com; quai du Maroc; ⊗ 8.30am-8pm) has regular ferries from Marseille to Corsica and Sardinia, plus routes to Algeria and Tunisia.

BUS

The **bus station** (Gare Routière; Map p160; ☑ 04 91 08 16 40; www.rtm.fr; 3 rue Honnorat;

MARSEILLE'S MARKETS

Farmers Market (Map p160; www.coursjulien.marsnet.org; cours Julien; ⊗ 8am-1pm Wed; Ⓜ Notre Dame du Mont) Every Wednesday morning the farmers market along cours Julien squawks with life, colour and accordion music as traders flog mounds of organic vegetables, jars of homemade fruit jam, hand-collected quail eggs and bouquets of fragrant herbs. Once your shopping bags are brimming, head to a nearby cafe and watch the mostly boho crowd haggle with the stallholders.

Fish Market (Map p166; quai du Port; ⊗ 8am-1pm; Ⓜ Vieux Port) You can still buy the fresh stuff here at the Vieux Port, among the vestiges of what would once have been a thriving quayside fish market.

Les Halles de la Major (Map p166; ☑ 04 91 45 80 10; www.leshallesdelamajor.com; 12 quai de la Tourette; mains €12-20; ⊗ 11am-2.45pm & 3-5pm Sun-Tue, 11am-2.45pm & 3-11pm Wed-Sat; 🚌 82) This upscale food market inside the renovated vaults of La Major Cathedral is great for foodies, self-caterers and browsers. Each stall serves a selection of small plated specialities such as local cheeses, freshly shucked oysters and Provençal 'tapas'. There's seating, a terrace and lovely views across the water.

Marché de la Joliette (Map p160; place de la Joliette; ⊗ 8am-1.30pm & 4-7pm Tue, 8am-1.30pm Wed-Sat; Ⓜ Joliette) This lively market sells a good range of fresh produce. The high-quality, all local producers' market on Tuesday afternoon is a highlight.

Marché des Capucins (Marché de Noailles; Map p166; place des Capucins; ⊗ 8am-7pm Mon-Sat; Ⓜ Noailles, 🚋 Canebière Garibaldi) Located one block south of La Canebière, this multicultural market has around 30 stalls selling fruit, veggies, fish and dried goods.

Marché Place Jean Jaurès (Marché de la Plaine; Map p160; place Jean Jaurès; ⊗ 7.30am-1.30pm Mon-Sat; Ⓜ Noailles) Fresh food, clothing, cheap gadgets and more on a large square. On Friday it's flowers.

Ⓜ Gare St-Charles) is located on the northern side of the train station. Buy tickets here or from the driver. Services to some destinations, including Cassis, use the **Castellane bus station** (Halte Routière Sud; Map p160; place Castellane; Ⓜ Castellane), south of the centre.

For most destinations along the Côte d'Azur, it's faster and easier to catch the train, but for some smaller towns and villages (especially inland), buses are an alternative. There are several different companies, but you can find comprehensive timetable information on the website Le Pilote (www.lepilote.com). Sample destinations:

Aix-en-Provence (€9, 40 minutes, every 10 minutes Monday to Saturday, less frequent Sunday) Cartreize line 50 express bus leaves from Gare St-Charles. Line 51 also runs frequently to Aix.

Barcelonette (€35, 4¼ hours, one direct daily) LER Line 28

Cassis (€2, 45 minutes, hourly Monday to Saturday) La Marcouline Line M06

Nice (€34, three to five hours, up to five per day) LER Line 20

Eurolines (Map p166; www.eurolines.com; 3 allées Léon Gambetta; Ⓜ Noailles) also has international services.

CAR

Most major car-rental firms have offices in or close to the train station.

TRAIN

Eurostar (www.eurostar.com) offers two to 10 weekly services between Marseille and London (from €213, seven hours) via Lille or Paris. As always, the earlier you book, the cheaper the fare.

Regular and TGV trains serve **Gare St-Charles** (☏ 04 91 08 16 40; www.rtm.fr; rue Jacques Bory; Ⓜ Gare St-Charles SNCF), which is a junction for both metro lines. The **left-luggage office** (Consignes Automatiques; ⊘ 8.15am-9pm) is next to platform A. Sample fares:

Avignon €22, 1¼ hours, hourly

Nice €38, 2½ hours, up to six per day

Paris Gare de Lyon from €76, 3½ hours, at least hourly

❶ Getting Around

TO/FROM THE AIRPORT

Navette Marseille (Map p160; www.lepilote. com; one way/return €8.30/14; ⊘ 4.30am-11.30pm) buses link the airport and Gare St-Charles (30 minutes) every 15 to 20 minutes.

The airport's train station has direct services to several cities including Arles and Avignon – a free shuttle bus runs to/from the airport terminal.

BICYCLE

With the **Le Vélo** (☏ English helpline 01 30 79 29 13; www.levelo-mpm.fr) bike-share scheme, you can pick up and drop off bikes from 100-plus stations across the city and along the coastal road to the beaches. Users must subscribe online first (per week/year €1/5) then the first 30 minutes of every hire is free, after which bikes cost €1 per hour. Stations only take credit cards with chips.

BOAT

Boats run from the old port to the **Îles du Frioul** (p163), as well as to the Parc National des Calanques. There's also a **ferry** (Map p166; one way €0.50; ⊘ 7.30am-8.30pm; Ⓜ Vieux Port) across the Vieux Port.

CAR

Trust us, you'll regret bringing a car into Marseille – car parks and on-street parking are very expensive, and competition is fierce for no-cost parking spaces in outer neighbourhoods. Central car parks include **Parking Indigo** (22 place du Général de Gaulle; ⊘ 24hr; Ⓜ Vieux Port), off La Canebière. Expect to pay around €3 per hour or €32 per 24 hours.

PUBLIC TRANSPORT

Marseille has two metro lines (Métro 1 and Métro 2), two tram lines (yellow and green) and an extensive bus network. Bus, metro or tram tickets (one/10 trips €1.70/14) are available from machines in the metro, at tram stops and on buses. Most buses start in front of the **Espace Infos RTM** (Map p166; ☏ 04 91 91 92 10; www.rtm. fr; 6 rue des Fabres; ⊘ 8.30am-6pm Mon-Fri; Ⓜ Vieux Port), where you can obtain information and tickets.

The metro runs from 5am to 10.30pm Monday to Thursday, and until 12.30am Friday to Sunday. Trams run 5am to 1am daily.

TAXI

Taxi Radio Marseille (☏ 04 91 02 20 20; www. taximarseille.com; ⊘ 24hr) One of Marseille's largest taxi companies.

AROUND MARSEILLE

Despite its size, Marseille quickly yields to lovely stretches of coast in both directions, sheltering national parks, charming towns and vineyards.

Les Calanques

It feels like a miracle to find a refuge such as the **Parc National des Calanques** (☏ 04 20 10 50 00; www.calanques-parcnational.fr; 141

av du Prado, Bâtiment A, Marseille) only a short distance from grimy, pressured Marseille. In parts of this diminutive 85-sq-km patch of scrubby, convoluted promontories, it's easy to believe you're miles from civilisation. Then a twist in a pine-clad gully reveals the entirety of France's second metropolis spread out within apparent touching distance; the *calanques* appear almost as its uninhabited suburbs.

But with their light-shifting geometry, rich plant and animal life and idyllic hidden coves, Les Calanques are much more than that. They are beloved by the Marseillais, who come for the sun and to hike over pine-strewn promontories, mess about on boats and generally refresh their souls. The region is hugely popular in summer, visited by boats and hikers who schlep hours to the secluded fishing villages.

⊙ Sights & Activities

Of the many *calanques* along the coastline, the most easily accessible are Calanque de Sormiou and Calanque de Morgiou, while remote inlets such as Calanque d'En Vau and Calanque de Port-Miou take dedication and time to reach – either on foot or by kayak.

Calanque de Morgiou   BAY
Rocky, pine-covered Cap Morgiou plunges to meet the Med at the eponymous Calanque de Morgiou – a pretty little port bobbing with fishing boats and sheer rock faces spangled with thrill-seeking climbers. An evening spent at its one (seasonal) restaurant, **Nautic Bar** (🗋 04 91 40 06 37; Calanque de Morgiou; mains €18-27; ⊙ noon-2.30pm & 7.30-9.30pm Apr-Oct), is dreamy.

The hair-raisingly steep, narrow road (3.5km) is open to motorists weekdays only from mid-April to May, and it's closed from June to September (when a one-hour distant car park is mandatory, although those with Nautic Bar reservations are allowed through).

En-Vau, Port-Pin & Port-Miou   BAY
To the east of the Parc National des Calanques, the stone-sculptured coast brings you to three remote *calanques:* En-Vau, Port-Pin and Port-Miou. A steep three-hour marked trail leads from the car park (closed July to mid-September) on the **Col de la Gardiole** to En-Vau, with a pebbly beach and emerald waters encased by cliffs. The slippery and sheer descents into the *calanque* are very

challenging. Its entrance is guarded by the Doigt de Dieu (God's Finger), a giant rock pinnacle.

Calanque de Sormiou   BAY
The largest *calanque* hit headlines in 1991 when diver Henri Cosquer from Cassis swam through a 150m-long passage 36m underwater and into a cave, only to find its interior adorned with wall paintings dating from around 20,000 BCE. Now named **Grotte Cosquer**, the cave is a protected historical monument and closed to the public.

To reach the *calanque,* take bus 23 from Marseilles' Rond-Point du Prado metro to the La Cayolle stop, from where it is a 3km walk.

Destination Calanques Kayak   KAYAKING
(🗋 06 07 15 63 86; www.destination-calanques.fr; half/full day €35/55; ⊙ Apr-Oct) By far the best way to explore the Parc National des Calanques is by sea kayak, ideally with an experienced local guide who can take you straight to all the best spots. Departures are from Port-Miou, Pointe-Rouge and Rouet beach.

Hiking
From October to June the best way to see the *calanques* (including the 500 sq km of the rugged inland **Massif des Calanques**) is to hike the many lined trails through the *maquis* (scrub). Marseille's tourist office (p176) leads guided walks (ages eight and over) and has information about trail and road closures. It also offers an excellent hiking map of the various *calanques,* as does Cassis' tourist office (p182).

From June to September trails may close due to fire danger.

Boating
The best way to reach the *calanques* is by sea – either by boat or by hiring a kayak from Marseille or Cassis. Operators such as Destination Calanques Kayak and Raskas Kayak (p163) organise sea-kayaking tours; local tourist offices have details of lots of other hire companies. **Calanc'O** (🗋 06 25 78 85 93; www.calanco-kayak-paddle.com; 9 ave Joseph Liautaud; half/full day €35/55; ⊙ 8am-8pm) also offers paddle boarding.

During July and August the only real option for accessing individual *calanques* is to take a boat tour with Croisières Marseille Calanques (p163) from Marseille or Cassis. Check in advance if you're hoping to be able to stop for a swim, as only a few tours allow this, such as the one offered by **Icard Mar-**

itime (Map p166; ☑ 04 91 33 36 79; www.visite-des-calanques.com; quai des Belges; adult/child from €23/18; Ⓜ Vieux Port).

✕ Eating

Le Château FRENCH €€
(☑ 04 91 25 08 69; www.lechateausormiou.fr; Calanque de Sormiou; mains €23-25; ☺ noon-2.30pm & 7.30-9.30pm Apr-Sep) This seasonal restaurant with excellent views has the best food in the Calanque de Sormiou. Reserve ahead – by phone – which allows you to drive your car to the *calanque* even when it is otherwise closed to traffic (June to September).

ⓘ Getting There & Away

Without a boat, you'll have to drive, cycle or take public transport to visit the *calanques*. Be warned that roads are rough, parking scarce and the going slow. The roads into each *calanque* are often closed to drivers, unless you have a reservation at one of the *calanque* restaurants. You must instead park at a public lot, then walk the rest of the way in.

For access to the *calanques* closest to Marseille, drive or take bus 19 from Marseille's Castellane bus station (p177) down the coast to its terminus at La Madrague, then switch to bus 20 to Callelongue (note that the road to Callelongue is only open to cars on weekdays from mid-April to May and closed entirely from June to September). From there you can walk to Calanque de la Mounine and Calanque de Marseilleveyre along spectacular trails over the cliff tops.

Calanque de Sugiton is also easy to access without a car. Take bus 21 from Castellane towards Luminy and get off at the last stop. From there follow the path (about a 45-minute walk).

Cassis

POP 7221

The charm of this fishing village, impeccably poised amongst the *calanques,* has hardly been dented by its great popularity. Yes, you're more likely to rub shoulders with crisply dressed Marseillais than sun-creased fisherfolk, and you'll need deep pockets to park anywhere central for any length of time, but Cassis is so beautiful, and so well-stocked with good bistros, bars and boutiques, that it's still well worth a side trip from Marseille.

To the east is a dramatic rocky outcrop crowned by a 14th-century château (now a hotel open only to guests), while the surrounding country is either pleasingly wild or quilted with wineries producing whites and

---

LOCAL KNOWLEDGE

TOP VIEWS

Europe's highest seaside cliff, the hollow limestone **Cap Canaille** (399m) towers above the southestern side of the **Baie de Cassis** (Bay of Cassis). From the top, captivating views unfold across the town and **Mont Puget** (564m), the highest point in the Massif de Calanques.

Offering equally jaw-dropping panoramas, the **Route des Crêtes** (D141; closed in high winds) snakes 16km along the cliff top from Cassis to La Ciotat.

---

rosés under the Cassis Appellation d'Origine Contrôlée (AOC).

⊙ Sights & Activities

The tourist office (p182) has information on rock climbing, deep-sea diving, sea kayaking and other activities, including a one-hour walking trail to **Calanque de Port-Pin** (take water and a map).

Twelve estates producing the Cassis appellation cover 210 hectares of the surrounding hillsides; the tourist office has a list of estates you can visit to taste and buy (most require advance reservation), as well as suggested itineraries. The office also offers guided tours throughout the village, stopping to taste local treats (per person €7, 90 minutes), and two-hour tours of the nearby *calanques* on electric bikes (per person €25). Tours are more frequent in high season; check with the office or online to book.

Les Bateliers Cassidains CRUISE
(☑ 06 86 55 86 70; www.cassis-calanques.com; quai St-Pierre; ☺ Feb-Nov) For most of the year, this company runs boat excursions from quai St-Pierre to the crenellated coast of the Parc National des Calanques. A 45-minute trip to three *calanques* (Port-Miou, Port-Pin and En-Vau) costs €16/9.50 per adult/child; a 65-minute trip covering these plus Oule and Devenson is €20/14. Buy tickets at the port-side kiosk.

🛏 Sleeping

Cassis Hostel HOSTEL €
(☑ 09 54 37 99 82; www.cassishostel.com; 4 av du Picouveau, Les Heures Claires; dm €30-35, d €85-95; P ⓡ ≋) On the hill above town, this small hostel is a very pleasant place for budgeteers, with two dorms (one six-bed, one four-bed)

LAVENDER

Pilgrims come from all over to follow the Routes de la Lavande (www.routes-lavande.com), tracking Provence's aromatic purple bloom. In flower from June to August, it usually hits peak splendour in late July.

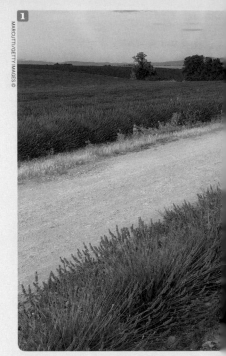

MARCUTTI/GETTY IMAGES ©

SAULT

1 The slopes of Mont Ventoux (p248), north of Lagarde d'Apt, make for prime high-altitude lavender. Aim to visit during the Fête de la Lavande (www.saultenprovence.com), usually on 15 August.

PLATEAU DE VALENSOLE

2 For sheer heady expansiveness, you can't beat the Plateau de Valensole's carpets of lavender, stretching, dreamlike, as far as the eye can see. Cruise across it on the D6 or D8 east of Manosque, and the A51.

ABBAYE NOTRE-DAME DE SÉNANQUE

3 Follow the winding D177 north of Gordes to this idyllic 12th-century Cistercian abbey (p261), tucked between hills and surrounded by brilliant fields of lavender. Resident monks tend the crops and stock their shop with monk-made goodies.

FORCALQUIER

4 Folks come from throughout the region for the booming Monday-morning market in Forcalquier (p279). An embarrassment of riches, the market has vendors selling lavender everything, plus mountain honey, creamy cheeses and handmade sausages.

CHÂTEAU DU BOIS

5 Provence is dotted with distilleries, but if you make it to tiny Lagarde d'Apt you're in for a treat: 80 hectares of Lavande des Alpes de Haute Provence, 'true lavender' (*Lavandula angustifolia*).

ROMRODINKA/GETTY IMAGES ©

1. Rows of lavender, Plateau de Valensole; **2.**Beehives in lavender fields, Plateau de Valensole; **3.**Lavender for sale

and a couple of doubles squeezed in under the eaves of the modern house. The pool, patio and kitchen complete a sweet package. Take the Cassis Casino bus from the station, get off at Belsunce and walk 200m.

Le Clos des Arômes
HOTEL €

(☏ 04 42 01 71 84; www.leclosdesaromes.fr; 10 rue Abbé Paul Mouton; s/d from €49/69; ❄ ☎) If you're keen to save some centimes, this old-fashioned hotel just five minutes' stroll from the waterfront is a decent bet. It's set around a lovely little garden, where breakfast is served in summer, but there's no getting around the fact that the rooms are looking a little worn. The on-site restaurant provides more-than-serviceable Provençal food.

Hôtel Cassitel
HOTEL €€

(☏ 04 42 01 83 44; www.cassitel.com; place Clémenceau; d €99-129; ❄ ☎) This Interhotel is all about location – you're right on Cassis' photogenic harbour-front, with clanking boats and port-side restaurants spread out beneath your window. While the burgundy-coloured rooms are plain, with MDF furniture and no-frills decor, they're perfectly serviceable. Online and breakfast-free bookings attract discounts.

✖ Eating & Drinking

Fleurs de Thym
PROVENCAL €€

(☏ 04 42 01 23 03; 5 rue Lamartine; lunch/dinner menu €20/34; ☺ noon-2pm & 7.30-10.30pm) With its open-sided fireplace and pretty, art-filled dining room, this small restaurant makes a good refuge from the harbour-side hustle. It also provides a no-nonsense grounding in Provençal flavours, from the complementary house-made tapenade to the *artichauts à la barigoule* (braised purple artichokes), monkfish bouillabaisse and authentically Marseillais *pieds paquets* (stewed lamb's feet and tripe).

COASTAL WALKS

From the tiny waterside **Port de la Redonne**, a single-track road climbs over to **Les Figuières** (1.5km), the **Petit Méjean** (1.7km) and the **Grand Méjean** (1.9km). In Grand Méjean you can pick up a stunning 2.1km-long coastal trail to **Calanque de l'Érevine**; it's worth hiking up the rock-embedded steps at the start of the trail for breathtaking views.

Poissonnerie Laurent
SEAFOOD €€

(☏ 04 42 01 71 56; 6 quai Jean Jacques Barthélemy; mains €23, menu €30; ☺ noon-2pm & 7.30-10pm) Run by brothers Laurent and Eric, this fish shop-cum-seafood restaurant has been a fixture on the Cassis waterfront for decades, and it shows no sign of losing its popularity (especially on sunny days, when the harbour terrace is always full). Expect fresh, simple seafood – perhaps steamed mussels (€14), fish plucked from the slab and expertly grilled, or bouillabaisse (€46).

★ La Villa Madie
GASTRONOMY €€€

(☏ 04 96 18 00 00; www.lavillamadie.com; av de Revestel-anse de Corton; mains €78, menus €95-155; ☺ noon-1.15pm Thu-Mon & 7-9.15pm Thu-Sat & Mon) This double Michelin-starred restaurant with fantastic coastal views has become one of the destination addresses on the Riviera, renowned for creative seafood and a refined setting. Top-drawer ingredients like Aubrac beef and locally caught sea urchins, turbot and blue lobster form the core of the menu, with more exotic ingredients such as kaffir lime making judicious appearances.

Le Chai Cassidain
WINE BAR

(☏ 04 42 01 99 80; 6 rue Dr Séverin Icard; ☺ 9.30am-1pm & 3-10pm Tue-Sun) This cosy *cave à vin* (wine cellar) offers a long wooden bar, red leather armchairs, vintage posters on the walls and a knowledgeable and affable owner – all up, a perfect setting for navigating an extensive list of local and French wines. There's plenty by the glass, bottles to take away, free nibbles and occasional tastings.

Clos Sainte Magdeleine
WINERY

(☏ 04 42 01 70 28; www.clossaintemagdeleine.fr; av du Revestel; ☺ 9.30am-12.30pm & 2.30-7pm Mon-Sat) Close to central Cassis, with a regularly open cellar door and a viticultural pedigree stretching back to the 1800s, this seaward-facing winery is a good place to acquaint yourself with the region's whites and rosés. Adjacent is the pebbly but spectacular beach of Anse de l'Arène.

ⓘ Information

Tourist Office (☏ 08 92 39 01 03; www.ot-cassis.com; quai des Moulins; ☺ 9am-6.30pm Mon-Sat, 9.30am-12.30pm & 3-6pm Sun May-Aug, shorter hours rest of year; ☎) Provides booking services, *calanque* maps (which can be very useful, given how hot, dry and rugged the hiking can get) and guided tours of the village and surrounds (€7, 90 minutes). There's another info point at the Gorguettes car park, with shorter hours.

❶ Getting There & Away

The M8 bus (€2.20, 40 minutes, up to seven daily) leaves from the **Castellane** (p177) stop in Marseille for Carnoux, stopping en route at the **Gendarmerie bus stop** (1-3 av du 11 Novembre 1918), a five-minute stroll from central Cassis. From Aubagne, take the 68 (€2.50, 30 minutes, up to 14 daily).

Cassis train station (av de la Gare), 3.5km north of the centre, is on the Marseille–Hyères line. The M1 bus connects it to the centre of town (€0.90, 15 minutes, 20 daily).

If you drive to Cassis during high season when town parking is scarce (and, as always, expensive) park at **Parking Relais des Gorguettes** (av de Gorguettes), the large lot at the northwestern entrance to town, and take the *navette* (shuttle) down to the harbour (return €1.60).

Côte Bleue

The Côte Bleue, the stretch of Mediterranean shore between Marseille and the Camargue, deserves more attention. Running 22km west of the city towards wave-washed Cap Couronne, the coast reveals a succession of limestone coves, crested with Aleppo pines, threaded with walking trails and sheltering unpretentious fishing villages-cum-holiday towns. The waters around the sandy cape are rich with marine life, protected by the **Parc Marin de la Côte Bleue** (Blue Coast Marine Park; ☎ 04 42 44 45 07; www.parcmarincotebleue.fr). Its natural beauty may not quite equal that of the nearby Parc National des Calanques, but it's plenty picturesque in its own right.

Now on the outskirts of Marseille's north-western sprawl, **L'Estaque** (www.estaque.com) once lured artists from the impressionist, Fauvist and cubist movements. Moving west you'll find *calanques* and towns such as Le Rove, Niolon, Méjean, Ensuès-la-Redonne, Carry-le-Rouet, Sausset-les-Pins and Martigues.

❶ Getting There & Away

Bus C8 runs several times per day from Marseille's Gare St-Charles to L'Estaque (25 minutes), Carry-le-Rouet (50 minutes) and Sausset-les-Pins (70 minutes). A one-hour ticket is €0.90. If your journey will exceed an hour, or you'll take a few on the same service, consider buying a *carnet* of 10 (€6.30) from the *billetterie* (ticket office) at the bus station. Single tickets are available on board.

❶ Getting Around

The Blue Coast Line, the commuter train between Marseille and Miramas via Port de Bouc, is an excellent way to traverse the Côte Bleue. It skirts along most of the 60km coast, passing through more than 20 tunnels and over sweeping bridges and viaducts. There are generally around 14 services per day, and a one-way adult fare is €10.80.

Carry-le-Rouet

POP 5908

Sleepy fishing port Carry-le-Rouet grew to a bustling settlement of several hundred after the arrival of the railway from Marseille. It is now defined more by pleasure-craft, holiday houses and seasonal bistros than the unglamorous drudgery of fishing. It has a château-turned-restaurant, swanky-looking yachts in the marina, and plenty of restaurants happy to trade on its reputation as one of the best places on earth to eat *oursins* – sea urchins. They can only be caught between September and April; fishing for them in summer, when they reproduce, is forbidden.

If this isn't to your taste, the hiking, diving and swimming around Carry is particularly good – it lies within the Parc Marin de la Côte Bleue, after all.

✦ Festivals & Events

Les Oursinades   FOOD & DRINK

(☉1st, 2nd & 3rd Sun in Feb) Every February since 1960, Carry-le-Rouet has come alive to *Les Oursinades,* a multiple-week celebration of the spiny *oursin,* of which only the lurid-orange gonad is eaten. *Oursin*-lovers descend over three Sundays of events, performances, dinners, art exhibitions and, of course, *oursins* by the bucketload.

LOCAL KNOWLEDGE

FÊTE DE LA TRANSHUMAN

Every spring throughout parts of southern France, an incredible migration known as the **Transhumance** (☉May/Jun) takes place as thousands of sheep are led from the coast to the mountains to summer on alpine pastures. The journey takes about six days, and sheep, goats and donkeys block many tertiary routes to the Alps, leading to the amusement or annoyance of many a tourist.

In St-Rémy-de-Provence on Pentecost Monday this tradition is honoured as shepherds in traditional dress lead about 6000 sheep through St-Rémy's streets on their way to the mountains, and market-day festivities fill the town.

42 13 20 36; www.otcarry
...ue; ☺ 9.30am-12.30pm
...0am-12.30pm Sun
& 2-5pm Tue-Sat Oct-
...iation on the ecology and
...ritime park.

ⓘ Getting There & Away

The C8 bus runs from Marseille's Gare St-Charles to Carry (€0.90, 50 minutes, three daily). There are also regular train services (€5.90, 30 minutes, every two hours).

Sausset-les-Pins

POP 7624

A sleepy fishing port with a devoted (mainly local) clientele of regular holidaymakers, Sausset is a quiet and unspectacular place that attempts none of the glitz of so many other places on the Provençal coastline. Fishing boats pull into the rock-walled harbour each day to offload their catch at the early-morning fish market (look for the sign *Ventes de poissons frais')*, and a block in from the water a trio of mouth-watering *poissonneries* (fishmongers) sell a heady choice of fish.

ⓘ Getting There & Away

Sausset has a stop on the train line from Marseille to Martigues (€6.30, 35 minutes, up to six daily).

PAYS D'AIX

Dominated by the elegance of Aix-en-Provence, picturesque Pays d'Aix ('Aix Country'), is a classic Provençal territory of wooded hills, prosperous farms and vineyards, and charismatic stone villages perched on the hillsides that once gave them defensive advantages. Made perhaps most famous by Paul Cézanne, who painted this landscape extensively (especially the iron-grey eminence of Montagne Ste-Victoire) it still draws locals and foreigners alike to its many delights. Hiking is a popular pastime here, and there are some fabulous restaurants just a short drive from Aix.

◉ Sights

Aqueduc de Roquefavour   HISTORIC SITE

The arches of the three-tiered Aqueduc de Roquefavour reach 83m in height, making it the world's largest stone aqueduct. Three hundred and seventy-five metres long, it was first planned in the 16th century to transport water from the River Durance to Marseille, but not built until 1847. To reach it take the D64 13km west of Aix.

Château de Vauvenargues   CHATEAU

(4 rue René Nicol, Vauvenargues) A stunning Pays d'Aix photo opportunity framed by Montagne Ste-Victoire, this 13th-century château is the final resting place of Pablo Picasso. Owned and augmented by a succession of notables, from the Archbishops of Aix to King René and finally the Picassos (who still own it), it's a dramatically sited fastness, partially screened by conifers. Unfortunately, it's not accessible to the public.

Aix-en-Provence

POP 142,668

A pocket of left-bank Parisian chic deep in Provence, Aix (pronounced like the letter X) is all class: its leafy boulevards and public squares are lined with 17th- and 18th-century mansions, punctuated by gurgling moss-covered fountains. Haughty stone lions guard its grandest avenue, cafe-laced cours Mirabeau, where fashionable Aixois pose on polished pavement terraces, sipping espresso. While Aix is a student hub, its upscale appeal makes it pricier than other Provençal towns.

The part-pedestrianised centre of Aix' old town is ringed by busy boulevards, with several large car parks dotted on the edge of town. Don't try and drive into the centre: roads are narrow and often one-way, traffic is abundant and there's no free parking.

History

Aix marks the spot where Roman forces enslaved the inhabitants of the Ligurian Celtic stronghold of Entremont, 3km north. In 123 BCE the military camp was named Aquae Sextiae (Waters of Sextius) for the thermal springs that still flow today. In the 12th century the counts of Provence proclaimed Aix their capital, which it remained until the Revolution, when it was supplanted by Marseille. The city became a centre of culture under arts patron King René (1409–80): painter Paul Cézanne and novelist Émile Zola are its most famous sons.

◉ Sights & Activities

Art, culture and architecture abound in Aix. Of special note are the town's many fountains. Some, like the 1860 **Fontaine de la**

WINERIES OF THE PAYS D'AIX

The countryside that spreads out from Aix in every direction, especially north, is rich with wineries and notable grape-growing areas. Head east into the tiny Palette microappellation, where you can visit boutique producers such as **Château Crémade** ([✍]04 42 66 76 80; www.chateaucremade.fr; rte de Langesse, Le Tholonet; ⊙9am-noon & 2-6pm; [P]; [🖿]13) and the larger **Château Simone** ([✍]04 42 66 92 58; www.chateau-simone.fr; chemin de la Simone; ⊙8am-noon & 2-6pm Mon-Fri, from 9am Sat; [P]; [🖿]13), both of which produce fine grenache, mourvèdre, syrah, cinsault and carignan.

Back through Aix, head north on the N296 for **Château de la Gaude** ([✍]04 13 91 05 33; www.chateaudelagaude.com; 60 rue de la Tramontane; ⊙9.30am-1pm & 2-6pm Mon-Fri), with its handsome 18th-century manor house and excellent rosés. Take the D63 south to cross A51 and join the D13, where **Domaine de la Brillane** ([✍]04 42 54 21 44; www. labrillane.com; 195 rte de Couteron; ⊙visits by appointment), another producer of superlative rosés, lies a few kilometres north. You'll need to arrange a visit ahead of time.

From here, you'll need to negotiate a few kilometres of narrow country road westwards, before finding the D14, after which it's a short drive north to **Château la Coste** ([✍]04 42 61 92 92; www.chateau-la-coste.com; 2750 Route de la Cride, Le Puy Sainte Réparade; art walk adult/child €15/12; ⊙cellar door 9am-7.30pm Mon-Sat, from 10am Sun May-Sep, to 6.30pm Oct-Apr). Art gallery, dining destination, fine winery: this is one of the loveliest estates in the Pays d'Aix.

If you haven't had enough (and can still safely drive), then it's worth dropping in on **Domaine Pey Blanc** ([✍]04 42 12 34 76; www.pey-blanc.fr; 1200 chemin du Vallon des Mourgues; ⊙9am-noon & 2-7pm Mon-Sat; [P]) as you wend your way south to Aix, via the D14, D63 and a few local roads.

Rotonde (pl du Général de Gaulle), are quite grand. Others have simpler charms, such as the 1819 **Fontaine du Roi René** (cours Mirabeau) and the 1734 **Fontaine d'Eau Chaude** (Mossy Fountain; cours Mirabeau) – the former features the king holding a bunch of grapes, while the latter has temperate 18°C water from a spring and is covered in moss.

★**Musée Granet** MUSEUM
([✍]04 42 52 88 32; www.museegranet-aixen provence.fr; place St-Jean de Malte; adult/child €5.50/free; ⊙10am-7pm Tue-Sun mid Jun–Sep, noon-6pm Tue-Sun Oct–mid-Jun) Aix established one of France's first public museums here, on the site of a former Hospitallers' priory, in 1838. Nearly 200 years of acquisitions (including bequests by the eponymous François Marius Granet, himself a painter of note) have resulted in a collection of more than 12,000 works, including pieces by Picasso, Léger, Matisse, Monet, Klee, Van Gogh and, crucially, nine pieces by local boy Cézanne. This fabulous art museum sits right near the top of France's artistic must-sees.

★**Caumont Centre d'Art** HISTORIC BUILDING
([✍]04 42 20 70 01; www.caumont-centredart.com; 3 rue Joseph Cabassol; adult/child €6.50/free; ⊙10am-7pm May-Sep, to 6pm Oct-Apr) The Cau-

mont is a stellar art space housed inside the Mazarin quarter's grandest 18th-century *hôtel particulier*. While there are three quality exhibitions each year, plus concerts and other events, it's the building itself that's the star of the show. Built from local honey-coloured stone, its palatial rooms are stuffed with antiques and objets d'art attesting to the opulence of the house's aristocratic past.

Vieil Aix HISTORIC SITE
One of Aix' great charms is its historical centre: ramble through it, drinking in divine streetscapes as you choose which historical, cultural or culinary highlight to sample next. North of the graceful cours Mirabeau, the city's main artery, is the oldest part of town; to the south, the 17th-century **Quartier Mazarin** is home to some of Aix' finest buildings and streets (including the **Place des Quatre Dauphins**, ennobled by a baroque fountain of the same name).

Fondation Victor Vasarely GALLERY
([✍]04 42 20 01 09; www.fondationvasarely.org; 1 av Marcel Pagnol; adult/child €9/4; ⊙10am-6pm; [P]) This gallery, 4km west of the city, was designed by Hungarian optical-art innovator Victor Vasarely (1906–97). An architectural masterpiece, it has 16 interconnecting,

ence

N 0 ———————— 200 m
   0 ———————— 0.1 miles

tel Paul
(50m)

Villa Gallici
(400m)

Bd Aristide Briand

R de la Roque

R Gaston de Saporta

3

Pl des
Martyrs de
la Résistance

R du Puis Neuf

R Boulegon

R Mignet

Cours St-Louis

14

Av des Thermes

R du Cancel

27

R Paul Bert

R Constantin

R Puits Juif

R de Suffren

Cours des Arts
et Métiers

Forum des
Cardeurs

Pl de l'Hôtel
de Ville

22

Pl des
Prêcheurs

Bd Carnot

R Van Loo

Pl des
Cardeurs

25

35

34

R de la Verrerie

Pl
Richelme

26

R Rifle Rafle

Cours Sextius

29

R des Cordeliers

R F Gaut

39

32

R de Vauvenargues

R d'Entrecasteaux

28

23

R Aumône
Vieille

Pl Ramus

Pl d'Albertas

10

Pl St-
Honoré

Pl de
Verdun

36

31

R Manuel

R Émeric David

TGV
(17km)

R Bruyès

21

R de la Fontaine

R des Tanneurs

R de la Couronne

R des

Pl Esparian

R Nazareth

R Marius Reynaud

R Fabrot

R Thiers

8

R Tournefort

Pl Forbin

R de l'Opéra

Av Napoléon Bonaparte

R Victor Leydet

R des
Bernardines

Pl Jeanne
d'Arc

Pl des
Augustins

17

R Clemenceau

33

R du Maréchal Joffre

Av Giuseppi
Verdi

Pl du Général
de Gaulle

R Paul
Doumer

6

Cours Mirabeau

4

7

Caumont
Centre
d'Art

1

R Mazarine

R Ferrand Dol

R d'Italie

37

Tourist Office

Mattéi
Sq

11

13

30

Cabassol

R Laroque

R du 4 Septembre

9

R Frédéric Mistral

Pl St-Jean
de Malte

15

5

**Musée
2 Granet**

R Lapierre

12

20

R Villars

R Cardinale

R Marcel
Guillaume

Av Victor Hugo

19

24

R Roux Alphéran

18

R Sallier

Grand
Théâtre de
Provence
(250m)

R Gustave Desplaces

16

Av Malherbe

**QUARTIER
MAZARIN**

Bd du Roi René

(100m)

City
Centre

R Gontard

Parc
Jourdan

Av du Parc

---

hexagonal galleries purpose-built to display and reflect the patterning of the artist's 44 acid-trip-ready, floor-to-ceiling geometric artworks. Take bus 2 to the Vasarely stop.

Cours Mirabeau STREET

No streetscape better epitomises Provence's most graceful city than this 440m-long, fountain-studded street, sprinkled with Renaissance *hôtels particuliers* (private mansions) and crowned with a summertime roof of leafy plane trees. It was laid out in the 1650s and later named after the Revolutionary hero the Comte de Mirabeau. Cézanne and Zola hung out at Les Deux Garçons (p191), one of a string of busy pavement cafes.

Église St-Jean de Malte CHURCH

(place St-Jean de Malte; ⊙10am-noon & 3-7pm Mon-Sat, 3-6pm Sun) This 13th-century Gothic church in Aix's Quartier Mazarin, built as a fortified place of worship by the Knights Hospitaller, was the first of its kind in Provence and was once the burial place of the medieval Counts of Provence. It sports a 67m tower, and its ancient priory has been converted into the wonderful Musée Granet (p185).

Aix-en-Provence

Cathédrale St-Sauveur　　　CATHEDRAL
(34 place des Martyrs-de-la-Résistance; ⊙ cathedral 8am-7.30pm, cloisters 10am-noon & 2-5.30pm) Built between 1285 and 1350 in a potpourri of styles, this cathedral includes a Romanesque 12th-century nave in its southern aisle, chapels from the 14th and 15th centuries, and a 5th-century sarcophagus in the apse. More recent additions include the 18th-century gilt Baroque organ. Acoustics make Sunday-afternoon Gregorian chants unforgettable. The entire ensemble sits over the vanished 1st-century Roman forum.

Thermes Sextius　　　SPA
(☑ 04 42 23 81 82; www.thermes-sextius.com; 55 av des Thermes; day pass from €110; ⊙ 8am-8pm Mon-Sat) These modern thermal spas are built on the site of Roman Aquae Sextiae's springs, the excavated remains of which are displayed beneath glass in the lobby.

☞ Tours

Guided Walking Tours　　　WALKING
(☑ 04 42 16 11 84; www.aixenprovencetourism. com; 300 av Giuseppe Verdi; adult/child €10/7; ⊞) The tourist office runs a few guided walking tours in English covering Cézanne and the many sights of the old town. There are about six per week between April and October, falling to one in November and December (if you speak French, your options multiply). Tours leave from the tourist office, usually at 10am, and should be booked in advance.

Mini-Tram　　　TOURS
(Compagnie des Petits Trains du Sud; ☑ 06 11 54 77 73; adult/child €8/3; ⊙ 11am-6pm late Mar–mid-Nov) Offering two routes – a circuit of the old town, and another following the life and locations of Cézanne　these multilingual (French and English) train tours depart from place du Général de Gaulle and wind through the Quartier Mazarin, along cours Mirabeau, and around Vieil Aix. There are more services from mid-April to mid-October.

✦ Festivals & Events

Festival d'Aix-en-Provence　　　MUSIC
(☑ 04 34 08 02 17; www.festival-aix.com; ⊙ Jul) Established in the spirit of rebirth following WWII, this world-renowned festival brings opera, orchestral works, chamber music and even buskers to Aix throughout July. The wonderfully atmospheric **Théâtre de l'Archevêché**, created for the first festival in 1948 and still its principal venue, occupies the courtyard of the former Archbishop's Palace.

AIX DISCOUNTS

The **Aix City Pass** (http://booking.aix enprovencetourism.com; adult 24/48/72hr €25/34/43, child 24/48/72hr €17/21/26) covers entry to all the major museums and Cézanne sights, plus public transport and a guided walking tour.

🛏 Sleeping

Hôtel Paul   HOTEL €
(📞 04 42 23 23 89; www.aix-en-provence.com/hotel paul; 10 av Pasteur; r from €71; 🅿 🛜) On the edge of Vieil Aix, this faded hotel is hardly luxurious, but it's a bit of a bargain as long as you can put up with the no-frills decor. There's a pleasant garden, and breakfast is a very reasonable €6.

⭐**Hôtel les Quatre Dauphins**   BOUTIQUE HOTEL €€
(📞 04 42 38 16 39; www.lesquatredauphins. fr; 54 rue Roux Alphéran; s/d €101/123; ❄🛜) This sweet 13-room hotel slumbers in a former 19th-century mansion in one of the loveliest parts of town. Rooms are fresh and clean, decorated with a great eye and equipped with excellent modern bathrooms. Those with sloping, beamed ceilings in the attic are quaint but not for those who don't pack light – the terracotta-tiled staircase is not suitcase friendly.

Hôtel des Augustins   HOTEL €€
(📞 04 42 27 28 59; www.hotel-augustins.com; 3 rue de la Masse; s/d €139/159; ❄🛜) Once a 15th-century Augustinian convent – the magnificent stone-vaulted lobby makes visible use of an earlier, 12th-century chapel – this charismatic hotel has volumes of history. Martin Luther even stayed here after his excommunication. Sadly, there's not so much heritage to be found in the modern rooms, though pricier suites have antique furniture and private terraces beneath the bell tower.

Hôtel Saint-Christophe   HOTEL €€
(📞 04 42 26 01 24; www.hotel-saintchristophe. com; 2 av Victor Hugo; r from €107; 🅿❄🛜) The Saint-Christophe is a proper hotel, with a big lobby, a central location, original artwork by Provençal painter Marcel Arnaud gracing the walls and an unbroken history of family ownership. Rooms nod to art-deco in their styling and have the standard mid-range amenities, including good bathrooms;

some have terraces, and some can sleep four. Parking can be reserved (€14).

Hôtel Cardinal   HOTEL €€
(📞 04 42 38 32 30; www.hotel-cardinal-aix.com; 24 rue Cardinale; s/d €80/100; 🛜) Pleasantly removed from the hustle of central Aix, yet close enough to walk to most sights, this 18th-century Mazarin quarter hotel is surprisingly elegant, considering the price, with heritage rooms featuring original fireplaces, antiques and swag curtains. There are also six suites in the annexe up the street, each with a kitchenette and dining room – ideal for longer stays.

Hôtel La Caravelle   HOTEL €€
(📞 04 42 21 53 05; www.lacaravelle-hotel.com; 29 bd du Roi René; s/d from €69/95; ❄🛜) On the southern side of the Mazarin luarter, this friendly family-run hotel represents super value in Aix – the rates hardly vary, making it a real bargain in summer. The decor's nothing to get excited about – white walls, grey bedspreads, functional bathrooms – but rooms are quite comfortable. Ask for one on the garden side if you're a light sleeper.

⭐**Villa Gallici**   HISTORIC HOTEL €€€
(📞 04 42 23 29 23; www.villagallici.com; 18 av de la Violette; r from €560; 🅿❄🛜🏊) Baroque and beautiful, this fabulous villa was built as a private residence in the 18th century and still feels marvellously opulent. Rooms are more like museum pieces, stuffed with gilded mirrors, toile de Jouy wallpaper and filigreed furniture. There's a lovely lavender-filled garden to breakfast in, plus a pool, a superb restaurant and a wine cellar.

Hôtel Cézanne   BOUTIQUE HOTEL €€€
(📞 04 42 91 11 11; www.hotelaix.com; 40 av Victor Hugo; d/ste €310/410; 🅿❄@🛜) This striking design hotel acknowledges Aix' painterly pedigree with a life-sized Cézanne figure, abstract sculptures and huge panels of modern art. The rooms perhaps don't justify the price (to which €20 per person is added for an admittedly outstanding breakfast), but fancy extras like iMacs, a brace of hip bars, free Nespresso refills and free parking tip the balance.

🍴 Eating

⭐**Farinoman Fou**   BAKERY €
(www.farinomanfou.fr; 3 rue Mignet; bread €1.40-3; ⏱7am-7pm Tue-Sat) To appeal to bread connoisseurs, in Aix as in any part of France, you need to know your dough. Judging by

the lines typically spilling out of this store onto place des Prêcheurs, artisanal *boulanger* Benoît Fradette clearly does. The bakery has no need to invest in a fancy shopfront – customers jostle for space with bread ovens and dough-mixing tubs.

Maison Nosh
CAFE €

(☑ 06 52 86 22 39; www.maison-nosh.com; 42-44 cours Sextius; lunch menus €10-12; ⊙ 10am-6pm Mon-Sat) Branching out from its original menu of posh hot dogs and gourmet English muffins, this breezy, youthful cafe now offers healthier breakfast, brunch and lunch options, and it's a pleasant place to linger over excellent coffee. Gourmet hot dogs and muffins still form the core of the lunchtime *formules*, however: for €10 you also get a dessert and a drink.

Le Bistrot
BISTRO €

(☑ 04 42 23 34 61; 5 Rue Campra; plat du jour €10, lunch menu €16, mains €15-16; ⊙ noon-2pm & 7.30-10pm) Locals pack into the tiny vaulted dining room of this hard-to-find place for the superb-value lunch *menus*. All the bistro boxes are ticked: red-and-white tablecloths, friendly old-school service, a chuffing coffee machine and menu classics like *daube provençal* (meat stew), chicken hotpot and grilled entrecôte. Extra points for the witty names: the chocolate mousse is called 'Look out, moustache-wearers'.

Chez Charlotte
BISTRO €

(☑ 04 42 26 77 56; 32 rue des Bernardines; 2-/3-course menus €17/22; ⊙ 12.30-2pm & 8-10.30pm Tue-Sat; 🐾) It's all very cosy at Charlotte, where everyone knows everyone. French classics like veal escalope and grilled entrecôte steak are mainstays, and there is always a vegetarian dish and a couple of imaginative *plats du jour*. In summer everything moves into the delightful, walled garden.

La Bidule
BISTRO €

(☑ 04 42 26 87 75; www.brasserielebidule.fr; 8 rue Lieutaud; mains €10-15, 2-course lunch menu €13; ⊙ noon-3pm & 7-11pm) Places come and go around the Forum des Cardeurs, but 'The Thingy' is an enduring, cheap and cheerful favourite, with flowery PVC tablecloths, a vast blackboard menu and a fairy-light-lit terrace presided over by a gnarled olive tree. Expect filling pastas, copious salads, big burgers and a classic *plat du jour*. Lunch *menus* include wine or coffee.

★ Jardin Mazarin
FRENCH €€

(☑ 04 28 31 08 36; www.jardinmazarin.com; 15 rue du 4 Septembre; lunch/dinner menus €23/29; ⊙ 9am-3pm & 7-10.30pm Mon-Sat) This elegant restaurant is set perfectly on the ground floor of a handsome 18th-century *hôtel particulier* in the Quartier Mazarin. Two salons sit beneath splendid beamed ceilings, but the real gem is the verdant fountain-centred garden, which comes into its own in summer. Expect knowledgeable treatment of local, seasonal produce (such as truffles and asparagus) from the kitchen.

★ Le Petit Verdot
PROVENCAL €€

(☑ 04 42 27 30 12; www.lepetitverdot.fr; 7 rue d'Entrecasteaux; mains €21-23; ⊙ 7pm-midnight Mon-Sat) It's all about hearty, honest dining here, with tabletops made out of old wine crates, and a lively chef-patron who runs the place with huge enthusiasm, happily showing how good Provençal food and wine can be. Expect dishes such as *onglet* (skirt-steak) in green-pepper sauce or Pata Negra pork with mustard and honey, accompanied by great wines and seasonal veggies.

Jacquou Le Croquant
PROVENCAL €€

(☑ 04 42 27 37 19; www.jacquoulecroquant.com; 2 rue de l'Aumône Vielle; mains €16-21, menus €20-38; ⊙ noon-2.30pm & 7-10.30pm) Smack bang in the centre of old Aix, this jolly little restaurant specialises in southwestern cuisine, which means copious amounts of duck,

---

MARKETS IN AIX

At the daily **food market** (place Richelme; ⊙ 7am-noon), trestle tables groan each morning under the weight of marinated olives, goat's cheese, garlic, lavender, honey, peaches, melons, cherries and a bounty of other sun-kissed fruit, veggies and seasonal food. Plane trees provide ample shade on the atmospheric T-shaped square, endowed with a couple of corner cafes where Aixois catch up on the gossip over *un café* once their shopping is done.

Flower markets fill place des Prêcheurs (Sunday morning) and place de l'Hôtel de Ville (Tuesday, Thursday and Saturday mornings).

The **flea market** (place de Verdun; ⊙ Tue, Thu & Sat mornings) has quirky vintage items three mornings a week.

rabbit and foie gras on the menu (with almost nothing for vegetarians and absolutely nothing for vegans). There's a pleasing patio for sunny days.

La Cantine CORSICAN €€
(☑ 04 42 67 29 66; 13 rue des Bouteilles; menus €16-29; ⊙ 10am-3pm & 6-11pm Tue-Sat; 🐾) The peasant flavours of Corsica are given free

rein at this backstreet bistro – from big platters of Corsican charcuterie to a wine list with some of the island's best vintages. Tartines, salads and summery Italian and Provençal dishes are also on offer if you're after something lighter. There's lots of seating on the pavement outside, perfect for late-lunch lingering.

BOUCHES-DU-RHÔNE AIX-EN-PROVENCE

SHADOWING CÉZANNE

Local lad Paul Cézanne (1839–1906) is revered in Aix. To see where he lived, ate, drank, studied and painted, follow the **Circuit de Cézanne** (Cézanne Trail), marked by bronze plaques embedded in the footpath. The essential English-language guide to the circuit, and other artist-related sites, *In the Steps of Cézanne,* is free at the **tourist office** (p191).

East of Aix rises Cézanne's favourite haunt, the magnificent silvery ridge of **Montagne Ste-Victoire** (www.grandsitesaintevictoire.com), its dry slopes carpeted in *garrigue* (scented scrub), bristling with pines, crossed by stone-walled paths and concealing sites such as the 17th-century Sainte-Victoire Priory. The burnt-orange soil supports Coteaux d'Aix-en-Provence vineyards, and hiking, mountain-biking and other activities can be arranged through the Aix tourist centre. Many hike the 1011m-mountain's north side, but the south side, though steeper, is quite beautiful.

If you take the D17 along the south side, pick up info on hiking and biking at the **Maison de Ste-Victoire** (☑ 04 13 31 94 70; D17, Saint-Antonin-sur-Bayon; ⊙ 10am-6pm Mon-Fri, to 7pm Sat & Sun; 🚌 110) in St-Antonin-sur-Bayon. The mountain is closed in July and August due to the threat of forest fire (though roads remain open). Driving the loop around Ste-Victoire is gorgeous, or catch bus 110 from La Rotonde in Aix to Payloubier/St-Antonin-sur-Bayon.

Cézanne's last studio, **Atelier Cézanne** (☑ 04 42 21 06 53; www.atelier-cezanne.com; 9 av Paul Cézanne; adult/child €6.50/free, audioguide €3; ⊙ 10am-6pm Jun-Sep, 10am-12.30pm & 2-6pm Apr & May, 10.30am-12.30pm & 2-5pm Oct-Mar, closed Sun Dec-Feb; 🚌 5, 12), where he worked from 1902 until his death four years later, has been painstakingly preserved. Some elements have been re-created: not all the tools and still-life models strewn around the room were his. Though the studio is inspiring, and home to periodic exhibitions, none of Cezanne's works actually hang there. It's a leisurely walk to the studio at Lauves hill, 1.5km north of central Aix, or you can take the bus.

Terrain des Peintres (www.terrain-des-peintres-aix-en-provence.fr; chemin de la Marguerite; 🚌 5, 12) is wonderful terraced garden perfect for a picnic, from where Cézanne, among others, painted the Montagne Ste-Victoire. The view of the jagged mountain is inspirational – Cézanne painted over 80 renditions of it, nine of which are immortalised in stone. The gardens are opposite 62 av Paul Cézanne. You'll find them a 10-minute walk uphill from the Atelier Cézanne stop (bus 5 or 12).

In 1859 Cézanne's father bought **Bastide du Jas de Bouffan** (☑ 04 42 16 11 61; www.cezanne-en-provence.com; 17 route de Galice; adult/child €6/free; ⊙ guided tours from 10.30am daily Jun-Sep, Tue, Thu & Sat May & Oct, Wed & Sat Nov-Mar) , an 18th-century country manor west of Aix where Cézanne painted furiously, producing 36 oils and 17 watercolours depicting the house, farm, chestnut alley, green park and so forth. The manor was closed for major renovations when we visited, and is expected to reopen in 2022. Check for updates with the tourist office in Aix..

In 1895 Cézanne rented a *cabanon* (cabin) at the **Carrières de Bibemus** (Bibémus Quarries; ☑ 04 42 16 11 61; www.cezanne-en-provence.com; 3090 chemin de Bibémus; adult/child €7.70/free; ⊙ English-language tours 11am Apr, May & Oct; 🅿) , east of Aix, where he painted 27 works. Atmospheric one-hour tours of the ochre quarry take visitors on foot through the dramatic burnt-orange rocks that Cézanne captured so vividly on canvas. Tours are mostly in French, though occasional tours are offered in English; book in advance at the tourist office, wear sturdy shoes and avoid wearing white. The ticket price includes a shuttle from the tourist office.

★ **La Table de Pierre Reboul** GASTRONOMY €€€

(☑ 04 42 52 27 27; www.chateaudelapioline.com; 260 rue Guillaume du Vair, Château de la Pioline; lunch/dinner menus from €51/72; ⊘ noon-2pm & 7-10pm) Pierre Reboul's renowned restaurant has moved from central Aix to the aristocratic Château de la Pioline, a suitably smart location for his high-class cuisine. The rich, indulgent French fare meets flavours and ingredients cherry-picked from across the globe (like tempura prawns, or the day's fish with goat's curd and spinach). Rooms are sumptuous too (doubles from €145).

🍸 Drinking & Nightlife

Le Brigand PUB

(17 place Richelme; ⊘ 11pm-2am) A diet of house, techno and electro is varied by theme nights and DJs playing more exotic styles.

Les Deux Garçons CAFE

(☑ 04 42 26 00 51; http://lesdeuxgarcons.fr; 53 cours Mirabeau; ⊘ 7am-2am) Cézanne and Zola once lingered in this classic brasserie-cafe, named for the eponymous two waiters who bought it from their former employer in 1880, and still doing a good line in snooty servers in waistcoats and a huge, chronically-overpriced menu of bistro standards. Ignore the slow service and just enjoy sipping a *petit café* or, better still, a pastis sundowner.

La Mado CAFE

(Chez Madeleine; ☑ 04 42 38 28 02; www.la-mado-aix.fr; 4 place des Prêcheurs; ⊘ 7am-2am) This smart cafe, with grey parasols and box-hedged terrace on a busy square, is unbeatable for coffee and fashionable-people watching. Its European food, a wide range of tartares, pastas, fish and meat (plat du jour €17, *menus* €24-38) is augmented by very decent sushi.

☆ Entertainment

Scat Club de Jazz LIVE MUSIC

(☑ 04 42 23 00 23; http://scatclub.free.fr/scatnet; 11 rue de la Verrerie; ⊘ 4pm-6am Tue, 11pm-6am Wed-Fri, 11pm-4am Sat) This cave-like bar is an old favourite for jazz, rock, funk, Brazilian or whatever regular band is booked that night. The music starts at 11pm and goes for three 45-minute sets, interspersed with DJs.

Grand Théâtre de Provence PERFORMING ARTS

(☑ 08 20 13 20 13; www.lestheatres.net; 380 av Max Juvénal) State-of-the-art theatre presenting music, drama and educational and outreach programs for youth.

Shopping

★ **Cave du Félibrige** WINE

(☑ 04 42 96 90 62; www.aix-en-provence.com/cave-felibrige; 8 rue des Cordeliers; ⊘ 10am-7pm Mon-Sat) Run by committed oenophiles Francois and Vincent, this trove of rare and delightful bottles aims to cover the many French styles and *terroirs*, paying particular attention to Provence. Deeper explorations of the cellar's contents take place at a nearby restaurant on the first Thursday of the month from February to June and October to November. Prebooking and a 50% deposit are mandatory.

★ **Book in Bar** BOOKSHOP

(☑ 04 42 26 60 07; www.bookinbar.com; 4 rue Joseph Cabassol; ⊘ 9am-7pm Mon-Sat) Bibliophiles rejoice: this brilliant Anglophile bookshop has a huge selection of English-language books for sale (amongst works in other languages) and a thoroughly pleasant tearoom to boot. Look out for occasional book readings, jazz evenings and an English-language book club on the last Thursday of the month (from 5.30pm).

La Chambre aux Confitures FOOD

(☑ 04 42 24 07 74; www.lachambreauxconfitures. com; 16bis rue d'Italie; ⊘ 10am-2pm & 3-7pm Mon-Fri, to 7.30pm Sat, to 1pm Sun) This pretty, orderly little shop sells delicious artisanal jams – including unexpected flavours like gooseberry, lavender, strawberries in champagne and bitter lemon – and other condiments for cheese and charcuterie. They're happy for you to mix-and-match and create your own gift packs.

ℹ Information

Tourist Office (☑ 04 42 16 11 61; www.aixen provencetourism.com; 300 av Giuseppe Verdi, Les Allées; ⊘ 8.30am-7pm Mon-Sat, 10am-1pm & 2-6pm Sun Apr-Sep, 8.30am-6pm Mon-Sat Oct-Mar; ☎) Located centrally in the Les Allées shopping centre, this well-resourced tourist office sells tickets for guided tours and cultural events, and it has a shop selling regional products and souvenirs. Touch screens add a high-tech air to the usual collection of brochures.

ℹ Getting There & Away

Consult www.lepilote.com for timetables, fares and itineraries for public transport journeys to/from Aix and www.navetteaixmarseille.com for shuttle buses to/from Marseille.

AIR

Aéroport Marseille-Provence (p329) is 25km southwest and served by regular shuttle buses (€8.20, 33 minutes, from 4.40am to 10.30pm).

BUS

Aix' **bus station** (Gare routière; ☎ 04 42 91 26 80, 08 91 02 40 25; 6 bd Coq) is a 10-minute walk southwest from La Rotonde. Sunday services are limited.

Most of the following services are run by LER (www.info-ler.fr):

Avignon (LER line 23, €18, 1¼ hours, six daily)

Marseille (Cartreize line 50, €9, 40 minutes, every 10 minutes Monday to Saturday, fewer on Sunday)

Nice (line 20, €30, 2¼ hours, five daily Monday to Saturday, three on Sunday)

Toulon (line 19, €14, 1¼ hours, seven daily)

TRAIN

The **city centre train station** (☎ 08 00 11 40 23; www.ter.sncf.com/paca; av Maurice Blondel; ◷ 5am-1am Mon-Sat, from 6am Sun), at the southern end of av Victor Hugo, serves Marseille (€8.30, 45 minutes).

Aix' **TGV station** (☎ 0892 35 35 35; www. gares-sncf.com; rte Départementale 9; ◷ 5.30am-1am), 15km from the centre, is a stop on the high-speed Paris–Marseille line. Destinations include Avignon (from €13, 25 minutes, one or two per hour), Lyon (from €33, 1½ hours, around hourly) and Dijon (from €77, 3¼ hours, one or two daily).

Bus 40 runs from the TGV station to Aix' bus station (€4.30, 15 minutes, every 15 minutes).

Note that the direct Eurostar that connects London, Lyon, Avignon and Marseille does not stop at Aix' TGV station; to get to Aix, you have to change onto a connecting TGV at Lille or Paris.

ⓘ Getting Around

BICYCLE

Opposite the train station, **AixenVelo** (☎ 04 42 39 90 37; www.aixenvelo.com; 12 rue Gustave Desplaces; per day €45; ◷ 10am-7pm Mon-Sat; ⊕) rents bikes with electrical motors and has mapped several itineraries around town.

SWEET SPECIALITIES

Aix' sweetest treat since King René's wedding banquet in 1473 is the marzipan-like local speciality, *calisson d'Aix*, a small, diamond-shaped, chewy delicacy made on a wafer base with ground almonds and fruit syrup, and glazed with icing sugar. Traditional *calissonniers* still make them, including **La Maison du Roy René** (www.calisson. com; 13 rue Gaston de Saporta; calisson boxes from €4.90; ◷ 8am-4.30pm Mon-Thu, to 11am Fri).

BUS

Aix en Bus (www.aixenbus.fr) runs local buses. Most run until 8pm. La Rotonde is the main hub. The tourist office has schedules.

Half-hourly shuttles link Aix' bus station and the TGV station (€4.30) with the airport (€8.20) from 4.40am to 10.30pm.

CAR & MOTORCYCLE

Circumnavigating the old town is a nightmare and metered street parking spaces are hard to find. Parking lots (around €15 to €18 per day) are plentiful, but if you're staying a few days and want to ditch your car, drop your bags at the hotel and park on the edge of town at **Parc Relais Route des Alpes** or **Parc Relais Hauts de Brunet** and take the free shuttle to the centre.

TAXI

Taxis can be found outside the bus station. Also try **Taxi Mirabeau** (☎ 04 42 21 61 61).

Ventabren

POP 5278 / ELEV 238M

Something of a secret, this delightful hilltop village, 15km west of Aix-en-Provence, provides the perfect lazy day out. It's the gorgeous medieval town itself, built as protection from Saracen raids from the 10th century, that's the attraction – that and its charming 360º views. Meander narrow cobbled lanes and take in the *maisons de village* of golden stone, with their faded wooden shutters and pretty green-leaf camouflage. Peep inside its 17th-century church, or hike uphill to enjoy panoramic views of Ste-Victoire (p190), Étang de Berre and northern Luberon from the ruins of **Château de la Reine Jeanne**.

✕ Eating

★**La Table de Ventabren** FRENCH €€€
(☎ 04 42 28 79 33; www.danb.fr; 1 rue Frédéric Mistral; menus €48-107; ◷ kitchen noon-1.15pm & 7.45-9.15pm Tue-Sun May-Sep, shorter hours rest of year) Many restaurants with stunning views rest on their laurels in the kitchen: not so La Table de Ventabren. This Michelin-starred restaurant – with a canvas-canopied terrace that's magical on summer evenings – serves exquisite food. Chef Dan Bessoudo creates inventive French dishes and out-of-this-world desserts.

ⓘ Getting There & Away

Bus L220 (€1, 15 minutes, up to 14 daily) runs from the bus station in Aix to Ventabren.

Drivers from Aix should take the D10 west, then the D64 to Ventabren (you'll have to park on the outskirts of the old town).

Salon-de-Provence

POP 44,836

Surrounded by precious olive groves, Salon-de-Provence was fortified in the 12th century, and today it retains much of its central medieval layout. With plenty of cafes, boutiques and delicatessens to poke around in, you could start your exploration from pretty place Crousillat, on the cusp of the old town, then explore twisting streets once wandered by prognosticator Nostradamus.

Also worth a visit is the 14th-century **Collégiale St-Laurent** (place St-Laurent; ⊙2-4.30pm Mon-Fri) and the town's two famous, long-lived *savonneries* (soap makers). Soap was an important industry thanks to Salon's abundance of olive oil and the palm and copra oils arriving from the French colonies. Perhaps the key sight, however, is the imposing **Château de l'Empéri** (☏04 90 44 72 80; Montée du Puech; adult/child €5/3.20, with Nostradamus House €7.50/5.50; ⊙9.30am-noon & 2-6pm Tue-Sun mid-Apr–Sep; 1.30-6pm Tue-Sat Oct–mid-Apr), an overwhelming fortified palace that's now an accessible museum of art and military history.

⊙ Sights

Maison de Nostradamus HISTORIC BUILDING
(Nostradamus House; ☏04 90 56 64 31; 11 rue Nostradamus; adult/child €5.10/3.30; ⊙9am-noon & 2-6pm Mon-Fri, 2-6pm Sat & Sun) Michel de Nostredame lived here from 1547 until his death in 1566. A physician and philosopher, he married a rich widow and churned out some of his most famous work here. Scrolls of his prophecies line the walls, while often macabre wax figures recreate key scenes from his life, accompanied by piped commentary in several languages (tell the front desk what language you'd like and they'll run it on the next available loop).

⊙ Getting There & Away

From the **train station** (av Émile Zola), a 1km walk from town, trains run to/from Marseille (€11, 30 minutes, frequent), Arles (€26, 2½ hours, up to eight per day) and Avignon (€12, one hour, frequent).

LES ALPILLES

A silvery chain of low, jagged mountains strung between the Rivers Durance and Rhône, the craggy limestone peaks of Les Alpilles rise impressively to the south of the

WORTH A TRIP

CAMP DES MILLES

Eight kilometres southwest of Aix is the town of Les Milles, where the imposing factory of **Camp des Milles** (☏04 42 39 17 11; www.campdesmilles.org; 40 chemin de la Badesse, Les Milles; adult/child €9.50/7.50; ⊙10am-7pm, ticket office to 6pm; P) produced bricks and tiles from 1882 until 31 August 1939, when it was turned into a concentration camp. The camp is now a movingly preserved memorial, with modern exhibits documenting how 10,000 prisoners from 38 countries were held here. Poignant paintings and prose inscribed on the walls by prisoners remain untouched, as does one of the wagons used to transport 2000 prisoners by rail from Les Milles to Auschwitz.

chic town of St-Rémy de Provence. Designated as the Parc Naturel Régional des Alpilles in 2007, the area's hill villages are best explored by car – or better still on foot, along one of the trails that wind amongst the peaks. While you walk, look out for eagles and Egyptian vultures soaring overhead.

Covered with scrubby *maquis* and wild almond and olive trees, the area was immortalised by Vincent van Gogh, who created many much-loved paintings here during the later period of his life – especially while he was a resident at the sanatorium of Monastère St-Paul de Mausole (p194).

St-Rémy-de-Provence

POP 10,826

Ravishing St-Rémy is about as cultured and chi-chi as Provence gets, and yet somehow – and in stark contrast to some of the flashier coastal towns (St-Tropez, we're looking at you) – it's managed to cling on to its heart and soul during the gentrification process. Built from honey-coloured stone, and centred on a lovely, plane-shaded square lined by cafes, St-Rémy is a favourite summer haunt of the jet-set – and yet, even in midsummer, it's possible to find pockets of peace and quiet along the streets of the old town.

South of town, the rugged hills of Les Alpilles rise along the horizon, and one of Provence's most impressive Roman ruins can be explored – the incredibly well-preserved ancient town of Glanum.

SALON'S SOAP

From the turn of the 20th century until the 1950s, soap was a buoyant business in Salon, making fortunes for manufacturers such as Marius Fabre. Run by three generations of the same family, the **Savonnerie Marius Fabre** (☑ 04 90 53 24 77; www.marius-fabre.fr; 148 av Paul Bourret; ☺ 9.30am-12.30pm & 2-7pm Mon-Sat Apr-Sep, to 6pm Oct-Mar, call for tour times) **FREE**, dating from 1900, paints a vivid portrait of the industry with its small museum. Naturally there's a shop – fragrant and artfully arranged.

Savonnerie Rampal-Latour (☑ 04 90 56 07 28; www.rampal-latour.com; 71 rue Félix Pyat; tours free; ☺ 9am-noon & 2-6pm Mon-Fri, call for tour times) has a century-old factory that also recalls the time when soap making was big business in Salon (now the real manufacturing is done elsewhere, on modern premises). Tours generally leave at 10am on weekdays and are more frequent in summer. You can also buy soap at factory prices in the beautiful 1907 boutique.

◉ Sights

★**Site Archéologique de Glanum** RUINS
(☑ 04 90 92 23 79; www.site-glanum.fr; rte des Baux-de-Provence; adult/child €7.50/free, parking €2.70; ☺ 9.30am-6.30pm Apr-Sep, 10am-5pm Oct-Mar, closed Mon Sep-Mar) It might lack the scale and ambition of some of Provence's better-known Roman monuments, but for a glimpse into everyday life in Gaul, this ancient town has no equal. A Roman colony founded around 27 CE, the remains of this once-thriving town have been excavated – complete with baths, forum, columns, marketplace, temples and houses.

Two monuments mark the entrance, 2km south of St-Rémy – a mausoleum (from around 30 BCE) and France's oldest triumphal arch, built around 20 CE.

Monastère St-Paul de Mausole HISTORIC SITE
(☑ 04 90 92 77 00; www.saintpauldemausole.fr; adult/child €5/free; ☺ 9.30am-6.45pm Apr-Sep, 10.15am-5.15pm Oct-Mar, closed Jan–mid-Feb) This monastery turned asylum is famous for one of its former residents – the ever-volatile Vincent van Gogh, who admitted himself in 1889. Safe within the monastery's cloistered walls, Vincent enjoyed his most productive period, completing 150-plus drawings and around 150 paintings, including his famous *Irises*. A reconstruction of his room is open to visitors, as are a Romanesque **cloister** and **gardens** growing flowers that feature in his work.

Hôtel de Sade MUSEUM
(☑ 04 90 92 64 04; www.hotel-de-sade.fr; 1 rue du Parage; adult/child €3.50/free; ☺ 9.30am-1pm & 2-6pm Jun-Sep, shorter hours Oct-May) Reopened after an expensive program of renovations, this impressive Renaissance *hôtel particulier* was built in 1513 by Balthazar de Sade

(ancestor of the much more notorious Marquis de Sade). Since the early 20th century it has housed the most important archaeological finds from the Roman town of Glanum – including an amazing array of sculptures discovered at the site, such as a striking bust of Livia, wife of Emperor Augustus, thought to have been made between 4 and 14 CE.

🛏 Sleeping

★**Sous les Figuiers** BOUTIQUE HOTEL €€
(☑ 04 32 60 15 40; www.hotelsouslesfiguiers.com; 3 av Gabriel St-René Taillandier; d €99-191; 🅿🌡🛜🞖) 'Under The Fig Trees' nicely captures the languid, leisurely, home-away-from-home feel of this charming, country-chic house a five-minute walk from the town centre. All the rooms are decorated with great style, blending distressed wood, warm colours and ethnic textiles; some are in the main house, others are in the gorgeous garden and have cute, private patios. Breakfast costs €15.

Le Sommeil des Fées B&B €
(☑ 04 90 92 17 66; www.angesetfees-stremy.com; 4 rue du 8 Mai 1945; s incl breakfast €55-70, d €70-90) Upstairs from La Cuisine des Anges, this cosy, colourful B&B has five rooms all named after characters from Arthurian legend, blending Provençal and Andalucian decorative details. It's bright, modern and – considering you're in St-Rémy, and that rates include breakfast – really quite a steal.

Le Mas des Carassins HOTEL €€€
(☑ 04 90 92 15 48; www.masdescarassins.com; 1 chemin Gaulois; d €152-234; 🅿@🞖) Arty owners have made this edge-of-town farmhouse a supremely elegant, relaxing and quietly luxurious retreat, with wonderful gardens and a brace of pools. Cool rooms are deco-

rated in china-blues and terracottas, with luxurious linens, wrought-iron beds and tiled floors, and the odd piece of modern art. Ground-floor rooms have small terraces leading onto the private garden.

✗ Eating

Michel Marshall PASTRIES €
(☑ 04 90 95 03 54; 2 place Joseph Hilaire; pastries €5-7; ☺9am-6pm Mon-Sat) St-Rémy's most refined patisserie is elegant for afternoon tea – accompanied by the most delicate of French fancies, *bien sûr.*

Da Peppe ITALIAN €
(☑ 04 90 92 11 56; 2 av Fauconnet; pizza €12-16, mains €14-22; ☺noon-2.30pm & 7-11pm Wed-Mon; 🖟) Excellent pizza and pasta with a Sicilian spin – but the wonderful rooftop terrace is the bit that seals the deal.

La Cuisine des Anges BISTRO €€
(☑ 04 90 92 17 66; www.angesetfees-stremy.com; 4 rue du 8 Mai 1945; 2-course menu €27-29, 3-course menu €32; ☺noon-2.30pm & 7.30-11pm Mon, Wed, Sat & Sun, 7.30-11pm Thu & Fri; 🖃 🖘) You can't really go too far wrong at the Angels' Kitchen – at least if you're looking for solid, no-nonsense Provençal cooking just like *grande-mère* would have made. Tuck into dishes like slow-cooked lamb, bream fillet, baked St-Marcellin cheese and duck pot-au-feu, and dine either in the courtyard or the stone-walled dining room. Fancy, no; flavoursome, yes.

Upstairs is a cute B&B, Le Sommeil des Fées.

L'Aile ou la Cuisse FRENCH €€
(☑ 0432620025;www.laile-ou-la-cuisse-restaurant-saint-remy-de-provence.com; 5 rue de la Commune; menu €29.90, mains €23-40; ☺noon-2.30pm & 7-10.30pm) As Gallic as a *tricolor* Citroën 2CV, this long-established address is run by the Ricci family, also proprietors of Gus and Da Peppe. With its burnished wood, chandeliers and bustling waiters, it's every inch the old-school brasserie – perfect for classics like lamb *en croûte,* honey-glazed pork, picture-worthy pastries and the house special, roast cockerel in foie gras sauce.

Gus BISTRO €€€
(☑ 04 90 90 27 61; www.gussaintremy.com; 31 bd Victor Hugo; mains from €19.50; ☺noon-2.30pm & 7-10.30pm Tue-Sat) This bright, breezy restaurant is a favourite for the chi-chi summer crowd, and with good reason: the food is classy and the ambience is buzzy, with overtones of a Parisian street cafe. It's par-ticularly good on seafood – big *fruits de mer* platters, lobsters and plates of oysters – but there's a blackboard of French specials too.

🔒 Shopping

St-Rémy's packed with boutiques and shops. Hours are reduced in winter, and some shops close for the season.

★ Joël Durand CHOCOLATE
(☑ 04 90 92 38 25; www.joeldurand-chocolatier. fr; 3 bd Victor Hugo; ☺9.30am-12.30pm & 2.30-7.30pm) Among France's top chocolatiers, using Provençal herbs and plants – lavender, rosemary, violet and thyme – with unexpected flavours such as Earl Grey.

La Cave aux Fromages CHEESE
(☑ 04 90 92 32 45; 1 place Joseph Hilaire; ☺10am-7pm, reduced hours Oct-Apr) Thrilling cheese shop with a 12th-century ripening cellar and cheese and charcuterie plates.

ⓘ Information

Tourist Office (☑ 04 90 92 05 22; www.saint remy-de-provence.com; place Jean Jaurès; ☺9.15am-12.30pm & 2-6.30pm Mon-Sat, 10am-12.30pm Sun mid-Apr–mid-Oct, longer hours Jul & Aug, shorter hours mid-Oct–mid-Apr) St-Rémy's tourist office is extremely efficient and well informed, with transport schedules, walking maps of town and Van Gogh sites, and summertime guided tours (book ahead). It does get very busy in summer, however.

ⓘ Getting There & Away

BICYCLE
Cycling is a great way to explore the area around St-Rémy – although you'll need strong legs if you want to make it all the way up into Les Alpilles.

There are several bike-rental companies around town, most of which will deliver within a 20km radius of St-Rémy: contact **Telecycles** (☑ 04 90 92 83 15; www.telecycles-location.fr; per day €20) or **Vélo-Passion** (☑ 04 90 92 49 43; www.velopassion.fr; per day €15).

Alternatively, battery-assisted electric bikes can be hired from **Sun e-Bike** (☑ 04 32 62 08 39; www.location-velo-provence.com; 16 bd Marceau; per day €36; ☺9am-6.30pm Apr-Sep, shorter hours Oct-Mar) and Vélo-Passion (from €35).

> ### ⓘ ST-RÉMY PASS
> Pick up the free Carte St-Rémy at the first sight you visit, get it stamped, then benefit from reduced admission at St-Rémy's other sights.

BUS

Allô Cartreize (☑ 08 10 00 13 26; www.lepilote. com) buses depart from place de la République.

Arles (50 minutes, €2.50, two daily) line 54; also stops in Cavaillon for onward travel into the Luberon Valley.

Avignon (€3.60, one hour, at least one every two hours).

CAR

St-Rémy gets packed in summer; there's parking by the tourist office (parking Jean-Jaurès) and north of the periphery (parking Général-de-Gaulle).

Les Baux-de-Provence

POP 436

Clinging precariously to an ancient limestone *baou* (Provençal for 'rocky spur'), this fortified hilltop village is one of the most visited in France (best seen as a day trip, and avoid the summer crowds if you can). It's easy to understand its popularity: narrow cobbled streets wend car-free past ancient houses, up to a splendid ruined castle.

◉ Sights

★**Carrières de Lumières**   GALLERY

(☑ 04 90 49 20 03; www.carrieres-lumieres.com; rte de Maillane; adult/child €12/10; ☺ 9.30am-7pm or 7.30pm Apr-Sep, 10am-6pm Oct-Dec & Mar) Inside the chilly galleries of a former limestone quarry, this intriguing attraction is like an underground audiovisual art gallery, with giant projections illuminating the walls, floor and ceiling, accompanied by oration and music. Programs change annually and there are joint tickets with the Château des Baux (adult/child €18/16 in summer). Dress warmly.

Château des Baux   CASTLE, RUIN

(☑ 04 90 49 20 02; www.chateau-baux-provence. com; adult/child Apr-Sep €10.50/8.50, Oct-Mar

€8.50/6.50; ☺ 9am-8pm Jul & Aug, to 7pm Apr-Jun & Sep, reduced hours Oct-Mar) Crowning the village of Les Baux, these dramatic, maze-like ruins date to the 10th century. The cliff top castle was largely destroyed in 1633, during the reign of Louis XIII, and is a thrilling place to explore – particularly for rambunctious kids. Climb crumbling towers for incredible views, descend into disused dungeons and flex your knightly prowess with giant medieval weapons dotting the open-air site. Medieval-themed entertainment and hands-on action – shows, duels, catapult demonstrations and so on – abound in summer.

✕ Eating

★**L'Oustau de Baumanière**   GASTRONOMY €€€

(☑ 04 90 54 33 07; www.baumaniere.com; menus €100-215, mains €65-100; ❀ ☎) Twice Michelin-starred and luxurious with a capital L, this legendary hotel-restaurant is the most exclusive – and expensive – place to dine in this corner of Provence. Head chef Jean-André Charial revels in the rich flavours of classic French cooking, and at one of the *table d'hôte* lunch sessions (€33) you can watch the chef work and share some food with him.

ⓘ Information

Tourist Office (☑ 04 90 54 34 39; www. lesbauxdeprovence.com; Maison du Roy; ☺ 9.30am-5pm Mon-Fri, 10am-5.30pm Sat & Sun) Central and helpful, but chronically overworked in summer.

ⓘ Getting There & Away

Bus services to Les Baux-de-Provence are nonexistent. Driving is easiest, but parking can be hellish. Find metered parking spaces (€5 per day) far down the hill at the village's edge; there's free parking outside Carrières de Lumières. Good luck.

OILS OF LES ALPILLES

Moulin Jean-Marie Cornille (☑ 04 90 54 32 37; www.moulin-cornille.com; rue Charloun Rieu, Maussane-les-Alpilles; ☺ 9.30am-6.30pm Mon-Sat, 11am-6pm Sun) This cooperative *moulin* (mill) produces 200,000L of Vallée des Baux-de-Provence AOC oil per year. June to September, you can tour the mill (free) at 11am Tuesday and Thursday.

Moulin Coopératif de Mouriès (☑ 04 90 47 53 86; www.moulincoop.com; Quartier du Mas Neuf, Mouriès; ☺ 9am-noon & 2-6pm Mon-Sat, 2-6pm Sun) At Mouriès, 6km southeast of Maussane, pop in for a tasting of exceptional oils milled at Moulin Coopératif.

Moulin à Huile du Calanquet (☑ 04 32 60 09 50; www.moulinducalanquet.fr; vieux chemin d'Arles; ☺ 9am-noon & 2-7pm Mon-Sat, 10am-noon & 3-6pm Sun Apr-Oct, 9am-noon & 2-6.30pm Mon-Sat Nov-Mar) Brother-and-sister-run olive-oil mill located 4.5km southwest of St-Rémy, with tastings and homemade tapenade, fruit juice and jam.

The Camargue

Best Places to Eat

➡ L'Atelier Jean-Luc Rabanel (p209)

➡ Le Gibolin (p208)

➡ Le Mazet du Vaccarès (p212)

➡ La Telline (p212)

➡ La Chassagnette (p213)

Best Places to Stay

➡ Le Cloître (p208)

➡ L'Hôtel Particulier (p208)

➡ Hôtel de l'Amphithéâtre (p207)

➡ Lodge Sainte Hélène (p216)

➡ Le Mas de Peint (p212)

Why Go?

Where the Petit Rhône and Grand Rhône meet the Mediterranean, the Camargue arises: 930 sq km of *sansouires* (salt flats), *étangs* (saltwater lakes), marshlands and farmland.

Forget all about time in this hauntingly beautiful part of Provence, roamed by black bulls, white horses and pink flamingos. This is slow-go country, a timeless wetland chequered with silver salt pans, waterlogged rice paddies and traditional *gardians* ('cowboys'). But birds are perhaps the delta's greatest feature – flamingos are the obvious star attraction, but there are countless other species to spot.

The main town of the region, Arles, is a show-stopper. Wander the golden-hued streets, the same ones that famously inspired Van Gogh, to find the town's lovely restored Roman amphitheatre, top-notch museums and world-class restaurants.

The Camargue's two largest towns are the seaside pilgrim's outpost Stes-Maries-de-la-Mer and, to the northwest, the walled town of Aigues-Mortes.

Driving Distances (km)

	Salin de Giraud	Le Sambuc	Stes-Maries-de-la-Mer	La Capelière	Aigues-Mortes
Le Sambuc	15				
Stes-Maries-de-la-Mer	61	59			
La Capelière	22	13	41		
Aigues-Mortes	70	62	33	56	
Arles	38	31	37	21	51

Camargue Highlights

1 Arles (p204)
Discovering the city's rich Roman remains and Van Gogh connections.

2 Parc Ornithologique du Pont de Gau (p216)
Watching rose-pink flamingos at this wondrous wetland park.

3 La Capelière (p213) Spotting local flora and fauna from the many nature trails of the Réserve Nationale de Camargue (p211).

4 Le Sambuc (p202) Feasting on fish and seafood at one of the area's excellent restaurants.

5 Domaine de la Palissade (p211) Galloping like the wind on the Camargue's iconic horses.

6 La Digue à la Mer (p216) Biking along the edge of the world to a 19th-century lighthouse.

7 Stes-Maries-de-la-Mer (p213) Tracing the footsteps of generations of pilgrims to this seaside port.

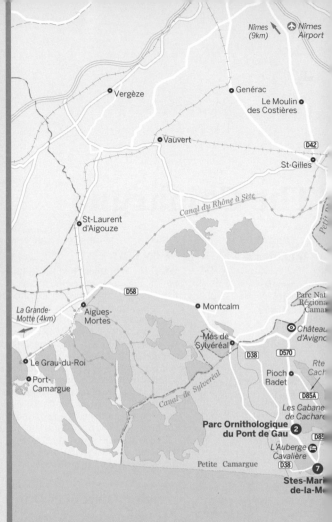

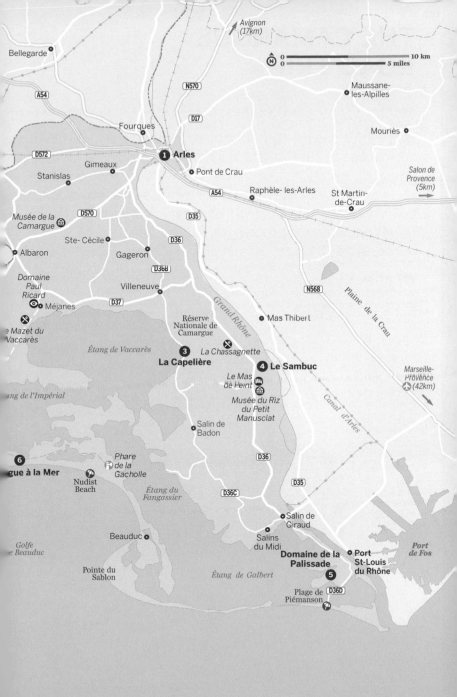

THE CAMARGUE ROAD TRIP

Leave Arles and the highway behind and suddenly you're surrounded by the Camargue's great yawning green, and an equally expansive sky. It won't be long until you spot your first field of cantering white horses, or face off with a black bull. This is not a long trip, but one that will plunge you into an utterly unique world of cowboys, fishers, beachcombers, the Roma, and all their enduring traditions.

❶ Arles

Befitting its role as gateway to the Camargue, Arles has a delightfully insouciant side. Long home to bohemians of all stripes, it's a great place to hang up your sightseeing hat for a few languorous hours (or days). Soak it in from the legendary bar at the **Hôtel Nord-Pinus** (p208), with its bullfighting trophies and enthralling photography collection, or

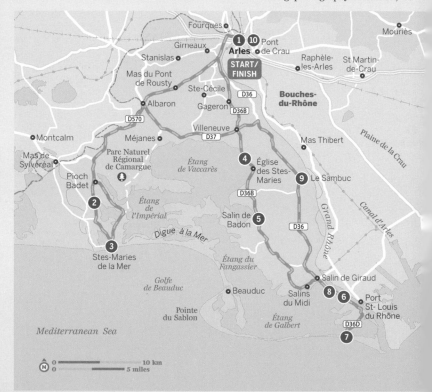

4 Days 190km / 118 miles

Great for ... Outdoors; Families

Best Time to Go May, July and September

pull up a table on lively place Paul Doumer, where Arles' new generation makes its mark. Make a beeline for the Saturday-morning market (bd des Lices) and pack a Camargue-worthy picnic basket with local goat's cheese, olives and *saucisson d'Arles* (bull-meat sausage), or do likewise on Wednesday mornings on bd Émile Combes.

With precious little parking within the old town, unless you're staying at a hotel with a garage (usually an expensive extra), opt for the secure municipal facilities on bd des Lices (€7 per day).

The Drive > Take the D35A across the Grand Rhône at the Pont de Trinquetaille, then follow signs to the D570 – you'll soon be in no doubt you've entered the Camargue. Continue south on the D570 until Pont de Gau, 4km before you hit the coast, around 30 minutes all up.

➊ Parc Ornithologique de Pont de Gau

Itching to get in among all that green? Parc Ornithologique de Pont de Gau (p216), a 60-hectare bird park, makes for a perfect pit stop. As you meander along 7km of trails, flamingos pirouette overhead; the pink birds can't help play diva. Secreted away in the marshes, though, is every bird species that calls the Camargue wetlands home, including herons, storks, egrets, teals and raptors.

The Drive > Continue south on the D570. The last stretch of road into Stes-Maries-de-la-Mer is dotted with stables – little-white-horse heaven, so get out your camera.

➌ Stes-Maries-de-la-Mer

Apart from a stretch of fine sand beaches – some 30km – the main attraction at this rough-and-tumble beach resort is the hauntingly beautiful Église des Stes-Maries (p216), a 12th-century church that's home to a statue of Sara-la-Kali, or black Sara. The crypt houses her alleged remains, along with those of Marie-Salomé and Marie-Jacobé, the Maries of the town's name. Shunned by the Vatican, this paleo-Christian trio has a powerful hold on the Provençal psyche, with a captivating back story involving a boat journey from Palestine and a cameo from Mary Magdalene. Sara is the patron saint of the *gitans* (Roma people), and on 24 and 25 May each year, thousands come to town to pay their respects and party hard. Don't miss the ex-voto paintings that line the smoke-stained walls, personal petitions to Sara that are touching and startlingly strange in turns.

This town is the easiest spot to organise *promenades à cheval* (horseback riding); look for Fédération Française d'Equitation (FFE) accredited places, such as the friendly Cabanes de Cacharel (☑ 04 90 97 84 10, 06 11 57 74 75; www.cabanesdecacharel.com; rte de Cacharel, D85A; horse trek per hour/day €22/70) on the easterly D85A.

The Drive > The scenic D85A rejoins the D570. After 10 minutes or so, turn right onto the D37. Stop at Méjanes for supplies or to visit the legendary fish restaurant Le Mazet du Caccarés. The D36B dramatically skims the eastern lakeshore; it's a 20-minute journey but is worth taking your time over.

➍ Étang de Vaccarès

This 600-sq-km lagoon, with its watery labyrinth of peninsulas and islands, is where the wetlands are at their most dense, almost primordial. Much of its tenuous shore forms the Réserve Nationale de Camargue and is off-limits, making the wonderful nature trails and wildlife observatories at La Capelière (p213) particularly precious. The 1.5km-long Sentier des Rainettes (Tree-Frog Trail) takes you through tamarisk woodlands and the grasses of brackish open meadows.

The Drive > Continue on the D36B past Fiélouse for around 10 minutes.

➎ Salin de Badon

Before you leave La Capelière, grab your permits for another outstanding reserve site, once the royal salt works (adult/child €3/1.50). Around the picturesque ruins are a number of observatories and 4.5km of wild trails – spy on flamingos wading through springtime iris. True birdwatchers mustn't miss a night in the **gîte** (www.snpn.com/re servedecamargue; off the D36B; dm €12) here, a bare-bones cottage in a priceless location.

The Drive > Continue south until you meet the D36, turning right. Stop in Salin de Giraud for bike hire and fuel (there's a 24/7 gas station) or visit the salt works. The D36 splits off to cross the Rhône via punt, but you continue south on the D36D, where it gets exciting: spectacular salt pans appear on your right, the river on your left.

⑥ Domaine de la Palissade

Along the D36D, **Domaine de la Palissade** (p211) organises horse treks (€19 per hour) where you'll find yourself wading across brackish lakes and through a purple haze of sea lavender. It will also take you around lagoons and scrubby glasswort on foot, or give you a free map of the estate's marked walking trails. Don't forget to rent binoculars; best €2 you'll spend this trip!

The Drive > The next 3.7km along the rte de la Mer is equally enchanting, with flocks of birds circling and salt crystals flashing in the sun. Stop when you hit the sea.

⑦ Plage de Piémanson

Just try to resist the urge to greet the Med with a wild dash into the waves at this lovely, windswept beach. Unusually, camping is allowed here from May to September, and hundreds of campervans line up along the dunes for the duration of the *belle saison*. It's a scene that's as polarising of opinion as it is spectacular. Basic facilities and a patrolled section of sand are right at the end of rte de la Mer; head east for the popular nudist beach.

The Drive > Backtrack north along the D36. Just before Salin de Giraud, look for a car park and a small black shack on your right.

⑧ Le Point de Vue

This lookout provides a rare vantage point to take in the stunning scene of pink-stained *salins* (salt pans) and soaring crystalline mountains. As fruitful as it is beguiling, this is Europe's largest salt works, producing some 800,000 tonnes per year. A small shop (the aforementioned black shack) sells *sel de Camargue* (Camargue salt) by the pot or sack, bull-meat sausages and tins of fragrant local olive oil.

The Drive > Heading north on D36 for 20 minutes, Le Mas de Peint is on your right before Le Sambuc, while La Chassagnette's fork and trowel shingle is on the left to its north.

⑨ Le Sambuc

This sleepy town's outskirts hide away one of the region's most luxurious places to stay, and one of its best restaurants. **Le Mas de Peint** (p212) is owned by the Le Bon family, who have been in the *gardian* (cowboy) business for decades. Along with superb Provençal food and lovely rooms, the hotel also offers flamenco, bull-herding and birdwatching weekends.

The Drive > Continue north on the D36, where you'll re-meet the D570 heading to Arles, a 25km stretch in all.

⑩ Arles

Back in Arles, last stop is **Les Arènes** (p204), the town's incredibly well-preserved Roman amphitheatre. Dating from around 90 CE, this great arena would once have held more than 21,000 baying spectators, and it's still used for many events. The structure itself hasn't survived the centuries entirely intact, but it's still an evocative insight into the Roman psyche. Entry is on the northern side.

BIENCHEN-S/S/SHUTTERSTOCK ©

1. Salins
Salt lakes are stained pink throughout the area.

2. Parc Ornithologique de Pont de Gau (p216)
Migrating storks can be spotted in this reserve.

3. Market shopping in Arles (p208)
Pick up local cheeses at the Saturday market.

MARC DOGGETT/SHUTTERSTOCK ©

SALPARADIS/SHUTTERSTOCK ©

ARLES

POP 52,886

Roman treasures, shady squares and plenty of Camarguais culture make Arles a seductive stepping stone into the Camargue. And if its colourful sun-baked houses evoke a sense of déjà vu, it's because you've seen them already on a Van Gogh canvas – the artist painted 200-odd works around town, though sadly his famous little 'yellow house' at 2 place Lamartine, which he painted in 1888, was destroyed during WWII.

Arles' Saturday market is also a must-see – it's one of Provence's best.

History

Long before Van Gogh captured starry nights over the Rhône, the Romans had been won over by the charms of the Greek colony Arelate. In 49 BCE Arles' prosperity and political standing rose meteorically when it backed a winner in Julius Caesar. After Caesar plundered Marseille, which had supported his rival Pompey the Great, Arles eclipsed Marseille as the region's major port. Soon its citizens were living the high life with gladiator fights and chariot races in magnificent open-air theatres. Still intact, the 12,000-seat theatre and 20,000-seat amphitheatre now stage events including Arles' famous *férias,* with their controversial lethal bullfights, less bloody *courses Camarguaises* (where the animals are still taunted) and three-day street parties.

◎ Sights & Activities

★ **Les Arènes**   ROMAN SITE

(Amphithéâtre; ☑ 08 91 70 03 70; www.arenes-arles.com; Rond-Point des Arènes; adult/child €6/free, incl Théâtre Antique €9/free; ☺ 9am-8pm Jul & Aug, to 7pm May, Jun & Sep, shorter hours Oct-Apr) In Roman Gaul, every important town had an amphitheatre, where gladiators and wild animals met their (usually grisly) ends. Few examples have survived, but Arles (like nearby Nîmes) has preserved its colosseum largely intact. At 136m long, 107m wide and 21m tall, built around 90 CE, the oval-shaped amphitheatre would have held 21,000 baying spectators. Though the structure has suffered down the centuries, it's still evocative of the might and capabilities of Roman civilisation. Entry is on the northern side.

Théâtre Antique   ROMAN SITE

(☑ 04 90 49 59 05; rue de la Calade; adult/child €9/free, incl entry to Les Arènes; ☺ 9am-7pm May-Sep, to 6pm Mar, Apr & Oct, 10am-5pm Nov-Feb) It's easy to admire the grace and engineering of this theatre – built at the behest of the unofficial first Roman Emperor, Augustus, in the 1st century BCE, despite a semi-ruinous state brought on by centuries of pilfering. It still serves as one of Arles' premier venues, staging summertime concerts and plays where lighting, seating for 10,000 and the few remaining pillars create a magical atmosphere. The entrance and ticket office is on rue de la Calade.

★ **Fondation Vincent Van Gogh**   GALLERY

(☑ 04 90 93 08 08; www.fondation-vincentvangogh-arles.org; 35ter rue du Docteur Fanton; adult/child €9/free; ☺ 10am-7pm Jul & Aug, from 11am Sep-Jun) Housed in a listed 15th-century manor, now twice repurposed (its other incarnation was as a bank), this Van Gogh–themed gallery is a must-see, as much for the architecture as the art. It has no permanent collection – rather, it hosts one or two excellent exhibitions a year, always with a Van Gogh theme and always including at least one Van Gogh masterpiece. Architectural highlights include the rooftop terrace and the coloured-glass bookshop ceiling. Look online for child- and family-centred programs.

★ **Musée Réattu**   GALLERY

(☑ 04 90 49 37 58; www.museereattu.arles.fr; 10 rue du Grand Prieuré; adult/child €8/free; ☺ 10am-6pm Tue-Sun, to 5pm Dec-Feb) This superb 150-year-old museum, housed in an exquisitely renovated 15th-century Hospitaller priory by the Rhône, might be assumed old-fashioned, yet its modern collection is truly top-notch. Among its holdings are works by 18th- and 19th-century Provençal artists, two paintings and 57 sketches by Picasso, and of course some works from its namesake, Jacques Réattu. It also stages wonderfully curated cutting-edge exhibitions.

Église St-Trophime   CHURCH

(6 place de la République; ☺ 8am-noon & 2-6pm Mon, Fri & Sat, to 5pm Tue-Thu, 2-5pm Sun) Named for Arles' semi-mythical first archbishop, this Romanesque-style church, built over a 5th-century basilica, was a cathedral until the bishopric moved to Aix in 1801. Built between the 12th and 15th centuries, it's considered a masterpiece of Provençal Romanesque. Look for the intricately sculpted western portal, topped by a tympanum depicting the Apocalypse (and St Trophime himself, brandishing his crozier). Inside, the treasury contains bone fragments of Arles' bishops. Occasional exhibitions are hosted in neighbouring cloister, **Cloître St-Trophime**.

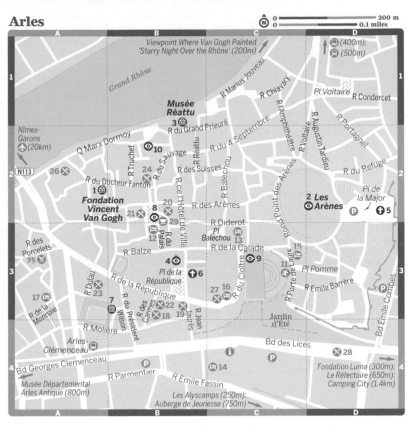

Arles

◎ Top Sights

◎ Sights

✈ Activities, Courses & Tours

🛏 Sleeping

✖ Eating

◉ Drinking & Nightlife

THE CAMARGUE ARLES

Musée Départemental Arles Antique

MUSEUM

(☑ 04 13 31 51 03; www.arles-antique.cg13.fr; av de la Première Division Française Libre; adult/child €8/free; ☺ 10am-6pm Wed-Mon; 🅿) This striking cobalt-blue museum perches on the edge of what used to be the Roman chariot-racing track (hippodrome), southwest of central Arles. The collection of pagan and Christian finds includes stunning mosaics and a wing of treasures highlighting Arles' commercial and maritime prominence. Permanent collections reach back to prehistory, through the arrival of the Greeks in 600 BCE to the Roman period and beyond. If you love a proper museum, full of artefacts and history, you'll love it.

Cryptoportiques

ROMAN SITE

(place de la République, Hôtel de Ville; adult/child €4.50/free; ☺ 10am-5pm Nov-Feb, 9am-6pm Mar, Apr & Oct, 9am-7pm May-Sep) The origins of these fascinating underground chambers, now sitting below the current city centre, go at least back to the first Roman colony in Arles in 46 BCE, and most likely extend to much older Greek caverns. It's a wonderfully literal 2000-year excursion to take the stairs from the gleaming administrative heart of modern Arles, down to three vaulted chambers that may have housed shops or storage cellars under the Roman forum.

Thermes de Constantin

ROMAN SITE

(☑ 04 90 49 59 05; rue du Grand Prieuré; adult/child €4/free; ☺ 9am-7pm May-Sep, to 6pm Mar, Apr & Oct) These partly preserved Roman baths were built for Emperor Constantin's private use in the 4th century. While much of the complex has been built over across the centuries, you can still see the hypocausts (under-floor heating), several plunge pools and the overall elegance of the construction.

Espace Van Gogh

GALLERY

(☑ 04 90 49 39 39; place Félix Rey; ☺ 8am-6pm) FREE The 16th-century hospital where Van Gogh had his ear stitched on and was later locked up hosts the occasional exhibition (which attracts an entry fee). At other times, its small garden, modelled on Van Gogh's *Le Jardin de l'Hôtel de Dieu*, is worth a peek.

Les Alyscamps

CEMETERY

(av des Alyscamps; adult/child €4.50/free; ☺ 9am-7pm May-Sep, shorter hours rest of year) Testa-

---

VAN GOGH IN ARLES

It's easy to forget that Vincent van Gogh was only 37 when he died, as he appears much older in some of his self-portraits. Born in 1853, the Dutch painter arrived in Arles in 1888 after living in Paris with his younger brother Theo, an art dealer who financially supported Vincent from his own modest income. In Paris he had become acquainted with seminal artists Edgar Degas, Camille Pissarro, Henri de Toulouse-Lautrec and Paul Gauguin.

Revelling in Arles' intense light and bright colours, Van Gogh painted with a burning fervour, unfazed by howling mistral winds. During a mistral he would kneel on his canvases and paint horizontally, or lash his easel to iron stakes driven deep into the ground. He sent paintings to Theo for him to try to sell, and dreamed of founding an artists colony in Arles, but only Gauguin accepted his invitation. Their differing artistic approaches (Gauguin believed in painting from imagination, Van Gogh in painting what he saw) and artistic temperaments came to a head with the argument in December 1888 that led to Van Gogh lopping off part of his own ear.

In May 1889 Van Gogh voluntarily entered an asylum, Monastère St-Paul de Mausole (p194) in St-Rémy de Provence. During his one year, one week and one day's confinement he painted 150-odd canvases, including masterpieces like *Starry Night* (not to be confused with *Starry Night over the Rhône*, painted in Arles).

In February 1890 Van Gogh's Arles-painted work *The Red Vines* (1888) was bought by Anne Boch, sister of his friend Eugene Boch, for 400 francs (around €50 today) – the only painting he sold in his lifetime. It now hangs in the Pushkin State Museum of Fine Arts.

On 16 May 1890 Van Gogh moved to Auvers-sur-Oise, just outside Paris, to be closer to Theo. But on 27 July that year he shot himself and died two days later, with Theo at his side. Theo subsequently had a breakdown, was committed and died, aged 33, just six months after Vincent. Less than a decade later, Van Gogh's talent started to achieve recognition, with major museums acquiring his work.

ment to the significance of Roman Arles, this grand processional avenue of tombs and sarcophagi holds more than 1500 years of corpses (which Roman custom insisted were buried outside the city). Van Gogh and Gauguin both painted this necropolis, at the eastern end of which stands the marvellously atmospheric, unfinished 11th-century St-Honorat chapel.

Église Notre Dame de la Major   CHURCH
(16 place de la Major) Complicated restoration projects mean this 12th-century church, dominating Arles from the highest point in the city, can only be admired from outside. Enduring a chequered history, including desacralisation during the Revolution, it's now the unofficial church of the *gardians* (Camargue cowboys).

Camargue Découverte   SAFARI
(06 86 35 10 04; www.camargue-decouverte.com; 24 rue Porte de Laure) Delve into the delta by 4WD jeep on safari-style half-day trips, which can be combined with horseback rambles.

★ Festivals & Events

Fête des Gardians   CULTURAL
(1 May) Mounted *gardians* (Camarguais cowboys) parade and hold games in central Arles during this festival, which affords a fascinating insight into the region's traditions. The show, put on by the Brotherhood of the Gardians, founded in 1512, culminates in the Arena d'Arles.

Les Suds   MUSIC
(04 90 96 06 27; www.suds-arles.com; Jul) This wonderfully imaginative and multi-faceted world music festival makes use of Arles venues as diverse as the Roman theatre and the abandoned industrial complex Parc des Ateliers. While the main festival occurs over a week in July, the organisers stay busy throughout the year with live events, workshops and more.

Fêtes d'Arles   CULTURAL
(www.festivarles.com; mid-Jun–early Jul) Races, parades, costumes, theatre and music come to Arles over several weeks from mid-June. Highlights include La Course de Satin – a bare-back race on pure-bred Camargue horses dating to 1529 – and the Pegoulado – a torchlight procession of participants dressed in traditional Provençal costume that has wended its way through town to the Roman theatre since at least 1830.

Les Rencontres d'Arles Photographie   ART
(www.rencontres-arles.com; adult/child from €28/23; Jul-Sep) This internationally renowned photography festival, with a pedigree stretching to 1969, makes great use of a number of heritage sites around Arles for its many exhibits, debates, performances and workshops.

🛏 Sleeping

Auberge de Jeunesse   HOSTEL €
(04 90 96 18 25; www.hifrance.org; 20 av Maréchal Foch; dm incl breakfast & linen €20.30; Mar-Oct) Modern, shiny and neat, this efficient if uninspiring hostel's drawcard is its location, 10 minutes' walk from the city centre. The usual Fédération Unie des Auberges de Jeunesse (FUAJ) facilities are on offer – kitchen, lounge, cafe and dorms of varying sizes, plus a bar. Bedding is provided, towels aren't, and the doors are locked at 11pm.

Camping City   CAMPGROUND €
(04 90 93 08 86; www.camping-city.com; 67 rte de Crau; 1-/2-person sites €18/20; Apr-Sep; P) On the road to Marseille, 1.5km southeast of town, Camping City is the closest camping ground to Arles. Bike hire and laundry facilities are available, and there are indoor and outdoor activities for kids. To get here, take bus 2 to the Hermite stop.

Hôtel de l'Amphithéâtre   HISTORIC HOTEL €€
(04 90 96 10 30; www.hotelamphitheatre.fr; 5-7 rue Diderot; s/d €89/109;) This elegant address across from the amphitheatre is quite a bargain: the standard of design here far outreaches the reasonable price tag. Antiques, rugs, fireplaces and staircases speak of the building's history, while minimal rooms nod to modern trends, and several have super views over Les Arènes and Arles' rooftops (although you'll pay for the privilege).

Le Calendal   HOTEL €€
(04 90 96 11 89; www.lecalendal.com; 5 rue Porte de Laure; s/d/tr €109/149/159; lunch noon-2.30pm, salon de thé 4-6pm;) Hotel, spa and restaurant, this cosy bolt-hole opposite the Théâtre Antique has bright rooms and an inviting stone-walled garden. Breakfast is a buffet in **Le Comptoir du Calendal** (04 90 96 11 89; www.lecalendal.com; 5 rue Porte de Laure; mains €12-18; 8am-8.30pm;). A massage in the spa is always a good idea.

DON'T MISS

ARLES' SATURDAY MARKET

Plan to be in Arles for the whopping Saturday morning **market** (☑ 04 90 49 36 36; bd des Lices; ☉ 8am-1pm Sat). You'll find all the Camargue's best produce: salt, rice, goat's cheese, *saucisson d'Arles* (bull-meat sausage) and so much more. Stalls line both sides of the street as visitors and locals alike browse, sample and buy everything from lavender honey to baby chicks.

★ **Hôtel Jules César**   DESIGN HOTEL €€€
(☑ 04 90 52 52 52; www.hotel-julescesar.fr; 9 bd des Lices; r from €226; ❋ 🛜 ⛱) It's not often you can say you've stayed somewhere designed from scratch by a world-famous fashion icon – but that's what you get at this luxe address (part of Sofitel's MGallery collection), renovated by couturier Christian Lacroix. Once a convent for Carmelite nuns, it's now a temple to fashion, glittering with over-the-top mirrors, Roman busts, modern art and trendy textiles.

★ **Grand Hôtel Nord Pinus**   HERITAGE HOTEL €€€
(☑ 04 90 93 44 44; www.nord-pinus.com; place du Forum; s/d €232/368; ❋ 🛜) This Arlésian landmark has housed everyone from Picasso and Hemingway to Cocteau and Fritz Lang. Its style is 1930s opulence: wrought-iron beds, art-deco sinks, designer furniture, vintage *féria* posters, black-and-white Peter Beard photographs and a chichi bar and restaurant. This is not the place to stay if you baulk at paying €25 for parking and €32 for breakfast.

★ **Le Cloître**   DESIGN HOTEL €€€
(☑ 04 88 09 10 00; www.hotelducloitre.com; 18 rue du Cloître; r €213; ❋ @ 🛜) The traditional Mediterranean courtyard that greets you on arrival at 'The Cloister' is charming enough, but doesn't betray the inventiveness of the warm, colourful design within. Its 19 rooms are all distinct, with Italian showers and unusual furniture that sacrifices no comfort. Rooms are €14 per person cheaper if you forgo breakfast, and there's a panoramic rooftop terrace.

L'Hôtel Particulier   BOUTIQUE HOTEL €€€
(☑ 04 90 52 51 40; www.hotel-particulier.com; 4 rue de la Monnaie; r/ste €392/452; ❋ 🛜 ⛱) It's hard to believe this former priory is in central Arles, it is so peaceful and secluded. It's all too easy to relax here amongst the manicured gardens, luminous all-white rooms, rococo detailing, original fireplaces, elegant staircase, inviting bar and gorgeous *hammam* (Turkish steambath). The restaurant is top-class, too.

✖ Eating

Glacier Arlelatis   ICE CREAM €
(☑ 06 50 05 74 39; 8 place du Forum; 1/2 scoops €2/4; ☉ 12.30-11pm) Thirty-eight flavours of artisanal ice cream and sorbet are the mainstays of this *glacier* on busy place du Forum. Buy a cone to take away or treat yourself to a magnificent whipped-cream-topped sundae sitting down. Flavours change but there are always a few distinctly Provençal ones: lavender honey, chestnut and so forth.

Fadoli et Fadola   CAFE €
(☑ 04 90 49 70 73; 44 rue des Arènes; sandwiches €5, salads €7; ☉ noon-2.30pm; 🍽) Well-stuffed sandwiches – made to order, *frotté à l'ail* (rubbed with garlic) and dripping with silken AOC Vallée des Baux olive oil – lure the crowds to this tiny sandwich shop with a hole-in-the-wall takeaway counter. It also sells olive oil by the litre (€12 to €25) and even sushi. Find it footsteps from central 'cafe' square, place du Forum.

L'Entrevue   MOROCCAN €
(☑ 04 90 93 37 28; www.lentrevue-restaurant. com; place Nina Berberova; plat du jour €13, mains €17-20; ☉ noon-2.30pm & 7-11pm Sep-Jun, noon-3.30pm & 7-10.30pm Jul & Aug; 🍽) There's a French portion to the menu at this popular Moroccan brasserie by the Rhône, but we strongly recommend you stick to wonderful Maghrebian favourites such as couscous, tajines and pastillas – they're excellent.

Comptoir du Sud   CAFE €
(☑ 04 90 96 22 17; 2 rue Jean Jaurès; sandwiches €4.50-6; ☉ 10.30am-4pm Tue-Fri) A great lunch option, with a counter brimming with picnicky treats – sandwiches filled with inventive ingredients such as Roquefort and *cèpe crème* (porcini cream), homemade pâtés, chutneys and cheeses, top-class charcuterie and fresh salads. There are a few bar stools to perch on, but most people order to go.

★ **Le Gibolin**   BISTRO €€
(☑ 04 88 65 43 14; 13 rue des Porcelets; 2-/3-course menus €27/34; ☉ 12.15-2pm & 8-10.30pm Tue-Sat Apr-Jul & Oct, shorter hours rest of year) After spending three decades plying Paris with

their passion for organic wines, owners Brigitte and Luc decided to head south and do the same for Arles. Unsurprisingly, it's become a much-loved local fixture, known for its hearty home cooking and peerless wine list (racked up temptingly behind the bar and mostly available by the glass).

★ L'Autruche
MODERN FRENCH €€

(☑ 04 90 49 73 63; 5 rue Dulau; menus €29; ⊙ noon-1.30pm & 7.30-9pm Thu-Sun, noon-1.30pm Wed) 'The Ostrich', run by husband-and-wife team Fabien and Ouria, is a family restaurant in the best tradition. Market-fresh produce is assured, as is the ability of their Michelin-experienced chef to treat it with skill – perhaps plaice with coco beans or silky asparagus soup with nuts. Extravagant desserts are a further treat.

L'Ouvre Boîte
TAPAS €€

(☑ 04 88 09 10 10; 22 rue du Cloître; dishes €8-10; ⊙ 6.30-9.30pm Mon-Fri, 11am-2pm & 6.30-9.30pm Sat & Sun) Alexandre's little joint (the 'Open Box') has become a firm Arlésian favourite for chilled evening eats in the courtyard of the Hôtel du Cloître. It specialises in shared tapas-like 'little plates' – oysters, octopus in herby-tomato sauce, pork in Asian broth – ordered to share. Arrive early for a prime table.

À Côté
BISTRO €€

(☑ 04 90 47 61 13; www.bistro-acote.com; 21 rue des Carmes; menus €32; ⊙ noon-1.30pm & 7.30-9pm Wed-Sun) A meal at Jean-Luc Rabanel's nearby flagship restaurant may be too expensive for some, but he knows how to do great bistro dining too. While bearing the Rabanel signature style, À Côté is reassuringly casual, with wooden chairs, terrace-style tables, and a blackboard menu of solid bistro classics – go for something like confit lamb shank or local terrine with condiments.

Le Galoubet
FRENCH €€

(☑ 04 90 93 18 11; 18 rue du Docteur Fanton; 2-/3-course menus €27/33; ⊙ noon-1.30pm & 7-9.30pm Tue-Sat) Eighteenth-century stone walls, a wooden bar, a fireplace, friendly staff and French/Provençal food that's not afraid to play with Asian ingredients like Thai basil – what's not to like about this romantic, reliable bistro? Céline works the magic in the kitchen, while husband Franck runs things out front. Try the *onglet* (skirt steak) with morel mushrooms.

Le Réfectoire
INTERNATIONAL €€

(☑ 04 90 47 11 67; 45 chemin des Minimes, La Grande Halle, ZAC des Ateliers; 2-/3-course menus €22/27; ⊙ 11am-6pm Fri-Tue; ☑) You won't find a much better lunch venue than this convivial canteen within the emergent cultural centre Luma. The food is light and colourful, with a strong emphasis on veggies and organic wholefoods. Expect dishes such as tabbouleh of carrots, lentils and celery, stuffed purple aubergines, quinoa salads, and more filling mains like roast Ventoux pork.

★ L'Atelier
Jean-Luc Rabanel
GASTRONOMY €€€

(☑ 04 90 91 07 69; www.rabanel.com; 7 rue des Carmes; menus €55-155; ⊙ noon-1pm & 8-9pm Thu-Sat, noon-1pm Sun, 8-9pm Wed) As much an artistic experience as a double-Michelin-starred adventure, this is the gastronomic flagship of charismatic chef Jean-Luc Rabanel. Many products are sourced from the chef's veggie patch, and wine pairings are an experience in themselves. Saturday-morning cooking classes are also available, working with the kitchen brigade (€200). Next door, Rabanel's À Côté offers bistro fare.

🍷 Drinking & Nightlife

Le Café Van Gogh
CAFE

(Le Café La Nuit; ☑ 04 90 96 44 56; www.restaurant-cafe-van-gogh.com; 11 place du Forum; ⊙ 11am-3pm & 6-11pm) Immortalised in Van Gogh's 1888 *Terrasse du Café le Soir,* this cafe trades on its plum spot on the place du Forum and its association with the adopted Arlésian painter. Shaded by plane trees, it turns into a giant terrace at lunch and dinner in summer.

ILLUMINATING THE FUTURE

In 2021 Arles' already-bulging cultural landscape welcomed the new cutting-edge gallery and arts centre **Luma Arles** (☑ 04 90 47 76 17; www.luma-arles.org; 45 chemin des Minimes; ⊙ Parc des Ateliers), rising inexorably on a defunct railway depot in the city's southeastern quarter. Funded by the Swiss-based Luma Foundation, and designed by Frank Gehry, the cultural centre is host to presentations, exhibitions and artists' residences. The building is an artwork in itself, a twisting, shimmering tower loosely inspired by Van Gogh's *Starry Night*, sitting on a sprawling 27-acres.

☆ Entertainment

**La Guinguette du
Patio de Camargue** LIVE MUSIC
(📱 04 90 49 51 76; www.chico.fr; 49 chemin de Barriol; ⏱11am-midnight) Established in 1995 by Chico, co-founder of the Gypsy Kings, on a patch of industrial wasteland by the banks of the Rhône, this is now a wonderful riverside grill and bar. It's quite festive, especially on Friday and Saturday nights when there's a special tapas, paella and barbecue menu and live music.

Every month or so the owner's new band, Chico and the Gypsies, performs at a dinner concert (from €70 including food and drink).

❶ Information

Tourist Office (📱 04 90 18 41 20; www.arlestourisme.com; 9 blvd des Lices; ⏱9am-6.45pm Apr-Sep, 9am-4.45pm Mon-Sat, 10am-1pm Sun Oct-Mar; 🐱) Sells Arles' two sightseeing passes, and also has some useful leaflets on cycling and walking itineraries.

❶ Getting There & Away

BUS

Buses leave from either the central **bus station** (Gare Routière; www.lepilote.com; av Paulin Talabot) near the train station, or the more central **stop on bd Clémenceau** (bd Clémenceau); many stop at both. There are three different companies, so for up-to-date timetables, consult www.lepilote.com, www.edgard-transport.fr or www.envia.fr. Destinations include the following:

Aix-en-Provence (Cartreize Line 18, €11, 1¼ hours, up to nine a day from Arles-Clémenceau)

Salon-de-Provence (Cartreize Line 29, €4.80, 1¼ hours, up to six per day from the central bus station)

Stes-Marie-de-la-Mer (Envia Line 20, €2.50, one hour, up to six per day from the central bus station Monday to Saturday)

TRAIN

The **train station** (av Paulin Talabot) has services to Nîmes (from €7.50, 30 minutes to one

hour, hourly), Marseille (€13, one hour, at least hourly) and Avignon (€6, 20 minutes, every one to two hours). The closest TGV stations are in Avignon and Nîmes.

❶ Getting Around

BICYCLE

1Véloc (📱 04 86 32 27 05; www.1veloc.fr; 12 rue de la Cavalerie; bike/ebike per day from €8/25; ⏱10am-12.30pm & 3-6pm Tue-Fri, 3-6pm Sat Sep-Jun, plus 10am-noon & 5-6pm Sun Jul & Aug) Rents bikes and runs tours.

BUS

Envia (📱 08 10 00 08 18; www.tout-envia.com; 24 bd Georges Clemenceau; 1/10 tickets €0.80/6.50; ⏱7am-6.30pm Mon-Fri, 7.30am-noon & 2-5.30pm Sat) Local buses run 6.30am to 7.30pm Monday to Saturday, and 9.30am to 5.30pm Sunday. Buy tickets on board.

Free minibuses circle most of the old city every 25 minutes from 7.10am to 7.15pm Monday to Saturday.

TAXI
Taxi (📱 04 90 96 90 03)

CAMARGUE COUNTRYSIDE

Travelling around the Camargue is tantamount to frolicking with a zillion mosquitoes in a giant nature park. Almost all the Camargue's wetlands are protected by the 850-sq-km Parc Naturel Régional de Camargue. The Maison du Parc, 4km north of Stes-Maries-de-la-Mer in Pont de Gau, is closed indefinitely, but you can pick up information on walking, birdwatching and other activities at the park-run **Musée de la Camargue** (Musée Camarguais; 📱 04 90 97 10 82; www.parc-camargue.fr; D570, Mas du Pont de Rousty; adult/child €5/free; ⏱9am-12.30pm & 1-6pm Apr-Sep, 10am-5.30pm Oct-Mar), 10km south of Arles on the D570.

On the periphery, the 600-sq-km lagoon **Étang de Vaccarès** and nearby peninsulas and islands form the 132-sq-km Réserve Nationale de Camargue. Get the full lowdown on the reserve and its activities at the information centre (p213) in La Capelière.

Another 20 sq km between Arles and Salin de Giraud is managed by the Conservatoire du Littoral (www.conservatoire-du-littoral.fr), France's coastal protection agency, which purchases threatened natural areas by the sea to restore and protect.

◉ Sights & Activities

★ Domaine de la Palissade   PARK
(☑ 04 42 86 81 28; www.palissade.fr; 36 chemin
Départemental; adult/child €3/free, horse trekking
per hour adult/child from €19/16; ⊙ 9am-6pm mid-
Jun–mid-Sep, to 5pm Mar–mid-Jun & mid-Sep–Oct,
9am-5pm Wed-Sun Feb & Nov; P) This remote
nature centre, 12km south of Salin de
Giraud, organises fantastic forays through
702 hectares of protected marshland, scrubby glasswort, flowering sea lavender (in
August) and lagoons, on foot and horseback
(call ahead to book horse treks). Before
hitting the scrub, rent binoculars (€2) and
grab a free map of the estate's three marked
walking trails (1km to 8km) from the office.
The tours are as educational as they are
enjoyable.

Réserve Nationale
de Camargue   NATIONAL PARK
(☑ 04 90 97 00 97; www.snpn.com/reservede
camargue; C134, rte de Fiélouse, La Capelière) One
of the oldest nature reserves in France (first
delineated in 1927 and given official protected status in 1975), it covers 132 sq km of wetlands, lagoons, islands, peninsulas and the
vast 600-sq-km Étang de Vaccarès. There's
an information centre at La Capelière (p213)
where you can access useful maps detailing recommended birdwatching areas and
balades naturalistes (nature walks).

Parc Naturel Régional
de Camargue   NATIONAL PARK
(PNRC; www.parc-camargue.fr) Enclosed by
the Petit Rhône and Grand Rhône rivers,
most of the Camargue wetlands fall within
the 850-sq-km Parc, established in 1970 to
preserve the area's fragile ecosystem, while
sustaining local agriculture. It's a stunning
and precious environment in which age-old
farming practices coexist with one of Europe's greatest havens for birdlife. If you are
a birdwatcher, you simply must come here.
The park's headquarters are housed in the
Musée de la Camargue, just outside Arles.

Manade des Baumelles   FARM
(☑ 04 90 97 84 14; www.manadedesbaumelles.
fr; D38; tour with/without lunch €45/25; ⊙ tours
10.30am Tue-Sun; P) Located on the Petit
Rhône, this *manade* (bull farm) lets visitors
enter the world of the *gardians* ('cowboys'),
watching their strenuous work from the
safety of a truck. The braver can ride horses, join in the farm-work, go canoeing and
play traditional *gardian* games. Tours end

FÉRIA D'ARLES

While it centres on the ethically ques-
tionable 'sport' of bullfighting, the Féria
d'Arles is also unavoidably one of the
highlights of the city's calendar. Or rather, two of them: one in Easter marking
the beginning of the bullfighting season,
and one in September, called the Féria
du Riz (Festival of Rice), but also involving bullfighting.

Over half a million visitors and bullfighting aficionados descend on Arles
for the Easter Féria, with 50,000 cram-
ming into the Roman amphitheatre Les
Arènes to see the fights (and the less
cruel bull-leaping). But it's in the streets
of Arles that the true Féria unfurls:
music, feasting, parties, traditional costumes and instruments are all abundant.

with an optional farm lunch (menus €25/37)
and a gift shop stocked with Camargue
specialities.

La Maison du Guide   OUTDOORS
(☑ 06 12 44 73 52, 04 66 73 52 30; www.maison
duguide.camargue.fr; 154 rue du Château de Montcalm, Montcalm; guided tours adult/child €20/
free, 4-person cottage per week €270-550; ⊙ office 9am-noon Mon; ⊕) Discovery weekends
by naturalist Jean-Marie Espuche embrace
birdwatching, cycling, horse riding and sunrise nature walks. You'll find 'secret' parts of
the Camargue and see much more birdlife
than you otherwise might. Jean-Marie also
rents a four-person cottage in Montcalm, a
useful base on the edge of the Camargue.

Manade Salierène   HORSE RIDING
(☑ 04 66 86 45 57; www.manadesalierene.com;
D37, Mas de Capellane; weeklong course €700,
gîte per night €80; ⊙ Apr-Aug; ⊕) Get a taste
of Camargue *gardian* ('cowboy') life with a
one-week *stage de monte gardiane*. Courses include riding, accommodation, meals
with the *manadier's* (herder's) family and
the chance to get involved. Surrounded by
wetlands, birdlife and a *manarde* (herd) of
horses and cattle, this may be the ultimate
way for travellers to experience this unique
part of France.

Kayak Vert Camargue   CANOEING
(☑ 04 66 73 57 17; www.kayakvert-camargue.fr;
rte départementale 202, Mas de Sylvéréal; kayak
per hour/day €10/35; ⊙ 9am-7pm Mar-Oct) For

CHÂTEAU DE TARASCON

Twenty kilometres north of Arles, the mighty walls of the 15th-century **Château de Taras-con** (✆ 04 90 91 01 93; www.tarascon.fr; adult/child 10-17yr €7.50/3.50; ☉ 9.30am-5.30pm Oct-May, to 6.30pm Jun-Sep, last entry 45min before close) rise straight out of the River Rhône, in the relaxed village of the same name. A beauty of a castle, the imposing fortress was built by Louis II to defend Provence's frontier. Today it's a great destination for a half-day trip. Cross the mossy inner courtyard and explore the dainty chapel, ancient pharmacy and carved grotesques as you make your way to the crenellated rooftop for stunning river views.

After losing battles and suffering a lengthy imprisonment, Louis' son King René (r 1409–80) turned away from politics and towards the arts, writing poetry, decorating the castle in rich Renaissance style, organising courtly tournaments and instigating the Fêtes de la Tarasque, an Easter parade to celebrate St Martha's taming of Tarasque, a monstrous lion-headed, tortoise-shelled, fish-bellied beast that legend says once lurked in the river. This colourful festival still takes place today.

canoeing and kayaking on the Petit Rhône, contact Kayak Vert Camargue, 14km north of Stes-Maries-de-la-Mer off the D38.

🛏 Sleeping

The most obvious base in the Camargue is Arles, which has a wealth of accommodation. Further out into the countryside hotels are less sophisticated, but there are some attractive B&Bs, cabins and rural camping grounds scattered around.

Ranch-style motel accommodation lines the D570 heading into Stes-Maries-de-la-Mer. The tourist offices can point you towards self-catering *cabanes de gardian* (traditional whitewashed cowboy cottages) and farmstays.

★ Cacharel Hotel   HOTEL €€

(✆ 04 90 97 95 44; www.hotel-cacharel.com; rte de Cacharel, D85A; s/d €151/164, horse riding per hour €30; @🛜🏊) This isolated farmstead, 400m down an unpaved track off the D85A just north of Stes-Maries-de-la-Mer, perfectly balances modern-day comforts with rural authenticity. Photographic portraits of the bull herder who created the hotel in 1955 (son Florian runs the three-star hotel with much love today) give the vintage dining room soul. Rooms sit snug in whitewashed cottages, some overlooking the water.

★ Mas de Calabrun   HOTEL €€€

(✆ 04 90 97 82 21; www.mas-de-calabrun.fr; rte de Cacherel, D85A; s/d/wagons €167/199/185; ☉ mid-Feb–mid-Nov; 🅿@🛜🏊) From the striking equestrian sculpture in its front courtyard to the swish pool, stylish restaurant terrace and fabulous views of open Camargue countryside, this hotel thoroughly deserves its three stars. There are 31 individually de-

signed rooms, but the icing on the cake is the trio of *roulottes* (old-fashioned 'gypsy' wagons), which promise the perfect romantic getaway. The breakfast buffet is €15.

★ Le Mas de Peint   BOUTIQUE HOTEL €€€

(✆ 04 90 97 20 62; www.masdepeint.com; rte de Salin de Giraud, Le Sambuc, Manade Jacques Bon; d €250; ☉ mid-Mar–mid-Nov; 🌡🛜🏊) This 17th-century farmhouse has managed to become an upmarket hotel without jettisoning design elements that nod to its rural roots: solid beams, wooden furniture, saddles on the walls, and a bull's head in the lobby. But it's the superb restaurant many come for – watch chefs work from the dining room, or eat on the lovely poolside terrace.

🍴 Eating

★ Le Mazet du Vaccarès   SEAFOOD €€

(Chez Hélène et Néné; ✆ 04 90 97 10 79; www.mazet-du-vaccares.fr; rte Albaron Villeneuve; fish/bouillabaisse menu €38/60; ☉ 10am-11pm Fri-Sun mid-Jan–mid-Aug & mid-Sep–mid-Dec; 🅿) Shuddering along the low ribbed road past flamingos and Camargue ponies is totally worth it for the seafood at this legendary lakeside cabin. Memorabilia from Hélène and Néné's days as lighthouse keepers in Beauduc fill the restaurant with soul. The jovial couple cook up one fixed *menu*, built from the catch of local fishers. Cash only.

★ La Telline   FRENCH €€

(✆ 04 90 97 01 75; www.restaurantlatelline.fr; Quarter Villeneuve, rte de Gageron, Villeneuve; mains €24-35; ☉ noon-1.15pm & 7.30-9pm Thu-Mon; 🅿) A true local favourite, this isolated cottage restaurant with sage-green wooden shutters is one of the best places to sample genuine Camargue food.

Summer dining is in a small and peaceful flower-filled garden, where straightforward starters such as *tellines* (molluscs), salad or terrine are followed by grilled fish or meat, or a beef or bull steak. No credit cards.

Chez Bob FRENCH €€
(☑ 04 90 97 00 29; www.restaurantbob.fr; Mas Petite Antonelle, rte du Sambuc, Villeneuve; menu €45; ⊙ noon-2pm & 7.30-9pm Wed-Sun; P) This house restaurant is an iconic address adored by Arlésians. Feast on grilled bull chops, mullet eggs and *anchoïade* (a powerful Provençal garlic and anchovy emulsion) beneath trees or inside between walls plastered in photos, posters and other memorabilia collected over the years by Jean-Guy, aka 'Bob'. It's 18km south of Arles; reserve ahead.

★**La Chassagnette** GASTRONOMY €€€
(☑ 04 90 97 26 96, www.chassagnette.fr; rte du Sambuc, Domaine de L'Armellière; menus €55-115; ⊙ noon-1.30pm & 7-9.30pm Jun-Sep, noon-1.30pm Thu-Sat Oct-May; ☑) Surrounded by a vast *potager* (kitchen garden), which supplies practically all the restaurant's produce, this renowned gourmet table is run by Armand Amal, a former pupil of Alain Ducasse. The multi-course *menus* are full of surprises, and the bucolic setting is among the loveliest anywhere in the Camargue. There's a vegetarian *menu* (unfortunately available only at lunch).

Le Mas de Peint Restaurant FRENCH €€€
(☑ 04 90 97 20 62; www.masdepeint.com; rte de Salin de Giraud, Manade Jacques Bon; menus lunch €39, dinner €41-69; ⊙ lunch & dinner Sat & Sun, lunch only Fri & Mon-Wed) Le Mas de Peint's gourmet restaurant, masterminded by highly credentialled chef Grégory Brousse, offers seasonal menus and Camarguais dishes in a choice of settings: In the rustic dining room or on the poolside terrace. Serving wonderful dishes such as estate-grown black rice with local seafood, it's also open to nonguests.

ⓘ Information

SNPN La Capelière (☑ 04 90 97 00 97; www.snpn.com/reservedecamargue; C134, rte de Fiélouse; permits adult/child €4/2; ⊙ 9am-1pm & 2-6pm Apr-Sep, to 5pm Wed-Mon Oct-Mar) Run by the Société Nationale de Protection de la Nature (SNPN), this is the information centre for the Réserve Nationale de Camargue (p211). It sells permits for the observatories and 4.5km of nature trails at the wild **Salin de Badon**, and is good for all kinds of advice. At La Capelière's 1.5km-long **Sentier des Rainettes** (Tree-Frog Trail) discover flora and fauna native to freshwater marshes.

ⓘ Getting There & Away

The rural bus network is a bit patchy, but there are links between most larger towns and villages.

Arles is the Camargue's principal point on the rail network, with connections to Marseille every hour or two (€17, one hour). You can also get a train from Nîmes to Aigues-Mortes (€16, 45 minutes to 1¼ hours, up to six daily).

For drivers, the A54 will get you from Nîmes to Arles in 35 minutes, while it's just over an hour on the A54 and A7 to Marseille.

ⓘ Getting Around

Touring the tiny roads criss-crossing this flat, wild region is best done by car or bicycle. The Bac de Barcarin provides a car ferry (€6) across the Grand Rhône from Salin de Giraud to Marseille.

BICYCLE

Bicycles are ideal on the Camargue's flat terrain. East of Stes-Maries-de-la-Mer, seafront paths like Digue à la Mer are reserved for walkers and cyclists. **Le Vélo Saintois** (p216), with an English-language list of cycling routes, rents bikes of all sizes. **Le Vélociste** (p216) rents and organises cycling and horse-riding (€36) or cycling and canoeing (€30) packages. Both deliver bikes for free to hotels throughout the Camargue.

STES-MARIES-DE-LA-MER

POP 2680

The saints who give their name to this whitewashed seaside town are Marie-Salomé and Marie-Jacobé, persecuted early Christians who escaped here from Palestine. With them, the legend says, was their handmaiden Sara, whose sanctification as Saint Sara the Black makes this a significant place of pilgrimage for Roma and other 'gypsy' peoples, whose patron she is. Stes-Maries has a rough-and-tumble holidaymaker feel, with salt-licked buildings crowding dusty streets. During its Roma pilgrimages, street-cooked pans of paella fuel chaotic crowds of carnivalesque guitarists, dancers and mounted cowboys.

ARLES DISCOUNT CARDS

Buy a pass for multiple sights at the Arles tourist office or any Roman site: the **Pass Avantage** (€16) covers the museums, theatres, baths, crypt, Les Alyscamps and the Cloître St-Trophime; the **Pass Liberté** (€12) gives you the choice of a total of six sights, including two museums.

BIRDLIFE OF THE CAMARGUE

The largest wetland in France, home (at least part of the year) to around two-thirds of Europe's bird species, the Camargue is an ornithological wonderland. A national park since 1970, it's a vital waypoint on migratory routes between Europe and Africa. Within the 930 sq km national park, coexisting with farms producing Camarguais rice, bulls and horses, lies a Unesco-protected biosphere of 131 sq km, in which over 300 bird species have been observed.

WHERE TO BIRDWATCH

Amongst the best sites for birdwatchers are Marais du Vigueirat, **Domaine de la Palissade** (p211), **Parc Ornothologique du Pont de Gau** (p216) and **La Capelière** (p213).

La Capelière, at 13 sq km, is the largest single reserve in the park, with a visitor centre open year-round. There's the chance to spot redshanks and reed warblers in summer, snipe and tufted ducks in winter, and migratory plovers and kingfishers throughout the year.

Palissade has varying trails from 1km to 8km through a section that hasn't been tamed by artificial embankments. You can see spectacled warblers in summer, greylag geese in winter, and migrating curlews and mallards year-round.

Pont de Gau is a 60-hectare sanctuary and veterinary centre with 7km of trails affording sightings of hoopoes in summer, marsh harriers in winter, and migrating storks and grey- and night-heron year-round.

Vigueirat offers 15km of trails through 11.2 sq km of marshland, with purple herons and great spotted cuckoos present in summer, booted eagles in winter, spoonbills and terns during migratory periods, and bitterns and egrets year-round

FLAMINGO SEASON

Each year in the Camargue some 10,000 pink or greater flamingo (*Phoenicopterus ruber*) couples nest on the Étang du Fangassier. This 4000-sq-m artificial island, constructed in 1970 as a flamingo-breeding colony, is one of the rare spots in Europe that guarantees the flamingo protection from predators.

This well-dressed bird stands between 1.5m and 2m tall and has an average wingspan of 1.9m. When the flamingo feels threatened, its loud hiss is similar to the warning sound made by a goose. Flamingo courtship starts in January, with mating taking place from March to May. Come the end of August or early September, thousands of birds take flight for Spain, Tunisia and Senegal where they winter in warmer climes before returning to the Camargue in February. Some 6000 to 7000 flamingos, however, remain in the Rhône delta year-round.

ONDREJ PROSICKY/SHUTTERSTOCK ©

WONDRY/SHUTTERSTOCK ©

DENNIS W DONOHUE/SHUTTERSTOCK ©

1. Spoonbill
2. Kingfisher
3. Flamingo

⊙ Sights & Activities

★ Parc Ornithologique du Pont de Gau
WILDLIFE RESERVE

(☑ 04 90 97 82 62; www.parcornithologique.com; D570, Pont du Gau; adult/child €7.50/5; ⊙ 9am-7pm Apr-Sep, 10am-6pm Oct-Mar; P 🐾) Flamingos are a dime a dozen in the Camargue, but this park is one of the best places to see the many other migratory and seasonal species that thrive in these wetlands. Herons, storks, egrets, teals, avocets and grebes are just some you may spot, depending on the time of year. The reserve has 7km of trails, giving you every chance to see its avian inhabitants, and a care centre for sick and injured birds. Follow the D570 4km north from Stes-Maries-de-la-Mer.

La Digue à la Mer
NATURAL FEATURE

This 2.5m-high dyke was built in the 19th century to cut the delta off from the sea, making the southern Camargue arable. A 20km-long walking and cycling track runs along its length, linking Stes-Maries with the solar-powered **Phare de la Gacholle** (1882), a lighthouse automated in the 1960s. Footpaths cut down to lovely sandy beaches and views of pink flamingos strutting across the marshy planes are second to none. Walking on the fragile sand dunes is forbidden, as is driving.

Église des Stes-Maries
CHURCH

(☑ 04 90 97 80 25; www.sanctuaire-des-saintes maries.fr; 2 place de l'Église; rooftop €2.50; ⊙ 10am-noon & 2-5pm Mon-Sat, 2-5pm Sun) Built on the potential first site of Christianity in the Camargue, this fortified church is of uncertain vintage, but probably hails from the 12th century. It draws legions of pilgrims to venerate the statue of Sara, their revered patron saint, during the **Pèlerinage des Gitans** (Roma pilgrimages; ⊙ 24-25 May). The relics of Sara and those of Marie-Salomé and Marie-Jacobé, all found in the crypt by King René in 1448, are enshrined in a wooden chest, stashed in the stone wall above the choir. Don't miss the panorama from the **rooftop terrace**.

Tiki III
BOATING

(☑ 04 90 97 81 68; www.tiki3.fr; chemin du Clos du Rhone, off D38; adult/child €13/7; ⊙ mid-Mar–Oct) This paddleboat is moored at the mouth of the Petit Rhône, 1.5km west of Stes-Maries-de-la-Mer next to Camping Le Clos du Rhône. Arrive 15 minutes before embarkation for a 90-minute circuit of the lower river.

Les Quatre Maries
BOATING

(☑ 04 90 97 70 10; www.bateaux-4maries.camargue. fr; 36bis av Théodore Aubanel; adult/child €12/6; ⊙ mid-Mar–Oct; 🐾) The 'Four Maries' (it's unclear who is the addition to the town's three revered Maries) takes passengers on a 1½-hour cruise out to sea then up the Petit Rhône.

Le Vélo Saintois
CYCLING

(☑ 04 90 97 74 56; www.levelosaintois.camargue. fr; 19 rue de la République; per day adult/child/ ebike €15/14/30; ⊙ 9am-7pm Mar-Nov) This bike-rental outlet has bikes of all sizes, including tandems and kids' wheels. Helmets cost an extra €1 per day. A free brochure details four circular cycling itineraries (26km to 44km, four hours to eight hours) starting in Stes-Maries-de-la-Mer. Free hotel delivery.

Le Vélociste
CYCLING

(☑ 04 90 97 83 26; www.levelociste.fr; 8 place Mireille; per day adult/child/ebike €15/14/30; ⊙ 9am-7pm Mar-Nov) This bike-rental shop rents wheels, advises on cycling itineraries (24km to 70km, four hours to nine hours) and organises fun one-day combined cycling and horse-riding (from €30) or cycling and canoeing (€30) packages. Free hotel delivery.

🛏 Sleeping

Camping Le Clos du Rhône
CAMPGROUND €

(☑ 04 90 97 85 99; www.camping-leclos.fr; rte d'Aigues Mortes; site €30, mobile home per week €847; ⊙ late Mar–mid-Nov; @ 🖥 🏊) Right by the beach (yet lavishly embellished with an onshore water park), this large and well-equipped camping ground sports the whole range of accommodation options: tent sites, wooden chalets and self-catering cottages. The pool, two-lane water slide, and beachside spa with Jacuzzi and *hammam,* plus more mundane services like a grocer, laundry and BBQ, make this a family favourite.

★ Lodge Sainte Hélène
BOUTIQUE HOTEL €€€

(☑ 04 90 97 83 29; www.lodge-saintehelene. com; chemin Bas des Launes; d for 2 nights €626; ❄ @ 🖥 🏊) These white terraced cottages on a peninsula on the Etang des Launes are prime real estate for birdwatchers and romance seekers. It's so quiet you can hear flamingos flapping past. Each room comes with a birdwatchers' guide and binoculars, and owner Benoît Noel is a font of local knowledge.

Mas de la Fouque
DESIGN HOTEL €€€

(☑ 04 90 97 81 02; www.masdelafouque.com; rte du Petit Rhône, D38; r €360; 🖥 🏊) This smartly refurbished eco-sensitive hotel on the Étang des Launes manages to feel deliciously remote. Decoration is a very 'now' combination of local *vide grenier* (car-boot sale) finds, posh

CAMARGUAIS CULTURE

The *course Camarguaise* is a Camargue variation of the bullfight, but one in which the bulls aren't harmed. It sees amateur *razeteurs* (from the word 'shave') wearing skin-tight white shirts and trousers get as close as they dare to the *taureau* (bull) to try to snatch rosettes and ribbons tied to the bull's horns, using a *crochet* (a razor-sharp comb). They leap over the arena's barrier as the bull charges, making spectators' hearts lurch.

Bulls are bred on a *manade* (bull farm) by *manadiers,* who are helped in their daily chores by *gardians* (Camargue cattle-herding cowboys). These mounted herdsmen parade through Arles during the **Fête des Gardians** (p207) in May.

Many *manades* also breed the creamy white *cheval de Camargue* (Camargue horse) and some welcome visitors; ask at tourist offices in **Arles** (p210) and **Stes-Maries-de-la-Mer**.

A calendar of *courses Camarguaises* is online at the **Fédération Française de la Course Camarguaise** (French Federation of Camargue Bullfights; ☑ 04 66 26 05 35; www.ffcc.info), with many occurring at the arena in Stes-Maries-de-la-Mer. *Recortadores* (where the aim is to leap safely over the charging bull, rather than wound or kill it) also happens during the bullfighting season (Easter to September).

---

midcentury pieces, and locally sourced linens. While there are indulgences like the spa, you can take comfort from the fact that the hotel uses solar and geothermal power sources.

**L'Auberge Cavalière
du Pont des Bannes** RESORT €€€
(☑ 04 90 97 88 88; www.aubergecavaliere.com; rte d'Arles, D570; r €220; P ❄ ☎) This classy resort-hotel fits perfectly into the lush Camargue wetlands 1.5km north of Stes-Maries, somehow unobtrusively blending in tennis courts, a spa, bars, restaurants, horse riding and anything else you may feel the need to indulge in. Some rooms overlook a bird-filled pond; the thatched cabins are cosily independent. On-site restaurant Pont de Barre offers four fantastic courses for €54.

✖ Eating

Lunch *sur la plage* (on the beach) never fails to seduce and Stes-Maries-de-la-Mer lives up to the promise with two hip and dandy beach restaurants, **Calypso – Lou Santen** (☑ 07 71 03 43 46; av Riquette Aubanel, Plage Ouest; lunch menu €20; ⊙ 10am-7pm May-Sep, to 11pm Sat Jul & Aug) and **La Playa** (☑ 06 29 48 82 01; www.laplaya-en-camargue.fr; Plage Est; small plates €18; ⊙ 10am-10pm May-Sep; ☎), both open May to September.

★ Ô Pica Pica SEAFOOD €€
(☑ 06 10 30 33 49; www.degustationcoquillages-les saintesmariesdelamer.com; 16-18 av Van Gogh; mains €17-25; ⊙ noon-3pm & 7-11pm Mar-Nov) Fish and shellfish don't come fresher than this. Watch them get gutted, filleted and grilled in the 'open' glass-walled kitchen, then devour your meal on the sea-facing terrace or out the back in the typically Mediterranean white-walled garden. Simplicity is king here: plastic glasses, fish grilled *à la plancha,* and shellfish platters. No coffee and no credit cards.

La Grange FRENCH €€
(☑ 04 90 97 98 05; 23 av Frédéric Mistral; mains €16-22, menus €19-30; ⊙ noon-2pm & 6.30-10pm Mar-Nov) If you've developed a desire to get closer to the Camargue's bulls by eating them, then head to the Grange, an ode to Camargue's *gardians,* with bull-herding memorabilia on the walls and plenty of *taureau* (bull meat) on the menu. Portions are copious, and you can begin with a Lou Gardian, the house *apéro,* mixing white wine and peach liqueur.

❶ Information

Tourist Office (☑ 04 90 97 82 55; www.saintes maries.com; 5 av Van Gogh; ⊙ 9am-8pm Jul & Aug, to 7pm Apr-Jun & Sep, to 6pm Oct, to 5pm Dec-Feb & Mar) Stocks a wealth of information on the attractions, flora, fauna, accommodation, festivals, food and traditions of the town and the Camargue, and offers a rich array of tours – on foot, horseback, and in 4WDs.

❶ Getting There & Away

Buses to/from Arles (Line L20, €2.90, one hour, four to eight daily) use the bus shelter at the northern entrance to town on av d'Arles (the continuation of rte d'Arles and the D570).

❶ Getting Around

Le Vélo Saintois and **Le Vélociste** hire bicycles.

THE CAMARGUE STES-MARIES-DE-LA-MER

AIGUES-MORTES

POP 8400

Set in flat marshland and encircled by high stone walls, the picturesque town of Aigues-Mortes was established in the mid-13th century by Louis IX to give the French crown a Mediterranean port under its direct control. Cobbled streets inside the walls are lined with restaurants, cafes and bars, giving the town a festive atmosphere and making it a charming spot from which to explore the Camargue. It's actually located over the border from Provence in the Gard *département*, 28km northwest of Stes-Maries-de-la-Mer at the western extremity of the Camargue.

Sights & Activities

Les Salins du Midi LANDMARK

(☎04 66 73 40 24; www.visitesalinaiguesmortes.com; rte du Grau-du-Roi; electric train adult/child €11/9, cycling tour €31; ⏲Mar-Nov) Glowing pink in the sunlight, the vast, flat salt pans that stretch southwards from Aigues-Mortes have for centuries produced the region's famous salt. It's still done in the traditional way, with *sauniers* (salt workers) harvesting the salt by hand in late summer. You can visit the salt pans either aboard an electric train (1¼ hours, up to 10 daily) or on a cycling tour (three hours, two per day). Reserve ahead.

Town Walls & Tour de Constance TOWER

(www.tourdeconstance.com; adult/child €8/free; ⏲10am-7pm May-Aug, to 5.30pm Sep-Apr; 👪) Scaling the ramparts of the picturesque town of Aigues-Mortes rewards you with sweeping views. Head to the top of the 13th-century Tour de Constance (in which persecuted Huguenots were imprisoned in the 16th century) to reach them. The 1.6km wall-top walk takes about one hour.

Croisière de Camargue BOATING

(Péniches Isles de Stel; ☎04 66 53 60 70, 06 10 90 16 68; 12 quai du Commerce, ave de la Tour de Constance; adult/child €15/7; ⏲Mar-Oct) A variety of different barges leave from the Quai du Commerce to tour through canals, reed-beds, salt flats and other sights surrounding Aigues-Mortes. Croisière de Camargue is one of the largest operators. It has a physical ticket office at 24 rue Jean Jaurès, and only accepts cash.

Sleeping & Eating

Hôtel L'Escale HOTEL €

(☎04 66 53 71 14; www.escale-hotel.fr; 3 av Tour de Constance; s/d €60/80; P 🛜) This simple 10-room hotel is a real bargain, offering some of the cheapest rooms anywhere in the Camargue – and while not luxurious, the family-run vibe, cheery decor and (often) sunny courtyard are thoroughly pleasant. There's a decent restaurant, too, serving local specialities (menus €14 at lunch, €25 at dinner).

L'Hermitage de St-Antoine B&B €

(☎06 03 04 34 05; www.lhermitagedestantoine.com; 9 bd Intérieur Nord; r incl breakfast €95; ❄🛜) Directly across from the town's northern bastion, this pocket-sized *chambre d'hôte* has four artfully appointed rooms, one with a small private terrace.

Information

Aigues Mortes Tourist Office (☎04 66 53 73 00; www.ot-aiguesmortes.fr; place St-Louis; ⏲9am-6pm) Excellent for accommodation, eating and activity suggestions, and information on the salt pans and the Camargue.

Getting There & Away

Bus 132 runs regularly between Aigues-Mortes and Nîmes (€1.50, 1 hour).

CATHOLICISM & THE CAMARGUE

Catholicism first reached European shores in what's now tiny Stes-Maries-de-la-Mer. The stories say that Stes Marie-Salomé and Marie-Jacobé (and some say Mary Magdalene) fled the Holy Land in a little boat and were caught in a storm, drifting until washing ashore here.

Provençal and Catholic lore diverge at this point: Catholicism relates that Sara, patron saint of the *gitans* (Roma people, also known as gypsies), travelled with the two Marys on the boat. Provençal legend says Sara was already here and was the first person to recognise their holiness. In 1448 skeletal remains said to belong to Sara and the two Marys were found in a crypt in Stes-Maries-de-la-Mer.

Gitans continue to make pilgrimages, **Pèlerinage des Gitans**, here on 24 and 25 May (often staying for up to three weeks), dancing and playing music in the streets, and parading a statue of Sara through town. The Sunday in October closest to the 22nd sees a second pilgrimage dedicated to the two Stes Maries; *courses Camarguaises* (p217) are also held at this time.

Vaucluse

Best Places to Eat

➜ Le Vivier (p257)

➜ Christian Etienne (p234)

➜ L'Oustalet (p246)

➜ Les Remparts (p259)

➜ Bistro du'O (p244)

Best Places to Stay

➜ Hôtel La Mirande (p231)

➜ La Prévôté (p256)

➜ Les Jardins de Baracane (p230)

➜ Metafort (p254)

➜ Les Remparts (p248)

Why Go?

Named after France's most powerful natural spring, which wells up outside Fontaine-de-Vaucluse, the Vaucluse *département* sits on Provence's west side, sandwiched between the rumpled mountains of the Hautes-Alpes and the rocky Var coastline. Crossed by three great rivers – the Rhône, the Durance and the Sorgue – Vaucluse is renowned for its lavender fields and its vineyards, including the legendary Châteauneuf-du-Pape. The area has been occupied since ancient times, but it was the Romans who left the greatest mark in the form of Orange's ancient theatre and the remains of two Roman towns, Glanum and Vasio Vocontiorum. Centuries later, Avignon became the seat of papal power, and its crenellated ramparts and monumental Palais des Papes provide a glimpse of medieval majesty.

These days visitors come to explore Vaucluse's hilltop villages, elegant towns and excellent restaurants – as well as the snowcapped summit of the *géant de Provence*, Mont Ventoux.

When to Go

	Salin de Giraud	Le Sambuc	Stes-Maries -de-la-Mer	La Capelière	Aigues-Mortes
Le Sambuc	15				
Stes-Maries-de-la-Mer	61	59			
La Capelière	22	13	41		
Aigues-Mortes	70	62	33	56	
Arles	38	31	37	21	51

Vaucluse Highlights

1 Avignon (p226) Wandering the hallways of the Palais des Papes with a histopad.

2 Châteauneuf-du-Pape (p238) Savouring the taste of one of Provence's greatest wines.

3 Orange (p240) Imagining yourself as a Roman spectator in the ancient theatre.

4 Dentelles de Montmirail (p245) Hiking or biking between hilltop villages.

5 Carpentras (p252) Tasting your way around the stalls of one of Provence's best markets.

6 Vaison-la-Romaine (p243) Climbing to the top of this medieval town for panoramic Provence views.

7 Fontaine-de-Vaucluse (p258) Seeing France's most powerful natural spring and the source of the River Sorgue.

8 Mont Ventoux (p248) Biking or hiking to the summit of Provence's highest mountain.

ROMAN PROVENCE ROAD TRIP

● ●

Provence was where Rome first truly flexed its imperial muscles. Follow Roman roads, cross Roman bridges and grab a seat at Roman theatres and arenas. Thrillingly, you'll discover that most of Provence's Roman ruins aren't ruins at all. Many are exceptionally well preserved, and some are also evocatively integrated into the modern city. With Provence's knockout landscape as a backdrop, history never looked so good!

❶ Nîmes

Although Nîmes isn't strictly speaking in modern Provence, a long, shared regional history means it has to feature in this Ro-

man tour. The city's bizarre coat of arms – a crocodile chained to a palm tree! – recalls the region's first, but definitely not last, horde of sun-worshipping retirees. Julius Caesar's

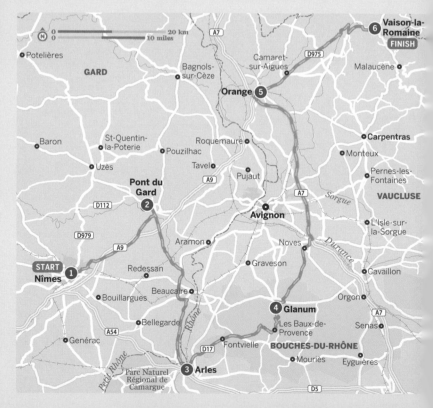

3 Days 205km / 127 miles

Great for ... Culture; Families

Best Time to Go All year, but avoid August's heat.

● ●

loyal legionnaires were granted land here to settle after hard years on the Nile campaigns. Two millennia later, their ambitious town blends seamlessly with the bustling, workaday French streetscapes of the modern city. **Les Arènes** (☑ 04 66 21 82 56; www.arenes-nimes. com; place des Arènes; adult/child incl audioguide €10/8; ⊙ 9am-8pm Jul & Aug, 9am-6.30pm Apr-Jun & Sep, 9am-6pm Mar & Oct, 9.30am-5pm Jan, Feb, Nov & Dec), an impressively intact 1st-century-CE amphitheatre, makes for a majestic traffic roundabout. Locals nonchalantly skateboard or window-shop on the elegant place that's home to a beautiful and preciously intact 1st-century-CE temple, the **Maison Carrée** (☑ 04 66 21 82 56; www.maisoncar ree.eu; place de la Maison Carrée; adult/child €6/5; ⊙ 9.30am-8pm Jul & Aug, 10am-6.30pm Apr-Jun & Sep, 10am-6pm Mar & Oct, 10am-1pm & 2-4.30pm Jan, Feb, Nov & Dec). Skip the 22-minute film and instead stroll over to the elegant Jardins de la Fontaine. The remains of the Temple de Diane are in its lower northwest corner and a 10-minute uphill walk brings you to the crumbling, 30m-high **Tour Magne** (quai de la Fontaine; adult/child €3.50/3, garden free; ⊙ 9am-8pm Jul & Aug, 9am-5pm Sep-Jun). Built in 15 BCE as a watchtower and display of imperial grunt, it is the only one that remains of several that once spanned the 7km-long ramparts.

The Drive > From Nîmes it takes 30 minutes on D6086 and then a short northward leg along the D981 to Pont du Gard.

② Pont du Gard

You'll get a glimpse of the **Pont du Gard** (☑ 04 66 37 50 99; www.pontdugard.fr; adult/child €8.50/6, Pass Aqueduc incl guided visit of topmost tier €11.50/6; ⊙ 9am-11pm Jul & Aug, to 10pm Jun & Sep, to 9pm May, to 8pm Apr & Oct, to 6pm Nov-Mar) as you approach. Nature (and clever placement of car parks and visitor centres) has created one bravura reveal. Spanning the gorge is a magnificent three-tiered aqueduct, a marvel of 1st-century engineering. During the Roman period, the Pont du Gard was (like Nîmes) part of the Roman province

of Gallia Narbonensis. It was built around 19 BCE by Agrippa, Augustus' deputy, and it's huge: the 275m-long upper tier, 50m above the Gard, has 35 arches. Each block (the largest weighs over 5 tonnes) was hauled in by cart or raft. It was once part of a 50km-long system that carried water from nearby Uzès down to thirsty Nîmes. It's a 400m wheelchair-accessible walk from car parks on both banks of the river to the bridge itself, with a shady cafe en route on the right. Swim upstream for unencumbered views, though downstream is also good for summer dips, with shaded wooden platforms set in the flatter banks. Want to make a day of it? There's Museo de la Romanité, an interactive, information-based museum, plus a children's area, and a peaceful 1.4km botanical walk, Mémoires de Garrigue.

The Drive > Kayaking to the next stop would be more fun, and more direct, but you'll need to return south via the D986L to Beaucaire, then the D90 and D15 to Arles.

❸ Arles

Arles, formerly known as Arelate, was part of the Roman Empire from as early as the 2nd century BCE. It wasn't until the 49–45 BCE civil war, however, when nearby Massalia (Marseille) supported Pompey (ie backed the wrong side), that it became a booming regional capital.

The town today is delightful, Roman cache or no, but what a living legacy it is. Its **Les Arènes** (p204) is not as large as Nîmes', but it is spectacularly sited and occasionally still sees blood spilled, just like in the old gladiatorial days (it hosts gory bullfights and *courses Camarguaises*, which is the local variation). Likewise, the 1st-century **Théâtre Antique** (p204) is still regularly used for alfresco performances.

Just as social, political and religious life revolved around the forum in Arelate, the busy plane-tree-shaded **place du Forum** (Map p205; place du Forum) buzzes with cafe life today. Sip a pastis here and spot the remains of a 2nd-century temple embedded in the facade of the Hôtel Nord-Pinus. Under your feet are **Cryptoportiques** (p206) – subterranean foundations and buried arcades. Access the underground galleries, 89m long and 59m wide, at the **Hôtel de Ville** (Town Hall; Map p205; place de la République).

Emperor Constantin's partly preserved 4th-century private baths, the **Thermes de Constantin** (p206), are a few minutes' stroll away, next to the *quai*. Southwest of the centre is **Les Alyscamps** (p206), a necropolis founded by the Romans and adopted by Christians in the 4th century. It contains the tombs of martyr St Genest and Arles' first bishops. You may recognise it: Van Gogh and Gauguin both captured the avenues of cypresses on canvas (though only melancholy old Van Gogh painted the empty sarcophagi).

The Drive > Take the D17 to Fontvielle, follow the D78F/D27A to Baux-de-Provence, then the D5. This detour takes you past beautiful dry white rocky hills dotted with scrubby pine; the trip will still only take around 45 minutes. There's on-site parking at Glanum. If heading into St-Rémy, there's parking by the tourist office (parking Jean-Jaurès) and north of the periphery (parking Général-de-Gaulle).

4 Glanum

Such is the glittering allure of the gourmet delis, interiors boutiques and smart restaurants that line St-Rémy-de-Provence's circling boulevards and place de la République that a visit to the **Site Archéologique de Glanum** (p194) is often an afterthought. But the triumphal arch (20 CE) that marks Glanum's entrance, 2km south of St-Rémy, is far from insignificant. It's pegged as one of France's oldest and is joined by a towering mausoleum (30–20 BCE). Walk down the main street and you'll pass the mainstays of Roman life: baths, a forum and marketplace, temples and town villas. And beneath all this Roman handiwork lies the remnants of an older Celtic and Hellenic settlement, built to take advantage of a sacred spring. Van Gogh, as a patient of the neighbouring asylum, painted the olive orchard that covered the site until its excavation in the 1920s.

The Drive > It's the A7 all the way to Orange, 50km of nondescript driving if you're not tempted by a detour to Avignon on the way.

5 Orange

It's often said if you can only see one Roman site in France, make it Orange. And yes, the town's Roman treasures are gobsmacking and unusually old; both are believed to have been built during Augustus Caesar's rule (27 BCE–14 CE). Plus, while Orange may not be the Provençal village of popular fantasy, it's a cruisy, decidedly untouristy town, making for good-value accommodation and hassle-free sightseeing (such as plentiful street parking one block back from the theatre).

At a massive 103m wide and 37m high, the stage wall of the **Théâtre Antique** (p240) dominates the surrounding streetscape. Minus a few mosaics, plus a new roof, it's one of three in the world still standing in their entirety, and originally seated 10,000 spectators. Admission includes an informative audioguide, and access to the **Musée d'Art et d'Histoire** (p240) across the road. Its collection includes friezes from the theatre with the Roman motifs we love: eagles holding garlands of bay leaves, and a cracking battle between cavalrymen and foot soldiers. Note that a major restoration project is currently underway to restore the theatre's limestone structure, which is degrading badly – so unfortunately some scaffolding will be inevitable until at least 2024.

For bird's-eye views of the theatre – and phenomenal vistas of rocky Mont Ventoux and the Dentelles – follow montée Philbert de Chalons, or montée Lambert, up Colline St-Eutrope, once the ever-vigilant Romans' lookout point.

To the town's north, the Arc de Triomphe stands on the ancient Via Agrippa (now the busy N7), 19m high and wide, and a stonking 8m thick. Restored in 2009, its richly animated reliefs commemorate 49 BCE Roman victories with images of battles, ships, trophies, and chained, naked and utterly subdued Gauls.

The Drive > Northeast, the D975 passes through gentle vineyard-lined valleys for 40 minutes, with views of the Dentelles de Montmirail's limestone ridges along the way (the D977 and D23 can be equally lovely). Parking in Vaison can be a trial; park by the tourist office (place du Chanoine Saute), or below the western walls of the Cité Médiévale, if you don't mind walking.

Pont du Gard (p223)

❻ Vaison-la-Romaine

Is there anything more telling of Rome's smarts than a sturdy, still-used Roman bridge? Vaison-la-Romaine's pretty little Pont Romain has stood the test of time and severe floods. Stand at its centre and gaze up at the walled, cobbled-street hilltop **Cité Médiévale** (p243), or down at the fast-flowing Ouvèze River.

Vaison-la-Romaine is tucked between seven valleys and has long been a place of trade. The ruined remains of Vasio Vocontiorum, the Roman city that flourished here between around 100 BCE and 450AD, fill two central **Gallo-Roman sites** (p243). Dual neighbourhoods lie on either side of the tourist office and av du Général-de-Gaulle. The Romans shopped at the colonnaded boutiques and bathed at La Villasse, where you'll find Maison au Dauphin, which has splendid marble-lined fish ponds.

In Puymin, see noblemen's houses, mosaics, a workmen's quarter, a temple, and the still-functioning 6000-seat Théâtre Antique (c 20 CE). To make sense of the remains (and gather your audioguide), head for the archaeological museum, which revives Vaison's Roman past with an incredible swag: superb mosaics, carved masks, and statues that include a 3rd-century silver bust and marble renderings of Hadrian and his wife, Sabina. Admission includes entry to the soothing 12th-century Romanesque cloister at **Cathédrale Notre-Dame de Nazareth** (p243), a five-minute walk west of La Villasse and, like much of Provence, built on Roman foundations.

AVIGNON

POP 91,250

Attention, quiz fans: name the city where the pope lived during the early 14th century. Answered Rome? Bzzz: sorry, wrong answer. For 70-odd years of the early 1300s, the Provençal town of Avignon was the centre of the Roman Catholic world, and though its stint as the seat of papal power only lasted a few decades, it's been left with an impressive legacy of ecclesiastical architecture, most notably the soaring, World Heritage–listed

Avignon

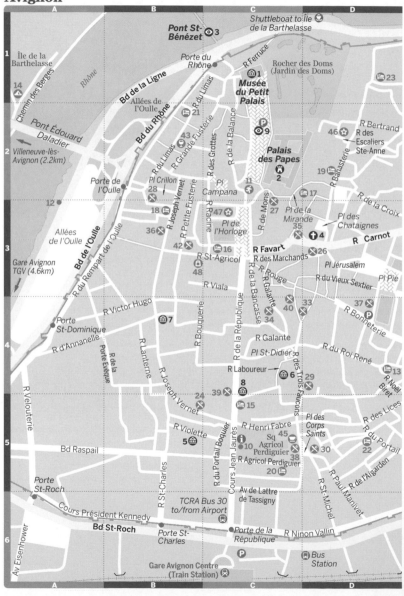

fortress-cum-palace known as the Palais des Papes.

Avignon is now best known for its annual arts festival, the largest in France, which spans several weeks in July. The rest of the year, its rampart-ringed old town, medieval

bridge, leafy squares and super restaurants are the main attractions.

History

Avignon first gained its ramparts – and reputation for arts and culture – during the 14th century, when Pope Clement V fled political turmoil in Rome. From 1309 to 1377, seven French-born popes invested huge sums in the papal palace and offered asylum to Jews and political dissidents. Pope Gregory XI left Avignon in 1376, but his death two years later led to the Great Schism (1378–1417), during which rival popes (up to three at one time) resided at Rome and Avignon, denouncing and excommunicating one another. Even after the matter was settled and an impartial pope, Martin V, established himself in Rome, Avignon remained under papal rule. Avignon and Comtat Venaissin (now the Vaucluse *département*) were ruled by papal legates until 1791.

◉ Sights & Activities

Ticket offices for sights close 30 to 60 minutes before overall closing time.

★**Palais des Papes** PALACE
(Papal Palace; ☑ tickets 04 32 74 32 74; www.palais-des-papes.com; place du Palais; adult/child €12/10, with Pont St-Bénézet €14.50/11.50; ☉ 9am-8pm Jul, to 8.30pm Aug, shorter hours Sep-Jun) The largest Gothic palace ever built, the Palais des Papes was erected by Pope Clement V, who abandoned Rome in 1309 in the wake of violent disorder after his election. Its immense scale illustrates the medieval might of the Roman Catholic church.

Ringed by 3m-thick walls, its cavernous halls, chapels and antechambers are largely bare today – but tickets now include tablet 'Histopads' revealing virtual-reality representations of how the building would have looked in all its papal pomp.

Place du Palais SQUARE
This impressive vast square surrounding the Palais des Papes provides knockout photo ops. On top of the Romanesque 17th-century cathedral stands a golden statue of the Virgin Mary (weighing 4.5 tonnes), while next to the cathedral, the hilltop **Rocher des Doms** gardens provide great views of the Rhône, Mont Ventoux and Les Alpilles. Opposite the palace is the 17th-century **Hôtel des Monnaies**, once the papal mint and festooned with elaborate carvings and heraldic beasts.

Avignon

★ **Pont St-Bénézet** BRIDGE
(☑ tickets 04 32 74 32 74; bd de la Ligne; adult/child 24hr ticket €5/4, with Palais des Papes €14.50/11.50; ◷ 9am-8pm Jul, to 8.30pm Aug, shorter hours Sep-Jun) Legend says Pastor Bénézet (a former shepherd) had three visions urging him to build a bridge across the Rhône. Completed in 1185, the 900m-long bridge linked Avignon with Villeneuve-lès-Avignon. It was rebuilt several times before all but four of its 22 spans were washed away in the 1600s, leaving the far side marooned in the middle of the Rhône. There are fine (and free) views from Rocher des Doms park, Pont Édouard Daladier, and Île de la Barthelasse's chemin des Berges.

★ **Musée du Petit Palais** MUSEUM
(☑ 04 90 86 44 58; www.petit-palais.org; place du Palais; adult/child €6/free; ◷ 10am-1pm & 2-6pm Wed-Mon) The archbishops' palace during the 14th and 15th centuries now houses outstanding collections of primitive, pre-Rennaissance,

13th- to 16th-century Italian religious paintings by artists including Botticelli, Carpaccio and Giovanni di Paolo – the most famous is Botticelli's *La Vierge et l'Enfant* (1470).

Musée Calvet GALLERY
(☑ 04 90 86 33 84; www.musee-calvet.org; 65 rue Joseph Vernet; adult/child €6/3, joint ticket with Musée Lapidaire €7/3.50; ◷ 10am-1pm & 2-6pm Wed-Mon) The elegant Hôtel de Ville-neuve-Martignan (built 1741-54) provides a fitting backdrop for Avignon's fine-arts museum, with 16th- to 20th-century oil paintings, compelling prehistoric pieces, 15th-century wrought iron, and the elongated landscapes of Avignonnais artist Joseph Vernet.

Collection Lambert GALLERY
(☑ 04 90 16 56 20; www.collectionlambert.fr; 5 rue Violette; adult/child €10/8; ◷ 11am-6pm Tue-Sun Sep-Jun, to 7pm daily Jul & Aug) Reopened in summer 2015 after significant renovation and expansion, Avignon's contemporary-arts

museum focuses on works from the 1960s to the present. Work spans from minimalist and conceptual to video and photography – in stark contrast to the classic 18th-century mansion housing it.

Musée Angladon   GALLERY
(☑ 04 90 82 29 03; www.angladon.com; 5 rue Laboureur; adult/child €8/6.50; ☺ 1-6pm Tue-Sun Apr-Sep, Tue-Sat Oct-Mar) Tiny Musée Angladon harbours an impressive collection of impressionist treasures, including works by Cézanne, Sisley, Manet, Modigliani, Degas and Picasso – but the star piece is Van Gogh's *Railway Wagons,* the only painting by the artist on display in Provence. Impress your friends by pointing out that the 'earth' isn't actually paint, but bare canvas.

Musée Lapidaire   MUSEUM
(☑ 04 90 85 75 38; www.musee-lapidaire.org; 27 rue de la République; adult/child €2/1, joint ticket with Musée Calvet €7/3.50; ☺ 10am-1pm & 2-6pm Tue-Sun) Housed inside the town's striking Jesuit Chapel is the archaeological collection of the Musée Calvet, displayed since 2015. There's a good display of Greek, Etruscan and Roman artefacts, but it's the Gaulish pieces that really draw the eye – including some grotesque masks and deeply strange figurines.

Basilique St-Pierre   CHURCH
(place St-Pierre; ☺ 8am-8pm Mon-Sat) Basilique St-Pierre, in the centre of the walled city of Avignon, was built between the 14th and 16th centuries in the Flamboyant Gothic style.

Le Carré du Palais   WINE TASTING
(☑ 04 90 27 24 00; www.carredupalais.fr; 1 place du Palais) The historic Hôtel Calvet de la Palun building in central Avignon has been renovated into a wine centre promoting and serving Côtes du Rhône and Vallée du Rhône appellations. Stop in to get a taste of the local vintages.

☞ Tours

Avignon Guided Tours   TOURS
(☑ reservations 04 32 74 32 74; www.avignon-tourisme.com; 41 cours Jean Jaurès; tours from €16.50) The tourist office (p236) runs year-round themed, guided walks exploring the city's past, both the obvious (architecture, art, history) and the esoteric (a behind-the-scenes tour of the palace's secret corners, and a fun tour exploring animals in papal art called 'The Popes and their Pets'). Most tours are in French only – ask about English-language tours when you reserve, either in person or online.

Les Grands Bateaux de Provence   BOATING
(☑ 04 90 85 62 25; http://bateauxdeprovence.fr; allées de l'Oulle; 1hr cruise €12) Runs hour-long boat cruises along the river, offering great views of the Palais des Papes and the Pont St-Bénézet. Also runs day-long boat tours to Arles, Châteauneuf-du-Pape and Tarascon, as well as dinner cruises.

Avignon Wine Tour   TOURS
(☑ 06 28 05 33 84; www.avignon-wine-tour.com; per person €95-110) Visit the region's vineyards with a knowledgeable guide, leaving you free to enjoy the wine. There are seven possible options, each exploring different wine areas.

✪ Festivals & Events

★ **Festival d'Avignon**   PERFORMING ARTS
(☑ box office 04 90 14 14 14; www.festival-avignon.com; ☺ Jul) The three week annual Festival d'Avignon is one of the world's great performing-arts festivals. Over 40 international works of dance and drama play to 100,000-plus spectators at venues around town. Tickets don't go on sale until springtime, but hotels sell out by February.

Festival Off   PERFORMING ARTS
(www.avignonleoff.com; ☺ Jul) The Festival d'Avignon is paralleled by a simultaneous fringe event, Festival Off, with eclectic experimental programming.

🛏 Sleeping

Avignon is an excellent place to base yourself, with a wide range of hotels and B&Bs. There is one major proviso, however: parking is pretty much nonexistent inside the city walls, so you'll have to drop off your luggage, leave your car at one of the large car parks on the edge of the city and walk.

A bit of a pain, but can't be helped. Many hotels offer discounted rates on the town's car parks.

ℹ AVIGNON PAS CHER
....

Avignon's beautiful maze of medieval streets, crammed with ancient buildings, independent shops, statues and murals, requires no spending. For postcard-perfect views of the palace and bridge, take the free **shuttle boat** (p237) across the Rhône to Île de la Barthelasse, then stroll left along the river bank (to the pontoon adjacent to Pont St-Bénézet).

Le Colbert
HOTEL €

(☎ 04 90 86 20 20; www.lecolbert-hotel.com; 7 rue Agricol Perdiguier; s €78-134, d €93-149; ⊗ Apr-Oct; ☎) One of several hotels on a shaded side street off rue de la République, this pleasant, old-fashioned hotel has 15 rooms decked out in art posters and zingy shades of yellow, terracotta and tangerine. Rooms are fairly standard, but it's the sweet interior patio that sells it – with a palm tree and a tinkling fountain, it's a dreamy setting for breakfast.

Péniche Le Hasard
HOUSEBOAT €

(☎ 06 12 07 47 17, 06 11 62 02 73; www.peniche-le-hasard.fr; chemin des Canotiers, Île de la Barthelasse; r incl breakfast €95; P ❀ ☎ ☎) Avast, landlubbers: how about spending a night on a riverboat? This lovingly restored *péniche* bobs on the river about 2km from the old town. Two rooms here: the boatman's wheelhouse and the captain's cabin, both quirkily decorated and squeezed into the boat's odd-angled architecture – and up top there's a lovely deck terrace and, believe it or not, a pool.

Hôtel Mignon
HOTEL €

(☎ 04 90 82 17 30; www.hotel-mignon.com; 12 rue Joseph Vernet; s €50-69, d €55-84, tr €75-99, q €105; ❀ @ ☎) Cute by name and nature, this little hotel is a sweet place to stay. Its slightly faded rooms are good value and the location on Avignon's smartest shopping street is great, but bathrooms are tiny, stairs are steep and the sound-proofing leaves something to be desired. Breakfast costs €8.

AVIGNON PASSION

An excellent-value discount card, Avignon Passion yields cheaper admission to big-hitter museums and monuments in Avignon and Villeneuve-lès-Avignon. The first site visited is full price, but each subsequent site is discounted. The reduction depends on each museum, but the discount is at least €1 (it gives you €2 off full price at the Palais des Papes, for example). For maximum savings, pay full price at one of the cheaper museums like the Musée Lapidaire, and benefit from the discount at more expensive ones such as the Palais des Papes and Pont St-Bénézet.

The pass is free and valid for 15 days. It covers a couple of tours too, and is available at the **tourist office** (p236) and at museums.

Camping Bagatelle
CAMPGROUND €

(☎ 04 90 86 30 39; www.campingbagatelle.com; Île de la Barthelasse; sites for tent, car & 2 people €15-30; ⊗ reception 8am-9pm; @) A family-friendly campsite that's shaded and just 20 minutes' walk from the city centre on an adjacent small island in the Rhône.

★ Les Jardins de Baracane
B&B €€

(☎ 06 11 14 88 54; www.lesjardinsdebaracane.fr; 12 rue Baracane; r €125-310; P ❀ ☎ ☎) This 18th-century house near place des Corps Saints is owned by an architect, so it's been sensitively and tastefully renovated. Wood beams, stone walls and period detailing feature in all rooms, but the best are the two suites, which are posh enough for a pope. There's a great pool, and breakfast is served in the garden under a huge wisteria tree.

Hôtel de l'Horloge
HOTEL €€

(☎ 04 90 16 42 00; www.hotel-avignon-horloge.com; place de l'Horloge; d €140-230; ❀ ☎) A refined choice: a spacious and well-run hotel in a lovely building near the town hall (and its clock, hence the name), handily placed just off Avignon's main thoroughfare. The decor is fairly standard – beige walls, tasteful prints – but the terrace rooms are worth the extra for their knockout views (room 505 overlooks the Palais des Papes).

Le Limas
B&B €€

(☎ 04 90 14 67 19; www.le-limas-avignon.com; 51 rue du Limas; ste €140-250; ❀ @ ☎) This chic B&B in an 18th-century town house, like something out of *Vogue Living*, is everything designers strive for when mixing old and new: state-of-the-art kitchen and minimalist white decor complementing antique fireplaces and 18th-century spiral stairs. Breakfast on the sun-drenched terrace is divine, darling.

Hotel Central
HOTEL €€

(☎ 04 90 86 07 81; www.hotel-central-avignon.com; 31 rue de la République; d €89-119) As its name suggests, this efficient hotel is right in the heart of things, smack bang beside the main thoroughfare of rue de la République. It's modern throughout, with small rooms and minimal clutter, but the drawback is the steep central stairs and lack of elevator. Ask for a room overlooking the interior courtyard.

La Banasterie
B&B €€

(☎ 06 87 72 96 36; www.labanasterie.com; 11 rue de la Banasterie; r €125-180; ❀ @ ☎) Heritage meets contemporary at this B&B, offering five spacious rooms in a building behind the Palais des Papes. It's stylish, and there are treats like in-room Nespresso machines and artisan teas, but the decor choices might not be everyone's cup of tea: some bathrooms are separated by a curtain rather than a door, and others just feel a bit stark.

Autour du Petit Paradis   APARTMENT €€
(☑ 04 90 81 00 42; www.autourdupetitparadis.com; 5 rue Noël Biret; apt from €95; ✴@ ⑨) Live like a local in a 17th-century stone house converted into a small apartment-hotel. Scrupulously maintained, each has a kitchenette, ideal for travellers who like style but want to cook their own local cuisine.

Villa de Margot   B&B €€
(☑ 04 90 82 62 34; www.demargot.fr; 24 rue des Trois Colombes; d €110-190; ✴⑨) A charming, quiet old-city address, this 19th-century private home, converted into an elegant guesthouse, has a walled garden and rooftop views. Rooms are styled like their names – Oriental, Royal, Art Deco and Romantic.

★ Hôtel La Mirande   HOTEL €€€
(☑ 04 90 14 20 20; www.la-mirande.fr; 4 place de la Mirande; d from €450; ✴@⑨) The address to sleep in Avignon *en luxe*. It's located literally in the shadow of the palace, and stepping inside feels more like entering an aristocrat's château than a hotel, with oriental rugs, gold-threaded tapestries, marble statues and oil paintings everywhere you look. Rooms are equally opulent, and the best overlook the interior garden where afternoon tea is served.

Its renowned restaurant, Le Marmiton (p235), offers cooking classes (from €90).

✖ Eating

★ Maison Violette   BAKERY €
(☑ 06 59 44 62 94; place des Corps Saints; ⊙ 7am-7.30pm Mon-Sat) We simply defy you to walk into this bakery and not instantly be tempted by the stacks of baguettes, *ficelles* and *pains de campagnes* loaded up on the counter, not to mention the orderly ranks of éclairs, *millefeuilles*, fruit tarts and cookies lined up irresistibly behind the glass. Go on, a little bit of what you fancy does you good, *non*?

Hygge   CAFE €
(☑ 04 65 81 06 87; 25 place des Carmes; 2-/3-course lunch €13.90/15.90; ⊙ 8am-3pm Mon-Wed, 8am-3pm & 6-10pm Thu-Sat) 🍴 Having worked at a smorgasbord of high-flying restaurants (including Copenhagen's Noma and Avignon's La Mirande), Jacques Pampiri opened his own place in Avignon, and it's a big hit with the locals. Hearty, wholesome organic food is dished up canteen-style to keep costs down, and the mix-and-match thrift-store decor is great fun. Arrive early for a prime table on the square.

Ginette et Marcel   CAFE €
(☑ 04 90 85 58 70; 27 place des Corps Saints; tartines €4.30-7.50; ⊙ 11am-11pm Wed-Mon; 🍴) Set on one of Avignon's most happening plane-tree-shaded squares, this vintage cafe styled like a 1950s grocery is a charming spot to hang out and people-watch over a *tartine* (open-face sandwich), tart, salad or other light dish – equally tasty for lunch or an early-evening *apéro*. Kids adore Ginette's cherry- and violet-flavoured cordials and Marcel's glass jars of old-fashioned sweets.

Le Barrio   BISTRO €
(☑ 04 90 27 00 45; 13 rue des Infirmières; 2-course weekday lunch €14.90, mains €10-20; ⊙ 11am-2.30pm & 7-10pm Tue-Sat) In the town's studenty quarter near elegant place des Carmes, this no-fuss hang-out is ideal for solid, unpretentious grub like stir-fries, crusted cod, burgers and hotpots. It attracts a young crowd – note the vintage vinyl hanging on the walls and shabby-chic tables – and there's a choice of inside or outside dining. Head here for a laid-back lunch.

Le Potard   BURGERS €
(☑ 04 90 82 34 19; www.lepotard.com; 19-21 place de la Principale; burgers €14-18; ⊙ noon-2.30pm Tue-Sat, 6.30-10pm Wed-Sat) Gourmet brioche-based burgers in a multitude of guises, loaded with tempting goodies from smoked bacon and St-Nectaire cheese to caramelised onions, crunchy rocket and sundried tomato caviar. There's also a range of salad plates served with mini-burgers. In case you're wondering, the name refers to the dial on a guitar (sometimes called a 'pot' in English).

E.A.T.   BISTRO €
(Estaminet, Arômes et Tentations; ☑ 04 90 83 46 74; www.restaurant-eat.com; 8 rue Mazan; lunch menu €16, mains €11-17; ⊙ noon-2pm & 7-9.45pm Thu-Tue) Weird name; great food. This back-alley bistro near place Crillon is a strong local's tip. It's very French, but borrows flavours and spices freely: smoked hake with pear compôte, perhaps, or one-pot veal in a rich, oozy sauce. There's not much space, though: definitely elbows-in dining. The €16 lunch

THEO, THERON/GETTY IMAGES ©

GERHARD ROETHLINGER/SHUTTERSTOCK ©

Châteauneuf-du-Pape (p238)
taste one of the world's great wines here, where
an ancient glacier created perfect wine-growing
conditions.

Théâtre Antique, Orange (p240)
explore one of France's most impressive Roman
sites.

Dentelles de Montmirail (p245)
network of footpaths offers hikers the chance to
see these strange rock formations up close.

Monastère St-Paul de Mausole
(p194), St-Remy-de-Provence
once used as an asylum, this monastery was
home to Vincent van Gogh during one of his most
productive periods.

L VALENCIA/GETTY IMAGES ©

menu includes two courses, a glass of wine and coffee.

Naka   JAPANESE €

(☑ 04 90 82 15 70; www.restaurantnaka.fr; 4 place de la Principle; lunch menu €13.50-14.50, dinner menu €13.50-22; ⊙ noon-2.30pm & 7-10.30pm Mon-Sat) When tastebuds tire of Provençal, consider this uber-cool Japanese restaurant. At home in a deconsecrated chapel on a beautiful stone-paved square in the old city, its setting is stunning. Take your pick of sushi, sashimi, maki, tempura and chirashi, or opt for an excellent-value *menu*.

★ Restaurant L'Essentiel   FRENCH €€

(☑ 04 90 85 87 12; www.restaurantlessentiel.com; 2 rue Petite Fusterie; menus €32-46; ⊙ noon-2pm & 7-9.45pm Tue-Sat) In the top tier of Avignon's restaurants for many a year, this elegant restaurant remains (as its name suggests) as essential as ever. First there's the setting: a lovely, honey-stoned *hôtel particulier* (mansion) with a sweet courtyard garden. Then there's the food: rich, sophisticated French dining of the first order, replete with the requisite foams, veloutés and reductions.

83.Vernet   MODERN FRENCH €€

(☑ 04 90 85 99 04; www.83vernet.com; 83 rue Joseph Vernet; 2-course lunch menu €17, 2-/3-course dinner menu €24/30; ⊙ noon-3pm & 7pm-1am Mon-Sat) Forget flowery French descriptions. The menu is straightforward and to the point at this bistro-bar, where the stark white furniture and studiously minimal decor counterpoints the heritage architecture of a medieval college. Expect bistro classics, with a modern flavour.

Numéro 75   MODERN FRENCH €€

(☑ 04 90 27 16 00; www.numero75.com; 75 rue Guillaume Puy; 2-/3-course menus from €31/38; ⊙ noon-2pm & 7.30-9.30pm Mon-Sat) The chic dining room, in the former mansion of absinthe inventor Jules Pernod, is a fitting backdrop to the stylised Mediterranean cooking. *Menus* change nightly and include just a handful of mains, but brevity guarantees freshness. On balmy nights, reserve a table in the elegant courtyard garden.

Au Jardin des Carmes   FRENCH €€

(☑ 09 54 25 10 67; 21 place des Carmes; 2-/3-course menu €28/33; ⊙ noon-10.30pm Tue-Sat) There's one standout reason to lunch at this homely restaurant, and that's the delightful courtyard garden, shaded by sails, tall bamboo and climbing plants. À la carte starters are

€11, mains €21, desserts €9, plus the *plat du jour* at €16. The food is honest rather than *haute cuisine,* but it's prettily presented and packed with flavour.

Fou de Fafa   BISTRO €€

(☑ 04 32 76 35 13; 17 rue des Trois Faucons; 2-/3-course menu €25/31; ⊙ 6.30-11pm Wed-Sun; 🖼) A typical French bistro, Fou de Fafa's strength lies in simplicity – fresh ingredients, bright flavours, convivial surroundings (and an early opening time handy for families with young children). Dining is between soft golden-stone walls and the chef gives a fresh spin to classics. *Magret de canard* (duck breast) in a strawberry and balsamic reduction, anyone?

Le Vintage   BISTRO €€

(☑ 04 86 65 48 54; 10 rue Galante; 2-course menu €18, mains €14-18; ⊙ noon-2.30pm & 6-9pm) Deep in the medieval quarter, this welcoming bistro is a fun place to dine. Zinc tables, well-worn furniture and a busy, noisy kitchen out back conjure up the air of a village bistro, something backed up by the trad French dishes. It's also one of the few places in town open daily – and the local wine selection is super.

Bar à Manger du Coin Caché   BISTRO €€

(☑ 04 32 76 27 16; 3 place des Chataignes; mains €12-15; ⊙ noon-3pm & 7-10pm) This place is pure charm. On cobbled-stone place des Chataignes (Chestnut Tree Square) it spills across to its ancient stone neighbour (Cloître St-Pierre). More bistro than bar, it cooks up seasonal dishes with a fusion twist. Kickstart the alfresco occasion with a sweet Vin de Noix de la St Jean, peachy Rinquinquin or other Provençal aperitif. No credit cards.

L'Épicerie   BISTRO €€

(☑ 04 90 82 74 22; www.restaurantlepicerie. fr; 10 place St-Pierre; lunch menu €15.90, dinner mains €18-23; ⊙ noon-2.30pm & 8-10pm) From the checked tablecloths to the booth seats, handwritten blackboards and vintage signs, this reliable bistro is a fine spot for hearty French dishes, from homemade foie gras to a mixed platter of Provençal produce (€19). Lots of local wines are available by the glass.

★ Christian Etienne   FRENCH €€€

(☑ 04 90 86 16 50; www.christian-etienne.fr; 10 rue de Mons; lunch/dinner menus from €35/75; ⊙ noon-2pm & 7.30-10pm Tue-Sat) If it's the full-blown, fine-dining French experience you're after, then Monsieur Etienne's much-vaunted (and Michelin-starred) restaurant is the place to go. It's the real deal: truffles and foie gras galore, and the kind of multi-course menus that demand a second mortgage. It's a bit dated inside: go for the lovely, leafy terrace for fine views of the medieval building.

Les 5 Sens   GASTRONOMY €€€
(☑ 04 90 85 26 51; www.restaurantles5sens.com; 18 rue Joseph Vernet; menus lunch €22.50/29, dinner €39-56; ⊙ noon-1.30pm & 7.30-11pm Fri-Tue) This gastronomic temple is a great option for a *très Français* fine-dining experience. Overseen by chef supremo Thierry Baucher, it's particularly known for its mix of Provençal and southwestern flavours – so expect contemporary spin on traditional dishes such as *cassoulet* (meat-and-bean stew), foie gras and *suprême de pintade* (guinea-fowl supreme).

Le Marmiton   FRENCH €€€
(4 place de la Mirande; menus €75-115, mains €35-40) Le Marmiton, the super-formal restaurant of Hôtel La Mirande (p231), offers cooking classes (from €90) and a twice-weekly chef's table (reservations essential). Afternoon tea is served (albeit slowly) in the glittering lobby.

Self-Catering

Les Halles   MARKET €
(www.avignon-leshalles.com; place Pie; ⊙ 6am-1.30pm Tue-Fri, to 2pm Sat & Sun) Over 40 food stalls showcase seasonal Provençal ingredients. Cooking demonstrations are held at 11am Saturday. Outside on place Pie, admire Patrick Blanc's marvellous vegetal wall.

Monoprix   SUPERMARKET €
(24 rue de la République; ⊙ 8am-9pm Mon-Sat) Catch-all supermarket in the centre of town.

🍷 Drinking & Nightlife

Chic yet laid-back Avignon is awash with gorgeous, tree-shaded pedestrian squares buzzing with cafe life. Favourite options, loaded with pavement terraces and drinking opportunities, include place Crillon, place Pie, place de l'Horloge and place des Corps Saints.

Students tend to favour the many bars dotted along the aptly named rue de la Verrerie (Glassware St).

Milk Shop   CAFE
(☑ 09 82 54 16 82; www.milkshop.fr; 26 place des Corps Saints; ⊙ 7.45am-7pm Mon-Fri, 9.30am-7pm Sat; 🛜) Keen to mingle with Avignon

LOCAL KNOWLEDGE

RUE DES TEINTURIERS

Canalside rue des Teinturiers (literally 'street of dyers') is a picturesque pedestrian street known for its alternative vibe in Avignon's old dyers' district. A hive of industrial activity until the 19th century, populated by weavers and tapestry-makers, the street today is renowned for its bohemian bistros, cafes and gallery-workshops. Stone 'benches' in the shade of ancient plane trees make the perfect perch to ponder the irresistible trickle of the River Sorgue, safeguarded since the 16th century by Chapelle des Pénitents Gris.

students? Make a beeline for this *salon au lait* ('milk bar') where super-thick ice-cream shakes (€4.50) are slurped through extra-wide straws. Bagels (€5 to €7), cupcakes and other American snacks create a deliberate US vibe, while comfy armchairs and wi-fi encourage hanging out.

L'Explo   CRAFT BEER
(2 rue des Teinturiers; ⊙ 5pm-midnight Tue-Sat) It's a sunny evening and your inner beer nerd is in the market for a dry rye, hoppy IPA or boozy Belgian wheatbeer. Well you're in luck: this groovy little bar on happening rue des Teinturiers serves a big range of artisanal beers, many made locally.

L'Esclave   LGBTIQ+
(☑ 04 90 85 14 91; 12 rue du Limas; ⊙ 11.30pm-7am Tue-Sun) Avignon's inner-city gay bar rocks well into the wee hours, pulling a clientele that is not always that quiet, based on dozens of neighbour-considerate 'be quiet' signs plastered outside.

⭐ Entertainment

Avignon is one of the premier cities for theatre in France; tickets for concerts and events are sold at the tourist office *billetterie* (box office).

La Manutention   ARTS CENTER
(☑ 04 90 86 86 77; 4 rue des Escaliers Ste-Anne; ⊙ noon-midnight) At the foot of a staircase just behind the Palais des Papes, this arts hub covers lots of bases: with a program of jazz, live gigs and film. The architecture is lovely, with tall windows and a courtyard garden, and the restaurant does fairly decent food, too.

Cinéma Utopia   CINEMA
(☎ 04 90 82 65 36; www.cinemas-utopia.org; La Manutention, 4 rue des Escaliers Ste-Anne) Four-screen art-house cinema at cultural centre La Manutention which shows films in their original language.

Opéra Théâtre d'Avignon   PERFORMING ARTS
(☎ 04 90 82 81 40; www.operagrandavignon.fr; place de l'Horloge; ☺ box office 11am-6pm Tue-Sat) Built in 1847, Avignon's main classical venue presents operas, plays, chamber music and ballet from October to June.

AJMI   JAZZ
(Association pour le Jazz & la Musique Improvisée; ☎ 04 90 86 08 61; www.jazzalajmi.com; La Manutention, 4 rue des Escaliers Ste-Anne) Inside La Manutention arts centre, AJMI showcases improvisational jazz at its intimate 2nd-floor (no elevator) black-box theatre.

Shopping

Find high-end antique shops along rue du Limas, mainstream shopping on rue de la République, and boutiques on its side streets, such as rue St-Agricol.

ℹ Information

Centre Hospitalier Avignon (☎ 04 32 75 33 33; www.ch-avignon.fr; 305 rue Raoul Follereau) Marked on maps as Hôpital Sud, 2.5km south of the central train station – take bus 2, 6 or 14.

Police Station (☎ 04 32 40 55 55; 14 bd St-Roch)

Tourist Office (☎ 04 32 74 32 74; www.avignon-tourisme.com; 41 cours Jean Jaurès; ☺ 9am-6pm Mon-Sat, 10am-5pm Sun Apr-Oct, shorter hours Nov-Mar) Offers a range of excellent **guided walking tours** (p229) covering the town's history, architecture and papal buildings. It can also book tickets for boat trips on the Rhône and wine-tasting trips to nearby vineyards.

Tourist Office Annexe (Gare Avignon TGV; ☺ Jun-Aug) During summer, Avignon has an information booth at the Avignon TGV station.

ℹ Getting There & Away

The TGV has pretty much eliminated the need to fly to Avignon from anywhere in mainland France; it's nearly always easier, cheaper (and in many cases faster) to take the train than fly.

AIR
Aéroport Avignon-Provence (p329) In Caumont, 8km southeast of Avignon. Direct flights to London, Birmingham and Southampton in the UK.

From the airport, TCRA bus 30 (www.tcra.fr; €1.40, 25 minutes, Monday to Saturday) goes to the post office and LER bus 22 (www.info-ler.fr; €1.50) goes to the Avignon bus station and TGV station.

Taxis cost about €35 to €40.

BUS
Avignon's **bus station** (bd St-Roch; ☺ information window 8am-7pm Mon-Fri, to 1pm Sat) is a major bus hub for the Vaucluse *département*. Long-haul companies **Linebus** (☎ 04 90 85 30 48; www.linebus.com) and **Eurolines** (☎ 04 90 85 27 60; www.eurolines.com) have offices at the far end of bus platforms and serve places like Barcelona. TransVaucluse (www.vaucluse.fr) offers regional bus services in the Avignon area.

Aix-en-Provence (€18, LER Line 23, 1¼ hours, six daily Monday to Saturday, two on Sunday)

Arles (€7.80, LER Line 18, 50 minutes, five daily)

Carpentras (€2.10, TransVaucluse Line 5, 45 minutes, 11 daily Monday to Saturday, six on Sunday)

Orange (€2.10, TransVaucluse Line 2, one hour, hourly Monday to Saturday, three on Sunday)

TRAIN
Avignon has two train stations: **Gare Avignon Centre** (42 bd St-Roch), on the southern edge of the walled town, and **Gare Avignon TGV** (Courtine), 4km southwest in Courtine.

Local shuttle trains link the two every 15 to 20 minutes (€1.60, six minutes, 6am to 11pm). Note that there is no luggage storage at the train station.

Eurostar (p330) services operate one to five times weekly between Avignon TGV and London St Pancras (from €78, 5¾ hours) en route to/from Marseille.

TGV Services
Aix-en-Provence (€12.50 to €21, 25 minutes)
Marseille (€12.50 to €19, 40 minutes)
Marseille-Provence airport (Vitrolles station, €12 to €21, one to 1½ hours)
Nice (€36 to €62, 3¼ hours)
Paris Gare du Lyon (€45 to €90, 3½ hours)

Non-TGV Services
Arles (€8, 17 minutes)
Nîmes (€9.90, 30 minutes)
Orange (€6.60, 22 minutes)

ℹ Getting Around

BICYCLE
Vélopop (☎ 08 10 45 64 56; www.velopop.fr; per half-hour €0.50) Shared-bicycle service,

with 17 stations around town. Membership is €1/5 per day/week.

Provence Bike (☑ 04 90 27 92 61; www. provence-bike.com; 7 av St-Ruf; bicycles per day/week from €12/65, scooters €25/150; ⊙9am-6.30pm Mon-Sat, plus 10am-1pm Sun Jul) Rents city bikes, mountain bikes, scooters and motorcycles.

BOAT
The free **shuttleboat** (Navette Fluviale; ⊙ mid-Feb–Dec) runs from near the base of Pont St-Bénézet to Île de la Barthelasse.

BUS
TCRA (Transports en Commun de la Région d'Avignon; ☑ 04 32 74 18 32; www.tcra.fr) tickets (€1.30) are sold on board. Buses run from 7am till about 8pm. The main transfer points are Poste (main post office) and place Pie. For Villeneuve-lès-Avignon, take bus 5.

Autocars Lieutaud (☑ 04 90 86 36 75; www. cars-lieutaud.fr; 36 bd St-Roch) runs tours to vineyards around Avignon.

CAR & MOTORCYCLE
Find car-hire agencies at both train stations (reserve ahead, especially in July). Narrow, one-way streets and impossible parking make driving within the ramparts an absolute horror: park outside the walls.

The most convenient car park for the town centre is **Parking Palais des Papes** (place du Palais; per hour €2, 24hr €18.80; ⊙24hr), but it tends to fill up quickly on busy summer days. Thankfully, there is plenty of free parking available: 900 free spaces at **Parking de L'Ile Piot**, and 1150 at **Parking des Italiens**, both under surveillance and served by the free **TCRA shuttle bus**.

On directional signs at intersections, 'P' in yellow means pay lots; 'P' in green, free lots. Pay **Parking Gare Centre** (☑ 04 90 80 74 40; bd St-Roch; ⊙24hr) is next to the central train station.

TAXI
Taxi-Radio Avignon (☑ 04 90 82 20 20)

AROUND AVIGNON

Villeneuve-lès-Avignon
POP 12,872

Across the Rhône from Avignon, compact Villeneuve-lès-Avignon has monuments to rival Avignon's but none of the crowds. Meander the cloisters of a medieval monastery, take in hilltop views from Fort St-André and

lose yourself in spectacular gardens at Abbaye St-André – reason enough to visit.

◉ Sights
The Avignon Passion (p230) discount pass is valid here.

★Abbaye et Jardins de l'Abbaye   MONASTERY, GARDENS
(☑ 04 90 25 55 95; www.abbayesaintandre.fr; Fort St-André, rue Montée du Fort; adult/child abbey €14/free, garden €7/free; ⊙10am-6pm Tue-Sun May-Sep, 10am-1pm & 2-5pm Tue-Sun Mar & Oct, to 6pm Apr) The resplendent vaulted halls of this 10th-century abbey, within Fort St-André, can only be visited by guided tour. The stunning terrace gardens, however – built atop the abbey vaults and classed among France's top 100 gardens – can be freely roamed. Pathways meander among fragrant roses, iris-studded olive groves, wisteria-covered pergolas and the ruins of three ancient churches. The views of Avignon and the Rhône are spectacular.

Fort St-André   FORT
(☑ 04 90 25 45 35; rue Montée du Fort; adult/child €6/free, joint ticket with Chartreuse du Val de Bénédiction €9/free; ⊙10am-6pm Jun-Sep, 10am-1pm & 2-5pm Oct-May) King Philip the Fair (aka Philippe le Bel) wasn't messing around when he built defensive 14th-century Fort St-André on the then border between France and the Holy Roman Empire: the walls are 2m thick! Today you can walk a small section of the ramparts and admire views from the **Tour des Masques** (Wizards' Tower) and **Tours Jumelles** (Twin Towers). You can also tour the Abbaye et Jardins de l'Abbaye.

Chartreuse du Val de Bénédiction   MONASTERY
(☑ 04 90 15 24 24; www.chartreuse.org; 58 rue de la République; adult/child €8/free, joint ticket with Fort St-André €9/free; ⊙9.30am-6.30pm May-Sep, to 5pm Oct-Mar) Shaded from the summer's heat, the three cloisters, 24 cells, church, chapels and nook-and-cranny gardens of the Chartreuse du Val de Bénédiction make up France's biggest Carthusian monastery, founded in 1352 by Pope Innocent VI, who was buried here 10 years later in an elaborate mausoleum.

Tour Philippe-le-Bel   LANDMARK
(☑ 04 32 70 08 57; montée de la Tour; adult/child €2.60/free; ⊙10am-12.30pm & 2-6pm Tue-Sun

May-Oct, 2-5pm Feb-Apr) King Philip commissioned the Tour Philippe-le-Bel, 500m outside Villeneuve, to control traffic over Pont St-Bénézet to and from Avignon. The steep steps spiralling to the top reward climbers with stunning river views.

Musée Pierre de Luxembourg MUSEUM
(☑ 04 90 27 49 66; 3 rue de la République; adult/child €3.60/free; ⊙10am-12.30pm & 2-6pm Tue-Sun May-Oct, 2-5pm Nov-Apr) Inside a 17th-century mansion, this museum's masterwork is Enguerrand Quarton's *The Crowning of the Virgin* (1453), in which angels wrest souls from purgatory. Rounding out the collection are 16th- to 18th-century paintings.

🛏 Sleeping & Eating

Find cafes and food shops around place Jean Jaurès, near Musée Pierre de Luxembourg.

YMCA-UCJG HOSTEL €
(☑ 04 90 25 46 20; www.ymca-avignon.fr; 7bis chemin de la Justice; dm €35-45, without bathroom €25-32; ⊙reception 8.30am-6pm, closed Nov-Dec; P 🛜 ⚊) There's no hostel in central Avignon, but budgeteers can catch TCRA bus 4 (Monteau stop) over to this place just outside Villeneuve-lès-Avignon. It's standard hostel style – basic but clean dorms, a few private rooms, a lounge, a kitchen – but the cracking pool is a definite plus. Sheets are included; towels cost €2.

★ Carré Cardinal B&B €€
(☑ 04 90 22 00 00; 57 rue de la République; d/tr/ste from €100/130/150; ❄ 🛜) Pretty rooms in this renovated historic building across from the Chartreuse du Val de Bénédiction are kitted out with creamy linens, flat-screen TVs and modern bathrooms. Two rooms let onto the internal courtyard; one is a two-storey suite.

Les Jardins de la Livrée B&B €€
(☑ 04 86 81 00 21; www.la-livree.fr; 4bis rue du Camp de Bataille; r from €100; ⊙closed Jan–mid-Mar & late Oct–mid-Dec; P ❄ 🛜 ⚊) The herb-themed rooms at this little town-centre B&B are simple, but the walled garden and lovely pool make it a relaxing refuge. Free parking.

ℹ Information

Tourist Office (☑ 04 90 25 61 33; www.ot-villeneuvelezavignon.fr; 1 place Charles David; ⊙9.30am-12.30pm & 2-5pm Mon-Fri, 9am-1pm Sat, slightly longer hours in summer) Guided English-language tours in July and August.

ℹ Getting There & Away

TCRA (p237) bus 5 links Villeneuve-lès-Avignon with Avignon (it's only 2km, but dull walking).

Châteauneuf-du-Pape

POP 2210

Even in the world of fine wines, Châteauneuf-du-Pape retains a special cachet. It's arguably the best-known of the Rhône appellations, prized by oenophiles the world over: mostly based on grenache, with dashes of syrah and mourvèdre sometimes added to the mix. Needless to say, there are numerous vineyards around town offering opportunities to taste.

As its name hints, the hilltop château after which the wine is named was originally built as a summer residence for Avignon's popes, but it's little more than a ruin now – plundered for stone after the Revolution, and bombed by Germany in WWII for good measure. Even so, the wraparound views of the surrounding Rhône valley are epic, stretching all the way to Mont Ventoux.

◉ Sights & Activities

Domaine de la Solitude WINE
(☑ 04 90 83 71 45; www.domaine-solitude.com; rte de Bédarides, D192; ⊙10am-6pm Mon-Fri, by appointment Sat & Sun) Two kilometres east of the village, appreciate Châteauneuf-du-Pape from this family-run estate, cultivated for 600 years by descendants of Pope Urbain VIII. Call ahead to receive a warm welcome, in English, as you discover elegant, rounded wines, with supple, never-harsh tannins. Tastings (free) include visits to the barrel cellar.

Château Mont-Redon WINE
(☑ 04 90 83 72 75; www.chateaumontredon.com; rte d'Orange, D88; ⊙9am-7pm Apr-Sep, reduced hours Oct-Mar) Three kilometres from Châteauneuf-du-Pape, Mont-Redon is gorgeously placed amid sweeping vineyards. Large, and easy for drop-ins, it can attract weekend crowds for its respectable wines, including an excellent, minerally white. Tastings free.

Caves du Verger des Papes WINE
(☑ 04 90 83 58 08; www.caveduverger.com; 4 montée du Château; ⊙10am-7pm Tue-Sat, to 4pm Sun Jul & Aug, reduced hours Sep-Jun) FREE Beneath the town's namesake château, these small, magnificent wine *caves* (cellars) date

WINE PRIMER: CHÂTEAUNEUF-DU-PAPE

Thank geology for these luscious wines: when glaciers receded, they left a thick layer of *galets* scattered atop the red-clay soil; these large pebbles trap the Provençal sun, releasing heat after sunset, helping grapes ripen with steady warmth.

The Romans first planted vines here 2000 years ago, but wine-growing took off after Pope John XXII built a castle in 1317, planting vineyards to provide the court with wine. From this papally endorsed beginning, wine production flourished.

Most Châteauneuf-du-Pape is red; only 6% is white (rosé is forbidden). Strict regulations – which formed the basis for the Appellation d'Origine Contrôlée (AOC) system – govern production. Reds come from 13 grape varieties – grenache is the biggie – and should age five years minimum. The full-bodied whites drink well young (except for all-roussanne varieties) and make an excellent, minerally aperitif that's hard to find elsewhere (but taste before buying; some may lack acidity).

back 2000 years. The bar carries 80 of the town's 250 labels. English is spoken.

École de Dégustation WINE
(Tasting School; ☏04 90 83 56 15; www.oenologie-mouriesse.com; 2 rue des Papes; 2hr class €40) This sophisticated wine-tasting school is the best place to learn more about the wines of the Châteauneuf-du-Pape area, and to refine your palate. There are regular classes on Friday evenings and Saturday mornings in French, or if you can get together a group, a bespoke course can be arranged in English.

Sleeping & Eating

Espace de l'Hers B&B €€
(☏06 22 65 41 18; www.espacedelhers.com; 5 Chemin de l'Hers; d €100-180; P🛜♨) This old wine estate makes a fittingly upmarket place to stay in the middle of the Rhône's most upmarket appellation. Renovated in 2015, it has four elegant rooms, blending period architecture with modern style, and all overlooking the estate's vineyards and a lovely swimming pool.

★**Le Verger des Papes** FRENCH €€
(☏04 90 83 50 40; www.vergerdespapes.com; 4 rue du Château; lunch/dinner menus €22/32; ⊙noon-2pm Tue-Sat, 7-9pm Thu-Sat) A working vineyard as well as an excellent restaurant, this friendly *domaine* is a favourite tip for Châteauneuf aficionados. Dine on typical Provençal country food, with a divine view over the town's rooftops, then educate yourself in the cellars.

La Mère Germaine FRENCH €€
(☏04 90 22 78 34; place de la Fontaine; lunch/dinner menus from €25/40; ⊙noon-2pm & 7-9pm

mid-Mar–Oct, closed Wed Nov–mid-Mar; P🌡🛜) Locals have been heading for this classic village *auberge* (country inn) for more than nine decades (since 1922, in fact). It's the kind of place where the owner knows everyone by name, and classic country dishes are served up with zero pretension. The vineyard views are lovely, and as you'd expect, the wine choice is super.

Shopping

Chocolaterie Bernard Castelain FOOD
(☏04 90 83 54 71; www.vin-chocolat-castelain.com; 1745 rte de Sorgues; ⊙9am-noon & 2-7pm Mon-Sat) The specialities at this artisan *chocolatier* include *picholines* (dark-chocolate-covered roasted almonds that look like Provençal olives) and *Palets des Papes* (Châteauneuf-du-Pape liquer-infused truffles).

Information

Châteauneuf-du-Pape Tourist Office (☏04 90 83 71 08; www.ot-chateauneuf-du-pape.mobi; place du Portail; ⊙9.30am-6pm Mon-Sat, closed lunch & Wed Oct-May) Has loads of advice on wine tasting and visiting local vineyards, including ones that offer English-language tours. It can also make appointments for you.

Getting There & Away

Buses stop at the intersection of av Louis Pasteur and rue de la Nouvelle Poste. The following are TransVaucluse (www.vaucluse.fr) services:

Avignon (Line 22, €2.10, 25 minutes, three daily Monday to Saturday)

Orange (Line 23, €2.10, 25 minutes, three daily Monday to Saturday)

Orange

POP 29,645

Two thousand years ago, Orange – then known as Arausio – was one of the major settlements in this sunbaked corner of the Gallo-Roman empire. To cement its status, townsfolk constructed an impressive series of structures, including the town's mighty ancient theatre – once the largest in Gaul, it still steals the show and is rightly (along with Orange's triumphal arch) a World Heritage site. Unfortunately, despite its massive scale, the limestone structure is surprisingly fragile, and a monumental eight-year restoration project is currently underway to preserve it for the future. Expect scaffold until at least 2024.

The modern town itself isn't quite as starry – in fact in places it looks positively unloved – so there's no real reason to spend the night unless you have to.

History

The House of Orange, the princely dynasty that had ruled Orange since the 12th century, made its mark on the history of the Netherlands through a 16th-century marriage with the German House of Nassau, and then English history through William of Orange. Orange was ceded to France in 1713 by the Treaty of Utrecht. To this day, many members of the royal house of the Netherlands are known as the princes and princesses of Orange-Nassau.

◉ Sights

★ **Théâtre Antique** ROMAN SITE
(Ancient Roman Theatre; ☑ 04 90 51 17 60; www.the atre-antique.com; rue Madeleine Roch; adult/child €9.50/7.50; ☺ 9am-7pm Jun-Aug, to 6pm Apr, May & Sep, 9.30am-5.30pm Mar & Oct, 9.30am-4.30pm Nov-Feb) Orange's monumental, Unesco-protected Roman theatre is unquestionably one of France's most impressive Roman sights. It's one of only three intact Roman theatres left in the world (the others are in Syria and Turkey), and its sheer size is awe-inspiring: designed to seat 10,000 spectators, its stage wall reaches 37m high, 103m wide and 1.8m thick. Little wonder that Louis XIV called it 'the finest wall in my kingdom'.

In its heyday the theatre would have been a sight to behold: covered in statues and carvings, and decorated in mosaics and marble slabs. Experiments have shown the wall was specially designed to focus and project sound.

Unfortunately, time has taken its toll on this most theatrical of structures, and an enormous preservation project was launched in 2016 to make sure it survives for future theatre-goers to enjoy. The local limestone from which it was built has weathered badly, and over eight years the most delicate parts of the building will undergo painstaking restoration using a variety of cutting-edge techniques, including laser-mapping and chemical preservation, as well as good old-fashioned stonemasonry. Different sections of the theatre are being restored each year, but this does mean you'll have to deal with scaffolding and construction until at least 2024.

Nevertheless, the theatre remains completely open to visitors, and still hosts its annual opera festival, **Chorégies d'Orange** (www.choregies.asso.fr; ☺ Jul & Aug).

You can book admission tickets in advance online. There's also a useful app available to download, which includes an 80-minute guided tour.

The entrance is on the theatre's west side.

★ **Colline St-Eutrope** GARDENS
For bird's-eye views of the theatre – and phenomenal vistas of Mont Ventoux and the Dentelles de Montmirail – follow montée Philbert de Chalons or montée Lambert up Colline St-Eutrope (St Eutrope Hill; elevation 97m), once the Romans' lookout point. En route, pass ruins of a 12th-century **château**, once the residence of the princes of Orange.

Musée d'Art et d'Histoire MUSEUM
(www.theatre-antique.com; rue Madeleine Roch; entry incl with Théâtre Antique; ☺ 9.15am-7pm Jun-Aug, to 6pm Apr, May & Sep, shorter hours Oct-Mar) This small museum contains various finds relating to the theatre's history, including plaques and friezes that once formed part of the scenery, a range of amphora, busts, columns and vases, and a room displaying three rare engraved *cadastres* (official surveys) dating from 77 BCE.

Arc de Triomphe HISTORIC SITE
Orange's 1st-century-CE monumental arch, the Arc de Triomphe – 19m high and wide, and 8m thick – stands on the Via Agrippa. Restored in 2009, its brilliant reliefs commemorate 49 BCE Roman victories with carvings of chained, naked Gauls.

Église St-Florent CHURCH
This Franciscan church was established in the 14th century and was the burial place of the princes of Baux. It was heavily damaged in the Wars of Religion.

Orange

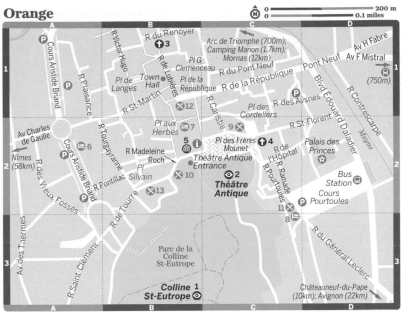

Orange

◎ Top Sights
1 Colline St-Eutrope	B3
2 Théâtre Antique	C2

◎ Sights
3 Cathédrale Notre-Dame de Nazareth	B1
4 Église St-Florent	C2
5 Musée d'Art et d'Histoire	B2

🛏 Sleeping
6 Hôtel Le Glacier	A2
7 Hôtel l'Herbier d'Orange	B2
8 Hôtel Saint Jean	C3

🍴 Eating
9 À la Maison	C2
10 La Grotte d'Auguste	B2
11 Le Parvis	C2
12 Les Artistes	B1
13 Les Saveurs du Marché	B2

Cathédrale Notre-Dame de Nazareth CHURCH
(⊙8am-7pm) Orange's oldest church was consecrated in the 12th century.

🛏 Sleeping

Hôtel Saint Jean HOTEL €
(⌨04 90 51 15 16; www.hotelsaint-jean.com; 1 cours Pourtoules; s/d/tr/q €75/85/105/125; P❄🤚) An attractive option with bags of Provençal character, half-built into the hillside of the Colline St-Eutrope. Inside, there are checked fabrics and cosy rooms, with windows overlooking a little patio; outside, the building is all yellow stone and pistachio-coloured shutters. A few of the rooms have walls cut straight into the hill.

Hôtel l'Herbier d'Orange HOTEL €
(⌨04 90 34 09 23; www.lherbierdorange.com; 8 place aux Herbes; s/d/tr/q €55/62/79/92; P❄@🤚) On a quiet, tree-shaded square, this simple hotel makes a pleasant-enough base in Orange, with 20 bright, colourful rooms, livened up with jolly fabrics and tiled floors. The stone-walled breakfast room is attractive too.

Camping Manon CAMPGROUND €
(⌨04 32 81 94 96; www.camping-manon.com; 1321 rue Alexis Carrel, Quartier Le Jonquier; sites for 2 people €14-28; ⊙Apr-Sep; @🤚🏊) This good camping ground has been recently overhauled and has a pool, hot tub, tennis, laundry and minimart. Camping sites are available both with and without electricity.

★ **Le Mas Julien**   B&B €€

(☑ 04 90 34 99 49; www.mas-julien.com; 704 chemin de St Jean; d €95-125, studio €110-180; P ✳ 🖥 🐾) Out in the countryside between Orange and Châteauneuf-du-Pape, this delightful farmhouse is the stuff of Provençal dreams: wisteria-clad facade, gorgeous pool, quiet location and rooms that blend contemporary style with rustic charm. There are four rooms and a self-contained studio. Owner Valère caters dinners on request.

Hôtel Le Glacier   HOTEL €€

(☑ 04 90 34 02 01; www.le-glacier.com; 46 cours Aristide Briand; d €79-150; ✳ @ 🖥) This hotel doesn't look like much from outside, but surprises await inside: all of the 33 rooms have a different feel, some in cool blues and checks, others in crimsons and yellows or country florals. It's part of the Logis umbrella, but family-owned, so there's plenty of personal service. There's easy parking in front of the hotel, and bike rental. Breakfast €10.

🍴 Eating

There are several cafes opposite the Roman theatre, but you'll eat better by heading further into the old town. Markets spill across streets in the town centre every Thursday.

À la Maison   BISTRO €

(☑ 04 90 60 98 83; 4 place des Cordeliers; 2-/3-course menu lunch €12.50/15, dinner €25/32; ☺ noon-2pm & 7-10pm Mon-Sat) For dinner on a warm summer night, 'At Home' has the pick of the settings of any of Orange's restaurants, on a side square next to a tinkling fountain shaded by plane trees. The food is fairly standard bistro fare – mainly steaks, salmon, salads and seafood – but it's a shame about the nasty plastic chairs.

Les Saveurs du Marché   FRENCH €

(☑ 06 14 44 26 63; 24 place Sylvain; 2-/3-/4-course lunch menu €13/16/24, dinner menu €29; ☺ noon-2pm Tue-Sun, 7-9pm Tue-Sat) As the name suggests, market flavours underpin the menu

here, from delicious homemade tapenades to pan-seared red mullet drizzled with olive oil and fragrant pesto. The menu changes regularly – the four-course lunch is a steal – but quality can suffer a bit when it gets over-busy, so arrive early.

Les Artistes   BISTRO, CAFE €

(place de la République; mains €8-15; ☺ 8am-2am) This catch-all, basic brasserie-bar is where everyone likes to hang out for an evening aperitif, perhaps followed by a simple dish of pasta or a quick steak. The location in the old square is great.

Le Parvis   FRENCH €€

(☑ 04 90 34 82 00; www.restaurant-le-parvis-orange.com; 55 cours Pourtoules; 2-/3-course menu lunch €24.50/29.50, dinner €39/49; ☺ noon-1.45pm & 7.30-9.15pm Tue-Sat) This top-class restaurant has been run by local chef Jean-Michel Bérengier for going on three decades, and it's firmly established itself for its classic Provençal food. The service is a little starchy, and the beamed dining room rather old-school, but if it's fine Provençal food you're after, you'll be well served here.

La Grotte d'Auguste   FRENCH €€

(☑ 04 90 60 22 54; www.restaurant-orange.fr; Théâtre Antique, rue Madeleine Roch; lunch/dinner menu from €16/21; ☺ noon-2pm & 7-10pm Tue-Sat) Old-school French dining is the order of the day at Auguste's Cave – an apt name, as the restaurant is half-built into the rocky hillside. Food-wise, expect hearty, meaty dishes presented with care, but few fireworks.

ℹ Information

Tourist Office (☑ 04 90 34 70 88; www.otorange.fr; place des Frères Mounet; ☺ 9am-6.30pm Mon-Sat, 9am-1pm & 2-6.30pm Sun, closed Sun Oct-Mar) Brochures and hotel bookings.

ℹ Getting There & Around

BICYCLE

Sport Aventure (☑ 04 90 34 75 08; 1 place de la République; half-day/day/week €12/18/69) Central bike shop; delivers within 20km radius.

BUS

Most buses depart from Orange's **bus station** (☑ 04 90 34 15 59; 201 cours Pourtoules).

Avignon (€2.10, TransVaucluse Line 2, one hour, hourly Monday to Saturday, three on Sunday)

Vaison-la-Romaine (€2, TransVaucluse Line 4, 45 minutes, eight daily Monday to Saturday, two on Sunday)

ROMAN PASS

The Roman Pass (Pass Romain; adult/child €18.50/14) is a joint ticket that allows access to Orange's Roman theatre and museum, plus Nîmes' Les Arènes, the Maison Carrée and Tour Magne. It's valid for seven days, and you can buy it at any of the venues.

TRAIN

Orange's **train station** (av Frédéric Mistral) is 1.5km east of the town centre.

Arles (€12.60, 40 minutes)
Avignon (€6.60, 22 minutes)
Marseille (€26.20, 1¾ hours)
Marseille-Provence airport (Vitrolles station; €23, 1¼ hours)

Vaison-la-Romaine

POP 6275

Tucked between seven hills, Vaison-la-Romaine has long been a traditional exchange centre, and it still has a thriving Tuesday market. The village's rich Roman legacy is obvious – 20th-century buildings rise alongside France's largest archaeological site. A Roman bridge crosses the River Ouvèze, dividing the contemporary town's pedestrianised centre and the spectacular walled, cobbled-street hilltop Cité Médiévale – one of Provence's most magical ancient villages – where the counts of Toulouse built their 12th-century castle. Vaison is a good base for jaunts into the Dentelles de Montmirail or Mont Ventoux, but tourists throng here in summer: reserve ahead.

👁 Sights & Activities

Vaison's position is ideal for village-hopping by bicycle. The tourist office stocks excellent brochures detailing multiple cycling circuits (www.escapado.fr), rated by difficulty, from 26km to 91km.

★ Gallo-Roman Ruins   RUINS

(☑04 90 36 50 48; www.provenceromaine.com; adult/child incl all ancient sites, museum & cathedral €8/4; ⊙9.30am-6.30pm Jun-Sep, to 6pm Apr & May, 10am-noon & 2-5.30pm Oct-Mar) The ruined remains of Vasio Vocontiorum, the Roman city that flourished here between the 6th and 2nd centuries BCE, fill two central Vaison sites. Two neighbourhoods of this once opulent city, Puymin and La Villasse, lie on either side of the tourist office and av du Général de Gaulle. Admission includes entry to the 12th-century Romanesque cloister at Cathédrale Notre-Dame de Nazareth, a five-minute walk west of La Villasse and a soothing refuge from the summer heat.

In **Puymin**, see houses of the nobility, mosaics, workers' quarters, a temple and the still-functioning, 6000-seat **Théâtre Antique** (c 20 CE). To make sense of the remains (and collect your audioguide; €3),

head for the **Musée Archéologique Gallo-Roman**, which revives Vaison's Roman past with incredible swag – superb mosaics, carved masks and statues that include a 3rd-century silver bust and marble renderings of Hadrian and wife Sabina.

The Romans shopped at the colonnaded boutiques and bathed at **La Villasse**, where you'll find **Maison au Dauphin**, which has splendid marble-lined fish ponds.

★ Cité Médiévale   HISTORIC SITE

Wandering around Vaison-la-Romaine's wonderful medieval quarter, you could be forgiven for thinking you've stepped into a forgotten set from *Monty Python and the Holy Grail*. Ringed by ramparts and accessed via the pretty **Pont Romain** (Roman Bridge), it's a fascinating place to explore, criss-crossed by cobbled alleyways. Look out for the elaborate carvings around many of the doorways as you climb up towards the 12th-century **château** and its wraparound vistas.

Cathédrale Notre-Dame
de Nazareth   CHURCH

(cloister only €1.50; ⊙10am-12.30pm & 2-6pm Mar-Dec) The peaceful 12th-century Romanesque cloister at Cathédrale Notre-Dame de Nazareth is a five-minute walk west of La Villasse – and a great spot to find refuge from the summer heat.

🎊 Festivals & Events

Festival de Vaison-la-Romaine   DANCE

(www.vaison-danses.com; ⊙Jul) Three-week-long dance festival held at the Roman Théâtre Antique. Book by April.

Festival des Chœurs Lauréats   MUSIC

(www.festivaldeschoeurslaureats.com; ⊙late Jul) The best choirs in Europe.

🛏 Sleeping

The tourist office has lists of *chambres d'hôte*, self-catering apartments and camping grounds.

★ Hôtel Burrhus   HOTEL €

(☑04 90 36 00 11; www.burrhus.com; 1 place de Montfort; d €65-96, apt €140; 🅿 ❋ 🛜) From the outside, this looks like a classic town hotel: shutters, stonework and a prime spot on the town square. But inside, surprises await: the arty owners have littered it with modern art, sculptures, funky furniture and colourful decorative details, although the white-walled rooms themselves sometimes feel stark. On

WORTH A TRIP

FORTERESSE DE MORNAS

Perched on some precipitous cliffs, the 11th- to 14th-century **Forteresse de Mornas** (☑ 04 90 37 01 26; www.forteresse-de-mornas.com; adult/child €5/3; ◷ 10.30am-5pm Mon-Fri Apr-Aug, 11am-5pm Mon-Fri Sep-Nov, 1.30-4pm daily Feb & Mar), 12km north of Orange, makes a dramatic backdrop for the pretty village below. Built by the medieval Counts of Toulouse, it commands outstanding views west to the Rhône and east to Mont Ventoux.

You can visit by yourself, or take one of the five guided tours (adult/child €9/7) available daily in July and August, or on weekends from April to June and in September.

sunny days, take breakfast on the plane-tree-shaded balcony overlooking the square.

For three days every December during the Supervues art festival (www.supervues.com), the hotel's rooms are occupied by artists who create work during their stay. Breakfast is €10.

L'École Buissonière
B&B €

(☑ 04 90 28 95 19; www.buissonniere-provence.com; D75, Buisson; s/d/tr/q from €55/68/83/100; 🛜) Five minutes north of Vaison, in the countryside between Buisson and Villedieu, hosts Monique and John have transformed their stone farmhouse into a tastefully decorated three-bedroom B&B, big on comfort. Breakfast features homemade jam, and there's an outdoor summer kitchen.

Camping du Théâtre Romain
CAMPGROUND €

(☑ 04 90 28 78 66; www.camping-theatre.com; chemin de Brusquet; sites per 2 people with tent & car €14.90-25.90; ◷ mid-Mar–mid-Nov; 🛜🏊) A large, well-run campsite opposite the Théâtre Antique. It gets lots of sun, and there's a pool.

Hostellerie Le Beffroi
HISTORIC HOTEL €€

(☑ 04 90 36 04 71; www.le-beffroi.com; rue de l'Évêché; d €105-195, tr €205-230; ◷ Apr-Jan; 🛜🏊) This hotel on the narrow streets of the old town wins hands-down for atmosphere, but you might not feel so enthusiastic once you've lugged your luggage up from the car park. Still, it's awash with history: the two buildings date from 1554 and 1690, and rooms feel appropriately old-fashioned. There's a delightful rose garden and (rather improbably) even a pool.

L'Évêché
B&B €€

(☑ 04 90 36 13 46; http://eveche.free.fr; rue de l'Évêché; r €90-165) There's atmosphere galore in this rambling, regal B&B in the old medieval city, once the bishop's residence. Rooms are huge and packed with period detail, from wonky beams to nooks and crannies. Owners Jean-Loup and Aude know practically everyone in town, and will happily lend you bikes.

Eating

Brasseries on place de Montfort vary in quality; restaurants on cours Taulignan are generally better. Dining in Cité Médiévale is limited and pricey.

Maison Lesage
BAKERY €

(2 rue de la République; sandwiches €4-6; ◷ 7am-1pm & 3-5pm Mon, Tue & Thu-Sat, 7am-1pm Sun) For picnics by the river, this excellent bakery has no shortage of foodie fare: big baguettes, homemade pastries and nougat, and the house speciality, bun-sized meringues in a rainbow of flavours.

★ Bistro du'O
BISTRO €€

(☑ 04 90 41 72 90; www.bistroduo.fr; rue du Château; lunch/dinner menus from €26/38; ◷ noon-2pm & 7.30-10pm Tue-Sat) For fine dining in Vaison, this is everyone's tip. The setting is full of atmosphere, in a vaulted cellar in the medieval city (once the château stables), and the chef Philippe Zemour takes his cue from Provençal flavours and daily market ingredients. Top-class food, top setting, tops all round.

La Lyriste
FRENCH €€

(☑ 04 90 36 04 67; 45 cours Taulignan; menus €14.50-28; ◷ noon-2.30pm & 7.15-10pm Tue-Fri, 7.15-10pm Sat; 🍴) Nothing world-changing here, but tasty regional food from *bourride* (fish stew) to *brandade de cabillaud* (cod kebabs), laced with lashings of olive oil, tomatoes and Provençal herbs. Unusually, there's generally a good choice of veggie options on offer. The plane-tree-shaded terrace tables are the ones to ask for.

Le Moulin à Huile
GASTRONOMY €€€

(☑ 04 90 36 20 67; www.lemoulinahuile84.fr; quai Maréchal Foch, rte de Malaucène; 2-/3-/4-course menu €29/38/45; ◷ noon-1.30pm & 7.15-9.30pm Mon, Tue, Fri & Sat, 7.15-9.30pm Thu, noon-1.30pm Sun) This renowned restaurant is still a destination address in Vaison, if only for its lovely riverside setting in a former olive-oil mill. The menus are affordable, and stocked with locally sourced goodies, such as river trout, wood pigeon, and lamb and pork from local farms.

Le Bateleur FRENCH €€€
(📞 04 90 36 28 04; www.restaurant-lebateleur.
com; 1 place Théodore Aubanel; 3-/4-course menu
€37/57; ⊙ noon-2pm & 7.15-10pm Tue-Sat) Run
by Nicolas and Andrea Bofelli, this is another superior, if rather cramped, address for
Provençal dishes like crusty pork belly and
roast veal. The odd-shaped dining room is a
bit claustrophobic; try to snag a table on the
little streetside terrace.

ⓘ Information

Tourist Office (📞 04 90 36 02 11; www.vaison-
ventoux-tourisme.com; place du Chanoine
Sautel; ⊙ 9.30am-noon & 2-5.45pm Mon-Sat
year-round, plus 9.30am-noon Sun mid-Mar–
mid-Oct, longer hours in summer) Helps book
rooms and organise activities, and sells concert
and event tickets.

ⓘ Getting There & Away

The bus stop is on av des Choralies, 400m east
of the tourist office. Several services are provided by **Cars Comtadin** (📞 04 90 67 20 25; www.
sudest-mobilites.fr).
Carpentras (TransVaucluse Line 11, €2.10, 45
minutes, five daily Monday to Saturday)
Vaison-la-Romaine (TransVaucluse Line 4, €2,
45 minutes, eight daily Monday to Saturday, two
on Sunday)

Dentelles de Montmirail

Rising like a set of dragon's teeth from the flat,
vineyard-cloaked plains about 20km north of
Carpentras, this 8km-long rocky ridge is an
imposing sight. Rather fancifully, the craggy
spires are named after the *dentelles* (lace)
they supposedly resemble. They're impressive
seen from afar, but you can also hike in for a
closer view thanks to a network of footpaths
that wind amongst them and, if you're so
inclined, some famous rock-climbing routes.

Around the ridge are lots of small villages
and many, many vineyards – but for safety's
sake, maybe it's best to save the wine-tasting
for a post-hike treat.

ⓘ Getting There & Around

Several of the small villages, including Gigondas,
Suzette and Beaumes-de-Venise, are served by
Trans'CoVe (📞 04 84 99 50 10; www.transcove.
com; 270 ave de la Gare) buses, most of which operate on an on-demand basis (phone a day ahead
to book a seat). Destinations cost a flat-rate €4.

Gigondas

POP 548

Wine cellars and cafes surround the
sun-dappled central square of Gigondas, famous for prestigious red wine. Wine tasting

---

PRECIOUS FUNGUS

Provence's cloak-and-dagger truffle trade is operated from the back of cars, with payment
exclusively in cash. Little-known Richerenches, 23km northwest of Vaison-la-Romaine, a
deceptively wealthy village with a medieval Templar fortress, hosts France's largest wholesale truffle market. It's lovely to visit year-round, but especially so on Saturday mornings
during truffle season (mid-November to mid-March), when the main street fills with furtive
rabassaïres (truffle hunters), selling to courtiers (brokers) representing dealers in Paris,
Germany, Italy and beyond. So covert are the transactions you'll likely never see a truffle
change hands at this wholesale market. Head to av de la Rabasse for the retail stalls.

Black truffles *(Tuber melanosporum)* cost up to €1000 per kilogram wholesale, up to
€4000 retail. Although *trufficulteurs* (truffle growers) try tricks like injecting spores into
oak roots, humankind has so far been unable to increase crops of this quasi-mystical
fungus. Only nature can dictate if it will be a good or bad year – weather is the major
determinant of yield.

Richerenches villagers celebrate an annual Truffle Mass in the village church, when pa-
rishioners place truffles instead of cash into the collection plate. Then they're auctioned
to support the church. The Mass falls on the Sunday nearest 17 January, feast day of St
Antoine, patron saint of truffle harvesters. Contact Richerenches' **tourist office** (📞 04
90 28 05 34; www.richerenches.fr; place Hugues de Bourbouton, Richerenches; ⊙ 10am-1.30pm
& 2-6pm Mon-Sat) for details.

If you want to unearth truffles yourself, Dominique and Eric Jaumard arrange seasonal
hunts and year-round walks on their truffle-rich land, 7km southwest of Carpentras,
in Monteux. Or buy truffles fresh, in season, at weekly regional markets, including Vaison-la-Romaine (Tuesday) and Carpentras (Friday).

here provides an excellent counterpoint to Châteauneuf-du-Pape: both use the same grapes, but the soil is different. In town, **Caveau de Gigondas** ([📞] 04 90 65 82 29; www.caveaudugigondas.com; place Gabrielle Andéol; ⊙ 10am-noon & 2-6.30pm) represents 100 small producers and offers free tastings – most bottles cost just €12 to €17. The tourist office has a complete list of wineries.

Above the central square, along the Cheminement de Sculptures, enigmatic outdoor sculptures line narrow pathways, leading ever upward to castle ruins, campanile, church and cemetery with stunning vistas.

🍽 Sleeping & Eating

⭐ Les Florets   HOTEL €€€
([📞] 04 90 65 85 01; www.hotel-lesflorets.com; 1243 rte des Florêts; r €120-175; [P][🛜][❄]) A super hotel 2km outside Gigondas, with a modern-meets-heritage feel blending burnished wood, antique armchairs, attractive decor and minimal clutter. You can choose from rooms in the main house or the small one-storey lodge by the pool – they're all elegant. The Provençal restaurant (menus €25 to €54) is extremely good too, with tree-shaded tables and a divine vineyard view.

⭐ L'Oustalet   FRENCH €€€
([📞] 04 90 65 85 30; www.loustalet-gigondas.com; 5 place Gabrielle Andéol; 2-/3-course menu from €36/42; ⊙ noon-2pm & 7-9pm Tue-Sat) For a slap-up spoil, this Michelin-starred wonder owned by the wine-making Perrin family is the place. Using produce from his own kitchen garden, chef Laurent Deconinck creates delicious, refined dishes rooted in the flavours of traditional Provençal cooking. The dining room is smart, decorated with modern art, but the gorgeous olive-shaded garden is where you want to eat. Reservations essential.

It's possible to overnight, too, with three sophisticated rooms (doubles €160 to €210) full of designer style, tasteful furniture and wooden floors. The family suite even has a mezzanine for the kids. There's also an on-site wine shop.

ℹ Information

Gigondas Tourist Office ([📞] 04 90 65 85 46; www.gigondas-dm.fr; rue du Portail; ⊙ 9am-12.30pm & 2.30-6.30pm Mon-Sat, 10am-1pm Sun Jul & Aug, shorter hours Sep-Jun) The Gigondas tourist office has lists of the area's famed wineries.

ℹ Getting There & Away

Gigondas is hard to get to by public transport, so having a car makes life way easier.

Séguret

POP 884 / ELEV 250M

Medieval Séguret clings to a hillside above undulating vineyards. Narrow, cobbled streets, lined with flowering vines, wend past a 15th-century fountain, a 12th-century church, and uphill to castle ruins (park below the village and walk). Séguret makes a good base for cyclists and hikers, and lovers of quiet countryside.

🛏 Sleeping

La Bastide Bleue   INN €
([📞] 04 90 46 83 43; www.bastidebleue.com; rte de Sablet; s/d/tr/q incl breakfast €62.50/81.50/109.50/135; [P][🛜][❄]) This humble inn is a real bargain, with seven pretty rooms in Provençal shades of blue, yellow, orange and green – including three family-sized rooms. It's endearingly rustic, with a terracotta-tiled roof, original beams and a lovely back garden. A *table d'hôte* dinner is served on request.

Domaine de Cabasse   INN €€
([📞] 04 90 46 91 12; www.cabasse.fr; rte de Sablet; d €140-180; ⊙ Apr-Oct; [P][❄][🛜][❄]) A working wine estate and part of the Logis chain, Domaine de Cabasse also offers a good range of rooms in its shuttered lodge building. It's definitely worth upgrading to the pricier

---

CHRISTMAS IN SÉGURET

At dusk on Christmas Eve, Provence celebrates the Cacho Fio. A log cut from a pear, olive or cherry tree is placed in the hearth, doused with fortified wine, blessed three times by the youngest and oldest family members, and then set alight. The fire must burn until Three Kings Day, January 6th.

The village of Séguret has a unique version of this tradition. Rather than taking place in the villagers' homes, everyone gathers in the Salle Delage (adjoining Chapelle Ste-Thecle on rue du Four) to burn a log together. Later, locals wend their way to 12th-century Église St-Denis where, during Li Bergié, real-life shepherds, lambs and a baby in a manger create a living nativity scene. Then all join a midnight Mass in Provençal.

Grand Cru rooms for more space and better views over the estate. The hotel also has a good country restaurant which offers half-board, and a fine pool in the grounds.

ⓘ Getting There & Away

Driving is the easiest way to get to Séguret, but you can organise on-demand bus travel with **Trans'CoVe** (p245) from Carpentras – although you need to arrange it a day ahead.

Suzette

POP 127 / ELEV 425M

Tiny Suzette sits high in the hills between Malaucène and Beaumes-de-Venise, with incredible views that provide perspective on the landscape and make the winding drive worthwhile. Get your bearings at the village-centre *table d'orientation* (orientation plaque).

🛏 Sleeping & Eating

⭐ **Ferme le Dégoutaud** B&B €
(☑ 04 90 62 99 29; www.degoutaud.fr; rte de Malaucène; s/d/tr/q €70/80/90/100, cottages per week €560-890; 🛜 🖳) ⯅ This 16th-century working farm, 2.5km northeast of Suzette, has simple, spotless rooms of stone and wood, and self-catering cottages surrounded by spectacular countryside. The farm produces olive oil, honey, jam and organic apricot and cherry juice – sample them at breakfast. Outside there's a summer kitchen and an infinity pool with knockout views. Tops for nature lovers.

Les Coquelicots PROVENCAL €
(☑ 04 90 65 06 94; www.restaurant-les-coquel icots.com; menu €27; ⊙ noon-2pm & 7-8.30pm Thu-Tue Jun-Aug, reduced hours Sep-May) Seasonal ingredients underpin everything at this charming village restaurant, so the menu changes throughout the year – but the flavours are always 100% Provençal. It's a sweet spot to dine, with a little terrace and a cracking view over Suzette's vineyards.

ⓘ Getting There & Away

The only public transport to Suzette is provided by irregular **Trans'CoVe buses** (p245) which operate on demand.

Le Barroux

POP 710 / ELEV 325M

There's not a great deal in tiny Le Barroux apart from its medieval castle, but it makes a pleasant rest stop on a day trip through the Dentelles.

⊙ Sights

Château du Barroux CHATEAU
(☑ 04 90 62 35 21; adult/child €5/free; ⊙ 10am-7pm Jul-Sep, 2-6pm Oct, 10am-7pm Sat & Sun Apr & May, 2.30-7pm Jun) Built in the 12th century to protect Le Barroux from Saracen invaders, Château du Barroux is one of Provence's few castles. Its fortunes rose and fell, but its last indignity was in WWII, when retreating Germans set it ablaze – it burned for 10 days. Only ghosts remain, but it's great fun to explore, especially for kids unaccustomed to such architectural drama.

Abbaye Ste-Madeleine CHURCH
(☑ 04 90 62 56 31; www.barroux.org) Two kilometres north of Le Barroux along thread-narrow lanes, this abbey hears Gregorian chants sung by Benedictine monks at 9.30am daily (10am Sundays and holidays). The Romanesque-style monastery, built in the 1980s, is surrounded by lavender. Its shop carries delicious monk-made almond cake. Hats, miniskirts, bare shoulders and mobile phones are forbidden.

✕ Eating

Les Géraniums FRENCH €€
(☑ 04 90 62 41 08; www.hotel-lesgeraniums.com; place de la Croix; lunch/dinner menus from €18/30; ⊙ 12.15-2pm & 7.15-9pm Jun-Oct; 🅿) The Geraniums makes a sweet spot for a country lunch (washed down with a glass of local wine, of course). It's a century-old old *auberge* – beamed inside, with a fine terrace outside – and the food is first-rate. Upstairs rooms are simple but good value (doubles from €85).

Beaumes-de-Venise

POP 2425 / ELEV 126M

Snugly sheltered from mistral winds, the small village of Beaumes-de-Venise is famous for its *or blanc* (white gold) – sweet muscat wines, best drunk young and cold (and, according to local tradition, accompanied by slices of melon). More recently the town has made a name for its rich Côtes du Rhône reds too. You can taste both at the village's excellent wine school.

🏃 Activities

⭐ **Caveau Balma Vénitia** WINE
(☑ 04 90 10 19 11; www.vbv.rhonea.fr; 228 rte de Carpentras; ⊙ 9am-7pm Apr-Sep, 10am-12.30pm

& 2-6pm Oct-Mar) Locally made wines from growers around Beaumes-de-Venise are on sale at this excellent wine shop, which also doubles as a tasting school. The staff are extremely knowledgeable, and can help guide your tasting; they can also organise local cellar visits and *grand cru* tastings, as well as guided walks in the Dentelles.

The centre's restaurant, La Cave à Manger, serves tapas-style lunch dishes, and also packs takeaway picnics.

🛏 Sleeping & Eating

There are a couple of pleasant restaurants in the village. For lunch, the restaurant at Caveau Balma Vénitia (p247) is a great option.

Château Juvenal　　　　　　B&B €€
(📞 04 90 62 31 76; www.chateaujuvenal.com; 120 chemin du Long-Serre, St-Hippolyte-le-Graveyron; d from €150; ❄🛜🏊) Five kilometres west of Beaumes-de-Venise, this wine estate is from a bygone age. Its grand rooms are a showpiece of 19th-century elegance, from their canopied beds to their fireplaces, and the rest of the house carries on in similar style (billiard room, *hammam*, music salon).

★ Les Remparts　　　　　　B&B €€€
(📞 04 90 62 75 49; www.lamaisondesremparts. com; 74 cours Louis Pasteur; d €200-290; 🛜🏊) A *grand cru* B&B to match Beaumes-de-Venise's finest wines. Built into the old town walls are five huge, luxurious rooms, each individually themed after saffron, ivory, cotton, mist and 'the legend of the Orient', complete with chandeliers, antiques, freestanding tubs and distressed wood. There's even a tiny pool – although it should be Olympic-sized considering the rates.

Le Clos Saint Sourde　　　　B&B €€€
(📞 04 90 37 35 20; www.leclossaintsaourde.com; 1769 rte de St Véran; r €180-250; 🅿🛜🏊) What a place: a ravishing marriage of modern style and rustic Provençal architecture (a couple of the cavernous rooms even have troglodyte-style walls built right into the rock). The 18th-century building has lots of intriguing features, from spiral staircases to original hearths, all updated with immensely good taste. The saltwater pool is fabulous.

🛍 Shopping

Moulin à Huile de la Balméenne　　FOOD
(📞 04 90 62 93 77; www.labalmeenne.fr; 82 av Jules Ferry; ⏱10am-12.30pm & 2-7pm

Mon-Sat, 10.30am-noon & 3-6pm Sun Apr-Sep, 10am-noon & 2-6pm Mon-Sat Oct-Mar) Alongside its wines, Beaumes-de-Venise also has a long tradition of olive-growing – and its oils are much-prized. This old mill, in business since 1867, makes a fine place to learn more about the process – and stock up on oils and other goodies to take home.

ℹ Information

Beaumes-de-Venise Tourist Office (📞 04 90 62 94 39; www.ot-beaumesdevenise.com; 122 place du Maré; ⏱9.30am-12.30pm & 2-6pm Mon-Sat Apr-Sep, to 5pm Oct-Mar) This excellent tourist office can help organise cellar visits and has lots of information on walking in the Dentelles.

ℹ Getting There & Away

Apart from the limited bus service run by **Trans'-CoVe** (p245), getting to Beaumes-de-Venise – and its vineyards – is best done by car or bike.

MONT VENTOUX

Visible for miles around, Mont Ventoux (1912m) stands like a sentinel over northern Provence. From its summit, accessible by road between May and October, vistas extend to the Alps and, on a clear day, the Camargue.

Because of the mountain's dimensions, every European climate type is represented here, from Mediterranean on its lower southern reaches to Arctic on its exposed northern ridge. As you climb, temperatures can plummet by 20°C, and the fierce mistral wind blows 130 days a year, sometimes at speeds of 250km/h. Bring warm clothes and rain gear, even in summer. You can ascend by road year-round, but you cannot traverse the summit from 15 November to 15 April.

The mountain's diverse fauna and flora have earned the mountain Unesco Biosphere Reserve status. Some species live nowhere else, including the rare snake eagle.

Three gateways – Bédoin, Malaucène and Sault – provide services in summer, but they're far apart.

🏃 Activities
Hiking

The GR4 crosses the Dentelles de Montmirail before scaling Mont Ventoux' northern face, where it meets the GR9. Both traverse the ridge. The GR4 branches eastwards to Gorges du Verdon; the GR9 crosses the Vaucluse Mountains to the Luberon. The essential map for the area is *3140ET Mont Ventoux,* by IGN (www.ign.fr). Bédoin's tourist office stocks maps and brochures detailing walks for all levels.

In July and August tourist offices in Bédoin and Malaucène facilitate night-time expeditions up the mountain to see the sunrise (participants must be over 15 years old).

Cycling

Tourist offices distribute *Les Itinéraires Ventoux,* a free map detailing 11 itineraries – graded easy to difficult – and highlighting artisanal farms en route. For more cycling trails, see www.lemontventoux.net. Most cycle-hire outfits also offer electric bikes.

Ventoux Bike Park   CYCLING
(🚲 04 90 61 84 55; www.facebook.com/Ventoux BikePark; Chalet Reynard; half/full day €10/14; ⊙ 10am-5pm Sat & Sun, hours variable Mon-Fri) Near the Mont Ventoux summit, at Chalet Reynard, mountain bikers ascend via rope tow (minimum age 10 years), then descend ramps and jumps down three trails (5km in total). In winter it's possible to mountain bike on snow. Bring bike, helmet and gloves or rent all gear at Chalet Reynard. Call to check opening times, which are highly weather dependent.

Bédoin Location   CYCLING
(🚲 04 90 65 94 53; www.bedoin-location.fr; 20 rte de Malaucène; mountain/road bike per day from €20/35, electric bike from €40; ⊙ 9am-7pm Mar-Nov) Opposite the tourist office in Bédoin, this sports shop rents and repairs mountain and road bikes, and delivers to the summit of Mont Ventoux.

La Route du Ventoux   CYCLING
(🚲 04 90 67 07 40; www.larouteduventoux.com; rte du Ventoux; road/mountain/tandem bikes per day from €35/25/50; ⊙ 8am-7pm Mon-Sat May-Aug, 9am-6pm Mar, Apr & Oct, plus 8am-12.30pm Sun Jul) Rents bicycles of many types in Bédoin.

Albion Cycles   CYCLING
(🚲 04 90 64 09 32; www.albioncycles.com; rte de St-Trinit; bike rental per day €29-30, e-bike €49; ⊙ 8am-7pm Jul & Aug, 8.30am-7pm Jun & Sep, 9am-7pm May & Oct, 9am-6pm Apr & Nov) Sault's bicycle-rental and sale outlet, including electric bikes. Will deliver.

VAUCLUSE MARKETS

To appreciate Provence's seasonal bounty, visit its markets (www. marches-provence.com); most run from 8am to noon. In Nîmes, the covered food market operates daily; Avignon's Les Halles (p235) operates Tuesday to Sunday.

Monday Bédoin, Fontvieille

Tuesday Tarascon, Vaison-la-Romaine (p243)

Wednesday Malaucène, Sault (p252), Valréas

Thursday Beaucaire, L'Isle-sur-la-Sorgue (small), Maillane, Maussane-les-Alpilles, Orange (p240), Villeneuve-lès-Avignon (p237)

Friday Carpentras (p252), Châteauneuf-du-Pape (p238)

Saturday Pernes-les-Fontaines (p255), Richerenches, Villeneuve-lès-Avignon (p237)

Sunday L'Isle-sur-la-Sorgue (large)

Skiing

Access **Chalet Reynard** (www.chalet-rey nard.fr) from Bédoin or Sault, not Malaucène, to sled or ski Mont Ventoux' south summit. Traverse the isolated back side, via the D974 from Malaucène, to reach the tiny north-facing ski area Mont Serein. It's fun for a few turns, but nothing serious. Snow melts by April.

❶ Getting There & Away

Getting up the mountain by public transport isn't feasible – you'll need a car or, if you're fit, a bike.

Bédoin

POP 3279 / ELEV 295M

On Mont Ventoux' southwestern flanks, peppy Bédoin is the most upbeat of the gateways, chock-a-block with cafes and shops. Its geographic position diminishes the mistral, which contributes to its popularity with cyclists. In July and August the tourist office (p252), an excellent information source on all regional activities, guides walks into the forest. Market day is Monday.

BARMALINI/SHUTTERSTOCK ©

1. Vines, Chateauneuf-du-Pape (p238)

Wine has been grown in this valley since the Romans first planted vines here 2000 years ago.

2. Site Archéologique de Glanum (p194)

St-Rémy-de-Provence offers a glimpse into everyday Roman life, and France's oldest triumphal arch.

3. Gallo-Roman Ruins, Vaison-la-Romaine (p243)

A Roman city flourished in Vaison-la-Romaine between the 6th and 2nd centuries BCE.

4. Dentelles de Montmirail (p245)

These teeth-like mountains rise above the vines of the Côtes du Rhône wine region.

HORST LIEBER/SHUTTERSTOCK ©

MATT MUNRO/LONELY PLANET ©

ERIC VALENNE GEOSTORY/SHUTTERSTOCK ©

🛏 Sleeping

Hôtel des Pins HOTEL €€
(📞 04 90 65 92 92; www.hotel-des-pins.fr; 171 chemin des Crans; r €90-130, ste €180-200; 🅿 🛜 🏊) An unexpected surprise near sleepy Bédoin: a smart, sophisticated hotel with a gorgeous garden and a fine outdoor pool. Rooms are a mixed bag, but more expensive ones have quirky touches; some have frilly bed canopies, others wooden sinks, and a few have private patios. The hotel's colourful restaurant, **L'Esprit Jardin** (mains €18 to €20), serves great Provençal food.

ℹ Information

Bédoin Tourist Office (📞 04 90 65 63 95; www.bedoin.org; Espace Marie-Louis Gravier, 1 rte de Malaucène; ⏰ 9.30am-12.30pm & 2-6pm Mon-Fri, 9.30am-12.30pm & 3-6pm Sat, 10am-12.30pm Sun mid-Apr–mid-Oct, reduced hours mid-Oct–mid-Apr) Excellent source of information on all regional activities; also helps with lodging.

ℹ Getting There & Around

Local buses are unreliable, so hiring a bike is the best way to get around.

Sault

POP 1301 / ELEV 800M

At the eastern end of the Mont Ventoux massif, drowsily charming Sault has incredible summertime vistas over lavender fields. Visit **André Boyer** (📞 04 90 64 00 23; www.nougat-boyer.fr; place de l'Europe) for honey-and-almond nougat, family-made since 1887. Sault's tourist office, a good resource for Mont Ventoux and Gorges de la Nesque, has lists of artisanal lavender producers such as **Les Lavandes Champelle** (📞 04 90 64 01 50; www.gaec-champelle.fr; rte de Ventoux) 🌿, a roadside farmstand northwest of town whose products include a great gift for cooks: *herbes de Provence*-infused *fleur de sel* (gourmet salt).

ℹ Information

Sault Tourist Office (📞 04 90 64 01 21; www.ventoux-sud.com; av de la Promenade; ⏰ 9.30am-12.30pm & 1.30-6.30pm Mon-Fri, 10am-12.30pm & 2-6.30pm Sat & Sun Jun-Aug, 9am-12.30pm & 2.30-5pm or 6pm Mon-Sat Sep-Mar) Good resource for Mont Ventoux information.

ℹ Getting Around

Your own transport is essential here.

CARPENTRAS

POP 29,600

Carpentras is a rather run-of-the-mill agricultural town, but it's worth a detour for one very compelling reason – an absolutely wonderful Provençal market, which takes over the entire town every Friday morning, with more than 350 stalls laden with bread, honey, cheese, olives, fruit and a rainbow of *berlingots*, Carpentras' striped, pillow-shaped hard-boiled sweets. In winter, it's also an important truffle-trading town.

◎ Sights & Activities

★ **Synagogue de Carpentras** SYNAGOGUE
(📞 04 90 63 39 97; place Juiverie; ⏰ 10am-noon & 3-4.30pm Mon-Thu, 10-11.30am & 3-3.30pm Fri) Carpentras' remarkable synagogue dates to 1367 and is the oldest still in use in France. Although Jews were initially welcomed into papal territory, by the 17th century they had to live in ghettos in Avignon, Carpentras, Cavaillon and L'Isle-sur-la-Sorgue: the synagogue is deliberately inconspicuous. The wood-panelled prayer hall was rebuilt in 18th-century baroque style; downstairs are bread-baking ovens, used until 1904. For access, ring the doorbell on the half-hour.

★ **Arc Romain** HISTORIC SITE
Hidden behind Cathédrale St-Siffrein, the Arc Romain was built under Augustus in the 1st century CE and is decorated with worn carvings of enslaved Gauls.

Cathédrale St-Siffrein CATHEDRAL
(place St-Siffrein; ⏰ 8am-noon & 2-6pm Mon-Sat) Carpentras' cathedral was built between 1405 and 1519 in meridional Gothic style but is crowned by a distinctive contemporary bell tower. Its **Trésor d'Art Sacré** (Treasury of Religious Art) holds precious 14th- to 19th-century religious relics that you can only see during the Foire de St-Siffrein (27 November) and on guided walks with the tourist office.

La Truffe du Ventoux OUTDOORS
(📞 04 90 66 82 21; www.truffes-ventoux.com; ⏰ Oct–mid-Mar) Glimpse the clandestine world of the 'black diamond' on a truffle hunt near Carpentras.

🛏 Sleeping

Le Malaga HOTEL €
(📞 06 16 59 85 59, 04 90 60 57 96; www.hotel-malaga-carpentras.fr; 37 place Maurice-Charretier; s/d/tr/q €43/49/65/75; 🛜) Plus points for this no-frills hotel: it's cheap as chips and dead

Carpentras

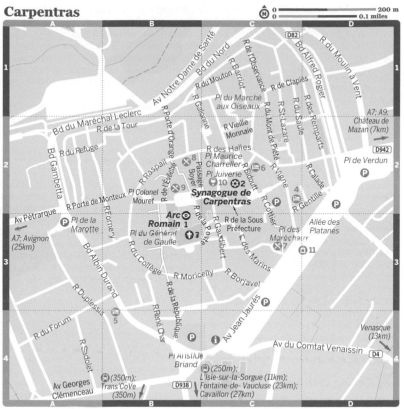

Carpentras

central. Minus points: rooms are basic bordering on spartan, and can be very prone to noise from the brasserie bar downstairs.

Hôtel du Fiacre HOTEL €€
(☏ 04 90 63 03 15; www.hotel-du-fiacre.com; 153 rue Vigne; d €70-140, f €105-140; 🅿🛜) Frills, swags and canopies abound at this grand old dame of a hotel, where the old-style de-

cor takes its cue from the 18th-century architecture. Contemporary it ain't, but charming it most surely is. The marble staircase is a thing of beauty, too.

Hotel le Comtadin HOTEL €€
(☏ 04 90 67 75 00; www.le-comtadin.com; 65 bd Albin Durand; d €90-110; 🌡🛜) Despite the heritage 18th-century facade, inside this former

mansion (now owned by Best Western) the rooms are fairly generic: comfy enough, but short on style. Pricier ones overlook the courtyard, cheaper ones face the street.

★**Metafort** B&B €€€

(☑ 04 90 34 46 84; www.metafort-provence.com; 31 Montée du Vieil Hôpital, Méthamis; d €145-195; ❉ ❈ ❊) Wow. This palatial pad pulls out all the stops in terms of architecture, design and out-and-out luxury. It's in a 17th-century village house in Méthamis, 17km southeast of Carpentras, but the design is unabashedly 21st-century: strikingly minimal rooms, modern art, Scandi-style furniture and an eye-popping rooftop pool overlooking the rocky, maquis-covered hills of the Nesque Valley. Stunning is an understatement.

Château de Mazan HOTEL €€€

(☑ 04 90 69 62 61; www.chateaudemazan.com; place Napoléon, Mazan; d €159-182, ste €300-450; ❉ Mar-Dec; ℙ ❈ ❊) A regal place to stay: an 18th-century mansion once owned by the licentious lothario Marquis de Sade. Today it's anything but seedy; the palatial rooms scream designer elegance, with tall arched windows, tiled floors, antique furniture and a sophisticated fine-dining restaurant – not to mention impeccable grounds. It's 7km east of Carpentras in the village of Mazan.

🍴 Eating & Drinking

It's all about the market in Carpentras – you'll find plenty of goodies to fill your belly on Friday. At other times of the week, there are a few bistros and restaurants to investigate around the town centre.

WORTH A TRIP

GORGES DU TOULOURENC

On hot days you can't beat this easy, family-friendly walk beneath Mont Ventoux' wild, northern face. Wear shorts and water shoes, and hike upstream, splashing in calf-deep water, and explore a spectacular, ever-narrowing limestone canyon. By bike, take the tiny road from Malaucène to the hamlet of Veaux (road signs say 'hameau de Veaux', maps say 'Veaux'); by car, the road via Entrechaux is less winding. Park at the blue bridge over the water. Two hours upstream, there's a Roman bridge – a good turnaround point. Carry food and water.

★**La Maison Jouvaud** PASTRIES €

(40 rue de l'Évêché; boxes of sweets from €10; ❉ 10am-7pm Mon, 8am-7pm Tue-Fri, 9am-7pm Sat & Sun) If you suffer from a sweet tooth, it's best not to even step inside this patisserie palace, where the glass cases brim with tempting things – from homemade chocolates, petits-fours and cakes to quite possibly the most impressive meringues you will ever see. It's vintage through and through – even the hot chocolate is à l'ancienne (old-fashioned).

Chez Serge FRENCH €€

(☑ 04 90 63 21 24; www.chez-serge.com; 90 rue Cottier; 2-/3-course dinner €29/39; ❉ noon-2pm & 7.30-10pm Jun-Sep, noon-1.30pm & 7.30-9.30pm Oct-May; ❈ ❊) Run by renowned sommelier Serge Ghokassian, this hip restaurant feels out of step with the rest of Carpentras: it's more Parisian chic than Provençal rustic, all sombre tones, swoopy plastic chairs, exposed stone and murals of crocodiles and elephants. The menu zings with southern flavours, and as you'd expect, the wine list is first-rate.

La Galusha FRENCH €€

(☑ 04 90 60 75 00, 06 62 79 25 42; www.galusha. fr; 30 place de l'Horloge; lunch/dinner menus from €16.50/27.50; ❉ noon-2pm Tue-Sun, 7-10pm Tue-Sat) Underneath Carpentras' 15th-century clock tower, this old village townhouse turns up surprises: a salon-style dining room decorated with Venetian lamps and whimsical Arcimboldo paintings, and a shady interior courtyard. Food is classy French.

Bistrot La Place WINE BAR

(☑ 04 90 61 37 54; 12 place de la Juiverie; ❉ 7.30am-9pm) This pleasant, central wine bar makes a good spot for an evening tipple, with a good selection of vins au verre (wines by the glass). The pavement tables under the plane trees fill up by early evening, so you might have to wait to bag a prime spot.

Simple brasserie dishes are also served.

ℹ Information

Tourist Office (☑ 04 90 63 00 78; www. carpentras-ventoux.com; 97 place du 25 Août 1944; ❉ 9.30am-12.30pm & 2-6pm Sat-Mon, 9.30am-12.30pm & 3-7pm Tue) Excellent website, guided tours in English, helpful staff and an adjoining boutique of local culinary products, like berlingots, honey and AOC Ventoux wine.

ℹ Getting There & Away

BUS

The **bus station** (place Terradou) is 150m southwest of the tourist office, which has schedules.

Voyages Arnaud (☑ 04 90 63 01 82; www.voy
ages-arnaud.com; 8 av Victor-Hugo) provides
several services as part of the TransVaucluse
network. Nearly all local destinations cost a
flat-rate €2.10.

Avignon (€2.10, TransVaucluse Line 5, 45 minutes, 11 daily Monday to Saturday, six on Sunday)

Orange (€2.10, TransVaucluse Line 10, 55
minutes, 10 daily Monday to Saturday)

Vaison-la-Romaine (€2.10, TransVaucluse Line
11, 45 minutes, five daily Monday to Saturday)

Marseille-Provence airport (€20.40, LER Line
17, two hours 25 minutes, three daily) Also
travels via L'Isle-sur-la-Sorgue, Cavaillon and
Aix-en-Provence.

Trans'CoVe (p245) also runs a number of local
buses to destinations including Gigondas,
Malaucène and the Venasque – but these are
mainly geared around school timetables, although you can reserve bus transport on most
routes by calling ahead a day in advance.

CAR

Free parking is northeast of the tourist office,
along av Jean Jaurès.

TRAIN

Local trains connect Carpentras' **train station**
(av de la Gare) to Avignon Centre station (€6.10,
32 minutes, hourly) and Avignon TGV station (38
minutes).

PERNES-LES-FONTAINES

POP 10,711

Once the capital of the Comtat Venaissin,
Pernes-les-Fontaines is now a sleepy village
of ancient buildings. It's known for its 40
fountains that splash and gurgle in shady
squares and narrow cobbled streets. Among
those not to missed: **Fontaine du Cormo-
ran** (pont Notre-Dame, 1761), **Fontaine
Reboul** (place Reboul, 15th century) and
Fontaine du Gigot (rue Victor-Hugo, 1757).

⊙ Sights & Activities

Maison du Costume Comtadin   MUSEUM
(☑ 04 90 61 31 04; www.costumescomtadin.com; rue
de la République; ⊙ 10am-12.30pm & 3-6.30pm Wed-
Mon Jul–mid-Sep, reduced hours mid-Sep–Jul) **FREE**
A 19th-century Provençal costume museum.

Town & Fountain Walk   WALKING
A free walking-tour map from the tourist
office details strolls through quaint streets
past such historic sights as the Maison du
Costume Comtadin, Maison Fléchier and a
fortified 11th-century church. Follow a rough
path to the top of the medieval clock tower
(*tour de l'horloge*) for panoramic views.

WORTH A TRIP

GORGES DE LA NESQUE

Abutting the Forêt de Venasque (and
connected via walking trail GR91), the
sheer-walled, 20km-long Gorges de la
Nesque is protected as a Unesco Biosphere Reserve. Other than driving or
hiking, a novel means of exploring this
spectacular limestone canyon (or nearby Mont Ventoux) is alongside a donkey
from **Les Ânes des Abeilles** (☑ 04
90 64 01 52; http://abeilles.ane-et-rando.
com; rte de la Gabelle, Col des Abeilles; day/
weekend from €50/95). Beasts carry up
to 40kg (ie small children or bags).

🛏 Sleeping & Eating

There's no compelling reason to make an
overnight stop in Pernes-les-Fontaines; Carpentras and L'Isle-sur-la-Sorgue make better
bases.

Mas de la Bonoty   PROVENCAL €€
(☑ 04 90 61 61 09; www.bonoty.com; chemin
de la Bonoty; lunch/dinner menus from €20/31;
⊙ 12.15-1.15pm & 7.30-9.15pm Tue-Sun; 🐾) It's
worth getting lost to find this 18th-century
farmhouse-hotel, which has earned its reputation as a laudable Provençal restaurant.
Menus feature hearty fare – thyme-roasted
duckling, foie gras and rack of lamb – served
on linen-dressed tables in an atmospheric
stone-walled dining room. Attractive, simple
rooms (doubles including breakfast €84 to
€94) are available with half-board.

ℹ Information

Tourist Office (☑ 04 90 61 31 04; www.
tourisme-pernes.fr; place Gabriel Moutte;
⊙ 10am-1pm & 2-6.30pm Mon-Fri, to 5pm Sat,
9.30am-12.30pm Sun Jul & Aug, reduced hours
Sep-Jun)

ℹ Getting There & Away

Bus 13 (€2.10, 10 daily Monday to Saturday)
between Carpentras and L'Isle-sur-la-Sorgue
stops in Pernes-les-Fontaines.

L'ISLE-SUR-LA-SORGUE

POP 19,395

The Island in the Sorgue is an apt name for
this ancient mid-river town, surrounded by
a moat of flowing water. L'Isle dates to the
12th century, when fishermen built huts
on stilts above what was then a marsh. By

DON'T MISS

PADDLING THE SORGUE

Kayaking and canoeing between Fontaine-de-Vaucluse and L'Isle-sur-la-Sorgue is very popular; most people start in Fontaine-de-Vaucluse and make the 8km trip downstream, but you can paddle in either direction.

Canoë Évasion (☑ 04 90 38 26 22; www.canoe-evasion.net; rte de Fontaine-de-Vaucluse/D24; adult/child €20/10) Next to Camping de la Coutelière on the D24 towards Lagnes.

Kayak Vert (☑ 04 90 20 35 44; www.canoe-france.com; Quartier la Baume; adult/child €20/10) By the aqueduct, 1km out of town on the D25 (direction Lagnes)

the 18th century, canals lined with 70 giant wheels powered silk factories and paper mills. Many of them have been left in place; you'll see them as you walk around the edge of the old town.

These days the 'Venice of Provence' is known for antiques. It's home to several antiques villages, housing 300 dealers between them. Sunday is the big market day, with antique vendors participating as well, while Thursday offers a smaller market through the village streets.

◉ Sights

The exceptional historic centre is contained within canals dotted by creaking water-wheels – the one by the tiny park at ave des Quatre Otages is particularly photogenic. The former Jewish quarter exists in name only: the ghetto's synagogue was destroyed in 1856. The ancient fishermen's quarter, a tangle of narrow passageways, dead-ends in L'Isle's eastern corner and retains a town-within-a-town feeling.

A tourist-office brochure details the attractions, and there's an app you can download.

Collégiale Notre Dame des Anges CHURCH (Our Lady of Angels; place de la Liberté; ⊙ 10am-noon & 3-6pm daily Jul-Sep, Tue-Sat Oct-Jun) In the very heart of the old town, the stately exterior of the Collégiale Notre Dame des Anges shows no sign of the baroque theatrics inside – 122 gold angels ushering forward the Virgin Mary, and a magnificent 1648-built organ, on the left as you face the altar (the pipes on the right are mute, there purely for visual symmetry).

Campredon Centre d'Art MUSEUM (☑ 04 90 38 17 41; www.campredoncentredart.com; 20 rue du Docteur Tallet; adult/child €6/free; ⊙ 10am-12.30pm & 2-5.30pm Tue-Sun) This 18th-century riverside mansion is a venue for seasonal contemporary art exhibitions. Opening hours may vary slightly according to exhibitions.

Partage des Eaux PARK (Parting of the Waters) A country lane runs riverside from the old town 2km east towards the serene *partage des eaux,* where the Sorgue splits into the channels that surround the town. It's a perfect spot for idling on grassy banks, skipping stones and watching birds. Waterside cafes sell ice cream.

Grottes de Thouzon CAVE (☑ 04 90 33 93 65; www.grottes-thouzon.com; 2083 rte d'Orange; ⊙ 10am-6.45pm Jul & Aug, 10.15am-12.15pm & 2-6pm Apr-Jun & Sep-Oct, 2-6pm Sun Mar) Following the course of a vanished underground river, this 230m-long cave was accidentally discovered in 1902 during mining works. Marvels include a mound of 5000-year-old bat poo, thousands of 'macaroni' stalactites, odd mineral formations like folds of waxy skin, and a 40-tonne flint boulder suspended from a limestone thread. Access is by a 45-minute guided tour, which runs every hour.

The cave is 2km outside the village of Le Thor on the D16, about 15 minutes' drive from L'Isle-sur-la-Sorgue.

⌨ Sleeping

Les Terrasses by David & Louisa HOTEL € (☑ 04 90 38 03 16; www.lesterrassesbydavidetlouisa.com; 2 av du Général de Gaulle; d €69-95; ☎ ✿) Riverside location, cute rooms, friendly owners and screamingly cheap rates – what's not to like about this little hotel? Okay, the rooms are small, but they're decorated with taste in shades of cappuccino, cream and taupe – and if you can get a river-view balcony, you really can't quibble. Meals (and breakfast) are served in the lovely waterside restaurant.

★**La Prévôté** B&B €€€ (☑ 04 90 38 57 29; www.la-prevote.fr; 4bis rue Jean-Jacques Rousseau; d €145-210; ⊙ closed late Feb–mid-Mar & mid-Nov–early Dec; ☎) If you're looking for inspiration on how to renovate a period building, this sexy *chambres d'hôte* is a case study. A 17th-century convent perched above a tributary of the Sorgue, it's been restored with great care and imagination, and the five rooms combine old architecture with zingy modern design, bright colours and carefully chosen *brocanteries* (antiques).

✕ Eating & Drinking

Most of the drinking goes on in the village's restaurants and cafes, but the vibe is generally sedate. For an evening aperitif, head for one of the canalside cafes.

Au Chineur   BISTRO €€
(☑ 04 90 38 33 54; 2 esplanade Robert-Vasse; 2-/3-course menu €13/16, mains €15-20; ☺ 7am-midnight) The best of the roll-call of bistros lining the canals, this quintessentially French bistro is a perfect place for lunch, complete with the checked tablecloths, chalkboard menus and classic dishes you'd expect to find – along with a collection of antique bric-a-brac to chat about. If in doubt, just go for the €10 'pdj' (*plat du jour;* dish of the day).

Le Cafe du Village   CAFE €€
(☑ 04 90 15 47 49; www.lecafeduvillage.fr; 2bis av de l'Égalité; menu €22, mains €14-18; ☺ 11am-3pm Fri-Mon) After a spot of weekend browsing in the antique markets, this convivial cafe is where everyone heads for a no-fuss lunch packed with French flavours. The food is hearty and unpretentious (steaks, grilled fish, *confit de canard*) and the vine-shaded terrace is definitely somewhere to linger after lunch with a glass or three of Côtes du Rhône.

Umami   FUSION, FRENCH €€
(☑ 04 90 20 82 12; www.restaurant-umami.fr; 33 rue Carnot; 2-/3-course lunch menu €14.90/17.90, dinner menu €27.90; ☺ noon-2pm & 7-10pm Wed-Sun) For something a bit different, try this local's tip little restaurant in the old town, which dabbles with ingredients like squid ink, tempura batter, spiced mango and edible flowers alongside the usual Provençal ingredients, and serves its dishes on striking black plates. There aren't many tables, so book ahead.

★ Le Vivier   GASTRONOMY €€€
(☑ 04 90 38 52 80; www.levivier-restaurant.com; 800 cours Fernande Peyre; 2-/3-course weekday menu €26/32, weekend dinner menu €58; ☺ noon-1.30pm Wed-Fri & Sun, 7.30-10pm Tue-Sun, closed Sun evening Oct-Apr) You couldn't really dream up a more romantic setting than at 'The Fishpond', with riverside tables shaded by weeping willows and overhanging oaks. But lovely as the location is, it's the Michelin-starred food that really steals the show here – creative, contemporary and surpris-

ingly good value. The €85 gourmet menu is served for the whole table to share.

La Prévôté   GASTRONOMY €€€
(☑ 04 90 38 57 29; www.la-prevote.fr; 4bis rue Jean-Jacques Rousseau; lunch/dinner menu €24/46; ☺ noon-1.30pm & 7.30-9.30pm Thu-Mon) Jean-Marie Alloin is the chef in charge at La Prévôté's primo – and deservedly popular – restaurant. The food here is modern, and occasionally experimental, but underscored by classic Provençal flavours: aubergines, olive oil, tomatoes, *herbes de Provence* and so on. You can dine in the old refectory or in the courtyard; both are delightful.

🛍 Shopping

Village des Antiquaires   ANTIQUES
(www.facebook.com/villagedesantiquaires; ☺ noon-6pm Fri, 10am-6pm Sat-Mon) If your manor house needs that perfect Louis XV chandelier, look no further. The former mills and factories along L'Isle-sur-la-Sorgue's main road contain seven fascinating-to-explore antiques villages with 300-plus high-end stalls. For bargains, it's better to come mid-August or Easter for the antiques fairs.

ℹ Information

Tourist Office (☑ 04 90 38 04 78; www.oti-delasorgue.fr; place de la Liberté; ☺ 9am-12.30pm & 2.30-5.30pm Mon-Sat, 9.30am-12.30pm Sun) In the centre of the old town, next to the Collegiale. Has leaflets on local bike rides and runs a separate cycling website (www.velo-provence.com).

ℹ Getting There & Around

BUS
L'Isle-sur-la-Sorgue is fairly well-served by buses. Destinations served by **Voyages Raoux** (www.voyages-raoux.fr):

Avignon (€2.10, TransVaucluse Line 6, 40 minutes, 12 daily Monday to Saturday, two on Sunday)

ℹ LAVENDER V LAVANDIN

When shopping for lavender, it's worth knowing that the most sought-after product is fine lavender (in French, *lavande fine;* in Latin, *Lavandula angustifolia, L vera, L officinalis*), not spike lavender (*L latifolia*) or the hybrid lavandin (*L hybrida*). The latter are high in camphor and are used in detergents and paint solvents, not perfume.

Carpentras (€2.10, TransVaucluse Line 13, 30 minutes, seven daily Monday to Saturday) Via Pernes-les-Fontaines. Travels to Cavaillon in the other direction.

Fontaine-de-Vaucluse (€1.60, 15 minutes, hourly during school term times)

TRAIN

L'Isle-sur-la-Sorgue–Fontaine de Vaucluse (av Julien Guigue, L'Isle-sur-la-Sorgue) is on the main train line between Marseille (€17.80, 1½ hours), Cavaillon (€2.90, seven minutes) and Avignon Centre (€5.20, 30 minutes).

BICYCLE

There are a couple of useful bike rental shops: **K-Vélo Rent** (☑ 04 90 38 59 30; www.kvelo-rent.com; 4 rue de la République; adult/child per day from €19/13; ☉ 9.30am-12.30pm & 2.30-6.30pm Tue-Sat, 10am-12.30pm Sun) in the old town, and **Trujibike Luberon** (☑ 09 83 75 97 18; www.truji-cycle.fr; 17 chemin du Bosquet; adult/child per day from €18/12; ☉ 9am-12.30pm & 2-7pm Tue-Sat) about 1km east. The tourist office has route suggestions and also runs its own cycling-dedicated website, Vélo Provence (www.velo-provence.com).

FONTAINE-DE-VAUCLUSE

POP 661

Since ancient times, the surging natural spring known as La Fontaine de Vaucluse has been a source of wonder and mystery: to prehistoric people it was a site of healing and mysticism, and even to their modern-day counterparts, it's an undeniably impressive sight. The miraculous appearance of this crystal-clear flood draws 1.5 million tourists each year – aim to arrive early in the morning before the trickle of visitors becomes a deluge.

As the origin of the River Sorgue, the village also makes a good base for kayaking

---

THE LEGEND OF ST VÉRAN

Il était une fois – once upon a time – Fontaine-de-Vaucluse was plagued by a vile half-dragon, half-serpent called the Couloubre. Enter St Véran, who slayed the beast and saved the town. A statue outside the village's 11th-century Romanesque church, **Église St-Véran**, commemorates the slaying. Follow the legend up the cliff to the 13th-century **ruins of a castle** built to protect the saint's tomb – views are as incredible as the tale.

---

and canoeing, with lots of activity providers around town.

The village was also once home to the Italian poet Petrarch (1304–74), who wrote his most famous works here: sonnets to his unrequited love, Laura.

◉ Sights

★**La Fontaine de Vaucluse**   SPRING
Beneath the limestone cliffs an easy 1km walk from the village, the magical spring after which the village is named gushes forth at an incredible rate – more than 90 cu metres per second, making it France's largest karst spring, and the fifth-largest on the planet. It's also the source of the River Sorgue.

The spring is most dazzling after heavy rain, when the water glows an ethereal azure blue. Arrive early in summer to avoid the crowds.

For centuries the spring was said to be bottomless. Jacques Cousteau was among those who attempted to plumb the spring's depths, before an unmanned submarine touched base (315m down) in 1985.

**Musée d'Histoire
Jean Garcin: 1939–1945**   MUSEUM
(☑ 04 90 20 24 00; chemin de la Fontaine; adult/child €3.50/free; ☉ 10am-6pm Wed-Mon Apr-Oct & Jan-Feb, Sat & Sun Mar, Nov & Dec) A small museum exploring the harsh realities of life in occupied France during WWII.

Maison de la Rose   PERFUMERY
(☑ 06 87 65 25 47; www.lesartsdelarose.com; ☉ 2-4pm) The facade of this eye-catching *hôtel particulier* dating from 1900 is pure romance. Sitting pretty in pink on the left as you walk from the car park to the village centre, the mansion's exquisitely sculpted floral facade shields an elegant interior dressed with original furnishings. Its boutique sells rose-scented cosmetics and other skin products crafted in the perfumery's laboratory, alongside edible rose products, rose plants and so on.

🛏 Sleeping & Eating

Hôtel du Poète   HISTORIC HOTEL €€
(☑ 04 90 20 34 05; www.hoteldupoete.com; d €98-240, ste €295-325; ☉ Mar-Nov; ❋ 🛜 ≋) A charming – if rather expensive – hotel in the middle of the village, renovated from a former mill. Rooms are attractive and rather feminine; more expensive ones come with sitting areas and balconies. Outside, there's a fine pool and a delightful garden, where you

can enjoy breakfast in summer – if you're happy to stretch to the €17 price tag.

Pétrarque et Laure   BRASSERIE €€
(☑ 04 90 20 31 48; www.petrarque-et-laure.com; place Colonne; lunch menu €14.80, 2-/3-course menu €22/23; ⊕ noon-3pm & 7-10pm; 🐾) Fontaine-de-Vaucluse's restaurants tend towards the *touristique;* this one is no exception, but it manages to serve reasonably priced, good-quality food (try the trout) on a wonderful tree-shaded terrace beside the river.

ℹ Information

Fontaine-de-Vaucluse Tourist Office (☑ 04 90 20 32 22; www.oti-delasorgue.fr; Résidence Jean Garcin; ⊕ 9am-1pm & 2.30-6pm Mon-Sat, 9.30am-1pm Sun) By the bridge, mid-village.

ℹ Getting There & Away

BICYCLE
A tourist-office brochure details three easy backroads biking routes. Bike shops in L'Isle-sur-la-Sorgue deliver to Fontaine.

BUS
Voyages Raoux (p257) runs buses to L'Isle-sur-la-Sorgue (€1.60, 15 minutes, hourly during school term-times, five daily during school holidays).

CAR & MOTORCYCLE
The narrow road to Gordes (14km, 20 minutes) from Fontaine-de-Vaucluse makes a scenic, less-travelled alternative to reach the Luberon. Parking in town costs €4.

PAYS DE VENASQUE

POP 1184 / ELEV 320M

The seldom-visited, beautiful 'Venasque Country' is perfect for a road trip: a rolling landscape of oak woodlands, dotted with villages atop rocky promontories and hundreds of *bories* (domed stone huts from the Bronze Age). The region is famous for its early-summer ruby-red cherries.

Tiny Venasque itself teeters on a rocky spur, its twisting streets and ancient buildings weathered by howling winds. Around it stretches the lovely Forêt de Venasque, with excellent walking.

◉ Sights

Forêt de Venasque   FOREST
The Forêt de Venasque, criss-crossed by walking trails (including long-distance

GR91), lies east of Venasque. Cross the Col de Murs mountain pass (627m) to pretty little Murs, and see remains of Le Mur de la Peste (the Plague Wall), built in 1720 in a vain attempt to stop the plague from entering papal territory.

You could also walk into the Luberon from here, calling at Gordes and Abbaye Notre-Dame de Sénanque. The map *Balades en forêts du Ventoux de Venasque et St-Lambert* (€8) outlines several family-friendly walks.

Église de Venasque   CHURCH
(Église Notre-Dame; ⊕ 9.15am-5pm) The village church contains the pride of the Pays de Venasque: an unusual late-Gothic *Crucifixion* painting (1498).

Baptistry   CHURCH
(☑ 04 90 66 62 01; place de l'Église; adult/child €3/free; ⊕ 9.15am-noon & 1-6.30pm, 9.15am-5pm winter) Tucked behind the Romanesque church, this baptistry was built in the 6th century on the site of a Roman temple.

🛏 Sleeping & Eating

There are rooms at Les Remparts, but the village can easily be visited on a day trip from Carpentras, Gordes or any of the Luberon villages.

★ Les Remparts   PROVENCAL €€
(☑ 04 90 66 02 79; www.hotellesremparts. com; 36 rue Haute; lunch/dinner menus from €22/27; ⊕ noon-1.30pm & 7.30-9.30pm Apr-Oct; P 🛜 🅿 👪) This rustic valley-view restaurant, built into Venasque's old ramparts, is almost worth the trip up to the village on its own. The Provençal dishes are delicious, they make their own cherry juice and, believe it or not, they even serve a vegetarian menu. Upstairs are eight sweet (if rather spartan) rooms (singles/doubles/triples/quads including breakfast €60/80/100/120).

ℹ Information
Venasque Tourist Office (☑ 04 90 66 11 66; www.tourisme-venasque.com; Grand Rue; ⊕ 10am-noon & 2-6pm Mon-Sat Apr-Oct) A good resource for hiking information.

ℹ Getting There & Away
There's no public transport to Venasque, so driving or cycling is the only way to visit – unless you're on a long-distance hike to the Luberon.

The Luberon

Best Places to Eat

➡ Le Sanglier Paresseux (p274)

➡ La Closerie (p277)

➡ La Table de Pablo (p269)

➡ La Petite Maison de Cucuron (p277)

Best Places to Stay

➡ Le Couvent (p272)

➡ Les Balcons du Luberon (p266)

➡ La Couleur des Vignes (p274)

➡ Maison Valvert (p275)

Why Go?

Named after the mountain range running east–west between Cavaillon and Manosque, the Luberon is a Provençal patchwork of hilltop villages, vineyards, ancient abbeys and mile after mile of fragrant lavender fields. It's a rural, traditional region that still makes time for the good things in life – particularly fine food and even finer wine. Nearly every village hosts its own weekly market, packed with stalls selling local specialities, especially olive oil, honey and lavender.

Covering some 600 sq km, the Luberon massif itself is divided into three areas: the craggy Petit Luberon in the west, the higher Grand Luberon mountains, and the smaller hills of the Luberon Oriental in the east. They're all worth exploring, but whatever you do, don't rush – part of the fun of exploring here is getting lost on the back lanes, stopping for lunch at a quiet village cafe, and taking as much time as you possibly can to soak up the scenery.

Driving Distances (km)

	Apt	Bonnieux	Cavaillon	Gordes	Lacoste
Bonnieux	10				
Cavaillon	35	25			
Gordes	21	19	17		
Lacoste	15	5	21	23	
Roussillon	13	10	28	9	14

ⓘ Getting There & Away

Long distance **LER buses** (Lignes Express Régionales; www.info-ler.fr) serve some areas of the Luberon. Apt is the main bus hub. The most useful route is Line 22, which travels from Avignon to Cavaillon, stops in Apt, and then continues on to Forcalquier and Digne-les-Bains.

To get north to Carpentras or south to Aix-en-Provence, you need to change to Line 17 in Cavaillon.

Several LER lines run from Marseille and Aix-en-Provence to Digne-les-Bains; to get to the Luberon, you need to change to Line 22 in La Brillane, or you can ride all the way to Digne-les-Bains and backtrack from there.

ⓘ Getting Around

The Luberon, an hour from Avignon, is just 60km in length. Having a car makes travel much easier, as bus services are limited. However, parking in some small villages can be a nightmare in summer.

The D900 bisects the valley from east to west. Secondary roads are slow and winding; watch out for roadside gullies.

BICYCLE

Don't be put off by the hills – the Luberon is a fantastic destination for cyclists. Several bike routes criss-cross the countryside, including **Les Ocres à Vélo**, a 51km route that takes in the ochre villages of Apt, Gargas, Rustrel, Roussillon and Villars, and the **Véloroute du Calavon**, a purpose-built bike path that follows the route of a disused railway line for 28km between Beaumettes in the west (near Coustellet), via Apt, to La Paraire in the west (near St-Martin-de-Castillon). Plans are underway to extend the trail all the way from Cavaillon to the foothills of the Alps, but it'll be a while before it's completed.

For longer trips, **Le Luberon à Vélo** (04 90 76 48 05; www.leluberonavelo.com) has mapped a 236km itinerary that takes in pretty much the whole Luberon. Tourist offices stock detailed route leaflets and can provide information on bike rental, luggage transport, accommodation and so on.

Several companies offer e-bikes, which have an electric motor. They're not scooters – you still have to pedal – but the motor helps on the ascents.

BUS

Most villages in the Luberon have a limited bus service that revolves around school term times. The main hub is Apt, which has buses to local villages, and a regular bus link to Cavaillon and Avignon. The Luberon Côte Sud (www.luberoncotesud.com) and Sudest Mobilité (www.sudest-mobilites.fr) websites have downloadable timetables.

Due to the relative paucity of bus services, many of the area's smaller villages are served by an on-demand minibus service, **line 109** (04 90 74 20 21; www.sudest-mobilites.fr). To use it, you need to reserve at least by 4pm the day before you want to travel: you can either telephone (in French) or reserve online.

The fare to all destinations is calculated by how far you travel; most local destinations cost a flat-rate €2.10, or €2.80 for longer distances.

Gordes

POP 2130

Arguably the scenic queen of the Luberon's hilltop villages, the tiered village of Gordes seems to teeter improbably on the edge of the sheer rock faces of the Vaucluse plateau from which it rises. A jumble of terracotta rooftops, church towers and winding lanes, it's a living postcard – but unfortunately it's also seethingly popular in summer, so arrive early or late to avoid the worst crowds. Better still, the village looks at its most beautiful as the sun sets and the village's honey-coloured stone glows like molten gold.

◉ Sights

★ Abbaye Notre-Dame de Sénanque
CHURCH

(04 90 72 05 72; www.abbayedesenanque.com; adult/child €7.50/3.50; 9-11.30am Mon-Sat Apr-Nov, shorter hours Dec-Mar, guided tours by reservation) If you're searching for that classic postcard shot of the medieval abbey surrounded by a sea of purple lavender, look no further. This sublime Cistercian abbey provides one of the most iconic shots of the Luberon, and it's equally popular these days for selfies. The best displays are usually in July and August. You can wander around the grounds on your own from 9.45am to 11am, but at other times (and to visit the abbey's cloistered interior) you must join a guided tour.

Village des Bories
ARCHITECTURE

(04 90 72 03 48; adult/child €6/4; 9am-8pm, shorter hours winter) Beehive-shaped *bories* (stone huts) bespeckle Provence and at the Village des Bories, 4km southwest of Gordes, an entire village of them can be explored. Constructed of slivered limestone, *bories* were built during the Bronze Age, inhabited by shepherds until 1839, then abandoned until their restoration in the 1970s. Visit early in the morning or just before sunset for the best light. Note that the lower car park is for buses; continue to the hilltop car park to avoid hiking uphill in the blazing heat.

The Luberon Highlights

1 Abbaye Notre-Dame de Sénanque (p261) Smelling the lavender (and taking plenty of photos) at this famous Provençal abbey.

2 Véloroute du Calavon (p261) Pedalling along a disused railway through the heart of the Luberon's loveliest countryside.

3 Gordes (p261) Snapping a sunset picture of this ravishing hilltop village.

4 Fôret des Cèdres (p274) Escaping the heat in this peaceful hilltop cedar forest.

5 Apt (p269) Shopping for ingredients at the fabulous Saturday-morning market.

6 Colorado Provençal (p268) Hiking through crimson landscapes formed by old ochre mines.

7 Musée de la Lavande (p266) Learning all about Provence's most fragrant export.

8 Gorges d'Oppedette (p273) Trekking through quiet canyons along the Calavon River.

9 Bonnieux (p274) Admiring the view from this lovely hilltop village.

10 Village des Bories (p261) Visiting ancient dwellings that have been a feature of the Provençal countryside for centuries.

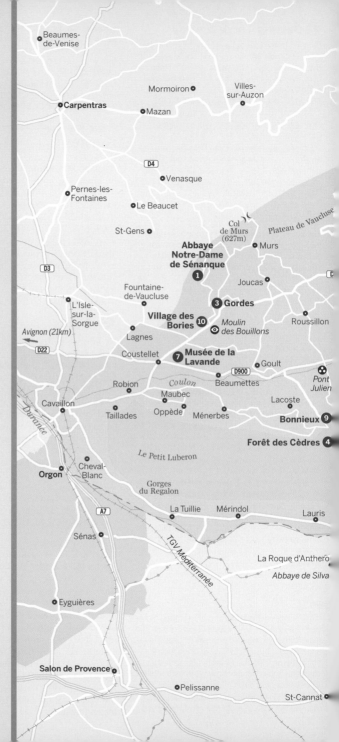

CYCLING IN VAUCLUSE & THE LUBERON

PRACTICALITIES

While it's certainly possible to bring your own bike, most people will probably end up hiring. There are lots of bike shops dotted throughout the region – there's usually at least one place in most sizeable towns where you can hire a bike by the half-day, day, week or even longer. You can usually choose between dedicated road bikes, VTT (*vélo à tout terrain,* otherwise known as mountain bikes) or hybrid bikes which are somewhere between the two. An increasing number of places are also starting to hire electronic or e-bikes, which have a small battery that charges up as you pedal and provides a boost when you're going up hill. Rental rates generally include helmet, lock, puncture repair kit and a local map of suggested routes.

Many bike shops will also deliver bikes within their local area (generally within about a 30km radius). Good operators include **Luberon Biking** (☑ 04 90 90 14 62; www.luberon-biking.fr; 90 chemin du Stade, Velleron; per day/week from €24/125) and **Sun-e-Bike** (www.location-velo-provence.com), but there are many more; the best idea is usually to ask in the local tourist office for details of nearby bike hire outlets.

If you do want to bring your own steed, most trains have limited spaces for carrying a few bikes in the luggage car (bike-friendly services are indicated by a little bike symbol on timetables). You don't usually need to book on local TER services, although it's always worth asking at the ticket office when you buy your ticket just in case. Reservations are compulsory on many intercity and all TGV trains; a small fee of €5 to €10 is payable at the same time when you buy your ticket.

RESOURCES

La Provence à Vélo (www.provence-cycling.co.uk) This fantastic website is a one-stop shop for cycling ideas in the Provence region. The site details a huge range of possible routes, grouped into areas including Mont Ventoux, the Luberon, Orange and Châteauneuf-du-Pâpe and L'Isle-sur-la-Sorgue, along with downloadable versions of route leaflets, which you can either save to your computer or print out (printed versions can also be picked up in local tourist offices). You can also select your ride by theme (lavender, villages, vineyards, waterside routes and so on). There's even a tool to plot your own custom route.

Véloloisir Provence (www.veloloisirprovence.com) Another great resource, with route ideas grouped into the Luberon and Verdon areas (there's a downloadable booklet for each area).

WHERE TO CYCLE

A number of dedicated bike routes crisscross through the countryside, and local tourist offices are well-stocked with leaflets, maps and booklets detailing a huge range of other potential routes, whether you're interested in mountain-biking or road-cycling. Just make sure you take time to stop and enjoy the view occasionally.

For the loveliest lavender fields, follow the 33km circular route around the Plateau de Sault.

A great option for families is the 14km Via Venassia *voie verte* (green way) route between Carpentras and Jonquières.

☆ **Mont Ventoux**

The *géant de Provence* is the main draw for mountain-bikers in Provence, with a network of groomed routes descending the hillsides, covering various levels of difficulty. The **Ventoux Bike Park** (p249) is a good place to start.

Pedalling up to Mont Ventoux' summit is another popular pastime (Ventoux is a legendary stage in the Tour de France). There are three possible routes from each of the gateway villages (Bedoin, Malaucène and Sault). The classic (and hardest) one is from Bédoin, covering 21km and an elevation gain of 1610m; experienced cyclists should manage it in two or three hours. The routes from Malaucène and Sault are a bit easier thanks to the slightly less punishing gradient.

There can be few more entertaining ways to enjoy the scenery of southern France than from the seat of your own *vélo*.

☆ The Luberon

With its hilltop villages and gorgeous countryside, the Luberon is unsurprisingly a popular place to cycle. A lovely long-distance trail, the Véloroute du Calavon (p261), follows the course of a disused railway line for 28km between Beaumettes (near Coustellet), via Apt, to La Paraire (near St-Martin-de-Castillon).

The countryside around Rustrel is another good area, with a dedicated route, **Les Ocres à Vélo**, that takes in the old ochre-mining valleys and villages. There are other organised routes that link together villages around Lourmarin, Gordes, Roussillon, Ménerbes and Ansouis; the 236km **Autour du Luberon** route is a long-distance loop that takes them all in.

☆ La Grande Traversée VTT de Vaucluse

For hardcore bikers, this long-distance trail from Mont Ventoux to the Luberon covers between 330km and 400km depending on the route you follow, via the Dentelles de Montmirail, the Plateau de Sault and the Luberon valley. Divided into nine stages between Savoillans and Mérindol, it's one of seven Grandes Traversées VTT (long-distance mountain-bike trails) officially recognised by the FFC, France's main cycling body. There's a downloadable leaflet available from Véloloisir Provence (www.veloloisirprovence.com/sites/default/files/itineraire/depliant_vtt_gde_traverse_vaucluse2016.pdf).

HEMIS/ALAMY STOCK PHOTO ©

Cyclists on Mont Ventoux (p249)

Musée de la Lavande
MUSEUM

(☑04 90 76 91 23; www.museedelalavande.com; D2; adult/child €6.80/free; ⊙9am-7pm May-Sep, 9am-noon & 2-6pm Oct-Apr) To get to grips with Provence's most prestigious crop, this excellent eco-museum makes an ideal first stop. An audioguide and video (in English) explain the lavender harvest, and giant copper stills reveal extraction methods. Afterwards you can take a guided tour of the fields (1pm and 5pm daily May to September). The onsite boutique is an excellent (if pricey) one-stop shop for top-quality lavender products.

Moulin des Bouillons
DISTILLERY

(☑04 90 72 22 11; www.moulindesbouillons.com; rte de St-Pantaléon; adult/child €5/3.50; ⊙10am-noon & 2-6pm Wed-Mon Apr-Oct) Heading 3.5km south from Gordes along rte de St-Pantaléon (D148), you hit this marvellous rural museum: an olive-oil mill with a 10m-long Gallo-Roman press weighing 7 tonnes – reputedly the world's oldest. The adjoining stained-glass museum showcases beautiful translucent mosaics; a joint ticket costs adult/child €7.50/5.50.

🛏 Sleeping

⭐ Auberge de Carcarille
HOTEL €€

(☑04 90 72 02 63; www.auberge-carcarille.com; rte d'Apt; d €83-150; P ❄ 🛜 🛖) Old outside, new inside: this country hotel marries the atmosphere of a traditional *bastide familiale* (family house) with spotless, modern rooms. There's a delightful garden to wander, and the restaurant serves superior Provençal food (three-course lunch/dinner *menu* €26/44); half-board deals are great value. It's 3km from Gordes, at the bottom of the valley.

⭐ Les Balcons du Luberon
B&B €€

(☑06 38 20 42 13; www.lesbalconsduluberon.fr; rte de Murs; d €110-180; 🛜 🛖) The 'Balconies of the Luberon' is an apt name for this lovely B&B: an 18th-century stone farmhouse with five simple, stylish rooms – the best of which have private patios overlooking epic Luberon scenery. Owner Étienne Marty (a trained chef) offers a sumptuous dinner by reservation (€35).

Le Mas de la Beaume
B&B €€

(☑04 90 72 02 96; www.labeaume.com; rte de Cavaillon; d €180-260; 🛜 🛖) This simple, homey *chambre d'hôte* is a very cosy option, with yellow paint-washed walls, bunches of dried lavender hanging from the ceiling and views over the quiet garden and the superb pool.

Bastide de Gordes
HERITAGE HOTEL €€€

(☑04 90 72 12 12; www.bastide-de-gordes.com; Le Village; r from €290; ❄ 🛜 🛖) Impeccably restored, this deluxe hotel is one of the Luberon's star turns, from the boater-wearing bellboys through to the beamed lobby stuffed with antiques, oil paintings and bookcases. Rooms are enormous and aristocratic (a valley view is essential); spa, gardens, an incredible pool and a trio of restaurants (one Michelin-starred) ice this most indulgent of cakes.

Le Jas de Gordes
B&B €€€

(☑04 90 72 00 75; www.jasdegordes.com; rte de Cavaillon; r €271; P 🛜 🛖) This sumptuous B&B manages to pull off a tricky balance between contemporary style and traditional architecture, with delightful, feminine rooms overlooking an impeccably-kept gar-

---

LUBERON MARKETS

If there's one thing you have to do in the Luberon, it's visit a local market. Luckily there's at least one every day of the week. They generally run from 8am to 1pm from April to September; some villages also host summer evening markets. If you only have time for one, Apt's Saturday morning Grand Marché is hard to beat for atmosphere.

Monday Cadenet, Cavaillon, Lauris

Tuesday Apt (p269), Cucuron, Gordes (p261), La Tour d'Aigues, Lacoste, St-Saturnin-lès-Apt (p268)

Wednesday Gargas, Mérindol, Pertuis, Rustrel (evening market), Viens

Thursday Céreste, Goult, Ménerbes (p275), Roussillon, Saignon (p273)

Friday Bonnieux (p274), Lourmarin (p276), Pertuis, St-Saturnin-lès-Apt (p268; Friday evening farmers market)

Saturday Apt (p272), Cadenet, Manosque, Oppède-le-Vieux, Pertuis, Vaugines

Sunday Coustellet, Vaugines, Villars

den filled with olive trees, fragrant shrubs, a fountain and a fine pool (garden rooms have little patios, top-floor rooms small balconies). The outside bar is a lovely place for an aperitif.

✗ Eating

La Boulangerie de Mamie Jane BAKERY €
(☑ 04 90 72 09 34; rue Baptistin Picca; dishes €7-10; ⊘ 6.30am-1pm & 2-6pm Thu-Tue) Those short of time or money in Gordes should follow the locals downhill along rue Baptistin Picca to this pocket-sized *boulangerie* (bakery), which has been in the same family for three generations. Mamie Jane cooks up outstanding bread, pastries, cakes and biscuits, including lavender-perfumed *navettes* and delicious peanut-and-almond brittle known as *écureuil* (from the French for squirrel). The baguettes are copious too.

Le Mas Tourteron GASTRONOMY €€€
(☑ 04 90 72 00 16; www.mastourteron.com; chemin de St-Blaise les Imberts; menu lunch/dinner €35/76; ⊘ 12.30-2pm Thu-Sun, 7.30-9.30pm Wed-Sat Apr-Oct) Another one of the Luberon's longstanding tables, overseen by bubbly Elisabeth Bourgeois. It's heavy on Provençal flavours: lots of stuffed aubergines, slow-roasted tomatoes and lashings of olive oil and *herbes de Provence*. The garden setting is lovely, and Elisabeth's husband Philippe handles wine choices. It's 3.5km south of Gordes off the D2.

ℹ Information

Tourist Office (☑ 04 90 72 02 75; contact@luberoncoeurdeprovence.com; place du Château; ⊘ 9am-12.30pm & 1.30-6pm Mon-Sat, from 10am Sun) Inside Gordes' medieval château.

ℹ Getting There & Away

TransVaucluse bus 17 (€2.10, four daily, two on Sunday) stops in Gordes on its way from Apt to Cavaillon. Other stops along the way include Bonnieux and Roussillon.

Roussillon

POP 1291

Red by name, red by nature, that's Roussillon – once the centre of local ochre mining, and still unmistakably marked by its crimson colour (villagers are required to paint their houses according to a prescribed palette of some 40 tints). Today it's home to artists' and ceramicists' workshops, and its charms are no secret: arrive early or late.

During WWII the village was the for playwright Samuel Beckett, who h the local Resistance by hiding explos at his house and sometimes going on rece missions.

Parking (€3 March to November) is 300m outside the village.

◉ Sights & Activities

Ôkhra Conservatoire
des Ocres et de la Couleur ARTS CENTRE
(L'Usine d'Ocre Mathieu; ☑ 04 90 05 66 69; www.okhra.com; rte d'Apt; tours adult/student €7/5.50; ⊘ 10am-7pm Jul & Aug, to 6pm Sep-Jun, closed Mon & Tue Jan & Feb; ⊛) This art centre is a great place to see ochre in action. Occupying a disused ochre factory on the D104 east of Roussillon, it explores the mineral's properties through hands-on workshops and guided tours of the factory. The shop upstairs stocks paint pigments and other artists' supplies.

Mines de Bruoux HISTORIC SITE
(☑ 04 90 06 22 59; www.minesdebruoux.fr; rte de Croagnes, Gargas; adult/child €8.10/6.50; ⊘ 10am-7pm Jul & Aug, to 6pm Apr-Jun, Sep & Oct) In Gargas, 7km east of Roussillon, this former mine has more than 40km of underground galleries where ochre was once extracted. Around 650m are open to the public, some of which is as much as 15m high. Visits are only by guided tour; reserve ahead as English-language tours are at set times.

★ Sentier des Ocres HIKING
(Ochre Trail; adult/child €2.50/free; ⊘ 9.30am-5.30pm; ⊛) In Roussillon village, groves of chestnut and pine surround sunset-coloured ochre formations, rising on a clifftop. Two circular trails, taking 30 or 50 minutes to complete, twist through mini-desert landscapes – it's like stepping into a Georgia O'Keeffe painting. Information panels highlight 26 types of flora to spot, the history of local ochre production, and so on. Wear walking shoes and avoid white!

⇔ Sleeping & Eating

Les Passiflores B&B €
(☑ 04 90 71 43 08; www.passiflores.fr; Les Huguets; d €78-88, q €138; ☎⊛) Quiet and friendly, this *chambre d'hôte* is hidden in the hamlet of Les Huguets, 4km south of Roussillon. Spotless rooms are decorated with pretty flourishes of country-Provençal prints. The four-person suite is excellent value. Outside, the 'pool' is a small filtered pond. *Table*

...O PROVENÇAL

...nges, scarlets and yellows, purples and crimsons – the fiery colours burned ...between Roussillon and Rustrel are astonishing. They're the result of the ...neral deposits, especially hydrated iron oxide, otherwise known as ochre, ...has been mined in this part of the Luberon since Roman times. Ochre was traditionally used to colour earthenware and paint buildings. Around the late 18th century, the extraction process was industrialised, and large mines and quarries sprang up. In 1929, at the peak of the ochre industry, some 40,000 tonnes of ochre was mined around Apt.

There are several ochre-themed sites to visit around Roussillon, but for the full technicolour experience, head for the **Colorado Provençal** (☑ 04 32 52 09 75; www.colorado-provencal.com; ☉ 9am-dusk), a quarry site where ochre was mined from the 1880s until 1956. With its weird rock formations and rainbow colours, it's like a little piece of the Southwest USA plonked down amongst the hills of Provence. The site is signposted south of Rustrel village, off the D22 to Banon.

For extra thrills, try the treetop assault courses on offer at nearby **Colorado Adventures** (☑ 06 78 26 68 91; www.colorado-adventures.fr; adult/child €19/14; ☉ 9.30am-7.30pm Jul & Aug, 10am-7pm Mar-Jun & Sep-Nov).

d'hôte (€29) by reservation, includes wine and coffee.

Clos de la Glycine   HOTEL €€
(☑ 04 90 05 60 13; www.luberon-hotel.fr; place de la Poste; d €135-280; ❋ ☎) You're paying a hefty premium for the view at this attractive hotel in the middle of Roussillon – but, boy, what a view! Rooms overlook your choice of ochre cliffs or the Luberon valley, and feel distinctively French, with artfully distressed paintwork and rococo furniture. The hotel's restaurant, David, is smart, but breakfast is very steep at €15.

Domaine des Finets   COTTAGE €€
(☑ 04 90 74 11 92; www.domainedesfinets.fr; Chemin des Finets, near Roussillon; per week Jul & Aug €700-800, Sep-Jun €500-620; ☎ ▣) Four cute cottages, tinted orange like the rest of Roussillon, and surrounded by grassy lawns. They're rustic in style, and all have self-contained kitchens, washing machines, log-burning stoves and barbecues. We particularly liked 'Les Ocres' with its mezzanine floor.

La Coquillade   FRENCH €€€
(☑ 04 90 74 71 71; www.coquillade.fr; Le Perrotet; menus lunch €42, dinner €75-95; ☉ 12.30-1.30pm & 7.30-9.30pm mid-Apr–mid-Oct) Overnighting at this luxurious hilltop estate won't suit everyone's budget, but everyone should try to fork out for the great-value Bistrot lunch menu. Michelin-starred and run by renowned chef Christophe Renaud, it'll be one of the most memorable meals you'll have in the Luberon. It's a 5km drive south of Roussillon on the D108; look out for signs.

ℹ️ Information

Tourist Office (☑ 04 90 05 60 25; http://otroussillon.pagesperso-orange.fr; place de la Poste; ☉ 9am-noon & 1.30-5.30pm Mon-Sat) General info on the village's history and suggestions for walking routes through the surrounding area.

ℹ️ Getting There & Away

Roussillon is served by TransVaucluse bus 17 (€2.10, four daily, two on Sunday) which stops in Apt, Bonnieux, Gordes and Cavaillon.

St-Saturnin-lès-Apt

POP 2479

About 9km north of Apt and 10km northeast of Roussillon, St-Saturnin-lès-Apt is refreshingly ungentrified and just beyond the tourist radar. Shops (not boutiques), cafes and bakeries line its cobbled streets. It has marvellous views of the surrounding Vaucluse plateau – climb to the ruins atop the village for knockout views. Or find the photogenic 17th-century windmill, Le Château les Moulins, 1km north, off the D943 towards Sault.

◎ Sights

Moulin à Huile Jullien   FARM
(☑ 04 90 75 56 24; www.moulin-huile-jullien.com; rte d'Apt; ☉ 10am-noon & 3-7pm Jul & Aug, 10am-noon & 2-6pm Sep-Jun, closed Sun year-round) **FREE** On the edge of the village, this working olive-oil mill allows you to follow the process from tree to bottle. Delicious honey is also made here. Tastings and mill tours are free.

🛏 Sleeping

Le Saint Hubert
HOTEL €

(📞 04 90 75 42 02; www.hotel-saint-hubert-luberon.com; rue de la République; d €57-63, tr €73) Charm personified, this quintessential village *auberge* (country inn) on the main street has welcomed travellers since the 18th century and is a gorgeous spot to stay. Rooms are simple but elegant, and the sweeping view of the southern Luberon from valley-facing rooms is breathtaking – especially considering the bargain-basement rates.

Le Mas Perréal
B&B €€

(📞 04 90 75 46 31; www.masperreal.com; Quartier la Fortune; d €140, studios €150; 🛜🖨) Surrounded by vineyards, lavender fields and cherry orchards, on a vast 7-hectare property outside St-Saturnin-lès-Apt, this farmhouse B&B offers a choice of cosy rooms or self-catering studios, both filled with country antiques and Provençal fabrics. There's a heavenly pool and big garden with mountain views. Elisabeth, a long-time French teacher, offers cooking and French lessons. It's 2km southwest of town along the D2.

Mas de Cink
APARTMENT €€

(📞 06 11 99 80 88; www.lemasdecink.com; Hameau des Blanchards; per week €700-1650; ❄🛜🖨) Apartments evocatively blend northern contemporary cool with earthy Provençal comfort in this sprawling old farmhouse and barn. All have fully equipped kitchens, and a couple are suitable for larger groups. Private terraces and trellised outdoor dining areas overlook a wild garden, lavender fields and vineyards. It's 2.5km west of St-Saturnin; follow the D2 and the signs.

Le Domaine Saint Jean
B&B €€

(📞 04 32 50 10 77; www.ledomainesaintjean.com; d €125-160, q €195; 🅿🛜🖨) This old farmstead in St-Saturnin-lès-Apt still has a pleasingly rural vibe – its rustic *gîtes* and B&B farmhouse are set around a courtyard that still has its old water pump and cattle trough. The style is country chic – a few florals here and there – but mostly cool and neutral. A couple of rooms have freestanding tubs.

🍴 Eating

L'Estrade
BISTRO €€

(📞 04 90 71 15 75; 6 av Victor Hugo; mains €14-28; ⊙ noon-2.30pm & 7.30-10.30pm Apr-Oct) Tiny and friendly, this village restaurant is a popular local's tip for solid, fuss-free Provençal cooking. Everything's cooked fresh on the day, so it's worth arriving early to make sure you have the full menu choice.

La Table de Pablo
MODERN FRENCH €€€

(📞 04 90 75 45 18; www.latabledepablo.com; Les Petits Cléments, Villars; menu €32-45; ⊙ 12.30-2pm & 7.30-9.30pm Mon, Tue, Fri & Sun, 7.30-9.30pm Thu & Sat) Run by top chef Thomas Gallardo, the contemporary feel of this renowned 'semi-gastronomic' restaurant belies its country setting. Funky globe bulbs, downlighters and wooden tables make the dining room look more suited to Paris than Provence – a contrast that's mirrored in the stylish, sophisticated food.

It's 5km east of St-Saturnin on the edge of the village of Villars: look out for the signs for Les-Petits-Cléments.

Apt

POP 11,500 / ELEV 250M

The Luberon's principal town, Apt is edged on three sides by sharply rising plateaux surrounding a river that runs through town. Its Saturday-morning market is full of local colour (and produce), but otherwise Apt is a place you pass through to get somewhere else. Nonetheless, it makes a decent base, if only for a night or two.

Apt is known throughout France for its *fruits confits* (candied fruits, sometimes also known as glacé or crystallised fruit). Strictly speaking, they're not sweets: they're made with real fruit, in which the water is removed and replaced with a sugar syrup to preserve them. As a result, they still look (and more importantly taste) like pieces of the original fruit. There are several makers around town where you can try and buy.

It's also a hub for the 1650-sq-km **Parc Naturel Régional du Luberon** (www.parcduluberon.fr), a regional nature park crisscrossed by hiking trails.

👁 Sights & Activities

Musée d'Apt
MUSEUM

(Industrial History Museum; 📞 04 90 74 95 30; 14 place du Postel; adult/child €5/free; ⊙ 10am-noon & 2-6.30pm Mon-Sat Jun-Sep, to 5.30pm Tue-Sat Oct-May) Apt's various industries – ochre-mining, *fruits confits* and faiences – are explored at this modest but well-curated museum in the middle of town. Exhibits include a reconstructed potter's workshop.

THE LUBERON APT

1

LOTTIE DAVIES/LONELY PLANET ©

VAGABOND54/SHUTTERSTOCK ©

1. Gordes (p261)
One of the Luberon's most scenic hilltop villages.

2. Roussillon (p267)
Red-painted shops lines the village's narrow streets.

3. Village des Bories (p261)
Near Gordes lies an entire village of *bories* (p316), beehive-shaped structures built in the Bronze Age.

4. St-Saturnin-lès-Apt (p268)
This quaint village offers stunning views of the surrounding Vaucluse plateau.

MARINA VN/SHUTTERSTOCK ©

Ancienne Cathédrale Ste-Anne
CHURCH

(rue Ste-Anne; ⊙9.30am-12.30pm & 2.30-6pm Mon-Fri, 2.30-6pm Sun) The 11th-century Ancienne Cathédrale Ste-Anne houses the relics of St Anne, and 11th- and 12th-century illuminated manuscripts.

Confiserie Kerry Aptunion
TOURS

(📋04 90 76 31 43; www.lesfleurons-apt.com; D900, Quartier Salignan; ⊙shop 9am-12.15pm & 1.30-6pm Mon-Sat, 9am-6pm Jul & Aug) Allegedly the largest *fruits confits* maker in the world, this factory 2.5km outside of Apt produces sweets under the prestigious Les Fleurons d'Apt brand. Free tastings are offered in the shop, and you can watch the process in action on guided factory tours; they run at 2.30pm Monday to Friday in July and August, with an extra tour at 10.30am in August. The rest of the year there's just one weekly tour, usually on Wednesday at 2.30pm; confirm ahead.

🛏 Sleeping

Hôtel le Palais
HOTEL €

(📋04 90 04 89 32; www.hotel-restaurant-apt.fr; 24bis place Gabriel-Péri; s/d/tr/q €55/67/80/90; 🛜) Don't go expecting many luxuries at this bargain-basement hotel above a pizza restaurant – but if price is more important than frills, it's a decent option. Rooms are small and very plain, but you're right in the middle of town, and breakfast is a bargain at €6.

★ Le Couvent
B&B €€

(📋04 90 04 55 36; www.loucouvent.com; 36 rue Louis Rousset; d €99-140; @🛜🏊) Hidden behind a wall in the old town, this enormous *maison d'hôte* occupies a 17th-century former convent. Staying here is as much architectural experience as accommodation: soaring ceilings, stonework, grand staircase, plus palatial rooms (one has a sink made from a baptismal font). There's a sweet garden with a little pool, and breakfast is served in the old convent refectory.

Hôtel Sainte-Anne
HOTEL €€

(📋04 90 74 18 04; www.apt-hotel.fr; 62 place Faubourg-du-Ballet; d €120-140; ❄@🛜) This pretty little hotel occupies a 19th-century house just outside the old town centre. Rooms aren't huge, but they're attractively appointed with a mix of period and modern furnishings. Breakfast has lots of nice touches, such as homemade jams and breads.

🍴 Eating

L'Auberge Espagnole
TAPAS €

(📋04 86 69 83 94; 1 rue de la Juiverie; tapas €4.50-8; ⊙noon-2pm & 5-10pm Mon-Sat) Simple tapas, cold beers and a nice location on a tree-shaded square – the 'Spanish Inn' makes a pleasant spot for a quick lunch or pre-dinner snacks.

L'Intramuros
FRENCH €€

(📋04 90 06 18 87; 120-124 rue de la République; mains €17-19.50; ⊙noon-2pm & 7-9pm Mon-Sat) What fun this place is: an offbeat French restaurant that's stocked to the gunwales with the owners' bric-a-brac finds, from vintage movie posters, antique shop signs and old radios to a collection of sardine cans. It's run by a father-and-son team, and food is filling – expect things like rabbit, duck breast and lamb, plus a choice of pastas.

Thym, Te Voilà
BISTRO €€

(📋04 90 74 28 25; www.thymtevoila.com; 59 place St-Martin; 2-/3-course menus lunch €17.90/23, dinner €23.50/28; ⊙noon-2pm & 7-9pm Tue-Sat; 🍴) *Cuisines du monde* is what's on offer at this charming little bistro – in other words, a little bit of everything, from a splash of Asian spice to a traditional Hungarian goulash. It's on a lovely square in the old town, with outside tables next to the tinkling fountain in summer.

🔒 Shopping

Fruits confits (candied fruits) are the speciality to buy in Apt – you'll find lots for sale at the market and at a couple of sweet shops in the old town. The **Saturday market** (⊙Sat) is one of the best in the Luberon, with tons of local produce for sale.

Confiserie Marcel Richaud
FOOD

(📋04 90 74 43 50; confiserie-marcel-richaud@wanadoo.fr; 112 quai de la Liberté; ⊙9am-noon & 2-5pm Tue-Sat) A small sweet shop selling locally made *fruits confits* (candied fruits) and *calissons d'Aix* (iced candied fruits). It's been in business for three generations.

ℹ Information

Tourist Office (📋04 90 74 03 18; www.luberon-apt.fr; 788 av Victor Hugo; ⊙9.30am-12.30pm & 2-6pm Mon-Sat, also 9.30am-12.30pm Sun Jul & Aug) Apt's tourist office has moved into premises in the town's former train station – which is handy if you're driving through, but not so handy if you're in the town centre. It has lots of information for activities, excursions, bike rides (including the Véloroute du Calavon) and walks.

Maison du Parc du Luberon (☑ 04 90 04 42 00; www.parcduluberon.fr; 60 place Jean Jaurès; ☉ 8.30am-noon & 1.30-6pm Mon-Fri, 9am-noon Sat Apr-Sep, shorter hours Oct-Mar) A central information source for the Parc Naturel Régional du Luberon, with maps, walking guides and general info. There's also a small fossil museum.

❶ Getting There & Away

The old train line that once passed through Apt has now been turned into the Véloroute du Calavon (p261) – so buses are the only public-transport option.

The **bus station** (250 av de la Libération) is just a few blocks east of the town centre. Lignes Express Régionales buses (www.info-ler.fr) operates local buses.

Avignon (€6.90, Line 22, 1½ hours, four daily Monday to Saturday, two on Sunday) Travels via Bonnieux, Cavaillon and Avignon's TGV station. In the opposite direction, travels to Forcalquier and Digne-les-Bains.

Bonnieux (€2.10, four daily) TransVaucluse Bus 17 stops in Bonnieux, Roussillon and Gordes before continuing to Cavaillon.

Le Grand Luberon

Divided from the hills of the Petit Luberon to the west by a deep river canyon, the Combe de Lourmarin, the scenic hills of the Grand Luberon are made for exploring. The main villages of note are Buoux, known for its small medieval fort, and Saignon, a sleepy place with impressive views. Take your time along the winding back roads: the scenery deserves to be savoured.

Buoux

POP 134

Dominated by the ruins of its eponymous Fort de Buoux, the tiny village of Buoux (the 'x' is pronounced) sits across the divide from Bonnieux, 8km south of Apt. The village itself is little more than a collection of a few tumbledown houses, but the valley has spectacular views. The sheer cliffs here are popular with local rock climbers.

◎ Sights

★ **Distillerie Les Agnels**   DISTILLERY
(☑ 04 90 74 34 60; www.lesagnels.com; rte de Buoux, btwn Buoux & Apt; adult/child €6/free; ☉ 10am-7pm Apr-Sep, to 5.30pm Oct-Mar) This

OFF THE BEATEN TRACK

GORGES D'OPPEDETTE

The Gorges du Verdon aren't the only canyons to explore in these parts. Lying 18km east of Rustrel, the Gorges d'Oppedette is a system of gorges gouged out from the limestone over the millennia by the Calavon River. Several marked trails wind though the gorges, lasting from around half an hour to three hours; the tourist office in Apt has route leaflets.

distillery on the edge of Buoux uses locally grown lavender, cypress and rosemary in its products. It also rents three gorgeous self-contained cottages (€1300 to €2000 per week) that share a glorious heated pool covered by a greenhouse roof.

Fort de Buoux   RUINS
(☑ 04 90 74 25 75; www.lefortdebuoux.e-monsite.com; adult/child €5/4; ☉ 10am-5pm Wed-Mon) Occupied since prehistoric times, the site of this clifftop fortress commands an incredible view over the surrounding valley. Abandoned in the 17th century, it's an atmospheric place to wander – but accessed by a winding, crumbling staircase, so take care as you hike up. Note that due to its exposed position, the fort is closed during heavy rain or high winds.

🛌 Sleeping

Auberge des Seguins   HOTEL €€
(☑ 04 90 74 16 37; www.aubergedesseguins.com; dm incl half-board €44, s €79-89, d €118-138, f €159-239; 🅿 🛜 🏊) Hunkered at the bottom of the valley 2.5km below Buoux, surrounded by sheer cliffs, this lovely old inn feels remarkably secluded. It offers simple, TV-less rooms (some with shared bathrooms) and a dorm in four stone-walled buildings, all with fine valley views. The Provençal restaurant (menu €25) is popular, especially for Sunday lunch; room rates include half-board.

Saignon

Even in a land of heart-stoppingly pretty villages, little Saignon still manages to raise an admiring eyebrow. Perched on a rocky flank, surrounded by lavender fields and overlooked by a crumbling medieval castle, its cobbled streets and central square

WORTH A TRIP

THE LAZY BOAR

There's one reason to make a detour to hilltop Caseneuve, 10km east of Saignon, and that's to eat at **Le Sanglier Paresseux** (The Lazy Boar; ☑ 04 90 75 17 70; www.sanglierparesseux. com; Caseneuve; 2-/3-/4-course menus €32/39/59; ⊙ 12.30-2.30pm & 7.30-9.30pm Wed-Sun May-Oct, plus Tue Jul & Aug, shorter hours Nov-Apr), one of the Luberon's most talked about tables. Cuisine is inventive, unfussy, seasonal and the perfect showcase for regional ingredients – and the view from the vine-shaded terrace is unforgettable. Reservations essential.

(complete with fountain) are the stuff of Provençal dreams.

A short trail leads up to the castle ruins and the aptly titled **Rocher de Bellevue**, a fabulous viewpoint overlooking the entire Luberon range all the way to Mont Ventoux.

🛏 Sleeping

L'Auberge du Presbytère　　　HOTEL €€
(☑ 04 32 52 15 28; www.laubergedupresbytere. com/en; place de la Fontaine; d €95-140, q €165-200; P 🖙 🕿) In the heart of the village, this ivy-covered beauty has comfortable rooms, which are spacious though rather lacking in personality. The terrace restaurant is a fine place to linger over a meal on clear days.

Le Petit Luberon

The westernmost extent of the Luberon massif, the Petit Luberon's craggy hills are interspersed with wooded valleys, vineyards and farms.

It's separated from the Grand Luberon by the slash of the Combe de Lourmarin, which cuts north–south through the mountains and is tracked by the D943 between Bonnieux and Lourmarin.

Bonnieux

POP 1,408

Settled during the Roman era, Bonnieux is another bewitching hilltop town that still preserves its medieval character. It's intertwined with alleys, cul-de-sacs and hidden staircases: from place de la Liberté, 86 steps

lead to 12th-century Église Vieille du Haut. Look out for the alarming crack in one of the walls, caused by an earthquake.

The pleasure here is just to wander – especially if you time your visit for the lively Friday market, which takes over most of the old town's streets.

◉ Sights & Activities

★**Forêt des Cèdres**　　　　　　　FOREST
(⊙ dawn-dusk) In the scrubby hills about 6km south of Bonnieux, a twisty back road slopes up to this wonderful cedar forest, whose spreading boughs provide welcome relief from Provence's punishing summer heat. Various paths wind through the woods, including a nature trail that's accessible for wheelchairs. The trip up to the forest is worth the drive by itself: the wraparound views of the Luberon valley and its *villages perchés* (hilltop towns) are out of this world.

Pont Julien　　　　　　　　　　BRIDGE
Situated 6km north of Bonnieux, near the junction of the D36 and D900, is one of the Luberon's most impressive Roman landmarks. Dating from around 3 BCE, the 85m-long Pont Julien was built to allow the region's main Roman road, the Via Domitia, to traverse the Calavon River. Amazingly, the bridge's three graceful tiers were still carrying cars as recently as 2005 – a testament to the ingenuity and skill of its engineers.

Musée de la Boulangerie　　　　MUSEUM
(☑ 04 90 75 88 34; 12 rue de la République; adult/student/child €3.50/1.50/free; ⊙ 10am-12:30pm & 2.30-6pm Wed-Mon Apr-Oct) A museum all about the history of breadmaking might not sound like a Bonnieux must-see, but it's actually an intriguing visit. Located in a 17th-century building that was used as a bakery until 1920, it explores the baker's art both in Bonnieux and further afield, with antique millstones, tools, vintage posters and various other bread-related exhibits.

🛏 Sleeping

★**La Couleur des Vignes**　　　　　B&B €€
(☑ 06 77 85 97 92; www.lacouleurdesvignes.com; r €130-150; P 🖙 🕿) On the northern edge of the village, this is the kind of place that inspires serious life envy. It feels wonderfully secluded, with fragrant lavender-filled gardens overlooking the Luberon hills, and five rooms named after local villages and stuffed with rustic-chic (thick walls, beams, tiles,

fireplaces). But it's the eye-popping 20m infinity pool that has the real wow factor.

Les Terrasses du Luberon   B&B €€
(☑04 90 75 87 40; www.lesterrassesduluberon.
fr; Quartier les Bruillères; r €155; P🅿🛜🏊) This
house on the edge of Bonnieux makes maximum use of its hillside location to provide
panoramic views, best appreciated with
something ice-cold next to the garden pool.
Rooms are bright, uncluttered and smart;
they're contemporary in style, and all have
their own private entrance, a nice luxury for
a B&B.

★ Maison Valvert   B&B €€€
(☑06 72 22 37 89; www.maisonvalvert.com; rte
de Marseille; d €205-250, treehouse €295; 🛜🏊)
Wow – for our money, this could well be
the most stylish B&B in the Luberon. On an
18th-century *mas* (farm) and lovingly renovated by Belgian owner Cathy, it's straight
out of a designer magazine: neutral-toned
rooms, natural fabrics, solar-heated pool
and fabulous buffet breakfast. For maximum
spoils, go for the ultra-romantic treehouse.

✕ Eating

Bonnieux has some lovely restaurants to
choose from, as well as a marvellous Friday
market.

★ L'Arôme   FRENCH €€€
(☑04 90 75 88 62; www.laromerestaurant.com;
2 rue Lucien Blanc; menus €35-45, mains €25-34;
⊗noon-2pm & 7-9.30pm Fri-Tue, 7-9.30pm Thu)
Lodged in a charming vaulted cellar in Bonnieux, L'Arôme is a pricey but prestigious
address, run by well-respected chef Jean-Michel Pagès. The menu revolves around
gourmet ingredients with impeccable local
provenance, dashed with spice and surprises, and the romantic stone-walled setting is
a winner.

Le Fournil   MODERN FRENCH €€€
(☑04 90 75 83 62; www.lefournil-bonnieux.com;
5 place Carnot; 2-/3-course menus lunch €24.90-
33.50, 2-/3-course dinner €36.50/42.80; ⊗12.30-
2pm & 7.30-9.30pm Wed-Sun) In the middle
of town next to the fountain, 'The Oven' is
another of Bonnieux' most consistent tables.
There's a choice of settings: the swish interior (carved straight into the hillside) or the
lovely terrace beside the village's 17th-century fountain. Either way, the menu's the
same: rich, delicious and very Mediterranean. It also has an ice-cream shop on the
same square.

ⓘ Information

Bonnieux Tourist Office (☑04 90 75 91 90;
www.tourisme-en-luberon.com; 7 place Carnot;
⊗9.30am-12.30pm & 2-6pm Mon-Fri, 2-6pm
Sat) Covers the entire Petit Luberon.

Ménerbes
POP 1144

Hilltop Ménerbes is another wonder for
wandering, with a maze of cobbled alleyways that afford sudden glimpses over the
surrounding valleys. It became famous as
the home of expat British author Peter Mayle, whose books *A Year in Provence* and *Toujours Provence* recounted his tales of renovating a farmhouse just outside the village
in the the late 1980s. He later moved to the
nearby villages of Lourmarin and Vaugines,
and died in 2018.

◉ Sights & Activities

Musée du Tire-Bouchon   MUSEUM
(☑04 90 72 41 58; www.domaine-citadelle.com;
adult/child €5/free; ⊗9am-noon & 2-7pm Apr-Oct,
10am-noon & 2-5pm Mon-Sat Nov-Mar) You have
to be a real wine buff to appreciate this museum – dedicated to the art of the humble
corkscrew. There are more than 1000 of
them on display at Domaine de la Citadelle,
a winery on the D3 toward Cavaillon, where
you can sample Côtes du Luberon.

Maison de la Truffe et du Vin   WINE
(House of Truffle & Wine; ☑04 90 72 38 37; www.
vin-truffe-luberon.com; place de l'Horloge; ⊗10am-
noon & 2.30-6pm daily Apr-Oct, Thu-Sat Nov-Mar)
In the middle of Ménerbes, opposite the
town's 12th-century church, this establishment is home to the Brotherhood of Truffles
and Wine of the Luberon, and represents
60 local *domaines*. From April to October,
there are free wine-tasting sessions daily,
and afterwards you can buy the goods at
bargain-basement prices. Winter brings
truffle workshops.

🛏 Sleeping & Eating

La Bastide de Marie   BOUTIQUE HOTEL €€€
(☑04 90 72 30 20; www.labastidedemarie.com;
64 chemin des Peirelles; d from €350; P🅿❄🛜🏊)
Run by renowned hotelier Jocelyne Sibuet,
this uber-luxurious Provençal bolt-hole oozes designer style from every corner, from the
effortlessly elegant rooms through to the
rustic charm of the restaurant. It's all spoils:
two-tiered swimming pool, four-poster beds
and an utterly lavish breakfast. There's even

a swanky villa and cute *roulotte* (gypsy caravan) for rent. It's about 5km east of Ménerbes along the D3.

Bistrot Le 5   BISTRO €€

(☑ 04 90 72 31 84; 5 place Albert Roure; mains €15-25; ⊗ noon-2.30pm & 7-9.30pm) Lunch with a view? *Mais oui* – and what a view. On the village's edge, this popular bistro boasts a grandstand, tree-shaded terrace overlooking classic Luberon countryside. The food is decent – mainly French bistro standards – and service can be slapdash, but on a warm summer's night, it'll be hard to take your attention away from the scenery anyway.

❶ Getting There & Away

TransVaucluse Line 18 (€2.10. three daily Monday to Saturday) runs from Apt to Bonnieux, Lacoste, Ménerbes and Oppède-le-Vieux en route to Cavaillon.

Lourmarin

POP 1145

As you pass through the Luberon massif via the deep, cliff-lined Combe de Lourmarin, the first village you'll strike is Lourmarin. Once a quiet farming town, it's now a chichi place, its streets lined with upmarket homewares shops and boutiques.

Apart from a walk around town, the main sight of note is the Renaissance Château de Lourmarin. Literary pilgrims might also want to peep into the town cemetery, the last resting place of Albert Camus (1913–60), who was living nearby when he was killed in a car accident in 1960, and the French author Henri Bosco (1888–1976).

◉ Sights

Château de Lourmarin   CASTLE

(☑ 04 90 68 15 23; www.chateau-de-lourmarin.com; adult/child €6.80/3; ⊗ 10am-6.30pm Jul & Aug, 10.30am-12.30pm & 2.30-5.30pm or 6.30pm Sep-Jun) This Renaissance château was the first of its kind in Provence. Built in the 16th century and later expanded, the castle has had a string of aristocratic owners, and is now owned by the Vibert family. Its rooms are filled with impressive antiques and objets d'art.

⌷ Sleeping

Lourmarin makes a good base for exploring the southern side of the Luberon, with several good B&Bs and hotels within easy reach

of town – although you'll need a car to reach most of them.

La Cordière   B&B €

(☑ 04 90 68 03 32; www.cordiere.com; rue Albert Camus; d per 3 nights €210-255, apt per week €450-495; 🖀) In Lourmarin's village centre, this character-rich house, built 1582, surrounds a tiny flower-bedecked courtyard, with adjoining summer kitchen for guests. Rooms are filled with atmospheric Provençal antiques and have spacious bathrooms, and some have self-contained kitchens.

Le Mas de Foncaudette   B&B €€

(☑ 04 90 08 42 51; www.foncaudette.com; d €95-130, tr €135-155, q €155-170; ⊗ Apr-Oct; 🖀🏊) A friendly base on the edge of Lourmarin, in a colourful 16th-century farmhouse surrounding a fig-shaded central courtyard. Rooms are cosy and feminine: we liked split-level Marius (good for families) and Paneloux, with its Moroccan-inspired decor. Owner Aline Edme is full of local knowledge, and the pool's a beauty. It's signposted off the D27 between Lourmarin and Puyvert.

✗ Eating

Market day in Lourmarin is Friday morning, and there's an evening market on Tuesday. The tourist office has a list of the many local wineries.

★ Café Gaby   CAFE €

(☑ 04 90 68 38 42; place de l'Ormeau; dishes €8-14; ⊗ 7am-midnight) There's a strip of cafes on pretty place de l'Orneau, but Café Gaby is the town's beating heart. It's busy throughout the day – from gentlemen stopping in for morning coffee right through to evening pastis – and the menu is full of tempting Provençal treats. It's a place just to sit and watch the south of France in full, fascinating flow.

★ Auberge La Fenière   GASTRONOMY €€€

(☑ 04 90 68 11 79; www.aubergelafeniere.com; rte de Lourmarin, Cadenet; restaurant 5-/7-/9-course menu €55/90/140, bistro mains €18-30; ⊗ restaurant noon-2pm & 7-9pm Thu-Mon, bistro noon-2pm Fri-Tue, 7-9pm Thu-Sat & Mon-Tue; 🖀) It doesn't get more Provençal than this wonderful farmhouse, run by Michelin-starred chef Reine Sammut, who is gradually handing the reins to her daughter, Nadia. The multi-course menus are hymns to Provençal produce, most of which is grown in the Sammuts' *potager* (kitchen garden). The restaurant is unsurprisingly expensive; diners on slighter budgets can opt for the bistro.

The farm also has a selection of lovely, elegant rooms which – considering the prestige of the place – are surprisingly affordable (doubles from €160 to €230). And if you want to learn from the maestros, half-day cooking classes start at €145, including lunch.

ℹ️ Information

Lourmarin Tourist Office (☑ 04 90 68 10 77; lourmarin@luberoncoeurdeprovence.com; place Henri Barthélémy; ⊘ 9am-12.30pm & 1.30-6pm Mon-Sat, 10am-12.30pm & 1.30-6pm Sun Apr-Sep, shorter hours Oct-Mar) A good source of information on both the town and the Luberon area; runs themed walks in season exploring Lourmarin's links to Albert Camus and Henri Bosco (usually in French).

ℹ️ Getting There & Away

TransVaucluse Line 19 (€2.10, every two hours Monday to Saturday) runs from Curcuron to Vaugines, Lourmarin and Cadenet.

From Cadenet, you can catch TransVaucluse bus 8 (flat rate €2.10, hourly Monday to Saturday, two on Sunday) on to Cavaillon.

Ansouis

POP 1100

Little changed in centuries, the part-fortified village of Ansouis has earned its place amongst France's *plus beaux villages* (most beautiful villages). Ramparts, watchtowers and gateways ring the village's old centre and the medieval Château d'Ansouis, which is now privately owned but can be visited on a guided tour. The village is also home to an oddball museum, the Musée Extraordinaire.

◉ Sights

Musée Extraordinaire MUSEUM
(☑ 04 90 09 82 64; www.musee-extraordinaire.fr; adult/child €3.50/1.50; ⊘ 10-7pm Jun-Sep, 2-6pm Oct-May; 🐾) This curious village museum was founded by Provençal painter and diver Georges Mazoyer, whose passion for the sea shows in the museum's fossil exhibits and oceanic art. It's a short walk from the town centre, off Rue du Vieux Moulin.

Château d'Ansouis CASTLE
(☑ 04 90 09 82 70; adult/child €10/1; ⊘ tours 3pm Thu-Mon mid-Apr–mid-Sep) The palatial Château d'Ansouis can be visited by guided tour, and in August it hosts classical-music

THE LUBERON ANSOUIS

WORTH A TRIP

THE LITTLE HOUSE OF CUCURON

If you feel like you've earned a post-hike dinner, you're in luck: Cucuron has its own Michelin-starred bistro, **La Petite Maison de Cucuron** (☑ 04 90 68 21 99; www.lapetitemaisondecucuron.com; place de l'Etang; menus €60-90; ⊘ 12.30-2pm & 8 10pm Wed-Sun), where chef Eric Sapet creates sumptuous things from produce sourced from local farms. It's very upmarket (high heels rather than hiking boots), and reservations are essential. Cooking classes (in French, €80) are held every Saturday morning.

concerts in its courtyard. Tours run at 3pm except on Tuesdays and Wednesdays; there's an extra tour at 4.30pm from mid-June to mid-September.

🍴 Eating

L'Art Glacier ICE CREAM €
(☑ 04 90 77 75 72; www.artglacier.com; Les Hautes Terres; ⊘ hours vary) Go off the beaten path to find ice cream that's an art. Michel and Sigrid Perrière handcraft mind-boggling varieties of the sweet stuff: from lavender to sesame to cassis. The ice-creamery sits between Ansouis and La Tour d'Aigues on a hilltop off the D9 (look for the signs posted on roundabouts).

★ La Closerie FRENCH €€€
(☑ 04 90 09 90 54; www.lacloserieansouis.com; bd des Platanes; lunch menu €35, dinner menus €52-75; ⊘ noon-2pm Fri-Tue, 7-10pm Mon, Tue, Fri & Sat) A renowned fine-dining establishment in Ansouis, overseen by chef Olivier and his wife Delphine. The food here is sophisticated but full of flavour and flair – which explains why it's practically impossible to get a table in season, especially for the excellent-value lunch menu. It feels surprisingly relaxed for a Michelin-starred place, too.

ℹ️ Getting There & Away

Buses to Ansouis are extremely limited, and revolve around the school timetable – so having a car (or bike) is pretty much essential to get here.

Ansouis is about 8km from Pertuis, 15km from Lauris. The only vaguely useful bus is TransVaucluse Line 8, which travels to Cavaillon (€2.10, hourly Monday to Saturday, two on Sunday) via Pertuis and Lauris.

Alpes-de-Haute-Provence

Best Places to Eat

➜ La Bastide de Moustiers (p289)

➜ Le Pesquier (p284)

➜ La Ferme Ste-Cécile (p289)

➜ La Treille Muscate (p289)

➜ Café de Niozelles (p284)

Best Places to Stay

➜ Le Jas du Boeuf (p285)

➜ Les Méans (p294)

➜ La Bastide de Moustiers (p289)

➜ La Fabrique (p288)

➜ Couvent des Minimes (p284)

Why Go?

Provence might conjure up images of rolling fields and gentle hills, but east of the Luberon you'll find yourself travelling through altogether more dramatic landscapes. Rising like a tooth-lined jawbone along the border with Italy, just an hour's drive north of Nice, lie the Alps – France's most famous mountain range, a haven for mountaineers, hikers and wildlife spotters, and home to some of the region's most unforgettable scenery.

Cloaked in snow well into springtime, the mountains of Haute-Provence are divided by six main valleys, connected by some of the highest and most hair-raising road passes anywhere in Europe – an absolute must for road-trippers. At the heart of the area sprawls the huge Parc National du Mercantour, home to a host of rare wildlife, sky-top villages and pristine natural habitats. Make sure you keep the camera close to hand: there's a picture around every corner.

Driving Distances (km)

	Barcelonnette	Castellane	Digne-les-Bains	Forcalquier
Castellane	75			
Digne-les-Bains	76	45		
Forcalquier	120	83	48	
Moustiers Ste-Marie	125	35	47	51

PAYS DE FORCALQUIER

An oft-overlooked area between the Luberon valley and the Alpine foothills, the Pays de Forcalquier is well off the main tourist radar, meaning that its hilltop villages and rolling farms are usually relatively tranquil even in high summer.

It's the portal to Haute-Provence from the Luberon, and the fastest way in from Marseille, too. At its heart lies namesake Forcalquier, famous for its market and absinthe. Saffron grows here, as well as swathes of lavender.

❶ Getting There & Away

Several LER (www.info-ler.com) buses run through the area, connecting Marseille and Aix-en-Provence with the main transport hub of Digne-les-Bains.

Forcalquier

The area's largest town, Forcalquier is an appealing country town with a super morning market, held every Monday. You'll see the town long before you reach it thanks to the gold-topped 'citadel' that crowns the hilltop on which the town sits.

Further afield, the surrounding countryside is great for leisurely exploring: wildflower-tinged countryside, isolated villages, lavender farms and the spectre of the mountains never too far away.

◉ Sights

★ **Prieuré de Salagon**   MONASTERY, GARDENS
(☑04 92 75 70 50; www.musee-de-salagon.com; adult/child €8/6; ◯10am-8pm Jun-Aug, to 7pm May & Sep, to 6pm Oct–mid-Dec & Feb-Apr; ♿) Situated 4km south of Forcalquier near Mane, this peaceful priory dates from the 13th century. It's well worth a visit to wander around

its medieval herb gardens. There's also a show garden of plants from around the world, and a *'jardin de senteurs'* that's been planted especially for its fragrances.

La Citadelle   AREA
To reach Forcalquier's citadel and its little octagonal chapel, it's a 20-minute walk uphill via shady backstreets and winding steps. At the top there's a viewing platform offering panoramic views. On the way back down, keep an eye out for some of the town's impressive wooden doorways, dating from the days when Forcalquier was the pre-Revolutionary seat of power for the Comtes de Provence.

Ecomusée l'Olivier   MUSEUM
(☑04 92 72 66 91; www.ecomusee-olivier.com; adult/child €4/free; ◯10am-1pm & 2-6pm Tue-Sat) 🏴 If all the olive groves around Provence have inspired your curiosity, head 15km southeast of Foraclquier to Volx, where this intriguing eco-museum explains the extraction process and the olive tree's importance to Mediterranean culture. There's also a posh shop where you can pick up souvenirs, and taste olive-oil varieties, as well as an excellent Provençal restaurant, **Les Petites Tables** (☑04 86 68 53 14; www.lespetitestables.net; mains €10-16; ◯noon-3pm Tue-Sat), perfect for lunch.

🛏 Sleeping & Eating

Relais d'Elle   B&B €
(☑06 75 42 33 72, 04 92 75 06 87; www.relaisdelle. com; rte de la Brillane, Niozelles; s/d/tr/q from €60/70/90/115; 🛜🏊) For peace and tranquillity, you can't really quibble with this cosy, farmhouse, surrounded by lovely gardens and a pool. The rooms err towards the traditional rather than the fashionable, with old furniture and dated decor – but the gorgeous grounds and friendly owners make up for what the house lacks in luxury.

ALPES-DE-HAUTE-PROVENCE FORCALQUIER

STARGAZING IN HAUTE-PROVENCE

Driving through the scrubby back roads south of Forcalquier, an unexpected sight appears on the hills: the **Observatoire de Haute-Provence** (☑04 92 70 64 00; www.obs-hp.fr; adult/child €5/3; ◯guided visits 2-5pm Tue-Thu Jul & Aug, 2.15-4pm Wed Sep-Jun), a small dome-shaped observatory built in 1937 near the village of St-Michel-Observatoire to take advantage of Haute-Provence's wonderfully clear night skies. Several times a week in summer (and on Wednesdays the rest of the year), you can take a guided tour of the observatory and learn more about its work. Sometimes, there are night-time star-spotting sessions, too.

Tickets are sold at the **tourist office** (☑04 92 76 69 09; astronomie@haute-provence-tour isme.com; place de la Fontaine; ◯9am-noon & 2-6pm Mon & Wed-Sat) in St-Michel-Observatoire. Tours are generally in French, but some guides speak some English: ask at the tourist office when you buy your ticket.

Alpes-de-Haute-Provence Highlights

1 **Gorges du Verdon** (p286) Tracing the unforgettable clifftop roads around Europe's Grand Canyon.

2 **Vesúbia** (p298) Trying out canyoning, climbing and caving at this stunning activity complex in St-Martin-Vésubie.

3 **Train des Pignes** (p296) Riding this historic railway through the mountains from Nice to Digne-les-Bains.

4 **Alpha** (p298) Watching semi-wild grey wolves at this fascinating wildlife reserve.

5 **Col de Restefond la Bonette** (p297) Tracing the

Tour de France over Europe's highest road pass.

6 **Gorges de Daluis** (p296) Motoring through a maze of scarlet canyons and rocky valleys.

7 **Manosque** (p285) Getting lost among the endless lavender fields.

8 **Vallée des Merveilles** (p300) Admiring the work of ancient rock artists.

9 **Les Grès d'Annot** (p292) Hiking up into a wonderland of cliffs, caves and boulders.

HIKING IN ALPES-DE-HAUTE-PROVENCE

WHERE TO HIKE

A vast 6200km network of trails snakes its way through the mountains, covering practically every type of scenery: soaring peaks, crystal lakes, plunging canyons, grassy lowlands and high pastures – and all within half a day's drive from Nice.

The majority of the trails are located inside the Parc National du Mercantour, a 685-sq-km national park split between seven main valleys: Roya, Tinée, Vésubie, L'Ubaye, Haut Verdon, Haut-Var and Bévéra. Each of the valleys has enough trails to fill a lifetime of walks, so the best idea is to pick one valley and use it as a launchpad to explore: St-Martin-Vésubie (in the Vallée de la Vésubie), Allos (in the Vallée du Haut Verdon), St-Sauveur-sur-Tinée (in the Vallée de la Tinée) or Barcelonnette (in the Vallée du Haut-Var).

Another popular area to hike is around the Gorges du Verdon (p286), France's 'Grand Canyon'. Accessed via the gateway towns of Moustiers-Ste-Marie to the west and Castellane to the east, it's home to some of Provence's most dramatic scenery, as well as a well-marked trail network.

Several long-distance routes (known in France as GR, or *grandes randonnées*) travel through the region, including the GR4 through the Gorges du Verdon, and the GR52 through Parc National du Mercantour.

☆ Classic Haute-Provence Hikes

Vallée des Merveilles (p300; 13km round-trip, Vallée de la Roya) Prehistoric rock-carvings in a mountain valley.

Le Mont Mounier (17.2km from Col de l'Espaule) Full-day ascent to the summit of a 2817m peak.

GR4 (Gorges du Verdon) Five-day trail through the Gallic Grand Canyon.

Lacs de Vens (15km, Vallée de la Tinée) High-level hike to a sparkling twinset of lakes.

Lac d'Allos (4.5km round-trip, Vallée du Haut-Var) Easy half-day hike to a stunning alpine lake.

RESOURCES

Rando Alpes Haute Provence (www.rando-alpes-haute-provence.fr) is one of the best resources with hundreds of route suggestions, pictures, maps and tips. The national park website for the Parc National du Mercantour (www.parc-mercantour.eu) is another useful starting point.

Most local tourist offices have leaflets and trail booklets for suggested walks in their area – for free or a small charge. They can also put you in contact with local mountain guides who lead regular hikes into the mountains, usually starting at around €25 to €30 per person.

If you're hiking without a guide, it's essential to carry a good map (and know how to use it). Main trails are usually well marked, but less-frequented routes can be much more challenging. France's national map-maker, IGN (www.ign.fr), publishes detailed topographical maps for the whole of Haute-Provence. The most useful for hikers are the 1:25,000, blue-backed Série Bleue maps, such as 3741OT Vallée de la Vésubie, 3442OT to the Gorges du Verdon/Moustiers Ste-Marie and 3540OT to the Barcelonnette/

Lac d'Allos (p295), Vallée du Haut Verdon

ELEMENTALIS/GETTY IMAGES ©

They might not have the all-out height of the Alps proper, but the mountains of Haute-Provence still pack a powerfully wild punch, and access to some of France's most awe-inspiring landscapes.

Allos area. All are also available as downloadable maps for GPS units and smartphones – but remember paper maps don't need a battery, and work even after they've been dropped in a puddle.

Though officially covering the neighbouring Alpes-Maritimes département, RandOxygène (www.randoxygene.departement06.fr) is a useful resource for planning hikes in the Parc National du Mercantour, as well as other activities like via ferrata, horse-riding and snowshoeing.

WHEN TO HIKE

Snow lingers long in the high valleys, often well into May, and often returns again in early October – so the hiking season is relatively short. June and September are the perfect months, and usually a lot quieter than the main season in July and August, when many hotels and gîtes (walkers' hostels) are likely to be full. It's also possible to hike in winter in many areas using raclettes (snowshoes) – although unless you're an experienced hiker, it's best to attempt this with a qualified guide due to the risk of avalanche and navigational error.

EQUIPMENT & CLOTHING

As always when you're walking in high places, it's important to be properly equipped. Even in summer, sudden weather systems can sweep through the mountains with surprising speed and ferocity, caused by the meeting of warm air from the south and colder air from the mountains, which often results in fierce summer thunderstorms.

Even in high summer, decent breathable waterproofs (e.g. Gore-tex) and good-quality, wicking fabrics are a must. Dressing in layers allows you to add and remove clothing according to the weather: a base-layer, mid-layer and waterproof shell should be sufficient, plus a warmer fleece in the shoulder months.

For footwear, sturdy, waterproof hiking boots are sensible, as they will cope with all terrains and weathers. Many people prefer the lighter weight of trail or approach shoes, but do be aware that since these lack ankle support, on rougher trails you are more prone to slipping and twisting an ankle. Many hikers carry walking poles to provide extra support.

A day-bag with a detachable cover is also essential, along with trail snacks, energy bars and medical kit, plus plenty of food and water.

CRISTIANO/LESSANDRO/GETTY IMAGES ©

Lacs de Vens, Parc National du Mercantour (p292)

Bergerie La Beaudine
B&B €

(✉ 04 92 75 01 52; www.gite-labeaudine.com; rte de Limans, Forcalquier; s/d/tr €60/75/99; 🛜 🖈) A quietly stylish B&B, with five rooms and a self-contained *gîte*, all decorated in colourful style. The lavender-blue La Béruguette and two-bedroom Sous les toits de Provence are good choices. Outside there's a pleasant pool and outdoor cooking facilities including a barbecue for guest use. It's 2km from town via the D950 toward Banon.

Couvent des Minimes
HOTEL €€€

(✉ 04 92 74 77 77; www.couventdesminimes-hotel spa.com; chemin des Jeux de Maï, Mane; r from €310; 🖈 🛜 🖈) This medieval convent has been turned into one of Provence's most indulgent country retreats courtesy of the luxury Occitane brand. It's a no-expense-spared affair: luminous rooms incorporating the building's ecclesiastical architecture, a wonderful spa and pool, a belt-buster Michelin-starred restaurant, **Le Cloître** (menus from €75) and a more affordable bistro, **Le Pesquier** (menus €35 to €45). It's in Mane, 3.5km south of Forcalquier on the D4100.

Café de Niozelles
PROVENCAL, ITALIAN €€

(✉ 04 92 73 10 17; www.bistrot-niozelles.fr; place du Village, Niozelles; set menu €26; ⏱ 12.30-2.30pm & 7-9pm Fri-Wed; 🖈) For just-like-mama-made-it French cuisine, it's worth the 5km drive from Forcalquier to this apologetically old-school bistro in Niozelles. You'll need an appetite, and a taste for all the traditional trimmings, like offal, tripe and sheep trotters, but you won't find a more authentic French meal in the Pays de Forcalquier.

Aux Deux Anges
BISTRO €€

(✉ 04 92 75 04 36; 3 place St-Michel, Forcalquier; menus from €17.50; ⏱ noon-1.30pm Wed-Sun, 7-10.30pm Wed-Mon) Beside a fountain in Forcalquier's old town, this homespun place is as traditional as it gets. All the dishes are made to timeworn recipes *comme à la maison* (like you'd have at home) – hearty stews, slow-cooked lamb and the like, simply served with vegetables. Far from fancy, but flavoursome – and the junk shop interior is fun.

ℹ Information

Forcalquier Tourist Office (✉ 04 92 75 10 02; www.haute-provence-tourisme.com; 13 place du Bourguet; ⏱ 9am-noon & 2-6pm Mon-Sat) The main source of information on the area; ask for leaflets on local walks and bike rides.

ℹ Getting There & Around

LER (www.info-ler.fr) operates buses to/from Forcalquier.

LER Bus 25 (four daily Monday to Saturday, two on Sunday) Runs direct from Marseille (€18.60, two hours) and Aix-en-Provence (€12, 1½ hours) to Forcalquier, stopping at Volx and Manosque.

LER Line 22 (four daily, one or two on Sundays) Travels to Avignon (€16.80, 2 hours 20 minutes), and to Digne-les-Bains (€9.80, one hour) in the opposite direction.

Bachelas Cycles (✉ 04 92 75 12 47; www. bachelas-cycles.com; 5 bd de la République; per day/week from €19/81; ⏱ 9am-12.30pm & 2-7pm Mon-Wed, Fri & Sat) rents mountain, road, tandem and electric bicycles.

Banon

POP 940 / ELEV 760M

The little village of Banon is famous for its eponymous cheese, *chèvre de Banon* – made from goat's milk, wrapped in a chestnut leaf and tied with raffia string. It's a prized local delicacy, eaten both fresh and cooked. You'll see it for sale at many local markets, including Banon's own on Tuesday morning. The town also hosts its own **cheese festival** in May.

◎ Sights

Fromagerie de Banon
FARM

(✉ 04 92 73 25 03; www.fromagerie-banon.fr; rte Carniol; ⏱ 2.30-5.30pm Mon-Fri Apr-Oct) This family-run cheese farm near Banon makes superb *chèvre de Banon* (Banon goat's cheese). It's about 3.5km south of the village along the D51; look for signs on the left as you head south.

✕ Eating

Les Vins au Vert
BISTRO €

(✉ 04 92 75 23 84; www.restaurant-caviste-ba non-04.fr; rue Pasteur; menus €13.50-15; ⏱ 10am-3pm & 5.30-11pm Thu-Sat, 10am-3pm Wed & Sun) The pick of the places to eat in Banon: an informal bistro-bar, which has a prodigious selection of local wines by the glass, partnered with delicious meat and cheese platters. It's all quite relaxed, with simple wooden tables and shelves lined with wine bottles.

Brindille Melchio
FOOD €

(✉ 04 92 73 23 05; place de la République; ⏱ 8am-12.30pm & 2.30-6.30pm Wed-Sun Sep-Jun, 8am-7pm daily Jul & Aug) Picnic supplies galore are on offer at this friendly grocer's on the village square. There's a great cheese selection, as well as homemade charcuterie and sausages.

ℹ️ Information

Tourist Office (☑ 04 92 72 19 40; www.haute provencepaysdebanon-tourisme.fr; place de la République; ⊙ 9am-12.30pm & 3-6pm Tue-Sat year-round, plus 10am-noon Sun Jul & Aug) The village's tourist office is on the main square.

VALLÉE DE LA DURANCE

Halfway between the Luberon and the high Alps lies the broad, flat floodplain of the River Durance. Centuries ago, this natural pass was crossed by the Via Domitia – the main road that enabled Roman legionnaries and traders to travel through the south of Gaul. It's now crossed by a more modern equivalent: the A8 motorway.

The area is also famous for its lavender fields, especially around **Manosque** and the nearby Plateau de Valensole. Many growers offer guided visits and sell products direct: ask in any local tourist office for one of the free *Routes de la Lavande* leaflets.

◉ Sights

Les Mées   ARCHAEOLOGICAL SITE
Travelling north from Forcalquier towards Sisteron, you can't miss the mysterious Rochers des Mées: rows and rows of rocky pinnacles, some as high as 100m. Legend claims they were once monks, turned to stone for lusting after Saracen women. A loop trail travels through the formations, taking around 3½ hours from end to end.

Monastère Notre Dame
de Ganagobie   MONASTERY
(☑ 04 92 68 00 04; www.ndganagobie.com; Ganagobie; ⊙ 3-5pm Tue-Sun, shop 10.30am-noon & 2.30-6pm Tue-Sun) Ganagobie's otherworldly monastery is an essential stop. Founded in the 10th century, it's still home to a working Benedictine community, whose products, including soap, honey, jam and beer, are all for sale in the monastery shop. The chapel (worth a visit for its fabulous 12th-century floor mosaics) is the only area open to the public, but you're free to wander around most of the grounds.

Citadelle de Sisteron   FORT
(☑ 04 92 61 27 57; www.citadelledesisteron.fr; Sisteron; adult/child €6.60/2.90; ⊙ 9am-6pm Apr-Oct, to 7.30pm Jul & Aug) For the finest views of the valley, head to Sisteron's hilltop citadel, perched on a rock high above the town. Built in stages between the 13th and 16th centuries, it was badly damaged by bombardment in August 1944 but has since been meticulously restored.

WORTH A TRIP

SEAT OF POWER

Forming part of the 12th-century fortified castle built by the Simiane-Agoult family, who were one of the region's most powerful medieval dynasties, **Château de Simiane-la-Rotonde** (www.simiane-la-rotonde.fr; Simiane-la-Rotonde; adult/12-18yr/under 12yr €5.50/3.50/free; ⊙ 10.30am-1pm & 2-7pm May-Aug, 1.30-6pm Wed-Sun Mar, Apr & Sep–mid-Nov) is notable for its magnificent central cupola, graced by a soaring dome, 12 supporting ribs and a forest of decorative columns and intricate stonework. It's a masterpiece of medieval engineering, and every August provides the unforgettable setting for classical-music festival **Les Riches Heures Musicales de la Rotonde**.

🛏️ Sleeping & Eating

⭐ **Le Jas du Boeuf**   B&B €€
(☑ 04 92 79 01 05; www.lejasduboeuf.fr; Lieu dit Parrot, Cruis; r €80-115, bungalow €90-135; 🅿 ❄ 🤚 🛜 ⛱) A ravishing pool, a beautiful stone farmhouse and impeccably styled rooms are the selling points at this B&B, run by Jérôme Mantel and Dana Silk. Despite the rural location near Cruis, the vibe is big-city boutique: two garden lodges, plus two rooms in the main house, all clean-lined and Scandi-sleek – and an absolute corker of a pool.

La Magnanerie   HOTEL €€
(☑ 04 92 62 60 11; www.la-magnanerie.net; N85, Aubignosc; r €81-113, menus €17-25; ⊙ restaurant noon-1.30pm & 7-9.30pm Wed-Sun; 🤚) This roadside hotel makes a pleasant stopover 9km southeast of Sisteron. The rooms are imaginatively decorated, with themes such as 'cinema' and 'city'; the more expensive suites have freestanding baths and modern furniture. The restaurant is good, too, with bistro-style dishes and an attractive garden.

ℹ️ Information

Sisteron Tourist Office (☑ 04 92 61 36 50; www.sisteron-tourisme.fr; 1 place de la République) Sisteron's tourist office.

ℹ️ Getting There & Away

LER Buses (Lignes Express Régionales; ☑ 08 21 20 22 03; www.info-ler.fr) connect Forcalquier, Mane and St-Michel l'Observatoire with Apt, Avignon, Digne-les-Bains, Sisteron, Manosque, Aix-en-Provence and Marseille.

WORTH A TRIP

THE ROAD OF TIME

The Route du Temps (Road of Time) is a signed route that winds through some of the area's most dramatic valleys, historical sites and rock formations; it starts just north of Sisteron and follows the D3 to St-Geniez, up and over Col de Font-Belle (1304m) to the medieval fortified village of Thoard.

Interpretive panels along the way explain what you're seeing, and if you fancy a closer look, various trails criss-cross their way into the surrounding hills.

In total, it's a journey of around two to three hours, depending on how many stops you make. For further information and a route map (€2), contact the Sisteron tourist office (p285).

GORGES DU VERDON

For sheer, jaw-dropping drama, few sights in France can match the epic Gorges du Verdon. The 'Grand Canyon of Europe' slices a 25km swath through Haute-Provence's limestone plateau all the way to the foothills of the Alps. Etched out over millions of years by the Verdon River, the gorges have formed the centrepiece of the Parc Naturel Régional du Verdon since 1997. With their sheer, plunging cliffs – in some places 700m high, twice the height of the Eiffel Tower – the gorges are a haven for birds, including a colony of reintroduced *vautours fauves* (griffon vultures).

The main gorge begins at Rougon, near the confluence of the Verdon and Jabron Rivers. The most useful jumping-off points are Moustiers Ste-Marie, in the west, and Castellane, in the east.

🏃 Activities

From the top of the cliffs, the Verdon River itself seems little more than a silver trickle, but down at gorge level it takes on a different character: it's one of France's best spots for white-water rafting. The canyon floors are only accessible by foot or raft, and it's worth experiencing the gorges from both bottom and top to get a proper sense of their brain-boggling size.

Cycling & Driving

A complete circuit of the Gorges du Verdon from Moustiers Ste-Marie involves 140km of driving, not to mention a relentless series of hairpin turns. There's a cliffside road on either side of the gorges, but passing spots are rare, roads are narrow and rockfalls are possible – so take it slow and enjoy the scenery.

Spring and autumn are ideal times to visit: the roads can be traffic-clogged in summer and icy in winter. The only village en route is La Palud-sur-Verdon (930m), so make sure you've got a full tank of gas before setting out.

⭐ **Route des Crêtes**   DRIVING TOUR
(D952 & D23; ⊘ mid-Mar–mid-Nov) A 23km-long loop with 14 lookouts along the northern rim with drop-dead vistas of the plunging Gorges du Verdon. En route the most thrilling view is from Belvédère de l'Escalès – one of the best places to spot vultures overhead.

You'll see signs for the route as you drive through La Palud-sur-Verdon. Note that the road is generally closed outside April to October due to snowfall.

Walking & Hiking

Dozens of blazed trails traverse the wild countryside around Castellane and Moustiers. Tourist offices carry the excellent, English-language *Canyon du Verdon* (€4.70), detailing 28 walks, as well as maps of five principal walks (€2.40).

Note that wild camping anywhere in the gorges is illegal. Don't cross the river, except at bridges, and always stay on marked trails, lest you get trapped when the upstream dam opens, which happens twice weekly. Check water levels and the weather forecast with local tourist offices before embarking.

⭐ **Verdon Nature**   WALKING
(☎ 06 82 23 21 71; www.verdon-nature.com; per person €25) Local man Laurent Pichard runs excellent guided walks into the gorges, including vulture-spotting trips, nature hikes and guided routes following several classic hiking paths. He also offers a sunset walk and a night sleeping under the stars including the gorges' highest summit, Le Grand Margès.

Outdoor Sports

Castellane is the main water-sports base (April to September); its tourist office has lists of local operators. Most charge similar rates for rafting, canyoning, kayaking and hydrospeed expeditions: around €35 for two hours, €55 for a half-day and €75 for a full day. Safety kit is provided, but you'll get (very) wet, so dress appropriately. Reservations are required.

Lac de Castillon's beaches are popular for swimming and paddle boating, while St-André-les-Alpes, on the lakeshore, is France's leading paragliding centre.

Des Guides pour l'Aventure   OUTDOORS
(☑06 85 94 46 61; www.guidesaventure.com) Offers activities including canyoning (from €50 per half-day), rock climbing (€45 for three hours), rafting (€45 for 2½ hours) and 'floating' (€50 for three hours) – which is like rafting, except you have a buoyancy aid instead of a boat.

Yeti Rafting   RAFTING
(www.verdon-rafting.com; 12 blvd de la République; ☺Apr-Sep) Rafting, cano-rafting, airboating, canyoning and plenty more besides. Activities start around €35 per day. Most guides speak some English.

Bureau des Guides de Canyon   RAFTING
(☑04 92 83 05 64; www.procanyon.com; 3 rue du Mazeau) This experienced outfit is a good one-stop shop for thrills and spills in the gorge, with packages including rafting, canyoning, climbing and via ferrata.

Latitude Challenge   ADVENTURE SPORTS
(☑04 91 09 04 10; www.latitude-challenge.fr; bungee jumps €130) Bungee jumps from Europe's highest bungee site, the 182m Pont de l'Artuby (Artuby Bridge). Also offers skydiving.

Wildlife Watching
Sortie de Découverte des Vautours du Verdon   WILDLIFE WATCHING
(☑04 92 83 61 14; adult/child €10/6; ☺9.30am & 6pm Tue, Wed & Fri mid-Jun–mid-Sep) Guided tours to watch vultures in the Gorges du Verdon. Book through the tourist office in Castellane.

ℹ Information

Castellane Tourist Office (☑04 92 83 61 14; www.castellane-verdontourisme.com; rue Nationale; ☺9am-7.30pm daily Jul & Aug, 9am-noon & 2-6pm Mon-Sat, 10am-1pm Sun May-Jun & Sep, closed Sun rest of year) On the east side of the gorges, Castellane's tourist office is the best source for info on river trips and climbing expeditions, as well as general info on the Gorges du Verdon.

Moustiers Ste-Marie Tourist Office (☑04 92 74 67 84; www.moustiers.eu; passage du Cloître; ☺9.30am-7pm Mon-Fri, 9.30am-12.30pm & 2-7pm Sat & Sun Jul & Aug, 10am-noon & 2-6pm Apr-Jun & Sep, closes around 5pm Oct-Mar; ⊚) This pretty town acts as the gateway point to the western side of the gorges, and

its tourist office is extremely well informed, organises activities and has free wi-fi too.

Verdon Tourisme (www.verdontourisme.com) Excellent online resource for exploring the gorges.

ℹ Getting There & Away

BUS
Public transport in the gorges is limited, but the useful **Navette des Gorges du Verdon** (☑04 92 34 22 90; autocars.delaye@orange.fr) shuttle bus links Castellane with Point Sublime, La Palud and La Maline (but not Moustiers). Services run twice daily in July and August and on weekends April to June and in September. The fare costs between €2 and €6.

There are also three daily **buses** (☑08 21 20 22 03; www.info-ler.fr) from Marseille to Riez (€17.50). At least one bus a day continues to Moustiers, La Palud and Castellane, then returns along the same route. The single fare from Moustiers to Castellane is €7.30.

TRAIN
The **Train des Pignes** (p296) travels north of the gorges: the nearest stops are at St-André-les-Alpes, 21km north of Castellane, and Barrême, 25km northwest.

ℹ Getting Around

Apart from the Navette des Gorges du Verdon shuttle bus, the only real way to properly explore the gorges is either to cycle or to drive – although be warned that traffic on the narrow roads can be extremely heavy in July and August – and reversing along some of the narrower, single-track roads is not for the faint-hearted.

Moustiers Ste-Marie
POP 710 / ELEV 634M

Huddled at the base of soaring cliffs, the picturesque village of Moustiers Ste-Marie is unquestionably the prettiest spot anywhere near the Gorges du Verdon, for which it serves as a useful gateway. Lining either side of a river valley, the village's main claim to fame is the Chapelle Notre Dame de Beauvoir, a 14th-century chapel that teeters precariously on the edge of a steep canyon. A winding staircase leads up to the church for epic views over the surrounding plains.

The village is also known for its long tradition of faience (fine pottery); you'll find endless shops round the village touting their wares. Avoid July and August if you can, when Moustiers' car parks are full to bursting, and the village's charms are smothered.

⊙ Sights

★ Chapelle Notre Dame de Beauvoir
CHURCH

High above the village, Moustiers' 14th-century church clings to a cliff ledge like an eagle's nest. A steep trail climbs beside a waterfall to the chapel, passing 14 stations of the cross en route. High above, a 227m-long chain bearing a shining gold star is stretched between the cliff walls – a tradition, legend has it, begun by the Knight of Blacas, in return for his safe return from the Crusades.

Musée de la Faïence
MUSEUM

(☑ 04 92 74 61 64; rue Seigneur de la Clue; adult/child €3/free; ⊙ 10am-12.30pm Jul & Aug, to 5pm or 6pm rest of year, closed Tue year-round) Moustiers' decorative faience (glazed earthenware) once graced the tables of Europe's most aristocratic houses. Today each of Moustiers' 15 ateliers has its own style, from representational to abstract. Antique masterpieces are housed in this little museum, adjacent to the town hall.

🛌 Sleeping

Clos des Iris
HOTEL €

(☑ 04 92 74 63 46; www.closdesiris.fr; chemin de Quinson; d €75-90, f €120-160; ⊙ Jan-Sep; 🅿🛜) The kind of pretty-as-a-picture French hotel that you thought just couldn't exist any more – shutters, pergolas, Provençal colours, verdant gardens and all. Each of the nine bedrooms has a little patio where you can enjoy breakfast. The owners also run a four-bed self-catering cottage down the road.

Ferme du Petit Ségriès
FARMSTAY €

(☑ 04 92 74 68 83; www.chambre-hote-verdon.com; d €79-89; 🛜) This rural, vine-covered farmhouse is a real bargain, with five pleasant rooms and a lovely location deep in the countryside, 5km west of Moustiers on the D952 to Riez. It's not fancy, but it's extremely good value considering that the rates include breakfast.

★ La Fabrique
B&B €€

(☑ 06 95 36 08 31; www.lafabrique04360.com; La Maladrerie, rte de Riez; d €98-135, f €135-150; 🅿🛜) If you enjoy architectural grand designs, you'll adore this wonderful B&B. Inside the handsome brick shell (a former factory) are gorgeous, clean-lined, screamingly elegant rooms, with industrial touches like exposed brick and industrial-style sliding doors. Downstairs is the former factory floor, now a design-mag dream, complete with steel staircase, floor-to-ceiling windows, pendant lights and a vast refectory table where breakfast is served.

★ La Ferme Rose
HOTEL €€

(☑ 04 92 75 75 75; www.lafermerose.com; chemin de Peyrengue; d €85-159; ❋🛜) The Pink Farm is quirkiness and charm personified. Inside its rosy-pink, Italianate facade, you'll find a treasure trove of collectables – from vintage soda siphons and antique film projectors to a display case of coffee grinders. Even bet-

---

WORTH A TRIP

LACS DE STE-CROIX & DE QUINSON

The largest of the lakes in Parc National Régional du Verdon, Lac de Ste-Croix (southwest of Moustiers Ste-Marie) is a reservoir formed in 1974. It has scads of watercraft – windsurfers, canoes, kayaks – to rent; try **L'Étoile** (☑ 04 94 70 22 48; single/double kayak per hour €8/15, 5-person pedalo €15; ⊙ 10am-6pm Apr-Sep). Pretty Bauduen sits on its southeastern banks.

Lac de Quinson lies at the southernmost foot of the lower Gorges du Verdon. In the village of Quinson, taxidermy-rich **Musée de la Préhistoire des Gorges du Verdon** (☑ 04 92 74 09 59; www.museeprehistoire.com; rte de Montmeyan; adult/child €8/6; ⊙ 10am-8pm Jul & Aug, to 6pm Wed-Mon low season, closed mid-Dec–end Jan; 🐾) explores the gorges' natural history and archaeological treasures. From March to October, it organises monthly expeditions to the Grotte de la Baume Bonne, a prehistoric cave.

Nearby Allemagne-en-Provence is named for Roman goddess of fertility Alemona. Her likeness appears on the village's focal point, the turret-topped 12th- to 16th-century **Château d'Allemagne** (☑ 04 92 77 46 78; www.chateaudallemagneprovence.com; Allemagne-en-Provence; guided tours adult/child €7/free; ⊙ tours 4pm & 5pm Tue-Sun Jul–mid-Sep, Sat & Sun only Easter-Jun & mid-Sep–Oct) – straight from a fairy tale.

Several campsites dot the lake shores, such as the **Domaine du Petit Lac** (☑ 04 92 74 67 11; www.lepetitlac.com; rte des Salles en Verdon; 2-person campsite for 4 nights from €38; ⊙ mid-Apr–mid-Oct; @🛜🏊) , a large activity-oriented campsite that also has wooden chalets and mobile homes. The nearest B&Bs, hotels and bus connections are in Moustiers Ste-Marie.

ter, the rooms (all colour-coded and themed accordingly) are charming, looking out onto dreamy, flower-filled gardens.

Eating

La Grignotière
PROVENCAL €

(☑ 04 92 74 69 12; rte de Ste-Anne; mains €10-35; ☺ 11.30am-10pm May-Sep, to 6pm Feb–mid-May) Hidden behind the soft-pink facade of Moustiers' Musée de la Faïence is this peaceful garden restaurant. Tables sit between olive trees and the colourful, eye-catching decor – including the handmade glassware – is the handiwork of talented, dynamic owner Sandrine. Cuisine is 'picnic chic', meaning lots of creative salads, tapenades, quiches and so on.

★ La Ferme Ste-Cécile
GASTRONOMY €€

(☑ 04 92 74 64 18; www.ferme-ste-cecile.com; D952; 2-/3-course menu €30/39; ☺ noon-2pm & 7.30-10pm Tue-Sat, noon-2pm Sun) Just outside Moustiers, this wonderful *ferme auberge* (country inn) immerses you in the full Provençal dining experience, from the sun-splashed terrace and locally picked wines right through to the chef's meticulous Mediterranean cuisine. It's about 1.2km from Moustiers; look out for the signs as you drive towards Castellane.

La Treille Muscate
PROVENCAL €€

(☑ 04 92 74 64 31; www.restaurant-latreillemus cate.fr; place de l'Église; lunch/dinner menus from €28/38; ☺ noon-2pm & 7.30-10.30pm Fri-Tue, noon-2pm Wed) The top place to eat in the village proper: classic Provençal cooking served with panache, either in the stone-walled dining room or on the terrace with valley views. Expect sophisticated, rather formal dishes, all heavy on the Provençal ingredients but treated with a light touch. Reservations recommended.

★ La Bastide de Moustiers
GASTRONOMY €€€

(☑ 04 92 70 47 47; www.bastide-moustiers.com; chemin de Quinson; menus €60-90; ☺ 12.30-1.30pm & 7.30-9pm, closed Oct-Feb) A legendary table of Provence, founded by chef supremo Alain Ducasse. As you'd expect from this Michelin-starred, much-lauded restaurant, it's a temple to French cuisine – from the playful *amuses bouches* to the rich, sauce-heavy mains and indulgent desserts. Much of the produce comes from the inn's own kitchen garden. Dress very smartly, and reserve well ahead.

❶ Getting There & Away

LER bus 27 (www.info-ler.fr) travels from Marseille and Aix-en-Provence direct to Moustiers Ste-Marie

(€18.90), then continues on to La Palud and Castellane before heading back the way it came.

Moustiers is also served by the **Navette des Gorges du Verdon** (p287).

Castellane
POP 1539 / ELEV 723M

At the eastern end of the gorges, Castellane is a run-of-the-mill town, teeming with visitors in summer and all but deserted out of season.

Its main feature is the amazing Chapelle Notre Dame du Roc – a truly impressive sight, perched high above the town on a 184m-high rock pillar. On 15 August (Assumption Day) pilgrims ascend by torchlight for Mass.

◉ Sights

Chapelle Notre Dame du Roc
CHURCH

This hillside chapel sits high above Castellane at an altitude of 903m, wedged into a cleft between the mountains and offering a panoramic view across the valley. There has been a chapel of some form since the 9th century, although the present structure largely dates from later reconstruction in the 18th century. The chapel is accessed via a steep, winding path from town; allow about an hour there and back, or a bit longer if you take it slow.

Musée Sirènes et Fossiles
MUSEUM

(☑ 04 92 83 19 23; place Marcel Sauvaire; adult/child €4/2; ☺ 10am-1pm & 3pm-6.30pm daily Apr, Jul & Aug, Wed, Sat & Sun only May, Jun & Sep, closed Oct-Mar; ⊞) Mermaids and fossils feature at this worthwhile paleontology museum, which explores the geological past of the Alps – hard to believe this whole mountain range once lay at the bottom of a vast temperate sea. It's worth combining with a walk along the 2km **Sentier des Siréniens** (Col des Lèques), which passes through areas of ancient fossils.

⌸ Sleeping

Mas du Verdon
B&B €

(☑ 04 92 83 73 20; www.masduverdon.com; Quartier d'Angles; r €65-79, apt €99-106; ☺ Apr-Oct; ☎) ✦ It's well worth heading a little east of town (1.5km to be precise) to find this attractive B&B, on a hillock with views over the Verdon's banks. It's lodged inside an attractive 18th-century farmhouse, and offers four rooms named after herbs and flowers, as well as three self-catering apartments. *Table d'hôte* (set menu) dinners cost €24 per person, or €30 with wine.

PHOTOGRAPHY BY BERT.DESIGN/GETTY IMAGES ©

JACQUES VANNI/SHUTTERSTOCK ©

PHILIP LEE HARVEY/LONELY PLANET ©

ELEMENTALS/SHUTTERSTOCK ©

3

1. Train des Pignes (p296)

This picturesque train track travels through more than 50 tunnels and over 16 viaducts.

2. Mont Ventoux (p248)

The 1912m summit of this Vaucluse mountain is visible for miles around.

3. Ibex, Parc National Du Mercantour (p292)

This vast national park is home to ibex, along with mouflon, golden eagles and wild grey wolves.

4. Route des Crêtes (p286)

Winding along the Gorges du Verdon, this driving tour offers jaw-dropping scenery.

Gîte de la Baume
HOSTEL, B&B €€

(☎04 92 83 70 82; www.gite-de-la-baume.com; La Baume; dm €25, d €75-90; P ☎) What a cracking retreat this is, 9km north of Castellane. It's a friendly *auberge* (country inn) which offers surprisingly smart rooms (nearly all with some kind of a view) and a delicious, rustic *table d'hôte* (set menu) dinner (€20) in its restaurant, Aux Delices du Verdon. Half-board rates are available if you're staying overnight, or you can just visit for supper.

Nouvel Hôtel du Commerce
HOTEL €€

(☎04 92 83 61 00; www.hotel-du-commerce-verdon. com; place Marcel Sauvaire; d €135-180, tr €195-270, f €260-370; ☺Apr-Oct; P ☎ ☎) By far the best of the town-centre hotels overlooking Castellane's main square, with rooms decorated in 'comfort' and 'superior' styles. Both are smart, with wooden floors and cool colour schemes; some overlook the square, others the garden. Rates include breakfast and free parking.

❶ Getting There & Away

LER (www.info-ler.fr) provides most of the useful buses to/from Castellane.

Bus 27 Travels from Marseille and Aix-en-Provence to Castellane (€26.70, daily, 3¾ hours), stopping at Moustiers Ste-Marie (€7.30) en route.

Bus 30 (€17.30, two daily, 2¼ hours) Travels from Nice to Castellane, then heads on to Digne-les-Bains, Sisteron and ultimately Grenoble.

PARC NATIONAL DU MERCANTOUR

This vast national park covers seven alpine valleys and an area of 685 sq km. Marked by deep valleys and jagged peaks, and dominated by the Cime du Gélas (3143m), it's a haven for outdoor activities: skiing and snowboarding in winter, and hiking and biking in summer.

It's also celebrated for its flora and fauna, including rare ibex, mouflon, golden eagles

> **WORTH A TRIP**
>
> ### LES GRÈS D'ANNOT
>
> A hike up to **Les Grès d'Annot** – massive, fractured stone blocks above the town of Annot – is well worth the effort. Caused by volcanic activity 35 million years ago, they've been sculpted into wondrous forms by millennia of erosion. The site covers an area of around 150 hectares crossed by several hiking trails.

and wild grey wolves, which you can see at the excellent Alpha wolf park (p298) near the mountain village of St-Martin-Vésubie. The park is at the forefront over the debate of the return of the wild wolf to France: after more than a century of absence, wolf numbers are increasing – a cause of celebration for conservationists, and of deep anger for local farmers.

❶ Information

The official online portal for the park (www.mercantour-parcnational.fr) has background information on activities, areas to visit and conservation issues. It's in French, but a less comprehensive English-language site can also be visited.

There are information centres in several villages, including **St-Étienne-de-Tinée** (p297), **St-Martin-Vésubie** (p299) and **Valberg** (p296), which can provide you with trail maps, weather updates, accommodation advice and more. The main park office is in **Nice** (Map p56; ☎04 93 16 78 88; www. mercantour-parcnational.fr; 23 rue d'Italie).

❶ Getting There & Away

High-sided gorges make for spectacular driving, especially along canyons such as the Gorges de Daluis, where mineral deposits glow red.

Most of the valleys are served by local buses, but often services only run once or twice a day. The **Train des Pignes** (p296) from Nice to Digne-les-Bains passes through the national park, stopping at Entrevaux and Annot.

Note that mountain passes connecting the valleys are usually closed by snow from October to May – roads leading up to the passes indicate whether they are open or closed to road traffic.

Digne-les-Bains
POP 17,680 / ELEV 608M

An ancient crossroads (named for its hot-spring spa, known to the Romans), Digne-les-Bains is the capital of the *département* of Alpes-de-Haute-Provence. It's the largest town around and an important lavender processing centre, but it's a little short on must-see sights. It's useful as a stop if you're travelling from the Luberon to the mountains, or as a gateway to the Parc National du Mercantour.

◉ Sights & Activities

★ **Musée Promenade**
MUSEUM

(☎04 92 36 70 70; www.museepromenade.com; 10 montée Bernard Dellacasagrande; adult/child €7/5; ☺9am-7pm Jul & Aug, 9am-noon & 2-5.30pm Apr-Jun & Sep-Nov, closed some weekends in low season) Situated 2km north of Digne-les-Bains in St-Bénoît, en route to Barle, this museum and park features four trails that explore the region's geology and natural history. Highlights include a sculpture park, a Japanese garden, a waterfall and the Jardin des Papillons (butterfly garden), which attracts more than half of France's butterfly species.

Musée de la Lavande   MUSEUM

(☑ 04 92 31 14 90; www.musee-lavande-digne.fr; 32 bd Gassendi; adult/child €5.50/free; ⊙ 10am-6pm daily Jul & Aug, noon-6pm Mon, 10am-6pm Tue-Sat Sep-Jun) Opened in 2015, this museum in Digne explores Provence's lavender-growing culture through multimedia displays, explanatory panels, archive materials and vintage equipment. There's some interesting testimony on industrialisation since the heyday of the 1920s. It also holds distilling displays in its courtyard during summer.

Musée Gassendi   MUSEUM

(☑ 04 92 31 45 29; www.musee-gassendi.org; 64 blvd Gassendi; adult/student €4/free; ⊙ 11am-7pm Apr-Sep, 9am-noon & 1.30-5.30pm Mon-Fri, 1.30-5.30pm Sat & Sun Oct-Mar) An oddball mix of exhibits are on show at Digne's main museum – from 19th-century Provençal paintings and natural history exhibits to contemporary art. The most interesting part lies outside the museum, where several outdoor sculptures by Goldsworthy have been placed in the surrounding hills, linked by a 10-day hike. It's collectively known as the **Refuge d'Art** (www.refugedart.fr), and the tourist office can provide a map if you want to find them.

Via Ferrata du Rocher
de Neuf Heures   CLIMBING

(www.ot-dignelesbains.fr; ⊙ 6am-8pm high season, 8am-5pm low season) Inspired by the system of fixed ladders and cables that Italian troops used to travel through the Dolomites in WWII, Digne's via ferrata course allows you all the thrill of rock climbing without the need for experience. If you've done it before, you can rent the necessary kit at the tourist office – or arrange a guide if it's your first time.

🛏 Sleeping & Eating

⭐ Hôtel Villa Gaïa   HISTORIC HOTEL €€

(☑ 04 92 31 21 60; www.hotel-villagaia-digne.com; 24 rte de Nice; s €65-120, d €84-150, f €140-180; ⊙ Apr-Oct; ℗ 🛜) Digne's hotels leave a lot to be desired, so it's worth heading 2km west of town to this lovely 19th-century villa, brimful of antiques. It feels like the private mansion it once was, with Italianate gardens, tennis court, library and grand dining room. *Tables d'hôte* by reservation. The gate shuts at 11pm.

WORTH A TRIP

HAUTE-PROVENCE
GEOLOGICAL RESERVE

Millions of years ago the Alps sat at the bottom of a vast temperate sea, leaving behind millions of fossils pressed into the rock – including ammonites, trilobites and even the footprints of prehistoric birds. Spread across the **Réserve Géologique de Haute-Provence**, they offer a window into the past – but you'll need a car (and the official map, available at tourist offices) to find them. Take a full day to cover the reserve's 18 sites – especially if you want to combine it with a visit to the Musée Promenade.

L'Olivier   FRENCH €€

(☑ 04 92 31 47 41; 1 rue des Monges; mains €10-18, 3-course menu €27; ⊙ noon-2pm & 7-10pm Thu-Mon) Classic French food, friendly service and a parasol-shaded street terrace make this one of Digne's better dining options. Expect dishes such as thyme-infused lamb and confit duck leg – and if in doubt, just plump for a bargain €10 *plat du jour* (dish of the day).

ℹ Information

Digne Tourist Office (☑ 04 92 36 62 62; www.ot-dignelesbains.fr; place du Tampinet; ⊙ 9am-noon & 2-6pm, closed weekends winter) One of the main information hubs for the region.

ℹ Getting There & Away

BUS

Digne is one of the most useful hubs for bus transport in the region. Most long-distance buses are run by LER (www.info-ler.com).

Avignon (Line 22; €28.80, 2½ hours, every two hours) Via Forcalquier and Apt.

Marseille (Line 28; €22.30, two hours, four to six daily Monday to Saturday) Via Aix-en-Provence, Volx and Manosque. In the opposite direction, one bus a day travels north to Barcelonnette.

Nice (Line 31; €23, 3½ hours, two daily)

TRAIN

The **Train des Pignes** (p296) serves Nice and stations in between, including Annot and Entrevaux.

Vallée de l'Ubaye

At the far northern edge of the Parc National du Mercantour, the Ubaye valley is probably the least-visited of the seven principal valleys, running east–west beneath snowcapped mountains, delimiting Haute-Provence from the Alps. It's a remote spot, and harder to reach than other areas of the national park. Most visitors come to ski: the popular resort of **Pra Loup** is just a short drive away from the valley's main town, **Barcelonnette**, which has a rather curious Mexican flavour thanks to the large number of Mexican immigrants who arrived here in the 18th century to work in the local silk and wool-weaving industries.

◉ Sights & Activities

There are fantastic walks in summer around the valley, and in winter you can try snow-shoeing and dog-sledding. Ask at the Barcelonnette tourist office for details, or contact the **Bureau des Guides de l'Ubaye** (☑06 86 67 38 73).

Fort de Tournoux   RUINS
(patrimoine@ubaye.com; adult/child €8.50/4; ☺ guided visits 10.30am & 2pm Jun-Sep) Originally built to protect the French border from invasion, and later used as part of the Maginot Line during WWII, this hillside fortress 18km northeast of Barcelonnette provides an evocative reminder of just how close you are to the French frontier here. Guided visits explore the fortifications, including gun batteries, casements and dugouts. There are several more military ruins to visit around the valley.

Musée de la Vallée   MUSEUM
(☑04 92 81 27 15; 10 av de la Libération, Barcelonnette; adult/10-18yr/under 10yr €4/2/free; ☺10am-noon & 2.30-6.30pm daily mid-Jul & Aug, 2.30-6pm Wed-Sat rest of year, closed mid-Nov–mid-Dec) Surrounded by a fine public park, this intriguing museum explores the valley's history. Highlights include a fascinating collection of Bronze Age arrowheads, axes, rings and bracelets, various exhibits relating to the adventurous naturalist Émile Chabrand, and some fine pieces of Mexican art.

Rando Passion   HIKING
(☑04 92 81 43 34; www.rando-passion.com; 31 rue Jules Béraud, Barcelonnette; guided walks €25) This experienced outfit leads treks into the mountains around Barcelonnette, including to picturesque local lakes and the best panoramas around the Ubaye valley. They also offer marmot-spotting trips, and in winter, lead snowshoeing expeditions.

🛏 Sleeping

Hotel de la Placette   HOTEL €€
(☑04 92 81 03 37; www.hotel-barcelonnette.fr; 14 rue Emile Donnadieu, Barcelonnette; d €74-95, f €102-129; 🛜) Right in the middle of Barcelonnette above a popular cafe, this central hotel offers smart (if rather small) rooms with fun design touches to liven things up (from mini deer's heads to motivational wall murals). Street noise can be an issue in midsummer.

Les Méans   B&B €€
(☑04 92 81 03 91; www.les-means.com; D900, Méolans-Revel; d €85-120, f from €125; 🛜) 🏼 Alpine atmosphere abounds at this attractive B&B 12km west of Barcelonnette, with five rustic rooms to choose from: we particularly liked the Alpages suite, with its original fireplace, and the wood-panelled Sommets suite (both also have private balconies and kitchenettes).

Villa Morelia   HISTORIC HOTEL €€€
(☑04 92 84 67 78; www.villa-morelia.com; Jausiers; €158-202, ste €246-308; P🅿🛜💺) In the hamlet of Jausiers, 10km northeast of Barcelonnette, this is a regal choice: a veritable mini-château, complete with turret, 18th-century furnishings and a gorgeous leafy park. The bedrooms are very elegant: some have rococo detailing and clawfoot baths, others are more modern in style.

🍴 Eating

Poivre d'Âne   FRENCH €€
(☑04 92 81 48 67; www.le-poivre-ane-barcelonnette.fr; 49 rue Manuel, Barcelonnette; menus €21-31; ☺12.30-2pm & 7.30-9.30pm) On Barcelonnette's main shopping street, the Donkey's Pepper is the place to stuff yourself silly with mountain sausages, cheesy *tartiflettes* (potatoes, cheese and bacon baked casseroles) and even cheesier fondues. With its cute shutters, vintage skis and other alpine ephemera, all it really lacks is the lonely goatherd.

ℹ Getting There & Away

LER Line 28 (www.info-ler.fr; €12.90, three daily Monday to Saturday, 1½ hours) buses shuttle from Barcelonnette to Digne-les-Bains, with onward connections to Aix-en-Provence and Marseille.

Vallée du Haut Verdon

It's only an hour or so's drive from Digne-les-Bains, but there's something about this valley that feels truly remote; especially the further north you travel, as the villages peter out, the mountains stack up along the horizon and the road draws ever closer to the dizzying **Col d'Allos** – the high mountain pass that connects this valley with the neighbouring Vallée de l'Ubaye, which runs in an east–west direction over the northern side of the pass. Unsurprisingly, at 2250m, the pass is usually snowbound between October and May.

In winter, there's skiiing around **Foux d'Allos** (www.valdallos.com), which shares pistes with **Pra Loup** (☎04 92 84 10 04; www.praloup.com), on the other side of the pass. In summer the whole area becomes a hiker's haven, but in the shoulder months the place feels decidedly quiet – bordering on deserted.

◉ Sights & Activities

Colmars-les-Alpes VILLAGE

With its towers, turrets and ramparts, this medieval village looks like a relic from a Monty Python film set. In the late 14th century, the valleys around Allos and Barcelonnette to the north were given to the Duchy of Savoy, and Colmars became an important border town, which meant it also required fortification. Despite additions by the military architect Vauban in the 18th century, the village looks largely as it would have during medieval times.

Lac d'Allos LAKE

It's worth the trek (and metered traffic) to reach Europe's largest alpine lake, Lac d'Allos (2226m; inaccessible fall to spring). From Allos, narrow, bumpy D226 climbs 12km to parking; then it's a 40-minute walk. Trail maps are available from the summer-only Parc National du Mercantour hut at the car park. Sited right beside the lake, the **Refuge du Lac d'Allos** (☎04 92 83 00 24; www.refugedulacdallos.com; menu €19.50; ⊗May-Sep) is an ideal spot for lunch, and has dorms if you're planning an overnight hike.

Retrouvance HIKING

(https://gitesetrandonnees.onf.fr/randonnee/circuit-randonnee-haut-verdon-val-dentraunes; 6-day hikes €580) Run by the Office Nationale des Fôrets, this fantastic multiday hike runs through the mountains from Thorame to Lac d'Allos, and includes an official guide as well as overnight accommodation in *gîtes* and farmhouses. Reservations can be made online or through Colmars' tourist office.

🛏 Sleeping

Les Transhumances B&B, APARTMENT €

(☎04 92 83 44 39; http://lestranshumances.pagesperso-orange.fr; Les Espiniers, Colmars-les-Alpes; s/d/tr/q €64/84/99/110, cottages per week €450-540; 🛰) 🖉 Named after the annual tradition of herding livestock up and down from the mountain pastures, this quiet 18th-century farm is equally pleasant if you're exploring by car or hiking the valley's trails. It's a simple, unpretentious place, with rustic, pine-panelled rooms offering sweeping mountain views – and breakfast is a treat.

Hotel Le France HOTEL €

(☎04 92 83 42 93; www.hotellefrance-colmarslesalpes.com; Colmars-les-Alpes; s €47-56, d €56-68, tr €70-90, f €70-90; P🛰) Situated right opposite the main gate of Colmars-les-Alpes, this simple, good-value hotel makes a decent base in the valley. It's far from luxurious, but the rooms are reasonable and the restaurant serves generous portions. There are also a couple of small apartments with kitchenettes.

🍴 Eating

Le Martagon HOTEL €

(☎04 92 83 14 26; www.le-martagon.com; Villars-Colmars, menu €29,90) A smart modern restaurant-with-rooms in the quiet village of Villars-Colmars, perfect for a lunch or dinner stop, with mountain specialities such as cheesy *tartiflette*, duck breast, locally cured ham and so on. Upstairs, small rooms (double €59 to €85) are enlivened by splashes of magenta, lime and brown; there are also timber camping pods (€90 to €113) in the hotel's grounds.

★ La Ferme Girerd-Potin FRENCH €€

(☎04 92 83 04 76; www.chambredhotes valdallos.com; rte de la Foux; meals around €25, r per person incl breakfast & dinner €50-59; ⊗by reservation Oct-Apr, Jul & Aug; 🐾) Five kilometres from Allos at an altitude of 1700m, this working farm is a wonderful spot to try true mountain food – all of it homegrown, farm-raised, self-baked or home-cooked, from vegetables to bread, meats and cheeses. The farm's 16th-century architecture is charming, and dinner is served in a beamed, candlelit dining room. You need to reserve a day ahead.

❶ Information

Colmars-les-Alpes Tourist Office (☎04 92 83 41 92; www.colmarslesalpes-verdontourisme.

DON'T MISS

TRAIN DES PIGNES

Zipping between mountains and sea, the narrow-gauge **Train des Pignes** (Pine Cone Train; www.trainprovence.com; single/return Nice to Digne €24.10/48.20; 🚇1 to Libération), is one of Provence's most picturesque trips. Conceived in 1861 and opened in 1911, the line was originally served by steam locomotives: a vintage train still puffs a few stops around **Puget-Théniers** on Sunday between spring and autumn.

Rising to 1000m in altitude, the 151km track passes through 50 tunnels and over 16 viaducts and 15 metal bridges along its cliff-hugging journey to Digne-les-Bains, stopping at nearly 50 villages en route. The mountain views on all sides are magnificent.

The entire trip from Nice to Digne-les-Bains takes 3¼ hours. There are usually five trains a day; if you don't have time for the whole journey, hop off at **Entrevaux**, 1½ hours from Nice (€11.80 one way), have a wander around the village, then catch the train back a couple of hours later.

Schedules are available at **Chemins de Fer de Provence** (📞04 97 03 80 80; www.trainprovence.com).

com; Ancienne Auberge Fleurie, Colmars-les-Alpes; ⊙9am-12.30pm & 2-6.30pm Jul & Aug, 10am-noon & 2-5pm Mon-Sat Sep-Jun) Colmar's tourist office provides advice on hiking, mountain biking, rafting and horse riding in the valley.

Val d'Allos Tourist Office (📞04 92 83 02 81; www.valdallos.com; place de la Coopérative, Allos; ⊙9.30am-noon & 2-6pm) Covers activities and accommodation around the entire Haut Verdon. The main office is in Allos; there's a small seasonal branch in Foux d'Allos, open during the ski season and in summer.

❶ Getting There & Away

Getting to the valley by public transport involves a combination approach: an SNCF train from Nice or Digne-les-Bains to Thorame, from where Haut Verdon Voyages (www.haut-verdon-voyages.fr) buses travel onwards to Colmars-les-Alpes and Allos (four daily, 50 minutes from Thorame). The combined return fare from Digne is €25, or €39 from Nice.

It's easier to arrive in ski season; LER (www.info-ler.fr) runs *navettes blanches* (ski shuttles) from the TGV station in Aix-en-Provence and Marseilles' train station direct to the Val d'Allos.

Vallée du Haut-Var

The Gorges du Verdon get the plaudits, but the Vallée du Haut-Var has its own spectacular twinset of valleys: the crimson Gorges de Daluis and the less-trafficked Gorges du Cians, which can be linked in a memorable 82km loop.

It makes a great (if long) day trip from Nice, but be prepared for narrow roads and a lot of driving. The best route is to take the D6202 west, then turn off onto the D902 towards Daluis and the gorges. On the D28, the ski town of **Valberg** and the small village of **Beuil** (elevation 1450m) make useful lunch stops before you return south along the D28 through the Gorges du Cians, then return to Nice.

◉ Sights & Activities

★ **Gorges de Daluis**   CANYON
This stunning network of scarlet gorges looks for all the world like it's been collected from Arizona and plonked down in Haute-Provence. Carved out over the millennia by the Var River, it runs for 6km between Guillaumes and Daluis, twisting high above the river past towering sandstone cliffs, weird rock formations and plunging waterfalls. It's best seen in a northbound direction on the D902/D2202, as tunnels on the southbound lane obscure most of the views.

Sentier du Point Sublime   HIKING
This 4km hiking trail starts at the Pont de Berthéou, 8km south of Guillaumes on the D2202. It climbs through oak-and-pine forest and scarlet rock forms to a famous panoramic viewpoint, aptly known as Point Sublime. It's a 90-minute hike there and back (longer in hot weather).

❶ Information

Maison du Parc National du Mercantour (📞04 93 02 58 23; varcians@mercantour-parcnational.fr; rue Jean Mineur, Valberg; ⊙9am-noon & 2-6pm Thu-Tue, plus Wed school holidays) General information on the Parc National du Mercantour, inside the Maison Valbergane.

Valberg Tourist Office (📞04 93 23 24 25; www.valberg.com; place du Quartier, Valberg;

⌚9am-noon & 2-5pm Mon-Sat, 10am-1pm Sun) Valberg's tourist office makes room reservations and organises local activities.

Getting There & Away

Lignes d'Azur (www.ligneesdazur.com) Line 770 buses run direct from Nice to Valberg (€1.50, three daily, two hours and 10 minutes).

Vallée de la Tinée

This steep, V-shaped valley runs north for 149km all the way from the pretty little town of St-Sauveur-sur-Tinée (elevation 490m) to the Vallée de l'Ubaye. En route, it climbs up and over the **Col de Restefond la Bonette**, Europe's highest road pass – and invariably the last one to open after the spring thaw (usually in late May but sometimes as late as early June). It's a favourite for road-trippers and motorbikers, and occasionally features on the Tour de France. During winter, the valley can only be accessed from the south.

At 1100m elevation, the sky-top village of **Roure** is also worth a detour thanks to its amazing alpine arboretum – as long as you can handle the hair-raisingly steep mountain road. From the 1920s until 1961, villagers used a 1850m-long cable to transport items up the mountain; the cable still remains.

Sights

★Arboretum Marcel Kroenlein GARDENS
(☎09 77 31 68 33; www.arboretum-roure.org; Roure; suggested donation adult/child €5/free; ⌚10am-6pm; 👪) This alpine garden is probably the last thing you'd expect in tiny Roure. It's a pet project of Monaco's Prince Rainier, who's covered 15 steep-sided hectares (ranging in altitude from 1200m to 1700m) with mountain flora, interspersed with sculptures by Niçois artists. If you're really lucky, you might even spot an eagle or a vulture wheeling over the garden terraces.

Sleeping & Eating

Hotel Edelweiss HOTEL €
(☎04 93 03 40 48; www.edelweissauron.com; place Centrale, Auron; d €75-85, tr €100, q €130; 📶) A small, traditional alpine hotel in the little village of Auron, about 8km south of St-Etienne-de-Tinée. Above a restaurant serving hearty mountain specialities, it's a cosy enough base, with yellow-washed walls, narrow corridors and small bathrooms. It's worth upping to the superior rooms as most of these have views.

Hostellerie du Randonneur HOTEL €€
(☎04 93 02 01 45; www.hostellerie-rimplas.fr; Rimplas; d/f €69/119; P📶) In the minuscule village of Rimplas, off the road connecting the Vésubie and Tinée valleys, this basic hotel is a favourite for hikers exploring the Mercantour. Built from solid stone with shuttered windows looking out onto the mountains, it's a simple place: rooms are quite spartan, but you're well off the beaten track and the mountains are on your doorstep.

Information

Mercantour National Park Office (☎04 93 02 42 27; mercantour@wanadoo.fr; Haute Vallée de le Tinée, St-Étienne-de-Tinée; ⌚10am-5pm Mon-Sat Jul-Aug) A small national park office in St-Étienne-de-Tinée that provides information on visiting the park.

St-Étienne-de-Tinée Tourist Office (☎04 93 02 41 96; www.saintetiennedetinee.fr; rue des Communes de France, St-Étienne-de-Tinée; ⌚9am-12.30pm & 2-5pm Mon-Sat Apr-Sep, shorter hours Oct-Mar) St-Étienne's small tourist office provides local information.

Getting There & Away

Lignes D'Azur (www.lignesdazur.com) is the main bus company here.

Line 740 (two daily Monday to Saturday, one on Sunday) runs from Nice up the Vallée de la Tinée, stopping at all the main villages including Rimplas, St-Sauveur, Roure, St-Étienne and Auron.

Vallée de la Vésubie

If you only have time to explore one mountain valley in Haute-Provence, make it the Vésubie. Dotted with hilltop mountain towns and flanked by craggy peaks, it's known as 'La Suisse Niçoise' for a reason. Once the private hunting reserve of King Victor Emmanuel II of Italy, it's now a hub for all manner of outdoor activities: hiking, biking, wildlife watching, paragliding and via ferrata, to name a few.

The main town, St-Martin-Vésubie (elevation 1000m) is a central place to base yourself for wider forays around the Mercantour, with plenty of hotels, restaurants and activity providers in the area – as well as a mountain activity centre, built at an eye-watering cost of €25 million and opened in 2017.

Sights

Roughly halfway along the valley, **St-Martin-Vésubie** has preserved much of its medieval character: you can still glimpse vestiges of its original ramparts and one of its town gates on its steep main street.

The hilltop villages of **Belvédère** (820m), 12km south of St-Martin-Vésubie, and **La Colmiane** (1795m), 7km west, are also well worth visiting for their wraparound mountain views.

★ Alpha WILDLIFE RESERVE

(☏ 04 93 02 33 69; www.alpha-loup.com; Le Boréon; adult/child €10/8; ⊙ 10am-5pm or 6pm Apr-Oct; ⚐) The grey wolf was hunted nearly to extinction in France by 1930, but in 1992 two 'funny-looking dogs' were spotted near Utelle, presumably from over the Italian border. Since then, the animals have made a comeback in the French Alps, and though they're hard to spot in the wild, you'll have a good chance of a sighting at this fascinating wolf reserve, where three packs live in semi-freedom.

La Madone de Fenestres CHURCH

At an altitude of 1904m, this impressively situated hilltop church was supposedly founded on the site where a local villager had a vision of the Virgin Mary; twice a year, on 15 August and 8 September, there's a solemn procession to commemorate the event. The statue of Mary inside is thought to have been carved from a Lebanese cedar in the 14th century. It's at the end of a winding 10km road leading east of St-Martin-Vésubie; look out for signs.

🏃 Activities

St-Martin-Vésubie is a hub for hiking, with 13 marked trails climbing through the surrounding mountains, intersecting with four GR *(grande randonnée)* paths.

★ Vesúbia ADVENTURE SPORTS

(☏ 04 93 23 20 30; www.vesubia-mountain-park. fr; allée du Docteur Fulconis, St-Martin-de-Vésubie; swimming €5, climbing €9.50, canyoning €14; ⊙ 9am-8.30pm or 9.30pm Jul & Aug, 2-8pm Mon-Fri, 9-8pm Sat, 9-7pm Sun Jun & Sep, ring ahead at other times) This hulking, gigantic mountain-activities centre looks rather like a supertanker that's marooned itself in the middle of St-Martin-de-Vésubie. Clad in timber, glass and a grass roof, and built at a vast budget of €25 million, it offers introductory sessions to climbing, canyoning and caving, using fibreglass models to simulate natural features – such as a 13m rock face and a cave system complete with pools and cascades. There's also a swimming pool, solarium and sauna.

Horse&Ventures HORSE RIDING

(☏ 06 22 29 58 86; www.horseandventures.com; Le Boréon; 2hr/full-day ride €35/75) English-speaking Denis Longfellow runs horseback trips from Le Boréon as well as longer tuition courses.

DRIVING IN HAUTE-PROVENCE

It might only be an hour or two north of Nice, but make no mistake: you're in the Alps proper in Haute-Provence. Heavy snowfall means the highest *cols* (passes) are usually only open between May and September. Access roads have signs indicating whether the pass is *ouvert* (open) or *fermé* (closed), or you can check in advance with local tourist offices.

A road map is indispensable: GPS units have a nasty habit of leading you up steep, narrow roads that really aren't designed for cars and frequently don't have guard rails. Also look out for deep gullies along the roadsides – if you run a front wheel into them you'll need a tow truck to get you out. Snow tyres are required on many roads during winter.

The main passes that close in winter are:

Col d'Allos (2250m) Links the north–south D126/D908 from Allos in the Vallée du Haut Verdon to Barcelonnette in the Vallée de l'Ubaye.

Col de la Cayolle (2326m) Links the Vallée du Haut Var with the Vallée de l'Ubaye along the D2202/D902, running north–south from St-Martin-d'Entraunes to Barcelonnette.

Col de Restefond la Bonette (2802m) Europe's highest mountain pass links the D64 from St-Étienne-de-Tinée in the Vallée de la Tinée to Barcelonnette in the Vallée de l'Ubaye.

Col des Champs (2095m) The east–west D2/D72 road connecting St-Martin-d'Entraunes in the Vallée du Haut Var with Colmars-les-Alpes in the Vallée d'Allos.

Thermes de
Berthemont-les-Bains   THERMAL BATHS
(☑04 93 03 47 00; www.valvital.eu; from €45;
☺Apr-Oct) A great place to soak weary bones
after a long hike, or just loll in luxury, the
Thermes de Berthemont-les-Bains offers a
range of massages and baths. It's about an
11km drive southeast of St-Martin-Vésubie.

🛏 Sleeping & Eating

There are a few traditional restaurants dotted along the main street of St-Martin-Vésubie, but for a proper three-course Provençal
dinner, the lovely restaurant at La Bonne
Auberge is the best bet in the village.

Le Boréon   HOTEL €
(☑04 93 03 20 35; www.hotel-boreon.com; d/tr/q
from €92/129/155, 2-course menus from €18.90;
☺closed Nov-Mar; 🅿🍴) Magical mountain
views unfurl from this large Swiss-chalet-
style hotel 8km north of St-Martin-Vésubie.
The rooms are nothing to write home about,
but you won't complain too much when you
look out the window. The restaurant serves
alpine specialities.

Moonlight Chalet   BOUTIQUE HOTEL €€
(☑06 89 25 36 74; www.moonlightchalet.com; 8
rue Rumplemeyer, St-Martin-Vésubie; r incl breakfast €120-130; 🏊) This B&B is quirky through
and through: its lodges and rooms are decorated with elements inspired by nature –
bathtubs made from river rocks, furniture
crafted from tree trunks (one room is even
built around a fir tree). It's a bucolic setting,
but the aesthetic might be a little too homespun for some.

La Bonne Auberge   HOTEL €€
(☑04 93 03 20 49; www.labonneauberge06.
fr; 98 allée du Verdun, St-Martin-Vésubie; s/d
from €51/69; ☺Feb–mid-Dec; 🍴) A classic,
old-fashioned family-run French hotel – in
the same hands since 1946. Upstairs are traditional, pine-clad rooms arranged along a
rather noisy corridor; downstairs, there's a
lovely restaurant (menus €25 to €31) that
serves wholesome mountain food in a dining room crammed with alpine ephemera
(boars' heads, snowshoes, hunting horns
and St-Martin's first TV set from 1960).

🛈 Information

Colmiane Tourist Office (☑04 93 23 25 90;
www.colmiane.com; ☺9am-noon & 2-6pm)
Small tourist office in the village of Colmiane.

Maison du Parc National du Mercantour
(☑04 93 03 23 15; vesubie@mercantour-parc-
national.fr; av Kellermann, St-Martin-Vésubie;
☺9am-noon & 2-6pm mid-Jun–mid-Sep)
Summer-only office staffed by park rangers.
St-Martin-Vésubie Tourist Office (☑04 93 03
21 28; www.saintmartinvesubie.fr; place Félix
Faure, St-Martin-Vésubie; ☺8.30am-12.30pm
& 2-7pm daily Jul & Aug, 9am-noon & 2-7pm
Mon-Sat Sep-Jun; 🕿) St-Martin's efficient tourist office organises walks and has lists of local
activity providers. A board outside the office
details local hikes with durations and routes.

🛈 Getting There & Away

Lignes d'Azur bus 730 (www.lignesdazur.com;
two daily, 1¾ hours) runs direct from Nice to
St-Martin-Vésubie.

Vallée de la Roya

Occupied by Italy during WWII, the Roya
only became part of France in 1947. Wedged
hard against the Italian border, the valley
runs all the way from the coast to Tende,
where a tunnel built in 1892 burrows under
the mountains into Italy. It's a great day trip
from Nice, either by car or aboard the grand-
ly titled Train des Merveilles (p300).

St-Dalmas-de-Tende and nearby Casterino are the main gateways from the east for
the prehistoric rock carvings of the Vallée
des Merveilles (p300).

◉ Sights

Monastère de Saorge   MONASTERY
(☑04 93 04 55 55; www.monastere-saorge.fr;
Saorge; adult/child €6/free; ☺10am-12.30pm
& 2.30-6.30pm daily Jun-Sep, Wed-Mon Feb-May
& Oct, closed Nov-Jan) Situated 9km north
of Breil-sur-Roya, the dramatic Gorges de
Saorge lead to the fortified village of Saorge
(elevation 520m). Perched on sheer cliffs,
the village is a maze of tangled streets, with
lots of 15th- to 17th-century houses, as well
as this Franciscan monastery, notable for its
baroque church, decorated with frescoes of
St Francis.

Sanctuaire Notre Dame
des Fontaines   CHURCH
(€2; ☺10am-12.30pm & 2-5.30pm May-Oct)
Dubbed the Sistine Chapel of the Southern
Alps, this church is famous for its wall-to-
wall 15th-century frescoes, created by Pied-
montese painters Jean Canavesio and Jean
Baleison. It's 4km east of La Brigue.

VALLÉE DES MERVEILLES

Wedged between the Vésubie and Roya valleys, this narrow, remote **canyon** (Valley of Wonders) is famous for its amazing Bronze Age petroglyphs – ancient pictures carved into rock. The valley contains more than 36,000 prehistoric carvings of figures, symbols and animals, thought to have been etched by members of a Ligurian cult between 1800 and 1500 BCE.

Most can only be seen on foot. Access to the valley from the south is on the D171 from the Vallée de la Vésubie, or from the west on the D91 from the Vallée de la Roya via Casterino. Trails remain snow-covered into late spring; the best time is June to October. Access is restricted without a guide, which you can arrange through the Parc National du Mercantour visitor centres or the **Bureau des Guides du Mercantour** (☑ 04 93 03 31 32; www.guidescapade.com; place du Maré, St-Martin-Vésubie; ⊙ Jul & Aug).

Musée des Merveilles MUSEUM
(☑ 04 93 04 32 50; av du 16 Sepembre 1947, Tende; ⊙ 10am-6pm May–mid-Oct, 10am-5pm mid-Oct–Apr, closed Tue Sep-Jun) FREE In Tende, this museum provides useful context if you're visiting the prehistoric carvings of the Vallée des Merveilles. Inside the striking modern building, exhibits explore the culture of the prehistoric people who called the valley home, with life-size models and archaeological finds.

🏃 Activities

Train des Merveilles RAIL
(Train of Marvels; www.tendemerveilles.com; return from Nice adult/child €16/10; ⊙ May-Oct) For fans of the iron horse, this scenic rail ride is a trip not to be missed. It runs north from Nice right through the Vallée de la Roya, passing hilltop villages, dramatic canyons and mountain vistas en route. You even get a commentary (in French) courtesy of the conductor.

Roya Évasion CYCLING, CANYONING
(☑ 04 93 04 91 46; www.royaevasion.com; 1 rue Pasteur, Breil-sur-Roya; rafting trips €38-45) Breil-sur-Roya is the valley's water-sports base. This experienced outfit organises kayaking, canyoning and rafting on the Roya River, plus hiking and mountain biking. It also conducts English-language rock-art tours to the Merveilles.

🛏 Sleeping & Eating

Le Prieuré HOTEL €
(☑ 04 93 04 75 70; www.leprieure.org; rue Jean Medecin, St-Dalmas-de-Tende; s/d/tr/q €79/85/95/105; 🛜) Once a priory, there's still a whiff of the monastical about this place – in the ecclesiastical architecture and the rather spartan decor. Still, if you can bag a

room overlooking the river, you'll be thoroughly blessed. The restaurant is great, too, with intriguing dishes like chestnut gnocchi and *soupe de pierres* (literally, 'friar's soup'; meat-and-veg stew).

Auberge du Col de Bruis INN €€
(☑ 04 93 55 30 88; www.coldebrouis.com; rue du Col de Brouis; d €75-35, f €100-125; 🅿 🛜) A long-standing hostelry for cross-border travellers, road-trippers and bikers, this hilltop auberge at the crest of the Col de Bruis makes a pleasant stop. The owner, Christina, serves filling and tasty mountain food, and there's a selection of plain, cosy rooms upstairs – most with mountain outlooks. It's on the D2204 between Sospel and Breil-sur-Roya.

ℹ Information

Sospel Tourist Office (☑ 04 93 04 15 80; www.sospel-tourisme.com; 19 av Jean Médecin, Sospel; ⊙ 10am-12.30pm & 1.30-6pm Mon, 9.30am-6pm Tue-Fri, 9.30am-4.45pm Sat, 10am-12.30pm Sun) Useful tourist office at the southern end of the valley.

Tende Tourist Office (☑ 04 93 04 73 71; www.tendemerveilles.com; av du 16 Sepembre 1947, Tende; ⊙ 9am-noon & 2-5pm Mon-Sat, 9am-noon Sun) Tende's tourist office provides details on guided archaeological walks and 4WD trips to Mont Bégo and the Vallée des Merveilles.

ℹ Getting There & Away

The tortuous mountain roads around Sospel (especially from the Vésubie) are scenic but not for the faint of heart. From Nice, the fastest route is to take the autoroute to Ventimiglia (across the Italian border), then follow it north back into France toward the Col de Tende (Italian signs read 'Colle di Tenda').

The **Train des Merveilles** runs from Nice through the valley to Tende.

Understand Provence & the Côte d'Azur

History

From prehistoric burial sites and cave paintings to Roman amphitheatres, medieval castles, Napoleonic roads and cutting-edge modern-art museums, Provence has more than 3000 years of compelling history to investigate. It's a long and varied tale that involves Celtic tribes and Roman legionaries, popes, princes and revolutionaries, impressionist painters and world-class writers – a microcosm of France, in fact, only with its own distinctly Provençal perspective.

Prehistoric Man

Provence was inhabited from an exceptionally early age: primitive stone tools more than a million years old were found near Roquebrune-Cap-Martin. Neanderthal hunters occupied the Mediterranean coast from about 90,000 BCE to 40,000 BCE, living in caves such as Grottes de l'Observatoire in Monaco. Modern man arrived with creative flair in 30,000 BCE. The ornate wall paintings inside the decorated Grotte Cosquer, near Marseille, date from 20,000 BCE, while the outstanding collection of 30,000 petroglyphs decorating Mont Bégo in the Vallée des Merveilles dates back to 1800 BCE to 1500 BCE.

Archaeologists have found that the people living around Châteauneuf-les-Martigues, northwest of Marseille, about 6000 to 4500 years ago were among the first ever to domesticate wild sheep, allowing them to shift from a nomadic to a settled lifestyle.

Top Prehistoric Sites

Grottes de l'Observatoire (Monaco)

Vallée des Merveilles

Musée de la Préhistoire des Gorges du Verdon

Village des Bories, near Gordes

Réserve Géologique de Haute-Provence (Digne-les-Bains)

Greeks to Romans

Massalia (Marseille) was colonised around 600 BCE by Greeks from Phocaea in Asia Minor; from the 4th century BCE they established more trading posts along the coast at Antipolis (Antibes), Olbia (Hyères), Athenopolis (St-Tropez), Nikaia (Nice), Monoïkos (Monaco) and Glanum (near St-Rémy-de-Provence). They brought olives and grapevines to the region.

While Hellenic civilisation was developing on the coast, the Celts penetrated northern Provence. They mingled with ancient Ligurians to create a Celto-Ligurian stronghold around Entremont; its influence extended as far south as Draguignan.

TIMELINE	c 90,000 BCE	600 BCE	125–126 BCE
	Neanderthal hunters occupy the Mediterranean coast; starting around 30,000 BCE Cro-Magnons start decorating their caves.	The Greeks colonise Massalia (now Marseille) and establish trading posts along the coast, bringing olive trees and grapevines to the region.	Romans create Provincia Gallia Transalpina, from which Provence gets its name, and Provence joins the Roman Empire.

In 125 BCE the Romans helped the Greeks defend Massalia against invading Celto-Ligurians. Their victory marked the start of the Gallo-Roman era and the creation of Gallia Narbonensis, the first Roman *provincia* (province), from which the name Provence is derived.

The Gallo-Romans

Gallia Narbonensis (also sometimes known as Provincia Gallia Transalpina), embraced all of southern France from the Alps to the Mediterranean and the Pyrenees. In 122 BCE the Romans destroyed the Ligurian capital of Entremont and established the Roman stronghold of Aquae Sextiae Salluviorum (Aix-en-Provence) at its foot. Around 188 BCE, they began construction of the Via Domitia, the first Roman road in Gaul, which stretched all the way from the Alps via the Durance Valley, Apt, Arles, Nîmes and Narbonne, where it intersected with the Via Aquitania to the Atlantic Coast.

The construction of the road helped Rome's further conquest of Gaul by enabling movement of troops and supplies, but it wasn't completely conquered until Julius Caesar's final victorious campaign from 58 BCE to 51 BCE. Massalia, which had retained its independence following the creation of Provincia, was incorporated by Caesar in 49 BCE. In 14 BCE the still-rebellious Ligurians were defeated by Augustus Caesar, who celebrated by building a monument at La Turbie in 6 BCE. Arelate (Arles) became the regional capital.

Under the emperor Augustus, vast amphitheatres were built at Arelate, Nemausus (Nîmes), Forum Julii (Fréjus) and Vasio Vocontiorum (Vaison-la-Romaine). Triumphal arches were raised at Arausio (Orange), Cabelio (Cavaillon), Carpentorate (Carpentras) and Glanum, and a series of aqueducts were constructed. The 275m-long Pont du Gard was part of a 50km-long system of canals built around 19 BCE by Agrippa, Augustus' deputy, to bring water from Uzès to Nîmes.

Christianity – brought to the region, according to Provençal legend, by Mary Magdalene, Marie-Jacobé and Marie-Salomé, who sailed into Stes-Maries-de-la-Mer in 40 CE – penetrated the region, was adopted by the Romans and continued to spread over the next few hundred years.

Top Roman Sights

....

Théâtre Antique (Orange)

....

Les Arènes & Théâtre Antique (Arles)

....

Glanum (St-Rémy-de-Provence)

....

Puymin & La Villasse (Vaison-la-Romaine)

Medieval Provence

After the collapse of the Roman Empire in 476 CE, Provence was invaded by various Germanic tribes. In the early 9th century the Saracens (an umbrella term adopted locally to describe Muslim invaders such as Turks, Moors and Arabs) emerged as a warrior force to be reckoned with. Attacks along the Maures coast, Niçois hinterland and more northern Alps persuaded villagers to take refuge in the hills. Many of Provence's hilltop villages date from this chaotic period. In 974 CE the Saracen fortress at La Garde Freinet was defeated by William the Liberator (Guillaume Le

400–900 CE	974–1032	1309–77	1481
The Roman Empire collapses and Germanic tribes invade Provence; Franks (hence the name 'France') encourage villagers to move uphill to avert Saracen attacks.	William the Liberator extends his feudal control over Provence, which becomes a marquisate and joins the Holy Roman Empire.	Pope Clément V moves the Holy Seat to Avignon, and nine pontiffs head the Roman Catholic church from there until 1377; 'home' is the Palais des Papes.	King of Naples, Good King René's nephew and successor, Charles III, dies heirless and Provence falls to Louis XI of France.

Libérateur), count of Arles, who consequently extended his feudal control over the entire region, marking the return of peace and unity to Provence, which became a marquisate. In 1032 it joined the Holy Roman Empire.

The marquisate of Provence was later split in two: the north fell to the counts of Toulouse from 1125 and the Catalan counts of Barcelona gained control of the southern part (stretching from the Rhône to the River Durance and from the Alps to the sea). This became the county of Provence (Comté de Provence). Raymond Bérenger V (1209–45) was the first Catalan count to reside permanently in Aix (the capital since 1186). In 1229 he conquered Nice and in 1232 he founded Barcelonnette. After Bérenger's death the county passed to the House of Anjou, under which it enjoyed great prosperity.

The French Riviera: A Cultural History by Julian Hale delves into the modern Côte d'Azur's vibrant past with panache and (Champagne) buckets of anecdotes.

The Popes

In 1274 Comtat Venaissin (Carpentras and its Vaucluse hinterland) was ceded to Pope Gregory X in Rome. In 1309 French-born Clément V (r 1305–14) moved the papal headquarters from feud-riven Rome to Avignon. A tour of the Papal palace illustrates how resplendent a period this was for the city, which hosted nine pontiffs between 1309 and 1376.

The death of Pope Gregory XI led to the Great Schism (1378–1417), during which rival popes resided at Rome and Avignon and spent most of their energies denouncing and excommunicating each other. Even after the schism was settled and a pope established in Rome, Avignon and the Comtat Venaissin remained under papal rule until 1792.

The arts in Provence flourished under the popes. A university was established in Avignon as early as 1303, followed by a university in Aix a century later. In 1327 Italian poet Petrarch (1304–74) encountered his muse, Laura, in Fontaine de Vaucluse. During the reign of Good King René, king of Naples (1434–80), French became the courtly language.

French Provence

In 1481 René's successor, his nephew Charles III, died heirless and Provence was ceded to Louis XI of France. In 1486 the state of Aix ratified Provence's union with France and the centralist policies of the French kings saw the region's autonomy greatly reduced. Aix Parliament, a French administrative body, was created in 1501.

A period of instability ensued, as a visit to the synagogue in Carpentras testifies: Jews living in French Provence fled to ghettos in Carpentras, Pernes-les-Fontaines, L'Isle-sur-la-Sorgue, Cavaillon or Avignon. All were part of the pontifical enclave of Comtat Venaissin, where papal protection remained assured until 1570.

The Luberon was an early victim of the Reformation that swept Europe in the 1530s and the consequent Wars of Religion (1562–98). In

1530s	1539	1545	1560
The Reformation sweeps through France, prompting the core of Catholicism to be questioned.	French (rather than Provençal) is made the official administrative language of Provence.	People of 11 Luberon villages are massacred under the terms of the Arrêt de Mérindol, a bill condemning anyone of Waldensian faith to death.	Nîmes native Jean Nicot (1530–1600) becomes the first to import tobacco into France from Portugal, hence the word 'nicotine'.

April 1545 the populations of 11 Waldensian (Vaudois) villages in the Luberon were massacred. Numerous clashes followed between the staunchly Catholic Comtat Venaissin and its Huguenot (Protestant) neighbours to the north around Orange.

In 1580, as in much of Europe, plague devastated the region, causing tens of thousands of deaths – a problem that continued to recur over the ensuing decades. The Edict of Nantes in 1598 (which recognised Protestant control of certain areas, including Lourmarin in the Luberon) brought an uneasy peace to the region – until its revocation by Louis XIV in 1685. Full-scale persecution of Protestants ensued.

In 1720, Marseille was hit by another devastating outbreak of plague. The disease spread from a merchant ship after the city's chief magistrate, owner of the ship's cargo, ignored quarantine measures to ensure his goods made it to the local fair. Half the city's population died.

The close of the century was marked by the French Revolution in 1789: as the National Guard from Marseille marched north to defend the Revolution, a merry tune composed in Strasbourg several months earlier for the war against Prussia – 'Chant de Guerre de l'Armée du Rhin (War Song of the Rhine Army)' – sprang from their lips. France's stirring national anthem, 'La Marseillaise', was born.

From France, to Italy & Back

Provence was divided into three *départements* (administrative divisions) in 1790: Var, Bouches du Rhône and the Basse-Alpes. Two years later papal Avignon and Comtat Venaissin were annexed by France, making way for the creation of Vaucluse.

In 1793 the Armée du Midi marched into Nice and declared it French territory. France also captured Monaco, until then a recognised independent state ruled by the Grimaldi family. When Toulon was occupied by the English, it was thanks to the efforts of a dashing young Corsican general named Napoléon Bonaparte (Napoléon I) that France recaptured it.

The Reign of Terror that swept through France between September 1793 and July 1794 saw religious freedoms revoked, churches desecrated and cathedrals turned into 'Temples of Reason'. In the secrecy of their homes, people hand-crafted thumbnail-sized biblical figurines, hence the inglorious creation of the *santon* (small clay image used in a Christmas crèche).

In 1814 France lost the territories it seized in 1793. The County of Nice was ceded to Victor Emmanuel I, King of Sardinia. It remained under Sardinian protectorship until 1860, when an agreement between Napoléon III and the House of Savoy helped drive the Austrians from northern Italy, prompting France to repossess Savoy and the area around Nice. In Monaco the Treaty of Paris restored the rights of the Grimaldi royal family; from 1817 until 1860 the principality was under the protection of Sardinia.

Top Religious Architecture

....

Palais des Papes (Avignon)

....

Chartreuse du Val de Bénédiction (Villeneuve-lès-Avignon)

....

Abbaye Notre-Dame de Sénanque (Gordes)

....

Monastère de la Verne (Collobrières)

....

Abbaye de Thoronet (Lorgues)

1562–98	1598	1720	1789–94
The Wars of Religion see numerous bloody clashes between French Catholics and Protestants (Huguenots).	Bourbon king Henry IV gives French Protestants freedom of conscience with the Edict of Nantes – to the horror of Catholic Paris and Roman Catholicism stronghold Avignon.	The Great Plague of Marseille eventually results in the death of more than half the city's population, and the building of Le Mur de la Peste (Plague Wall).	Revolutionaries storm the Bastille, leading to the beheading of Louis XVI and Marie-Antoinette, the Reign of Terror, and the revocation of religious freedoms.

Meanwhile, the Allied restoration of the House of Bourbon to the French throne at the Congress of Vienna (1814–15), following Napoléon I's abdication and exile to Elba, was rudely interrupted by the return of the emperor. Following his escape from Elba in 1815, Napoléon landed at Golfe-Juan on 1 March with a 1200-strong army. He proceeded northwards, passing through Cannes, Grasse, Castellane, Digne-les-Bains and Sisteron en route to his triumphal return to Paris on 20 May. Napoléon's glorious 'Hundred Days' back in power ended with the Battle of Waterloo and his return to exile. He died in 1821.

The Belle Époque

The Second Empire (1852–70) brought to the region a revival in all things Provençal, a movement spearheaded by Maillane-born poet Frédéric Mistral. Rapid economic growth was another hallmark: Nice, which had become part of France in 1860, became Europe's fastest-growing city thanks to its booming tourism. The city was particularly popular with the English aristocracy, who followed their queen's example of wintering on the Riviera's shores. European royalty followed soon after. The train line reached Toulon in 1856, followed by Nice in 1864, the same year work started on a coastal road from Nice to Monaco.

In neighbouring Monaco the Grimaldi family gave up its claim over its former territories of Menton and Roquebrune in 1861 in exchange for France's recognition of its status as an independent principality. Four years later Monte Carlo Casino opened and Monaco leapt from being Europe's poorest state to one of its richest.

The Third Republic ushered in the glittering belle époque, with art nouveau architecture, a whole field of artistic 'isms', including impressionism, and advances in science and engineering. Wealthy French, English, American and Russian tourists and tuberculosis sufferers (for whom the only cure was sunlight and sea air) discovered the coast. The intensity and clarity of the region's colours and light appealed to many painters.

Top Belle Époque Sights

Casino de Monte Carlo (Monaco)

Hôtel Negresco (Nice)

Musée Masséna (Nice)

Excelsior-Regina (Nice)

Carlton Interconti-nental (Cannes)

WWI & the Roaring Twenties

No blood was spilled on southern French soil during WWI. Soldiers were conscripted from the region, however, and the human losses included two out of every 10 Frenchmen between 20 and 45 years of age. With its primarily tourist-based economy, the Côte d'Azur recovered more quickly from the postwar financial crisis than France's more industrial north.

The Côte d'Azur sparkled as an avant-garde centre in the 1920s and 1930s, with artists pushing into the new fields of cubism and surrealism, Le Corbusier rewriting the architectural textbook and foreign writers thronging to the liberal coast.

1790–92	1815	1848	1860
Provence is divided into three *départements* (which still exist today); Papal Avignon and Comtat Venaissin are annexed by France and Vaucluse is created.	Exiled Napoléon Bonaparte escapes Elba and journeys in secret over the mountains near Digne-les-Bains and Gap to reclaim his title in Paris – it'll only last 100 days.	In 1848 French revolutionaries adopt the red, white and blue tricolour of Martigues near Marseille as their own. France's national flag is born.	The County of Nice becomes part of French Provence. Meanwhile, European royalty winters in Nice, Europe's fastest-growing city.

The coast's nightlife gained a reputation for being cutting edge. Rail and road access to the south improved: the railway line between Digne-les-Bains and Nice was completed, and in 1922 the luxurious Train Bleu made its first run from Calais, via Paris, to the coast. The train only had 1st-class carriages and was quickly dubbed the 'train to paradise'.

The roaring twenties hailed the start of the summer season on the Côte d'Azur. Outdoor swimming pools were built, sandy beaches cleared of seaweed, and sunbathing sprang into fashion after a bronzed Coco Chanel appeared on the coast in 1923, draped over the arm of the Duke of Westminster. France lifted its ban on gambling, prompting the first casino to open on the coast in the Palais de la Méditerranée (today a hotel) on Nice's Promenade des Anglais in 1927. With the advent of paid holidays for all French workers in 1936, even more tourists flocked to the region. Second- and 3rd-class seating were added to the Train Bleu.

Greatly affected by the plague of phylloxera in the 1880s, vineyards were replanted but struggled: France was overproducing and WWI soldiers preferred red wine to rosé for their rations. With the introduction of AOC labels in the 1930s, which allowed each area to control and market their own regional wines, Provence's wine industry began to take off in earnest.

WWII

With the onset of war, the Côte d'Azur's glory days turned grey. On 3 September 1939 France and Britain declared war on Germany. But following the armistice treaty agreed with Hitler on 22 June 1940, southern France fell into the 'free' Vichy France zone, although Menton and the Vallée de la Roya were occupied by Italians. The Côte d'Azur – particularly Nice – immediately became a safe haven from war-torn occupied France; by 1942 some 43,000 Jews had descended on the coast to seek refuge. Monaco remained neutral for the duration of WWII.

On 11 November 1942 Nazi Germany invaded Vichy France. Provence was at war. At Toulon 73 ships, cruisers, destroyers and submarines – the major part of the French fleet – were scuttled by their crews to prevent the Germans seizing them. Almost immediately, Toulon was overcome by the Germans and Nice was occupied by the Italians. In January 1943 the Marseille quarter of Le Panier was razed, its 40,000 inhabitants being given less than a day's notice to pack up and leave. Those who didn't were sent to Nazi concentration camps. The Resistance movement, particularly strong in Provence, was known in the region as *maquis,* after the Provençal scrub in which people hid.

Two months after D-Day, on 15 August 1944, Allied forces landed on the southern coast at beaches including Le Dramont near St-Raphaël, Cavalaire, Pampelonne and the St-Tropez peninsula. St-Tropez and Provence's hinterland were almost immediately liberated, but it was only after five days of heavy fighting that Allied troops freed Marseille on 28 August (three days after the liberation of Paris). Toulon was liberated on 26 August, a week after French troops first attacked the port. Italian-occupied areas in the Vallée de la Roya were only returned to France in 1947.

1914–18	**1939–45**	**1946**	**1947**
The human cost of WWI is enormous: of the eight million French men called to arms, 1.3 million are killed and almost one million crippled.	Nazi Germany occupies France, establishing a puppet state led by ageing WWI hero General Pétain in Vichy; Provence is liberated two months after D-Day.	The first international film festival opens at Cannes' old casino, and is a smashing success, helping revive postwar life on the coast.	Vallée de La Roya, in eastern Provence, which had been occupied by the Italians during WWII, is returned to France.

Les 30 Glorieuses: France's Golden Decades

The 30-odd years following WWII saw unprecedented growth, creativity and optimism in France, and Provence and the Côte d'Azur were no exception. After a false start, Cannes' 1946 international film festival heralded the return of party madness. The 1950s and 1960s saw a succession of society events: the fairy-tale marriage of Monaco's prince to Hollywood film-legend Grace Kelly in 1956; Vadim's filming of *Et Dieu Créa la Femme* (And God Created Woman) with a smouldering Brigitte Bardot in St-Tropez the same year; the creation of the bikini; the advent of topless sunbathing (and consequent nipple-covering with bottle tops to prevent arrest for indecent exposure); and Miles Davis, Ella Fitzgerald and Ray Charles appearing at the 1961 Juan-les-Pins jazz festival.

Rapid industrialisation marked the 1960s. A string of five hydroelectric plants was constructed on the banks of the River Durance and in 1964 Électricité de France (EDF), the French electricity company, dug a canal from Manosque to the Étang de Berre. The following year construction work began on a 100-sq-km petrochemical zone and an industrial plant at Fos-sur-Mer, southern Europe's most important. The first metro line opened in Marseille in 1977 and TGV high-speed trains reached the city in 1981.

From the 1970s mainstream tourism started making inroads into Provence's rural heart. The small flow of foreigners that had trickled into Provence backwaters to buy crumbling old *mas* (Provençal farmhouses) in the late 1970s had become an uncontrollable torrent by the 1980s. By the turn of the new millennium, the region was welcoming nine million tourists annually.

Modern Politics

Writer Somerset Maugham had famously described Monaco as 'a sunny place for shady people', but over the course of the 1980s and 1990s many increasingly felt that this could apply to the region as a whole. Although it was well-known that the Italian, Russian and Corsican mafias all operated on the coast, their true extent was revealed after a series of corruption scandals, none more dramatic than the assassination of *député* (member of parliament) Yann Piat in 1994: she was shot in her Hyères constituency following her public denunciation of the Riviera mafia.

The same year, former Nice mayor Jacques Médecin, who had run the city from 1966 to 1990, was found guilty of income-tax evasion and misuse of public funds after being extradited from Uruguay where he'd fled. And in 1995, Bernard Tapie, the flamboyant owner of Olympique de Marseille football club, was found guilty of match fixing and sentenced to two years in jail.

1953	1956	1981	2000
A 17-year-old Brigitte Bardot dons a bikini at the Cannes Film Festival, and starts a new fashion trend on the Côte d'Azur.	Rainier Louis Henri Maxence Bertrand Grimaldi, Count of Polignac, aka Prince Rainier III of Monaco, weds his fairy-tale princess, Hollywood film legend Grace Kelly.	The superfast TGV makes its first commercial journey from Paris to Lyon, breaking all speed records to complete the train journey in two hours instead of six.	European leaders meet in Nice to thrash out future EU expansion. Not without controversy, they establish a new system of voting in the Council of Ministers.

Many now think that it was these high-profile corruption cases, combined with economic recession and growing unemployment, that helped fuel the rise of the extreme-right Front National (FN). Led by firebrand Jean-Marie Le Pen, infamous for having described the Holocaust as a 'detail of history', the FN won municipal elections in Toulon, Orange and Marignane in 1995, and Vitrolles in 1997. The party also gained 15.5% of the vote in regional elections in 1998 and 14.7% in 2004.

The FN never succeeded in securing the presidency of the Provence-Alpes-Côte d'Azur *région,* but Le Pen's success in the first round of presidential elections in 2002 – he landed 16.86% of the vote, with his main support base in the south of France – shocked many people. He eventually lost in the second round, after a massive 80% turnout at the ballot boxes, and 82% of the vote in favour of his opponent, Jacques Chirac.

The far right continues to exert a strong pull over the region's political fortunes. Now known as Rassemblement National and run by Jean-Marie's daughter, Marine Le Pen, the party has continued to poll strongly in several important elections – including the presidential elections of 2017, when the party took four out of the six Provençal *départements* during the first round of voting, only to ultimately fail to win any during the second-round run-off against Emmanuel Macron. The movement was dealt another blow in 2017 when its young figurehead in Provence, Marion Maréchal-Le-Pen, the niece of current leader Marine Le-Pen, announced her decision to resign from politics, just five years after being elected the country's youngest parliamentarian.

The popularity of the far right can perhaps be explained by several thorny issues that continue to dog Provençal politics. Poverty, high unemployment and immigration remain perennial topics here, as does the threat of terrorism – especially in the wake of the brutal Bastille Day attack of 14 July 2016, when a 14-tonne truck was deliberately driven into crowds on Nice's Promenade des Anglais, killing 86 people and injuring 458 more. Subsequent investigations revealed the driver to be Mohamed Lahouaiej-Bouhlel, a Tunisian resident of France who had professed support for the Islamic State. Lahouaiej-Bouhlel was shot by police, and six accomplices were subsequently charged with terrorist offences.

Like the rest of France, Provence has had to come to terms both with the consequences of the attack itself, and the grim reality of planning for future terrorist incidents. Police presence has been strengthened at stations, airports and popular tourist areas, and while Provence is statistically no more dangerous than the rest of France, there's nevertheless something profoundly unsettling about the sight of armed police patrolling the Côte d'Azur, a place synonymous with fun, happiness and the good life.

Top Museums

Musée des Civilisations de l'Europe et de la Méditerranée (Marseille)

Musée d'Archéologie Méditerranée (Marseille)

Musée Archéologique (Fréjus)

Musée Départemental Arles Antique (Arles)

Hôtel de Sade (St-Rémy-de-Provence)

HISTORY MODERN POLITICS

2005	2016	2017	2021
After the end of a three-month mourning period for his father, Prince Albert II of Monaco is crowned monarch of the world's second-smallest country.	On Bastille Day, a man drives a truck into crowds along the Promenade des Anglais, killing 86 people in Provence's worst-ever terrorist attack.	Serious wildfires ravage many parts of Provence and the Côte d'Azur, causing large-scale emergency evacuations of thousands of people.	The sprawling Luma Arles, a 27-acre art and cultural campus opens in Arles. Its pièce de résistance is a shimmering tower designed by Frank Gehry.

Painters in Provence

Whether it was the search for a refuge, light or more clement weather, it seems that the painters who settled in Provence came here looking for something – and found a lot more than they'd hoped for.

The Impressionists
Van Gogh

Above Atelier Cézanne (p190), Aix-en-Provence

Vincent van Gogh (1853–90) arrived in Arles from Paris in 1888, keen to escape the excesses of the capital. He found inspiration amid the region's landscapes, customs and, above all, the intense quality of the light. By the time he left Arles a year later, he'd completed more than 200 oil paintings – including masterpieces such as *Bedroom in Arles* (1888) and *Still Life: Vase with Twelve Sunflowers* (1888).

Throughout his life, Van Gogh was wracked with self-doubt and depression, conditions that were compounded by his lack of commercial success – famously, he sold just a single painting during his entire career, and never received any kind of serious critical acclaim. He was prone to fits of manic depression, including the famous incident in December 1888, when he cut off part of his left ear following a spat with Paul Gauguin.

In May 1889, he voluntarily committed himself to an asylum in St-Rémy-de-Provence; despite his illness, he continued to work at a feverish pace, producing many key works including *Starry Night* (1889) and several haunting self-portraits. Van Gogh left St-Rémy in May 1890 to join his brother Theo in Auvers-sur-Oise; he shot himself two months later, aged just 37.

Van Gogh is now acknowledged as one of the 20th century's greatest painters. Most of his works now reside in international museums, although a few have stayed in Provence – notably at Musée Angladon (p229) in Avignon and Musée Granet (p185) in Aix-en-Provence.

Cézanne

Paul Cézanne (1839–1906) is perhaps the most Provençal of all the impressionists. His work is generally credited with providing a translation from 'traditional' 19th-century art to the radical new art forms of the 20th century, notably cubism.

Cézanne was born in Aix-en-Provence and spent most of his life there, save for a decade in Paris and another ferrying between Provence and the capital. He met writer Émile Zola at school in Aix and the pair remained friends for years – until Zola used Cézanne as the main inspiration for his character Claude Lantet, a failed painter, in his novel *L'Oeuvre* (The Work; 1886).

Provence was Cézanne's chief inspiration: the seaside village of L'Estaque, the Bibémus quarries near Aix (said to have inspired his cubist trials by their geometric character) and the family house, Jas de Bouffan, in Aix appear in dozens of paintings. But it was the Montagne Ste-Victoire (p190) that captivated him the most, its radiance, shape and colours depicted in no fewer than 30 oil paintings and 45 watercolours.

Sadly, Cézanne's admiration for Provence was not mutual: few of Aix's conservative bourgeoisie appreciated Cézanne's departure from the creed of classical painting and there were even calls for him to leave the city.

In 1902, Cézanne moved into a purpose-built studio, Les Lauves, from where he did much of his painting until his death in 1906. The studio has been left untouched and is one of the most poignant insights into his art.

Renoir

In 1892, Pierre-Auguste Renoir (1841–1919), started to develop rheumatoid arthritis. The condition gradually worsened, and in 1907 doctors ordered Renoir to move to the sunny climes of Cagnes-sur-Mer in a bid to alleviate his pains.

In 1909, Renoir bought a farm in Cagnes-sur-Mer called Les Colettes, where he lived until his death. Far from being a retirement home, however, Renoir enjoyed a new lease of life in the south of France and painted vigorously throughout his twilight years. Although he had to adapt his painting technique – he was wheelchair-bound and suffered from ankylosis in his shoulder – many credit his late works with displaying the same joy and radiance that were the hallmark of his earlier (and most famous) works.

Renoir's house at Les Colettes is now the Musée Renoir (p74), where you can see the artist's studios, his gorgeous garden and several of his works.

Van Gogh's Ear by Bernadette Murphy traces the truth about the artist's notorious act of self-mutilation, exploring the artist's life and times along the way and characters including his brother Theo and fellow artist Paul Gauguin.

PAINTERS IN PROVENCE THE IMPRESSIONISTS

Cézanne Sights

Atelier Cézanne (Aix-en-Provence)

Le Jas de Bouffan (Aix-en-Provence)

Carrières de Bibemus (Aix-en-Provence)

L'Estaque

Matisse

Originally from drab northern France, leading Fauvist exponent Henri Matisse (1869–1954) spent his most creative years lapping up the sunlight and vivacity of the coast in and around Nice.

Matisse travelled to southern France on a number of occasions, including a visit to impressionist Paul Signac in St-Tropez, which inspired one of his most famous works: *Luxe, Calme et Volupté* (Luxury, Calm and Tranquillity; 1904). But it was a trip to Nice to cure bronchitis in 1917 that left Matisse smitten – he never really looked back.

Matisse settled in Cimiez, in the hills north of Nice's centre, and it was here that he started experimenting with his *gouaches découpées* (collages of painted paper cutouts) in the 1940s, after an operation. The famous *Blue Nude* series and *The Snail* epitomise this period.

Matisse's ill health was also a key factor in the creation of his masterpiece, the Chapelle du Rosaire (p75) in Vence. The artist had been looked after by a nun during his convalescence and the chapel was his mark of gratitude. Matisse designed everything, from the stained-glass windows to the altar, the structure of the chapel and the robes of the priests. The chapel took four years to complete and was finished in 1951.

Matisse died in Nice in 1954 and is buried in Cimiez' cemetery.

Matisse Sights

Musée Matisse *(Nice)*

Chapelle du Rosaire *(Vence)*

Cemetery at Monastère de Cimiez *(Nice)*

Picasso

Although Pablo Picasso (1881–1973) moved to the Côte d'Azur rather late in life (the Spanish artist was in his mid-sixties when he moved to Golfe-Juan with his lover Françoise Gilot in 1946), his influence over the region and the region's influence on him were significant.

Vauvenargues & Mougins

In 1959, Picasso bought the Château de Vauvenargues (p184) near Aix-en-Provence. The castle slumbered at the foot of the Montagne Ste-Victoire, depicted so often by Cézanne, whom Picasso greatly admired. It was Cézanne's early studies on cubism that had led Picasso and his peers to launch the cubist movement (which seeks to deconstruct the subject into a system of intersecting planes and present various aspects of it simultaneously); Picasso was also an avid collector of Cézanne's works.

In 1961, Picasso moved to Mougins with his second wife, Jacqueline Roque. He had many friends in the area, including photographer André Villers, to whom Picasso gave his first camera and who in turn took numerous portraits of the artist.

Picasso died in Mougins in 1973 and is buried in Château de Vauvenargues, which remains the property of his family.

Picasso Sights

Musée Picasso *(Antibes)*

Musée National Picasso 'La Guerre et La Paix' *(Vallauris)*

Château de Vauvenargues

Musée de la Photographie André Villers *(Mougins)*

Antibes & Vallauris

It was following an offer from the curator of Antibes' Château Grimaldi – now the Musée Picasso (p83) – that Picasso set up a studio on the 3rd floor of the historic building. Works from this period are characterised by an extraordinary *joie de vivre* and a fascination with Mediterranean mythology.

It was that same year that Picasso visited the nearby potters' village of Vallauris and discovered ceramics. Picasso loved the three-dimensional aspect of the art and experimented endlessly. His method was somewhat unorthodox: he melted clay, used unglazed ceramics and decorated various pieces with relief motifs; he also eschewed traditional floral decorations for a bestiary of his favourite mythological creatures.

Picasso settled in Vallauris in 1948, and although he left in 1955, he carried on working with ceramics until his death. His time in Vallauris wasn't only dedicated to ceramics, however; it was here that Picasso got

Musée Matisse (p54), Nice

'his chapel' (arch-rival Matisse had finished his in 1951). It was the chapel of the town's castle, in which he painted *War and Peace* (1952), the last of his monumental creations dedicated to peace, after *Guernica* (1937) and *Massacre in Korea* (1951).

There are talks of a new museum dedicated to Picasso being established in Aix-en-Provence, by the artist's step-daughter, Catherine Hutin-Blay. If the museum comes to frution it will house 2000 Picasso works – the largest collection in the world.

Modern Art
Chagall

Belorussian painter Marc Chagall (1887–1985) moved to Paris from Russia in 1922. He was well-known for his dazzling palette and the biblical messages in his later works (inspired by his Jewish upbringing in Russia and trips to Palestine). Chagall managed to escape to the US during WWII, and it was upon his return to France in the early 1950s that he settled in St-Paul de Vence on the Côte d'Azur. Both Matisse and Picasso lived in the area at the time, and many artists regularly visited; it was this sense of 'artistic colony' that attracted Chagall.

Though Provence and the Côte d'Azur never featured explicitly in Chagall's works, he was clearly fascinated by the region's light and colour – something that becomes obvious looking at the luminous works on display at the Musée National Marc Chagall (p54) in Nice. Chagall is buried in St-Paul de Vence.

School of Nice

Provence and the Côte d'Azur produced a spate of artists at the forefront of modern art in the middle of the 20th century. Most famous perhaps

Hungarian-born Victor Vasarely (1908–97), best-known for his bold, colourful geometrical forms and shifting perspectives, had a summer house in Gordes from 1948. He opened a first museum there in 1970 (which closed in 1996) and a second one, Fondation Vasarely, in Aix-en-Provence in 1976, which you can still visit.

Musée d'Art Moderne et d'Art Contemporain (p54), Nice

was Nice-born Yves Klein (1928–62), who stood out for his series of daring monochrome paintings, the distinctive blue he used in many of his works (supposedly inspired by the colour of the Mediterranean) and his experiments in paint-application techniques: in his series *Anthropométrie,* paint was 'applied' by women covered from head to toe in paint and writhing naked on the canvas.

Also making a splash in modern-art circles was native Niçois Arman (1928–2005), who became known for his trash-can portraits, made by framing the litter found in the subject's rubbish bin, and Martial Raysse, born in Golfe-Juan in 1936, renowned for pioneering the use of neon in art: his 1964 portrait of *Nissa Bella* (Beautiful Nice) – a flashing blue heart on a human face – is typical.

Klein, Arman and Raysse were among the nine people to found New Realism in 1960. The movement was one of several avant-garde trends of the time and was often perceived as the French interpretation of American pop art. In 1961, another prominent Provençal artist, Marseillais César Baldaccini (1921–98), known for his crushed cars and scrap metal art, joined the New Realists' rank, as did Niki de Saint Phalle (1930–2002), famous for her huge, colourful papier mâché sculptures.

Nice's Musée d'Art Moderne et d'Art Contemporain (p54) has one of the best collections of New Realist artists' works; the building itself is a work of art too.

Yves Klein's famous blue became more than a signature colour: it was actually patented. It is now known in art circles as International Klein Blue (or IKB), a deep, bright hue close to ultramarine.

Cinema & the Arts

The artistic pace in this pocket of southern France has always been fast and furious, fuelled by a constant flux of new arrivals who brought with them new ideas, traditions and artistic know-how. From the novels of Fitzgerald to the films of the Nouvelle Vague (New Wave), this is a region where creativity and inspiration go hand in hand.

Cinema

Provence and cinema have had a thing going on for more than a century: one of the world's first motion pictures, by the Lumière brothers, premiered in La Ciotat (between Marseille and Toulon) in September 1895. The series of two-minute reels, entitled *L'Arrivée d'un Train en Gare de La Ciotat* (The Arrival of a Train at La Ciotat Station), made the audience leap out of their seats as the steam train rocketed forward.

Jacques Audiard's searing film *Un Prophète* (2009) explored the world of an Arab prisoner struggling to survive in a southern French jail. Not for the faint-hearted.

Early Days

French film flourished in the 1920s, Nice being catapulted to stardom by Hollywood director Rex Ingram, who bought the city's Victorine film studios in 1925 and transformed them overnight into the hub of European film-making.

A big name in the 1930s and '40s was Aubagne-born writer and film-maker Marcel Pagnol (1895–1974), whose career kicked off in 1931 with *Marius,* the first part of his Fanny trilogy, portraying pre-war Marseille. Pagnol's work was famous for its endearing depiction of Provençal people, and he remains a local icon.

Cannes & St-Tropez

With the Cannes Film Festival taking off after WWII, French cinema started to diversify. Jean Cocteau (1889–1963) eschewed realism with two masterpieces of cinema: *La Belle et la Bête* (Beauty and the Beast; 1945) and *Orphée* (Orpheus; 1950). The director's life and work is explored at the fantastic Musée Jean Cocteau Collection Séverin Wunderman in Menton.

Nouvelle Vague (New Wave) directors made films without big budgets, extravagant sets or big-name stars. Roger Vadim turned St-Tropez into the hot spot with his *Et Dieu Créa la Femme* (And God Created Woman; 1956), starring Brigitte Bardot. Jacques Démy's *La Baie des Anges* (The Bay of Angels; 1962) is set in Nice, while François Truffaut filmed part of *La Nuit Américaine* (The American Night; 1972) in the Victorine studios, the Niçois hinterland and the Vésubie valley.

Le Gendarme de St-Tropez (1964) is a knockabout comedy caper, worth watching for the period St-Tropez locations.

Contemporary Cinema

Provence and the Côte d'Azur continue to inspire and play host to hundreds of films. For a classic vision of sun-dappled Provence, it's hard to beat Claude Berri's dreamy double-bill, *Jean de Florette* and *Manon des Sources,* adapted from the classic books by Marcel Pagnol.

More action-packed tales such as *The Transporter* (starring Jason Statham) and the *Taxi* trilogy (by Luc Besson, complete with a home-grown rap soundtrack) were set on the Riviera and in Marseille respectively, while James Bond drops by Monaco in *GoldenEye*. The cult comedy *Bienvenu Chez les Ch'tis* tells the story of a Provençal public servant being relocated – shock horror – to northern France, and was a huge national hit.

The highlight of the calendar is Cannes' famous film festival, when major stars descend on the town to celebrate *la septième art* (the '7th art', as the French call cinema). The year's top film is awarded the Palme d'Or.

Architecture

Antiquity

Although there is plenty of evidence suggesting the region was inhabited several thousand years ago, early populations left little in the way of architecture. It was the Massiliots (Greeks) who, from 600 BCE, really started building across Provence; the Romans, however, took it to a whole new level. Their colossal architectural legacy includes amphitheatres, aqueducts, arches, temples and baths.

A distinctive feature to look out for in rural Provence are *bories,* small dome-shaped buildings made of stone and usually used as store-houses and sometimes as dwellings. Their design stretches back into prehistory, but the same essential shape was still being used by local farmers right up to the 20th century. A small village of restored *bories* can be seen near Gordes in the Luberon.

Romanesque to Renaissance

A religious revival in the 11th century ushered in Romanesque architecture, so-called because of the Gallo-Roman architectural elements it adopted. Round arches, heavy walls with few windows, and a lack of ornamentation were characteristics of this style, Provence's most famous examples being the 12th-century abbeys in Sénanque and Le Thoronet.

Gothic architecture swapped roundness and simplicity for ribbed vaults, pointed arches, slender verticals, chapels along the nave and chancel, refined decoration and large stained-glass windows. Provence's most important examples of this period are Avignon's Palais des Papes and the Chartreuse du Val de Bénédiction in Villeneuve-lès-Avignon.

The French Renaissance scarcely touched the region – unlike mighty citadel architect Sébastien Le Prestre de Vauban (1633–1707), who notably reshaped Antibes' star-shaped Fort Carré and Île Ste Marguerite's Fort Royal.

Classical to Modern

Classical architecture fused with painting and sculpture from the end of the 16th to late 18th centuries to create stunning Baroque structures with interiors of great subtlety, refinement and elegance: Chapelle de la Miséricorde in Nice and Marseille's Centre de la Vieille Charité are classics.

Neoclassicism came into its own under Napoleon III, the Palais de Justice and Palais Masséna in Nice demonstrating its the renewed interest in classical forms. The true showcase of this era, though, is the 1878 Monte Carlo Casino, designed by French architect Charles Garnier (1825–98). Elegant Aix-en-Provence's fountains and *hôtels particuliers* (private mansions) date from this period too, as do the intricate wrought-iron campaniles.

The belle époque heralded an eclecticism of decorative stucco friezes, *trompe l'œil* paintings, glittering wall mosaics, brightly coloured Moorish minarets and Turkish towers. Anything went.

The three decades following WWII were marked, as in much of Europe, by the rise of modernist architecture – concrete blocks and high-rise towers

Coco Before Chanel is a 2009 film starring Audrey Tautou as the legendary French designer Coco Chanel and exploring her early life before fashion fame and acclaim.

The 2003 film *Swimming Pool* stars Charlotte Rampling as crime novelist Sarah Morton, who travels to the south of France, and strikes up an unlikely and tempestuous relationship with wild-child Julie, played by Ludivine Sagnier.

– partly as a response to pressing housing needs. Marseille's notorious suburbs, Monaco's forest of skyscrapers and the emblematic pyramidal Marina Baie des Anges in Villeneuve-Loubet all date back to this era. Many now bemoan the flurry of postwar construction, often built for speed and cost rather than aesthetic value.

Contemporary Architecture

As with every other art form, Provence and the Côte d'Azur have kept innovating in architecture. Mouans-Sartoux' 2004 lime-green Espace de l'Art Concret, designed by Swiss-based architects Annette Gigon and Mike Guyer to complement the village's 16th-century château, has to be among the boldest examples.

Another famous contemporary architect to have left his print on Provence–Côte d'Azur is British master Sir Norman Foster, who designed Nîmes' steel-and-glass Carré d'Art, the Musée de la Préhistoire des Gorges du Verdon in Quinson and the five-storey building for Monaco Yacht Club, which opened in the summer of 2014. His firm is also leading the redevelopment and extension of Marseille's airport.

In 2017 Renzo Piano Building Workshop also designed a flashy building in Provence, the sail-topped Château La Coste Art Gallery in a vineyard near Aix-en-Provence.

There are lots more new buildings of note, though their architects aren't quite household names yet – like the Musée Jean Cocteau in Menton by Rudy Ricciotti, who also designed the Pavillon Noir in Aix-en-Provence. The cow-print-like seafront building couldn't contrast more with the old town's Italianate architecture and is an ode to Cocteau's own surrealist style. Contemporary French architects Elisabeth and Christian de Portzamparc are also making waves with their design for the Musée de la Romanité in Nîmes, the latest in a long line of landmark urban projects for the pair.

Literature
Courtly Love to Nostradamus

Lyric poems of courtly love, written by troubadours solely in the Occitan language, dominated medieval Provençal literature.

Provençal life featured in the works of Italian poet Petrarch (1304–74), exiled in 1327 to Avignon, where he met Laura, to whom he dedicated his life's works. Petrarch lived in Fontaine de Vaucluse from 1337 to 1353, where he wrote poems and letters about local shepherds,

LE CORBUSIER

It was rather late in life that Swiss-born Charles-Édouard Jeanneret (1887–1965), alias Le Corbusier, turned to the south of France. He first came to visit his friends Eileen Gray, an Irish designer, and Romanian-born architect Jean Badovici in the 1930s. Gray and Badovici had a very modern seaside villa, E-1027, on Cap-Martin, and Le Corbusier was a frequent guest.

However, following a spat with Gray in 1938, Le Corbusier built his own holiday pad, Le Cabanon. It remained his summer cabin until his death in 1965 (he died of a heart attack while swimming).

Le Cabanon is unique because it is a project that Le Corbusier built for himself, but his most revolutionary design is undoubtedly the Marseille concrete apartment block L'Unité d'Habitation. Built between 1947 and 1952 as a low-cost housing project, it comprised 337 apartments arranged inside an elongated block on stilts; deeply controversial at the time, it's been protected as a historical monument since 1986.

Le Corbusier is buried with his wife in section J of Roquebrune-Cap-Martin cemetery.

fishermen he met on the banks of the Sorgue, and his pioneering ascent up Mont Ventoux.

In 1555 the philosopher and visionary writer from St-Rémy-de-Provence, Nostradamus (1503–66), published (in Latin) his prophetic *Centuries* in Salon de Provence, where he lived until his death (from gout, as he had predicted).

Mistral to Mayle

The 19th century witnessed a revival in Provençal literature, thanks to poet Frédéric Mistral (1830–1914). Mistral set up the literary movement Le Félibrige with six other young Provençal poets in a bid to revive the Provençal dialect and codify its orthography. The result was Provençal dictionary *Lou Trésor dou Félibrige*.

Numerous writers passed through or settled in Provence over the course of the 20th century. Colette (1873–1954) lived in St-Tropez from 1927 until 1938; her novel *La Naissance du Jour* (Break of Day) evokes an unspoilt St-Tropez. F Scott Fitzgerald enjoyed several stays in the inter-war years; playwright Samuel Beckett sought refuge in Roussillon during WWII; Lawrence Durrell (1912–90) settled in Somières, near Nîmes; and Graham Greene lived in Antibes for many years and even wrote an incendiary pamphlet about political corruption in the 1980s.

Most famous perhaps is Peter Mayle (1939–2018), whose novels about life as an Englishman in Provence have greatly contributed to the popularity of the region. He wrote a string of highly successful novels, beginning with the bestselling memoir *A Year in Provence* in 1989, which inspired countless Brits to follow in his footsteps in search of the Provençal good life as well as a string of bestselling sequels. He died aged 78 in 2018.

Never Mind (Edward St Aubyn; 1992) is the first of five semi-autobiographical books featuring the author's alter-ego Patrick Melrose and his dysfunctional, deeply unpleasant aristocratic English family. Much of the book is set in their country retreat in southern France.

Music

Traditional Provençal music is based on polyphonic chants; as a music form, they have gone out of fashion, although they remain part and parcel of traditional celebrations, notably Christmas and Easter.

Where Provence has really made a contribution to the French contemporary music scene is in rap, jazz and world music, with Marseille's multicultural background proving an inspiration to many artists.

The phenomenal hip-hop lyrics of 1991 smash-hit album, *de la Planète Mars* ('From Planet Mars', Mars being short for Marseille) by rapping legends IAM – France's best-known rap group from Marseille – nudged rap into the mainstream. IAM have since gone on to collaborate with everyone from Beyoncé to film-director Luc Besson.

Since that time, the city's music scene has transcended its rap roots. Cheb Khaled, Cheb Aïssa and Cheb Mami – all from Marseille – have contributed hugely to the development of Algerian *raï* and have encouraged other world-music talents such as Iranian percussionist Bijan Chemiranito, who plays the *zarb* (Persian goblet drum).

The Riviera has also fostered a special relationship with jazz music over the years. Nice launched its jazz festival in 1948; Antibes-Juan-les-Pins followed in 1960 after legendary saxophonist Sidney Bechet settled there in the 1950s. Numerous jazz greats have played here since – including Ella Fitzgerald, Miles Davis and Ray Charles, as well as modern artists like Jamie Cullum.

Provençal Living

Life in Provence has much in common with the rest of France – not least a love of food, family, wine and good living. But make no mistake: this is a region that's fiercely proud of its history, heritage and culture, and it's important to get to grips with Provençal passions if you want to understand what makes its people tick.

A Question of Identité

Young or old, people in the south tend to share a staunch loyalty to the hamlet, village, town or city in which they live. People in Marseille have a particularly passionate attachment to their city, a port known for its stereotyped rough-and-tumble inhabitants, who are famed among the French for their exaggerations and imaginative fancies, such as the tale about the sardine that blocked Marseille port.

Markedly more Latin in outlook and temperament, Niçois exhibit a zest for the good life in common with their Italian neighbours; law-abiding Monégasques dress up to the nines, and don't break the law or gossip. In rural pastures where family trees go back several generations and occupations remain firmly implanted in the soil, identity is deeply rooted in tradition.

Affluent outsiders buying up the region are prompting some traditional village communities to question their own (shifting) identities. With 20% of privately owned homes being *résidences secondaires* (second homes), everyday shops in some villages are struggling to stay open year-round, while property prices in many places have spiralled out of reach of local salaries.

The list of Provence–Côte d'Azur's most famous residents is long and always shifting. Angelina Jolie and Brad Pitt own Château de Miraval in Correns. The Beckhams have a villa in Bargemon, John Malkovich has one in the Luberon and singer Bono has one in Èze-sur-Mer.

Le Weekend

The working week in Provence is much like any working week in any other developed country: plagued with routine, commuting and getting the children to school, albeit with more sunshine than in many places.

The weekend, however, is when living in Provence comes into its own. Going to the local market on Saturday or Sunday morning is a must, not only to pick the finest ingredients for a delicious lunch or dinner, but also to catch up on gossip at the stalls or stop for a coffee at the village cafe.

Sport is another weekend favourite; football, cycling, trekking, sailing, skiing and scuba-diving are all popular in the region. Between April and October many people head to the beach for the afternoon.

Weekends also mean going out, whatever your age. Young people pile into the region's bars and nightclubs (the latter don't open until 11pm, so partying generally finishes in the wee hours of the morning); older generations dress up to go out for dinner at a restaurant or a friend's house, working their way through aperitif, three courses, coffee and *digestif*.

Along with its sing-song quality, *L'accent du midi's* most distinctive aspects are the addition of a 'g' sound for words ending in nasal sounds (so 'pain' sounds more like 'pang') and a silent 'e' at the end of a word becoming a full-on 'euh'.

Pétanque

If there's one image that sums up the Provençal lifestyle, it's a game of *pétanque* being played on a patch of dusty ground in the evening sunshine.

PROVENCE BETWEEN PAGES

No titles provide better insight into Provençal living, past and present, than these:

Everybody Was So Young (Amanda Vaill; 1998) Beautiful evocation of an American couple and their glam literary friends in the jazzy 1920s.

Côte d'Azur: Inventing the French Riviera (Mary Blume; 1992) Fabulous portrait of Riviera life: fantasy, escapism, pleasure, fame, eccentricity...

Provence A–Z (Peter Mayle; 2006) The best, the quirkiest, the most curious moments of the 20-odd years this best-selling author has spent in Provence.

Provençal Escapes (Caroline Clifton-Mogg; 2005) Image-driven snoop around beautiful homes in Provence.

Words in a French Life: Lessons in Love and Language from the South of France (Kristin Espinasse; 2006) Daily life in Provence through a series of French words.

Pétanque (known in the rest of France as boules) was invented in La Ciotat, near Marseille, in 1910 when arthritis-crippled Jules Le Noir could no longer take the running strides prior to aiming demanded by the *longue boule* game. The local champion thus stood with his feet firmly on the ground – a style that became known as *pieds tanques* (Provençal for 'tied feet', from which *'pétanque'* emerged).

To have a spin yourself (or watch the drama unfold on the village square), here are the rules:

➡ Two to six people, split into two teams, can play. Each player has three solid metal boules (balls).

➡ Each team takes it in turn to aim a boule at a tiny wooden ball called a *cochonnet* (jack), the idea being to land the boule as close as possible to it. The team with the closest boule wins the round; points are allocated by totting up how many boules the winner's team has closest to the marker (one point for each boule). The first to notch up 13 wins the match.

➡ The team throwing the *cochonnet* (initially decided by a coin toss) has to throw it from a small circle scratched in the gravel. It must be hurled 6m to 10m away. Each player aiming a boule must likewise stand in this circle, with both feet planted firmly on the ground.

➡ Underarm throwing is compulsory. Beyond that, players can roll the boule along the ground (known as *pointer*, literally 'to point') or hurl it high into the air in the hope of its landing smack-bang on top of an opponent's boule and sending it flying out of position. This flamboyant tactic, called *tirer* (literally 'to shoot'), can turn an entire game around in seconds.

It's estimated that fewer than 100,000 people speak Provençal, the region's traditional language, a remarkable fact considering most locals didn't learn French until the beginning of the 20th century. Universal primary education cemented French as the country's lingua franca. You're most likely to see Provençal used on road signs.

Olympique de Marseille

Long the stronghold, not to mention heart and soul, of French football, Olympique de Marseille (OM; www.om.net) was national champion for four consecutive years between 1989 and 1992, and in 2010, but the team's fortunes have been mixed since. In 2016, US businessman Frank McCourt – formerly the owner of the LA Dodgers – acquired the club and vowed to restore the club's glory days.

The club has a die-hard fan base and the city has spawned many football greats, chief among them Zinedine Zidane, aka Zizou, who captained France to victory in the 1998 World Cup. The most important match of the year is Le Classique, played against arch-rivals Paris St-Germain.

Arsenal manager Arsène Wenger and star striker Thierry Henry both began their careers with the region's other strong club, AS Monaco (ASM).

Survival Guide

Directory A–Z

Accessible Travel

France is slowly improving access for travellers with disabilities (*visiteurs handicapés*), but inevitably there are problems – narrow streets, cobbles, a lack of kerb ramps and a lack of elevators in old hotels, to name a few. For guidance, download Lonely Planet's free Accessible Travel guides from https://shop.lonelyplanet.com/categories/accessible-travel.com.

➡ Check carefully whether your hotel or B&B has an elevator and is fully accessible – steps and small bathrooms are common pitfalls.

➡ Most parking areas have dedicated sections for drivers with disabilities (bring your parking placard).

➡ Some beaches are wheelchair accessible – flagged *handiplages* on city maps – in Cannes, Marseille, Nice, Hyères, Ste-Maxime and Monaco.

➡ Michelin's *Guide Rouge* and Gîtes de France (www.gites-de-france-paca.com) flag wheelchair access in their listings.

➡ Most SNCF trains are wheelchair accessible; major train stations will have staff who can assist you as you get on board.

➡ Detailed information is available on the SNCF Accessibilité website (www.accessibilite.sncf.com).

Climate

Marseille

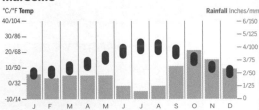

Accommodation

For information on accommodation in Provence and the Côte d'Azur, see p24.

Customs Regulations

Goods imported and exported within the EU incur no additional taxes, provided duty has already been paid somewhere within the EU and the goods are for personal consumption. Duty-free shopping is only available if you are leaving the EU. For full details, see www.douane.gouv.fr.

Coming from non-EU countries, duty-free adult allowances are as follows:

➡ 200 cigarettes

➡ 50 cigars

➡ 1L of spirits

➡ 2L of wine

➡ 50mL of perfume

➡ 250mL of eau de toilette

Discount Cards

Many museums and monuments sell *billets jumelés* (combination tickets). Some cities, such as Aix-en-Provence, Arles and Avignon, have museum passes. Seniors over 60 or 65 are entitled

---

PLAN YOUR STAY ONLINE

For more accommodation reviews by Lonely Planet authors, check out www.lonelyplanet.com. You'll find independent reviews, as well as recommendations on the best places to stay

to discounts on public transport, museums and cinemas. Train discounts are available.

French Riviera Pass (www. frenchrivierapass.com) Allows admission to all Nice's paying attractions, plus many nearby.

Electricity

➡ Plugs have two round pins; electrical current is 220V/50Hz AC.

Type C
220V/50Hz

Type E
220V/50Hz

EATING PRICE RANGES

·······················

The following prices refer to two-course *menus* – appetiser and main, or main and dessert.

€ less than €20

€€ €20–40

€€€ more than €40

Embassies & Consulates

All embassies are in Paris, but several countries have consulates in Marseille or Nice.

Australian Embassy (☑01 40 59 33 00; www.france.embassy. gov.au; 4 rue Jean Rey, 15e; Ⓜ Bir Hakeim)

Canadian Embassy (☑01 44 43 29 00; www.amb-canada.fr; 35 av Montaigne, 8e; Ⓜ Franklin D Roosevelt)

Dutch Consulate (☑04 91 25 66 64; www.amb-pays-bas.fr; 146 rue Paradis, Marseille; ☒41)

German Consulate (☑04 91 16 75 20; www.marseille.diplo.de; 10 place de la Joliette, Marseille; ☉8.30-11.30am Mon Fri; Ⓜ Joliette)

New Zealand Embassy (☑01 45 01 43 43; www.mfat.govt. nz; 103 rue de Grenelle, 7e; Ⓜ Varenne)

UK Consulate (☑04 91 15 72 10; www.gov.uk; 1st fl, 10 place de la Joliette, Marseille; ☉9.30am-12.30pm Mon, Wed & Fri; ☒35, 82)

US Consulate (☑01 43 12 48 85; https://fr.usembassy.gov; place Varian Fry, Marseille; ☉9am-noon & 2-5pm Mon-Fri; Ⓜ Estrangin Préfecture)

Food

For information on food in Provence and the Côte d'Azur, see p37.

Health

Health care in France is of an extremely high standard, with major hospitals near every major city, supple-

mented by many smaller regional hospitals. EU citizens are guaranteed reciprocal healthcare, but other travellers should take out appropriate health insurance.

Before You Go

No vaccinations are required for France, but the World Health Organization recommends travellers be vaccinated against diphtheria, tetanus, measles, mumps, rubella and polio, regardless of destination.

Availability & Cost of Health Care

➡ For emergencies, dial 15 for ambulance (SAMU) or urgent house call. Or find the nearest *hôpital* or *salles des urgence*. Doctors' offices are *cabinets médicals*.

➡ For medical referrals and minor illnesses, pharmacists dispense advice and sell medications; look for green neon crosses.

➡ Doctor visits cost about €25.

➡ Emergency contraception is available by prescription. Condoms (*préservatifs*) are commonly available.

➡ If your problem is not sufficiently serious to call SAMU but you still need to consult a doctor at night, call the 24-hour doctor service, operational in most towns in the region.

Insurance

Medical Insurance

EU citizens and those from Switzerland, Iceland, Norway and Liechtenstein are covered for emergencies by the

European Health Insurance Card (EHIC), but not for non-emergencies or repatriation. Every family member needs a card. Seek care from state providers (conventionnés); private health care is not covered. Pay directly and keep receipts for reimbursement.

If you're not from Europe you need to determine whether your country has reciprocity with France for free medical care. If you need health insurance, strongly consider a policy that covers worst-case scenarios, including emergency medical evacuation. Determine in advance if your insurance pays directly for overseas expenditures or reimburses you later (it's probably the latter). Keep all documentation.

Travel Insurance

We recommend travel insurance covering theft, loss and medical problems. Some policies exclude dangerous activities, including diving, motorcycling and mountaineering. Read the fine print.

Purchasing airline tickets with a credit card may provide limited travel-accident insurance. Ask your credit-card company.

Internet Access

➔ Wi-fi (pronounced wee-fee) is offered by many hotels, cafes and some tourist offices. If you need the password, ask for le code.

➔ Wi-fi is also available in many public spaces; check coverage at www.journaldunet.com/wifi.

➔ 3G is widely available in urban areas, but check roaming rates with your provider before you switch it on.

➔ Internet cafes provide access for €4 to €6 per hour but are becoming rare – it's a better idea just to head for the nearest bar or cafe.

Language Courses

The government site www.diplomatie.gouv.fr (under 'Francophony') and www.europa-pages.com/france list language schools.

Centre Méditerranéen d'Études Françaises (www.cmef-monaco.fr; av Prince Rainier III de Monaco, chemin des Oliviers, Cap d'Ail) Côte d'Azur language school since 1952.

Legal Matters

➔ French police have wide powers of search and seizure, and may demand identification at any time, regardless of 'probable cause'.

➔ Foreigners must be able to prove immigration status (eg passport, visa, residency permit).

➔ Verbally (or physically) abusing police officers carries hefty fines, even imprisonment.

➔ You may refuse to sign a police statement, and you have the right to request a copy.

➔ Those arrested are innocent until proven guilty but may be held until trial. The website www.service-public.fr details rights.

➔ French police are ultra-strict with security. Never leave baggage unattended at airports or stations: suspicious objects may be destroyed.

➔ French law makes no distinction between 'hard' and 'soft' drugs.

➔ The penalty for personal use of stupéfiants (including cannabis) can be a one-year jail sentence and a €3750 fine but may be lessened to a stern talking-to or compulsory rehab.

➔ Public drunkenness (ivresse) is punishable by a €150 fine. It's illegal to drive with a blood-alcohol concentration (BAC) over 0.05%. Police conduct random breathalyser tests.

➔ Smoking is illegal in public interiors, including restaurants and bars.

LGBTIQ+ Travellers

France is liberal about LGBT matters, but, as always, rural Provence tends to be more conservative than its big cities. Aix-en-Provence, Nice and Cannes have gay bars, while Marseille has the region's biggest gay community and hosts the **Lesbian & Gay Parade** (⊘Jul).

Centre Évolutif Lilith (CEL; Map p160; ☑06 99 55 06 02; http://celmrs.free.fr; 93 La Canebière) Lesbian socialising, activism.

Gay Provence (☑04 91 84 08 96; www.gay-provence.org) Hotel listings.

Gay Map Marseille (www.gaymapmarseille.com) Entertainment in Aix and Marseille.

Maps

Driving, cycling and hiking maps are widely available at maisons de la presse (newsagencies), papeteries (stationery shops), tourist offices, bookshops and petrol stations. Quality maps cost about €7 or €8. The website http://fr.mappy.com has online maps and a journey planner, including tolls and petrol costs.

Free street plans (maps) distributed by tourist offices range from superb to useless.

FFRP (www.ffrandonnee.fr) Topographic hiking maps.

Institut Géographique National (www.ign.fr) France's definitive map publishers, great for hiking and cycling.

Michelin (www.viamichelin.com, www.michelin-boutique.com) Brilliant atlases and driving maps.

Money

The euro (€) is the only legal tender in France and Monaco. ATMs are widely available, and most hotels and restaurants take credit cards.

ATMs

ATMs (distributeurs automatiques de billets or points d'argent) are the easiest means of obtaining cash, but banks charge foreign-transaction fees (usually 2% to 3%), plus a per-use ATM charge. Check with your bank. Cirrus and Maestro networks are common.

Credit & Debit Cards

Credit and debit cards are widely accepted, although some restaurants and B&Bs may only accept cash.

➡ North American cards with magnetic strips don't work on (certain) autoroutes or at unattended 24-hour petrol stations – which can leave you in a sticky situation if you have no alternative method of payment.

➡ Nearly everywhere requires a card with a chip and PIN. Notify your bank/card provider before departure to avoid a block on your account.

➡ Visa (Carte Bleue – or CB – in France) and MasterCard (Access or Eurocard) are common. American Express is less so, but Amex offices provide exchange and travel services.

➡ Credit cards generally incur a more favourable exchange rate than debit cards, but it depends entirely on your bank/credit-card provider.

➡ Most credit cards charge a foreign-transaction fee (generally around 2.5%), but again it depends on the provider. Some credit cards charge a 0% fee for overseas use.

➡ Consider getting a prepaid currency card, which you can load with currency before departure. You won't incur a foreign-transaction fee, and if it's lost you just cancel the card and order a replacement. Most importantly, you don't lose the funds.

Moneychangers

➡ Banks usually charge stiff €3 to €5 fees per foreign-currency transaction – if they change money at all.

➡ Bureaux de change (exchange bureaux) are faster and easier, are open longer and usually have better rates.

➡ To track rates and find local exchange bureaux, see http://travelmoney.moneysavingexpert.com.

➡ Some post offices exchange travellers cheques and banknotes but charge a €5 commission for cash; most won't take US$100 bills.

Travellers Cheques

Secure and fee-free, but places where they are accepted are becoming extremely rare. Must be converted at exchange bureaux, and rates aren't always favourable.

Opening Hours

Most businesses, sights and museums close over lunch between noon and 2pm. In rural Provence, many places open only from Pâques (Easter) to Toussaint (1 November). Standard hours are as follows:

Banks 9am–noon and 2pm–5pm Monday to Friday

Cafes 8am–11pm Monday to Saturday

Post offices 8.30am–5pm Monday to Friday, 8am–noon Saturday

Restaurants Lunch noon–2.30pm, dinner 7pm–11pm

Shops 10am–noon and 2pm–6.30pm Monday or Tuesday to Saturday

Supermarkets 8.30am–7pm Monday to Saturday, 8.30am–12.30pm Sunday

Public Holidays

French Public Holidays

The following jours fériés (public holidays) are observed in France:

New Year's Day (Jour de l'An) 1 January

Easter Sunday & Monday (Pâques & lundi de Pâques) late March/April

May Day (Fête du Travail) 1 May

TIPPING

By law, restaurants and cafes are service compris (15% service included), thus there's no need to leave a pourboire (tip). If satisfied with the service, leave a euro or two on the table.

Bar Round to nearest euro

Hotel housekeepers €1 to €1.50 per day

Porters €1 to €1.50 per bag

Restaurants Generally 2% to 5%

Taxis 10% to 15%

Toilet attendant €0.20 to €0.50

Tour guide €1 to €2 per person

PRACTICALITIES

Weights and measures France uses the metric system. To convert kilometres to miles, multiply by 0.6; miles to kilometres, multiply by 1.6.

Radio Regional news and chat airs in English on Monte Carlo–based Riviera Radio (www.rivieraradio.mc).

Newspapers French-language regional newspapers are *Nice Matin* (www.nicematin.fr) and *La Provence* (www.laprovence.com). English-language regional newspapers are the *Riviera Reporter* (www.riviera-reporter.com) and *Riviera Times* (www.rivieratimes.com).

TV French TV networks broadcast a second audio in the program's original language, often English, so fiddle with your remote.

Victoire 1945 8 May – celebrates the Allied victory that ended WWII

Ascension Thursday (L'Ascension) May – the 40th day after Easter

Pentecost/Whit Sunday & Whit Monday (Pentecôte & lundi de Pentecôte) mid-May to mid-June – celebrated seventh Sunday after Easter

Bastille Day/National Day (Fête Nationale) 14 July

Assumption Day (L'Assomption) 15 August

All Saints' Day (La Toussaint) 1 November

Remembrance Day (L'onze Novembre) 11 November – marks WWI armistice

Christmas (Noël) 25 December

Monégasque Public Holidays

Monaco shares the same holidays, except 8 May, 14 July and 11 November. Additionally:

Feast of Ste-Dévote 27 January – Monaco's saint's day

Corpus Christi June – three weeks after Ascension

National Day (Fête Nationale) 19 November

Immaculate Conception 8 December

Safe Travel

In general, Provence is a safe destination. Petty theft and burglary are the main problems – especially in touristy cities such as Marseille and Nice – but assault is rare.

Beaches & Rivers

➔ Watch for pale-purple jellyfish on beaches.

➔ Major rivers are often connected to hydroelectric stations and flood suddenly when dams open. Ask tourist offices about *l'ouverture des barrages* – commonplace in summer.

➔ Swimming is prohibited in reservoirs with unstable banks (eg Lac de Ste-Croix, southwest of Gorges du Verdon; Lac de Castillon; and Lac de Chaudanne, northeast of the gorges). Sailing, windsurfing and canoeing are restricted to flagged areas.

Extreme Weather

Thunderstorms – sometimes violent and dangerous – are common in August and September. Check weather (*la météo*) before embarking on hikes. Carry pocket rain gear and extra layers to prevent hypothermia. Year-round, *mistral* winds can be maddening.

Forest Fires

➔ In fire emergency, dial 18. Forest fires are common in July and August, and spread incredibly fast. July to mid-September, high-risk trails close. Never walk in closed zones.

➔ Forests are criss-crossed by fire roads. Signposted DFCI (forest-fire defence team) tracks are closed to motorists but open to walkers.

➔ Campfires are forbidden. Barbecues are forbidden in many areas in July and August.

Theft

It's sensible to take the usual precautions: don't flash money around, keep expensive electronics and camera equipment concealed, and beware of pickpockets in busy areas (rucksacks are a favourite target).

➔ Mobile-phone theft is now probably the most common theft of all – tourists wandering around following directions on Google Maps are favourite targets. Try not to wander round city streets and train stations staring at your phone, and keep it hidden when not using it.

➔ Theft from luggage, pockets, cars, trains and laundrettes is widespread, particularly along the Côte d'Azur. Beware pickpockets in crowded tourist areas.

➔ If you carry a rucksack in very crowded areas, slinging it across your front makes it harder for pickpockets to undo the zips without you noticing.

➔ Keep close watch on bags, especially in markets, at train and bus stations, at outdoor cafes, on beaches and during overnight train rides (lock your compartment door).

➔ If travelling on trains, don't leave laptops, tablets and smartphones on display. If you go to the toilet or plan to sleep, lock your compartment door.

➔ If you're worried, lock your passport in your safe,

or ask at reception to use the hotel's safe if your room doesn't have one. Don't forget it when you leave!

➔ Carry your passport number (or a photocopy) and your driver's licence for ID.

➔ Email yourself scans, or upload cloud copies of important documents such as passports, travel insurance documents, driving licences and so on. They're much easier to replace if you have copies. Photocopies are a useful back-up.

➔ When swimming, don't leave valuables unattended – you might have to take turns. On the Prado beaches in Marseille, consider placing valuables in one of the free (staffed) lockers.

➔ Break-ins on unattended vehicles are a big problem – leave nothing of value inside.

➔ Aggressive theft from cars stopped at red lights is an occasional problem in Marseille, Nice and larger cities; keep doors locked and windows up when idling.

➔ Common cons: thief finds a gold ring in your path, or lays a newspaper on your restaurant table, or approaches to ask if you speak English. Ignore children with clipboards, especially those playing deaf.

Telephone
Dialling Codes

Calling France (or Monaco) from home Dial your country's international-access code, then 33 for France (or 377 for Monaco), then the 10-digit number, without the initial zero.

Calling abroad from France Dial 00 for international access, then the country code (1 for US, 44 UK, 16 Australia), then the area code and local number, minus any initial zeros.

Mobile Phones

➔ French mobile-phone numbers begin with 06 or 07.

➔ Most modern smartphones will be able to pick up a signal from one of France's main carriers: Bouygues (www.bouyguestelecom.fr), Orange (www.orange.fr) and SFR (www.sfr.com).

➔ For EU travellers, roaming charges are now standardised across the EU area, meaning you can use your calls, texts and data package as you would back home for no extra cost. You'll probably receive a text message reminding you when you first switch on your phone.

➔ For non-EU travellers, phone and data roaming is likely to be more expensive (often substantially more expensive), although many providers now offer contracts that include certain overseas destinations; check before you travel.

➔ Some providers offer call and data packages that cover travel in other European countries for a fixed daily fee; check before you leave.

➔ If you are a pay-as-you-go user, or your provider doesn't offer overseas roaming packages, then it may be cheaper to buy a French SIM card or a French pay-as-you-go handset than to use your own phone. If so, buy when you land in Paris, where more salespeople speak English than in Provence.

➔ Remember that SMS texting is always cheaper than making a call – and using wi-fi in a cafe or tourist office combined with a message or calling service such as WhatsApp is completely free.

➔ For help in English with all Orange services, see www.

orange.com or call 09 69 36 39 00.

Phonecards & Payments

Public payphones are becoming rarer by the day, but assuming you can find one, it's almost certain to only accept credit cards or phonecards (available at tobacconists and super-markets). Rates are likely to be very high for both.

Useful Numbers & Codes

Emergency numbers Free from payphones and mobiles.

International access code 00

France country code 33

Monaco country code 377

Directory enquiries 12 or 11 87 12 (€1, plus €0.23 per minute). Not all operators speak English.

International directory enquiries 11 87 00

Time

France uses the 24-hour clock (eg 20.00 is 8pm) and Central European Time, one hour ahead of GMT/UTC. During daylight saving (last Sunday in March to last Sunday in October), France is two hours ahead of GMT/UTC.

Toilets

➔ Public toilets are signposted *toilettes* or WC. In towns, look for public toilets near the town hall, port, public squares or parking areas.

➔ Mechanical, coin-operated toilets are free or €0.20. (Never dodge in after the previous user or you'll be doused with disinfectant!) If you exceed 15 minutes, the door automatically opens. Green means *libre* (available); red *occupé* (busy).

→ A few older cafes and petrol stations still have hole-in-the-floor squat toilets. Provided you hover, they're hygienic, but stand clear when flushing.

→ The French are used to unisex facilities.

Tourist Information

Nearly every city, town and village – even the smallest ones – usually has a tourist office where you can pop in and pick up a wealth of local information, ranging from accommodation to transport schedules and nearby activities. In larger towns, there's nearly always at least one staff member who can speak English.

Tourisme PACA (www.tourisme paca.fr) The region's main tourist portal, packed with high-level information.

Côte d'Azur (www.cote dazur-tourisme.com) Similar general info for the Riviera towns.

Visas

The new European Travel Information and Authorisation System (ETIAS) is slated to go into effect by the end of 2022 or 2023. Some nationalities (including US, Canadian, Australian and New Zealand passport holders) will need to fill out the ETIAS registration form and pay a fee online in order to obtain an ETIAS visa waiver. Negotiations are still underway, but UK travellers may also need an ETIAS visa waiver. Other nationalities will require a Schengen visa.

For up-to-date information on visa requirements see www.etiasvisa.com and http://france-visas.gouv.fr.

→ EU nationals and citizens of Iceland, Liechtenstein, Norway and Switzerland need only their passport to enter France and work. However, nationals of the 12 countries that joined the EU in 2004 and 2007 are subject to residency and work limitations.

→ Citizens of the US, Australia, Canada, New Zealand, Bosnia & Herzegovina, Hong Kong (China), Israel, Japan, Malaysia, Moldova, Serbia, Singapore, South Korea, the UAE and many Latin American countries will need to to apply for an ETIAS visa waiver. UK visitors may also be required to apply. Check www.etiasvisa.com for details. Visitors must fill out an online ETIAS registration form and pay the fee for stays shorter than 90 days.

→ The ETIAS visa waiver is valid for multiple visits over a three-year period. Stays must not exceed 90 days within a 180-day time frame.

→ Others must apply for a Schengen visa, allowing unlimited travel throughout 26 European countries for a 90-day period. Apply at the consulate of the country that's your first port of entry or will be your principal destination. Among other particulars, you must provide proof of travel and repatriation insurance, and prove you have sufficient money to support yourself.

→ ETIAS visa waivers cannot be extended, except in emergencies (such as medical problems).

Transport

GETTING THERE & AWAY

Entering Provence & the Côte d'Azur

With the exception of travellers coming from the UK, the Channel Islands and Andorra, there are no checkpoints between European countries. Arriving in France from any non EU countries, you'll need to show a valid passport and your ETIAS visa waiver (or visa, if applicable) to clear customs.

Air

Airports & Airlines

Air France (www.airfrance.com) is the main national carrier, and provides the most links between French cities – although it's often cheaper and faster to catch a TGV. Budget airlines (including easyJet, Flybe, Cityjet and Ryanair) serve various European destinations.

Provence has two major airports: Marseille-Provence and Nice-Côte d'Azur. The much smaller regional airports in Avignon, Nîmes and Toulon offer seasonal flights.

Aéroport Avignon-Provence (AVN; ✆04 90 81 51 51; www.avignon.aeroport.fr; Caumont) Eight kilometres southeast of Avignon. Currently only served by budget carrier Flybe (Southampton and Birmingham).

Aéroport Marseille-Provence (Aéroport Marseille-Marignane; MRS; ✆08 20 81 14 14; www.marseille.aeroport.fr) Twenty-five kilometres northeast of Marseille. Year-round flights around France, Europe, North Africa, the Middle East and Canada.

Nice-Côte d'Azur Airport (NCE; ✆08 20 42 33 33; www.nice.aeroport.fr; ☎; ☒98, 99, ☒2) Six kilometres west of Nice. Year-round flights to most European cities, plus North Africa, the Middle East, New York and Quebec.

Aéroport de Nîmes Alès Camargue Cévennes (FNI; ✆04 66 70 49 49; www.aeroport-nimes.fr; St-Gilles) Fifteen kilometres south of Nîmes. Served by Ryanair, with current flights to London Stansted, Brussels and Fez (in Morocco).

Toulon-Hyères Airport (TLN; ✆08 25 01 83 87; www.toulon hyeres aeroport fr; bd de la Marine; ☎) Twenty-five kilometres east of Toulon. The next best option after Marseille and Nice, with daily flights to Paris, as well as seasonal flights to other cities including Lyon, Bordeaux, Brest, Strasbourg and Bastia and Ajaccio (in Corsica). There are also flights to Copenhagen, Rotterdam, Geneva, Brussels, London and Southampton.

CLIMATE CHANGE & TRAVEL

Every form of transport that relies on carbon-based fuel generates CO_2, the main cause of human-induced climate change. Modern travel is dependent on aeroplanes, which might use less fuel per kilometre per person than most cars but travel much greater distances. The altitude at which aircraft emit gases (including CO_2) and particles also contributes to their climate change impact. Many websites offer 'carbon calculators' that allow people to estimate the carbon emissions generated by their journey and, for those who wish to do so, to offset the impact of the greenhouse gases emitted with contributions to portfolios of climate-friendly initiatives throughout the world. Lonely Planet offsets the carbon footprint of all staff and author travel.

Land

Bicycle

European Bike Express
(☑+44 01430-422 111; www.
bike-express.co.uk) Transports
cyclists and bikes from the UK to
destinations across France.

Bus

Europe's largest international bus network, **Eurolines**
(☑08 92 89 90 91; www.euro
lines.com) has routes be-
tween major cities, including
Nice, Marseille and Avignon,
and the rest of Europe.
Buses operate daily in summer, several times a week
in winter; advance tickets
required.

From within France – and
often from other nearby
countries such as Spain and
Italy – it's easiest to reach
Provence by train.

Car & Motorcycle

From Paris, consider rid-
ing the high-speed TGV to
Avignon or Marseille, then
picking up a rental car; this
shaves four hours off travel
time to Provence and dodges
tolls and driving time.

To bring your own vehicle,
you'll need the registration
papers, proof of third-party
(liability) insurance and a
valid driving licence. Vehicles
entering France must display
a sticker identifying country
of registration.

Between the UK and
France, high-speed Auto-
Trains run by **Eurotunnel**
(☑France 08 10 63 03 04,
UK 08 443 35 35 35; www.
eurotunnel.com) transport
vehicles through the Channel
Tunnel between Folkestone
and Coquelles (35 minutes,
24 hours, up to four hourly),
5km southwest of Calais.
Note: LPG and CNG tanks
are not permitted, and
campers and caravans must
take ferries.

Train

Rail Europe (☑in Canada 1
800 361 7245, in the UK 0844
848 5848, in the USA 1 800

622 8600; www.raileurope.
com) Offers online booking and
general advice on European rail
travel.

The Man in Seat 61 (www.
seat61.com) Another great
resource, with timetables and
insider tips.

FROM THE REST OF
FRANCE

France's pride and joy is the
state-owned **SNCF** (www.
oui.sncf.com), which runs
the country's entire rail
network.

The SNCF's flagship train
service is the high-speed,
formidably punctual TGV
(*train à grande vitesse*),
which is capable of carrying
you all the way from Paris to
the Côte d'Azur in under four
hours. The route runs from
Paris' Gare du Nord via destinations including Orange,
Avignon, Aix-en-Provence
and Marseille (unfortunately,
a second proposed route
to Nice has been shelved).
Note that the TGV stations
are several kilometres from
the town centre but are
linked by trains or shuttle
buses.

➡ You can choose to travel
in 1st or 2nd class; 1st has
bigger seats, better food
and free wi-fi.

➡ Booking online in advance
is always cheaper than
buying on the day, especially
for intercity services.
Travelling off-peak gets a
considerable discount.

➡ You can also buy tickets
direct from mainline train
stations, or SNCF ticket
centres (boutiques).

➡ As a rough guide, a single
2nd-class fare from Paris to
Marseille starts at around
€90 and the trip takes
just under 3½ hours – but
booking early non-flexible
tickets can sometimes bring
fares down as low as €38.

➡ An important note
if you buy online with
a foreign credit card:
SNCF automated ticket
machines often have trouble

recognising overseas cards,
so you will probably have to
collect your tickets from the
ticket office instead (just
show them your reservation
receipt or reservation
number).

WITH A BICYCLE

On certain trains (flagged
with bike symbols on timetables), bikes are allowed in
luggage vans without being
packed; you don't have to reserve space except on TGVs,
but space is limited, so it's
often wise to book space
along with your ticket for a
small fee (between free and
€10 for standard trains, €10
for TGVs). See www.sncf.
com/sncv1/en/services/
travelling-with-your-bike.

The useful **Bagages à
domicile** (☑00 33 892 35 35
35; https://bagages.oui.sncf)
luggage service transports
bicycles door to door in
France. Small bags (with
combined dimensions of up
to 2.5m) cost €38, larger
bags €80; the maximum
weight is 25kg. Delivery
takes 48 hours, excluding
Saturday afternoon, Sunday
and holidays.

FROM THE UK

The **Eurostar** (www.eurostar.
com) whisks you between
London and Paris in 2¼
hours, with onward trains
across the rest of France.
Eurostar's integrated service
to the south of France runs
direct from London to Lyon
(4¾ hours), Avignon (5¾
hours) and Marseille (6½
hours). All trains travel via
Lille, where you are required
to leave the train briefly for
security and immigration
checks. Standard single
fares start at £99.

For other destinations in
the south (including Aix-en-
Provence), you can catch the
Eurostar to Paris, and then
catch a high-speed TGV –
although it's worth noting
that this requires a schlep
on the metro across Paris
from the Gare du Nord to the
Gare du Lyon, which can be

a real pain if you have lots of luggage.

FROM ITALY & SPAIN

Nice is the major rail hub along the busy Barcelona–Rome line. Prices vary widely according to times and dates; those given are a very general guide.

Nice–Rome from around €69.90, nine hours

Nice–Barcelona from around €103, 10 hours

Sea

Ferries cross from Nice, Marseille and Toulon to Corsica (France), Sardinia (Italy) and North Africa. Vehicles can be taken; reservations essential.

From Corsica (France)

Ferries from Corsica to Provençal ports are operated by the following companies. Depending on the departure and arrival ports, journeys take between 5½ and 15½ hours. Fares vary depending on demand and sailing times, but expect to pay between €30 and €100 for a foot passenger.

Corsica Ferries (☑04 95 32 95 95; www.corsicaferries.com) Ferries from Nice and Toulon to Ajaccio, Bastia, Calvi and Île Rousse.

Corsica Linea (Marseille,☑08 25 80 76 26; www.corsicalinea. com) Ferries from Marseille to Bastia, Ajaccio, Porto Vecchio, Île Rousse and Propriano.

La Méridionale (☑08 10 20 13 20; www.lameridionale.fr) Ferries from Marseille to Bastia and Ajaccio.

From Sardinia (Italy)

La Méridionale (☑08 10 20 13 20; www.lameridionale. fr) runs an overnight ferry between Marseille and Sardinia (adult one-way €66.30, with car €150.04).

From the UK & Ireland

There are no direct ferries to Provence, but year-round ferries connect the UK with French ports, including Calais, Roscoff, Cherbourg, Dunkerque and St-Malo. Dover to Calais is shortest. There are lots of companies, including big players **Brittany Ferries** (☑08 25 82 88 28; www.brittany-ferries.co.uk) and **P&O Ferries** (www.poferries. com).

Check out online booking agencies such as **Ferry Savers** (☑0844-371 8021; www. ferrysavers.co.uk) for cheap fares; phone bookings incur fees.

GETTING AROUND

Public transport in Provence, as in the rest of France, is generally good value and reasonably reliable.

The excellent French-language website **PACA Mobilité** (www.pacamobilite.fr) offers handy planning tools for getting around by public transport in the PACA region.

Car Allows maximum freedom, especially in rural areas. Cars can be hired in most towns and cities. Driving is on the right, but automatic transmissions are rare. *Autoroutes* (motorways) are fast, but many charge tolls. Beware the *priorité à droite* rule, which means you have to give way to vehicles entering on the right.

Train France's state-owned trains are fast, efficient and great value. High-speed TGVs connect major cities; smaller towns are served by slower TER trains, sometimes supplemented by buses. Remember to time-stamp your ticket before boarding.

Bus Useful for remote villages that aren't serviced by trains, but timetables revolve around school-term times; fewer

READING SCHEDULES

Transport schedules use abbreviations. The most common:

tlj (tous les jours) daily

sauf except

lun Monday

mar Tuesday

mer Wednesday

jeu Thursday

ven Friday

sam Saturday

dim Sunday

jours fériés (jf) holidays

services run on weekends and school holidays.

Bicycle

Provence, particularly the Luberon, is great for cycling, with quiet back roads and a number of dedicated bike paths – although it's worth considering summer temperatures when planning your expedition.

By law, bicycles must have two functioning brakes, bell, red reflector on the back and yellow reflectors on the pedals. After sunset, and when visibility is poor, cyclists must illuminate with a white light in front and a red light in rear. Cyclists must ride single file when being overtaken by vehicles or other cyclists. Cycling off-road in national parks is forbidden.

The **Fédération Française de Cyclisme** (☑01 49 35 69 00; www.ffc.fr) is a useful resource.

Most towns have bike-rental outlets; the daily cost is €18 to €25.

Boat

Ferries connect the mainland with offshore islands, notably to/from St-Tropez and St-Raphaël, Port Grimaud and Ste-Maxime in warmer months (generally April to October).

Canal boating is a popular pastime in France. The Canal du Midi – France's most popular – stretches 240km east from Toulouse toward the Camargue and the Canal du Rhône. West of Toulouse, the Canal du Midi connects with the River Garonne, leading west to the Atlantic Ocean. Anyone over 18 can pilot a houseboat or barge, but first-timers must undergo brief training to obtain a temporary pleasure-craft permit (carte de plaisance). The speed limit is 6km/h in canals, 10km/h on rivers.

Prices range from €450 to over €3000 per week. A few online rental agencies:

H2olidays (Barging in France; www.barginginfrance.com)

Le Boat (☑in France 04 68 94 42 80, in the UK 0844 463 3594; www.leboat.net)

Rive de France (☑04 67 37 14 60)

Bus

Services and routes are extremely limited in rural areas, where buses primarily transport school children. Bus transport is useful only if you have no car, and trains don't go where you want, but you may get stuck until the next day. Tourist offices always have schedules.

Autocars (regional buses) are operated by multiple companies, which have offices at gares routières (bus stations) in larger towns.

Car & Motorcycle

Your own vehicle is essential for exploring Provence's smaller towns, many inaccessible by public transport.

Autumn to spring, driving is easy along the Côte d'Azur, but not in July and August, when intense traffic chokes all roads and it takes hours to go a few kilometres. For English-language traffic reports, tune to 107.7MHz FM, which updates every 30 minutes in summer.

There are four types of intercity roads, each with alphanumeric designation:

Autoroutes (eg A8) High-speed multi-lane highways with péages (tolls)

Routes Nationales (N, RN) National highways

Routes Départementales (D) County roads

Routes Communales (C, V) Tertiary routes

Autoroutes are always fastest (summer traffic notwithstanding), but they're expensive due to tolls – Marseille to Nice costs €17.60, Paris to Nice €77.10.

Pay close attention at toll booths: 'CB' (Carte Bleue) indicates credit-card lanes; yellow arrows are exclusively for prepaid drivers; green arrows are for cash. If you choose the wrong lane, you'll have to back up – nearly impossible in summer.

For traffic information, see www.autoroutes.fr.

Calculate toll and fuel costs at www.viamichelin.com and www.mappy.fr.

Fuel & Spare Parts

Essence (petrol or gasoline), also called carburant (fuel), costs roughly €1.50 a litre. You'll pay somewhere in the region of €1.42 a litre for diesel. Autoroute service areas (aires) are priciest but open 24 hours; hypermarkets are cheapest.

➜ Unleaded (sans plomb) pump handles are usually green; diesel (diesel, gazoil or gazole) pumps are yellow or black.

➜ Many service stations close Saturday afternoon and Sunday, and during lunch in small towns.

➜ Some petrol pumps dispense fuel after hours, but only with chip-and-PIN credit cards.

➜ North American credit cards (with magnetic strip instead of chip and PIN) do not work at 24-hour pumps. To purchase fuel at night with magnetic-strip cards, take the autoroute.

➜ When travelling in mountain regions, keep the tank full.

➜ If your car is en panne (broken down), you'll need services for your particular marque (make). Peugeot, Renault and Citroën garages are common, but you may have trouble in remote areas finding mechanics to service foreign cars.

Hire

All the major car-hire firms (including Hertz, Avis, Europcar, Budget and Sixt) have a presence at airports, TGV stations and major town centres. Smaller French firms like ADA and DLM sometimes offer cheaper rates.

Most companies require drivers to be at least 21, to have had a driving licence for at least a year, and to pay with an international credit card. Drivers under 25 usually pay a surcharge.

Online comparison services such as **Auto Europe** (☑1 888 223 5555, from France 800 223 55555; www.autoeurope.com), **Holiday Autos** (www.holidayautos.com) and **Moneymaxim** (www.moneymaxim.co.uk) offer good discounts, especially for longer hire periods, but make sure you check very carefully what's included in the package – especially insurance, breakdown cover, tax, unlimited mileage (kilométrage limité or illimité) and, most importantly, the excess.

Extra points:

➜ Automatic transmissions are rare: reserve well ahead.

➜ French rental cars have distinctive licence plates, making them a target for thieves. Don't leave any valuables inside.

➜ Remember to check whether the car takes *gazole* (diesel) or *sans plomb* (unleaded), and whether it was supplied with a full or empty tank when you picked it up.

➜ Rental cars should come with registration papers (usually in the glove compartment), but double-check before you drive off.

MAJOR HIRE FIRMS

ADA (www.ada.fr)

Avis (☏08 20 05 05 05; www. avis.com)

Budget (☏08 25 00 35 64; www.budget.com)

Easycar (www.easycar.com)

Enterprise Rent-a-Car (☏08 25 16 12 12; www.enterprise.fr)

Europcar (www.europcar.com)

Hertz (☏08 25 09 13 13; www. hertz.com)

Purchase-Repurchase Plans

If you live outside the EU and will be in France (or Europe) from one to six months (up to a year, if studying), by far the cheapest option is to 'purchase' a brand-new car, then 'sell' it back – called *achat-rachat*. You only pay for the time it's in your possession, but the 'temporary transit' (TT) paperwork makes the car legally yours – and it's exempt from huge taxes. Such cars carry red licence plates, instantly identifying drivers as foreigners.

Eligibility is restricted to non-EU residents (EU citizens are eligible only if they reside outside the EU); minimum age is 18 (sometimes 21). You must order at minimum six weeks ahead and prepay your balance before

---

PRIORITÉ À DROITE

The key road rule that catches foreign drivers out in France is *priorité à droite*. This means that, unless otherwise indicated, any car entering at an intersection (eg via a slip road onto a motorway) has the right of way. Drivers may shoot out from intersections directly in front of you: approach with caution!

Sometimes intersections are marked *vous n'avez pas la priorité* (you do not have right of way) or *cédez le passage* (yield); follow the rules accordingly.

Priorité à droite is suspended on priority roads, which are marked by a yellow diamond with a white border; it's reinstated when you see a black bar through the yellow diamond.

---

the factory builds your car – and you get to pick the model. Diesel (*gasoil*) vehicles are more expensive up front, but you pay less for fuel. All plans include unlimited kilometres, 24-hour towing and breakdown service, and comprehensive insurance with zero deductible/excess.

Companies offering *achat-rachat* are Citroën (www.citroen-europass. com), Peugeot (www. peugeot-openeurope. com) and Renault (www. renault-eurodrive.com).

Insurance

Car-hire companies provide mandatory third-party liability insurance, but other important insurances cost extra, including collision-damage waiver (CDW, *assurance tous risques*), which covers the cost of the vehicle in the event of accident or theft.

Most hire agreements come with a hefty excess (known as the *franchise* or *déductible*, and usually between €750 and €1500, depending on the size of the vehicle). This is the maximum sum for which you will be liable if you have an accident or bring the car back damaged.

All car-hire firms will offer you the chance to reduce this excess to zero, but it is nearly always very expensive – often adding between €5 and

€20 extra to the daily hire rate. It's up to you whether you take it out, but it's worth remembering that even a minor scrape will often incur a hefty bill.

An alternative is to take out separate excess insurance – if you damage the car, you pay the agreed excess when you return the vehicle, and then claim the sum back from your insurance provider (take photos and keep hold of all relevant documents such as accident reports, damage sheets and so on). It's more complicated but works out much, much cheaper than the rental firms. Some credit-card providers also cover CDW if you pay using their card; check their terms before you travel.

If you don't have a zero-excess contract, most rental firms will preload a sum onto your credit card to cover the excess when you pick up the vehicle. Make sure you have enough available credit on your card to cover this amount.

Parking

Provence's ancient villages and cities can be hellish on drivers, with narrow streets, confusing one-way systems and limited parking. Many hotels have no garages: guests drop off bags, then either claim a resident's parking permit from the hotel (if available at all) and find street parking or hunt down a garage. Ask when reserving.

In city centres, look for 'P' signs to locate parking (often underground); expect to pay about €2.50/20 per hour/day.

Road Rules

Enforcement of French traffic laws (visit www. securite-routiere.gouv.fr) has been stepped up considerably. Speed cameras are common and hard to spot (they're the small grey boxes you'll see by the roadside). Sometimes the presence of a speed camera is indicated by signs (reading *Contrôles Radar Fréquents*) – but not always.

Mobile radar traps, unmarked police vehicles and roadside drug tests are also commonplace. If you see a flash, you've probably been caught. If you're driving a rental car, tickets are usually charged to your credit card, often with a hefty administration charge. If you're driving your own vehicle, you might receive a ticket in the mail, or you might not – minor infractions may not be worth the trouble for police to pursue, but there are no hard-and-fast rules.

Fines for many infractions are given on the spot; serious violations can lead to confiscation of licence and vehicle. If you have an accident, you will be drug tested.

Key points:

➜ Blood-alcohol limit is 0.05% (0.5g per litre of blood) – roughly the equivalent of two glasses of wine for a 75kg adult. Stick to one glass to be on the safe side.

➜ All passengers must wear seatbelts.

➜ Children less than 10kg must travel in backward-facing child seats; children up to 36kg must travel in child seats in the vehicle's rear seat.

➜ UK and Irish vehicles must fit headlight reflectors to avoid dazzling oncoming traffic.

➜ Only hands-free, speaker-phone mobiles are allowed – no handsets, no texting.

➜ US and Canadian drivers, note: turning right at a red light is illegal.

➜ All vehicles in France must carry a high-visibility safety vest (stored inside the vehicle, not the trunk) and a reflective warning triangle. The recent law mandating a single-use breathalyser kit has effectively been shelved; in theory you are still supposed to carry one, but you can't be fined for not doing so.

➜ Drivers of two-wheeled motorised vehicles (except electric bicycles) must wear helmets. No special licence is required for motorbikes under 50cc.

➜ Some roads in Haute-Provence require the use of snow chains in winter.

➜ In forested areas, fire roads signposted DFCI (Défense de la Forêt Contre l'Incendie) are strictly off limits to private vehicles.

Taxi

Find taxi ranks at train and bus stations, or telephone for radio taxis. Fares are metered, with minimum fare €6; rates are roughly €1.60 per kilometre for one-way journeys.

Train

SNCF's regional train network is served by TER (Trains Express Régionales) trains; bookings and timetables are handled by the SNCF. A popular journey is the narrow-gauge **Train des Pignes** (Pine Cone Train; www.trainprovence.com; single/return Nice to Digne €26/52; 🚋1 to Libération), which links Nice with Digne-les-Bains.

Reservations are not mandatory on most regional trains, but advance purchase is a good idea in summer.

Classes & Costs

Passes are sold at student travel agencies, major train stations within Europe, and at **Rail Europe** (🖥in Canada 1 800 361 7245, in the UK 0844 848 5848, in the USA 1 800 622 8600; www.raileurope.com).

SNCF DISCOUNT FARES & PASSES

Train fares vary widely according to demand and your chosen times and dates of travel. Generally the further in advance you book, the cheaper the fare.

The **Ouigo** (www.ouigo.com) service allows cut-price travel on certain TGVs (including some to Aix-en-Provence and Avignon). Tickets must be purchased from three weeks to four hours prior to departure; tickets are sent by email and must be printed out, or downloaded via the Ouigo app (Android and iPhone). You're allowed one piece

---

SPEED LIMITS

Populated areas 50km/h

Undivided N and D highways 90km/h (80km/h if raining)

Non-autoroute divided highways 110km/h (100km/h if raining)

Autoroutes 130km/h (110km/h if raining, 60km/h if icy)

of cabin luggage and one piece of hand luggage and a pushchair; you can buy extra bags for €5 in advance, or a hefty €20 on the day of travel.

➡ Booking via the website of **SNCF** (www.oui.sncf. com) is the easiest way to compare fares. A 1st-class fare costs 20% to 30% more than a 2nd-class one.

➡ The cheapest fares are Prem's, which are non-amendable and non-refundable. Flexible tickets always cost more.

➡ Children under four travel free. Ages four to 11 travel half-price.

➡ Travellers aged 12 to 25 and those aged over 60 receive discounts.

➡ *Bons plans* are last-minute tickets advertised on the SNCF website (http://www. voyages-sncf.com/bons-plans/derniere-minute).

TRAIN PASSES

Guaranteed discounts of 25% (last-minute booking) to 60% (advance bookings for low-volume 'blue periods') are available with several cards:

Carte Jeune (€50) For travellers aged 12 to 27.

Carte Enfant+ (€75) For one to four adults travelling with a child aged four to 11.

Carte Week-end (€75) For travellers aged 26 to 59, booking return journeys of at least 200km that include weekend-only travel, or a Saturday night away.

Carte Sénior+ (€60) For travellers over 60.

Two regional passes are also available:

Pass Zou! (www.ter.sncf.com/paca/offres/cartes-abonnements/zou-50-75; adult over 26/under 26 €30/15) Offers discounts of up to 75% on TER trains in the PACA region.

STAMP IT!

You must time-stamp your ticket in a *composteur* (freestanding yellow post at the entrance to train platforms) immediately before boarding, or you'll incur a hefty fine. Smartphones displaying barcode boarding passes are exempt.

Pass Isabelle (www.ter.sncf.com/paca/offres/pass-promos/pass-isabelle-famille; family of 4 €35) Covers one-day of travel on TER trains for families (two adults and two children) within the Alpes-Maritime *département*.

Language

Standard French is taught and spoken throughout France. The heavy southern accent is an important part of regional identity in Provence, but you'll have no trouble being understood anywhere if you stick to standard French, which we've also used in the phrases in this chapter.

The sounds used in spoken French can almost all be found in English. There are a couple of exceptions: nasal vowels (represented in our pronunciation guides by o or u followed by an almost inaudible nasal consonant sound m, n or ng), the 'funny' u (ew in our guides) and the deep-in-the-throat r. Bearing these few points in mind and reading our pronunciation guides below as if they were English, you'll be understood just fine.

BASICS

French has two words for 'you' – use the polite form *vous* unless you're talking to close friends or children in which case you'd use the informal *tu*. You can also use *tu* when a person invites you to use *tu*.

All nouns in French are either masculine or feminine, and so are the adjectives, articles *le/la* (the) and *un/une* (a), and possessives *mon/ma* (my), *ton/ta* (your) and *son/sa* (his, her) that go with the nouns. In this chapter we have included masculine and femine forms where necessary, separated by a slash and indicated with 'm/f'.

Hello.	Bonjour.	bon·zhoor
Goodbye.	Au revoir.	o·rer·vwa
Excuse me.	Excusez-moi.	ek·skew·zay·mwa

WANT MORE?

For in-depth language information and handy phrases, check out Lonely Planet's *French Phrasebook*. You'll find it at **shop.lonelyplanet.com**, or you can buy Lonely Planet's Fast Talk app at the Apple App Store.

Sorry.	Pardon.	par·don
Yes.	Oui.	wee
No.	Non.	non
Please.	S'il vous plaît.	seel voo play
Thank you.	Merci.	mair·see
You're welcome.	De rien.	der ree·en

How are you?
Comment allez-vous? — ko·mon ta·lay·voo

Fine, and you?
Bien, merci. Et vous? — byun mair·see ay voo

You're welcome.
De rien. — der ree·en

My name is ...
Je m'appelle ... — zher ma·pel ...

What's your name?
Comment vous appelez-vous? — ko·mon voo·za·play voo

Do you speak English?
Parlez-vous anglais? — par·lay·voo ong·glay

I don't understand.
Je ne comprends pas. — zher ner kom·pron pa

ACCOMMODATION

Do you have any rooms available?
Est-ce que vous avez des chambres libres? — es·ker voo za·vay day shom·brer lee·brer

How much is it per night/person?
Quel est le prix par nuit/personne? — kel ay ler pree par nwee/per·son

Is breakfast included?
Est-ce que le petit déjeuner est inclus? — es·ker ler per·tee day·zher·nay ayt en·klew

campsite	camping	kom·peeng
dorm	dortoir	dor·twar
guest house	pension	pon·syon
hotel	hôtel	o·tel
youth hostel	auberge de jeunesse	o·berzh der zher·nes

PROVENÇAL

Despite the bilingual signs that visitors see when they enter most towns and villages, the region's mother tongue – Provençal – is scarcely heard on the street or in the home. Just a handful of older people in rural Provence (Prouvènço) keep alive the rich lyrics and poetic language of their ancestors.

Provençal (*prouvençau* in Provençal) is a dialect of the *langue d'oc* (Occitan), the traditional language of southern France. Its grammar is closer to Catalan (spoken in Spain) than to French. In the grand age of courtly love – the period between the 12th and 14th centuries – Provençal was the literary language of France and northern Spain and was even used as far afield as Italy. Medieval troubadours and poets created melodies and elegant poems, and Provençal blossomed.

The 19th century witnessed a revival of Provençal after its rapid displacement by the *langue d'oïl*, the language of northern France which originated from the vernacular Latin spoken by the Gallo-Romans and gave birth to modern French (*francés* in Provençal). The revival of Provençal was spearheaded by Frédéric Mistral (1830–1914), a poet from Vaucluse, whose works in Provençal won him the 1904 Nobel Prize for Literature.

a ... room	*une chambre ...*	ewn shom·brer ...
single	*à un lit*	a un lee
double	*avec un grand lit*	a·vek un gron lee
twin	*avec des lits jumeaux*	a·vek day lee zhew·mo
with (a)...	*avec ...*	a·vek ...
air-con	*climatiseur*	klee·ma·tee·zer
bathroom	*une salle de bains*	ewn sal der bun
window	*fenêtre*	fer·nay·trer

DIRECTIONS

Where's ...?
Où est ...? oo ay ...

What's the address?
Quelle est l'adresse? kel ay la·dres

Could you write the address, please?
Est-ce que vous pourriez écrire l'adresse, s'il vous plaît? es·ker voo poo·ryay ay·kreer la·dres seel voo play

Can you show me (on the map)?
Pouvez-vous m'indiquer (sur la carte)? poo·vay·voo mun·dee·kay (sewr la kart)

at the corner	*au coin*	o kwun
at the traffic lights	*aux feux*	o fer
behind	*derrière*	dair·ryair
in front of	*devant*	der·von
far (from)	*loin (de)*	lwun (der)
left	*gauche*	gosh
near (to)	*près (de)*	pray (der)
next to	*à côté de*	a ko·tay der
opposite	*en face de*	on fas der

right	*droite*	drwat
straight ahead	*tout droit*	too drwa

EATING & DRINKING

What would you recommend?
Qu'est-ce que vous conseillez? kes·ker voo kon·say·yay

What's in that dish?
Quels sont les ingrédients? kel son lay zun·gray·dyon

I'm a vegetarian.
Je suis végétarien/ végétarienne. zher swee vay·zhay·ta·ryun/ vay·zhay·ta·ryen (m/f)

I don't eat ...
Je ne mange pas ... zher ner monzh pa ...

Cheers!
Santé! son·tay

That was delicious.
C'était délicieux! say·lay day·lee·syer

Please bring the bill.
Apportez-moi l'addition, s'il vous plaît. a·por·tay·mwa la·dee·syon seel voo play

I'd like to reserve a table for ...	*Je voudrais réserver une table pour ...*	zher voo·dray ray·zair·vay ewn ta·bler poor ...
(eight) o'clock	*(vingt) heures*	(vungt) er
(two) people	*(deux) personnes*	(der) pair·son

Key Words

appetiser	*entrée*	on·tray
bottle	*bouteille*	boo·tay
breakfast	*petit déjeuner*	per·tee day·zher·nay

LANGUAGE EATING & DRINKING

QUESTION WORDS

How?	*Comment?*	ko·mon
What?	*Quoi?*	kwa
When?	*Quand?*	kon
Where?	*Où?*	oo
Who?	*Qui?*	kee
Why?	*Pourquoi?*	poor·kwa

children's menu	*menu pour enfants*	mer·new poor on·fon
cold	*froid*	frwa
delicatessen	*traiteur*	tray·ter
dinner	*dîner*	dee·nay
dish	*plat*	pla
food	*nourriture*	noo·ree·tewr
fork	*fourchette*	foor·shet
glass	*verre*	vair
grocery store	*épicerie*	ay·pees·ree
highchair	*chaise haute*	shay zot
hot	*chaud*	sho
knife	*couteau*	koo·to
local speciality	*spécialité locale*	spay·sya·lee·tay lo·kal
lunch	*déjeuner*	day·zher·nay
main course	*plat principal*	pla prun·see·pal
market	*marché*	mar·shay
menu (in English)	*carte (en anglais)*	kart (on ong·glay)
plate	*assiette*	a·syet
spoon	*cuillère*	kwee·yair
wine list	*carte des vins*	kart day vun
with/without	*avec/sans*	a·vek/son

Meat & Fish

beef	*bœuf*	berf
chicken	*poulet*	poo·lay
crab	*crabe*	krab
lamb	*agneau*	a·nyo
oyster	*huître*	wee·trer
pork	*porc*	por
snail	*escargot*	es·kar·go
squid	*calmar*	kal·mar
turkey	*dinde*	dund
veal	*veau*	vo

Fruit & Vegetables

apple	*pomme*	pom
apricot	*abricot*	ab·ree·ko
asparagus	*asperge*	a·spairzh
beans	*haricots*	a·ree·ko
beetroot	*betterave*	be·trav
cabbage	*chou*	shoo
cherry	*cerise*	ser·reez
corn	*maïs*	ma·ees
cucumber	*concombre*	kong·kom·brer
grape	*raisin*	ray·zun
lemon	*citron*	see·tron
lettuce	*laitue*	lay·tew
mushroom	*champignon*	shom·pee·nyon
peach	*pêche*	pesh
peas	*petit pois*	per·tee pwa
(red/green) pepper	*poivron (rouge/vert)*	pwa·vron (roozh/vair)
pineapple	*ananas*	a·na·nas
plum	*prune*	prewn
potato	*pomme de terre*	pom der tair
prune	*pruneau*	prew·no
pumpkin	*citrouille*	see·troo·yer
shallot	*échalote*	eh·sha·lot
spinach	*épinards*	eh·pee·nar
strawberry	*fraise*	frez
tomato	*tomate*	to·mat
vegetable	*légume*	lay·gewm

Other

bread	*pain*	pun
butter	*beurre*	ber
cheese	*fromage*	fro·mazh
egg	*œuf*	erf
honey	*miel*	myel
jam	*confiture*	kon·fee·tewr
lentils	*lentilles*	lon·tee·yer
pasta/noodles	*pâtes*	pat
pepper	*poivre*	pwa·vrer
rice	*riz*	ree
salt	*sel*	sel
sugar	*sucre*	sew·krer
vinegar	*vinaigre*	vee·nay·grer

Drinks

beer	*bière*	bee·yair
coffee	*café*	ka·fay
(orange) juice	*jus (d'orange)*	zhew (do·ronzh)
milk	*lait*	lay
tea	*thé*	tay

(mineral) water	*eau (minérale)*	o (mee·nay·ral)
(red) wine	*vin (rouge)*	vun (roozh)
(white) wine	*vin (blanc)*	vun (blong)

EMERGENCIES

Help!
Au secours! — o skoor

I'm lost.
Je suis perdu/perdue. — zhe swee·pair·dew (m/f)

Leave me alone!
Fichez-moi la paix! — fee·shay·mwa la pay

There's been an accident.
Il y a eu un accident. — eel ya ew un ak·see·don

Call a doctor.
Appelez un médecin. — a·play un mayd·sun

Call the police.
Appelez la police. — a·play la po·lees

I'm ill.
Je suis malade. — zher swee ma·lad

It hurts here.
J'ai une douleur ici. — zhay ewn doo·ler ee·see

I'm allergic to ...
Je suis allergique ... — zher swee za·lair·zheek ...

SHOPPING & SERVICES

I'd like to buy ...
Je voudrais acheter ... — zher voo·dray ash·tay ...

May I look at it?
Est-ce que je peux le voir? — es·ker zher per ler vwar

I'm just looking.
Je regarde. — zher rer·gard

I don't like it.
Cela ne me plaît pas. — ser·la ner mer play pa

How much is it?
C'est combien? — say kom·byun

It's too expensive.
C'est trop cher. — say tro shair

Can you lower the price?
Vous pouvez baisser le prix? — voo poo·vay bay·say ler pree

There's a mistake in the bill.
Il y a une erreur dans la note. — eel ya ewn ay·rer don la not

ATM	*guichet automatique de banque*	gee·shay o·to·ma·teek der bonk
credit card	*carte de crédit*	kart der kray·dee
internet cafe	*cybercafé*	see·bair·ka·fay
post office	*bureau de poste*	bew·ro der post
tourist office	*office de tourisme*	o·fees der too·rees·mer

TIME & DATES

What time is it?
Quelle heure est-il? — kel er ay til

It's (eight) o'clock.
Il est (huit) heures. — il ay (weet) er

It's half past (10).
Il est (dix) heures et demie. — il ay (deez) er ay day·mee

morning	*matin*	ma·tun
afternoon	*après-midi*	a·pray·mee·dee
evening	*soir*	swar
yesterday	*hier*	yair
today	*aujourd'hui*	o·zhoor·dwee
tomorrow	*demain*	der·mun

Monday	*lundi*	lun·dee
Tuesday	*mardi*	mar·dee
Wednesday	*mercredi*	mair krer doo
Thursday	*jeudi*	zher·dee
Friday	*vendredi*	von·drer·dee
Saturday	*samedi*	sam·dee
Sunday	*dimanche*	dee·monsh

January	*janvier*	zhon·vyay
February	*février*	fayv·ryay
March	*mars*	mars
April	*avril*	a·vreel
May	*mai*	may
June	*juin*	zhwun
July	*juillet*	zhwee·yay
August	*août*	oot
September	*septembre*	sep·tom·brer
October	*octobre*	ok·to·brer
November	*novembre*	no·vom·brer
December	*décembre*	day·som·brer

SIGNS

Entrée	Entrance
Femmes	Women
Fermé	Closed
Hommes	Men
Interdit	Prohibited
Ouvert	Open
Renseignements	Information
Sortie	Exit
Toilettes/WC	Toilets

TRANSPORT

Public Transport

boat	*bateau*	ba·to
bus	*bus*	bews
plane	*avion*	a·vyon
train	*train*	trun

I want to go to ...
Je voudrais aller à ...   zher voo·dray a·lay a ...

Does it stop at (Amboise)?
Est-ce qu'il s'arrête à   es·kil sa·ret a
(Amboise)?   (om·bwaz)

At what time does it leave/arrive?
À quelle heure est-ce   a kel er es
qu'il part/arrive?   kil par/a·reev

Can you tell me when we get to ...?
Pouvez-vous me   poo·vay·voo mer
dire quand   deer kon
nous arrivons à ...?   noo za·ree·von a ...

I want to get off here.
Je veux descendre   zher ver day·son·drer
ici.   ee·see

first	*premier*	prer·myay
last	*dernier*	dair·nyay
next	*prochain*	pro·shun

NUMBERS

1	*un*	un
2	*deux*	der
3	*trois*	trwa
4	*quatre*	ka·trer
5	*cinq*	sungk
6	*six*	sees
7	*sept*	set
8	*huit*	weet
9	*neuf*	nerf
10	*dix*	dees
20	*vingt*	vung
30	*trente*	tront
40	*quarante*	ka·ront
50	*cinquante*	sung·kont
60	*soixante*	swa·sont
70	*soixante-dix*	swa·son·dees
80	*quatre-vingts*	ka·trer·vung
90	*quatre-vingt-dix*	ka·trer·vung·dees
100	*cent*	son
1000	*mille*	meel

a ... ticket	*un billet ...*	un bee·yay ...
1st-class	*de première classe*	der prem·yair klas
2nd-class	*de deuxième classe*	der der·zyem las
one-way	*simple*	sum·pler
return	*aller et retour*	a·lay ay rer·toor

aisle seat	*côté couloir*	ko·tay kool·war
delayed	*en retard*	on rer·tar
cancelled	*annulé*	a·new·lay
platform	*quai*	kay
ticket office	*guichet*	gee·shay
timetable	*horaire*	o·rair
train station	*gare*	gar
window seat	*côté fenêtre*	ko·tay fe·ne·trer

Driving & Cycling

I'd like to hire a ...	*Je voudrais louer ...*	zher voo·dray loo·way ...
4WD	*un quatre-quatre*	un kat·kat
car	*une voiture*	ewn vwa·tewr
bicycle	*un vélo*	un vay·lo
motorcycle	*une moto*	ewn mo·to

child seat	*siège-enfant*	syezh·on·fon
diesel	*diesel*	dyay·zel
helmet	*casque*	kask
mechanic	*mécanicien*	may·ka·nee·syun
petrol/gas	*essence*	ay·sons
service station	*station-service*	sta·syon·ser·vees

Is this the road to ...?
C'est la route pour ...?   say la root poor ...

(How long) Can I park here?
(Combien de temps)   (kom·byun der tom)
Est-ce que je peux   es·ker zher per
stationner ici?   sta·syo·nay ee·see

The car/motorbike has broken down (at ...).
La voiture/moto est   la vwa·tewr/mo·to ay
tombée en panne (à ...).   tom·bay on pan (a ...)

I have a flat tyre.
Mon pneu est à plat.   mom pner ay ta pla

I've run out of petrol.
Je suis en panne   zher swee zon pan
d'essence.   day·sons

I've lost my car keys.
J'ai perdu les clés de   zhay per·dew lay klay der
ma voiture.   ma vwa·tewr

GLOSSARY

Word gender is indicated as (m) masculine or (f) feminine; (pl) indicates plural.

abbaye (f) – abbey

AOP – Appellation d'Origine Protégée (formerly Appellation d'Origine Contrôlée [AOC], still commonly used in France); wines and olive oils that have met stringent government regulations governing where, how and under what conditions the grapes or olives are grown and the wines and olive oils are fermented and bottled

arrondissement (m) – one of several districts into which large cities, such as Marseille, are split

atelier (m) – artisan's workshop

auberge (f) – inn

autoroute (f) – motorway or highway

baie (f) – bay

bastide (f) – country house

billetterie (f) – ticket office or counter

borie (f) – primitive beehive-shaped dwelling, built from dry limestone around 3500 BCE

boulangerie (f) – bread shop or bakery

calanque (f) – rocky inlet

carnet (m) – a book of five or 10 bus, tram or metro tickets sold at a reduced rate

cave (f) – wine or cheese cellar

centre (de) hospitalier (m) – hospital

chambre d'hôte (f) – B&B accommodation, usually in a private home

charcuterie (f) – pork butcher's shop and delicatessen; also cold meat

château (m) – castle or stately home

chèvre (f) – goat; also goat's-milk cheese

col (m) – mountain pass

conseil général (m) – general council

corniche (f) – coastal or cliff road

corrida (f) – bullfight

cour (f) – courtyard

course Camarguaise (f) – Camargue-style bullfight

dégustation (f) – the fine art of tasting wine, cheese, olive oil or seafood

département (m) – administrative area (department)

DFCI – Défense de la Forêt Contre l'Incendie; fire road (public access forbidden)

digue (f) – dike

domaine (m) – an estate producing wines

église (f) – church

épicerie (f) – grocery shop

étang (m) – lagoon, pond or lake

faïence (f) – earthenware

féria (f) – bullfighting festival

ferme auberge (f) – family-run inn attached to a farm or *château*; farmhouse restaurant

fête (f) – party or festival

formule (f) – fixed main course plus starter or dessert

fromagerie (f) – cheese shop

galets (m) – large smooth stones covering Châteauneuf du Pape vineyards

gardian (m) – Camargue horseman or cattle-herding cowboy

gare (f) – train station

gare maritime (f) – ferry terminal

gare routière (f) – bus station

garrigue (f) – ground cover of aromatic scrub; see also *maquis*

gitan (m) – Roma Gitano person, gypsy

golfe (m) – gulf

grotte (f) – cave

halles (f pl) – covered market; central food market

hôtel de ville (m) – town hall

hôtel particulier (m) – private mansion

jardin (botanique) (m) – (botanic) garden

mairie (f) – town hall

manade (f) – bull farm

maquis (m) – aromatic Provençal scrub; name given to the French Resistance movement; see also *garrigue*

marché (m) – market

mas (m) – Provençal farmhouse

menu (m) – meal at a fixed price with two or more courses

mistral (m) – incessant north wind

monastère (m) – monastery

Monégasque – native of Monaco

moulin à huile (m) – oil mill

musée (m) – museum

navette (f) – shuttle bus, train or boat

Niçois – native of Nice

office du tourisme, office de tourisme (m) – tourist office (run by a unit of local government)

ONF – Office National des Forêts; National Forests Office

parc national (m) – national park

parc naturel régional (m) – regional nature park

pétanque (f) – a Provençal game of boules, similar to lawn bowls

pic (m) – mountain peak

place (f) – square

plage (f) – beach

plan (m) – city map

plat du jour (m) – dish of the day

pont (m) – bridge

porte (f) – gate or door; old-town entrance

préfecture (f) – main town of a *département*

presqu'île (f) – peninsula

prieuré (m) – priory

quai (m) – quay or railway platform
quartier (m) – quarter or district
rade (f) – gulf or harbour
région (m) – administrative region
rond-point (m) – roundabout

salin (m) – salt marsh
santon (m) – traditional Provençal figurine

sentier (m) – trail, footpath
sentier littoral (m) – coastal path
SNCF – Société Nationale des Chemins de Fer Français; state-owned railway company
SNCM – Société Nationale Maritime Corse-Méditerranée; state-owned ferry company linking Corsica and mainland France
stade (m) – stadium

tabac (m) – tobacconist (also sells newspapers, bus tickets etc)
TGV – Train à Grande Vitesse; high-speed train
théâtre antique (m) – Roman theatre

vendange (f) – grape harvest
vieille ville (f) – old town
vieux port (m) – old port
vigneron (m) – winegrower

Behind the Scenes

SEND US YOUR FEEDBACK

We love to hear from travellers – your comments keep us on our toes and help make our books better. Our well-travelled team reads every word on what you loved or loathed about this book. Although we cannot reply individually to your submissions, we always guarantee that your feedback goes straight to the appropriate authors, in time for the next edition. Each person who sends us information is thanked in the next edition – the most useful submissions are rewarded with a selection of digital PDF chapters.

Visit **lonelyplanet.com/contact** to submit your updates and suggestions or to ask for help. Our award-winning website also features inspirational travel stories, news and discussions.

Note: We may edit, reproduce and incorporate your comments in Lonely Planet products such as guidebooks, websites and digital products, so let us know if you don't want your comments reproduced or your name acknowledged. For a copy of our privacy policy visit lonelyplanet.com/privacy.

WRITER THANKS

Hugh McNaughtan

As always, I must thank Tasmin, Maise and Willa, my endlessly patient family, plus my editor Dan, and the support team at Lonely Planet. I'd also like to thank Audrey, Isabelle and the many kind people in Provence who made this project a success and a pleasure.

Oliver Berry

A big *merci* to everyone who helped me with my research in Provence this time 'round, including Jérome Coustellet, Marie Lafarge, Sophie Casticci, James Clarke, Agnès Caron and Aurelie Martin. Back home, thanks to Rosie Hillier for putting up with long days and nights of write-up, and to everyone in the Lonely Planet team putting the project together, especially destination editor Dan Fahey for fielding myriad questions about taxonomy, topography, Typefi and plenty more besides. *Un grand merci à tous!*

Gregor Clark

Merci beaucoup to the many French and Monégasque locals who shared their insights about France and Monaco with me, especially Marion Pansiot, Clara Diaz Campuzano, Lucie Richard, Did Kwo, Claire Bouvrot, Bruno Rouganne and Eric Demeester. Back home, hugs to Gaen, Meigan and Chloe, who always make coming home the best part of the trip.

ACKNOWLEDGEMENTS

Climate map data adapted from Peel MC, Finlayson BL & McMahon TA (2007) 'Updated World Map of the Köppen-Geiger Climate Classification', *Hydrology and Earth System Sciences*, 11, 1633–44.

Cover photograph: Sunflower and lavender field, Provence, Navinpeep/Getty Images©

Illustrations p118–19, p164–5 by Javier Zarracina.

THIS BOOK

This 10th edition of Lonely Planet's *Provence & the Côte d'Azur* guidebook was researched and written by Oliver Berry, Gregor Clark, Hugh McNaughtan and Regis St Louis.

This guidebook was produced by the following:

Destination Editor Daniel Fahey

Senior Product Editors Daniel Bolger, Genna Patterson

Product Editors Hannah Cartmel, Heather Champion

Senior Cartographer Mark Griffiths

Cartographer Corey Hutchison

Book Designers Hannah Blackie, Gwen Cotter

Assisting Editors Michelle Bennett, Andrea Dobbin, Samantha Forge, Cath Lanigan, Charlotte Orr, Monique Perrin, Gabrielle Stefanos, Sarah Stewart, Fionnuala Twomey, Simon Williamson

Assisting Book Designer Jessica Rose

Cover Researcher Brendan Dempsey-Spencer

Thanks to Frank Gelok, Sonia Kapoor, Sandie Kestell, Claire Naylor, Karyn Noble, Andre Pfanner, Matt Phillips, James Smart, Stevie Taylor

Index

INDEX B-C

Map Pages **000**
Photo Pages **000**

Map Legend

Sights

- Beach
- Bird Sanctuary
- Buddhist
- Castle/Palace
- Christian
- Confucian
- Hindu
- Islamic
- Jain
- Jewish
- Monument
- Museum/Gallery/Historic Building
- Ruin
- Shinto
- Sikh
- Taoist
- Winery/Vineyard
- Zoo/Wildlife Sanctuary
- Other Sight

Activities, Courses & Tours

- Bodysurfing
- Diving
- Canoeing/Kayaking
- Course/Tour
- Sento Hot Baths/Onsen
- Skiing
- Snorkelling
- Surfing
- Swimming/Pool
- Walking
- Windsurfing
- Other Activity

Sleeping

- Sleeping
- Camping
- Hut/Shelter

Eating

- Eating

Drinking & Nightlife

- Drinking & Nightlife
- Cafe

Entertainment

- Entertainment

Shopping

- Shopping

Information

- Bank
- Embassy/Consulate
- Hospital/Medical
- Internet
- Police
- Post Office
- Telephone
- Toilet
- Tourist Information
- Other Information

Geographic

- Beach
- Gate
- Hut/Shelter
- Lighthouse
- Lookout
- Mountain/Volcano
- Oasis
- Park
- Pass
- Picnic Area
- Waterfall

Population

- Capital (National)
- Capital (State/Province)
- City/Large Town
- Town/Village

Transport

- Airport
- Border crossing
- Bus
- Cable car/Funicular
- Cycling
- Ferry
- Metro station
- Monorail
- Parking
- Petrol station
- Subway station
- Taxi
- Train station/Railway
- Tram
- Underground station
- Other Transport

Routes

- Tollway
- Freeway
- Primary
- Secondary
- Tertiary
- Lane
- Unsealed road
- Road under construction
- Plaza/Mall
- Steps
- Tunnel
- Pedestrian overpass
- Walking Tour
- Walking Tour detour
- Path/Walking Trail

Boundaries

- International
- State/Province
- Disputed
- Regional/Suburb
- Marine Park
- Cliff
- Wall

Hydrography

- River, Creek
- Intermittent River
- Canal
- Water
- Dry/Salt/Intermittent Lake
- Reef

Areas

- Airport/Runway
- Beach/Desert
- Cemetery (Christian)
- Cemetery (Other)
- Glacier
- Mudflat
- Park/Forest
- Sight (Building)
- Sportsground
- Swamp/Mangrove

Note: Not all symbols displayed above appear on the maps in this book

OUR STORY

A beat-up old car, a few dollars in the pocket and a sense of adventure. In 1972 that's all Tony and Maureen Wheeler needed for the trip of a lifetime – across Europe and Asia overland to Australia. It took several months, and at the end – broke but inspired – they sat at their kitchen table writing and stapling together their first travel guide, *Across Asia on the Cheap*. Within a week they'd sold 1500 copies. Lonely Planet was born.

Today, Lonely Planet has offices in the US, Ireland and China, with a network of over 2000 contributors in every corner of the globe. We share Tony's belief that 'a great guidebook should do three things: inform, educate and amuse'.

OUR WRITERS

Hugh McNaughtan

A former English lecturer, Hugh swapped grant applications for visa applications, and turned his love of travel into a full-time thing. Having done a bit of restaurant-reviewing in his home town (Melbourne, Australia) he's now eaten his way across four continents. He's never happier than when on the road with his two daughters. Except perhaps on the cricket field...

Oliver Berry

Oliver is a writer and photographer from Cornwall. He has worked for Lonely Planet for more than a decade, covering destinations from Cornwall to the Cook Islands, and has worked on more than 30 guidebooks. He is also a regular contributor to many newspapers and magazines. His writing has won several awards, including *The Guardian* Young Travel Writer of the Year and the *TNT Magazine* People's Choice Award. His latest work is published at www.oliverberry.com.

Gregor Clark

Gregor is a US-based writer whose love of languages and curiosity about what's around the next bend have taken him to dozens of countries on five continents. Since 2000, Gregor has regularly contributed to Lonely Planet guides, with a focus on Europe and the Americas. Titles include *Italy*, *France*, *Portugal*, *Montreal & Quebec City*, *France's Best Trips*, cycling guides to Italy and California and coffee-table pictorials such as *Food Trails*, *The USA Book* and *The LP Guide to the Middle of Nowhere*. Gregor was born in New York City, and lived in California, France, Spain and Italy prior to settling with his wife and two daughters in his current home state of Vermont.

Regis St Louis

Regis grew up in a small town in the American Midwest – the kind of place that fuels big dreams of travel – and he developed an early fascination with foreign dialects and world cultures. He spent his formative years learning Russian and a handful of Romance languages, which served him well on journeys across much of the globe. Regis has contributed to more than 50 Lonely Planet titles, covering destinations across six continents. His travels have taken him from the mountains of Kamchatka to remote island villages in Melanesia, and to many grand urban landscapes. When not on the road, he lives in New Orleans. Follow him on www.instagram.com/regisstlouis.

Published by Lonely Planet Global Limited
CRN 554153
10th edition – January 2022
ISBN 978 1 78868 041 7
© Lonely Planet 2022   Photographs © as indicated 2022
10 9 8 7 6 5 4 3 2 1
Printed in China

Although the authors and Lonely Planet have taken all reasonable care in preparing this book, we make no warranty about the accuracy or completeness of its content and, to the maximum extent permitted, disclaim all liability arising from its use.

All rights reserved. No part of this publication may be copied, stored in a retrieval system, or transmitted in any form by any means, electronic, mechanical, recording or otherwise, except brief extracts for the purpose of review, and no part of this publication may be sold or hired, without the written permission of the publisher. Lonely Planet and the Lonely Planet logo are trademarks of Lonely Planet and are registered in the US Patent and Trademark Office and in other countries. Lonely Planet does not allow its name or logo to be appropriated by commercial establishments, such as retailers, restaurants or hotels. Please let us know of any misuses: lonelyplanet.com/ip.